ANNALS OF
AMERICAN LITERATURE
1602–1983

ANNALS OF AMERICAN LITERATURE

1602–1983

EDITED BY

Richard M. Ludwig

Clifford A. Nault, Jr.

NEW YORK   OXFORD

Oxford University Press

1986

Oxford University Press

Oxford   New York   Toronto
Delhi   Bombay   Calcutta   Madras   Karachi
Petaling Jaya   Singapore   Hong Kong   Tokyo
Nairobi   Dar es Salaam   Cape Town
Melbourne   Auckland

and associated companies in
Beirut   Berlin   Ibadan   Nicosia

Copyright © 1986 by Oxford University Press, Inc.

Published by Oxford University Press, Inc.,
200 Madison Avenue, New York 10016

Oxford is a registered trademark of Oxford University Press

Library of Congress Cataloging-in-Publication Data
Ludwig, Richard M., 1920–
Annals of American literature, 1602–1983.
Includes index.
1. American literature—Chronology.
I. Nault, Clifford A., 1926–.   II. Title.
PS94.L83   1986   810.2′02   85-15405
ISBN 0-19-503970-X

Printing (last digit): 9 8 7 6 5 4 3 2 1

Printed in the United States of America
on acid-free paper

PREFACE

In 1935, the first edition of *Annals of English Literature 1475–1925* appeared in England, calling itself a "little book" designed "to give the student, at a glance, the main literary output of any year or series of years; to show what books people were likely to be reading at any time, and with what rivals a candidate for literary fame had to reckon." The success of the work led to a second edition, in 1961, with numerous corrections in the whole text and the addition of a new section covering the years 1925–50. A new edition is in preparation.

Publication of *Annals of American Literature 1602–1983* has been long overdue. The usefulness of the English volume, with its copious index, has been apparent for decades, and readers have discovered that browsing for pleasure has also been a part of the charm of that reference work. Its American counterpart, therefore, follows basically the same format, with one major alteration and a few minor changes.

The first book printed in the American colonies is known as the *Bay Psalm Book,* translated from the Hebrew by Richard Mather and others, printed by Stephen Daye in Cambridge, Mass., in 1640. Why then begin these annals with the year 1602 rather than, let us say, 1588 when Thomas Hariot published his justly famous *Briefe and True Report of the New-Found Land of Virginia* after spending two years there on Sir Richard Grenville's second expedition? The reason is simply that Hariot antedates by fourteen years any sizable quantity of publications which, although printed in Europe, reflect the growing concern with the settlement of North America. The fifty-two titles listed between 1602 and 1639 are accounts of early explorations (John Brierton, Samuel de Champlain, James Rosier, John Smith, et al.), sermons and pamphlets by emigrant religious leaders (John Cotton, Richard Mather, John Winthrop, Thomas Hooker, et al.), and papers by political figures in the colonies (William Bradford and John Winthrop). From 1640 to the end of the century, the ratio of American to British publications increases so rapidly in these lists that by the early years of the eighteenth century the annals are wholly American and remain so to the last page. Unlike our British model, which extends the provenance of authors writing in English to include Australia, Canada, India, New Zealand, South Africa, and the United States of America, we chose to be parochial. This is our one major alteration.

General guidelines and minor changes are few in number, but they need to be described here in detail so that the reader will know what to look for to facilitate easy reference as well as what he should expect to find if he is familiar with the English *Annals.*

Running heads. From 1602 to 1774, the reigning British monarchs appear as running heads on each page. From 1789 to the present, the American presidents take their place.

The first census in the United States was taken in 1790, and these data appear as running heads from 1790 on, updated at ten-year intervals.

Author's name. It is printed in full for every entry.

Date of birth. Following the author's name, the date of birth is given in parentheses to remind the reader that, for example, Benjamin Franklin was only twenty-seven when he began publishing *Poor Richard's Almanack,* Nathaniel Hawthorne was fifty-six when he published his last novel, *The Marble Faun,* and Lillian Hellman saw her last book through the press at age seventy-five. Posthumous works are indicated by placing the author's death date in parentheses.

Date of publication. We have used in general the date of the book, not of the serial or magazine, publication. If the title page is one year later than the copyright date, we used the latter since publishers frequently postdate books published near the end of the calendar year. Dramatic works are entered in the year of production or publication, whichever came first. If the script was published after the year of production, its publication date is given in parentheses following the title. Since there are many sources of confusion in dating American publications, general agreement is not easily arrived at.

Coverage. To keep this book to a manageable size it has been necessary to omit as well as include. For the major authors we have listed every well-known title and a selection of the lesser works; for the minor authors we have chosen the more influential publications. Among the dramatists, we have excluded screen and radio writers as well as the librettists of musicals and operas. It is clearly not our intention to produce an inclusive bibliography. That work has been published at great length elsewhere.

Genre designations. Following the title, one of four letters indicates the genre of the work. F = fiction; NF = non-fiction; D = drama; V = poetry. We have not used the letter P in order to avoid the inevitable confusion of poetry with prose in the reader's mind.

Pseudonyms. Unlike real names, pseudonyms are not listed last name first. Mark Twain, for example, is listed in quotation marks from his first to last entry and is alphabetized yearly under the M's, not the T's. In the index, however, he is entered three times: under the C's (as Clemens, Samuel Langhorne ["Mark Twain"], 1835–1910.), under the M's (as "Mark Twain." See Clemens, Samuel Langhorne.), and under the T's.

In 1951, Feike Feikema, an Iowa-born author of Frisian ancestry, adopted Frederick Manfred as his pen name. Before that date his work is found under Feikema. After 1951, titles are listed under Manfred, Frederick (Feike Feikema) (1912). In 1965, LeRoi Jones, a New Jersey author, changed his name to Imamu Amiri Baraka. In 1970, he began using his new name on title pages. He is thereafter listed as Baraka, Imamu Amiri (LeRoi Jones) (1934). Authors using two names are listed under both names in the index.

An entry such as "William Wharton" (?) indicates that we have not ascertained his birthdate. Since we also do not know his real name, he is listed in the index only as "William Wharton."

Because of space limitations in the side-columns, we use only the surnames of foreign authors including those writing under pseudonyms. Fielding is Fielding, naturally; but Voltaire is Voltaire, not "Voltaire." The case is likewise for Molière, Stendhal, Sand, Ouida, Gorky, Dinesen, Mishima, and scores of other pseudonymous authors. Since none of these literary entries are listed in the index, we do not have to confront there the Twain-Feikema-Wharton problems.

Change of nationality. Even though T. S. Eliot became a British subject in 1927, he is included throughout the main entries because of his family and professional ties with the United States. W. H. Auden, Christopher Isherwood, and Vladimir Nabokov appear in the main entries because they became American citizens at least midway in their careers.

Social history, journals, and foreign literature. Under each year we have provided in the side-column a list of historical events, the founding of newspapers and periodicals, the birth and death of authors, and the appearance of major foreign literature. Surnames only are used in these literary entries unless two authors published under the same surname (Huxley, Waugh, Lawrence, Wilson, Thomas, Shaffer, et al.). Again, space considerations dictated a modest number of side-column entries for the seventeenth century; the twentieth century errs perhaps in the other direction. Commencing in 1783 (with the signing of the Treaty of Paris), the list is divided by a rule: American events above, foreign events below. Unlike the lists in the English *Annals,* our side-column entries include titles in Slavic, Scandinavian, and Oriental languages as well as the more familiar French, German, Italian, Spanish, and of course titles in English published outside the United States. It would be foolish to translate titles such as Hitler's *Mein Kampf,* Cocteau's *Les Enfants Terribles,* or Fuentes's *Terra Nostra,* but the vast majority of foreign titles are given in English at the risk of purists' objections. Granted it is easy to recognize *The School for Wives* or *The Sorrows of Young Werther* in their original language, but what does one do with Tolstoy's *Voskresenie,* Ibsen's *Gengangere,* or Kawabata's *Yukiguni?* Foreign works, however, are listed in the year of first publication, not in the year of availability in English.

Abbreviations. The following abbreviations have been used throughout.

adap.	adaptation	N.H.	New Hampshire
Ala.	Alabama	N.J.	New Jersey
attrib.	attributed to	N.M.	New Mexico
b.	born	N.Y.	New York
coll.	collected	Okla.	Oklahoma
Calif.	California	Penna.	Pennsylvania
Conn.	Connecticut	R.I.	Rhode Island
cont.	continuation of	S.C.	South Carolina
d.	died	Phila.	Philadelphia
D.C.	District of Columbia	posth.	posthumous
ed.	edited	prod.	produced
enl.	enlarged	pub.	published
Ga.	Georgia	repr.	reprinted
Ill.	Illinois	repub.	republished
Ind.	Indiana	rev.	revised
Kan.	Kansas	ser.	series
Mass.	Massachusetts	Tenn.	Tennessee
Me.	Maine	trans.	translation, translated
Mont.	Montana	Va.	Virginia
N.C.	North Carolina		

All reference works are by their very nature cooperative enterprises. This book is no exception. We leaned heavily on three major American publications in making our selections—the *American Bibliography* [1639–1800] (ed. Charles Evans et al., 13 vols., 1903–55); the *Literary History of the United States* (ed. Robert E. Spiller et al., 4th edition, 2 vols., 1974); and James D. Hart's *Oxford Companion to American Literature* (5th edition, 1983)—as well as the libraries and their staffs at Princeton University and at Indiana University-Purdue University at Fort Wayne. Errors and omissions are ours, of course. We hope the readers of this book will report their discoveries or queries to the publisher for correction in future editions.

Princeton, N.J.   *R. M. L.*
Fort Wayne, Ind.   *C. A. N.*
May 1985

MONARCHS AND PRESIDENTS
1602–1983

Elizabeth I, 1558–1603
James I, 1603–1625
Charles I, 1625–1649
Commonwealth, 1649–1660
Charles II, 1660–1685
James II, 1685–1688
William III and Mary II, 1689–1694
William III, 1694–1702
Anne, 1702–1714
George I, 1714–1727
George II, 1727–1760
George III, 1760–1820

George Washington, 1789–1797
John Adams, 1797–1801
Thomas Jefferson, 1801–1809
James Madison, 1809–1817
James Monroe, 1817–1825
John Quincy Adams, 1825–1829
Andrew Jackson, 1829–1837
Martin Van Buren, 1837–1841
William Henry Harrison, 1841
John Tyler, 1841–1845
James K. Polk, 1845–1849
Zachary Taylor, 1849–1850
Millard Fillmore, 1850–1853
Franklin Pierce, 1853–1857

James Buchanan, 1857–1861
Abraham Lincoln, 1861–1865
Andrew Johnson, 1865–1869
Ulysses S. Grant, 1869–1877
Rutherford B. Hayes, 1877–1881
James A. Garfield, 1881
Chester A. Arthur, 1881–1885
Grover Cleveland, 1885–1889
Benjamin Harrison, 1889–1893
Grover Cleveland, 1893–1897
William McKinley, 1897–1901
Theodore Roosevelt, 1901–1909
William Howard Taft, 1909–1913
Woodrow Wilson, 1913–1921
Warren G. Harding, 1921–1923
Calvin Coolidge, 1923–1929
Herbert Hoover, 1929–1933
Franklin D. Roosevelt, 1933–1945
Harry S Truman, 1945–1953
Dwight D. Eisenhower, 1953–1961
John F. Kennedy, 1961–1963
Lyndon B. Johnson, 1963–1969
Richard M. Nixon, 1969–1974
Gerald R. Ford, 1974–1977
Jimmy Carter, 1977–1981
Ronald Reagan, 1981–

ANNALS OF
AMERICAN LITERATURE
1602–1983

1602

Brierton, John (fl. 1572–1619), A Briefe and True Relation of the Discouerie of the North Part of Virginia. NF

Bartholomew Gosnold's expedition to New England coast.
Shakespeare's *Hamlet; Troilus and Cressida*.
Dekker's *Satiro-mastix* (with John Marston).

1603

Champlain, Samuel de (c. 1567), Des sauvages; ou, voyage de Samuel Champlain de Brouage fait en la France nouvelle. NF

Death of Elizabeth I; accession of James I.
Daniel's *A Defence of Ryme*.
Thomas Heywood's *A Woman Killed with Kindness*.
Florio's trans. of Montaigne's *Essais*.

1604

French settlement in Nova Scotia.
Hampton Court Conference (High Church vs. Puritans).
Shakespeare's *Measure for Measure; Othello*.

1605

Rosier, James (c. 1575), A True Relation of the Most Prosperous Voyage Made This Present Yeere 1605 by Captaine George Waymouth. NF

Guy Fawkes and "Gunpowder Plot.'
Repression of English Puritans and Catholics.
Bacon's *Advancement of Learning*.
Cervantes's *Don Quixote* (1605–15).

1606

Percy, George (1580), Observations gathered out of a Discourse of the Plantation of the Southerne Colonie in Virginia by the English (pub. by Samuel Purchas, 1625). NF

The London and the Plymouth Companies chartered to found colonies in America.
Shakespeare's *King Lear*.
Jonson's *Volpone*.

1607

Jamestown first permanent English settlement in America.
Shakespeare's *Antony and Cleopatra*.
Tourneur's *The Revenger's Tragedy*.
Chapman's *Bussy d'Ambois*.

1608

Smith, John (1580), A True Relation of such occurrences and accidents of noate as hath hapned in Virginia since the first planting of that Collony. NF

Henry Hudson searched for Northwest Passage.
Shakespeare's *Coriolanus; Pericles*.
Webster's *The White Devil*.
Joseph Hall's *Characters of Virtues and Vices*.

1609

Gray, Robert (fl. 1609), Good Speed to Virginia. NF
Jonson, Robert (fl. 1609–12), Nova Britannia: offering most excellent Fruites by Planting in Virginia. NF

Henry Hudson discovered Hudson River, claimed New Netherland.
Galileo built telescope.
Shakespeare's *Sonnets*.
Jonson's *Epicoene*.
Bacon's *De sapientia veterum*.
Beaumont's *The Knight of the Burning Pestle*.

1610

Rich, Richard (fl. 1609–10), Newes from Virginia. V
Villagrá, Gaspar Pérez de (c. 1555), Historia de la Nueva
Mexico (prose trans., History of New Mexico, pub. 1933). V

Spanish founded Santa Fe, N.M.
Jonson's *The Alchemist.*
Donne's *Pseudo-Martyr.*
John Fletcher's *The Faithful
Shepherdess.*

1611

De La Warr, Thomas West, Baron (1577), The relation of the
Right Honourable the Lord De-La-Warre, lord gouernour &
captaine generall of the colonie, planted in Virginea. NF

James I dissolved Parliament.
"Authorized Version" of the Bible.
Jonson's *Catiline his Conspiracy.*
Davies's *The Scourge of Folly.*

1612

Jonson, Robert (fl. 1609–12), The New Life of Virginia
(attrib.). NF
Smith, John (1580), A Map of Virginia, with a Description of
the Country. NF
Strachey, William (fl. 1606–18), For the Colony of Virginea
Britannia: Lawes Divine, Morall, and Martiall. NF

John Rolfe cultivated tobacco in
Virginia.
Anne Bradstreet b.
Daniel's *The Historie of England*
(1612–18).

1613

Purchas, Samuel (1575?), Purchas his Pilgrimage; or, Relations
of the World and the Religions observed in all Ages and places
discovered, from the Creation unto this Present. NF
Whitaker, Alexander (1585), Good News from Virginia. NF

Globe Theatre burned.
Drayton's *Poly-Olbion* (1613–22).
Campion's *Two Books of Ayres.*
Shakespeare's *Henry VIII* (with John
Fletcher).

1614

Captain John Smith explored New
England.
Dutch traders in New York and Long
Island.
Jonson's *Bartholomew Fayre.*

1615

William Baffin piloted exploration for
Northwest Passage.
St. Peter's Basilica in Rome completed
(1506–1615).
Rowlands's *The Melancholie Knight.*

1616

Smith, John (1580), A Description of New England: or the
Observations and Discoveries of Captain John Smith . . . .
NF

William Harvey discovered circulation
of the blood.
William Shakespeare d.
Miguel de Cervantes d.
Jonson's *Works* (2nd edition, 1640; 3rd
edition, 1692).

1617

English criminals transported to
Virginia.
Tobacco major New World export.
Middleton's *A Faire Quarrell* (with
William Rowley).

1618

Strachey, William (fl. 1606–18), The Historie of Travaile into
Virginia Britannia . . . (pub. 1849). NF

Sir Walter Ralegh beheaded for treason.
Revolt in Bohemia began Thirty Years'
War, devastating Central Europe.
Chapman's trans. of Hesiod's *Works
and Days* (pub. as *Georgicks*).

1619

Purchas, Samuel (1575?), Purchas his Pilgrim. Microcosmus, or the histories of Man. NF

A General Assembly met for the first time in Jamestown, Va.
Dutch sold Negro slaves to Jamestown colonists.
John Fletcher's The Humorous Lieutenant.

1620

Smith, John (1580), New Englands Trials. NF

Pilgrims landed at Plymouth, Mass.
Mayflower Compact set up a "civil body politic."
Congregational (Calvinist) Church established in Plymouth.
Bacon's Novum organum.

1621

William Bradford elected governor of Plymouth Colony.
Dutch West India Co. founded.
Burton's The Anatomy of Melancholy.
Middleton's Women Beware Women.

1622

Bradford, William (1590), A Relation or Journall of the Beginning and Proceedings of the English Plantation Setled at Plimoth in New England (commonly known as Mourt's Relation; attrib. to Bradford and Edward Winslow). NF

James I dissolved Parliament.
Bacon's The Historie of the Raigne of King Henry the Seventh.
Sir Richard Hawkins's Observations . . . in his Voiage into the South Sea.

1623

Colonists expanded settlements to Portsmouth, N.H.
Shakespeare's Comedies, Histories, and Tragedies [First Folio].
Middleton's The Changeling (with William Rowley).

1624

Smith, John (1580), The Generall Historie of Virginia, New England, and the Summer Isles. NF
Winslow, Edward (1595), Good News from New England. NF

Dutch established New Netherland Colony in America.
Donne's Devotions Upon Emergent Occasions.
Wotton's The Elements of Architecture.
Middleton's A Game at Chesse.

1625

Morrell, William (fl. 1623–25), Nova Anglia (New-England, or a Briefe Enarration). V
Purchas, Samuel (1575?), Hakluytus Posthumus, or Purchas his Pilgrimes, contayning a History of the World in Sea Voyages and Lande Travells, by Englishmen and others. NF

Death of James I; accession of Charles I.
Huguenot revolt in France.
Ford's 'Tis Pity She's a Whore.

1626

Sandys, George (1578), Ovid's Metamorphosis Englished by G.S. V
Smith, John (1580), An Accidence: or, The Pathway to Experience Necessary for All Young Seamen. NF
Vaughan, Sir William (1577), The Golden Fleece. NF, V
Wilson, John (c. 1591), A Song, or Story, for the Lasting

Peter Minuit arrived in New Netherland, bought Manhattan Island from the Indians, renamed it New Amsterdam (1626–31).
Massinger's The Roman Actor.
Donne's Five Sermons.

Remembrance of Divers Famous Works (repub. as A Song of
Deliverance, 1680). V

1627

French, Dutch, English settlers in West
 Indies.
Drayton's *The Battaile of Agincourt*.
Phineas Fletcher's *The Locusts or
 Apollyonists*.

1628

John Endecott led Puritans to
 Massachusetts Bay, settled in Salem,
 became first governor of the colony.
Cardinal Richelieu became first
 minister to Louis XIII.
Harvey's *Essay on the Motion of the
 Heart and the Blood*.
Coke's *Institutes of the Laws of England*
 (1628–44).

1629

Hooker, Thomas (1586), The Poore Douting Christian. NF

Salem became first Puritan settlement
 to build a church.
French began trading with Canada.
D'Avenant's *The Cruel Brother*.
Corneille's *Mélite*.

1630

Benavides, Alonzo de (fl. 1600–34), Memorial (rev. edition,
 1634). NF
Cotton, John (1584), Gods Promise to His Plantation. NF
Higginson, Francis (1586), New-Englands Plantation. NF
Smith, John (1580), The True Travels, Adventures, and
 Observations of Captaine John Smith in Europe, Asia, Africa,
 and America, from . . . 1593 to 1629 . . . . NF
Vaughan, Sir William (1577), The Newlander's Cure. NF
White, John (1575), The Planter's Plea. NF
Winthrop, John (1588), The Humble Request of . . . the
 Company Late Gone for New England (with others). NF; "A
 Modell of Christian Charity." NF

John Winthrop and 700 Puritans settled
 in Shawmut (now Boston).
Quarles's *Divine Poems*.
Shirley's *The Gratefull Servant*.

1631

Smith, John (1580), Advertisements for the Unexperienced
 Planters of New England, or Anywhere; or, The Pathway to
 Erect a Plantation. NF

"Great Migration" of Puritans
 continued for a decade.
Maryland began tobacco cultivation.
John Donne d.
Captain John Smith d.
Chapman's *Caesar and Pompey*.
Shirley's *The Traitor*.

1632

Champlain, Samuel de (c. 1567), Voyages de la nouvelle
 France. NF
Hooker, Thomas (1586), The Soules Preparation for Christ.
 NF; The Equall Ways of God. NF

Boston became capital of
 Massachusetts Bay Colony.
Shakespeare's *Comedies, Histories, and
 Tragedies* [Second Folio].
Ralegh's *Instructions to His Son*
 (posth.).
Shirley's *Hyde Park*.
Corneille's *Clitandre*.

1633

Dutch settlers constructed Fort Good
    Hope (now Hartford, Conn.).
Donne's *Poems* (posth.).
Herbert's *The Temple*.
Prynne's *Histrio-Mastix*.

1634

Wood, William (fl. 1629–35), New Englands Prospect. NF

First school in New Amsterdam (now
    New York City).
Bubonic plague struck Canada.
First Oberammergau Passion Play.
Milton's *A Maske Presented at Ludlow
    Castle* [*Comus*].

1635

John Winthrop (the Younger) led
    settlement of Connecticut.
Boston Latin School founded.
Académie Française incorporated.
Quarles's *Emblems*.
Corneille's *Medea*.

1636

Roger Williams banished from Salem,
    founded Seekonk (now Providence,
    R.I.).
Thomas Hooker moved his
    congregation from Massachusetts to
    found the Connecticut Colony.
Harvard College founded.

1637

Hooker, Thomas (1586), The Soules Humiliation. NF; The
    Soules Implantation. NF; The Soules Ingrafting into Christ.
    NF; The Soules Effectuall Calling to Christ. NF
Morton, Thomas (1590?), New English Canaan. NF

English at war with Pequot Indians in
    Connecticut.
Ferdinand III became Holy Roman
    Emperor.
Ben Jonson d.
Descartes's *Discourse on Method*.
Corneille's *The Cid*.

1638

Hooker, Thomas (1586), The Soules Exaltation. NF; Heaven's
    Treasury Opened, in a Faithful Exposition of the Lord's
    Prayer. NF; The Unbeleevers Preparing for Christ. NF; Foure
    Godly and Learned Treatises. NF
Underhill, John (c. 1597), Newes from America. NF

John Davenport founded New Haven
    colony.
Anne Hutchinson banished from
    Massachusetts, fled to Rhode Island.
Stephen Daye set up a printing press in
    Cambridge, Mass.
Sir William D'Avenant named poet
    laureate of England.
Milton's *Lycidas*.

1639

John Wheelwright and Antinomian
    followers signed the Exeter (N.H.)
    Compact.
Oath of a Free-man, Stephen Daye's
    broadside, first printing in America.

1640

Hooker, Thomas (1586), The Christians Two Chiefe Lessons.
    NF
Mather, Richard (1596), The Whole Booke of Psalmes
    Faithfully Translated into English Metre (trans. with John Eliot

Charles I summoned the Long
    Parliament (1640–60).
Jonson's *Timber* (posth.).
Walton's *The Life and Death of Dr.
    [John] Donne*.

and Thomas Weld; commonly known as the Bay Psalm Book). V

Shepard, Thomas (1605), The Sincere Convert, Discovering the Paucity of True Believers. NF

Dacres's trans. of Machiavelli's *The Prince.*
Pascal's *Treatise on Conic Sections.*
Calderón's *The Mayor of Zalamea.*

1641

Cotton, John (1584), An Abstract of the Lawes of New England. NF

Hooker, Thomas (1586), The Danger of Desertion. NF

Body of Liberties: first written laws of Massachusetts.
Irish Rebellion; massacre of Protestants in Ulster.
The Episcopacy Controversy in England.
Day's *The Parliament of Bees* (posth.).

1642

Cotton, John (1584), A Briefe Exposition of the Whole Book of Canticles. NF; The Powrring Out of the Seven Vials. NF

Sir William Berkeley became governor of Virginia (1642–52; 1660–77).
French settlers arrived in Montreal.
Civil War in England (1642–46).
Galileo Galilei d.
Denham's *Cooper's Hill.*
Milton's *An Apology . . .* [for] *Smectymnuus.*
Thomas Fuller's *The Holy State and the Profane State.*

1643

Cotton, John (1584), A Letter . . . to Mr. Williams. NF

Mather, Richard (1596), Church-Government and Church-Covenant Discussed. NF

Peter (Peters?), Hugh (1598), New Englands First Fruits (with Thomas Weld). NF

Williams, Roger (c. 1603), A Key into the Language of America. NF

Massachusetts Bay, Plymouth, Connecticut, and New Haven colonies formed New England Confederation.
Browne's *Religio Medici* (authorized edition).
Milton's *The Doctrine and Discipline of Divorce.*
Prynne's *The Sovereign Power of Parliaments and Kingdoms.*

1644

Cotton, John (1584), The Keyes of the Kingdom of Heaven. NF

Parker, Thomas (1595), True Copy of a Letter written by Mr. T. Parker. . . . NF

Weld, Thomas (1595), An Answer to W. R. [William Rathband] . . . . NF

Williams, Roger (c. 1603), Mr. Cottons Letter Lately Printed, Examined, and Answered. NF; The Bloudy Tenent of Persecution, for Cause of Conscience, Discussed. NF; Queries of Highest Consideration. NF

Winthrop, John (1588), A Short Story of the Rise, Reign, and Ruine of the Antinomians . . . . NF

First ironworks built in America.
Globe Theatre razed in London.
Battle of Marston Moor (Cromwell defeated Cavaliers).
Milton's *Aeropagitica.*
Descartes's *Principles of Philosophy.*

1645

Cotton, John (1584), The Covenant of Gods Free Grace. NF; The Way of the Churches of Christ in New-England. NF

Hooker, Thomas (1586), The Saints Guide. NF

Shepard, Thomas (1605), New Englands Lamentation for Old Englands Present Errours. NF; The Sound Beleever. NF

Roxbury Latin School founded, near Boston.
Charles I defeated at Battle of Naseby.
Milton's *Poems.*
Waller's *Poems.*

Weld, Thomas (1595), A Brief Narration of the Practices of the Churches in New-England. NF

Wheelwright, John (c. 1592), Mercurius Americanus. NF

Williams, Roger (c. 1603), Christenings Make Not Christians. NF

Winthrop, John (1588), A Declaration of Former Passages and Proceedings Betwixt the English and Narrowgansets. NF

Thomas Fuller's *Good Thoughts in Bad Times*.
Scarron's *Jodelet*.

1646

Cotton, John (1584), The Controversie Concerning Liberty of Conscience in Matters of Religion. NF; Milk for Babes, Drawn out of the Breasts of Both Testaments. NF

Gorton, Samuel (c. 1592), Simplicities Defence against Seven-Headed Policy. NF

Parker, Thomas (1595), The Visions and Prophecies of Daniel expounded. NF

Winslow, Edward (1595), Hypocrisie Unmasked. NF

Massachusetts heresy laws.
Charles I surrendered to Scots.
Vaughan's *Poems*.
Crashaw's *Steps to the Temple*.
Browne's *Pseudodoxia epidemica* [*Vulgar Errors*].

1647

Child, John (?), New-Englands Jonas Cast Up at London. NF

Cotton, John (1584), The Bloudy Tenent, Washed, and Made White in the Bloud of the Lambe. NF

Gorges, Sir Ferdinando (c. 1566), The Briefe Narration of the Original Undertakings of the Advancement of Plantations into Parts of America. NF

Shepard, Thomas (1605), The Day-Breaking. NF

Ward, Nathaniel (1578?), The Simple Cobler of Aggawam in America. NF; A Religious Retreat Sounded to a Religious Army. NF; A Word to Mr. Peters. NF

Winslow, Edward (1595), New Englands Salamander [John Child] Discovered by an Irreligious and Scornfull Pamphlet. NF

Peter Stuyvesant became governor of New Netherland.
Thomas Hooker d.
Cowley's *The Mistress*.
May's *History of the* [Long] *Parliament*.
Cleveland's *The Character of a London-Diurnall*.

1648

Bradford, William (1590), "A Dialogue, or the Sum of a Conference Between Some Young Man Born in New England and Sundry Ancient Men That Came Out of Holland and Old England" (pub. 1841). NF

Cotton, John (1584), The Way of Congregational Churches Cleared. NF; A Survey of the Summe of Church-Discipline (cont. of Hooker, below). NF

Hooker, Thomas (d. 1647), A Survey of the Summe of Church-Discipline. NF

Norton, John (1606), Responsio ad Guliel. NF

Shepard, Thomas (1605), Certain Select Cases Resolved. NF; The Clear Sun-shine of the Gospel Breaking Forth upon the Indians. NF; The First Principles of the Oracles of God. NF

Cambridge Platform adopted by Massachusetts and Connecticut Congregationalists.
George Fox founded the first Quaker society in England (1648–50).
Peace of Westphalia ended Thirty Years War.
Herrick's *Hesperides*.

1649

Eliot, John (1604), The Glorious Progress of the Gospel Amongst the Indians (with Thomas Mayhew). NF

Hooker, Thomas (d. 1647), The Covenant of Grace Opened. NF

Charles I beheaded at Whitehall.
Commonwealth formed; Oliver Cromwell became commander-in-chief of the army.

Mather, Richard (1596), A Platform of Church Discipline (commonly known as the Cambridge Platform). NF
Shepard, Thomas (1605), Theses Sabbaticae. NF

Society for Propagation of the Gospel in New England founded in London.
John Winthrop d.
Milton's *The Tenure of Kings and Magistrates.*
Descartes's *Treatise on the Passions.*

1650

Baxter, Richard (1615), The Saints Everlasting Rest. NF
Bradford, William (1590), ''A Descriptive and Historical Account of New England in Verse'' (pub. 1794). V
Bradstreet, Anne (1612?), The Tenth Muse Lately Sprung Up in America. V

First export of iron from Massachusetts to England.
Jeremy Taylor's *The Rule and Exercises of Holy Living.*
Hobbes's *Human Nature*
Vaughn's *Silex Scintillans.*

1651

Bradford, William (1590), History of Plimmoth Plantation (written 1630–51; first pub., 1856; ed. in modern English, 1952). NF
Cotton, John (1584), Christ the Fountaine of Life. NF
Hooker, Thomas (d.1647), The Saints Dignitie, and Duty. NF
Shepard, Thomas (d. 1649), Four Necessary Cases of Conscience. NF

Charles II proclaimed king in Scotland (1650), defeated by Cromwell in England, escaped to France (1651).
Parliament prohibited trade with the colonies.
Hobbes's *Leviathan.*
Jeremy Taylor's *The Rule and Exercises of Holy Dying.*

1652

Clarke, John (1609), Ill News from New England. NF
Eliot, John (1604), Tears of Repentance (with Thomas Mayhew). NF
Mather, Richard (1596), The Summe of Certain Sermons Upon Genes. 15.6. NF
Shepard, Thomas (d. 1649), A Defence of the Answer (with John Allin). NF; Subjection to Christ. NF
Stone, Samuel (1602), A Congregational Church Is a Catholike Visible Church. NF
Williams, Roger (c. 1603), The Bloody Tenent Yet More Bloody . . . . NF; The Fourth Paper Presented by Major Butler. NF; The Hireling Ministry None of Christs. NF; Experiments of Spiritual Life and Health. NF

Maine declared legal part of Massachusetts Bay Colony.
England at war with the Dutch (1652–54).
John Cotton d.
Donne's *Paradoxes, Problems, Essays, Characters* (posth.).
Herbert's *Remains.*
Scarron's *Don Japhet.*

1653

Norton, John (1606), A Discussion of that Great Point in Divinity, the Sufferings of Christ. NF

Peter Stuyvesant forced to grant self-government to New Amsterdam.
Oliver Cromwell became Lord Protector of the Commonwealth.
Walton's *The Compleat Angler.*

1654

Cotton, John (d. 1652), A Briefe Exposition . . . of Ecclesiastes. NF; The New Covenant. NF
Eliot, John (1604), A Primer or Catechism in the Massachusetts Indian Language (Eng. title). NF
Johnson, Edward (1598), The Wonder-Working Providence of Sions Saviour in New England. NF
Shepard, Thomas (d. 1649), A Short Catechism. NF

Russia at war with Poland.
Madeleine de Scudéry's *Clélie* (1654–60).
Georges de Scudéry's *Alaric.*
Cyrano de Bergerac's *The Pedant Tricked.*

1655

Chauncy, Charles (1592), God's Mercy, Shewed to His People. NF

Cotton, John (d. 1652), An Exposition upon the Thirteenth Chapter of the Revelation. NF; The Covenant of Grace. NF; A Brief Exposition . . . of Canticles. NF

Eliot, John (1604), A Late and Further Manifestation of the Progress of the Gospel Amongst the Indians in New England. NF

Gorton, Samuel (c. 1592), Saltmarsh Returned from the Dead. NF

Dutch occupied Fort Casimir (now Newcastle) on the Delware, ending Swedish rule in North America.
Oliver Cromwell dissolved Parliament.
Thomas Fuller's *The Church History of Britain*.

1656

Cotton, John (d. 1652), A Practical Commentary . . . upon the First Epistle Generall of John. NF; Spiritual Milk for Boston Babes in Either England. NF

Hammond, John (fl. 1635–56), Leah and Rachel: or, The Two Fruitfull Sisters, Virginia and Maryland. NF

Hooker, Thomas (d. 1647), The Application of Redemption. NF

English Quakers arrived in Boston, were imprisoned and deported.
Cowley's *Poems*.
Hobbes's *Questions Concerning Liberty, Necessity and Chance*.
Pascal's *Provincial Letters* (1656–57).

1657

Fiske, John (1601), The Watering of the Olive Plant in Christs Garden. NF

Gorton, Samuel (c. 1592), An Antidote against the Common Plague of the World. NF

Mather, Richard (1596), A Farewel-Exhortation to the Church and People of Dorchester in New-England. NF

Quakers arriving in New Amsterdam sent to Rhode Island.
Oliver Cromwell refused the crown.
First school of science founded, in Italy.
Taylor's *Discourse of . . . Friendship*.

1658

Gorges, Ferdinando (1630), America Painted to the Life (1658–59). NF

Norton, John (1606), Abel Being Dead Yet Speaketh; or, The Life and Death of . . . John Cotton. NF

Pierson, Abraham (1608), Some Helps for the Indians. NF

Typhoid epidemic in New Amsterdam.
Oliver Cromwell died, son Richard proclaimed Lord Protector.
Browne's *Hydriotaphia: Urne-Buriall*.

1659

Eliot, John (1604), The Christian Commonwealth. NF; A Further Accompt of the Progresse of the Gospel Amongst the Indians. NF

Norton, John (1606), The Heart of N-England rent at the Blasphemies of the Present Generation. NF

Steendam, Jacob (c. 1616), Complaint of New Amsterdam in New Netherland (Eng. title; trans. from Dutch). V

Two Quakers hanged in Boston.
Richard Cromwell forced to resign; Commonwealth reestablished.
Milton's *A Treatise of Civil Power in Ecclesiastical Causes*.
Molière's *The Ridiculous Snobs*.

1660

Maverick, Samuel (c. 1602), A Briefe Description of New England and the Severall Townes Therein. NF

Norton, John (1606), A Brief Catechisme Containing the Doctrine of Godlines, or of Living Unto God. NF

Shepard, Thomas (d. 1649), The Parable of the Ten Virgins Opened and Applied. NF

First Indian churches established in Massachusetts.
Accession of Charles II.
London theatres reopened.
Milton's *The Ready and Easy Way to Establish a Free Commonwealth*.
Boyle's *New Experiments Physico-Mechanical*.

1661

Eliot, John (1604), The New Testament . . . Translated into the Indian Language. NF

Steendam, Jacob (c. 1616), Praise of New Netherland (Eng. title; trans. from Dutch). V

Charles II's first (Cavalier) Parliament.
Thomas Fuller d.
Dryden's *To His Sacred Majesty.*
Molière's *The School for Husbands.*

1662

Steendam, Jacob (c. 1616), "Spurring Verses" (Eng. title; trans. from Dutch). V

Wigglesworth, Michael (1631), The Day of Doom: or, A Poetical Description of the Great and Last Judgement. V

Richard Mather and the Half-Way Covenant.
Cavalier Parliament passed Act of Uniformity.
The Book of Common Prayer (final text).
Poor Robin's Almanack (anon.; 1662–76).
Fuller's *The History of the Worthies of England* (posth.).
Molière's *The School for Wives.*

1663

Cotton, Seaborn (1633), A Brief Summe of the Chief Articles of Our Christian Faith. NF

Davenport, John (1597), A Discourse about Civil Government in a New Plantation Whose Design is Religion. NF

Eliot, John (1604), The Holy Bible . . . Translated into the Indian Language. NF

Higginson, John (1616), The Cause of God and His People in New-England. NF

Shepard, Thomas (d. 1649), The Church-Membership of Children and Their Right to Baptisme. NF

Drury Lane Theatre opened.
The Intelligencer (London), 1663–66.
Butler's *Hudibras* (1663–78).
Shakespeare's *Comedies, Histories, and Tragedies* [Third Folio; 2nd issue, 1664].
Boyle's *The Usefulness of Experimental Natural Philosophy.*

1664

Allin, John (1596), Animadversions upon the Antisynodalia Americana. NF

Norton, John (1606), Three Choice and Profitable Sermons Upon Severall Texts of Scripture. NF

Whiting, Samuel (1597), A Discourse of the Last Judgment: or, Short Notes Upon Mat. XXV. NF

British troops seized New Amsterdam (renamed New York) and Fort Orange (renamed Albany) from the Dutch.
Etherege's *The Comical Revenge, or Love in a Tub.*
Racine's *The Thebiad.*
Molière's *Tartuffe,* prod. at Versailles, then banned.

1665

Darby, William (?), Ye Bare and Ye Cubb (with Cornelius Watkinson and Philip Howard; title also given as Ye Beare and Ye Club; prod. but not pub.). D

Eliot, John (1604), Communion of Churches: or, The Divine Management of Gospel-Churches by the Ordinance of Councils (the first privately printed American book). NF

Colony of New Jersey founded
New Haven Colony united with Connecticut Colony.
Great plague of London began.
The Oxford Gazette (renamed *The London Gazette*), 1665–.
Bunyan's *The Holy City: or the New Jerusalem.*
La Rochefoucauld's *Maxims.*

1666

Alsop, George (1638), A Character of the Province of Mary-Land. NF, V

Great Fire of London.
Boyle's *Origin of Forms and Qualities.*

Eliot, John (1604), The Indian Grammar Begun. NF
Whiting, Samuel (1597), Abraham's Humble Intercession for
Sodom, and the Lord's Gracious Concessions in Answer
Thereunto. NF

Bunyan's *Grace Abounding to the
Chief of Sinners.*
Boileau's *Satires* (1666–1711).
Molière's *The Misanthropist.*

1667

Wilcox, Thomas (1622), A Choice Drop of Honey from the Rock
Christ; or, A Short Word of Advice to All Saints and Sinners.
NF

End of Anglo-Dutch War in America.
Milton's *Paradise Lost.*
Dryden's *Annus Mirabilis.*
Racine's *Andromache.*

1668

Pain, Philip (?), Daily Meditations. V
Penn, William (1644), The Sandy Foundation Shaken. NF
Shepard, Thomas (d. 1649), Wine for Gospel Wantons. NF
Vincent, Thomas (1634), God's Terrible Voice in the City of
London Wherein You Have Narration of the Two Dreadful
Judgements of Plague and Fire. NF

French established Jesuit mission in
Michigan.
John Dryden named poet laureate of
England.
Dryden's *Essay of Dramatick Poesie.*
La Fontaine's *Fables* (1668–94).

1669

Davenport, John (1597), A Catechism Printed for the Use of the
First Church in Boston. NF; Gods Call to His People to Turn
Unto Him. NF
Eliot, John (1604), The Indian Primer: or, The Way of Training
Up Our Indian Youth in the Good Knowledge of God. NF
Mather, Increase (1639), The Mystery of Israel's Salvation. NF
Morton, Nathaniel (1613), New Englands Memoriall. NF
Penn, William (1644), No Cross, No Crown. NF
Walley, Thomas (1616), Balm in Gilead to Heal Sions Wounds.
NF

Christopher Wren appointed surveyor
general of England.
Académie Royale de Musique founded,
in Paris.
William Prynne d.
Milton's *Latin Grammar.*
Ban on Molière's *Tartuffe* lifted.

1670

Denton, Daniel (fl. 1670–96), A Brief Description of New-York.
NF
Mather, Increase (1639), The Life and Death of . . . Richard
Mather. NF
Oxenbridge, John (1609), A Quickening Word for the Hastening
a Sluggish Soul to a Seasonable Answer to the Divine Call. NF
Penn, William (1644), The Great Cause of Liberty of
Conscience. NF
Stoughton, William (1631), New-Englands True Interest. NF
Wigglesworth, Michael (1631), Meat Out of the Eater. V

English established colony in
Charleston, S.C.
Hudson's Bay Co. chartered in
England.
Wren began rebuilding 51 London
churches.
Dryden's *The Conquest of Granada.*
Pascal's *Pensées.*
Molière's *The Would-Be Gentleman.*
Racine's *Bérénice.*

1671

Danforth, Samuel (1626), A Brief Recognition of New-Englands
Errand into the Wilderness. NF
Eliot, John (1604), A Brief Narrative of the Progress of the
Gospel Among the Indians in New England. NF; Indian
Dialogues for Their Instruction in That Great Service of Christ.
NF
Mitchel, Jonathan (1624), Nehemiah on the Wall in
Troublesome Times. NF

Milton's *Paradise Regained; Samson
Agonistes.*
Buckingham's *The Rehearsal.*
Wycherley's *Love in a Wood.*
Molière's *The Cheats of Scapin.*

1672

Allin, John (d. 1671), The Spouse of Christ Coming Out of Affliction, Leaning Upon Her Beloved. NF

Denys, Nicolas (1598), Description géographique et historique des costes de l'Amérique Septentrionale (repub. as The Description and Natural History of the Coasts of North America, 1908). NF

Eliot, John (1604), The Logick Primer. Some Logical Notions to Initiate the Indians in the Knowledge of the Rule of Reason. NF

Fitch, James (1622), Peace the End of the Perfect and Upright. NF

Josselyn, John (fl. 1638–75), New-Englands Rarities Discovered. NF

Penn, William (1644), Quakerism: A New Nick-Name for Old Christianity. NF

Third Anglo-Dutch War in America.
Comte de Frontenac became governor of New France (1672–82; 1689–98).
Royal African Co. founded (English slave trade).
Anne Bradstreet d.
Dryden's *Marriage à la Mode.*
Molière's *The Learned Ladies.*

1673

Dod, John (d. 1645), Old Mr. Dod's Sayings; or, A Poesie Gathered Out of Mr. Dod's Garden. NF

Mather, Increase (1639), Wo to Drunkards. NF

Mucklow, William (1631), The Spirit of the Hat: or, The Government of the Quakers Among Themselves. NF

Oakes, Urian (1631), New-England Pleaded With, and Pressed to Consider the Things Which Concern Her Peace. NF

Oxenbridge, John (1609), New-England Freemen Warned and Warmed. NF

Shepard, Thomas (1635), Eye-Salve, or A Watch-Word from Our Lord Iesus Christ Unto His Churches. NF

French expedition discovered the upper Mississippi.
Parliament passed the Test Act (hobbling Roman Catholics).
Racine's *Mithridates.*
Molière's *The Imaginary Invalid.*

1674

Fitch, James (1622), An Holy Connexion or a True Agreement. NF

Josselyn, John (fl. 1638–75), An Account of Two Voyages to New-England. NF

Mather, Increase (1639), Some Important Truths About Conversion. NF

Oakes, Urian (1631), The Unconquerable, All-Conquering & More-Than-Conquering Souldier. NF

Sewall, Samuel (1652), Diary (1674–77, 1685–1729; pub. 1878–82). NF

Torrey, Samuel (1632), An Exhortation unto Reformation. NF

Treaty of Westminister restored New York to the English.
Sir Edmund Andros appointed governor of New York.
Holy Roman Empire declared war on France.
John Milton d.
Boileau's *The Art of Poetry.*
Racine's *Iphigenia.*

1675

Mather, Increase (1639), The Times of Men Are in the Hand of God. NF; The Wicked Mans Portion. NF; A Discourse Concerning the Subject of Baptisme. NF; The First Principles of New-England Concerning the Subject of Baptisme & Communion of Churches. NF

King Philip's War (Iroquois Confederacy vs. New England Confederacy, 1675–76).
The City Mercury (London), 1675–81.
Dryden's *Aureng-Zebe.*
Wycherley's *The Country Wife.*
Otway's *Alcibiades.*
Traherne's *Christian Ethics.*

1676

Folger, Peter (1617), A Looking-Glass for the Times. V
Hubbard, William (c. 1621), The Happiness of a People in the Wisdome of their Rulers. NF
Mather, Increase (1639), A Brief History of the Warr with the Indians in New-England. NF
Tompson, Benjamin (1642), New Englands Crisis. Or a Brief Narrative, of New-Englands Lamentable Estate at Present . . . (repr. for the most part in New-Englands Tears for Her Present Miseries, 1676). V
Williams, Roger (c. 1603), George Fox Digg'd out of his Burrows. NF

Nathaniel Bacon's Rebellion (against Governor Berkeley) and Indian rampages, in Virginia.
Etherege's *The Man of Mode.*
Otway's *Don Carlos.*
Wycherley's *The Plain Dealer*

1677

Hooker, Samuel (1635), Righteousness Rained from Heaven. NF
Hubbard, William (c. 1621), A Narrative of the Troubles with the Indians in New-England. NF
Mather, Increase (1639), A Relation of the Troubles Which Have Hapned in New-England (incl. an account of John Mason, c. 1600–72). NF
Oakes, Urian (1631), An Elegie Upon the Death of the Reverend Mr. Thomas Shepard. V
Thacher, Thomas (1620), A Brief Rule to Guide the Common People of New-England How to Order Themselves and Theirs in the Small Pocks, or Measels (first medical treatise published in America). NF

English Quakers settled in New Jersey.
Dryden's *All for Love*
Behn's *The Rover* (1677–81).
Otway's *Titus and Berenice.*
Racine's *Phaedra.*
Spinoza's *Ethics* (posth.).

1678

Barclay, Robert (1648), An Apology for the True Christian Divinity, As the Same Is Held Forth and Preached by the People Called, in Scorn, Quakers (Eng. title; trans. from Latin). NF
Bradstreet, Anne (d. 1672), Several Poems Compiled with Great Variety of Wit and Learning. V
Eliot, John (1604), The Harmony of the Gospels. NF
Mather, Increase (1639), Pray for the Rising Generation. NF
Nowell, Samuel (1634), Abraham in Arms. NF
Thacher, Thomas (1620), A Fast of Gods Chusing. NF
Williams, Roger (c. 1603), An Answer to a Letter Sent from Mr. Coddington . . . . NF

Sieur Duluth claimed upper Mississippi for France.
The Popish Plot (false threat against Charles II's life).
A Pacquet of Advice from Rome (London), 1678–83.
Bunyan's *The Pilgrim's Progress.*
La Fayette's *The Princess of Cleves.*

1679

Bridge, William (d. 1670), A Word to the Aged. NF
Eliot, John (1604), A Brief Answer to a Small Book Written by John Norcot Against Infant-Baptisme. NF
Fitch, James (1622), The First Principles of the Doctrine of Christ. NF
Hardy, Samuel (1636), A Guide to Heaven, from the Word. NF
Mather, Increase (1639), A Call from Heaven to the Present and Succeeding Generations. NF
Richardson, John (1647), The Necessity of a Well Experienced Souldiery. NF

England proclaimed New Hampshire a separate colony.
Cavalier Parliament dissolved.
Habeas Corpus Act passed in England.
The Domestick Intelligence (London), 1679–80.
Burnet's *The History of the Reformation of the Church of England* (1679–1714).

1680

Hoar, Leonard (d. 1675), The Sting of Death and Death Unstung. NF
Hubbard, William (c. 1621), A General History of New England from the Discovery to MDCLXXX (pub. 1815). NF
Willard, Samuel (1640), The Duty of a People That Have Renewed Their Covenant With God. NF
Wilson, John (d. 1667), A Song of Deliverance for the Lasting Remembrance of God's Wonderful Works. NF

London established the "penny post."
Comédie Française founded.
Otway's *The Orphan*.
Rochester's *Poems on Several Occasions* (posth.).

1681

Corbet, John (d. 1680), Self-Employment in Secret. NF
Goodhue, Sarah (1641), Valedictory and Monitory-Writing. NF
Mather, Increase (1639), Heavens Alarm to the World. NF
Willard, Samuel (1640), Ne sutor ultra crepidam. Or Brief Animadversions Upon the New-England Anabaptists Late Fallacious Narrative. NF

Charles II granted William Penn a charter for his "holy experiment," Pennsylvania.
The Observator (London), 1681–87.
Dryden's *Absalom and Achitophel* (1681–82).
Marvell's *Miscellaneous Poems* (posth.).

1682

Mather, Cotton (1663), A Poem Dedicated to the Memory of . . . Urian Oakes. V
Oakes, Urian (d. 1681), The Soveraign Efficacy of Divine Providence. NF
Penn, William (1644), A Brief Account of the Province of Pennsylvania. NF
Rowlandson, Mary (d. 1678?), The Sovereignty & Goodness of God, Together with the Faithfulness of His Promises Displayed; Being a Narrative of the Captivity [by the Indians] and Restauration of Mrs. Mary Rowlandson. NF
Willard, Samuel (1640), Covenant-Keeping the Way to Blessedness. NF

Philadelphia became capital of Penn's Quaker colony.
Sieur de La Salle descended the Mississippi from Canada, took possession of the valley, named it Louisiana for Louis XIV.
Otway's *Venice Preserv'd*.
Bunyan's *The Holy War*.
Dryden's *Religio Laici; Mac Flecknoe*.

1683

Fitch, James (1622), An Explanation of the Solemn Advice Recommended by the Council in Connecticut Colony. NF
Hennepin, Louis (1640), Déscription de la Louisiane. NF
Keach, Benjamin (1640), Sion in Distress, or The Groans of the Protestant Church. V
Mather, Increase (1639), Kometographia; or, A Discourse Concerning Comets. NF
Torrey, Samuel (1632), A Plea for the Life of Dying Religion. NF
Willard, Samuel (1640), The High Esteem Which God Hath of the Death of His Saints. NF

Rye House Plot to assassinate Charles II.
Siege of Vienna by the Turks.
Henry Purcell's first chamber music published.
Oldham's *Poems and Translations*.
Otway's *The Atheist*.

1684

Gage, Thomas (d. 1656), The English-American: His Travail by Sea and Land. NF
Mather, Increase (1639), An Arrow Against Profane and Promiscuous Dancing. NF; The Doctrine of Divine Providence, Opened and Applyed. NF; An Essay for the Recording of Illustrious Providences (commonly known as Remarkable Providences). NF

England revoked charter of the Massachusetts Bay Co.
Pierre Corneille d.
Dryden's *Miscellany Poems* (with others).
Southerne's *The Disappointment*.

Pastorius, Francis Daniel (1651), Copia, eines von einem Sohn an seine Eltern aus America, abgelossenen Brieffes . . . . NF; Sichere Nachricht auss America, wegen der Landschafft Pennsylvania . . . . . NF

Penn, William (1644), Information and Direction to Such Persons as Are Inclined to America. NF

Stone, Samuel (d. 1663), A Short Catechism Drawn Out of the Word of God. NF

Willard, Samuel (1640), Mercy Magnified on a Penitent Prodigal. NF

1685

Adams, William (1650), God's Eye on the Contrite. NF

Budd, Thomas (?), Good Order Established in Pennsylvania and New Jersey. NF

Mather, Cotton (1663), An Elegy . . . on Nathanael Collins. V

Moodey, Joshua (1633), A Practical Discourse Concerning the Choice Benefit of Communion with God. NF

Wakeman, Samuel (1635), Sound Repentance the Right Way to Escape Deserved Ruine. NF

Death of Charles II; accession of James II.
La Salle explored east Texas.
Edict of Nantes revoked; French Huguenots settled in America.
Shakespeare's *Comedies, Histories, and Tragedies* [Fourth Folio].
Charles Cotton's trans. of Montaigne's *Essais*.

1686

Higginson, John (1616), Our Dying Saviour's Legacy of Peace. NF

Mather, Increase (1639), A Brief Discourse Concerning the Unlawfulness of the Common-Prayer-Worship. NF

Willard, Samuel (1640), A Brief Discourse of Justification. NF; Heavenly Merchandize: or, The Purchasing of Truth Recommended. NF

Sir Edmund Andros appointed vice-regent of the Dominion of New England.
Dryden's *To the Pious Memory of . . . Mrs. Anne Killigrew*.
John Ray's *Historia plantarum* (1686–1704).
Leibniz's *Discourse on Metaphysics* (pub. 1846).

1687   .

Cotton, John (1640), Poem Occasioned by the Death of . . . John Alden. V

Harris, Benjamin (fl. 1673–1716), The New England Primer (compiler). V, NF

Mather, Cotton (1663), Military Duties, Recommended to an Artillery Company. NF

Mather, Increase (1639), A Testimony Against Several Prophane and Superstitious Customs. NF

Penn, William (1644), The Excellent Privilege of Liberty and Property. NF

First Anglican church service in Boston.
Yamassee Indian revolt in Florida.
Charles II's Declaration of Liberty of Conscience (indulgence to Catholics and dissenters).
Newton's *Principia mathematica* (first English trans., 1727).
Dryden's *The Hind and the Panther*.

1688

Baxter, Richard (1615), The Lawfulness of Swearing, Laying the Hand on the Bible. NF

Leeds, Daniel (1652), The Temple of Wisdom For the Little World, in Two Parts (editor). NF

Mather, Increase (1639), De successu evangelii apud Indos in Nova-Anglia. NF; A Narrative of the Miseries of New England. NF

King's Chapel, Boston, first Anglican church in New England.
Whigs and Tories induced Prince William of Orange to seize the throne of England.
James II escaped to France.
Halifax's *The Character of a Trimmer*.

1689

Bulkeley, Gershom (1636), The People's Right to Election or Alteration of Government in Connecticut. NF

Byfield, Nathaniel (1653), An Account of the Late Revolution in New-England. NF; Seasonable Motives. To Our Duty and Allegiance. NF

Keith, George (1638?), The Presbyterian and Independent Visible Churches in New-England. NF

Mather, Cotton (1663), The Declaration of the Gentlemen, Merchants, and Inhabitants of Boston. NF; Memorable Providences, Relating to Witchcrafts and Possessions. NF

Mather, Increase (1639), A Brief Relation of the State of New England. NF

Wigglesworth, Michael (1631), Riddles Unriddled; or, Christian Paradoxes (pub. in the 4th edition of Meat Out of the Eater, 1689). V

Colonists in Boston rebelled against the Andros regime, forcing his recall.

Accession of William III and Mary II as joint sovereigns.

King William's War (French vs. English in America, 1689–97).

Peter I crowned czar of Russia.

Thomas Shadwell named poet laureate of England.

Locke's *Letter Concerning Toleration*.

1690

Lee, Samuel (1625), Contemplations on Mortality. NF

Mather, Cotton (1663), The Present State of New England. NF; The Way to Prosperity. NF; The Wonderful Works of God Commemorated. NF

Mather, Increase (1639), A Vindication of New England. Containing the First Petition of the Boston Episcopalians. NF

Monmouth, James Scott, Duke of (d. 1685), An Abridgment of the English Military Discipline (the first military work printed in America). NF

Pastorius, Francis Daniel (1651), Vier kleine doch ungemeine und sehr nützliche Tractätlein . . . . NF

French and Indians destroy English settlements in New York and Maine.

Publick Occurrences (Boston), first colonial newspaper, suppressed after one issue.

John Eliot d.

Dryden's *Amphitryon; Don Sebastian*.

Locke's *Essay Concerning Human Understanding; Two Treatises of Government*.

1691

Mather, Cotton (1663), Little Flocks Guarded Against Grievous Wolves. NF; Some Considerations on the Bills of Credit. NF; The Triumphs of the Reformed Religion, in America (repub. as The Life and Death of the Renown'd Mr. John Eliot, 1691). NF

Mather, Increase (1639), A Brief Account Concerning Several of the Agents of New-England. NF

Savage, Thomas (1608), An Account of the Late Action . . . Against the French at Canada. NF

Scottow, Joshua (1618), Old Mens Tears for Their Own Declensions. NF

Sewall, Samuel (1652), The Revolution in New England Justified (with Edward Rawson). NF

Willard, Samuel (1640), The Barren Fig Trees Doom. NF

Thomas Neale granted monopoly for a postal system in America.

Sir George Etherege d.

The Athenian Gazette (London), 1691–97.

Dryden's *King Arthur*.

1692

Frame, Richard (?), A Short Description of Pennsilvania. NF

Keith, George (1638?), The Christian Faith of the People of God, Called in Scorn, Quakers in Rhode Island. NF; False Judgments Reprehended (with Thomas Budd). NF

Lee, Samuel (1625), Great Day of Judgment. NF

Mather, Cotton (1663), Fair Weather. NF; A Midnight Cry. NF; Ornaments for the Daughters of Zion. NF; The Return of Several Ministers. NF; Political Fables (pub. 1868). NF

Sir Edmund Andros appointed governor of Virginia.

Salem witchcraft trials condemned 20 persons to death.

Nahum Tate named poet laureate of England.

Rymer's *A Short View of Tragedy*.

Locke's *Third Letter on Toleration*.

Willard, Samuel (1640), Some Miscellany Observations on Our Present Debates Respecting Witchcrafts. NF

L'Estrange's trans. of the *Fables of Aesop* (1692–99).

1693

Bayard, Nicholas (1664?), A Narrative of an Attempt Made by the French of Canada Upon the Mohaques Country (with Charles Lodowick). NF

Keith, George (1638?), Exhortation and Caution to Friends. NF

Mather, Cotton (1663), Winter-Meditations. NF; The Wonders of the Invisible World. NF

Mather, Increase (1639), Cases of Conscience Concerning Evil Spirits Personating Men. NF; The Great Blessing of Primitive Counsellours. NF

Penn, William (1644), Some Fruits of Solitude. NF; Fruits of a Father's Love. NF; An Essay Towards the Present and Future Peace of Europe. NF

Willard, Samuel (1640), The Doctrine of the Covenant of Redemption. NF

William Bradford established a printing press in New York.
Postal service between New York and Philadelphia.
College of William and Mary founded.
Locke's *Some Thoughts Concerning Education.*
Congreve's *The Double Dealer.*

1694

Makemie, Francis (c. 1658), An Answer to George Keith's Libel. NF

Mather, Cotton (1663), The Short History of New England. NF

Penn, William (1644), An Account of W. Penn's Travails in Holland and Germany. NF

Scottow, Joshua (1618), A Narrative of the Planting of the Massachusetts Colony Anno 1628, With the Lords Signal Presence the First Thirty Years. NF

Willard, Samuel (1640), The Character of a Good Ruler. NF

Death of Mary II.
Bank of England founded.
Dictionary of the French Academy published.
Voltaire b.
Southerne's *The Fatal Marriage.*
Racine's *Spiritual Hymns.*
Bashō's *The Narrow Road to the Deep North.*

1695

Mather, Cotton (1663), Durable Riches. NF; Johannes in Eremo. NF

Mather, Increase (1639), Solemn Advice to Young Men, Not to Walk in the Wayes of Their Heart. NF

Penn, William (1644), A Brief Account of the Rise and Progress of the People Called Quakers. NF

Torrey, Samuel (1632), Man's Extremity, God's Opportunity. NF

Licensing Act lapsed in England.
The Post Boy (London), 1695–1736.
Congreve's *Love for Love.*
Locke's *The Reasonableness of Christianity.*

1696

Mather, Cotton (1663), A Cry Against Oppression. NF; Things for a Distress'd People to Think Upon. NF

Mather, Increase (1639), Angelographia. NF

Penn, William (1644), The Harmony of Divine and Heavenly Doctrines. NF; Primitive Christianity Revived. NF

Thacher, Peter (1651), The Saints' Victory and Triumph Over Sin and Death. NF

Walter, Nehemiah (1663), Unfaithful Hearers Detected & Warned. NF

Plot to assassinate William III thwarted.
Cibber's *Love's Last Shift.*
Aubrey's *Miscellanies.*
Vanbrugh's *The Relapse.*
Dryden's *An Ode on the Death of Mr. Henry Purcell.*

1697

Blair, James (1655), The Present State of Virginia, and the College (with Henry Hartwell and Edward Chilton; pub. 1727). NF
Hennepin, Louis (1640), Nouvelle découverte. NF
Mather, Cotton (1663), Humiliations Follow'd with Deliverances. NF; Pietas in Patriam: The Life of His Excellency, Sir William Phips. NF
Pastorius, Francis Daniel (1651), Ein Send-Brieff offenhertziger Liebsbezeugung an die sogennante Pietisten in Hoch-Teutschland. NF; Henry Bernhard Koster, William Davis, Thomas Rutter and Thomas Bowyer: Four Boasting Disputers of this World Briefly Rebuked . . . . NF
Sewall, Samuel (1652), Phænomena quædam apocalyptica. NF

James Blair, Virginia clergyman, forced the second recall of Governor Andros to England.
Treaty of Ryswick ended King William's War.
Vanbrugh's *The Provok'd Wife.*
Dryden's *Alexander's Feast.*
Defoe's *An Essay Upon Projects.*
Bayle's *Historical and Critical Dictionary* (1697–1702).
Perrault's *Mother Goose Tales.*

1698

Bradford, William (1663), The Secretary's Guide; or, Young Man's Companion. NF
Hennepin, Louis (1640), Nouveau voyage. NF
Mather, Cotton (1663), Eleutheria; or, An Idea of the Reformation in England. NF; The Boston Ebenezer. Some Historical Remarks on the State of Boston. NF
Pastorius, Francis Daniel (1651), A New Primmer or Methodical Directions to Attain the True Spelling, Reading, and Writing of English. NF

Bay Psalm Book newly edited with music.
Whitehall Palace (London) burned.
Society for Promoting Christian Knowledge founded in London.
The London Spy, 1698–1709.
Collier's *A Short View of the Immorality and Profaneness of the English Stage.*
Defoe's *An Enquiry into the Occasional Conformity of Dissenters.*

1699

Keith, George (1638?), The Deism of William Penn and His Brethren. NF
Makemie, Francis (c. 1658), Truths in a True Light. NF
Mather, Cotton (1663), Decennium luctuosum. NF; A Family Well-Ordered. NF; La fe del Christiano. NF; Pillars of Salt. NF
Mather, Increase (1639), The Surest Way to the Greatest Honour. NF
Penn, William (1644), The Christian Quaker and His Divine Testimony. NF
Willard, Samuel (1640), The Man of War. NF
Williams, John (1664), Warning to the Unclean. A Discourse Preacht . . . at the Execution of Sarah Smith. NF

Old Biloxi first white settlement in Louisiana.
"Captain Kidd" arrested as a pirate in New England, returned to London, executed in 1701.
The History of the Works of the Learned (London), 1699–1712.
Farquhar's *The Constant Couple.*
Fénélon's *Telemachus.*

1700

Calef, Robert (1648), More Wonders of the Invisible World. NF
Leeds, Daniel (1652), A Challenge to Caleb Pusey and a Check to His Lyes and Forgeries. NF
Mather, Cotton (1663), The Everlasting Gospel. NF; Reasonable Religion. NF
Mather, Increase (1639), The Order of the Gospel. NF
Pastorius, Francis Daniel (1651), Umständige geographische Beschreibung der zu allerletzt erfundenen Provintz Pensylvaniae. NF
Pusey, Caleb (1650), Satan's Harbinger Encountered. NF
Sewall, Samuel (1652), The Selling of Joseph. NF
Stoddard, Solomon (1643), The Doctrine of Instituted Churches. NF

Catholic priests banned in Massachusetts.
John Dryden d.
James Thomson b.
Congreve's *The Way of the World.*
Dryden's *Fables, Ancient and Modern.*
Motteux's trans. of *Don Quixote* (1700–03).

Willard, Samuel (1640), Love's Pedigree. NF; Morality Not to
Be Relied on For Life. NF

1701

Leeds, Daniel (1652), A Cage of Unclean Birds. NF
Mather, Cotton (1663), Some Few Remarks upon a Scandalous
Book . . . by One Robert Calef (with others).
NF; Consolations. V
Penn, William (1644), The Governour's Speech to the Assembly,
at Philadelphia. NF
Rogers, John (1666), Death the Certain Wages of Sin to the
Impenitent. NF

Antoine de la Mothe Cadillac settled
French colony (near Detroit).
Yale College founded.
War of the Spanish Succession
(England vs. France, Spain).
Collier's *Historical, Geographical,
Genealogical, and Poetical
Dictionary* (1701–21).

1702

Danforth, John (1660), The Right Christian Temper in Every
Condition. NF
Hale, John (1636), A Modest Enquiry into the Nature of
Witchcraft. NF
Mather, Cotton (1663), Christianus per ignem. NF; Magnalia
Christi Americana; or, The Ecclesiastical History of New-
England. NF
Mather, Increase (1639), The Excellency of a Publick Spirit.
NF; Ichabod. NF
Pusey, Caleb (1650), Daniel Leeds, Justly Rebuked for Abusing
William Penn. NF

Death of William III; accession of
Anne.
Queen Anne's War (1702–13); English
troops burned St. Augustine.
The Daily Courant (London), 1702–35,
first English daily newspaper.
Defoe's *The Shortest Way with the
Dissenters.*
Clarendon's *The History of the
Rebellion and Civil Wars in England.*

1703

Keith, George (1638?), The Spirit of Railing Shimei and of
Baal's Four Hundred Lying Prophets Entered into Caleb Pusey
and His Quaker Brethren in Pennsylvania, Who Approve Him.
NF
Lahontan, Louis-Armand, Baron de (1666), Nouveaux
voyages. NF
Leeds, Daniel (1652), The Rebuker Rebuked in a Brief Answer
to Caleb Pusey. NF
Mather, Cotton (1663), Meat Out of the Eater: or, Funeral
Discourses Occasioned by the Death of Several Relatives. NF
Pusey, Caleb (1650), George Keith Once More Brought to the
Test. NF
Stoddard, Solomon (1643), God's Frown in the Death of Usefull
Men. NF

First professional actors in the colonies,
in Charleston, S.C.
Samuel Pepys d.
Defoe's *A Hymn to the Pillory.*
Ward's *The London Spy* (coll. edition).
Rowe's *The Fair Penitent* (adap.).

1704

Knight, Sarah Kemble (1666), The Journal of Madam Knight
(pub. 1825). NF
Leeds, Daniel (1652), A Little Olive Leaf Put in the Mouth of
That (So Called) Noah's Dove. NF
Mather, Cotton (1663), Le vrai patron des saines paroles.
NF; The Nets of Salvation. NF
Pusey, Caleb (1650), False News from Gath Rejected. NF

French and Indians sacked Deerfield,
Mass.
English attacked Port Royal, Nova
Scotia.
The Boston News-Letter, 1704–76, first
successful American newspaper.
Swift's *A Tale of a Tub; The Battle of
the Books.*
Newton's *Optiks.*

1705

Beverley, Robert (c. 1673), The History and Present State of
Virginia (enl. edition, 1722). NF
Dunton, John (1659), Life and Errors of John Dunton. NF
Mather, Cotton (1663), A Faithful Man Described and
Rewarded. NF
Mather, Increase (1639), A Letter About the Present State of
Christianity, Among the Christianized Indians of New-England
(with others). NF
Pusey, Caleb (1650), The Bomb Search'd and Found Stuff'd
with False Ingredients. NF

John Vanbrugh commissioned to design
Blenheim Palace.
Michael Wigglesworth d.
Ward's *Hudibras Redivivus* (1705–07).
Halley's *Astronomiae cometicae
synopsis*.
Vanbrugh's *The Confederacy*.

1706

Keith, George (1638?), A Journal of Travels from New-
Hampshire to Caratuck. NF
Mather, Cotton (1663), The Negro Christianized. NF; Free-
Grace, Maintained and Improved. NF
Mather, Increase (1639), A Discourse Concerning Earthquakes.
NF
Pemberton, Ebenezer (1671), Ill-Boding Symptoms on a
Professing People. NF
Willard, Samuel (1640), The Just Man's Prerogative. NF

First presbytery established in America,
in Philadelphia.
England seized the Spanish
Netherlands.
Benjamin Franklin b.
Farquhar's *The Recruiting Officer*.
Rowe's *Ulysses*.
Defoe's *A True Relation of the
Apparition of One Mrs. Veal*.

1707

Colman, Benjamin (1673), The Government and Improvement
of Mirth. NF; A Poem on Elijah's Translation. V
Mather, Cotton (1663), A Memorial of the Present Deplorable
State of New England. NF; A Treacle Fetch'd Out of a Viper.
NF
Moody, Samuel (1676), The Vain Youth Summoned to Appear at
Christ's Bar. NF
Walter, Nehemiah (1663), The Body of Death Anatomized. NF
Williams, John (1664), The Redeemed Captive, Returning to
Zion (with Cotton Mather). NF
Williams, William (1665), The Danger of Not Reforming Known
Evils. NF

Union of Scotland and England as
Great Britain.
English attacked French in Nova Scotia.
The Muses Mercury (London) 1707–
08.
Farquhar's *The Beaux' Stratagem*.
Watts's *Hymns and Spiritual Songs*.
Lesage's *The Devil on Two Sticks*.

1708

Cook, Ebenezer (fl. 1708–32), The Sot-Weed Factor. V
Doolittle, Thomas (1632?), A Treatise Concerning the Lord's
Supper. NF
Mather, Cotton (1663), Corderius Americanus: An Essay upon
the Good Education of Children. NF; The Deplorable State of
New-England. NF; Winthropi justa. NF
Oldmixon, John (1673), The British Empire in America. NF
Stoddard, Solomon (1643), The Inexcusableness of Neglecting
the Worship of God, Under a Pretense of Being in an
Unconverted Condition. NF
Tompson, Benjamin (1642), The Grammarian's Funeral. V

Saybrook Platform accepted by
Connecticut Congregationalists.
Collier's *The Ecclesiastical History of
Great Britain* (1708–14).
Swift's *Predictions for the Year 1708*.
Regnard's *The Residuary Legatee*.

1709

Byrd, William (1674), The Secret Diary . . . (1709–12, 1717–
21, 1739–41; pub. 1941, 1942, 1958). NF

Quakers established first mental
hospital, in Philadelphia.

Cheever, Ezekiel (d. 1708), A Short Introduction to the Latin Tongue. NF
Lawson, John (d. 1711), A New Voyage to Carolina (repub. as The History of Carolina, 1714, 1718). NF
Mayhew, Experience (1673), Massachusee Psalter. V
Rawson, Grindall (1659), The Necessity of a Speedy and Thorough Reformation. NF
Stoddard, Solomon (1643), An Appeal to the Learned. NF

The Tatler (London), 1709–11.
Swift's A Project for the Advancement of Religion.
Prior's Poems on Several Occasions.
Defoe's History of the Union of Great Britain.
Rowe's edition of Shakespeare's Works.

1710

Danforth, John (1660), The Blackness of Sins Against Light. NF
Mather, Cotton (1663), Theopolis Americana. NF; Nehemiah. A Brief Essay on Divine Consolations. NF; Bonifacius (commonly known as Essays To Do Good). NF
Moody, Samuel (1676), The Gospel Way of Escaping the Doleful State of the Damned. NF
Wadsworth, Benjamin (1670), An Essay To Do Good: By a Dissuasive from Tavern-H[a]unting and Excessive Drinking. NF
Wise, John (1652), The Churches Quarrel Espoused. NF

English took Port Royal from the French.
First English copyright laws.
The Examiner (London), 1710–14.
Berkeley's Principles of Human Knowledge.
Swift's A Meditation upon a Broomstick.
Demaizeaux's edition of Bayle's Dictionary.
Leibniz's Theodicy.

1711

Colman, Benjamin (1673), The Duty and Honour of Aged Women. NF
Kino, Eusebio Francisco (d. 1711), Favores Celestiales (trans. and pub. 1919). NF
Mather, Increase (1639), Meditations on the Glory of the Heavenly World. NF
Shepard, Jeremiah (1648), A Sort of Believers Never Saved. NF

Tuscorora War (N.C. settlers vs. Indians), 1711–13.
St. Paul's Cathedral (London) rebuilt.
The Spectator (London), 1711–12, 1714.
Pope's An Essay on Criticism.
Shaftesbury's Characteristics.
Swift's Miscellanies.
Crébillon's Rhadamiste and Zenobia.

1712

Cheever, Samuel (1639), Gods Sovereign Government Among the Nations. NF
Mather, Cotton (1663), Curiosa Americana (1712–24). NF; Thoughts for the Day of Rain. NF; Grata brevitas. NF; The Young Man Spoken To. NF
Maule, Thomas (1645), Tribute to Caesar, How Paid by the Best Christians, and To What Purpose. NF
Penn, William (1644), Gospel-Times, or Oaths Forbidden Under the Gospel (with others). NF
Wadsworth, Benjamin (1670), Fraud and Injustice Detected and Condemned. NF

Negro slave rebellion in New York City.
Jean-Jacques Rousseau b.
Arbuthnot's The History of John Bull.
Swift's Proposals for Correcting . . . the English Tongue.
Pope's The Rape of the Lock (enl. edition, 1714).

1713

Mather, Cotton (1663), The Curbed Sinner. NF; Golgotha. A Lively Description of Death. NF; Nepenthes Evangelicum. NF
Morgan, Joseph (1671), The Portsmouth Disputation Examined. NF
Sewall, Samuel (1652), Proposals Touching the Accomplishment of Prophecies. NF
Stoddard, Solomon (1643), The Efficacy of the Fear of Hell to Restrain Men from Sin. NF

Treaty of Utrecht ended Queen Anne's War.
Scriblerus Club (Pope, Swift, Congreve, et al.).
The Guardian (London), 1713.
The Englishman (London), 1713–15.
Addison's Cato.
Pope's Windsor Forest.

Thacher, Peter (1651), The Perpetual Covenant. NF
Wise, John (1652), The Churches Quarrel Espoused, or a Reply in Satyre, to Certain Proposals Made, in Answer to This Question. NF

1714

Danforth, John (1660), A Poem, Upon the Much Honoured . . . Mrs. Maria Mather. V
Dudley, Paul (1675), Objections to the Bank of Credit Lately Projected at Boston. NF
Hunter, Robert (fl. 1710–19), Androboros. A Biographical Farce (the first pub. American play; prod.?). D
Mather, Cotton (1663), Duodecennium luctuosum. NF; Insanabilia; or, An Essay Upon Incurables. NF
Stoddard, Solomon (1643), A Guide to Christ. NF

Death of Anne; accession of George I.
End of War of the Spanish Succession.
Mandeville's *The Fable of the Bees.*
Rowe's *The Tragedy of Jane Shore.*
Gay's *The Shepherd's Week.*

1715

Colman, Benjamin (1673), The Blessing and Honour of Fruitful Mothers. NF
Mather, Cotton (1662), Durable Riches. NF; A Monitor for Communicants. NF; Shaking Dispensations. NF
Moody, Samuel (1676), The Debtor's Monitor, Directory and Comforter. NF
Shepard, Jeremiah (1648), God's Conduct of His Church Through the Wilderness. NF

Yamassee Indians massacred settlers in South Carolina.
First Jacobite rebellion in Scotland.
Death of Louis XIV; accession of Louis XV.
Nicholas Rowe named poet laureate of England.
Pope's trans. of *The Iliad* (1715–20).
Lesage's *Gil Blas* (1715–35).

1716

Church, Thomas (1673), Entertaining Passages Relating to Philip's War Which Began in the Month of June, 1675. NF
Colman, Benjamin (1673), The Honour and Happiness of the Vertuous Woman. NF
Mather, Cotton (1663), Fair Dealing. NF
Mather, Increase (1639), A Disquisition Concerning Ecclesiastical Councils. NF
Wadsworth, Benjamin (1670), Rulers Feeding, and Guiding Their People, with Integrity and Skilfulness. NF

British Septennial Act assured dominance of the Whig Party.
Banque Générale, first in France, founded.
William Wycherley d.
Gottfried Wilhelm von Leibniz d.
The Historical Register (London), 1716–38.
Mercurius Politicus (London), 1716–20.
Gay's *Trivia.*

1717

Colman, Benjamin (1673), A Holy Walk with God. NF
Cutler, Timothy (1684), The Firm Union of a People Represented. NF
Field, John (1652), The Christianity of the People, Called Quakers, Asserted by George Keith. NF
Mather, Cotton (1663), Febrifugium. An Essay for the Cure of Ungoverned Anger. NF
Sewall, Joseph (1688), Precious Treasure in Earthen Vessels. NF
Wadsworth, Benjamin (1670), The Bonds of Baptism. NF
Wise, John (1652), A Vindication of the Government of New-England Churches. NF

Bangorian Controversy (Anglican Church on succession of George I).
John Law's Mississippi Co. established trade rights in Louisiana; failed in 1720.
Horace Walpole b.
Pope's *Collected Works.*
Garth's edition of Ovid's *Metamorphoses.*

1718

Colman, Benjamin (1673), The Religious Regards We Owe to Our Country. NF
Foxcroft, Thomas (1697), A Practical Discourse Relating to the Gospel Ministry. NF
Keimer, Samuel (1688), A Brand Plucked from the Burning. NF; A Search After Religion. NF
Mather, Cotton (1663), Psalterium Americanum. V
Mather, Increase (1639), Practical Truths, Plainly Delivered. NF
Sewall, Joseph (1688), A Caveat Against Covetousness. NF
Wadsworth, Benjamin (1670), Fervent Zeal Against Flagrant Wickedness. NF

New Orleans founded.
Quadruple Alliance (England, France, Netherlands, Holy Roman Empire), against Spain.
Laurence Eusden named poet laureate of England.
Prior's *Poems on Several Occasions.*
Voltaire's *Oedipus.*
Fénélon's *Dialogues on Eloquence.*

1719

Colman, Benjamin (1673), Some Reasons and Arguments Offered to the Good People of Boston, and Adjacent Places for the Setting Up of Markets in Boston. NF
Hodder, James (?), Hodder's Arithmetic; or, That Necessary Art Made Most Easy (first pub. in London, 1661). NF
Mather, Cotton (1663), Concio ad populum. NF; Mirabilia Dei. NF
Stoddard, Solomon (1643), A Treatise Concerning the Nature of Saving Conversion. NF
Wadsworth, Benjamin (1670), Vicious Courses, Procuring Poverty. NF

French Mississippi Co. began settlements in America.
The Boston Gazette, 1719–98.
The American Weekly Mercury (Phila.), 1719–46.
The Daily Post (London), 1719–46?
Defoe's *Robinson Crusoe.*

1720

Blair, Thomas (?), Some Short and Easy Rules, Teaching the Pronunciation of the French Language. NF
Colman, Benjamin (1673), A Vindication of the New-North-Church in Boston, From Several Falsehoods. NF
Homes, William (1663), A Discourse Concerning the Publick Reading of the Holy Scriptures. NF
Mather, Cotton (1663), The Right Way to Shake Off a Viper. NF
Mather, Increase (1639), A Seasonable Testimony to Good Order in the Churches of the Faithful. NF
Neal, Daniel (1678), A History of New England . . . to . . . 1700. NF
Rogers, John (1648), The Book of the Revelation of Jesus Christ. NF
Walter, Thomas (1696), A Choice Dialogue Between John Faustus, a Conjuror, and Jack Tory, His Friend. NF

French Canadian settlers in Illinois; Spanish in Texas.
The South Sea Bubble (English investment mania).
Defoe's *Captain Singleton; Memoirs of a Cavalier.*
Collins's *The Baronettage of England.*
Prior's *The Conversation.*
Leibniz's *Monadology* (posth.).

1721

Boylston, Zabdiel (1680), Some Account of What Is Said of Inoculating or Transplanting the Small Pox. NF
Dummer, Jeremiah (c. 1679), Defence of the New England Charters. NF
Mather, Cotton (1663), The Accomplished Singer. NF; The Christian Philosopher. NF; India Christiana. NF; Sentiments on the Small Pox Inoculated. NF
Mather, Increase (1639), Several Reasons Proving that Inoculating . . . the Small Pox Is a Lawful Practice. NF
Rawle, Francis (1660), Some Remedies Proposed for the Restoring the Sunk Credit of the Province of Pennsylvania. NF

First smallpox inoculations, in Boston.
Sir Robert Walpole became first prime minister of England (1721–42).
Tobias Smollett b.
The New England Courant (Boston), 1721–26.
Swift's *A Letter to a Young Gentleman, Lately Entered into Holy Orders.*
Bailey's *Universal Etymological English Dictionary.*
Montesquieu's *Persian Letters.*

Sewall, Samuel (1652), A Memorial Relating to the Kennebeck Indians. NF
Walter, Thomas (1696), The Grounds and Rules of Musick Explained; or, An Introduction to the Art of Singing by Note. NF
Wise, John (1652), A Word of Comfort to a Melancholy Country. NF

1722

Blair, James (1655), Upon Our Saviour's Divine Sermon on the Mount. NF
Franklin, Benjamin (1706), The Dogood Papers. NF
Mather, Cotton (1663), An Account . . . of the Inoculating the Small-Pox. NF; The Angel of Bethesda. NF
Mayhew, Experience (1673), Observations on the Indian Language (pub. 1884). NF
Stoddard, Solomon (1643), An Answer to Some Cases of Conscience Respecting the Country. NF
Symmes, Thomas (1678), A Discourse Concerning Prejudice in Matters of Religion. NF
Wadsworth, Benjamin (1670), True Piety the Best Policy for Times of War. NF
Walter, Thomas (1696), The Sweet Psalmist of Israel. V

Iroquois Confederation of Six Nations signed treaty with Virginia settlers.
Samuel Adams b.
Defoe's *Moll Flanders; Colonel Jack; A Journal of the Plague Year, 1665.*
Steele's *The Conscious Lovers.*
Parnell's *Poems on Several Occasions.*

1723

Barclay, Robert (d. 1690), The Antient Testimony of the People Called Quakers, Reviv'd. NF
Colman, Benjamin (1673), God Deals with Us as Rational Creatures. NF; David's Dying Charge to the Rulers and People of Israel. NF
Keimer, Samuel (1688), Elegy on the Much Lamented Death of . . . Aquila Rose. V
Knapp, Francis (1672), Gloria Britannorum; or, The British Worthies (attrib.). V
Stoddard, Solomon (1643), Question Whether God Is Not Angry with the Country for Doing So Little Towards the Conversion of the Indians? NF
Symmes, Thomas (1678), Utile Dulci. Or, A Joco-Serious Dialogue, Concerning Regular Singing. NF

Boston built Christ Church (Old North Church), established a police force.
Johann Sebastian Bach's *St. John Passion,* in Leipzig.
Increase Mather d.
Voltaire's *The League.*

1724

Dickinson, Jonathan (1688), A Defence of Presbyterian Ordination. NF
Foxcroft, Thomas (1697), God's Face Set Against an Incorrigible People. NF
Jones, Hugh (c. 1670), An Accidence to the English Tongue. NF; The Present State of Virginia. NF
Mather, Cotton (1663), Parentator. Memoirs of Remarkables in the Life and Death of . . . Dr. Increase Mather. NF; Tela Prævisa. A Short Essay on Troubles To Be Look'd For. NF

First permanent white settlement in Vermont.
Defoe's *Roxanna.*
Swift's *The Drapier's Letters* (1724–35).
Bishop Burnet's *History of My Own Times* (1724–34; posth.).

1725

Ames, Nathaniel (1708), An Astronomical Diary, or An Almanack (annually, 1725–64). NF

First church of Colored Baptists, in Williamsbsburg, Va.

Dwight, Josiah (1671), An Essay to Silence the Outcry That Has Been Made in Some Places Against Regular Singing. NF

Franklin, Benjamin (1706), A Dissertation on Liberty and Necessity, Pleasure and Pain. NF

Gay, Ebenezer (1696), Ministers Are Men of Like Passions with Others. NF

Mather, Cotton (1663), Une grande voix du ciel à la France. NF; Christodulus. A Good Reward of a Good Servant. NF

Mayhew, Experience (1673), All Mankind, By Nature, Equally Under Sin. NF

Rawle, Francis (c. 1662), Ways and Means for the Inhabitants of Delaware to Become Rich. NF

Symmes, Thomas (1678), Historical Memoirs of the Late Fight at Piggwacket. NF

Wolcott, Roger (1679), Poetical Meditations, Being the Improvement of Some Vacant Hours. V

Friction between French and British in Maine.
The New York Gazette, 1725–44, first New York City newspaper.
Pope's trans. of *The Odyssey* (1725–26); edition of Shakespeare's *Works.*

1726

Colman, Benjamin (1673), It Is a Fearful Thing To Fall into the Hands of the Living God. A Sermon Preached to Some Miserable Pirates. NF

Franklin, Benjamin (1706), Journal of a Voyage from London to Philadelphia. NF

Greenwood, Isaac (1702), An Experimental Course on Mechanical Philosophy. NF

Mather, Cotton (1663), Manuductio ad ministerium. NF; Ratio disciplinæ fratrum Nov-Anglorum. NF; The Vial Poured Out of the Sea. NF

Penhallow, Samuel (1665), The History of the Wars of New-England with the Eastern Indians. NF

Willard, Samuel (d. 1707), A Compleat Body of Divinity. NF

Voltaire banished from France.
Sir John Vanbrugh d.
The Craftsman (London), 1726–50?
Swift's *Gulliver's Travels.*
Theobald's *Shakespeare Restored.*
William Law's *The Absolute Unlawfulness of the Stage Entertainment.*
Dennis's *The Stage Defended.*

1727

Byles, Mather (1707), A Poem on the Death of His Late Majesty King George, of Glorious Memory, and the Accession of Our Present Sovereign, King George II, to the British Throne. V

Colden, Cadwallader (1688), The History of the Five Indian Nations Depending on the Province of New-York in America. NF

Hoadly, Benjamin (1676), An Enquiry into the Reasons of the Conduct of Great Britain, with Relation to the State of Affairs in Europe. NF

Mather, Cotton (1663), Agricola, or The Religious Husbandman. NF; Boanerges. NF; Ignorantia scientifica. NF

Mayhew, Experience (1673), Indian Converts. NF

Prince, Thomas (1687), Earthquakes Are the Works of God and Tokens of His Just Displeasure. NF; A Sermon on the Sorrowful Occasion of the Death of His Late Majesty King George. NF

Death of George I; accession of George II.
Sir Isaac Newton d.
The Maryland Gazette (Annapolis), 1727–34; 1745–1839.
The New England Weekly Journal (Boston), 1727–41.
Gay's *Fables* (1727–38).
Defoe's *Essay on the History and Reality of Apparitions.*
Pope, Swift, Arbuthnot's *Miscellanies.*

1728

Appleton, Nathaniel (1693), The Wisdom of God in the Redemption of Fallen Man. NF

Burgess, Daniel (d. 1713), The Sure Way to Wealth, or An

John Bartram planted first botanical gardens, near Philadelphia.
Cotton Mather d.

Infallible Directory to Get and Keep Riches, Even While Taxes
Rise and Trades Sink. NF

Chauncey, Nathaniel (1681), Regular Singing Defended. NF

Cotton, John (1693), God's Awful Determination Against a
People That Will Not Obey His Voice. NF

Franklin, Benjamin (1706), Articles of Belief and Acts of
Religion. NF; Rules for a Club. NF

Gee, Joshua (1698), Israel's Mourning for Aaron's Death. A
Sermon Preached . . . After the Death of . . . Cotton
Mather. NF

Lewis, Richard (1699?), Muscipula (trans. of Edward
Holdsworth's Latin satire on the Welsh). V

Sewel, William (d. 1720), The History of the Rise, Increase, and
Progress of the Christian People Called Quakers. NF

The Pennsylvania Gazette (Phila.),
1728–1815.
Gay's *The Beggar's Opera.*
Pope's *The Dunciad* (pub. anon.).
Chambers's *Cyclopaedia.*
Voltaire's *The Henriad.*

1729

Byles, Mather (1707), The Character of the Perfect and Upright
Man. NF

Byrd, William (1674), History of the Dividing Line Betwixt
Virginia and North Carolina (pub. 1841). NF

Franklin, Benjamin (1706), Busybody Papers. NF; A Modest
Enquiry into the Nature and Necessity of a Paper Currency. NF

Gee, Joshua (1698), The Strait Gate and the Narrow Way. NF

Mather, Samuel (1706), The Life of the Very Reverend and
Learned Cotton Mather. NF

Baltimore founded.
'John and Charles Wesley formed a
religious society at Oxford.
Edward Taylor d.
Gay's *Polly.*
Swift's *A Modest Proposal.*
Samber's trans. of Perrault's *Mother
Goose Tales.*

1730

Aston, Anthony (fl. 1703–30), The Fool's Opera; or, The Taste
of the Age. D

Cook, Ebenezer (fl. 1708), Sotweed Redivivus: Or the Planter's
Looking-Glass (attrib.). V

Douglass, William (1691?), A Dissertation Concerning
Inoculation of the Small-Pox. NF

Foxcroft, Thomas (1697), Observations, Historical and Practical,
on the Rise and Primitive State of New-England. NF

Franklin, Benjamin (1706), A Dialogue Between Philocles and
Horatio. NF; A Second Dialogue . . . . NF; A Witch Trial at
Mount Holly. NF

Gay, Ebenezer (1696), The Duty of People to Pray For and
Praise Their Rulers. NF

Mollineux, Mary Southworth (1651?), Fruits of Retirement. V

Smith, Josiah (1704), Solomon's Caution Against the Cup. NF

Whittelsey, Samuel (1686), The Regards Due to Such As Have
Been Eminent and Useful. NF

French constructed a fort on Lake
Champlain, N.Y.
Community of Dunkards founded at
Ephrata, Penna.
Colley Cibber named poet laureate of
England.
The Grub Street Journal (London),
1730–37.
The Daily Advertiser (London), 1730–
1808?
James Thomson's *The Seasons* (rev.
edition, 1744).
Fielding's *Tom Thumb, a Tragedy;
Rape Upon Rape.*

1731

Catesby, Mark (c. 1679), The Natural History of Carolina,
Florida, and the Bahama Islands (1731–43). NF

Chauncy, Charles (1705), Man's Life Considered Under the
Similitude of a Vapour. NF

Cook, Ebenezer (fl. 1708–32), ''The History of Colonel
Nathaniel Bacon's Rebellion in Virginia'' (attrib.; pub. in The
Maryland Muse). V

Dudley, Paul (1675), An Essay on the Merchandize of Slaves and
Souls of Men. NF

Thomas Kean and Walter Murray
produced plays in Philadelphia.
Benjamin Franklin founded first
circulating library, in Philadelphia.
Treaty of Vienna (England and Holy
Roman Empire).
The Weekly Rehearsal (Boston), 1731–
35.
The Gentleman's Magazine (London),
1731–1907.

Edwards, Jonathan (1703), God Glorified in the Work of
Redemption. . . . NF
Franklin, Benjamin (1706), An Apology for Printers. NF
Prince, Thomas (1687), The Vade Mecum for America; or, A
Companion for Traders and Travellers. NF
Seccomb, John (1708), "Father Abbey's Will." V; "A Letter of
Courtship." V

Pope's *Moral Essays* (1731–35).
Lillo's *The London Merchant.*
Abbé Prévost's *Manon Lescaut.*
Voltaire's *The History of Charles XII.*

1732

Byles, Mather (1707), A Discourse on the Present Vileness of the
Body, and Its Future Glorious Change by Christ. NF
Byrd, William (1674), A Progress to the Mines (pub. 1841). NF
Cooper, William (1694), Divine Teaching To Be Sought. NF
Dickinson, Jonathan (1688), The Reasonableness of
Christianity. NF
Lewis, Richard (1699?), "A Description of Spring." V;
"Carmen Saeculare." V; "A Rhapsody" (attrib.). V
Neal, Daniel (1678), A History of the Puritans (4 vols., 1732–
38). NF
Oglethorpe, James Edward (1696), A New and Accurate
Account of the Provinces of South-Carolina and Georgia. NF

English settlers arrived in Georgia.
The New Theatre opened in New York
City.
The Covent Garden Theatre opened in
London.
George Washington b.
The London Magazine, 1732–85.
Neal's *The History of the Puritans*
(1732–38).
Berkeley's *Alciphron, or the Minute
Philosopher.*
Voltaire's *Zaïre.*

1733

Appleton, Nathaniel (1693), The Origin of War. NF
Brattle, William (1706), Sundry Rules and Regulations for
Drawing Up a Regiment. NF
Byrd, William (1674), A Journey to the Land of Eden (pub.
1841). NF
Checkley, Samuel (1696), Murder a Great and Crying Sin. NF
Dickinson, Jonathan (1688), The Scripture-Bishop Vindicated.
NF
Franklin, Benjamin (1706), Poor Richard's Almanack (annually,
1733–58). NF
Morgan, Joseph (1671), The Temporal Interest of North
America. NF
Wigglesworth, Samuel (1689), An Essay for Reviving Religion.
NF

Molasses Act (duties on imports from
non-British Caribbean islands).
James Edward Oglethorpe founded
Savannah.
The New York Weekly Journal, 1733–
52.
Pope's *Essay on Man* (1733–34).

1734

Anderson, James (1680), The Constitutions of the Free-Masons.
NF
Barnard, John (1681), The Throne Established by
Righteousness. NF
Cotton, John (1693), Ministers of the Gospel Should Speak, Not
as Pleasing Men, But God Who Tries Their Heart. NF
Edwards, Jonathan (1703), A Divine and Supernatural Light.
NF
Greenwood, Isaac (1702), Prospectus of Explanatory Lectures on
the Orrery . . . and Other Machines . . . Made Use of by
Astronomers. NF
Monis, Judah (1683), Proposals for Printing by Subscription a
Hebrew Grammar. NF
Stone, Nathanael (1667), Serious Reflections on Late Public
Concernments in These Churches. NF

Jonathan Edwards led "The Great
Awakening" (evangelical religious
revival).
French settled on the Wabash River in
Indiana.
Pope's *An Epistle to Dr. Arbuthnot.*
Theobald's edition of *The Plays of
Shakespeare.*
Montesquieu's *Grandeur and
Decadence of the Romans.*

1735

Adams, Eliphalet (1677), God Sometimes Answers His People by Terrible Things in Righteousness. NF

Brattle, William (d. 1717), Compendium logicæ secundum principia D. Renati Cartesii. NF

Colman, Benjamin (1673), Reliquiæ Turellæ, et lachrymæ paternæ. NF

Franklin, Benjamin (1706), Essay on Human Vanity (attrib.). NF

Gregory, Francis (d. 1707), Nomenclatura brevis. Anglo-Latino in usum scholarum. NF

Logan, James (1674), Cato's Moral Distichs (translator). V

Monis, Judah (1683), Dickdook Leshon Gnebreet. A Grammar of the Hebrew Tongue. NF

Tennent, Gilbert (1703), A Solemn Warning to the Secure World from the God of Terrible Majesty. NF

Wigglesworth, Edward (1693), A Seasonable Caveat Against Believing Every Spirit. NF

John Peter Zenger (ed. *New York Weekly Journal*) tried for seditious libel and acquitted.

John Wesley at Methodist mission in Georgia.

Moravian (United Brethren) community established in Savannah.

The Boston Evening Post, 1735–75.

The Daily Gazetteer (London), 1735–48.

Lillo's *The Christian Hero.*

Collins's *The Peerage of England.*

Marivaux's *The Upstart Peasant* (1735–36).

1736

Byles, Mather (1707), To His Excellency Governeur Belcher, on the Death of His Lady. An Epistle. V

Dawson, William (1704), Poems on Several Occasions. V

Douglass, William (c. 1691), The Practical History of a New Epidemical Eruptive Military Fever. NF

Mason, John (d. 1672?), A Brief History of the Pequot War . . . in 1637. NF

Prince, Thomas (1687), A Chronological History of New England in the Form of Annals. NF

Zenger, John Peter (1697), A Brief Narrative of the Case and Tryal of John Peter Zenger, Printer of the New-York Weekly Journal. NF

New England rum trade hobbled by Molasses Act.

The Virginia Gazette (Williamsburg), 1736–73.

Fielding's *Pasquin.*

Lillo's *The Fatal Curiosity.*

Warburton's *The Alliance Between Church and State.*

Voltaire's *Alzire.*

1737

Edwards, Jonathan (1703), A Faithful Narrative of the Surprising Work of God. NF

Holyoke, Edward (1689), Obedience and Submission to the Pastoral Watch and Rule Over the Church of Christ. NF

Wesley, John (1703) and **Charles Wesley** (1707), A Collection of Psalms and Hymns. V

Williams, William (1688), Martial Wisdom Recommended. NF

William Byrd laid out plans for Richmond, Va.

Copper money issued in Connecticut.

Fielding's *The Historical Register for the Year 1736.*

1738

Adams, Eliphalet (1677), A Sermon Preached on the Occasion of the Execution of Katherine Garret, an Indian-Servant (Who Was Condemned for the Murder of Her Spurious Child). NF

Byles, Mather (1707), On the Death of the Queen. V

Dickinson, Jonathan (1688), The Reasonableness of Nonconformity to the Church of England. NF

Edwards, Jonathan (1703), Discourses on Various Important Subjects. NF; Charity and Its Fruits. NF

George Whitefield's first visit to American Methodists.

Treaty of Vienna (ended War of the Polish Succession).

Johnson's *London.*

James Thomson's *Agamemnon.*

Swift's *Collection of Genteel . . . Conversation.*

Voltaire's *Discourse on Man.*

Eliot, Jared (1685), Give Caesar His Due; or, The Obligation That Subjects Are Under to Their Civil Rulers. NF

Gay, Ebenezer (1696), Well-Accomplish'd Soldiers, A Glory to Their King. NF

Mather, Samuel (1706), An Apology for the Liberties of the Churches in New England. NF

Pemberton, Ebenezer (1705), Sermons on Several Subjects. NF

Rowe, Elizabeth Singer (d. 1737), Devout Exercises of the Heart in Meditation and Soliloquy. NF

1739

Beckwith, George (1703), Whatsoever God Doeth Is Well Done. NF

Callender, John (1706), An Historical Discourse on the Civil and Religious Affairs of the Colony of Rhode-Island and Providence Plantations. NF

Dickinson, Jonathan (1688), The Danger of Schisms and Contentions. NF

Douglass, William (c. 1691), A Discourse Concerning the Currencies of the British Plantations in America . . . . NF

Mather, Samuel (1706), War Is Lawful and Arms Are To Be Proved. NF

Rowe, Elizabeth Singer (d. 1737), The History of Joseph. V

Whitefield, George (1714), A Journal of a Voyage from Gibraltar to Georgia. NF; The Almost Christian . . . A Sermon. With a Poem, on His Design for Georgia. V, NF

The War of Jenkin's Ear (England vs. Spain, 1739–42).
George Lillo d.
The Champion (London), 1739–43?
Hume's *A Treatise of Human Nature* (1739–40).
Swift's *Verses on the Death of Dr. Swift.*
John Wesley's *Journal* (1739–91; pub. 1909–16).

1740

Byles, Mather (1706), Affections on Things Above. NF

Colman, Benjamin (1673), A Humble Discourse of the Incomprehensibleness of God. NF

Dickinson, Jonathan (1688), Observations on That Terrible Disease Vulgarly Called the Throat-Distemper. NF; The Witness of the Spirit. NF

Edwards, Jonathan (1703), "Personal Narrative" (written c. 1740; pub. posth. 1765). NF

Hutchinson, Thomas (1711), A Discourse Concerning the Currencies of the British Plantations in America. NF

Rose, Aquila (d. 1723), Poems on Several Occasions. V

Seward, William (?), Journal of a Voyage from Savannah to Philadelphia, and from Philadelphia to England in 1740. NF

Tennent, Gilbert (1703), The Danger of an Unconverted Ministry. NF

Gen. Oglethorpe failed to seize St. Augustine from the Spanish.
James Boswell b.
Richardson's *Pamela* (1740–41).
Cibber's *Apology for the Life of Mr. Colley Cibber, Comedian.*
Somerville's *Hobbinal.*

1741

Chauncy, Charles (1705), An Unbridled Tongue a Sure Evidence That Our Religion Is Hypocritical and Vain. NF

Cooke, Samuel (1687), Divine Sovereignty in the Salvation of Sinners. NF

Dickinson, Jonathan (1688), The True Scripture-Doctrine Concerning Some Important Points of Christian Faith. NF

Edwards, Jonathan (1703), The Distinguishing Marks of a Work of the Spirit of God. NF; Sinners in the Hands of an Angry God. NF

Finley, Samuel (1715), Christ Triumphing and Satan Raging. NF

Capt. Vitus Bering (Danish navigator) discovered Alaska.
David Garrick's debut in London.
The General Magazine (Phila.), 1741.
The American Magazine (Phila.), 1741.
Fielding's *Shamela.*
Hume's *Essays Moral and Political.*
Arbuthnot, Pope, et al., *Memoirs of Martinus Scriblerus.*

Haven, Elias (1714), Youthful Pleasures Must Be Accounted For, at the Day of Judgment. NF
Phillips, Samuel (1690), Soldiers Counselled and Encouraged. NF
Tailfer, Patrick (fl. 1741), A True and Historical Narrative of the Colony of Georgia (with others). NF
Todd, Jonathan (1713), The Young People Warned. NF
Whitefield, George (1714), Free Grace Indeed! A Letter to the Reverend Mr. John Wesley (attrib.). NF

1742

Appleton, Nathaniel (1693), The Great Blessing of Good Rulers Depends Upon God's Giving His Judgment & Righteousness to Them. NF
Blair, Samuel (1712), The Doctrine of Predestination Truly & Fairly Stated. NF
Chauncy, Charles (1705), Enthusiasm Described and Caution'd Against. NF
Dickinson, Jonathan (1688), A Display of God's Special Grace. NF
Edwards, Jonathan (1703), Some Thoughts Concerning the Present Revival of Religion in New-England. NF
McGregore, David (1710), The Spirits of the Present Day Tried. NF
Prince, Nathan (1698), The Constitution and Government of Harvard College, From Its Foundation in 1636 to 1742. NF

Spanish troops attacked Georgia without success.
Faneuil Hall built in Boston (1740–42).
Handel's *Messiah*, in Dublin.
Fielding's *Joseph Andrews*.
Edward Young's *The Complaint, or Night Thoughts* (1742–48).
William Collins's *Persian Eclogues*.
Voltaire's *Mohammed*.

1743

Barnard, Thomas (1716), Tyranny and Slavery in Matters of Religion. NF
Blair, Samuel (1712), A Persuasive to Repentance. NF
Bland, Humphrey (1686?), An Abstract of Military Discipline. NF
Chauncy, Charles (1705), Seasonable Thoughts on the State of Religion in New-England. NF
Doolittle, Benjamin (1695), An Enquiry into Enthusiasm. NF
Edwards, Jonathan (1703), The Great Concern of a Watchman for Souls. NF
Franklin, Benjamin (1706), A Proposal for Promoting Useful Knowledge Among the British Plantations in America. NF
Seccombe, Joseph (1706), Business and Diversion Inoffensive to God, and Necessary for the Comfort and Support of Human Society. NF
Stiles, Isaac (1697), A Looking-glass for Changlings. NF

American Philosophical Society founded, in Philadelphia.
Thomas Jefferson b.
The American Magazine and Historical Chronicle (Boston), 1743–46.
Old England (London), 1743–53.
Fielding's *Jonathan Wild*.
Pope's *The Dunciad* (final edition).
Voltaire's *Merope*.

1744

Armstrong, John (1709?), The Art of Preserving Health. V
Balch, William (1704), The Duty of Ministers to Aim at Promoting and Being Partakers of the Gospel. NF
Byles, Mather (1707), Poems on Several Occasions. V; The Comet. V
Colman, Benjamin(1673), The Case of Satan's Fiery Darts in Blasphemous Suggestions and Hellish Annoyances. NF
Eliot, Andrew(1718), An Inordinate Love of the World, Inconsistent with the Love of God. NF
Franklin, Benjamin (1706), An Account of the New Invented

Moravians established a Collegium Musicum, in Bethlehem, Penna.
King George's War (French and British, for mastery of North American continent, 1744–48).
William Byrd d.
Alexander Pope d.
Johnson's *Life of Richard Savage*.
Akenside's *The Pleasures of the Imagination*.
Sarah Fielding's *David Simple*.

Pennsylvanian Fire-Places. NF; A Catalogue of Choice and
Valuable Books. NF
Hamilton, Dr. Alexander (1712), Itinerarium. NF
Horsmanden, Daniel (1694), A Journal of the Proceedings in the
Detection of the Conspiracy Formed by Some White People, in
Conjunction with Negro and Other Slaves. NF
Logan, James (1674), M. T. Cicero's Cato Major (translator).
NF
Mayhew, Experience (1673), Grace Defended, in a Modest Plea
for an Important Truth. NF
Prince, Thomas (1687), The Christian History (1744–45). NF

1745

Cadwalader, Thomas (1708), An Essay on the West-Indian Dry-
Gripes, with the Method of Preventing and Curing That Cruel
Distemper. NF
Cleaveland, John (1722), A Twig of Birch for Billy's Breech.
NF
Colden, Cadwallader (1688), An Explication of the First Causes
of Action in Matter, and of the Cause of Gravitation. NF
Dickinson, Jonathan (1688), Familiar Letters to a Gentleman
Upon a Variety of . . . Subjects in Religion. NF
Eliot, Jared (1685), God's Marvellous Kindness. NF
Franklin, Benjamin (1706), Advice to a Young Man on
Choosing a Mistress. NF
Jones, Hugh (1669), A Protest Against Popery. NF
Niles, Samuel (1674), Tristitiae Ecclesiarum, or a Brief and
Sorrowful Account of the Present State of the Churches of
New-England. NF
Walter, Nathaniel (1711?), The Character of a True Patriot. NF

Second Jacobite Rebellion (1745–46),
the last Stuart effort.
Jonathan Swift d.
The True Patriot (London), 1745–46.
Johnson's *Observations on Macbeth.*
Akenside's *Odes on Several Subjects.*
James Thomson's *Tancred and
Sigismunda.*

1746

Barnard, John (1690), The Presence of the Great God in the
Assembly of Political Rulers. NF
Brainerd, David (1718), Mirabilia Dei Inter Indicos. NF; Divine
Grace Displayed. NF
Browne, Arthur (1699), The Folly and Perjury of the Rebellion
in Scotland Display'd. NF
Burgh, James (1714), Britain's Remembrancer: or, The Danger
Not Over. Being Some Thoughts on the Proper Improvement
of the Present Juncture. NF
Edwards, Jonathan (1703), A Treatise Concerning Religious
Affections. NF; A Vindication of the Gospel Doctrine of
Justifying Faith. NF
Franklin, Benjamin (1706), Reflections on Courtship and
Marriage. NF
Johnson, Samuel (1696), Ethices Elementa (enl. as Elementa
Philosophica, 1752). NF
Prince, Thomas (1687), The Pious Cry of the Lord for Help
When the Godly & Faithful Fail Among Them. NF
Whitefield, George (1714), Britain's Mercies and Britain's
Duties. NF

College of New Jersey founded (now
Princeton University).
Thomas Southerne d.
The Museum (London), 1746–47.
William Collins's *Odes on Several
Descriptive and Allegoric Subjects.*
Diderot's *Philosophic Thoughts.*

1747

Chalkley, Thomas (d. 1741), Journal. NF
Edwards, Jonathan (1703), An Humble Attempt to Promote
Visible Union of God's People. NF

New York Bar Association established.
The Jacobite Journal (London), 1747–
48.

Franklin, Benjamin (1706), Plain Truth, or Serious
Considerations on the Present State of the City of Philadelphia.
NF
Livingston, William (1723), Philosophic Solitude; or, The
Choice of a Rural Life: A Poem. V
Niles, Samuel (1674), A Brief and Plain Essay on God's Wonder
Working Providence for New-England in the Reduction of
Louisburg and Fortresses Thereto Belonging on Cape Breton.
V
Shepard, Thomas (d. 1649), Three Valuable Pieces. NF
Stith, William (1707), The History of the First Discovery and
Settlement of Virginia. NF
Wetmore, James (1695), A Vindication of the Professors of the
Church of England in Connecticut. NF

Richardson's *Clarissa* (1747–48).
Gray's *Ode on a Distant Prospect of
Eton College.*
Johnson's *Plan of a Dictionary of the
English Language.*
Voltaire's *Zadig.*

1748

Appleton, Nathaniel (1693), The Cry of Oppression Where
Judgment Is Looked For. NF
Davies, Samuel (1724), A Sermon on Man's Primitive State. NF
Dickinson, Jonathan (d. 1747), A Second Vindication of God's
Sovereign Free Grace. NF
Edwards, Jonathan (1703), A Strong Road Broken and
Withered. NF
Hobart, Noah (1706), A Serious Address to the Members of the
Episcopal Separation in New-England. NF
How, Nehemiah (d. 1747), A Narrative of the Captivity of
Nehemiah How Who Was Taken by the Indians. . . . NF
Norton, John (1716), The Redeemed Captive [of the French and
Indians]. NF

Treaty of Aix-la-Chapelle restored
status quo in French and British
colonies.
Smollett's *Roderick Random.*
Hume's *Philosophical Essays
Concerning Human Understanding.*
James Thomson's *Castle of Indolence.*
Montesquieu's *The Spirit of the Laws.*
Klopstock's *The Messiah* (1748–73).
Voltaire's *Semiramis.*

1749

Briant, Lemuel (1722), The Absurdity and Blasphemy of
Depreciating Moral Virtue. NF
Colden, Cadwallader (1688), Plantae Coldenghamiae (1749,
1751). NF
Douglass, William (c. 1691), A Summary, Historical and
Political . . . of the British Settlements in North America
(1749–51). NF
Edwards, Jonathan (1703), An Account of the Life of the Late
Reverend Mr. David Brainerd. NF; An Humble Inquiry into
the Rules of the Word of God Concerning . . . Communion.
NF
Franklin, Benjamin (1706), Proposals Relating to the Education
of Youth in Pensilvania. NF
Morgan, Joseph (1671), Love to Our Neighbour Recommended.
NF
Prince, Thomas (1687), The Natural and Moral Government and
Agency of God in Causing Droughts and Rains. NF
Turell, Ebenezer (1702), The Life and Character of the Reverend
Benjamin Colman. NF

The Ohio Co. formed by Virginia
planters extended settlements
westward.
Washington and Lee University
founded.
Benjamin Franklin invented the
lightning rod.
The Monthly Review (London), 1749–
1844.
Fielding's *Tom Jones.*
Johnson's *The Vanity of Human
Wishes; Irene.*
Hartley's *Observations on Man.*

1750

Alleine, Richard (d. 1681), A Companion for Prayer in Times of
Extraordinary Danger. NF
Bellamy, Joseph (1719), True Religion Delineated. NF
Dickinson, Moses (1695), An Inquiry into the Consequences

Jonathan Edwards dismissed from his
Northampton church.
Murray and Kean produced 24 plays in
New York City.

Both of Calvinistic and Arminian Principles Compared
Together. NF
Doolittle, Benjamin (d. 1749), A Short Narrative of Mischief
Done By the French and Indian Enemy. NF
Edwards, Jonathan (1703), Christ the Great Example of Gospel
Ministers. NF
Lennox, Charlotte Ramsay (c. 1720), The Life of Harriot
Stuart. F
Mayhew, Jonathan (1720), A Discourse Concerning Unlimited
Submission and Non-Resistance to the Higher Powers. NF

Blue Stocking parties in vogue in
London.
The Rambler (London), 1750–52.
The Student (Oxford), 1750–51.
Rousseau's *Discourses on the Sciences
and Arts.*

1751

Bartram, John (1699), Observations on the Inhabitants, Climate,
Soil, Rivers . . . Made by Mr. John Bartram in His Travels
from Pensilvania to . . . Lake Ontario. NF
Beach, John (1700), A Continuation of the Calm and
Dispassionate Vindication of the Professors of the Church of
England. NF
Davies, Samuel (1724), The State of Religion Among the
Protestant Dissenters in Virginia. NF
Edwards, Jonathan (1703), A Farewell Sermon Preached at the
First Precinct in Northampton. NF
Franklin, Benjamin (1706), Experiments and Observations on
Electricity (1751–53). NF; The Idea of the English School.
NF
Hobart, Noah (1706), Civil Government the Foundation of
Social Happiness. NF
Peters, Richard (1704), A Sermon on Education. NF
Welsteed, William (1695), The Dignity and Duty of the Civil
Magistrate. NF
Williams, Solomon (1700), The Sad Tendency of Divisions and
Contentions in Churches. NF

British colonization of the Ohio Valley.
Benjamin Franklin helped found an
academy in Philadelphia (now
University of Pennsylvania).
Professional theatre built in
Williamsburg, Va.
Smollett's *Peregrine Pickle.*
Gray's *Elegy in a Country Churchyard.*
Fielding's *Amelia.*
Hume's *An Enquiry Concerning the
Principles of Morals.*
Diderot et al., *Encyclopédie* (1751–80).
Voltaire's *The Age of Louis XIV.*

1752

Chauncy, Charles (1705), The Idle-Poor Secluded from the
Bread of Charity by the Christian Law. NF
Davies, Samuel (1724), Miscellaneous Poems, Chiefly on Divine
Subjects. V
Edwards, Jonathan (1703), Misrepresentations Corrected, and
Truth Vindicated. NF
Gay, Ebenezer (1696), The Mystery of the Seven Stars in
Christ's Right Hand. NF
Judson, David (1715), Timely Warning Against Surfeiting and
Drunkenness. NF
Lennox, Charlotte Ramsay (c. 1720), The Female Quixote; or,
The Adventures of Arabella. F
Ross, Robert (1726), A Complete Introduction to the Latin
Tongue. NF
Sterling, James (1701?), An Epistle to the Hon. Arthur Dobbs.
NF
Stith, William (1707), The Sinfulness and Pernicious Nature of
Gaming. NF
Williams, Nathaniel (d. 1738), The Method of Practice in the
Small-Pox. NF

Gregorian Calendar ("New Style")
adopted in Great Britain.
Philip Freneau b.
The Independent Reflector (New York),
1752–53.
The Covent Garden Journal (London),
1752.
Hume's *Political Discourses.*
Bolingbroke's *Letters on the Study and
Use of History.*

1753

Bellamy, Joseph (1719), The Great Evil of Sin, As It Is Committed Against God. NF

Cotton, John (1693), Wisdom, Knowledge, and the Fear of God. NF

Edwards, Jonathan (1703), True Grace, Distinguished from the Experience of Devils. NF

Hopkins, Samuel (1693), Historical Memoirs, Relating to the Housatunnuk Indians. NF

Lennox, Charlotte Ramsay (c. 1720), Shakespear Illustrated. NF

Lining, John (1708), A Description of the American Yellow Fever. NF

Smith, William (1727), A General Idea of the College of Mirania, with a Sketch of the Method of Teaching Science and Religion. NF; A Poem on Visiting the Academy of Philadelphia. V

British Museum chartered in London.
Benjamin Franklin became a Fellow of the Royal Society of London.
The World (London), 1753–56.
Smollett's Ferdinand Court Fathom.
Richardson's Sir Charles Grandison (1753–54).
Edward Moore's The Gamester (with David Garrick).

1754

Chauncy, Charles (1705), The Horrid Nature and Enormous Guilt of Murder. NF

Edwards, Jonathan (1703), A Careful and Strict Enquiry into the Modern Prevailing Notions of that Freedom of Will, Which Is Supposed to Be Essential to Moral Agency, Vertue and Vice, Reward and Punishment, Praise and Blame (commonly known as Freedom of Will). NF

Finley, Samuel (1715), The Madness of Mankind. NF

Franklin, Benjamin (1706), Some Account of the Pennsylvania Hospital. NF

McGregore, David (1710), The Christian Soldier. NF

Shirley, William (1694), The Antigonian and Bostonian Beauties: A Poem. V

Washington, George (1732), The Journal of Major George Washington. NF

Woolman, John (1720), Some Considerations on the Keeping of Negroes (2nd part., 1762). NF

French and Indian War (1754–63).
French built Fort Duquesne (now Pittsburgh).
King's College chartered (now Columbia University).
Henry Fielding d.
Hume's History of Great Britain (1754–63).
Diderot's The Interpretation of Nature.

1755

Browne, Arthur (1699), Universal Love Recommended in a Sermon Before the . . . Free Masons. NF

Burr, Aaron (1716), A Discourse Delivered at New-Ark in New Jersey . . . on Account of the Late Encroachments of the French, and Their Designs Against the British Colonies in America. NF

Byles, Mather (1707), The Conflagration. V

Clarke, William (?), Observations on the Late and Present Conduct of the French. NF

Evans, Lewis (1700), Geographical, Historical, Political, Philosophical, and Mechanical Essays. NF

Franklin, Benjamin (1706), An Act for the Better Ordering and Regulating . . . for Military Purposes. NF; A Dialogue Between X, Y, and Z. NF

Hopkins, Stephen (1707), A True Representation of the Plan Formed at Albany for Uniting All the British Northern Colonies. NF

Acadians deported from Canada.
Baron de Montesquieu d.
The Connecticut Gazette (New Haven), 1755–68.
The Monitor (London) 1755–65?
The Edinburgh Review, 1755–56.
Johnson's A Dictionary of the English Language.
Fielding's Voyage to Lisbon (posth.).
Lessing's Miss Sara Sampson.
Rousseau's Discourse on the Origin and Bases of Inequality among Men.

Mitchell, John (fl. 1755–68), Map of the British and French Dominions in North America. NF
Sterling, James (1701?), Zeal Against the Enemies of Our Country Pathetically Recommended. NF
Stiles, Isaac (1697), The Character and Duty of Soldiers. NF

1756

Bellamy, Joseph (1719), The Law, Our School-Master. NF
Burr, Aaron (1716), A Sermon Preached Before the Synod of New-York. NF
Davies, Samuel (1724), Virginia's Danger and Remedy. NF
Duché, Jacob (1737), Pennsylvania: A Poem. V
Franklin, Benjamin (1706), A Plan for Settling the Western Colonies. NF
Tilden, Samuel (1690), Tilden's Miscellaneous Poems, on Divers Occasions, Chiefly to Animate and Rouse the Soldiers. V

Seven Years' War began (England vs. France).
Independence Hall built in Philadelphia (1732–56).
Stagecoach line established between New York and Philadelphia.
The New Hampshire Gazette (Portsmouth), 1756–1942.
The Critical Review (London), 1756–1817).
Burke's *A Vindication of Natural Society*.
Voltaire's *Essay on Morals*.

1757

Church, Benjamin (1734), The Choice. V
Franklin, Benjamin (1706), The Way to Wealth. NF
Livingston, William (1723), A Review of the Military Operations in North America . . . 1753–1756. NF; A Funeral E[u]logium, on the Reverend Aaron Burr. NF
Wigglesworth, Edward (1693), Some Thoughts on the Spirit of Infallibility, Claimed by the Church of Rome. NF

William Whitehead named poet laureate of England.
The London Chronicle, 1757–1823.
Hume's *The Natural History of Religion*.
Burke's *Origin of Our Ideas of the Sublime and Beautiful*.

1758

Amherst, Jeffrey (1717), A Journal of the Landing of His Majesty's Forces on the Island of Cape-Breton. NF
Bolles, John (1677), Persecutions in Boston and Connecticut Governments. NF
Edwards, Jonathan (1703), The Great Christian Doctrine of Original Sin Defended. NF
Lennox, Charlotte Ramsay (c. 1720), The History of Henrietta. F; Angelica; or, Quixote in Petticoats [adapted from her novel The Female Quixote (1752)]. D
Maylem, John (1739), The Conquest of Louisburg. V; Gallic Perfidy. V
Prince, Thomas (1687), The Psalms, Hymns, & Spiritual Songs of the Old and New Testaments. V
Shirley, William (1694), Memoirs of the Principal Transactions of the Last War Between the English and French in North-America (attrib.). NF
Ulloa, Antonio de (1716), Relación histórica del viage a la América Meridional (Eng. title: A Voyage to South America). NF
Woolman, John (1720), Considerations on Pure Wisdom and Human Policy. NF

First Indian reservation established, in New Jersey.
School for Negroes founded in Philadelphia.
The Annual Register (London), 1758–.
The Idler (London), 1758–60.
Goldsmith's *The Memoirs of a Protestant* (trans. from French).
Walpole's *Catalogue of Royal and Noble Authors*.
Diderot's *The Father of the Family*.

1759

Acrelius, Israel (1714), Beskrifning om . . . Nya Swerige
[Description of . . . New Sweden]. NF
Benezet, Anthony (1713), Observations on the Inslaving,
Importing, and Purchasing of Negroes. NF
Bowdoin, James (1726), A Paraphrase on Part of the Economy of
Human Life. NF
Davies, Samuel (1724), The Curse of Cowardice. NF
Franklin, Benjamin (1706), Some Account of the Success of
Inoculation for the Small-Pox in England and America. NF
Keteltas, Abraham (1732), The Religious Soldier. NF
Lockwood, James (1714), The Worth & Excellence of Civil
Freedom & Liberty Illustrated. NF

Wolfe defeated Montcalm at Plains of
Abraham; Quebec surrendered to the
British.
Johnson's *The Prince of Abissinia* (first
pub. as *Rasselas* in Phila., 1768).
Goldsmith's *Enquiry into the Present
State of Polite Learning in Europe.*
Adam Smith's *Theory of the Moral
Sentiments.*
Voltaire's *Candide.*

1760

Franklin, Benjamin (1706), The Interest of Great Britain
Considered with Regard to Her Colonies. NF
Hammon, Jupiter (c. 1720), An Evening Thought. V
Langdon, Samuel (1723), Joy and Gratitude to God for the Long
Life of a Good King. NF
Lucas, Richard (d. 1715), Rules Relating to Success in Trade.
NF
Otis, James (1725), The Rudiments of Latin Prosody . . . and
the Principles of Harmony in Poetic and Prosaic Composition.
NF
Smith, William (1727), A Discourse Concerning the Conversion
of the Heathen Americans. NF

Canada surrendered to the British.
Death of George II; accession of
George III.
The British Magazine (London), 1760–
67.
Sterne's *Tristram Shandy* (1760–67).
Voltaire's *Tancred.*

1761

Bolles, Joseph (1701), A Relation of the Opposition Which Some
Baptist People Met With at Norwich, 1761. NF
Davies, Samuel (1724), An Ode on the Prospect of Peace. V
Fordyce, James (1720), The Folly, Infamy and Misery of
Unlawful Pleasure. NF
Hopkinson, Francis (1737), An Exercise, Containing a Dialogue
and Ode Sacred to the Memory of . . . George II. V; The
Treaty. V
Lyon, James (1735), Urania, or A Choice Collection of Psalm-
Tunes, Anthems, and Hymns. V
Mayhew, Jonathan (1720), A Discourse Occasioned by the
Death of King George II, and the Happy Accession of His
Majesty King George III. NF
Smith, William (1727), The Great Duty of Public Worship. NF
Stiles, Ezra (1727), A Discourse on the Christian Union. NF
Winthrop, John (1714), Relation of the Voyage from Boston to
Newfoundland for the Observation of the Transit of Venus. NF

St. Cecilia Society (Charleston, S.C.)
first musical organization in America.
Samuel Richardson d.
Gibbon's *Essai sur l'étude de la
littérature* (pub. in French).
Charles Churchill's *The Rosciad.*
Murphy's *All in the Wrong.*
Rousseau's *Julia, or The New Eloisa.*

1762

Benezet, Anthony (1713), A Short Account of That Part of
Africa Inhabited by the Negroes. NF
Eliot, Jared (1685), An Essay on the Invention, or Art, of
Making Very Good, If Not the Best Iron, from Black Sea-
Sand. NF

Treaty of Fontainebleau (France ceded
the Louisiana Territory to Spain).
Peter III became czar of Russia,
assassinated same year; accession of
Catherine the Great.

Franklin, Benjamin (1706), Advice to a Young Tradesman,
   Written by an Old One. NF
Godfrey, Thomas (1736), The Court of Fancy: A Poem. V
Hopkinson, Francis (1737), An Exercise. V; Science: A Poem.
   V; A Collection of Psalm Tunes. V
Hutchinson, Thomas (1711), A Projection for Regulating the
   Value of Gold and Silver Coins. NF
Lennox, Charlotte Ramsay (c. 1720), Sophia. F
Otis, James (1725), A Vindication of the Conduct of the House
   of Representatives. . . . NF
Ross, Robert (1726), A Plain Address to the Quakers,
   Moravians, Separatists, Separate-Baptists, Rogerenes, and
   Other Enthusiasts. NF

Goldsmith's *The Citizen of the World.*
Smollett's *Sir Launcelot Greaves.*
Macpherson's *Fingal . . . with Other*
   Poems.
Rousseau's *The Social Contract; Emile.*

1763

Bellamy, Joseph (1719), A Blow at the Root of the Refined
   Antinomianism of the Present Age. NF
Catesby, Mark (d. 1749), Hortus Britanno-Americanus (1763–
   67). NF
Hopkinson, Francis (1737), Errata; or, The Art of Printing
   Incorrectly. NF
Lyon, James (1735), The Lawfulness, Excellency, and
   Advantage of Instrumental Musick, in the Publick Worship of
   God. NF
Mayhew, Jonathan (1720), Christian Sobriety. NF
Sewall, Stephen (1734), A Hebrew Grammar (compiler and
   editor). NF
Todd, John (1719), A Humble Attempt Towards the
   Improvement of Psalmody. NF
Wheelock, Eleazar (1711), Plain and Faithful Narrative of the
   . . . Indian Charity-School at Lebanon. NF
Wigglesworth, Edward (1693), The Doctrine of Reprobation
   Briefly Considered. NF

Treaty of Paris (ended French and
   Indian War).
Pontiac's Rebellion (Indians vs. British,
   1763–65).
First American synagogue, in Newport,
   R.I.
Mason-Dixon survey (1763–67) settled
   Pennsylvania-Maryland boundaries.
Montagu's *Letters* (1763–67; posth.).
Voltaire's *Treatise on Tolerance.*

1764

Apthorp, East (1733), Of Sacred Poetry and Music. NF
Dickinson, John (1732), A Protest Against the Appointment of
   Benjamin Franklin. NF; A Reply to the Speech of Joseph
   Galloway. NF; A Petition to the King from the Inhabitants of
   Pennsylvania. NF
Fitch, Thomas (1700?), Reasons Why the British Colonies in
   America Should Not Be Charged with Internal Taxes. NF
Franklin, Benjamin (1706), A Parable Against Persecution.
   NF; Cool Thoughts on the Present Situation of Our Public
   Affairs. NF; Preface to the Speech of Joseph Galloway. NF
Hunt, Isaac (c. 1742), A Letter from a Gentleman in Transilvania
   to His Friend in America. NF
Hutchinson, Thomas (1711), The History of the Colony of
   Massachusetts Bay, from Its First Settlement in 1628 to the
   Year 1750 (2 vols., 1764–67). NF
Kinnersly, Ebenezer (1711), A Course of Experiments, in That
   Curious and Entertaining Branch of Natural Philosophy, Called
   Electricity. NF
Mayhew, Jonathan (1720), Letter of Reproof to Mr. John
   Cleaveland. NF
Otis, James (1725), The Rights of the British Colonies Asserted
   and Proved. NF

St. Louis founded.
Smallpox epidemic in Boston.
Rhode Island College founded (now
   Brown University).
England passed the Sugar Act and the
   Colonial Currency Act.
The Connecticut Courant (Hartford),
   1764–.
Goldsmith's *The Traveller.*
Reid's *Inquiry into the Human Mind on
   the Principles of Common Sense.*
Charles Churchill's *The Duellist.*
Voltaire's *Philosophical Dictionary.*

Pownall, Thomas (1722), The Administration of the Colonies. NF

Prime, Benjamin Youngs (1733), The Patriotic Muse. V

Sandeman, Robert (1718), Some Thoughts on Christianity. NF

1765

Church, Benjamin (1734), The Times. V; Liberty and Property Vindicated and the St[am]pm[a]n Burnt. NF

Clap, Thomas (1703), An Essay on the Nature and Foundation of Moral Virtue. NF

Dickinson, John (1732), The Resolutions and Declarations of Rights Adopted by the Stamp Act Congress. NF; A Petition to the King from the Stamp Act Congress. NF: The Late Regulations Respecting the British Colonies on the Continent of America Considered. NF

Dulany, Daniel (1722), Considerations on the Propriety of Imposing Taxes in the British Colonies. NF

Edwards, Jonathan (d. 1758), Two Dissertations: I. Concerning the End for Which God Created the World; II. The Nature of True Virtue. NF

Godfrey, Thomas (d. 1763), Juvenile Poems on Various Subjects. With The Prince of Parthia, A Tragedy (prod. 1767). V, D

Hopkins, Samuel (1721), The Life and Character of the Late Reverend Mr. Jonathan Edwards. NF

Hopkins, Stephen (1707), The Rights of Colonies Examined. NF

Howard, Martin (fl. 1765–81), A Letter from a Gentleman at Halifax to His Friend in Rhode Island. NF; A Defense of the Letter from a Gentleman at Halifax to His Friend in Rhode Island. NF

Hunt, Isaac (1742?), A Humble Attempt at Scurrility in Imitation of Those Great Masters of the Art (attrib.). NF

Morgan, John (1735), A Discourse upon the Institution of Medical Schools in America. NF

Otis, James (1725), Considerations on Behalf of the Colonists, in a Letter to a Noble Lord. NF: Brief Remarks on the Defence of the Halifax Libel on the British-American Colonies. NF

Rogers, Robert (1731), Journals. NF; A Concise Account of North America. NF

Smith, Samuel (1720), The History of the Colony of Nova-Caesaria, or New Jersey . . . to the Year 1721. NF

Wheelock, Eleazar (1711), A Continuation of the Narrative of the State, & of the Indian Charity-School, at Lebanon, in Connecticut. NF

Great Britain levied first direct tax on the colonies (Stamp Act).

Stamp Act Congress (New York City) adopted Declaration of Rights and Grievances.

First American medical school (College of Philadelphia).

Johnson's edition of The Plays of William Shakespeare.

Walpole's The Castle of Otranto.

Blackstone's Commentaries on the Laws of England. (1765–69).

Percy's Reliques of Ancient English Poetry.

Leibniz's New Essays Concerning Human Understanding (posth.).

1766

Benezet, Anthony (1713), A Caution and Warning to Great-Britain and Her Colonies, in a Short Representation of the Calamitous State of the Enslaved Negroes in the British Dominions. NF

Bland, Richard (1710), An Enquiry into the Rights of the British Colonies. NF

Chauncy, Charles (1705), A Discourse on "the Good News from a Far Country." NF

Clap, Thomas (1703), The Annals or History of Yale-College, in New Haven. NF

Dickinson, John (1732), An Address to the Committee of Correspondence in Barbados. NF

British repealed Stamp Act, passed Declaratory Act (determination of colonial laws).

Queen's College chartered (now Rutgers University).

Thomas Malthus b.

Goldsmith's The Vicar of Wakefield.

Smollett's Travels through France and Italy.

Lessing's Laocoön.

Wieland's Story of Agathon (1766–67).

Franklin, Benjamin (1706), The Examination of Dr. Benjamin Franklin Before an August Assembly Relating to the Repeal of the Stamp Act. NF; Physical and Meteorological Observations. NF

Hopkinson, Francis (1737), A Psalm of Thanksgiving. V

Letchworth, Thomas, (1739), A Morning and Evening's Meditation; or, A Descant on the Times. V

Mayhew, Jonathan (1720), The Snare Broken. A Thanksgiving Discourse. NF

Morgan, John (1735), Four Dissertations on the Reciprocal Advantages of a Perpetual Union Between Great-Britain and Her American Colonies (with others). NF

Rogers, Robert (1731), Ponteach, or the Savages of America. D

Stillman, Samuel (1738), Good News from a Far Country . . . Upon the Arrival of the Important News of the Repeal of the Stamp-Act. NF

1767

Appleton, Nathaniel (1693), Considerations on Slavery. NF

Backus, Isaac (1724), True Faith Will Produce Good Works. NF

Chalmers, Lionel (1715?), An Essay on Fevers. NF

Chandler, Thomas Bradbury (1726), An Appeal to the Public, in Behalf of the Church of England in America. NF

Forrest, Thomas (?), The Disappointment; or, The Force of Credulity. D

Franklin, Benjamin (1706), Remarks and Facts Concerning American Paper Money. NF

Hopkinson, Francis (1737), The Psalms of David . . . in Metre. V

Phillips, Samuel (1690), The Sin of Suicide Contrary to Nature. NF

Tans'ur, William (1699?), The Royal Melody Complete; or, The New Harmony of Zion Containing a New and Correct Introduction to the Grounds of Musick. NF

British Parliament passed Townshend Acts (import duties).
Daniel Boone's first explorations west of Appalachia.
David Rittenhouse built a workable orrery.
The Pennsylvania Chronicle (Phila.), 1767–74.
Lessing's *Minna of Barnhelm.*
Beaumarchais's *Eugenia.*
Herder's *Fragments* (beginning of "Sturm und Drang" period).

1768

Adams, John (1735), An Essay on Canon and Feudal Law. NF

Chauncy, Charles (1705), The Appeal to the Public Answered, in Behalf of the Non-Episcopal Churches in America. NF

Clark, Jonas (1730), The Importance of Military Skill, Measures for Defence and a Martial Spirit, in a Time of Peace. NF

Dickinson, John (1732), Letters from a Farmer in Pennsylvania to the Inhabitants of the British Colonies. NF; "A Song for American Freedom (Liberty Song)." V; An Address Read at a Meeting of Merchants to Consider Non-Importation. NF

Franklin, Benjamin (1706), Causes of the American Discontent Before 1768. NF; Preface to Dickinson's Letters from a Farmer . . . (see above). NF; The Art of Swimming. NF; A Scheme for a New Alphabet. NF

Lee, Arthur (1740), "The Monitor's Letters." NF

Priestley, Joseph (1733), An Essay on the First Principles of Government. NF

Witherspoon, John (1723), Practical Discourses on the Leading Truths of the Gospel. NF

Woolman, John (1720), Considerations on Pure Wisdom and Human Policy; On Labour; On Schools. . . . NF

Colonial objections to Townshend Acts.
American troops sent to Boston.
Laurence Sterne d.
Encyclopedia Britannica (Edinburgh, London, Chicago), 1768–.
Goldsmith's *The Good-Natur'd Man.*
Sterne's *A Sentimental Journey through France and Italy.*
Boswell's *An Account of Corsica.*
Kelly's *False Delicacy* (with David Garrick).
Gray's *Poems.*
Priestley's *Essay on the First Principles of Government.*

1769

Adams, Samuel (1722), An Appeal to the World; or, A
Vindication of the Town of Boston from Many False and
Malicious Aspersions. NF

Bard, Samuel (1742), A Discourse Upon the Duties of a
Physician, with Some Sentiments on the Usefulness and
Necessity of a Public Hospital. NF

Bellamy, Joseph (1719), The Half-Way Covenant: A Dialogue.
NF

Hutchinson, Thomas (1711), A Collection of Original Papers
Relative to the History of the Colony of Massachusetts-Bay.
NF

Lennox, Charlotte Ramsay (c. 1720), The Sister [adapted from
her novel The History of Henrietta (1758)]. D

Virginia Association banned
importation of British goods.
Dartmouth College chartered.
First Californian Franciscan missions
founded.
The "Junius" Letters (in *The Public
Advertiser*), 1769–71.
Burke's *Observations on "The Present
State of the Nation."*
Smollett's *The History and Adventures
of an Atom.*

1770

Billings, William (1746), The New England Psalm-Singer. V

Champion, Judah (1729), A Brief View of the Distresses,
Hardships and Dangers Our Ancestors Encounter'd in Settling
New-England. NF

Clark, Jonas (1730), The Use and Excellency of Vocal Music in
Public Worship. NF

Dana, James (1735), An Examination of the Late Reverend
President Edwards's Enquiry on Freedom of Will. NF

Kalm, Peter (1716), Travels into North America . . . (Eng.
trans.; first pub. in Sweden, 1753–61).

Livingston, William (1723), A Soliloquy. V; America: or, A
Poem on the Settlement of the British Colonies. V; A Review
of the Military Operations in North America from . . . 1753
. . . to 1756. NF

Raynal, Guillaume Thomas François (1713), L'histoire
philosophique et politique des établissements et du commerce
des Européens dans les deux Indes (with others). NF

Robertson, William (1721), The History of the Reign of Charles
the Fifth, Emperor of Germany. NF

Trumbull, John (1750), An Essay on the Uses and Advantages
of the Fine Arts. NF, V

Woolman, John (1720), Considerations on the True Harmony of
Mankind. NF

Boston Massacre (British troops killed
Boston civilians).
Parliament repealed all Townshend
duties except tea.
College of Charleston (S.C.) founded.
Thomas Gainsborough's "The Blue
Boy."
William Wordsworth b.
Friedrich Hölderlin b.
The Massachusetts Spy (Boston;
Worcester), 1770–1904.
Goldsmith's *The Deserted Village; The
Life of Thomas Parnell.*
Burke's *Thoughts on . . . the Present
Discontents.*

1771

Adams, Zabdiel (1739), The Nature, Pleasure, and Advantages
of Church Musick. NF

Bard, Samuel (1742), An Enquiry into the Nature, Cause, and
Cure of the Angina Suffocativa, or, Sore Throat Distemper.
NF

Benezet, Anthony (1713), Some Historical Account of Guinea,
Its Situation, Produce, and the General Disposition of Its
Inhabitants. NF

Cadogan, William (1711), A Dissertation on the Gout. NF

Chauncy, Charles (1705), A Compleat View of Episcopacy. NF

Frisbie, Levi (1748), A Poem on the Rise and Progress of Moor's
Indian Charity School. V

Lathrop, John (1739?), Innocent Blood Crying to God from the
Streets of Boston . . . The Horrid Murder . . . by a Party of
Troops . . . on the Fifth of March, 1770. NF

Violence in North Carolina over lack of
representation in colonial
government.
Tobias Smollett d.
Charles Brockden Brown b.
Walter Scott b.
*Transactions of the American
Philosophical Society* (Phila.), 1771–.
*The Pennsylvania Packet or General
Advertiser* (Phila.), 1771–1839.
Smollett's *Humphrey Clinker.*
Mackenzie's *The Man of Feeling.*
Cumberland's *The West Indian.*
Klopstock's *Odes.*

Trumbull, John (1750), An Elegy on the Death of Mr.
Buckingham St. John. V

1772

Benezet, Anthony (1713), A Mite Cast into the Treasury; or,
Observations on Slave-Keeping (attrib.). NF
Brackenridge, Hugh Henry (1748), A Poem on the Rising Glory
of America (with Philip Freneau). V
Dwight, Timothy (1752), A Dissertation on the History,
Eloquence, and Poetry of the Bible. NF
Evans, Nathaniel (d. 1767), Poems on Several Occasions, with
Some Other Compositions. V
Freneau, Philip (1752), The American Village. To Which Are
Added Several Other Original Pieces in Verse. V
Gordon, William (1728), The Plan of a Society for Making
Provisions for Widows. NF
Hopkinson, Francis (1737), "Dirtilla." V
Hutchinson, Thomas (1711), The Hutchinson Letters. NF
Oliver, Andrew, Junior (1731), An Essay on Comets. NF
Paine, Thomas (1737), The Case of the Officers of Excise
(printed in 1772; pub. in 1793). NF
Rush, Benjamin (1745), Sermons to Gentlemen Upon
Temperance and Exercise. NF
Trumbull, John (1750), The Progress of Dulness (3 parts, 1772–
73). NF
Woolman, John (1720), An Epistle to the Quarterly and Monthly
Meetings of Friends. NF

British customs schooner *Gaspee*
burned off Rhode Island.
Samuel Adams's Committee of
Correspondence voiced colonists'
rights.
Charles Willson Peale's first portrait of
George Washington.
John Woolman d.
Samuel Taylor Coleridge b.
The Morning Post (London), 1772–
1937.
Cumberland's *The Fashionable Lover.*
Lessing's *Emilia Galotti.*
Herder's *Essay on the Origin of
Language.*

1773

Backus, Isaac (1724), An Appeal to the Public for Religious
Liberty. NF
Church, Benjamin (1734), An Oration . . . to Commemorate
the Bloody Tragedy of the Fifth of March, 1770. NF
Dickinson, John (1732), Two Letters on the Tea-Tax. NF
Franklin, Benjamin (1706), An Edict of the King of Prussia.
NF; Rules by Which a Great Empire May Be Reduced to a
Small One. NF
Hutchinson, Thomas (1711), Copy of Letters Sent to Great
Britain . . . [on] the Fatal Source of the Confusion and
Bloodshed in Which This Province [Massachusetts] Especially
Has Been Involved and Which Threatened Total Destruction to
the Liberties of All America. NF
Mather, Samuel (1706), Attempt to Shew That America Must Be
Known to the Ancients. NF; The Sacred Minister. V
Rush, Benjamin (1745), An Address to the Inhabitants of the
British Settlements in America, Upon Slave-Keeping. NF
Sharp, Granville (1735), An Essay on Slavery. NF
Skillman, Isaac (1740), The American Alarm, or The Bostonian
Plea for the Rights and Liberties of the People. NF
Warren, Mercy Otis (1728), The Adulateur. D
Wheatley, Phillis (1753?), Poems on Various Subjects. V

British Parliament passed Tea Act
(May).
Boston Tea Party (Dec.) demonstrated
colonists' refusal to be taxed.
Rivington's New York Gazetteer,
1773–83.
Goldsmith's *She Stoops to Conquer.*
Kelly's *The School for Wives.*
Mackenzie's *The Man of the World.*
James Cook's *An Account of a Voyage
Round the World.*
Goethe's *Götz of Berlichingen.*
Herder's *On German Character and
Art.*

1774

Adams, John (1735), History of the Dispute with America. NF
Anon., The First Book of the American Chronicles of the Times
(1774–75). NF

British Parliament passed Coercive Acts
to punish colonists.
First Continental Congress met (Sept.–
Oct.) in Philadelphia.

Brackenridge, Hugh Henry (1748), A Poem on Divine Revelation. V

Chauncy, Charles (1705), A Letter to a Friend. Giving a Concise, But Just, Representation of the Hardships and Sufferings the Town of Boston Is Exposed To. NF

Cooper, Myles (1735), The American Querist: or, Some Questions Proposed Relative to the Present Dispute Between Great Britain and Her American Colonies. NF; A Friendly Address to All Reasonable Americans. NF

Dickinson, John (1732), Address of Congress to the Inhabitants of the Province of Quebec. NF; An Essay on the Constitutional Power of Great-Britain over the Colonies in America. NF

Duché, Jacob (1737), Observations on a Variety of Subjects, Literary, Moral, and Religious (commonly known as Caspipina's Letters). NF

Galloway, Joseph (c. 1731), Plan of a Proposed Union Between Great Britain and the Colonies. NF

Hamilton, Alexander (1757), A Full Vindication of the Measures of the Congress from the Calumnies of Their Enemies. NF

Hopkinson, Francis (1737), A Pretty Story: Written in the Year of Our Lord 2774 . . . by Peter Grievous, Esq. F

Jay, John (1745), An Address to the People of Great Britain. NF

Jefferson, Thomas (1743), A Summary View of the Rights of British America. NF

Lee, Arthur (1740), An Appeal to the Justice and Interests of the People of Great Britain. NF

Livingston, Philip (1716), The Other Side of the Question: or, A Defence of the Liberties of North-America. NF

Occom, Samuel (1723), A Choice Collection of Hymns and Spiritual Songs (editor). V

Quincy, Josiah (1744), Observations on the Act of Parliament Commonly Called the Boston Port-Bill. NF

Rush, Benjamin (1745), An Inquiry into the Natural History of Medicine Among the Indians of North America. NF

Seabury, Samuel (1729), Free Thoughts on the Proceedings of the Continental Congress . . . Wherein Their Errors Are Exhibited, Their Reasonings Confuted. NF; The Congress Canvassed. NF; A View of the Controversy Between Great Britain and Her Colonies. NF

Trumbull, John (1750), An Elegy on the Times. V

Wilson, James (1742), Considerations on the Nature and Extent of the Legislative Authority of the British Parliament. NF

Woolman, John (d. 1772), A Journal of the Life, Gospel Labours, and Christian Experiences of . . . John Woolman. NF

Edmund Burke's speech on American taxation.

Louis XVI became king of France.

Oliver Goldsmith d.

The Royal American Magazine (Boston), 1774–75.

Chesterfield's *Letters to His Son, Philip Stanhope* (posth.).

Wartons's *The History of English Poetry* (1774–81).

Goethe's *The Sorrows of Young Werther.*

Wieland's *The Aberdites.*

Herder's *Another Philosophy of History.*

1775

Adair, James (c. 1709), The History of the American Indians. NF

Burgoyne, John (1722), The Blockade. D

Dickinson, John (1732), A Declaration by the Representatives of the United Colonies. NF

Digges, Thomas Atwood (1741?), Adventures of Alonso: Containing Some Striking Anecdotes of the Present Prior Minister of Portugal (attrib.). F

Duché, Jacob (1737), "The Duty of Standing Fast in Our Spiritual and Temporal Liberties." NF

Franklin, Benjamin (1706), An Account of Negotiations in London. NF; Articles of Confederation. NF

American Revolution (1775–83).

Battles of Lexington and Concord; capture of Fort Ticonderoga by Green Mountain Boys.

Second Continental Congress, in Philadelphia.

Washington named commander in chief of Continental Army.

British victory at Battle of Bunker Hill.

Gen. Richard Montgomery's expedition against Quebec.

The Pennsylvania Evening Post (Phila)., 1775–84, first American daily newspaper.

Freneau, Philip (1752), General Gage's Soliloquy. V; General Gage's Confession. V; A Voyage to Boston. V; American Liberty. V; A Political Litany. V

Galloway, Joseph (c. 1731), A Candid Examination of the Mutual Claims of Great Britain and Her Colonies with a Plan of Accommodation on Constitutional Principles. NF

Hamilton, Alexander (1757), The Farmer Refuted. NF

Hart, Levi (1738), Liberty Described and Recommended. NF

Hunt, Isaac (c. 1742), The Political Family: or, A Discourse Pointing Out the Reciprocal Advantages Which Flow from an Uninterrupted Union Between Great Britain and Her Colonies. NF

Langdon, Samuel (1723), Government Corrupted by Vice, and Recovered by Righteousness. NF

Lee, Arthur (1740), A Second Appeal. NF

Noble, Oliver (1734), Some Strictures Upon the Sacred Story Recorded in the Book of Esther. NF

Romans, Bernard (c. 1720), A Concise Natural History of East and West Florida. NF

Seabury, Samuel (1729), An Alarm to the Legislature of the Province of New York. NF

Smith, William (1727), A Sermon on the Present Situation of American Affairs. NF

Warren, Mercy Otis (1728), The Group. A Farce. D

"Yankee Doodle" became popular song.

Sheridan's The Rivals.

Johnson's A Journey to the Western Islands of Scotland.

Burke's Speech on Conciliation with the Colonies.

Beaumarchais's The Barber of Seville.

1776

Adams, John (1735), Thoughts on Government Applicable to the Present State of the American Colonies. NF

Brackenridge, Hugh Henry (1748), The Battle of Bunkers-Hill. D

Cartwright, John (1740), American Independence the Interest and Glory of Great Britain. NF

Clark, Jonas (1730), The Fate of Blood-Thirsty Oppressors, and God's Tender Care for His Distressed People. NF

Dalrymple, Sir John (1726), The Rights of Great Britain Asserted Against the Claims of America (attrib.). NF

Dickinson, John (1732), An Essay for a Frame of Government in Pennsylvania. NF

Fiske, Nathan (1733), Remarkable Providences Recollected. NF

Freneau, Philip (1752), "The Beauties of Santa Cruz" (pub. 1786). V; "The Jamaica Funeral" (pub. 1786). V

Green, Jacob (1722), Observations on the Reconciliation of Great-Britain and the Colonies. NF

Hopkinson, Francis (1737), A Prophecy. NF; Two Letters. NF

Jefferson, Thomas (1743), The Declaration of Independence. NF

Leacock, John (?), The Fall of British Tyranny; or, American Liberty Triumphant (attrib.). D

Loudon, Samuel (c. 1727), The Deceiver Unmasked; or, Loyalty and Interest United. NF

Morgan, John (1735), A Recommendation of Inoculation. . . . NF

Odell, Jonathan (1737), "A Birthday Song." V

Paine, Thomas (1737), Common Sense. NF; The American Crisis (13 pamphlets; 1776–83). NF

Price, Richard (1723), Observations on the Nature of Civil Liberty . . . and the Justice and Policy of the War with America. NF

Smith, William (1727), Plain Truth: . . . Remarks on a Late

British forces evacuated Boston (March).

France and Spain offered secret aid to colonists.

Congress adopted Declaration of Independence (July).

Gen. William Howe captured New York City (Sept.); Washington defeated Hessians at Trenton (Dec.).

Phi Beta Kappa founded at College of William and Mary.

David Hume d.

The Independent Chronicle (Boston), 1776–1819.

Gibbon's Decline and Fall of the Roman Empire (1776–88).

Adam Smith's The Wealth of Nations.

Charles Burney's A General History of Music (1776–89).

Bentham's A Fragment on Government.

Goethe's Stella.

Pamphlet, Entitled Common Sense. Wherein Are Shewn That
the Scheme of Independence Is Ruinous, Delusive, and
Impracticable. NF

Witherspoon, John (1723), The Dominion of Providence over
the Passions of Men. NF

1777

Backus, Isaac (1724), A History of New England, with Particular
Reference to the Denomination of Christians Called Baptists
(1777–96). NF

Brackenridge, Hugh Henry (1748), The Death of General
Montgomery at the Siege of Quebec. D

Dawes, Thomas (1757), The Law Given at Sinai. V

French, Jonathan (1740), A Practical Discourse Against
Extortion. NF

Hopkinson, Francis (1737), Letter Written by a Foreigner on the
Character of the English Nation. NF; A Political Catechism.
NF; "Camp Ballad." V; Answer to General Burgoyne's
Proclamation. NF

Inglis, Charles (1734), The Christian Soldier's Duty Briefly
Delineated. NF

Robertson, William (1721), The History of America (1777–96).
NF

Rush, Benjamin (1745), Observations Upon the Present
Government of Pennsylvania. NF

Whitaker, Nathaniel (1730), An Antidote Against Toryism. NF

Whitney, Peter (1744), American Independence Vindicated. NF

Washington defeated British at
Princeton (Jan.).
Congress reconvened in Philadelphia
(March), adopted the Thirteen
Articles of the Confederation (Nov.).
British controlled Philadelphia (Sept.);
Washington encamped at Valley
Forge (Dec.).
Journal de Paris, 1777–1840, first
French newspaper.
Sheridan's *The School for Scandal*.
Hume's *Two Essays* ("Of Suicide"; "Of
the Immortality of the Soul"; posth.).

1778

Allen, Ethan (1738), An Animadversory Address to the
Inhabitants of the State of Vermont. NF

Backus, Isaac (1724), Government and Liberty Described: and
Ecclesiastical Tyranny Exposed. NF

Barlow, Joel (1754), The Prospect of Peace. V

Benezet, Anthony (1713), Some Necessary Remarks on the
Education of the Youth. NF

Billings, William (1746), Chester. V; The Singing Master's
Assistant, or Key to Practical Music. NF

Brackenridge, Hugh Henry (1748), Six Political Discourses. NF

Carver, Jonathan (1701), Travels Through the Interior Part of
North America. NF

Cushing, Jacob (1730), Divine Judgments Upon Tyrants and
Compassion to the Oppressed. NF

Franklin, Benjamin (1706), The Ephemera. NF

Hopkinson, Francis (1737), "The Battle of the Kegs."
V; "Date Obolum Bellisario." V; "The Birds, the Beasts,
and the Bat." V; Letter to Joseph Galloway. NF

Keteltas, Abraham (1732), Reflections on Extortion. NF

Ramsay, David (1749), An Oration on the Advantages of
American Independence. NF

Rush, Benjamin (1745), Directions for Preserving the Health of
Soldiers. NF

Franco-American alliance (May).
French and British at war (June).
British evacuated Philadelphia;
Washington victorious at Battle of
Monmouth; Savannah fell to the
British.
Phillips Academy founded, in Andover,
Mass.
Voltaire d.
Jean-Jacques Rousseau d.
Fanny Burney's *Evelina*.
Burke's *Two Letters to Gentlemen in
the City of Bristol on Ireland*.
Herder's *Folk Songs* (1778–79).

1779

Allen, Ethan (1738), A Narrative of Colonel Ethan Allen's
Captivity . . . from 1775 to 1778. NF

Colonial attempt to recapture Savannah
failed.

Backus, Isaac (1724), Policy, as Well as Honesty, Forbids the Use of Secular Force in Religious Affairs. NF
Brackenridge, Hugh Henry (1748), An Eulogium of the Brave Men Who Have Fallen in the Contest with Great Britain. NF
Dickinson, John (1732), Address of Congress to the Several States on the Present Situation of Affairs. NF
Duché, Jacob (1737), Discourses on Various Subjects. NF
Franklin, Benjamin (1706), The Morals of Chess. NF; The Whistle. NF
Freneau, Philip (1752), "The House of Night" (enl. 1786). V
Hewat, Alexander (c.1745), An Historical Account of the Rise and Progress of the Colonies of South Carolina and Georgia. NF
Morris, Gouverneur (1752), Observations on the American Revolution. NF
Morris, Robert (1734), To the Citizens of Philadelphia [Defending His Management of Public Accounts]. NF
Odell, Jonathan (1737), "Word of Congress." V
Warren, Mercy Otis (1728), The Motley Assembly (attrib.). NF
Webster, Pelatiah (1725), An Essay on Free Trade and Finance. NF
Wharton, Charles Henry (1748), A Poetical Epistle to His Excellency George Washington. V

Capt. John Paul Jones and the *Bonhomme Richard* defeated the *Serapis* off coast of England.
Spain declared war on Great Britain.
David Garrick d.
Sheridan's *The Critic.*
Johnson's *The Lives of the English Poets* (1779–81).
Hume's *Dialogues Concerning Natural Religion* (posth.).
Cowper's *Olney Hymns* (with John Newton).
Lessing's *Nathan the Wise.*

1780

André, John (1751), Cow-Chace, in Three Cantos, Published on Occasion of the Rebel General Wayne's Attack of the Refugees Block-House on Hudson's River, on Friday the 21st of July, 1780. V
Barlow, Joel (1754), An Elegy on the Late Honorable Titus Hosmer. V
Dexter, Samuel (1761), The Progress of Science. V
Dwight, Timothy (1752), America: or, A Poem on the Settlement of the British Colonies (attrib.). V
Foster, Isaac (1725), A Defence of Religious Liberty. NF
Franklin, Benjamin (1706), Dialogue Between Franklin and the Gout. NF; The Handsome and the Deformed Leg. NF
Humphreys, David (1752), A Poem Addressed to the Armies of the United States. V
Odell, Jonathan (1737), "The American Times" (attrib.). V
Paine, Thomas (1737), Public Good, NF; The Crisis Extraordinary. NF
Webster, Pelatiah (1725), A Fourth Essay on Free Trade and Finance. NF

British troops captured Charleston.
Gen. Benedict Arnold defected and joined the British.
The American Academy of Arts and Sciences organized, in Boston.
The British Gazette and Sunday Monitor (London), 1780–1829, first Sunday newspaper.
Burke's *Speech on . . . a Plan for Economical Reformation.*
Wieland's *Oberon.*
Lessing's *The Education of the Human Race.*

1781

Barton, William (1754), Observations on the Nature and Use of Paper-Credit. NF
Billings, William (1746), The Psalm-Singers Amusement, Containing a Number of Fuging Pieces and Anthems. NF
Freneau, Philip (1752), The British Prison-Ship: A Poem. V
Hayley, William (1745), The Triumphs of Temper: A Poem. V
Hopkinson, Francis (1737), The Temple of Minerva. V
Peters, Samuel Andrew (1735), General History of Connecticut, by a Gentleman of the Province. NF
Raynal, Guillaume Thomas François (1713), The Revolution of America. NF
Rush, Benjamin (1745), The New Method of Inoculating for the Smallpox. NF

French fleet blockaded the British in Chesapeake Bay.
Siege of Yorktown; Gen. Charles Cornwallis's surrender to Washington.
Articles of Confederation and Perpetual Union ratified.
Continental Congress became "The United States in Congress Assembled."
Rousseau's *Confessions* (1781–88; posth.).
Kant's *Critique of Pure Reason.*

Seward, Anna (1742), Monody on Major André. V
Wharton, Samuel (1732), Plain Facts: Being an Examination
   into the Rights of the Indian Nations of America to Their
   Respective Countries. NF

1782

Adams, John (1735), A Collection of State Papers. NF
Allen, Ethan (1738), The Present State of the Controversy
   Between the States of New-York and New-Hampshire on the
   One Part and the State of Vermont on the Other. NF
Crèvecoeur, Michel-Guillaume Jean de (1735), Letters from an
   American Farmer. NF
Eckley, Joseph (1750), Divine Glory, Brought to View, in the
   Condemnation of the Ungodly. NF
Franklin, Benjamin (1706), Journal of the Negotiations for
   Peace. NF
Paine, Thomas (1737), Letter Addressed to the Abbé Raynal on
   the Affairs of North-America. NF
Trumbull, John (1750), M'Fingal: A Modern Epic Poem in Four
   Cantos. V

Fall of Lord North's Ministry.
Peace talks began in Paris.
The Netherlands recognized American
   independence.
Fanny Burney's Cecilia.
Cowper's Poems.
Burke's Letter . . . on the Penal Laws.
Priestley's The Corruptions of
   Christianity.
Leclos's Dangerous Liaisons.

1783

Brackenridge, Hugh Henry (1748), Narrative of a Late
   Expedition Against the Indians. NF
Clinton, Sir Henry (1738?), Narrative . . . Relative to His
   Conduct During Part of His Command of the King's Troops in
   North America. NF
Cooper, David (1725), A Serious Address to the Rulers of
   America, or the Inconsistency of Their Conduct Respecting
   Slavery (attrib.). NF
Edwards, Jonathan (1745), The Faithful Manifestation of the
   Truth. NF
Humphreys, David (1752), The Glory of America; or, Peace
   Triumphant over War. V; Poem on the Industry of the United
   States of America. V
Ledyard, John (1751), A Journal of Captain Cook's Last Voyage
   to the Pacific Ocean. NF
McClure, David (1748), An Oration on the Advantages of an
   Early Education. NF
Moore, John (1729), A View of Society and Manners in France,
   Switzerland, Germany and Italy. NF
Sheridan, Thomas (1719), A Rhetorical Grammar of the English
   Language. NF
Stiles, Ezra (1727), The United States Elevated to Glory and
   Honor. A Sermon. . . . NF
Webster, Noah (1758), A Grammatical Institute of the English
   Language Designed for Use of English Schools in America
   (1783-85). NF
Webster, Pelatiah (1725), A Dissertation on the Political Union
   and Constitution of the Thirteen United States of North-
   America. NF

Treaty of Paris (Sept.) ended
   Revolution.
British troops left New York City (Nov.).
Washington resigned as commander in
   chief (Dec.).
Phillips Exeter Academy founded, in
   N.H.
Washington Irving b.
The New York Independent Journal,
   1783–88.

William Pitt named British prime
   minister (1783–1801).
Blake's Poetical Sketches.
Crabbe's The Village.
Beckford's Dreams, Waking Thoughts
   and Incidents.

1784

Adams, Hannah (1755), Alphabetical Compendium of the
   Various Sects. NF
Allen, Ethan (1738), Reason the Only Oracle of Man, or a
   Compendious System of Natural Religion. NF

New York City became temporary
   capital of the U.S.
North Carolina ceded its western lands
   to the U.S.

Belknap, Jeremy (1744), The History of New Hampshire (1784–92). NF

Blair, Hugh (1718), Lectures on Rhetoric and Belles Lettres. NF

Brockway, Thomas (1745), America Saved, or Divine Glory Displayed in the Late War with Great-Britain. NF

Carroll, John (1735), An Address to the Roman Catholics of the United States of America. NF

Davidson, Robert (1750), Geography Epitomized; or A Tour Round the World. NF

Filson, John (1747?), The Discovery, Settlement, and Present State of Kentucke. NF

Franklin, Benjamin (1706), Information to Those Who Would Remove to America. NF; Remarks Concerning the Savages of North Amerca. NF

Hamilton, Alexander (1757), Letters from "Phocion." NF

Hopkinson, Francis (1737), "Modern Learning Exemplified." NF

Hutchins, Thomas (1730), An Historical Narrative and Topographical Description of Louisiana, and West-Florida. NF

Jefferson, Thomas (1743), Notes on the Establishment of a Money Unit and of a Coinage for the United States. NF; Notes on the State of Virginia (1784–85). NF

Markoe, Peter (c. 1752), The Patriot Chief. D

Morse, Jedidiah (1761), Geography Made Easy. NF

Strong, Nehemiah (1729), Astronomy Improved; or, A New Theory of the Harmonious Regularity Observable in the Mechanisms or Movements of the Planetary System. NF

Thomas Jefferson's territorial ordinance adopted as temporary government in the West.

Opening of the China trade.

First theological school, in New Brunswick, N.J.

American Mercury (Hartford), 1784–1833.

John Wesley ordained two ministers as missionaries to America.

Samuel Johnson d.

Burke's *Speech on . . . Fox's East India Bill.*

James Cook's *A Voyage to the Pacific Ocean.*

Schiller's *Love and Intrigue.*

Beaumarchais's *The Marriage of Figaro.*

1785

Backus, Isaac (1724), Godliness Excludes Slavery. NF

Bingham, Caleb (1757), The Young Lady's Accidence; or, A Short and Easy Introduction to English Grammar. NF

Brockway, Thomas (1745), The European Traveller in America (attrib.). NF

Dwight, Timothy (1752), The Conquest of Canaan; A Poem in Eleven Books. V

Edwards, Jonathan (1745), The Necessity of Atonement. NF

Franklin, Benjamin (1706), Maritime Observations. NF; Observations on the Causes and Cure of Smoky Chimneys. NF

Hopkins, Samuel (1721), A Dialogue Concerning the Slavery of the Africans. NF

Marshall, Humphrey (1722), Arbustrum Americanun: The American Grove. NF

More, Hannah (1745), Sensibility: A Poetical Epistle. V

Ramsay, David (1749), A History of the Revolution of South Carolina, from a British to an Independent State. NF

Stiles, Ezra (1727), An Account of the Settlement of Bristol, Rhode Island. NF

Webster, Noah (1758), Sketches of American Policy. NF

John Adams appointed minister to Great Britain; Thomas Jefferson, minister to France.

U.S. signed commerce treaty with Prussia.

Commercial relations abroad plagued Congress.

The Pennsylvania Evening Herald (Phila.), 1785–88.

Thomas Warton named poet laureate of England.

The Times (London), 1785–.

Cowper's *The Task.*

Boswell's *Journal of a Tour to the Hebrides.*

Paley's *The Principles of Moral and Political Philosophy.*

1786

Austin, Benjamin (1752), Observations on the Pernicious Practice of the Law. NF

Franklin, Benjamin (1706), The Art of Procuring Pleasant Dreams. NF

U.S. and Britain continued debt negotiations.

Adoption of Virginia Statute for Religious Freedom.

Freneau, Philip (1752), The Poems of Philip Freneau, Written Chiefly During the Late War. V

Hitchcock, Enos (1745), A Discourse on the Causes of National Prosperity. NF

Hopkins, Lemuel (1750), The Anarchiad (with David Humphreys, Joel Barlow, Timothy Dwight and John Trumbull, 1786–87). V

Hopkinson, Francis (1737), "A Plan for the Improvement of the Art of Paper War." NF

Humphreys, David (1752), A Poem, on the Happiness of America. V

Ladd, Joseph Brown (1764), The Poems of Arouet. V

More, Hannah (1745), Essays on Various Subjects, Principally Designed for Young Ladies. NF

Paine, Thomas (1737), Dissertations on Government, the Affairs of the Bank, the Paper-Money. NF

Parke, John (1754), The Lyric Works of Horace . . . to Which Are Added a Number of Original Poems. . . . V, D, NF

Rowson, Susanna (c. 1762), Victoria. F

Rush, Benjamin (1745), A Plan for the Establishment of Public Schools . . . in Pennsylvania. NF

Witherspoon, John (1723), An Essay on Money as a Medium of Commerce. NF

Shays's Rebellion (Massachusetts farmers vs. state legislature).
Treaty with Morocco over Mediterranean pirates and U.S. shipping.
The Columbian Magazine (Phila.), 1786–92.

Frederick the Great d.
Burke's *Articles of Charge . . . Against Warren Hastings.*
Beckford's *An Arabian Tale* (in English; pub. as *Vathek* in French).
Burns's *Poems Chiefly in Scottish Dialect.*

1787

Adams, John (1735), A Defence of the Constitutions of Government of the United States of America (1787–88). NF

Barlow, Joel (1754), The Vision of Columbus (rev. as The Columbiad, 1807). V

Beattie, James (1735), Poems on Several Occasions. V

Chastellux, François Jean, Marquis de (1734), Travels in North-America, in the Years 1780, 1781, and 1782. . . . NF

Freneau, Philip (1752), A Journey from Philadelphia to New York. NF

Hamilton, Alexander (1757), The Federalist (with James Madison and John Jay, 1787-88). NF

Hammon, Jupiter (c. 1720), An Address to the Negroes of the State of New York. NF

Harrison, Ralph (1748), Rudiments of English Grammar. NF

Lee, Richard Henry (1732), Observations Leading to a Fair Examination of the System of Government Proposed by the Late Convention. NF

Markoe, Peter (c. 1752), The Algerine Spy in Pennsylvania (attrib.). F

Paine, Thomas (1737), Prospects on the Rubicon. NF

Pinckney, Charles (1758), Observations on the Plan of Government Submitted to the Federal Convention. NF

Rush, Benjamin (1745), An Enquiry into the Effects of Public Punishments Upon Criminals, and Upon Society.
NF; Thoughts Upon Female Education, Accommodated to the Present State of Society, Manners, and Government in the United States of America. NF

Stevens, John (1749), Observations on Government (attrib.). NF

Tyler, Royall (1757), The Contrast (pub. 1790). D

Opening of Federal Constitutional Convention (Phila., May).
Signing of the Constitution by the 39 delegates (Sept.).
Northwest Ordinance established government of territory east of the Mississippi and north of the Ohio rivers.
John Fitch launched first American steamboat.
The American Museum (Phila.), 1787–92.

R. B. Sheridan's speech in Parliament against Warren Hastings.
Goethe's *Iphigenia in Tauris.*
Schiller's *Don Carlos.*

1788

Clarkson, Thomas (1760), An Essay on the Impolicy of the African Slave Trade. NF

Dickinson, John (1732), The Letters of Fabius . . . (1st ser.). NF

Dwight, Timothy (1752), The Triumph of Infidelity: A Poem. V

Edwards, Jonathan (1745), Observations on the Language of the Muhhekaneew Indians. NF

Freneau, Philip (1752), The Miscellaneous Works of Mr. Philip Freneau, Containing His Essays and Additional Poems. NF, V

Gordon, William (1728), The History of the Rise, Progress, and Establishment of the Independence of the United States of America. NF

Hopkinson, Francis (1737), Account of the Grand Federal Procession, Philadelphia, July 4, 1788. NF; An Ode [in Honor of the Adoption of the Constitution]. V; Seven Songs, for the Harpsichord or Forte-Piano. V

Humphreys, David (1752), Essay on the Life of the Honorable Major-General Israel Putnam. NF

Lee, Richard Henry (1748), An Additional Number of Letters from the Federal Farmer . . . Leading to a Fair Examination of the System of Government Proposed by the Late Convention. NF

Markoe, Peter (c. 1752), The Times. V; The Storm (attrib.). V

Minot, George Richards (1758), The History of the Insurrections, in Massachusetts, in the Year 1786. NF

Ramsay, David (1749), An Address to the Freemen of South-Carolina on the Subject of the Federal Constitution. NF

Roscoe, William (1753), The Wrongs of Africa. A Poem. V

Rowson, Susanna (c. 1762), The Inquisitor; or, Invisible Rambler. F; Poems on Various Subjects. V; A Trip to Parnassus. V

Tucker, St. George (1752), Liberty, A Poem on the Independence of America. V

Eleven states ratified Constitution.
Antifederalists urged Bill of Rights and other amendments.
Maryland and Virginia ceded land on Potomac for federal capital.
Philological Society founded, in New York City.

Temporary insanity of George III; regency contemplated.
Trial of Warren Hastings (1788–95).
Hannah More's *Thoughts on the Importance of the Manners of the Great.*
Goethe's *Egmont.*
Kant's *Critique of Practical Reason.*

1789

Adams, John (1735), Twenty-six Letters, upon Interesting Subjects Respecting the Revolution in America. NF

Blair, Hugh (1718), Essays on Rhetoric: Abridged Chiefly from Dr. Blair's Lectures on That Science. NF

Brown, William Hill (1765), The Power of Sympathy; or, The Triumph of Nature. F

Dunlap, William (1766), The Father; or American Shandyism (rev. as The Father of an Only Child, 1806). D; Darby's Return. D

Fitch, Elijah (1746), The Beauties of Religion. A Poem, Addressed to Youth. V

Franklin, Benjamin (1706), Observations Relative to . . . the Academy in Philadelphia. NF

Hopkinson, Francis (1737), An Oration. NF; Judgments in the Admiralty in Philadelphia. NF

Keate, George (1729), An Account of the Pelew Islands, Situated in the Western Part of the Pacific Ocean. NF

Morse, Jedidiah (1761), The American Geography; or, A View of the Present Situation of the United States of America. NF

Ramsay, David (1749), The History of the American Revolution. NF

Rowson, Susanna (c. 1762), Mary; or, The Test of Honour. F

Washington and Adams inaugurated in New York City.
Bill of Rights proposed by Congress.
North Carolina and Rhode Island ratified the Constitution.
John Jay appointed first chief justice of the Supreme Court.
Gazette of the United States (New York; Phila.), 1789–1847.

Paris mobs stormed the Bastille; royal family confined to the Tuileries Palace.
Blake's *Songs of Innocence.*
Bentham's *Principles of Morals and Legislation.*

Tench, Watkin (1759?), A Narrative of the Expedition to Botany Bay, with an Account of New South Wales. NF
Webster, Noah (1758), Dissertations on the English Language. NF

1790

Adams, John (1735), Discourses on Davila (written in 1790 and pub. in the Gazette of the United States; book pub., 1805). NF
Belsham, William (1752), An Essay on the African Slave Trade. NF
Daggett, David (1764), The Life and Extraordinary Adventures of Joseph Mountain, a Negro, Who was Executed at New-Haven . . . for a Rape. NF
Hamilton, Alexander (1757), Report on Public Credit. NF
Hitchcock, Enos (1744), Memoirs of the Bloomsgrove Family. F
Humphreys, David (1752), The Widow of Malabar. D
Leland, John (1754), The Virginia Chronicle with Judicious and Critical Remarks, under XXIV Heads. NF
Lennox, Charlotte Ramsay (c. 1720), Euphemia. F
Markoe, Peter (c. 1752), The Reconciliation; or, The Triumph of Nature (unprod. opera). V
Morton, Sarah Wentworth (1759), Ouâbi: or The Virtues of Nature. An Indian Tale. V
Ramsay, David (1749), A Dissertation on the Means of Preserving Health in Charleston, and the Adjacent Low Country. NF
Warren, Mercy Otis (1728), Poems, Dramatic and Miscellaneous. V, D
Winthrop, John (d. 1649), Journal (first 2 parts; repub. complete as The History of New England, 1825–26). NF

Philadelphia became the nation's capital (until 1800).
Alexander Hamilton's fiscal program split North and South delegates.
Benjamin Franklin d.
The New York Magazine, 1790–97.

French National Assembly drafted a constitution; Louis XVI a king without powers.
Henry James Pye named poet laureate of England.
Blake's *The Marriage of Heaven and Hell.*
Burke's *Reflections on the Revolution in France.*
Malone's edition of *The Plays and Poems of Shakespeare.*
Goethe's *Torquato Tasso.*

1791

Adams, John Quincy (1767), An Answer to Paine's Rights of Man (serial pub. in the Columbian Sentinel, signed "Publicola"; book pub. 1793). NF
Alsop, Richard (1761), The Echo (with Theodore Dwight, Lemuel Hopkins, Elihu Hubbard Smith, and Mason Cogswell, 1791–1805). V
Austin, David (1760), The American Preacher; or, A Collection of Sermons from Some of the Most Eminent Preachers Now Living in the United States (editor; 1791–93). NF
Barton, William (1739), Observations on the Progress of Population, and the Probabilities of the Duration of Human Life, in the United States of America. NF
Bartram, William (1739), Travels Through North & South Carolina, Georgia, East & West Florida, the Cherokee Country, the Extensive Territories of the Muscogulges, or Creek Confederacy, and the Country of the Chactaws. NF
Dana, James (1735), The African Slave Trade. A Discourse. NF
Dwight, Timothy (1752), Virtuous Rulers a Natural Blessing. NF
Edwards, Jonathan (1745), The Injustice and Impolicy of the Slave Trade, and of the Slavery of the Africans. NF
Franklin, Benjamin (d. 1790), Mémoires de la vie privée . . . écrits par lui-même (1st American edition of the Autobiography, 1818). NF
Hamilton, Alexander (1757), Report on Manufactures. NF; The Argument of the Secretary of the Treasury upon the Constitutionality of a National Bank. NF

Vermont admitted to the Union.
Bill of Rights ratified (10 amendments to the Constitution).
Pro-British Federalists and Hamilton opposed pro-French Republicans and Jefferson.
First Bank of the U.S. incorporated.
The National Gazette (Phila.), 1791–93.

The Observer (London), 1791–.
Boswell's *The Life of Samuel Johnson.*
Radcliffe's *The Romance of the Forest.*
Burke's *Two Letters on the French Revolution.*
Sade's *Justine.*
Schiller's *History of the Thirty Years' War* (1791–93).

Morris, Thomas (fl. 1741–67), Miscellanies in Prose and Verse. V, NF

Paine, Thomas (1737), The Rights of Man (1791–92). NF

Priestley, Joseph (1733), Letters to . . . Edmund Burke. NF

Prime, Benjamin Youngs (1733), Columbia's Glory, or British Pride Humbled. V

Rowson, Susanna (c. 1762), Charlotte Temple: A Tale of Truth. F; Mentoria: or, The Young Lady's Friend. F

Seabury, Samuel (1729), Discourses on Several Subjects (1791–98). NF

Webster, Noah (1758), The Prompter; or A Commentary on Common Sayings and Subjects. NF

1792

Barlow, Joel (1754), A Letter to the National Convention of France. NF; Advice to the Privileged Orders in the Several States of Europe (1792–93). NF

Belknap, Jeremy (1744), The Foresters, an American Tale: Being a Sequel to The History of John Bull the Clothier. F

Bingham, Caleb (1757), The Child's Companion; Being a Concise Spelling Book. NF

Brackenridge, Hugh Henry (1748), Modern Chivalry (1792–97). F

Ford, Timothy (1762), An Enquiry into the Constitutional Authority of the Supreme Federal Court over the Several States. NF

Gookin, Daniel (d. 1687), Historical Collections of the Indians in New England. NF

Hamilton, Alexander (1757), Letters by "An American." NF

Hazard, Ebenezer (1744), Historical Collections Consisting of State Papers and Other Authentic Documents (editor; 1792–94). NF

Hopkinson, Francis (d. 1791), The Miscellaneous Essays and Occasional Writings of Francis Hopkinson. NF, V

Imlay, Gilbert (c. 1754), A Topographical Description of the Western Territory of North America. NF

Odiorne, Thomas (1769), The Progress of Refinement. V

Paine, Thomas (1737), A Letter Addressed to the Addressers. NF

Rush, Benjamin (1745), Considerations on the Injustice and Impolicy of Punishing Murder by Death. NF

Smith, William (1727), Eulogium on Benjamin Franklin. NF

Kentucky admitted to the Union.
Militia Act to cope with Indian unrest in Northwest Territory.
New York Stock Exchange opened.
The White House cornerstone laid.

Prime Minister Pitt's attack on the slave trade.
France declared a republic.
Francis II became last Holy Roman Emperor.
Holcroft's *The Road to Ruin*.
Arthur Young's *Travels in France* (1792–94).
Wollstonecraft's *A Vindication of the Rights of Woman*.

1793

Alsop, Richard (1761), American Poems. V

Anon., The Hapless Orphan; or, Innocent Victim of Revenge. F

Bleecker, Ann Eliza (d. 1783), The Posthumous Works of Ann Eliza Bleecker (with Margarette Faugères's A Collection of Essays, Prose and Poetical). NF, V

Bradford, William (1755), An Enquiry How Far the Punishment of Death Is Necessary in Pennsylvania. NF

Hamilton, Alexander (1757), "Pacificus" Letters. NF

Hitchcock, Enos (1744), The Farmer's Friend; or, The History of Mr. Charles Worthy. NF

Hopkins, Samuel (1721), The System of Doctrines Contained in Divine Revelation. . . . NF; A Treatise on the Millenium. NF

Lathrop, John (1739?), A Discourse on the Errors of Popery. NF

Washington proclaimed neutrality in French-British war.
Citizen Genêt Affair.
Fugitive slave law passed.
Yellow fever epidemic in Philadelphia.
Charles Bulfinch drew plans for the Franklin Crescent in Boston.
The Farmer's Almanack (Boston et al.), 1793–.
The Farmer's Weekly Museum (Walpole, N.H.), 1793–1810.

France declared war on Great Britain.
Louis XVI, Marie Antoinette executed.
Reign of Terror in France (1793–94).

Paine, Thomas (1737), Reasons for Wishing to Preserve the Life of Louis Capet. NF

Reid, Thomas (1710), Essays on the Intellectual and Active Powers of Man. NF

Smith, Elihu Hubbard (1771), American Poems (editor). V

Taylor, John (1753), An Examination of the Late Proceedings in Congress Respecting the Official Conduct of the Secretary of the Treasury (attrib.). NF

Woolman, John (d. 1772), A Word of Remembrance and Caution to the Rich (also known as A Plea for the Poor). NF

Blake's *America: A Prophecy.*
Wordsworth's "An Evening Walk"; "Descriptive Sketches."
Godwin's *Political Justice.*
Schiller's *On Grace and Dignity.*

1794

Aikin, John (1747), Letters from a Father to His Son; on Various Topics, Relative to Literature and the Conduct of Life. NF

Belknap, Jeremy (1744), American Biography (1794–98). NF

Bingham, Caleb (1757), The American Preceptor; Being a New Selection of Lessons for Reading and Speaking. NF

Cobbett, William (1763), Observations on the Emigration of Dr. Joseph Priestley. NF

Dunlap, William (1766), The Fatal Deception; or, The Progress of Guilt (pub. as Leicester, 1807). D

Dwight, Timothy (1752), Greenfield Hill: A Poem in Seven Parts. V

Freneau, Philip (1752), The Village Merchant. V

Guthrie, William (d. 1770), A New System of Modern Geography (1794–95). NF

Hamilton, Alexander (1757), "Americanus" Letters. NF

Hopkinson, Francis (d. 1791), Ode from Ossian's Poems. V

Paine, Thomas (1737), The Age of Reason (1794–95). NF

Rowson, Susanna (c. 1762), Rebecca; or, The Fille de Chambre. F; Slaves in Algiers, or A Struggle for Freedom. D

Stiles, Ezra (1727), A History of Three of the Judges of King Charles I. NF

Taylor, John (1753), An Enquiry into the Principles and Tendency of Certain Public Measures. NF

Whisky Rebellion quelled (Pennsylvania farmers vs. excise tax).
Jay's Treaty (British evacuation of Northwest military posts).
Bowdoin College founded.
The Federal Orrery (Boston), 1794–96.

Great Britain suspended Habeas Corpus Act.
French occupied Belgium.
Blake's *Songs of Innocence and of Experience.*
Radcliffe's *The Mysteries of Udolpho.*
Godwin's *Caleb Williams.*
Paley's *Evidences of Christianity.*
Fichte's *Foundation of the Complete Theory of Knowledge.*

1795

Brackenridge, Hugh Henry (1748), Incidents of the Insurrection in the Western Parts of Pennsylvania. NF

Bradford, Ebenezer (1746), The Art of Courting (attrib.). F

Cobbett, William (1763), A Bone to Gnaw for the Democrats. NF; A Kick for a Bite; or, Review upon Review, with a Critical Essay on the Works of Mrs. S[usanna] Rowson. NF

Dunlap, William (1766), Fontainville Abbey (pub. 1806). D

Freneau, Philip (1752), Poems Written Between the Years 1768 and 1794. V

Hamilton, Alexander (1757), A Defence of the Treaty of Amity, Commerce, and Navigation . . . as It Appeared in the Papers under the Signature of Camillus (with Rufus King and John Jay). NF

Murdock, John (1748), The Triumphs of Love, or Happy Reconciliation. D

Murray, Lindley (1745), English Grammar (rev. edition, 1818). NF

Ogden, Uzal (1744), Antidote to Deism. The Deist

Treaty of San Lorenzo (U.S. and Spain) settled Florida boundary.
Naturalization Act (requirements for citizenship).
Yazoo frauds (Georgia land speculations).

French occupied the Netherlands.
End of the Reign of Terror; Third French Constitution formed the Directory.
John Keats b.
Thomas Carlyle b.
Blake's *The Book of Los.*
Chatterton's *The Revenge* (posth.).
Goethe's *Wilhelm Meister's Apprenticeship* (1795–96).
Jean Paul's *Hesperus.*

Unmasked; or An Ample Refutation of All the Objections of
Thomas Paine, Against the Christian Religion. NF
Paine, Robert Treat (1773), "The Invention of Letters." V
Paine, Thomas (1737), Dissertation on First-Principles of
Government. NF
Rowson, Susanna (c. 1762), The Volunteers. D; The Female
Patriot. D; Trials of the Human Heart. F
Story, Isaac (1774), Liberty. V
Sumner, Charles Pinckney (1776), The Compass. V

1796

Austin, David (1760), The Voice of God to the People of These
United States. NF
Barlow, Joel (1754), The Hasty-Pudding. V; The Political
Writings of Joel Barlow. NF
Cliffton, William (1772), The Group; or, An Elegant
Representation. V
Cobbett, William (1763), The Scare-Crow, Being an Infamous
Letter . . . . NF; The Life of Thomas Paine. NF; The Life
and Adventures of Peter Porcupine. NF
Dennie, Joseph (1768), The Lay Preacher; or, Short Sermons for
Idle Readers. NF
Dunlap, William (1766), The Archers; or, Mountaineers of
Switzerland. D; The Mysterious Monk (pub. as
Ribbemont; or, The Feudal Baron, 1803). D
Fulton, Robert (1765), Treatise on the Improvement of Canal
Navigation. NF
Hopkins, Lemuel (1750), The Guillotina, or a Democratic Dirge.
V
Hopkins, Samuel (1721), The Life and Character of Miss
Susanna Anthony (compiler). NF
Linn, John Blair (1777), The Poetical Wanderer. V
MacKenzie, Henry (1745), An Answer to Paine's Rights of
Man. NF
Morris, Thomas (fl. 1741–67), Quashy; or, The Coal-Black
Maid. V
Paine, Robert Treat (1773), "The Ruling Passion." V
Paine, Thomas (1737), The Decline and Fall of the English
System of Finance. NF; A Letter to George Washington. NF
Priestley, Joseph (1733), Unitarianism Explained and Defended.
NF
Smith, Elihu Hubbard (1771), Edwin and Angelina. D
Story, Isaac (1774), All the World's a Stage. V
Thompson, Benjamin (1753), Essays, Political, Economical, and
Philosophical (1796–1802). NF
Tucker, St. George (1752), Dissertation on Slavery. NF; The
Probationary Odes of Jonathan Pindar. V
Turnbull, Robert James (1775), A Visit to the Philadelphia
Prison. NF
Washington, George (1732), The Speech of George Washington,
Esq., Late President of the United States of America: on His
Resignation of That Important Office. NF

Tennessee admitted to the Union.
Rising strength of the Democratic-
Republican Party.
Washington's *Farewell Address*
published, not delivered.
William Hickling Prescott b.

Napoleon's Italian campaign (1796–
97).
Spain joined France against Britain.
Robert Burns d.
Lewis's *The Monk.*
Fanny Burney's *Camilla.*
Coleridge's *Poems on Various Subjects.*
Southey's *Joan of Arc.*
Burke's *Letter to a Noble Lord.*
Goethe and Schiller's *Xenien.*

1797

Bingham, Caleb (1757), The Columbian Orator. NF
Bleecker, Ann Eliza (d. 1783), The History of Maria Kittle. F
Boucher, Jonathan (1738), A View of the Causes and
Consequences of the American Revolution. NF
Brown, William Hill (1765), West Point Preserved. D

Deteriorating relations with France over
Jay's Treaty.
XYZ Affair (Talleyrand's attempt to
extort money from U.S.
commissioners).

Burk, John Daly (c. 1775), Bunker Hill, or the Death of General Warren. D

Butler, James (1775?), Fortune's Foot-ball; or, The Adventures of Mercutio (1797–98). F

Dickinson, John (1732), The Letters of Fabius . . . (2nd. ser.). NF

Dunlap, William (1766), The Knight's Adventure (pub. 1807). D

Foster, Hannah Webster (1759), The Coquette. F

Linn, John Blair (1777), Bourville Castle. D

Morton, Sarah Wentworth (1759), Beacon Hill: A Local Poem, Historic and Descriptive. V

Paine, Thomas (1737), Agrarian Justice. NF; Letter to the People of France and the French Armies. NF

Proud, Robert (1728), The History of Pennsylvania (1797–98). NF

Sampson, Deborah (1760), The Female Review; or, Life of Deborah Sampson. NF

Trumbull, Benjamin (1735), A Complete History of Connecticut (rev. edition, 1818). NF

Tyler, Royall (1757), The Georgia Spec; or, Land in the Moon. D; The Algerine Captive; or, The Life and Adventures of Doctor Updike Underhill. F

The Medical Repository (New York), 1797–1824).

France proclaimed Cisalpine and Ligurian republics in Italy.
The Anti-Jacobin (London), 1797–98.
Edmund Burke d.
Horace Walpole d.
Southey's *Poems.*
Radcliffe's *The Italian.*
Goethe's *Hermann and Dorothea.*
Hölderlin's *Hyperion* (1797–99).
Sade's *Juliette.*

1798

Alsop, Richard (1761), The Political Greenhouse (with Lemuel Hopkins and Theodore Dwight). V

Austin, William (1778), Strictures on Harvard University. NF

Brown, Charles Brockden (1771), Alcuin: A Dialogue. NF; Wieland; or, The Transformation. F

Burk, John Daly (c. 1775), Female Patriotism, or the Death of Joan d'Arc. D

Dunlap, William (1766), André. A Tragedy. D

Dwight, Timothy (1752), The True Means of Establishing Public Happiness, Two Discourses on the Nature and Danger of Infidel Philosophy. NF; The Duty of Americans, at the Present Crisis. NF

Foster, Hannah Webster (1759), The Boarding School; or, Lessons of a Preceptress to her Pupils. NF

Hopkinson, Joseph (1770), Hail Columbia. V

Munford, Robert (d. 1784), The Candidates; or, The Humours of a Virginia Election (written 1770?; prod.?). D; The Patriots (written 1779?; prod.?). D

Munford, William (1775), Prose on Several Occasions. NF, V

Murray, Judith Sargent (1751), The Gleaner. D, V, NF

Paine, Robert Treat (1773), "Adams and Liberty." V

Rowson, Susanna (c. 1762), Reuben and Rachel; or, Tales of Old Times. F.

Sewall, Jonathan Mitchell (1748), Versification of President Washington's Excellent Farewell-Address. V

Vancouver, George (1758?), Voyage of Discovery to the North Pacific Ocean, and Round the World. NF

11th Amendment (protection of states against suits) ratified.
Congress amended Naturalization Act, passed Alien and Sedition acts.
Creation of Mississippi Territory.
Undeclared naval war with France (1798–1800).

French troops occupied Rome.
Napoleon's Egyptian campaign (1798–99).
Lord Nelson destroyed French fleet near Alexandria.
Wordsworth and Coleridge's *Lyrical Ballads.*
Malthus's *An Essay on the Principle of Population.*
Schiller's *Wallenstein's Camp.*

1799

Adams, Hannah (1755), A Summary History of New England. NF

Baldwin, Thomas (1753), A Brief Account of the Late Revivals of Religion in . . . the New-England States. NF

Brown, Charles Brockden (1771), Ormond; or, The Secret

Death of Washington at Mt. Vernon.
President Adams avoided war with France.
Charles Bulfinch designed Boston State House.

Witness. F; Arthur Mervyn; or, Memoirs of the Year 1793.
F; Edgar Huntly; or, Memoirs of a Sleep-Walker. F
Carey, Mathew (1760), The Porcupiniad. A Hudibrastic Poem.
V
Cooper, Thomas (1759), Political Essays. NF
Dunlap, William (1766), The Italian Father (pub. 1810). D
Freneau, Philip (1752), Letters on Various Interesting and
Important Subjects. NF
Knox, Samuel (1756), An Essay on the Best System of Liberal
Education. NF
Lee, Harriet (1757), Constantia de Valmont. F
Morton, Sarah Wentworth (1759), The Virtues of Society. V
Murray, Lindley (1745), Extracts from the Writings of Divers
Eminent Authors . . . Representing the Evils and Pernicious
Effects of Stage Plays, and Other Vain Amusements (editor).
NF; The English Reader; or, Pieces in Prose and Poetry
Selected from the Best Writers (editor). F, NF, V
Rush, Benjamin (1745), Three Lectures upon Animal Life. NF
Smith, James (c. 1737), An Account of Remarkable Occurrences
in the Life and Travels of Col. James Smith. NF
Thompson, Benjamin (1753), Proposals for Forming . . . a
Public Institution . . . for the Application of Science to the
Common Purposes of Life. NF
Wells, Helena (fl. 1799–1800), The Stepmother. F

Napoleon overthrew the Directory,
became first consul.
British suppressed Irish rebellion.
Thomas Hood b.
Sheridan's *Pizarro* (adap.).
Godwin's *St. Leon.*
Park's *Travels in the Interior of Africa.*
Hannah More's *On the Modern System
of Female Education.*
Schiller's *Wallenstein's Death.*
Friedrich von Schlegel's *Lucinde.*

1800

Alsop, Richard (1761), A Poem, Sacred to the Memory of
George Washington. V
Caldwell, Charles (1772), An Elegiac Poem on the Death of
General Washington. V
Davis, John (1775), The Farmer of New Jersey; or, A Picture of
Domestic Life. F
Gallatin, Albert (1761), Views of the Public Debt, Receipts, &
Expenditures of the United States. NF
Hamilton, Alexander (1757), Letter . . . Concerning the Public
Conduct and Character of John Adams. NF
Jefferson, Thomas (1743), An Appendix to the Notes on
Virginia Relative to the Murder of Logan's Family. NF
Linn, John Blair (1777), The Death of George Washington.
V; Serious Considerations on the Election of a President. NF
Sewall, Jonathan Mitchell (1748), Eulogy on the Late General
Washington. V
Smalley, John (1734), On the Evils of a Weak Government. NF
Weems, Mason Locke (1759), Hymen's Recruiting-Serjeant; or,
The New Matrimonial Tatoo for the Old Bachelors. NF; The
Life and Memorable Actions of George Washington (cherry-
tree episode in 5th edition, 1806). NF
Wells, Helena (fl. 1799–1800), Constantia Neville; or, The West
Indian. F
Wood, Sarah Sayward Barrell Keating (1759), Julia, and the
Illuminated Baron. F

Washington, D.C., became U.S.
capital.
Northwest Territory divided into Ohio
and Indiana Territories.
Library of Congress founded.
*National Intelligencer and Washington
Advertiser,* (1800–70).

Spain ceded Louisiana Territory to
France.
Napoleon occupied Italy.
Robert Owen began social reforms in
English mills.
Morton's *Speed the Plough.*
Edgeworth's *Castle Rackrent.*
Schiller's *Maria Stuart.*
Novalis's *Hymns to the Night.*
Cuvier's *Lessons in Comparative
Anatomy* (1800–05).

1801

Allen, Paul (1775), Original Poems, Serious and Entertaining. V
Boudinot, Elias (1740), The Age of Revelation. NF
Brown, Charles Brockden (1771), Clara Howard. F; Jane
Talbot. F

Tripoli at war with U.S.
Benjamin Latrobe and Greek revival
architecture.
New York Evening Post, 1801–.

Crèvecoeur, Michel-Guillaume Jean de (1735), Voyage dans la Haute-Pennsylvanie et dans l'état de New-York. NF
Davis, John (1775), The Wanderings of William. F
Fiske, Nathan (d. 1799), The Moral Monitor. NF
Hamilton, Alexander (1757), An Address to the Electors of the State of New-York. NF
Ingersoll, Charles Jared (1782), Edwy and Elgiva. D
Jefferson, Thomas (1743), A Manual of Parliamentary Practice. NF
Linn, John Blair (1777), The Powers of Genius. V
Paine, Thomas (1737), Compact Maritime. NF
Sewall, Jonathan Mitchell (1748), Miscellaneous Poems. V
Story, Isaac (1774), A Parnassian Shop, Opened in the Pindaric Stile; by Peter Quince, Esq. V
Tenney, Tabitha (1762), Female Quixotism. F
Wood, Sarah Sayward Barrell Keating (1759), Dorval; or, The Speculator. F

United Kingdom of Great Britain and Ireland established.
Czar Paul I assassinated; Alexander I crowned.
Edgeworth's Belinda.
Southey's Thalaba.
Chateaubriand's Atala.
Schiller's The Maid of Orleans.

1802

Bowditch, Nathaniel (1773), The New American Practical Navigator. NF
Brackenridge, Hugh Henry (1748), The Standard of Liberty. NF
Cheetham, James (1772), View of the Political Conduct of Aaron Burr. NF
Dexter, Timothy (1747), A Pickle for the Knowing Ones. NF
Hamilton, Alexander (1757), The Examination of the President's Message . . . 1801. NF
Irving, Washington (1783), Letters of Jonathan Oldstyle, Gent. (1802–03). NF
Morris, Thomas (fl. 1741–67), Songs Political and Convivial. V
Paine, Thomas (1737), Letters to the Citizens of the United States of America (1802–03). NF
Thompson, Benjamin (1753), Philosophical Papers. NF
Wood, Sarah Sayward Barrell Keating (1759), Amelia; or, the Influence of Virtue. F

Georgia ceded its western territory to U.S.
U.S. Military Academy founded.

Jeremy Bentham introduced theory of utilitariansim.
Cobbett's Political Register (London), 1802–36.
The Edinburgh Review, 1802–1929.
Scott's Minstrelsy of the Scottish Border (1802–03).
Paley's Natural Theology.
de Staël's Delphine.
Chateaubriand's The Spirit of Christianity.

1803

Davis, John (1775), Travels of Four Years and a Half in the United States. NF
Dickinson, John (1732), An Address on the Past, Present, and Eventual Relations of the United States to France. NF
Duane, William (1760), The Mississippi Question. NF
Dunlap, William (1766), The Glory of Columbia; Her Yeomanry [revision of André (1798); pub. 1817]. D
Fessenden, Thomas Green (1771), Terrible Tractoration! V
Wirt, William (1772), Letters of the British Spy. NF

Ohio admitted to the Union.
Napoleon sold Louisiana Territory to U.S. for $15 million.
Marbury vs. Madison (affirmed the doctrine of judicial review).
The Literary Magazine and American Register (Phila.), 1803–07.

Britain renewed war with France.
Godwin's A Life of Chaucer.
Kleist's The Schroffenstein Family.

1804

Adams, Hannah (1755), The Truth and Excellence of the Christian Religion Exhibited. NF
Adams, John Quincy (1767), Letters on Silesia. NF
"Anthony Pasquin" (1761), The Hamiltoniad. V

12th Amendment (presidential elector ballots) ratified.
Aaron Burr killed Alexander Hamilton in a duel.

Austin, William (1778), Letters from London. NF
Ballou, Hosea (1771), Notes on the Parables. NF
Fessenden, Thomas Green (1771), Original Poems. V
Morse, Jedidiah (1761), A Compendious History of New
   England (with Elijah Parish). NF
Paine, Thomas (1737), Letter to the People of England. NF
Rowson, Susanna (c. 1762), Miscellaneous Poems. V
Wirt, William (1772), The Rainbow. NF
Wood, Sarah Sayward Barrell Keating (1759), Ferdinand and
   Elmira: A Russian Story. F

Lewis and Clark explored west of the
   Mississippi (1804–06).
Nathaniel Hawthorne b.
The Richmond Enquirer, 1804–77.

Napoleon crowned himself emperor of
   France.
British and Foreign Bible Society
   founded, in London.
Immanuel Kant d.
Blake's *Jerusalem* (1804–20); *Milton*
   (1804–08).
Edgeworth's *Popular Tales.*
Schiller's *Wilhelm Tell.*

1805

Ballou, Hosea (1771), A Treatise on Atonement. NF
Brackenridge, Hugh Henry (1748), Modern Chivalry (rev.
   edition). F
Davis, John (1775), The Post Captain. F; The First Settlers of
   Virginia. F
Fessenden, Thomas Green (1771), Democracy Unveiled. V
Ioor, William (fl. 1780–1830), Independence, or Which Do You
   Like Best, the Peer or the Farmer? D
Linn, John Blair (d. 1804), Valerian. V
Warren, Caroline Matilda (1787?), The Gamesters; or, Ruins
   of Innocence. F
Warren, Mercy Otis (1728), History of the Rise, Progress, and
   Termination of the American Revolution. NF
Wilson, Alexander (1766), The Foresters. V

U.S. signed peace treaty with Tripoli.
Creation of the Michigan Territory.
Zebulon Pike explored the Upper
   Mississippi River.
Boston Athenaeum founded.
Philadelphia Academy of the Fine Arts
   opened.

Napoleon crowned king of Italy.
Lord Nelson defeated French at
   Trafalgar.
Friedrich von Schiller d.
Scott's *The Lay of the Last Minstrel.*
Hazlitt's *Principles of Human Action.*
Chateaubriand's *René.*

1806

Anon., Adventures in a Castle. F
Assolini, Paolo (1759), Observations on the Disease Called the
   Plague. NF
Barlow, Joel (1754), Prospectus of a National Institution to be
   Established in the United States. NF
Bonnycastle, John (1750?), An Introduction to Algebra. NF
Ewell, Thomas (1785), Plain Discourses on the Laws or
   Properties of Matter. NF
Latrobe, Benjamin (1764), A Private Letter to the Individual
   Members of Congress. NF
Lee, Chauncey (1763), The Trial of Virtue. V
Littell, William (1768), An Epistle from William, Surnamed
   Littell, to the People of the Realm of Kentucky. NF
Morris, Gouverneur (1752), An Answer to War in Disguise; or,
   Remarks Upon the New Doctrine of England Concerning
   Neutral Trade (attrib.). NF
Payne, John Howard (1791), Julia; or, The Wanderer. D
Webster, Noah (1758), A Compendious Dictionary of the
   English Language. NF

President Jefferson ordered arrest of
   Aaron Burr.
Benjamin Latrobe designed first
   American Roman Catholic cathedral,
   in Baltimore.
Gas streetlights introduced in Newport,
   R.I.
William Gilmore Simms b.

Francis II renounced title of Holy
   Roman Emperor.
Prussia declared war on France.
John Stuart Mill b.
Elizabeth Barrett b.
Bryon's *Fugitive Pieces.*
Scott's *Ballads and Lyrical Pieces.*
Thomas Moore's *Epistles, Odes and
   Other Poems.*
Hazlitt's *Free Thoughts on Public
   Affairs.*

1807

Anon., Margaretta; or, The Intricacies of the Heart. F
Anon., The Vain Cottager; or, The History of Lucy Franklin. F
Barker, James Nelson (1784), Tears and Smiles. D

Congress passed Embargo Act.
Aaron Burr tried for treason and
   acquitted.

Barlow, Joel (1754), The Columbiad (revision of The Vision of Columbus, 1787). V

Brown, William Hill (d. 1793), Ira and Isabella; or, The Natural Children. F

Ioor, William (fl. 1780–1830), The Battle of Eutaw Springs (prod. 1813). D

Irving, Washington (1783), Salmagundi; or, The Whim-Whams and Opinions of Launcelot Langstaff, Esq., and Others (with others). NF

Manvill, Mrs. P. D. (?), Lucinda; or, The Mountain Mourner. F

Mease, James (1771), A Geological Account of the United States. NF

Paine, Thomas (1737), Examination of the Passages in the New Testament Quoted from the Old. NF

Peters, Samuel Andrew (1735), A History of the Reverend Hugh Peters. NF

Sampson, Ezra (1749), The Youth's Companion; or, An Historical Dictionary. NF

Trumbull, Benjamin (1735), An Address to the Public . . . on the Subjects of Prayer and Family Religion. NF

Robert Fulton launched his steamboat *Clermont*.
Henry Wadsworth Longfellow b.
John Greenleaf Whittier b.

———

Napoleon signed treaties with Russia and Prussia.
Wordsworth's *Poems in Two Volumes*.
Byron's *Poems on Various Occasions*.
Charles and Mary Lamb's *Tales from Shakespeare*.
Southey's *Letters from England*.
de Staël's *Corinne*.
Hegel's *The Phenomenology of Mind*.

1808

Ashe, Thomas (1770), Travels in America . . . for the Purpose of Exploring the Rivers Alleghany, Monongahela, Ohio, and Mississippi. NF

Bard, Samuel (1742), A Compendium of the Theory and Practice of Midwifery. NF

Barker, James Nelson (1784), The Embargo; or, What News? D; The Indian Princess; or, La Belle Sauvage. D

Bryant, William Cullen (1794), The Embargo; or, Sketches of the Times. V

Davis, John (1775), Walter Kennedy. F

Grant, Anne McVickar (1755), Memoirs of an American Lady. NF

Hassal, Mary (?), Secret History; or, The Horrors of St. Domingo, in a Series of Letters. F

Hitchcock, David (1773), A Poetical Dictionary; or, Popular Terms Illustrated in Rhyme. V, NF

Jenks, William (1778), Memoir of the Northern Kingdom (attrib.). F

Surr, Thomas Skinner (1770), A Winter in London, or Sketches of Fashion. F

Watterston, George (1783), The Lawyer; or, Man as He Ought Not to Be (attrib.). F

Wilson, Alexander (1766), American Ornithology (9 vols., 1808–14). NF

Congress prohibited importation of African slaves.
John Jacob Astor established American Fur Co.
John Dickinson d.
American Law Journal (Phila. et al.), 1808–17.

———

Napoleon occupied Spain.
The Examiner (London), 1808–81.
Scott's *Marmion*.
Charles Lamb's *Specimens of English Dramatic Poets*.
Thomas Moore's *A Selection of Irish Melodies* (1808–34).
Goethe's *Faust, Part I*.
Kleist's *Penthesilea*.

1809

Adams, John (1735), The Inadmissible Principles. NF

Allen, William (1784), American Biographical and Historical Dictionary (compiler). NF

Ames, Fisher (d. 1808), Works. NF

Campbell, Thomas (1777), Gertrude of Wyoming. V

Cheetham, James (1772), Life of Thomas Paine. NF

Freneau, Philip (1752), Poems . . . Third Edition. V

Irving, Washington (1791), A History of New York, From the Beginning of the World to the End of the Dutch Dynasty, by Diedrich Knickerbocker. F

Congress repealed Embargo Act.
Creation of the Illinois Territory.
First geological survey of the U.S. published.
Thomas Paine d.
Abraham Lincoln b.
Edgar Allan Poe b.

———

Russia annexed Finland.
Napoleon annexed the Papal States.
Alfred Tennyson b.

Payne, John Howard (1791), Lovers' Vows. D
Ramsay, David (1749), History of South Carolina from Its First
  Settlement in 1670 to the Year 1808. NF
Smith, Samuel Stanhope (1750), Lectures on the Evidences of
  the Christian Religion. NF
Tyler, Royall (1757), The Yankey in London. F

Byron's *English Bards and Scotch
  Reviewers.*
Chateaubriand's *Martyrs.*
Goethe's *The Elective Affinities.*
Friedrich von Schlegel's *On Dramatic
  Art and Literature.*

1810

Cooper, William (d. 1809), A Guide in the Wilderness. NF
Crafts, William (1787), The Raciad and Other Occasional
  Poems. V
Duane, William (1760), A Military Dictionary. NF
Hare, Robert (1781), Brief View of the Policies and Resources
  of the United States. NF
Ingersoll, Charles Jared (1782), Inchiquin, the Jesuit's Letters.
  . . . NF
Irving, Washington (1783), Biographical Sketch of Thomas
  Campbell (in The Poetical Works of Thomas Campbell). NF
Paine, Thomas (d. 1809), On the Origin of Freemasonry. NF
Pike, Zebulon Montgomery (1779), Account of Expeditions to
  the Sources of the Mississippi and through the Western Parts of
  Louisiana. NF
Thomas, Isaiah (1749), History of Printing in America. NF
Trumbull, Benjamin (1735), General History of the United
  States. NF
Worcester, Noah (1758), Bible News. . . . NF

U.S. annexed West Florida.
Macon's Bill No. 2 (trade with France
  and Britain).
Charles Brockden Brown d.
Margaret Fuller b.

Napoleon annexed Holland.
Scott's *The Lady of the Lake.*
Crabbe's *The Borough.*
Southey's *The Curse of Kehama.*
Goethe's *On the Theory of Colors.*
Kleist's *Kätchen from Heilbronn.*

1811

Bigland, John (1750), A Geographical and Historical View of the
  World. NF
Brackenridge, Hugh Henry (1748), An Epistle to Walter Scott
  on Reading "The Lady of the Lake." NF
Cole, John (1774), The Minstrel: A Collection of Celebrated
  Songs Set to Music (editor). V
Duane, William (1760), An Epitome of the Arts and Sciences.
  NF
Hoyt, Epaphras (1765), Practical Instructions for Military
  Officers. NF
Jackson, Daniel (fl. 1790–1811), Alonzo and Melissa, or The
  Unfeeling Father (plagiarized from Isaac Mitchell; see below).
  F
Lowell, John (1769), An Appeal to the People on the Causes and
  Consequences of a War with Great Britain (attrib.). NF
Mitchell, Isaac (c. 1759), The Asylum; or, Alonzo and Melissa.
  F
Montefiore, Joshua (1762), The American Trader's
  Compendium, Containing the Laws, Customs, and Regulations
  of the United States. NF
Williamson, Hugh (1735), Observations on the Climate in
  Different Parts of America. NF
Worcester, Noah (1758), A Respectful Address to the Trinitarian
  Clergy Relating to Their Manner of Treating Opponents. NF

Battle of Tippecanoe (Gen. William
  Henry Harrison defeated the
  Indians).
First steamboat service on the
  Mississippi River.
Harriet Beecher Stowe b.
Niles' Weekly Register (Baltimore),
  1811–49.

George, Prince of Wales, became
  prince regent (1811–20).
John Nash designed Regent's Park,
  London.
William Makepeace Thackeray b.
Théophile Gautier b.
Austen's *Sense and Sensibility.*
Scott's *The Vision of Don Roderick.*
Shelley's *The Necessity of Atheism.*
Fouqué's *Undine.*
Goethe's *Poetry and Truth* (1811–32).

1812

Adams, Hannah (1755), The History of the Jews. NF
Barker, James Nelson (1784), Marmion; or, The Battle of
  Flodden Field (pub. 1816). D

U.S. declared war on Great Britain
  (1812–14).
Louisiana admitted to the Union.

Dunlap, William (1766), Yankee Chronology; or, Huzza for the Constitution! D
Melish, John (1771), Travels in the United States. NF
Murray, John (1741), Letters and Sketches of Sermons (1812–13). NF
Noah, Mordecai Manuel (1785), Paul and Alexis (retitled The Wandering Boys, 1821). D
Paine, Robert Treat (d. 1811), Works. V
Paulding, James Kirke (1778), The Diverting History of John Bull and Brother Jonathan. NF
Pierpont, John (1785), The Portrait. V
Rush, Benjamin (1745), Medical Inquiries and Observations Upon Diseases of the Mind. NF
Smith, James (c. 1737), A Treatise on the Mode and Manner of Indian War. NF
Smith, Samuel Stanhope (1750), Lectures . . . on the Subjects of Moral and Political Philosophy. NF
Wirt, William (1772), The Old Bachelor (with others). NF

Creation of the Missouri Territory.
American Antiquarian Society founded, in Worcester, Mass.
First life insurance company, in Philadelphia.

Napoleon invaded Russia, destroyed Smolensk, occupied Moscow, retreated in disarray.
Roxburghe Club founded in England.
Byron's *Childe Harold's Pilgrimage* (1812–18).
Combe's *Dr. Syntax in Search of the Picturesque*.
Brothers Grimm's *Fairy Tales* (1812–14).
Hegel's *Logic* (1812–16).

1813

Allston, Washington (1779), The Sylphs of the Seasons. V
Anon., St. Herbert: A Tale. F
Dunlap, William (1766), Memoirs of George Fred. Cooke. NF
Fowler, George (?), A Flight to the Moon; or, The Vision of Randalthus. F
Heriot, George (1766), Travels Through the Canadas. NF
Holland, Edwin Clifford (c. 1794), Odes, Naval Songs, and Other Occasional Poems. V
Kilty, William (1757), The Vision of Don Croker (attrib.). V
Paulding, James Kirke (1778), The Lay of the Scottish Fiddle: A Tale of Havre de Grace, Supposed to Be Written by Walter Scott, Esq. F
Rowson, Susanna (c. 1762), Sarah; or, The Exemplary Wife. F
Sampson, William (1764), The Catholic Question in America. NF
Trotter, Thomas (1760), An Essay, Medical, Philosophical, and Chemical, on Drunkenness and Its Effects on the Human Body. NF
Watterston, George (1783), The Scenes of Youth. V

British blockade of U.S. coastal ports.
Burning of Buffalo.
Methodist Missionary Society founded.
First recorded use of "Uncle Sam."
Boston Daily Advertiser, 1813–1929.
The Christian Disciple (Boston), 1813–23.

Duke of Wellington invaded France.
Robert Southey named poet laureate of England.
Austen's *Pride and Prejudice*.
Shelley's *Queen Mab*.
Coleridge's *Remorse*.
de Staël's *On Germany*.

1814

Allen, Paul (1775), History of the Expedition of Captains Lewis and Clark (with Nicholas Biddle). NF
Brackenridge, Henry Marie (1786), Views of Louisiana. NF
Brackenridge, Hugh Henry (1748), Law Miscellanies. NF
Carey, Mathew (1760), The Olive Branch, NF
Dunlap, William (1766), A Narrative of the Events Which Followed Bonaparte's Campaign in Russia. NF
Humphreys, David (1752), The Yankey in England. D
Key, Francis Scott (1779), "The Star-Spangled Banner." V
Littell, William (1768), Festoons of Fancy: Consisting of Compositions Amatory, Sentimental, and Humorous in Verse and Prose. V, F
Taylor, John (1753), An Inquiry into the Principles and Policy of the Government of the United States. NF
Worcester, Noah (1758), A Solemn Review of the Custom of War. NF

British burned the White House and the Capitol, attacked Baltimore.
End of the Creek Indian War.
Emma Willard opened Middlebury Female Seminary.
Francis Scott Key's "The Star-Spangled Banner."

Napoleon abdicated; exiled to Elba.
Louis XVIII restored to French throne.
Edmund Kean's debut in London.
Austen's *Mansfield Park*.
Scott's *Waverley*.
Wordsworth's *The Excursion*.
Shelley's *A Refutation of Deism*.
Hoffmann's *Fantasy Pieces* (1814–15).

1815

Brackenridge, Hugh Henry (1748), Modern Chivalry (final edition). F

Crocker, Hannah Mather (1752), Series of Letters on Free Masonry. NF

Drake, Daniel (1785), Picture of Cincinnati in 1815. NF

Dunlap, William (1766), The Life of Charles Brockden Brown. NF

Dwight, Timothy (1752), Remarks on the Review of Inchiquin's Letters. NF

Freneau, Philip (1752), A Collection of Poems. V

Paulding, James Kirke (1778), The United States and England. NF

Payne, John Howard (1791), The Maid and the Magpie. D

Porter, David (1780), Journal of a Cruise Made to the Pacific Ocean. NF

Sigourney, Lydia Huntley (1791), Moral Pieces in Prose and Verse. NF, V

Verplanck, Gulian Crommelin (1786), A Fable for Statesman and Politicians. NF

Weems, Mason Locke (1759), God's Revenge Against Adultery. NF

Andrew Jackson routed British in New Orleans.
Benjamin Latrobe began rebuilding the White House (1815–17).
Stephan Decatur's expedition against the Dey of Algiers.
The North American Review (Boston; New York), 1815–1939.

Napoleon's return: "The Hundred Days."
Wellington's victory at Waterloo.
Napoleon's second exile, to St. Helena.
Scott's *Guy Mannering*.
Malthus's *An Inquiry into . . . Rent*.

1816

Ballou, Hosea (1771), A Series of Letters in Defense of Divine Revelation. NF

Channing, William Ellery (1780), A Sermon on War. NF

"Frederick Augustus Fidfaddy" (?), The Adventures of Uncle Sam, in Search After His Lost Honor. F

Gilmer, Francis Walker (1790), Sketches of American Orators. NF

Kneeland, Abner (1774), A Series of Letters in Defense of Divine Revelation (response to Ballou, above). NF

Ogilvie, James (1775), Philosophical Essays. NF

Payne, John Howard (1791), Accusation. D

Pickering, John (1777), Vocabulary of Words and Phrases Peculiar to the United States. NF

Pierpont, John (1785), Airs of Palestine. V

Ramsay, David (d. 1815), History of the United States (3 vols., 1816–17; completed by Samuel Stanhope Smith). NF

Tucker, George (1775), Letters from Virginia. NF

Wilson, Alexander (1776), Poems; Chiefly in the Scottish Dialect V

Woodworth, Samuel (1785), The Champions of Freedom. F

Indiana admitted to the Union.
Second Bank of the United States (1816–36).
First savings banks chartered, in Boston and Philadelphia.
American Bible Society founded, in New York City.
Hugh Henry Brackenridge d.

Typhus epidemic in Ireland.
Richard Brinsley Sheridan d.
Austen's *Emma*.
Shelley's *Alastor*.
Byron's *The Prisoner of Chillon*.
Peacock's *Headlong Hall*.
Coleridge's *Christabel, Kubla Khan, The Pains of Sleep*.
Goethe's *Italian Journey* (1816–17).
Hoffmann's *Night Pieces* (1816–17).

1817

Barker, James Nelson (1784), The Armourer's Escape; or, Three Years at Nootka Sound. D; How to Try a Lover. D

Birkbeck, Morris (1764), Notes on a Journey . . . to the Territory of Illinois. NF

Brackenridge, Henry Marie (1786), South America. NF

Bryant, William Cullen (1794), "Thanatopsis." V

Delano, Amasa (1763), A Narrative of Voyages and Travels in the Northern and Southern Hemispheres. NF

Dennie, Joseph (d. 1812), The Lay Preacher (new ser.). NF

Du Ponceau, Pierre Etienne (1760), English Phonology. NF

Mississippi admitted to the Union.
Creation of the Alabama Territory.
Construction began on Erie Canal.
Henry David Thoreau b.

Blackwood's Edinburgh Magazine (1817–1980).
Jane Austen d.
Mme. de Staël d.
Keats's *Poems*.
Coleridge's *Biographia Literaria*.

Neal, John (1793), Keep Cool. F
Paulding, James Kirke (1778), Letters from the South. NF
Wirt, William (1772), Life of Patrick Henry. NF

Byron's *Manfred*.
Scott's *Rob Roy*.
Thomas Moore's *Lalla Rookh*.

1818

Bancroft, Aaron (1755), A Discourse on Conversion. NF
Bristed, John (1778), The Resources of the United States of America. NF
Bryant, William Cullen (1794), "To a Waterfowl." V
Cobbett, William (1763), A Year's Residence in the United States of America. NF
Crocker, Hannah Mather (1752), Observations on the Real Rights of Women. NF
Dearborn, Henry (1751), An Account of the Battle of Bunker Hill. NF
Dwight, Timothy (d. 1817), Theology, Explained and Defended (1818–19). NF
"Guy Mannering" (?), Rosalvo Delmonmort. F
Kennedy, John Pendleton (1795), The Red Book (1818–19). NF
Latrobe, Christian Ignatius (1758), Journal of a Visit to South Africa in 1815 and 1816. NF
Neal, John (1793), "Battle of Niagara." V; "Goldau, or, the Maniac Harper." V
Norton, Andrews (1786), A Discourse on Religious Education. NF
Nuttall, Thomas (1786), The Genera of North American Plants. NF
"Obadiah Benjamin Franklin Bloomfield" (?), The Life and Adventures of Obadiah Benjamin Franklin Bloomfield, M. D. F
Paulding, James Kirke (1778), The Backwoodsman: A Poem. V
Payne, John Howard (1791), Brutus; or, The Fall of Tarquin. D
Woodworth, Samuel (1785), The Poems, Odes, Songs, and Other Metrical Effusions. . . . V

Illinois admitted to the Union.
U.S. and Britain established Canadian boundary.
General Andrew Jackson invaded Florida, began First Seminole War.

Austen's *Northanger Abbey; Persuasion*.
Keats's *Endymion*.
Mary Shelley's *Frankenstein*.
Scott's *The Heart of Midlothian*.
Byron's *Beppo*.
Peacock's *Nightmare Abbey*.
Grillparzer's *Sappho*.

1819

Adams, John (1735), Novanglus and Massachusettensis; or, Political Essays. NF
Allen, Paul (1775), History of the American Revolution (largely revised by John Neal). NF
Brackenridge, Henry Marie (1786), Voyage to South America. NF
Channing, William Ellery (1780), A Sermon Delivered at the Ordination of the Rev. Jared Sparks (commonly known as "Unitarian Christianity" or "Baltimore Sermon"). NF
Halleck, Fitz-Greene (1790), Poems, by Croaker, Croaker & Co., and Croaker Jun. (with Joseph Rodman Drake). V; Fanny. V
Heckewelder, John Gottlieb Ernestus (1743), An Account of the History, Manners, and Customs of the Indian Nations Who Once Inhabited Pennsylvania. NF
Hillhouse, James Abraham (1789), Percy's Masque. D
Irving, Washington (1783), The Sketch Book of Geoffrey Crayon, Gent. (1819–20). NF, F
Melish, John (1771), Information and Advice to Emigrants to the United States. NF

Alabama admitted to the Union.
East Florida ceded to U.S. by Spain.
Creation of the Arkansas Territory.
Financial panic in U.S.
McCulloch vs. Maryland (constitutionality of the Second Bank).
Herman Melville b.
Walt Whitman b.
New York American, 1819–45.

Peterloo Massacre (Manchester, England; repeal of corn laws).
Simon Bolívar became president of Venezuela.
National Museum of the Prado opened in Madrid.
John Ruskin b.
Byron's *Don Juan* (1819–24).
Scott's *Ivanhoe*.
Shelley's *The Cenci*.
Schopenhauer's *The World as Will and Idea*.

Neal, John (1793), Otho. D
Noah, Mordecai Manuel (1785), She Would Be a Soldier.
  D; Travels in England, France, Spain, and the Barbary States.
  NF
Paine, Thomas (d. 1809), Miscellaneous Poems. V
Paulding, James Kirke (1778), Salmagundi: Second Series
  (1819–20). NF
Ramsay, David (d. 1815), Universal History Americanized (12
  vols.). NF
Verplanck, Gulian Crommelin (1786), The State Triumvirate.
  NF
Walsh, Robert (1784), An Appeal from the Judgments of Great
  Britain Respecting the United States of America. NF
Wilde, Richard Henry (1789), "The Lament of the Captive." V
Willard, Emma (1787), Address . . . Proposing a Plan for
  Improving Female Education. NF
Wright, Frances (1795), Altorf. D

Hoffmann's *Tomcat Murr* (1819–22).

1820

Brooks, Maria Gowen (c. 1794), Judith, Esther, and Other
  Poems. V
Channing, William Ellery (1780), The Moral Argument Against
  Calvinism. NF
Cooper, James Fenimore (1789), Precaution: A Novel. F
Crafts, William (1787), Sullivan's Island and Other Poems. V
Force, Peter (1790), National Calendar and Annals of the United
  States (1820–24, 1828–36). NF
Hall, James (1793), Trial and Defense of First Lieutenant James
  Hall. NF
Heckewelder, John Gottlieb Ernestus (1743), A Narrative of
  the Mission of the United Brethern among the Delaware and
  Mohegan Indians. NF
Irving, Peter (1771), Giovanni Sbogarro. F
Noah, Mordecai Manuel (1785), The Siege of Tripoli. D
Raymond, Daniel (1786), Thoughts on Political Economy. NF
Sands, Robert C. (1799), Yamoyden (with James Wallis
  Eastburn). V
Taylor, John (1753), Construction Construed and Constitutions
  Vindicated. NF
Tudor, William (1779), Letters on the Eastern States. NF
Ware, Henry (1764), Letters to Trinitarians and Calvinists. NF

Maine admitted to the Union.
Missouri Compromise (on slavery in
  Louisiana Territory).

George IV crowned king of England.
Trial of Queen Caroline in London.
Venus de Milo discovered on Melos.
Shelley's *Prometheus Unbound.*
Keats's *Lamia and Other Poems.*
Maturin's *Melmoth the Wanderer.*
Pushkin's *Ruslan and Ludmila.*
Lamartine's *Meditations on Poetry.*

1821

Adams, John Quincy (1767), Report on Weights and Measures.
  NF
Allen, Paul (1775), Noah (rev. by John Neal). V
Bryant, William Cullen (1794), "The Ages." V; Poems. V
Channing, William Ellery (1780), A Discourse on the Evidences
  of Revealed Religion. NF
Cobbett, William (1763), The American Gardener. NF
Cooper, James Fenimore (1789), The Spy: A Tale of the Neutral
  Ground. F
Doddridge, Joseph (1769), Logan. D
Drayton, William Henry (d. 1779), Memoirs of the American
  Revolution. NF
Dwight, Timothy (d. 1817), Travels in New-England and New-
  York (1821–22). NF

Missouri admitted to the Union.
Andrew Jackson named military
  governor of Florida.
First public high school, in Boston.
The Saturday Evening Post (Phila.),
  1821–1969.

The Manchester Guardian, 1821–.
John Keats d.
Napoleon Bonaparte d.
Shelley's *Adonais; A Defence of Poetry.*
Scott's *Kenilworth.*
James Mill's *Elements of Political
  Economy.*
Southey's *A Vision of Judgment.*

Noah, Mordecai Manuel (1785), Marion; or, The Hero of Lake George. D
Payne, John Howard (1791), Thérèse, the Orphan of Geneva. D
Percival, James Gates (1795), Poems. V
Schoolcraft, Henry Rowe (1793), Narrative Journal of Travels through the Northwestern Regions of the United States . . . . NF
Tudor, William (1779), Miscellanies. NF
Wright, Frances (1795), Views of Society and Manners in America. NF

Goethe's *Wilhelm Meister's Travels* (1821, 1829).
Hegel's *The Philosophy of Right.*

1822

Ainslie, Hew (1792), A Pilgrimage to the Land of Burns. NF, V
Clarke, McDonald (1798), The Elixir of Moonshine . . . by the Mad Poet. V
Everett, Alexander Hill (1790), Europe. NF
Fairfield, Sumner Lincoln (1803), The Siege of Constantinople. V
Irving, Washington (1783), Bracebridge Hall; or, The Humorists. NF, F
Lawson, James (1799), Ontwa, the Son of the Forest. V
McHenry, James (1785), The Pleasures of Friendship. V
Morse, Jedidiah (1761), Report to the Secretary of War . . . on Indian Affairs. NF
Neal, John (1793), Logan, A Family History. F
Noah, Mordecai Manuel (1785), The Grecian Captive. D
Paulding, James Kirke (1778), A Sketch of Old England, by a New England Man. NF
Payne, John Howard (1791), Adeline, the Victim of Seduction. D
Percival, James Gates (1795), Clio (1822–27). V
Sedgwick, Catharine Maria (1789), A New-England Tale. F
Taylor, John (1753), Tyranny Unmasked. NF
Wright, Frances (1795), A Few Days in Athens. F

Florida organized as a territory, beset by Indian wars.
U.S. recognition of first Latin American independent republics.
Stephen Fuller Austin established first settlement of Anglo-Americans in Texas.

The Sunday Times (London), 1822–.
Percy Bysshe Shelley d.
Matthew Arnold b.
Byron's *The Vision of Judgment.*
De Quincey's *Confessions of an English Opium Eater.*
Peacock's *Maid Marian.*
Wordsworth's *Ecclesiastical Sketches* [Sonnets].
Heine's *Poems.*
Pushkin's *The Prisoner in the Caucasus.*

1823

Bancroft, George (1800), Poems. V
Cooper, James Fenimore (1789), The Pioneers; or, The Sources of the Susquehanna: A Descriptive Tale. F; Tales for Fifteen. F; The Pilot: A Tale of the Sea. F
McHenry, James (1785), Waltham. V; The Wilderness; or, Braddock's Time. F; The Spectre of the Forest. F
Moore, Clement Clarke (1779), "A Visit from St. Nicholas" (commonly known as " 'Twas the Night Before Christmas"). V
Morton, Sarah Wentworth (1759), My Mind and Its Thoughts. NF, V
Neal, John (1793), Errata; or, The Works of Will. Adams. F; Seventy-Six. F; Randolph. F
Paulding, James Kirke (1778), Koningsmarke: The Long Finne, A Story of the New World. F
Payne, John Howard (1791), Ali Pacha, or The Signet Ring. D; Clari; or, The Maid of Milan. D
Taylor, John (1753), New Views of the Constitution. NF
Thacher, James (1754), A Military Journal During the American Revolutionary War. NF
Tudor, William (1779), The Life of James Otis of Massachusetts. NF

Monroe Doctrine announced in president's message to Congress.
Francis Parkman b.
The New York Mirror, 1823–60.
John Howard Payne's "Home Sweet Home."

John Stuart Mill formed Utilitarian Society (1823–26).
William Wilberforce formed an antislavery society, in England.
Rugby football introduced, in England.
Scott's *Quentin Durward.*
Charles Lamb's *The Essays of Elia.*
Hazlitt's *Liber Amoris.*
Lamartine's *New Mediations on Poetry.*

1824

Austin, William (1778), "Peter Rugg, the Missing Man." F
Barker, James Nelson (1784), Superstition; or, The Fanatic
  Father (pub. 1826). D
Brainard, John Gardiner Calkins (1796), Letters Found in the
  Ruins of Fort Bradford. F
Bryant, William Cullen (1794), "Monument Mountain."
  V; "Mutation." V
Child, Lydia Maria (1802), Hobomok. F
Doddridge, Joseph (1769), Notes on the Settlement and Indian
  Wars of Virginia and Pennsylvania from 1763 to 1783. NF
Irving, Washington (1783), Tales of a Traveller. F
Morse, Jedidiah (1761), Annals of the American Revolution. NF
Neal, John (1793), American Writers (1824–25; coll. 1937). NF
Payne, John Howard (1791), Charles the Second; or, The Merry
  Monarch (with Washington Irving). D
Rafinesque, Constantine Samuel (1783), A History of
  Kentucky. NF
Seaver, James E. (1787), A Narrative of the Life of Mrs. Mary
  Jemison. NF
Sedgwick, Catharine Maria (1789), Redwood. F
Smith, Margaret Bayard (1778), A Winter in Washington. F
Tucker, George (1775), The Valley of Shenandoah. F
Tyler, Royall (1757), The Chestnut Tree (pub. 1931). V
Woodworth, Samuel (1785), LaFayette. D

James Bridger discovered Great Salt
  Lake.
First college of science and engineering
  founded (now Rensselaer
  Polytechnic Institute).
American Sunday School Union
  established, in Philadelphia.
The Christian Examiner (Boston),
  1824–69.

Charles X succeeded Louis XVIII in
  France.
National Gallery established in
  London.
The Westminster Review (London),
  1824–1914.
Lord Byron d.
Godwin's *A History of the
  Commonwealth of England* (1824–
  28)
Landor's *Imaginary Conversations*
  (1824 29).
Shelley's *Posthumous Poems* (ed. Mary
  Shelley).

1825

Brainard, John Gardiner Calkins (1796), Occasional Pieces of
  Poetry. V
Bryant, William Cullen (1794), "A Forest Hymn." V; "The
  Death of the Flowers." V
Child, Lydia Maria (1802), The Rebels, or, Boston before the
  Revolution. F
Cooper, James Fenimore (1789), Lionel Lincoln; or, The
  Leaguer of Boston. F
Dwight, Theodore (1764), The Northern Traveller. NF
Follen, Charles (1796), Hymns for Children. V
Halleck, Fitz-Greene (1790), Marco Bozzaris. V
Hentz, Nicholas Marcellus (1797), Tadeuskund, the Last King
  of the Lenape. F
Hillhouse, James Abraham (1789), Hadad. D
Jones, James Athearn (1791), The Refugee. F
Leggett, William (1801), Leisure Hours at Sea. V
Neal, John (1793), Brother Jonathan. F
Paulding, James Kirke (1778), John Bull in America; or, The
  New Munchausen. NF
Pinkney, Edward Coote (1802), Poems. V
Smith, Richard Penn (1799), The Divorce. D
Woodworth, Samuel (1785), The Forest Rose. D; The Widow's
  Son. D

Texas opened for settlement by
  American citizens.
Erie Canal completed.
Robert Owen's social community in
  New Harmony, Ind.
Hudson River School of landscape
  painting rebelled against 18th-
  century tradition.

Czar Nicholas I crushed Decembrist
  uprising.
Bolshoi Ballet established in Moscow.
Beginning of British labor unions.
Milton's *De Doctrina Christiana*
  (posth.).
Pepys's *Diary* (posth.; ed. Lord
  Braybrook).
Coleridge's *Aids to Reflection.*
Manzoni's *The Betrothed* (1825–27).

1826

Channing, William Ellery (1780), Unitarian Christianity Most
  Favorable to Piety. NF

U.S. Mission to Panama Congress
  failed.

Cooper, James Fenimore (1789), The Last of the Mohicans: A Narrative of 1757. F
Duane, William (1760), A Visit to Colombia. NF
Gilmer, Francis Walker (1790), Sketches, Essays and Translations. NF
Kent, James (1763), Commentaries on American Law (1826–30). NF
Leggett, William (1801), Journals of the Ocean. V
Morris, George Pope (1802), Brier Cliff. D
Murray, Lindley (1745), Memoirs. NF
Paulding, James Kirke (1778), The Merry Tales of the Three Wise Men of Gotham. F
Payne, John Howard (1791), Richelieu: A Domestic Tragedy (with Washington Irving). D
Pickering, John (1777), Comprehensive Lexicon of the Greek Language. NF
Reed, Sampson (1800), Observations on the Growth of the Mind. NF
Royall, Anne Newport (1769), Sketches of History, Life, and Manners in the United States. NF
Woodworth, Samuel (1785), Melodies, Duets, Trios, Songs, and Ballads. V

Thomas Jefferson d.
John Adams d.
National Academy of Design founded, in New York City.
Graham's Magazine (Phila.), 1826–58.

Benjamin Disraeli's *Vivian Grey* (1826–27).
E. B. Browning's *Essay on Mind, with Other Poems.*
Hazlitt's *Journey through France and Italy.*
Mary Shelley's *The Last Man.*
Heine's *Travel Sketches* (1826–31).
Vigny's *Poems Ancient and Modern.*

1827

Audubon, John James (1785), The Birds of America from Original Drawings (folio edition, 1827–38). NF
Bird, Robert Montgomery (1806), The Cowled Lover (pub. 1941). D; Caridorf; or, The Avenger (pub. 1941). D; News of the Night; or, A Trip to Niagara (pub. 1941). D; 'Twas All for the Best; or, 'Tis All a Notion (pub. 1941). D
Cooper, James Fenimore (1789), The Prairie: A Tale. F; The Red Rover: A Tale. F
Custis, George Washington Parke (1781), The Indian Prophecy, a National Drama in Two Acts, Founded on . . . the Life of George Washington. D
Drake, Benjamin (1795), Cincinnati in 1826 (with Edward D. Mansfield). NF
Everett, Alexander Hill (1790), America. NF
Fairfield, Sumner Lincoln (1803), The Cities of the Plain. V
Goodrich, Samuel Griswold (1793), The Tales of Peter Parley about America. F
Hale, Sarah Josepha (1788), Northwood, A Tale of New England. F
Halleck, Fitz-Greene (1790), Alnwick Castle, with Other Poems. V
Poe, Edgar Allan (1809), Tamerlane and Other Poems. V
Royall, Anne Newport (1769), The Tennessean. F
Sealsfield, Charles (1793), The United States of North America as They Are. . . . NF
Sedgwick, Catharine Maria (1789), Hope Leslie; or Early Times in Massachusetts. F
Simms, William Gilmore (1806), Lyrical and Other Poems. V; Early Lays. V
Tucker, George (1775), A Voyage to the Moon. F
Willis, N. P. (1806), Sketches. V
Wood, Sarah Sayward Barrell Keating (1759), Tales of the Night. F

Revival of tariff question, splitting North and South.
U.S. and Britain shared occupation of Oregon Territory.
First passenger railroad line incorporated (Baltimore and Ohio). ·
Freedom's Journal (New York), 1827–29, first Negro newspaper.

The Evening Standard (London), 1827–.
William Blake d.
Alfred and Charles Tennyson's *Poems by Two Brothers.*
De Quincey's *On Murder Considered as One of the Fine Arts.*
Thomas Moore's *The Epicurean.*
Hugo's *Cromwell.*
Heine's *Book of Songs.*

1828

Beecher, Lyman (1775), Letters of the Rev. Dr. Beecher and Rev. Mr. Nettleton on the "New Measures" in Conducting Revivals of Religion. NF

Bird, Robert Montgomery (1806), The City Looking Glass: A Philadelphia Comedy (pub. 1933). D

Channing, William Ellery (1780), Sermons and Tracts, Including the Analysis of the Character of Napoleon, and Remarks on the Life and Writings of John Milton. NF

Cooper, James Fenimore (1789), Notions of the Americans, Picked Up by a Travelling Bachelor. NF

Dewey, Orville (1794), Letter of an English Traveller to His Friend in England on the "Revivals of Religion" in America. NF

Dunlap, William (1766), A Trip to Niagara; or, Travellers in America (pub. 1830). D

Embury, Emma Catherine (1806), Guido. F

Hall, James (1793), Letters from the West. NF

Hawthorne, Nathaniel (1804), Fanshawe: A Tale. F

Heath, James Ewell (1792), Edge-Hill. F

Howe, Samuel Gridley (1801), An Historical Sketch of the Greek Revolution. NF

Irving, Washington (1783), A History of the Life and Voyages of Christopher Columbus. NF

Mellen, Grenville (1799), Sad Tales and Glad Tales. F

Neal, John (1793), Rachel Dyer. F

Olney, Jesse (1798), Practical System of Modern Geography. NF

Paulding, James Kirke (1778), The New Mirror for Travellers, and a Guide to the Springs. NF

Rowson, Susanna (d. 1824), Charlotte's Daughter; or. The Three Orphans (commonly known as Lucy Temple). F

Royall, Anne Newport (1769), The Black Book. . . . (3 vols. 1828–29). FN

Sealsfield, Charles (1793), The Americans As They Are . . . . NF; Austria As It Is . . . .NF; Tokeah; or, The White Rose . . . . F

Smith, Margaret Bayard (1778), What Is Gentility? F

Sparks, Jared (1789), Life of John Ledyard. NF

Thacher, James (1754), American Medical Biography. NF

Webster, Noah (1758), An American Dictionary of the English Language. NF

Wilcox, Carlos (d. 1827), Remains. NF, V

Democratic Party formed by Jackson-Calhoun faction.

Tariff of Abominations split Northern mercantile and Southern agrarian supporters.

Thomas Rice's "Jim Crow," a minstrel show.

The Ladies' Magazine (Boston), 1828–36.

Duke of Wellington named prime minister of Great Britain.

Sir Robert Peel founded London's Metropolitan Police Force ("bobbies").

The Spectator (London), 1828–.

The Athenaeum (London, 1828–1921.

George Meredith b.

Bulwer-Lytton's *Pelham.*

Hunt's *Lord Byron and Some of His Contemporaries.*

Napier's *History of the War in the Peninsula* (1828–40).

1829

Apes, William (1798), A Son of the Forest. NF

Carey, Mathew (1760), Autobiographical Sketches. NF

Cobbett, William (1763), Advice to Young Men. NF

Cooper, James Fenimore (1789), The Wept of Wish-ton-Wish: A Tale. F

Dwight, Theodore (1764), Sketches of Scenery and Manners in the United States. NF

Hale, Sarah Joseph (1788), Sketches of American Character. F

Haliburton, Thomas Chandler (1796), An Historical and Statistical Account of Nova Scotia. NF

Hall, James (1793), Winter Evenings. F

Irving, Washington (1783), A Chronicle of the Conquest of Granada. NF

Jones, James Athearn (1791), Tales of an Indian Camp. F

President Jackson's "Kitchen Cabinet" and the "spoils system."

Workingmen's Party founded, in New York.

Encyclopedia Americana published in Philadelphia.

Struggle began to free Ireland from British union.

First Oxford-Cambridge boat race, at Henley.

Revue des Deux Mondes (Paris), 1829–1940.

Carlyle's *Signs of the Times.*

Southey's *Sir Thomas More.*

Kettell, Samuel (1800), Specimens of American Poetry (editor). V

Knapp, Samuel Lorenzo (1783), Lectures on American Literature. NF

Leggett, William (1801), Tales and Sketches. By a Country Schoolmaster. F

Marsh, James (1794), S. T. Coleridge's Aids to Reflection (editor). NF

Paulding, James Kirke (1778), Tales of the Good Woman. F

Poe, Edgar Allan (1809), Al Aaraaf, Tamerlane and Minor Poems. V

Simms, William Gilmore (1806), The Vision of Cortes, Cain, and Other Poems. V

Smith, Richard Penn (1799), William Penn, or The Elm Tree. D; The Eighth of January. D; The Disowned. D; The Sentinels, or The Two Sergeants. D

Sparks, Jared (1789), The Diplomatic Correspondence of the American Revolution (editor; 12 vols., 1829–30). NF

Stone, John Augustus (1800), Metamora, or, The Last of the Wampanoags. D

Tudor, William (1779), Gebel Teir. F

Willis, N. P. (1806), Fugitive Poetry. V

Wright, Frances (1795), Course of Popular Lectures (1829, 1836). NF

Marryat's *Frank Mildmay*.
Balzac's *The Chouans* (beginning of *La Comédie Humaine* [1829–42]).
Saint-Simon's *Memoirs* (posth.; 21 vols., 1829–30).

1830

Alcott, Bronson (1799), Observations on the Principles and Methods of Infant Instruction. NF

Bird, Robert Montgomery (1806), Pelopidas (pub. 1919). D

Brainard, John Gardiner Calkins (d. 1828), Fugitive Tales. F

Carey, Mathew (1760), Miscellaneous Essays. NF

Channing, William Ellery (1780), ''The Importance and Means of a National Literature.'' NF

Cooper, James Fenimore (1798), The Water-Witch; or, The Skimmer of the Seas. F

Custis, George Washington Parke (1781), Pocahontas. D; The Railroad. D

Hale, Sarah Josepha (1788), Poems for Our Children. V

Holbrook, Josiah (1788), Scientific Tracts Designed for Instruction and Entertainment . . . (1830ff.). NF

Holmes, Oliver Wendell (1809), ''Old Ironsides.'' V

Lawson, James (1799), Tales and Sketches, by a Cosmopolite. F

Longfellow, Henry Wadsworth (1807), Elements of a French Grammar. NF; French Exercises. NF; Novelas Españolas (editor). F; Manuel de proverbes dramatiques (editor). NF

Murat, Achille (1801), Lettres sur les États-Unis. NF

Neal, John (1793), Authorship. F

Paulding, James Kirke (1778), Chronicles of the City of Gotham from the Papers of a Retired Common Councilman. F; The Lion of the West (pub. 1954). D

Pickering, John (1777), A Grammar of the Cherokee Language. NF

Royall, Anne Newport (1796), Letters from Alabama. NF

Sands, Robert C. (1799), Life and Correspondence of John Paul Jones. NF

Sedgwick, Catharine Maria (1789), Clarence; or, A Tale of Our Own Times. F

Smith, Joseph (1805), The Book of Mormon. NF

Smith, Richard Penn (1799), The Triumph at Plattsburg. D; The Deformed (revision of The Divorce). D; The Water Witch [adapted from James Fenimore Cooper's novel (1830)]. D

Webster-Hayne Debate (states' rights vs. federal government).
Joseph Smith founded Church of Jesus Christ of Latter-Day Saints (Mormons).
Boston Evening Transcript, 1830–1941.
Godey's Lady's Book (Phila., New York), 1830–98.

William IV crowned king of England.
Charles X forced to abdicate; Louis Philippe elected king of France.
Fraser's Magazine (London), 1830–82.
Cobbett's *Rural Rides*.
Tennyson's *Poems, Chiefly Lyrical*.
Lyell's *Principles of Geology* (1830–33).
Hugo's *Hernani*.

Snelling, William Joseph (1804), Tales of the Northeast; or, Sketches of Indian Life and Character. NF

Worcester, Joseph Emerson (1784), Comprehensive Pronouncing and Explanatory Dictionary of the English Language. NF

1831

Audubon, John James (1785), Ornithological Biography; or, An Account of the Habits of the Birds of the United States of America (5 vols. 1831–39). NF

Bacon, Delia Salter (1811), Tales of the Puritans. F

Bernard, William Bayle (1807), The Dumb Belle. D

Bird, Robert Montgomery (1806), The Gladiator (pub. 1919). D

Bryant, William Cullen (1794), "Song of Marion's Men." V

Cooper, James Fenimore (1789), The Bravo: A Tale. F; A Letter . . . to General Lafayette. NF

Deering, Nathaniel (1791), Carabasset. D

Holmes, Oliver Wendell (1809), "The Last Leaf." V; "My Aunt." V

Ingersoll, Charles Jared (1782), Julian. D

Irving, Washington (1783), Voyages and Discoveries of the Companions of Columbus. NF

Jones, James Athearn (1791), Haverhill; or, Memoirs of an Officer in the Army of Wolfe. F

Mason, Lowell (1792), Church Psalmody. V

Osborn, Laughton (c. 1809), Sixty Years of the Life of Jeremy Levis. F

Pattie, James Ohio (1804), Personal Narrative (ed. by Timothy Flint). NF

Paulding, Hiram (1797), Journal of a Cruise of the United States Schooner Dolphin. NF

Paulding, James Kirke (1778), The Dutchman's Fireside: A Tale. F

Peale, Rembrandt (1778), Notes on Italy. NF

Peck, John Mason (1789), Guide for Emigrants. NF

Poe, Edgar Allan (1809), Poems. V

Scott, Job (d. 1793), Works. NF

Smith, Richard Penn (1799), Caius Marius. D; The Forsaken. F

Smith, Samuel Francis (1808), "America." V

Snelling, William Joseph (1804), Truth: A New Year's Gift for Scribblers. V

Stone, John Augustus (1800), Tancred: King of Sicily. D; The Demoniac; or, The Prophet's Bride. D; The Lion of the West [revision of James Kirke Paulding's play (1830)]. D

Wheaton, Henry (1785), History of the Northmen. NF

Whittier, John Greenleaf (1807), Legends of New-England in Prose and Verse. F, V

Willard, Emma (1787), The Fulfillment of Promise. V

Willis, N. P. (1806), Poem Delivered Before the Society of United Brothers. V

President Jackson's break with John Calhoun.

Peggy Eaton affair and Cabinet reorganization.

Nat Turner's Rebellion (slaves vs. whites in Virginia).

Anti-Masonic Party met (first "third party").

The Floating Theatre, first showboat.

Spirit of the Times (New York), 1831–61.

Leopold I crowned king of the Belgians.

Workers' uprisings in France.

Charles Darwin's voyage on HMS Beagle (1831–36).

G. W. F. Hegel d.

Peacock's Crotchet Castle.

Pushkin's Boris Godunov.

Hugo's The Hunchback of Notre Dame.

Stendhal's The Red and the Black.

1832

Abbott, Jacob (1803), The Young Christian. NF

Bernard, William Bayle (1807), Rip Van Winkle [adapted from Washington Irving's short story (1819–20)]. D

Bird, Robert Montgomery (1806), Oralloossa (publ 1919). D

Bryant, William Cullen (1794), Poems. V

Black Hawk Indian War (Illinois and Wisconsin).

Boston Academy of Music founded.

First horsedrawn streetcars, in New York City.

Channing, William Ellery (1780), Discourses. NF
Chivers, Thomas Holley (1809), The Path of Sorrow. V
Conrad, Robert Taylor (1810), Conrad, King of Naples. D
Cooper, James Fenimore (1789), The Heidenmauer; or, The
    Benedictines: A Legend of the Rhine. F
Drake, Daniel (1785), Practical Essays on Medical Education and
    the Medical Profession in the United States. NF
Dunlap, William (1766), The History of the American Theatre.
    NF
Emerson, Ralph Waldo (1803), Letter . . . to the Second
    Church and Society. NF
Fairfield, Sumner Lincoln (1803), The Last Night of Pompeii. V
Fay, Theodore Sedgwick (1807), Dreams and Reveries of a
    Quiet Man. NF
Garrison, William Lloyd (1805), Thoughts on African
    Colonization. NF
Hall, James (1793), Legends of the West. F
Hawthorne, Nathaniel (1804), "Roger Malvin's Burial."
    F; "My Kinsman, Major Molineux." F
Irving, Washington (1783), The Alhambra. NF, F
Jones, Joseph Stevens (1809), The Liberty Tree. D
Kennedy, John Pendleton (1795), Swallow Barn; or, A Sojurn
    in the Old Dominion. F
Longfellow, Henry Wadsworth (1807), Syllabus de la
    grammaire Italienne. NF; Saggi de' novellieri Italiani. NF
Luther, Seth (fl. 1817–46), An Address to the Working-Men of
    New England. NF
Mason, Lowell (1792), The Choir (compiler). V
Murat, Achille (1801), Esquisse morale et politique des États-
    Unis. NF
Paulding, James Kirke (1778), Westward Ho! F
Richardson, John (1796), Wacousta, or The Prophecy: A Tale of
    the Canadas. F
Simms, William Gilmore (1806), Atalantis. V
Story, Joseph (1779), Commentaries (1832–45). NF
Stuart, Charles (1783), The West India Question: Immediate
    Emancipation Safe and Practical. NF
Thatcher, Benjamin Bussey (1809), Indian Biography. NF
Whittier, John Greenleaf (1807), Moll Pitcher. V

Philip Freneau d.
Louisa May Alcott b.

Great Cholera Epidemic (India to
    Scotland).
Reform Bill redistributed British
    Parliamentary seats.
Giuseppe Mazzini sought unification of
    Italy.
Sir Walter Scott d.
Johann Wolfgang von Goethe d.
Disraeli's *Contarini Fleming*.
Harriet Martineau's *Illustrations of
    Political Economy* (1832–34).
Bulwer-Lytton's *Eugene Aram*.
Hunt's *Poetical Works*.
Goethe's *Faust, Part II*
Sand's *Indiana*.

1833

Apes, William (1798), The Experiences of Five Christian
    Indians. NF
Bernard, William Bayle (1807), The Kentuckian; or, A Trip to
    New York [revision of James Kirke Paulding's The Lion of the
    West (1830)]. D
Black Hawk (1767), Autobiography. NF
Brooks, Maria Gowen (c. 1794), Zóphiël. V
Child, Lydia Maria (1802), An Appeal in Favor of that Class of
    Americans Called Africans. NF
Cooper, James Fenimore (1789), The Headsman; or, The
    Abbaye des Vignerons: A Tale. F
Cox, William (1805?), Crayon Sketches. F
Crockett, Davy (1786), Sketches and Eccentricities of Col.
    David Crockett (attrib.). NF
Custis, George Washington Parke (1781), North Point. D
Dana, Richard Henry, Sr. (1787), Poems and Prose Writings
    (enl. 1850). NF, V
Davis, Charles Augustus (1795?), Letters Written During the

President Jackson vs. Bank of the
    United States over public fund
    deposits.
American Anti-Slavery Society
    founded.
Oberlin College founded, admitting
    men and women.
The Knickerbocker Magazine (New
    York) 1833–65.
The New York Sun, 1833–1950.

The Oxford Movement (begun with
    John Keble's sermon "On National
    Apostasy").
Tracts for the Times (Newman, Keble,
    Froude, et al.), 1833–41.
Charles Lamb's *Last Essays of Elia*.
Tennyson's *Poems*.
Robert Browning's *Pauline*.
Pushkin's *Eugene Onegin*.

President's Tour, "Down East," by Myself, Major Jack
Downing, of Downingville. F

Dwight, Theodore (1764), History of the Hartford Convention.
NF

Greene, Asa (1789), Travels in America by George Fibbleton.
F; The Life and Adventures of Dr. Dodimus Duckworth. F; A
Yankee Among the Nullifers. F

Hall, James (1793), The Soldier's Bride and Other Tales. F; The
Harpe's Head: A Legend of Kentucky. F

Halleck, Fitz-Greene (1790), The Recorder, with Other Poems.
V

Holmes, Oliver Wendell (1809), The Harbinger: A May-Gift. V

Leslie, Eliza (1787), Pencil Sketches; or, Outlines of Character
and Manners (1833, 1835, 1837). F

Lockwood, Ralph Ingersoll (1798), Rosine Laval. F

Longfellow, Henry Wadsworth (1807), Coplas de Don Jorge
Manrique. V, NF; Outre-Mer: A Pilgrimage Beyond the Sea
(1833–34). NF

Luther, Seth (fl. 1817–46), An Address on the Right of Free
Suffrage. NF

Mellen, Grenville (1799), The Martyr's Triumph. V

Murat, Achille (1801), Exposition des principes du
gouvernement républicain, tel qu'il a été perfectionné en
Amérique. NF

Neal, John (1793), The Down-Easters. F

Poe, Edgar Allan (1809), "Ms. Found in a Bottle." F; "The
Coliseum." V

Sealsfield, Charles (1793), Der Legitime und die Republikaner
[revision of Tokeah; or, The White Rose (1828)].

Simms, William Gilmore (1806), The Remains of Maynard
Davis Richardson. NF; The Book of My Lady. F; Martin
Faber: The Story of a Criminal. F

Smith, Richard Penn (1799), Is She a Brigand? D

Smith, Seba (1792), The Life and Writings of Major Jack
Downing of Downingville. F

Stone, John Augustus (1800), The Ancient Briton. D

Story, Joseph (1779), On the Constitution. NF

Thatcher, Benjamin Bussey (1809), Indian Traits. NF

Thomas, Frederick William (1806), The Emigrant. V

Verplanck, Gulian Crommelin (1786), Discourses and
Addresses on Subjects of American History, Arts, and
Literature. NF

Whittier, John Greenleaf (1807), Justice and Expediency. NF

Balzac's *Eugénie Grandet.*
Sand's *Lélia.*

1834

Bancroft, George (1800), A History of the United States, from
the Discovery of the American Continent (10 vols., 1834–75).
NF

Bird, Robert Montgomery (1806), The Broker of Bogota (pub.
1917). D; Calavar; or, The Knight of the Conquest. F

Brackenridge, Henry Marie (1786), Recollections of Persons
and Places in the West. NF

Bryant, William Cullen (1794), Poems. V

Caruthers, William Alexander (1802), The Kentuckian in New
York. F; The Cavaliers of Virginia (1834–35). F

Chivers, Thomas Holley (1809), Conrad and Eudora. D

Cooper, James Fenimore (1789), A Letter to His Countrymen.
NF

Whig Party (anti-Jacksonian) formed
out of National Republicans.
Anti-abolition riots in New York and
Philadelphia.
Seminole Indians forced out of Florida.
Cyrus McCormick patented a reaper.
The Southern Literary Messenger
(Richmond), 1834–64.

Spanish Civil War (1834–39).
Quadruple Alliance (Great Britain,
France, Spain, Portugal) in support of
Isabella II.
Slavery abolished in the British
colonies.

Crockett, Davy (1786), A Narrative of the Life of David Crockett, of the State of Tennessee (attrib.). NF

Custis, George Washington Parke (1781), The Eighth of January. D

Davis, Charles Augustus (1795?), Letters of J. Downing, Major, Downingville Militia . . . to Mr. Dwight of the New York Daily Advertiser. F

Dunlap, William (1766), A History of the Rise and Progress of the Arts of Design in the United States. NF

Du Ponceau, Pierre Etienne (1760), A Discourse on the Necessity and Means of Making Our National Literature Independent . . . . NF

Gilman, Caroline Howard (1794), Recollections of a Housekeeper. NF

Greene, Asa (1789), The Perils of Pearl Street. F

Hall, James (1793), Sketches of History, Life, and Manners in the West. NF

Hart, Joseph C. (1798), Miriam Coffin; or, The Whale-Fishermen. F

Hawthorne, Nathaniel (1804), "Mr. Higginbotham's Catastrophe." F

Key, Francis Scott (1779), The Power of Literature and Its Connection with Religion. NF

Leggett, William (1801), Naval Stories. F

Logan, Cornelius Ambrosius (1806), Yankee Land; or, The Foundling of the Apple Orchard. D

Luther, Seth (fl. 1817–46), An Address on the Origin and Progress of Avarice. NF

Nott, Henry Junius (1797), Novelettes of a Traveller; or, Odds and Ends from the Knapsack of Thomas Singularity, Journeyman Printer. F

Paulding, Hiram (1797), Bolivar in His Camp. NF

Pike, Albert (1809), Prose Sketches and Poems, Written in the Western Country. NF, V

Schoolcraft, Henry Rowe (1793), Narrative of an Expedition through the Upper Mississippi . . . . NF

Sealsfield, Charles (1793), George Howard's Esq. Brautfahrt. F; Christophorus Bärenhäuter. F

Sedgwick, Susan (1789), Allen Prescott; or, The Fortunes of a New England Boy. F

Simms, William Gilmore (1806), Guy Rivers: A Tale of Georgia. F

Sparks, Jared (1789), The Writings of George Washington (editor; 12 vols., 1834–37). NF

Stone, William Leete (1792), Tales and Sketches. F

Stowe, Harriet Beecher (1811), Prize Tale: A New England Sketch. F

Thatcher, Benjamin Bussey (1809), Memoir of Phillis Wheatley. NF

Samuel Taylor Coleridge d.
Charles Lamb d.
Bulwer-Lytton's The Last Days of Pompeii.
Marryat's Peter Simple; Jacob Faithful.
Pushkin's The Queen of Spades.
Balzac's Father Goriot.
Mickiewicz's Master Thaddeus.

1835

Abbott, Jacob (1803), Rollo Series (28 vols., 1835 ff). F

Bird, Robert Montgomery (1806), The Infidel; or, The Fall of Mexico. F; The Hawks of Hawk-Hollow. F

Carey, Henry Charles (1793), Essay on the Rate of Wages. NF

Channing, William Ellery (1780), Slavery. NF

Colton, Walter (1797), Ship and Shore. NF

Conrad, Robert Taylor (1810), Jack Cade, The Captain of the Commons. D

Cooper, James Fenimore (1789), The Monikins. F

Attempted assassination of President Jackson.
Second Seminole Indian War (1835–42).
Armed clashes between Mexico and Texas.
Oberlin College admitted Negro students.
Samuel Langhorne Clemens b.
The New York Herald, 1835–1966.

Crockett, Davy (1786), An Account of Col. Crockett's Tour to the North and Down East (attrib.). NF; The Life of Martin Van Buren (attrib.). NF

Drake, Joseph Rodman (d. 1820), The Culprit Fay and Other Poems. V

Emerson, Ralph Waldo (1803), A Historical Discourse Delivered Before the Citizens of Concord, 12th September, 1835. NF

Fay, Theodore Sedgwick (1807), Norman Leslie: A Tale of the Present Times. F

Gallagher, William Davis (1808), Erato (1835–37). V

Hall, James (1793), Tales of the Border. F

Hawthorne, Nathaniel (1804), "The Ambitious Guest." F "Young Goodman Brown." F

Herbert, Henry William (1807), The Brothers: A Tale of the Fronde. F

Hoffman, Charles Fenno (1806), A Winter in the West. NF

Irving, John Treat (1812), Indian Sketches. NF

Irving, Washington (1783), The Crayon Miscellany (A Tour of the Prairies; Legends of the Conquest of Spain; Abbotsford and Newstead Abbey). NF

Kemble, Frances Anne (Fanny) (1809), Journal of Frances Anne Butler. NF

Kennedy, John Pendleton (1795), Horse-Shoe Robinson. F

Lockwood, Ralph Ingersoll (1798), The Insurgents. F

Logan, Cornelius Ambrosius (1806), The Wag of Maine. D

Longstreet, Augustus Baldwin (1790), Georgia Scenes, Characters, Incidents, &c. in the First Half Century of the Republic. F

Paulding, James Kirke (1778), A Life of Washington. NF

Peabody, Elizabeth Palmer (1804), Record of a School, Exemplifying the General Principles of Spiritual Culture. NF

Poe, Edgar Allan (1809), Politian: A Tragedy (1835–36, unfinished; pub. 1923). D; "Bernice." F "Morella." F

Porter, David (1780), Constantinople and Its Environs. NF

Sealsfield, Charles (1793), Morton, oder die grosse Tour. F; Ralph Doughby's Esq. Brautfahrt. F

Sedgwick, Catharine Maria (1789), The Linwoods; or, "Sixty Years Since" in America. F

Simms, William Gilmore (1806), The Yemassee: A Romance of Carolina. F; The Partisan: A Tale of the Revolution. F

Stone, William Leete (1792), The Mysterious Bridal and Other Tales. F

Stowe, Calvin Ellis (1802), Introduction to the Criticism and Interpretation of the Bible. NF

Thomas, Frederick William (1806), Clinton Bradshaw; or, The Adventures of a Lawyer. F

Thompson, Daniel Pierce (1795), The Adventures of Timothy Peacock, Esquire. F

Willis, N. P. (1806), Melanie, and Other Poems. V; Pencillings by the Way (1835–44). NF

Worcester, Joseph Emerson (1784), A Gross Literary Fraud Exposed. NF

Southern Literary Journal (Charleston), 1835–38.
The Western Messenger (Cincinnati; Louisville), 1835–41.

Attempted assassination of King Louis Philippe.
Robert Browning's *Paracelsus*.
Bulwer-Lytton's *Rienzi*.
Wordsworth's *Yarrow Revisited*.
Büchner's *Danton's Death*.
Andersen's *Fairy Tales* (1835–72).
Musset's *New Poems* (1835–52).
Vigny's *Chatterton*.
Krasinski's *The Undivine Comedy*.

1836

Alcott, Bronson (1799), The Doctrine and Discipline of Human Culture. NF; Conversations with Children on the Gospels (1836–37). NF

Arkansas admitted to the Union.
Creation of the Wisconsin Territory.
Siege of the Alamo; Battle of San

Apes, William (1798), Eulogy on King Philip of the Pequot Tribe. NF

Bird, Robert Montgomery (1806), Sheppard Lee. F

Brownson, Orestes (1803), New Views of Christianity, Society, and the Church. NF

Bryant, William Cullen (1794), Poems. V

Chandler, Elizabeth Margaret (d. 1834), Essays, Philosophical and Moral. NF; Poetical Works. V

Child, Lydia Maria (1802), Philothea. F

Cooper, James Fenimore (1789), Sketches of Switzerland. NF; Sketches of Switzerland: Part Second. NF

Crockett, Davy (d. 1836), Col. Crockett's Exploits and Adventures in Texas (attrib.). NF

Dunlap, William (1766), Thirty Years Ago; or, The Memoirs of a Water Drinker. F

Emerson, Ralph Waldo (1803), Nature. NF

Force, Peter (1790), Tracts and Other Papers, Relating Principally to the Origin, Settlement, and Progress of Colonies in North America (editor; 4 vols., 1836–46). NF

Gallatin, Albert (1761), Synopsis of the Indian Tribes . . . of North America. NF

Gilman, Caroline Howard (1794), Recollections of a Southern Matron. NF

Gookin, Daniel (d. 1687), An Historical Account of the Doings and Sufferings of the Christian Indians. NF

Gould, Edward Sherman (1805), American Criticism of American Literature. NF

Hall, James (1793), A Memoir of the Public Services of William Henry Harrison of Ohio. NF; Statistics of the West. NF; History of the Indian Tribes of North America (3 vols., 1836–44, with Thomas L. McKenney). NF

Hawthorne, Nathaniel (1804), "The Maypole of Merrymount." F; "The Minister's Black Veil." F

Hildreth, Richard (1807), The Slave; or, Memoirs of Archy Moore. F

Holmes, Oliver Wendell (1809), Poems. V

Ingraham, Joseph Holt (1809), Lafitte; or The Pirate of the Gulf. F

Irving, Washington (1783), Astoria. NF

Monk, Maria (c. 1817), Awful Disclosures. NF

Paulding, James Kirke (1778), Slavery in the United States. NF; The Book of Saint Nicholas. F

Rafinesque, Constantine Samuel (1783), A Life of Travels and Researches in North America and South Europe. NF; The American Nations (incl. trans. of "Walam Olum"). NF

Ripley, George (1802), Discourses on the Philosophy of Religion. NF

Sealsfield, Charles (1793), Pflanzerleben. F; Die Farbigen. F

Sedgwick, Susan (1789), The Young Emigrants. F

Simms, William Gilmore (1806), Mellichampe: A Legend of the Santee. F

Smith, Richard Penn (1799), The Daughter. D; The Actress of Padua. D; The Actress of Padua and Other Tales. F; Col. Crockett's Exploits and Adventures in Texas (attrib.; see Crockett above). NF

Sparks, Jared (1789), The Works of Benjamin Franklin (editor; 10 vols., 1836–40). NF

Story, Joseph (1779), Equity Jurisprudence. NF

Thomas, Frederick William (1806), East and West. F

Tucker, Nathaniel Beverley (1784), George Balcombe. F; The Partisan Leader. F

Walsh, Robert (1784), Didactics: Social, Literary and Political. NF

Jacinto; Sam Houston elected president of the republic of Texas. *The Philadelphia Public Ledger*, 1836–1934.

University of London founded. *The Dublin Review* (London), 1836–1969. William Godwin d. Dickens's *Sketches by "Boz."* Carlyle's *Sartor Resartus* (pub. in Boston). Marryat's *Mr. Midshipman Easy.* Gogol's *The Inspector General.* Heine's *The Romantic School.* Pushkin's *The Captain's Daughter.*

Wheaton, Henry (1785), Elements of International Law. NF
Whittier, John Greenleaf (1807), Mogg Megone. F
Willis, N. P. (1806), Inklings of Adventure. NF

1837

Bannister, Nathaniel Harrington (1813), England's Iron Days. D
Barnes, Charlotte Mary Sanford (1818), Octavia Bragaldi (pub. 1848). D
Beecher, Catharine Esther (1800), An Essay on Slavery and Abolitionism. NF
Bird, Robert Montgomery (1806), Nick of the Woods; or, The Jibbenainosay: A Tale of Kentucky. F
Carey, Henry Charles (1793), Principles of Political Economy (1837–40). NF
Channing, William Ellery (1780), A Letter to the Abolitionists. NF; A Letter to the Hon. Henry Clay, on the Annexation of Texas to the United States. NF; Character of Napoleon, and Other Essays, Literary and Philosophical. NF
Chivers, Thomas Holley (1809), Nacoochee. V
Cooper, James Fenimore (1789), Gleanings in Europe (1837–38). NF
Dana, James Dwight (1813), System of Mineralogy. NF
Dunlap, William (1766), A History of New York, for Schools. NF
Emerson, Ralph Waldo (1803), The American Scholar. NF
Force, Peter (1790), American Archives (editor; 9 vols., 1837–53). NF
Grund, Francis Joseph (1798), The Americans in Their Moral, Social and Political Relations. NF
Haliburton, Thomas Chandler (1796), The Clockmaker; or, The Sayings and Doings of Samuel Slick, of Slickville (1st ser.; 2nd, 1838; 3rd, 1840). F
Hawthorne, Nathaniel (1804), Peter Parley's Universal History (compiler). NF; Twice-Told Tales (enl., 1842). F
Irving, John Treat (1812), The Hawk Chief, A Tale of the Indian Country (also titled The Hunters of the Prairie). NF
Irving, Washington (1793), The Adventures of Captain Bonneville, U.S.A. NF; The Rocky Mountains. NF
Monk, Maria (c. 1817), Further Disclosures. NF
Norton, Andrews (1786), The Evidences of the Genuineness of the Gospels (1837–44). NF
Owen, Robert Dale (1801), Pocahontas. D
Peale, Rembrandt (1778), Portfolio of an Artist. NF, V
Sargent, Epes (1813), The Bride of Genoa. D; Velasco. D
Sealsfield, Charles (1793), Nathan, der Squatter-Regulator. F
Shelton, Frederick William (1815), The Trollopiad; or Travelling Gentlemen in America. V
Smith, Richard Penn (1799), The Bravo [adapted from James Fenimore Cooper's novel (1831)]. D
Snelling, William Joseph (1804), The Rat-Trap; or, Cogitations of a Convict in the House of Correction. NF
Stephens, John Lloyd (1805), Incidents of Travel in Egypt, Arabia Petraea, and the Holy Land. NF
Stowe, Calvin Ellis (1802), Report on Elementary Public Instruction in Europe. NF
Tucker, George (1775), The Life of Thomas Jefferson. NF; The Law of Wages, Profits, and Rent Investigated. NF
Ware, William (1797), Letters . . . from Palmyra (repub. as Zenobia, 1838). F
Weld, Theodore Dwight (1803), The Bible Against Slavery. NF

Michigan admitted to the Union.
Economic panic persisted until 1843.
Supreme Court enlarged to nine members.
Mount Holyoke Female Seminary founded by Mary Lyon.
William Dean Howells b.
The Baltimore Sun, 1837–.
United States Magazine and Democratic Review (Washington), 1837–59.

Death of William IV; accession of Victoria.
Friedrich Fröbel opened the first kindergarten, in Germany.
Dickens's *The Pickwick Papers*.
Carlyle's *The French Revolution*.
Disraeli's *Henrietta Temple*.
James Mill's *The Principles of Toleration*.
Harriet Martineau's *Society in America*.
Pushkin's *The Bronze Horseman*.

Whittier, John Greenleaf (1807), Poems Written During the Progress of the Abolition Question. V

Willis, N. P. (1806), Bianca Visconti; or, The Heart Overtasked (pub. 1839). D

1838

Bird, Robert Montgomery (1806), Peter Pilgrim; or, A Rambler's Recollections. F

Brooks, Charles T. (1813), William Tell (trans. from German). D

Channing, William Ellery (1780), Self-Culture. NF

Cooper, James Fenimore (1789), The American Democrat, or Hints on the Social and Civic Relations of the United States of America. NF; Homeward Bound; or, The Chase: A Tale of the Sea. F; Home as Found. F; Chronicles of Cooperstown. NF

Drake, Benjamin (1795), Tales and Sketches from the Queen City. NF; The Life and Adventures of Black Hawk. NF

Du Ponceau, Pierre Étienne (1760), Grammatical System of Some of the Languages of the Indian Nations of North America. NF

Embury, Emma Catherine (1806), Constance Latimer; or, The Blind Girl. F

Emerson, Ralph Waldo (1803), An Address Delivered Before the Senior Class in Divinity College, Cambridge. . . . NF; An Oration Delivered Before the Literary Societies of Dartmouth College. NF

Gilman, Caroline Howard (1794), The Poetry of Travelling in the United States. NF

Hawthorne, Nathaniel (1804), "Lady Eleanore's Mantle." F

Ingraham, Joseph Holt (1809), Burton; or, The Sieges. F

Judd, Sylvester (1813), A Young Man's Account of His Conversion from Calvinism. NF

Kemble, Frances Anne (Fanny) (1809), Journal of a Residence on a Georgian Plantation (1838–39; pub. 1863). NF

Kennedy, John Pendleton (1795), Rob of the Bowl. F

Lee, Eliza Buckminster (c. 1788), Sketches of a New England Village. F

Lieber, Francis (1800), Manual of Political Ethics. NF

Marsh, George Perkins (1801), A Compendious Grammar of the Old-Northern or Icelandic Language. NF

Mathews, Cornelius (1817), The Motley Book: A Series of Tales and Sketches. F

Morris, George Pope (1802), The Deserted Bride and Other Poems. V

Neal, Joseph Clay (1807), Charcoal Sketches; or, Scenes in a Metropolis. F

Osborn, Laughton (c. 1809), The Vision of Rubeta. F

Parker, Samuel (1779), Journal of an Exploring Tour Beyond the Rocky Mountains. NF

Paulding, James Kirke (1778), A Gift from Fairy-Land. F

Poe, Edgar Allan (1809), The Narrative of Arthur Gordon Pym, of Nantucket. F; "Ligeia." F

Prescott, William Hickling (1796), History of the Reign of Ferdinand and Isabella. NF

Rynning, Ole (1809), A True Account of America for the Information and Help of Peasant and Commoner (Eng. title; trans. from Norwegian). NF

Sanderson, John (1783), Sketches of Paris: In Familiar Letters to His Friends. NF

Simms, William Gilmore (1806), Slavery in America. NF; Richard Hurdis; or, The Avenger of Blood. F; Pelayo: A Story of the Goth. F; Carl Werner: An Imaginative Story. F

Creation of the Iowa Territory.

Beginning of Underground Railroad (flight of slaves northward).

Samuel F.B. Morse introduced telegraphic code.

Henry Adams b.

Proceedings of the American Philosophical Society (Phila.), 1838–.

Chartists (British political reformers) began agitation (1838–48).

Auguste Comte gave name to the science of sociology.

Jenny Lind's debut in *Der Freischütz*, in Stockholm.

Dickens's *Oliver Twist*.

Bulwer-Lytton's *The Lady of Lyons*.

E. B. Browning's *The Seraphim and Other Poems*.

Harriet Martineau's *Retrospect of Western Travel*.

Newman's *Lectures on Justification*.

Frances Trollope's *The Widow Barnaby*.

Hugo's *Ruy Blas*.

Stephens, John Lloyd (1805), Incidents of Travel in Greece, Turkey, Russia, and Poland. NF
Stone, William Leete (1792), Life of Joseph Brant. NF
Ware, William (1797), Probus (repub. as Aurelian, 1848). F
Whittier, John Greenleaf (1807), Narrative of James Williams. F

1839

Audubon, John James (1785), A Synopsis of the Birds of America. NF
Bacon, Delia Salter (1811), The Bride of Fort Edward. D
Bernard, William Bayle (1807), His Last Legs. D
Bird, Robert Montgomery (1806), The Adventures of Robin Day. F
Birney, James Gillespie (1792), Letter on the Political Obligations of Abolitionists. NF
Briggs, Charles Frederick (1804), The Adventures of Harry Franco. F
Bryant, William Cullen (1794), Poems. V
Channing, William Ellery (1780), Remarks on the Slavery Question. NF; Lecture on War. NF
Cooper, James Fenimore (1789), The History of the Navy of the United States of America. NF
Dana, Richard Henry, Jr. (1815), "Cruelty to Seamen." NF
Dawes, Rufus (1803), Geraldine, Athenia of Damascus, and Miscellaneous Poems. D, V; Nix's Mate. F
Dunlap, William (1766), History of the New Netherlands, Province of New York, and State of New York (1839–40). NF
Dwight, Theodore (1764), The Character of Thomas Jefferson. NF
Emerson, Ralph Waldo (1803), "Each and All." V; "The Humble-Bee." V; "The Rhodora." V
Fay, Theodore Sedgwick (1807), Sydney Clifton; or, Vicissitudes in Both Hemispheres. F
Follen, Charles (1796), Poems. V
Grund, Francis Joseph (1798), Aristocracy in America. NF
Heath, James Ewell (1792), Whigs and Democrats. D
Hillhouse, James Abraham (1789), Demetria. D
Hoffman, Charles Fenno (1806), Wild Scenes in the Forest and Prairie. NF
Jones, Joseph Stevens (1809), The People's Lawyer. D
Kirkland, Caroline Stansbury (1801), A New Home—Who'll Follow? or, Glimpses of Western Life (repub. as Our New Home in the West, 1874). NF
Leonard, Zenas (1809), Narrative of the Adventures of Zenas Leonard. NF
Lieber, Francis (1800), Legal and Political Hermeneutics. NF
Longfellow, Henry Wadsworth (1807), Hyperion: A Romance. V, F; Voice of the Night. V
Mathews, Cornelius (1817), Behemoth: A Legend of the Mound-Builders. F; The True Aims of Life. NF
Morris, George Pope (1802), The Little Frenchman and His Water Lots, with Other Sketches of the Times. F
Motley, John Lothrop (1814), Morton's Hope; or, The Memoirs of a Provincial. F
Norton, Andrews (1786), On the Latest Form of Infidelity. NF
Parker, Theodore (1810), The . . . Question between Mr. Andrews Norton and His Alumni. . . . NF
Poe, Edgar Allan (1809), "The Haunted Palace." V; "The Fall of the House of Usher." F; "William Wilson." F

Liberty Party formed (antislavery).
First normal school, in Lexington, Mass.
Harvard Astronomical Observatory opened.
Charles Goodyear accidentally vulcanized rubber.

Chartist riots after rejection by British Parliament.
First Opium War (Great Britain and China).
Carlyle's *Chartism*.
Dickens's *Nicholas Nickleby*.
Darwin's *Journal of Researches* . . . [on the] *HMS Beagle*.
Shelley's *Poetical Works* (posth.; ed. Mary Shelley).
Harriet Martineau's *Deerbrook*.
Marryat's *The Phantom Ship*.
Bulwer-Lytton's *Richelieu*.
Stendhal's *The Charterhouse of Parma*.

Reynolds, J. N. (1799?), "Mocha Dick; or, The White Whale of the Pacific." NF
Rouquette, François Dominique (1810), Les Meschacébéennes. V
Schoolcraft, Henry Rowe (1793), Algic Researches. NF
Sealsfield, Charles (1793), Die deutsch-amerikanischen Wahlverwandtschaften. (1839–40). NF
Simms, William Gilmore (1806), Southern Passages and Pictures. V; The Damsel of Darien. F
Smith, Seba (1792), John Smith's Letters with "Picters" to Match. F
Thompson, Daniel Pierce (1795), The Green Mountain Boys. F
Tucker, George (1775), The Theory of Money and Banks Investigated. NF
Very, Jones (1813), Essays and Poems. NF, V
Weld, Theodore Dwight (1803), American Slavery as It Is. NF
Willis, N. P. (1806), Tortesa; or, The Usurer Matched. D

1840

Adams, Abigail (d. 1818), Letters of Mrs. Adams, the Wife of John Adams. NF
Alcott, Bronson (1799), "Orphic Sayings." NF
Audubon, John James (1785), The Birds of America from Drawings Made in the United States and Their Territories (octavo edition, 1840–44). NF
Brisbane, Albert (1809), Social Destiny of Man. NF
Brownson, Orestes (1803), Charles Elwood; or, the Infidel Converted. F
Channing, William Ellery (1780), Emancipation. NF; Lectures on the Elevation of the Labouring Portion of the Community. NF
Cooke, Philip Pendleton (1816), "Florence Vane." V
Cooper, James Fenimore (1789), The Pathfinder; or, The Inland Sea. F; Mercedes of Castile; or, The Voyage of Cathay. F
Dana, Richard Henry, Jr. (1815), Two Years Before the Mast. NF
Evans, George Henry (1805), History of the . . . Working Men's Party. NF
Fay, Theodore Sedgwick (1807), The Countess Ida: A Tale of Berlin. F
Hoffman, Charles Fenno (1806), Greyslaer, A Romance of the Mohawk. F
Irving, Washington (1783), The Life of Oliver Goldsmith with Selections from His Writings. NF
Jones, Joseph Stevens (1809), The Carpenter of Rouen. D
Kennedy, John Pendleton (1795), Quodlibet: Containing Some Annals Thereof . . . by Solomon Secondthoughts, Schoolmaster. F
Lee, Eliza Buckminster (c. 1788), Delusion; or, The Witch of New England. F
Leggett, William (d. 1839), Political Writings. NF
Logan, Cornelius Ambrosius (1806), The Vermont Wool Dealer. D
Mathews, Cornelius (1817), The Politians: A Comedy. D
Meek, Alexander Beaufort (1814), The Southwest. NF
Osgood, Frances Sargent (1811), The Casket of Fate. V
Poe, Edgar Allan (1809), "The Journal of Julius Rodman." F; Tales of the Grotesque and Arabesque. F
Quincy, Josiah (1772), The History of Harvard University. NF

Independent Treasury Act (established federal depositories).
The Dial (Boston), 1840–44.
National Anti-Slavery Standard (New York), 1840–72.

Marriage of Queen Victoria and Prince Albert.
Great Britain annexed New Zealand.
London Library founded.
Samuel Cunard founded transatlantic steamship line.
Penny Post established throughout Great Britain.
Max Schneckenburger's "Die Wacht am Rhein."
Thomas Hardy b.
Emile Zola b.
Robert Browning's *Sordello.*
Bulwer-Lytton's *Money.*
Carlyle's *Chartism.*
Hunt's *A Legend of Florence.*
Sainte-Beuve's *History of Port-Royal* (1840–48).
Lermontov's *A Hero of Our Time.*

Ripley, George (1802), Letters on the Latest Form of Infidelity. NF

Simms, William Gilmore (1806), Border Beagles: A Tale of Mississippi. F; The History of South Carolina. NF

Thomas, Frederick William (1806), Howard Pinckney. F

Willis, N. P. (1806), Loiterings of Travel. NF; American Scenery. NF

1841

Allston, Washington (1779), Monaldi. F

Bryant, William Cullen (1794), Popular Considerations on Homoeopathia. NF

Catlin, George (1796), The Manners, Customs, and Condition of the North American Indians. NF

Channing, William Ellery (1780), The Works of William E. Channing (6 vols., 1841–43). NF

Cooper, James Fenimore (1789), The Deerslayer; or, The First War-Path. F

Dana, Richard Henry, Jr. (1815), The Seaman's Friend (pub. in London as The Seaman's Manual). NF

Drake, Benjamin (1795), The Life of Tecumseh and His Brother. NF

Dwight, Theodore (1764), The History of Connecticut. NF

Emerson, Ralph Waldo (1803), The Method of Nature. NF; Essays. NF; "Compensation." V; "The Sphinx." V

Fairfield, Sumner Lincoln (1803), Poems and Prose Writings. V, NF

Follen, Charles (d. 1840), Works (1841–42). V, NF

Gallagher, William Davis (1808), Selections from the Poetical Literature of the West (editor). V

Hawthorne, Nathaniel (1804), Grandfather's Chair. F; Famous Old People, Being the Second Epoch of Grandfather's Chair. F; Liberty Tree, with the Last Words of Grandfather's Chair. F

Jones, John Beauchamp (1810), Wild Western Scenes. F

Lowell, James Russell (1819), A Year's Life, and Other Poems. V

Mathews, Cornelius (1817), Wakondah, The Master of Life: A Poem. V; The Career of Puffer Hopkins (1841–42). F

Osgood, Frances Sargent (1811), The Poetry of Flowers and the Flowers of Poetry. V

Parker, Theodore (1810), "The Transient and Permanent in Christianity." NF

Poe, Edgar Allan (1809), "A Descent into the Maelstrom." F; "The Murders in the Rue Morgue." F

Robinson, Solon (1803), The Will: A Tale of the Lake of the Red Cedars and Shabbona. F

Rouquette, Adrien Emmanuel (1813), Les savanes. V

Sargent, Epes (1813), American Adventure by Land and Sea. NF

Sealsfield, Charles (1793), Das Cajütenbuch, oder nationale Charakteristiken. F

Sigourney, Lydia Huntley (1791), Pocahontas and Other Poems. V; Poems, Religious and Elegiac. V

Simms, William Gilmore (1806), The Kinsmen; or, The Black Riders of Congaree. F; Confession; or, The Blind Heart. F

Smith, Seba (1792), Powhatan. V

Stephens, John Lloyd (1805), Incidents of Travel in Central America, Chiapas and Yucatan. NF

President Harrison died one month after inauguration.
Repeal of Independent Treasury Act.
President Tyler's Cabinet (except Daniel Webster) resigned.
Brook Farm, cooperative community, founded in West Roxbury, Mass.
The New York Tribune, 1841–1966.
The Brooklyn Eagle, 1841–1955.

Punch (London), 1841–.
Newman's last Tract for the Times (No. 90).
Dicken's Barnaby Rudge; The Old Curiosity Shop.
Marryat's Masterman Ready.
Robert Browning's Bells and Pomegranates (1841–46).
Carlyle's On Heroes, Hero-Worship, and the Heroic in History.
Harriet Martineau's The Hour and the Man.
Merimée's Colomba.
Scribe's A Chain.

Stone, William Leete (1792), Life and Times of Red Jacket.
NF; The Poetry and History of Wyoming. NF
Thorpe, T. B. (1815), "The Big Bear of Arkansas." F
Trumbull, John (1756), Autobiography, Reminiscences and
Letters of John Trumbull. NF
Valentine, David Thomas (1801), Manual of the Corporation of
the City of New York (annually, 1841–67). NF
Ware, William (1797), Julian. F
Young, Alexander (1800), Chronicles of the Pilgrim Fathers
. . . from 1602 to 1625 (editor). NF

1842

Bidwell, John (1819), A Journey to California. NF
Brooks, Charles T. (1813), Songs and Ballads (trans. of various
German poets). V
Brownson, Orestes (1803), The Mediatorial Life of Jesus. NF
Bryant, William Cullen (1794), The Fountain and Other Poems.
V
Channing, William Ellery (1780), The Duty of Free States; or,
Remarks Suggested by the Case of the Creole. NF
Clay, Henry (1777), Speeches of the Hon. Henry Clay, of the
Congress of the United States (ed. by Richard Chambers). NF
Cooper, James Fenimore (1789), The Two Admirals: A Tale.
F; The Wing-and-Wing; or, Le Feu-Follet: A Tale. NF
Emerson, Ralph Waldo (1803), Man the Reformer. NF "Saadi."
V
Griswold, Rufus Wilmot (1815), The Poets and Poetry of
America (editor). NF, V
Hawthorne, Nathaniel (1804), Biographical Stories for Children.
F
Hoffman, Charles Fenno (1806), The Vigil of Faith. V
Holmes, Oliver Wendell (1809), Homoeopathy, and Its Kindred
Delusions. NF
Irving, John Treat (1812), The Quod Correspondence, or The
Attorney. F
Kirkland, Caroline Stansbury (1801), Forest Life. NF
Longfellow, Henry Wadsworth (1807), Ballads and Other
Poems. V; Poems on Slavery. V
Morris, George Pope (1802), The Maid of Saxony. D
Parker, Theodore (1810), A Discourse of Matters Pertaining to
Religion. NF
Poe, Edgar Allan (1809), "Eleonora." F; "The Masque of the
Red Death." F; "The Mystery of Marie Roget." F
Richardson, John (1796), War of 1812. NF
Sealsfield, Charles (1793), Süden und Norden (1842–43). F
Simms, William Gilmore (1806), Beauchampe; or, The
Kentucky Tragedy. F
Smith, Elizabeth Oakes (1806), The Western Captive. F
Stone, William Leete (1792), Uncas and Miantonomoh. NF
Street, Alfred Billings (1811), The Burning of Schenectady. V
Thompson, Zadock (1796), History of Vermont, Natural, Civil
and Statistical. NF
Whitman, Walt (1819), Franklin Evans; or, The Inebriate: A
Tale of the Times. F
Wilde, Richard Henry (1789), Conjectures Concerning . . .
Tasso. V

Dorr Rebellion (against new Rhode
Island constitution).
Webster-Ashburton Treaty (established
U.S.-Canadian border).
P.T. Barnum opened his American
Museum, in New York City.
Edwin P. Christy founded the Christy
Minstrels in Buffalo, N.Y.
William Ellery Channing d.
The Southern Quarterly Review
(Charleston), 1842–57.

Treaty of Nanking (China ceded Hong
Kong to Great Britain).
Illustrated London News, 1842–.
Stéphane Mallarmé b.
Tennyson's *Poems*.
Thackeray's *The Fitz-Boodle Papers*
(1842–43).
Wordsworth's *Poems, Chiefly of Early
and Late Years*.
Marryat's *Percival Keene*.
Sue's *The Mysteries of Paris* (1842–43).
Scribe's *A Glass of Water*.

1843

Arthur, Timothy Shay (1809), Temperance Tales. F
Brooks, Maria Gowen (c. 1794), Idomen; or, The Vale of Yumuri. F
Bryant, William Cullen (1794), An Address to the People of the United States in Behalf of the American Copyright Club. NF
Calhoun, John C. (1782), Speeches of John C. Calhoun. NF
Channing, William Ellery (1818), Poems. V
Cooper, James Fenimore (1789), Le Mouchoir: An Autobiographical Romance (repub. as Autobiography of a Pocket-Handkerchief, 1897). F; Wyandotté; or, The Hutted Knoll: A Tale. F; Ned Myers; or, A Life Before the Mast. F
Darley, Felix Octavius Carr (1822), Scenes in Indian Life. NF
Dix, Dorothea Lynde (1802), Memorial to the Legislature of Massachusetts. NF
English, Thomas Dunn (1819), "Ben Bolt." V
Fay, Theodore Sedgwick (1807), Hoboken. F
Garrison, William Lloyd (1805), Sonnets. V
Godwin, Parke (1816), Democracy, Constructive and Pacific. NF
Haliburton, Thomas Chandler (1796), The Attaché; or Sam Slick in England (2nd ser., 1844). F; The Old Judge; or, Life in a Colony. F
Hawthorne, Nathaniel (1804), "The Birthmark." F; "The Celestial Railroad." F; "The Hall of Fantasy." F
Holmes, Oliver Wendell (1809), The Contagiousness of Puerperal Fever. NF
Jarves, James Jackson (1818), Scenes and Scenery in the Sandwich Islands. NF
Kennedy, John Pendleton (1795), A Defense of the Whigs. NF
Longfellow, Henry Wadsworth (1807), The Spanish Student: A Play in Three Acts. D
Marsh, George Perkins (1801), The Goths in New-England. NF
Mathews, Cornelius (1817), Poems on Man in His Various Aspects under the American Republic. V
Neal, Joseph Clay (1807), In Town and About. F
Nichols, Thomas Low (1815), Ellen Ramsay. F
Percival, James Gates (1795), The Dream of a Day. V
Pierpont, John (1785), The Anti-Slavery Poems of John Pierpont. V
Poe, Edgar Allan (1809), "The Black Cat." F; "The Gold Bug." F; "The Pit and the Pendulum." F; "The Tell-Tale Heart." F; "Notes on English Verse" (repub. as "The Rationale of Verse," 1848). NF
Prescott, William Hickling (1796), History of the Conquest of Mexico. NF
Stephens, Ann Sophia (1813), High Life in New York. F
Stephens, John Lloyd (1805), Incidents of Travel in Yucatán. NF
Stone, William Leete (1792), Border Wars of the American Revolution. NF
Stowe, Harriet Beecher (1811), The Mayflower; or, Sketches of Scenes and Characters Among the Descendants of the Pilgrims. F
Thompson, William Tappan (1812), Major Jones's Courtship (enl. 1844). F
Tucker, George (1775), Progress of the United States . . . . NF
Whittier, John Greenleaf (1807), Lays of My Home and Other Poems. V; "Massachusetts to Virginia." V

Settlers moved westward over Oregon Trail.
Debates over potential annexation of Texas.
Congress assisted Samuel F.B. Morse with telegraph line.
Henry James b.
Miss Leslie's Magazine (New York), 1843–46.

Isabella II crowned queen of Spain.
William Wordsworth named poet laureate of England.
The Economist (London), 1843–.
Robert Southey d.
Dickens's *A Christmas Carol.*
Ruskin's *Modern Painters* (1843–60).
Carlyle's *Past and Present.*
Hood's "The Song of the Shirt."
John Stuart Mill's *A System of Logic.*
Spencer's *The Proper Sphere of Government.*
Thackeray's *The Irish Sketch-Book.*
Heine's *Atta Troll: A Summer Night's Dream.*

Willis, N. P. (1806), The Sacred Poems. V; Poems of Passion.
V; The Lady Jane and Other Poems. V

1844

Bannister, Nathaniel Harrington (1813), Putnam. D
Beecher, Henry Ward (1813), Seven Lectures to Young Men.
NF
Briggs, Charles Frederick (1804), Working a Passage. F
Bryant, William Cullen (1794), The White-Footed Deer and
Other Poems. V
Cannon, Charles James (1800), Mora Carmody; or, Woman's
Influence. F
Clark, Willis Gaylord (d. 1841), Literary Remains . . .
Including the Ollipodiana Papers. NF
Clarke, James Freeman (1810), Hymn Book for the Church of
the Disciples. (enl. 1852). V
Cooper, James Fenimore (1789), Afloat and Ashore. F; Miles
Wallingford. F
Cranch, Christopher Pearse (1813), Poems. V
Dwight, Marianne (1816), Letters from Brook Farm, 1844–1847
(pub. 1928). NF
Emerson, Ralph Waldo (1803), The Young American.
NF; Nature: An Essay, and Lectures of the Times. NF; An
Address Delivered in . . . Concord . . . . NF; Essays:
Second Series. NF; Orations, Lectures and Addresses. NF
Farley, Harriet (1817), Mind Amongst the Spindles (editor). NF
Fuller, Margaret (1810), Summer on the Lakes in 1843. NF
Godwin, Parke (1816), A Popular View of the Doctrines of
Charles Fourier. NF
Gregg, Josiah (1806), Commerce on the Prairies. NF
Hawthorne, Nathaniel (1804), "The Artist of the Beautiful."
F; "Rappaccini's Daughter." F
Hoffman, Charles Fenno (1806), The Echo. V
Holmes, Oliver Wendell (1809), The Position and Prospects of
the Medical Student. NF
Hosmer, William H. C. (1814), Yonnondio, or Warriors of the
Genesee. V
Kendall, George Wilkins (1809), Narrative of the Texan Santa
Fe Expedition. NF
Lewis, Sarah Anna (1824), Records of the Heart. V
Lippard, George (1822), The Monks of Monk Hall (repub. as
The Quaker City; or, The Monks of Monk Hall, 1844). F
Lowell, James Russell (1819), Poems. V
Mowatt, Anna Cora (1819), The Fortune Hunter. F
Neal, Joseph Clay (1807), Peter Ploddy and Other Oddities. F
Nichols, Thomas Low (1815), The Lady in Black. F
Poe, Edgar Allan (1809), "The Balloon Hoax." F; "The
Raven." V
Schoolcraft, Henry Rowe (1793), Oneóta, or Characteristics of
the Red Race of America (1844–45). NF
Sedgwick, Susan (1789), Alida; or, Town and Country. F
Simms, William Gilmore (1806), Castle Dismal; or, the
Bachelor's Christmas. F; The Prima Donna: A Passage from
City Life. F; The Life of Francis Marion. NF
Smith, William Henry (1806), The Drunkard; or The Fallen
Saved. D
Stephens, Ann Sophia (1810), Alice Copley: A Tale of Queen
Mary's Time. F

Annexation of Texas.
Oregon boundary dispute with Great
Britain.
Bronson Alcott's Fruitlands, a
cooperative community, founded at
Harvard, Mass.
Samuel F.B. Morse transmitted first
telegraphic message.
The Living Age (Boston), 1844–1941.
Brownson's Quarterly Review (Boston),
1844–75.
Stephen Foster's "Open Thy Lattice,
Love."

George Williams founded YMCA, in
England.
North British Review (Edinburgh),
1844–71.
Gerard Manley Hopkins b.
Lives of the English Saints (ed. John
Henry Newman).
Disraeli's *Coningsby*.
E.B. Browning's *Poems*.
Dickens's *Martin Chuzzlewit*.
Darwin's *Geological Observations on
the Volcanic Islands*.
Hebbel's *Maria Magdalena*.
Dumas père's *The Count of Monte
Cristo; The Three Musketeers*.
Heine's *New Poems*.

Taylor, Bayard (1825), Ximena; or, The Battle of the Sierra
Morena and Other Poems. V
Willis, N. P. (1800), Lecture on Fashion. NF

1845

Audubon, John James (1785), The Viviparous Quadrupeds of
North America (with John Bachman; folio edition, 1845–54).
NF
Bennett, Emerson (1822), The League of the Miami. F
Bridge, Horatio (1806), Journal of an African Cruiser. NF
Carey, Henry Charles (1793), Commercial Associations in
France and England. NF
Caruthers, William Alexander (1802), The Knights of the
Horse-Shoe. F
Chivers, Thomas Holley (1809), The Lost Pleiad and Other
Poems. V
Cooper, James Fenimore (1789), Satanstoe; or, The Littlepage
Manuscripts: A Tale of the Colony. F; The Chainbearer; or,
The Littlepage Manuscripts. F
Douglass, Frederick (1817), Narrative of the Life of Frederick
Douglass (rev. edition, 1892). NF
Everett, Alexander Hill (1790), Essays, Critical and
Miscellaneous (1845–46). NF
Fuller, Margaret (1810), Woman in the Nineteenth Century. NF
Gough, John Bartholomew (1817), Autobiography (rev. edition,
1869). NF
Hirst, Henry Beck (1817), The Coming of the Mammoth. V
Hooper, Johnson Jones (1815), Some Adventures of Captain
Simon Suggs, Late of the Tallapoosa Volunteers. F
Judd, Sylvester (1813), Margaret: A Tale of the Real and Ideal.
F
Kirkland, Caroline Stansbury (1801), Western Clearings. F
Longfellow, Henry Wadsworth (1807), The Belfry of Bruges
and Other Poems. V
Lord, William Wilberforce (1819), Poems. V
Mann, Horace (1796), Lectures on Education. NF
Mathews, Cornelius (1817), Big Abel and the Little Manhattan.
F
Mowatt, Anna Cora (1819), Fashion; or, Life in New York
(pub. 1850). D; Evelyn; or, A Heart Unmasked. F
Nichols, Thomas Low (1815), Raffle for a Wife. F
Noah, Mordecai Manuel (1785), Gleanings from a Gathered
Harvest. NF
Poe, Edgar Allan (1809), Tales. F; The Raven and Other
Poems. V
Prescott, William Hickling (1796), Biographical and Critical
Miscellanies. NF
Sargent, Epes (1813), Change Makes Change. D
Simms, William Gilmore (1806), Helen Halsey; or, The Swamp
State of Conelachita. F; Count Julian; or, The Last Days of the
Goth. F; The Wigwam and the Cabin: First Series. F; The
Wigwam and the Cabin: Second Series. F; Grouped Thoughts
and Scattered Fancies. V; The Views and Reviews in
American Literature, History, and Fiction. NF
Smith, Seba (1792), May-Day in New York (repub. as Jack
Downing's Letters, 1845). F
Thompson, William Tappan (1812), Chronicles of Pineville
(repub. as Scenes in Georgia, 1858). F
Wheaton, Henry (1785), History of the Law of Nations. NF

Texas and Florida admitted to the
Union.
"Manifest Destiny" first used to
describe Federal expansion.
U.S. Naval Academy opened.
Industrial Congress of the U.S. formed,
in New York City.
The National Police Gazette (New
York), 1845–1933.
Scientific American (New York), 1845–.
The American Whig Review (New
York), 1845–52.

The Great Famine in Ireland.
Anti–Corn Laws agitation in England.
Oxford Movement reached its apogee.
John Henry Newman joined the
Church of Rome.
Richard Wagner's *Tannhäuser*.
Disraeli's *Sybil*.
Dickens's *The Cricket on the Hearth*.
Jerrold's *Time Works Wonders*.
Engels's *The Condition of the Working
Class in England*.

Willis, N. P. (1806), Dashes at Life with a Free Pencil. F; Poems, Sacred, Passionate, and Humorous. V

1846

Beecher, Catharine Esther (1800), The Evils Suffered by American Women and . . . Children. NF

Browne, J. Ross (1821), Etchings of a Whaling Cruise. NF

Clapp, Henry (1814), The Pioneer; or, Leaves from an Editor's Portfolio. NF

Cooper, James Fenimore (1789), Lives of Distinguished American Naval Officers. NF; The Redskins; or, Indian and Injin: Being the Conclusion of the Littlepage Manuscripts. F

Fuller, Margaret (1810), Papers on Literature and Art. NF

Gallatin, Albert (1761), The Oregon Question. NF

Hall, James (1793), The Wilderness and the War Path. NF

Hawthorne, Nathaniel (1804), Mosses from an Old Manse. F

Herbert, Henry William (1807), My Shooting Box. F

Holmes, Oliver Wendell (1809), Urania: A Rhymed Lesson. V; Poems. V

Hopkins, Mark (1802), Lectures on the Evidences of Christianity. NF

Ingraham, Joseph Holt (1809), Leisler; or, The Rebel and the King's Man. F

James, Thomas (1782), Three Years Among the Indians and Mexicans. NF

Kellogg, Elijah (1813), "Spartacus to the Gladiators." V

Lippard, George (1822), Blanche of Brandywine. F

Mathews, Cornelius (1817), Witchcraft; or, The Martyrs of Salem (pub. 1852). D

May, Samuel Joseph (1797), The Rights and Condition of Women. NF

Melville, Herman (1819), Typee. F

Morford, Henry (1823), The Rest of Don Juan. V

Paulding, James Kirke (1778), The Old Continental; or, The Price of Liberty. F

Saxe, John Godfrey (1816), Progress: A Satirical Poem. V

Smith, Solomon Franklin (1801), The Theatrical Apprenticeship . . . of Sol Smith. F, NF

Stephens, Ann Sophia (1813), The Diamond Necklace, and Other Tales. F

Taylor, Bayard (1825), Views A-foot; or, Europe Seen with Knapsack and Staff. NF

Thorpe, T. B. (1815), The Mysteries of the Backwoods. F; Our Army on the Rio Grande. NF

Tuckerman, Henry Theodore (1813), Thoughts on the Poets. NF

Whittier, John Greenleaf (1807), Voices of Freedom. V

Young, Alexander (1800), Chronicle of the First Planters of the Colony of Massachusetts Bay from 1623 to 1636 (editor). NF

Iowa admitted to the Union.
Oregon Treaty gave U.S. claim to Pacific Northwest.
War with Mexico (1846–48).
Wilmot Proviso (banning slavery in land acquired from Mexico) failed to pass.
Donner Party (emigrants to California).
James Renwick designed Smithsonian Institution.
William T.G. Morton first used ether in a surgical operation.
The Home Journal (New York), 1846–1901.

Great Britain repealed Corn Laws.
Hakluyt Society founded, in England.
The Daily News (London), 1846–1930.
The Guardian (London), 1846–1951.
Lear's *A Book of Nonsense*.
Marryat's *The Privateer's-Man*.
Dostoevsky's *Poor Folk; The Double*.
Mérimée's *Carmen*.

1847

Briggs, Charles Frederick (1804), The Trippings of Tom Pepper: The Results of Romancing. An Autobiography by Harry Franco (2 vols., 1847–50). F

Brougham, John (1810), Metamora; or, The Last of the Pollywoags. D

American troops occupied Mexico City; Antonio López de Santa Anna renounced the presidency.
Peace negotiations begun with Mexico.
American Medical Association founded, in Philadelphia.

Bushnell, Horace (1802), Christian Nurture. NF
Channing, William Ellery (1818), Poems, Second Series. V
Cooke, Philip Pendleton (1816), Froissart's Ballads. V
Copway, George (1818), Life, History, and Travels. NF
Davis, Andrew Jackson (1826), Principles of Nature, Her Divine
    Revelations, and A Voice of Mankind. NF
Emerson, Ralph Waldo (1803), Poems. V
Farley, Harriet (1817), Shells from the Strand of the Sea of
    Genius. NF
Field, Joseph M. (1810), The Drama in Pokerville. F
Griswold, Rufus Wilmot (1815), The Prose Writers of America
    (editor). F. NF
Halleck, Fitz-Greene (1790), The Poetical Works of Fitz-Greene
    Halleck. V
Hoffman, Charles Fenno (1806), Love's Calendar; Lays of the
    Hudson and Other Poems. V
Kemble, Frances Anne (Fanny) (1809), A Year of Consolation.
    NF
Lippard, George (1822), Legends of Mexico. F
Longfellow, Henry Wadsworth (1807), Evangeline: A Tale of
    Acadie. V
Melville, Herman (1819), Omoo: A Narrative of Adventures in
    the South Seas. F
Mowatt, Anna Cora (1819), Armand, the Child of the People. D
Noyes, John Humphrey (1811), The Berean. NF
Palmer, Joel (1810), Journal of Travels over the Rocky
    Mountains. NF
Paulding, James Kirke (1778), The Bucktails; or, Americans in
    England. D
Peck, John Mason (1789), Life of Daniel Boone. NF
Prescott, William Hickling (1796), History of the Conquest of
    Peru. NF
Robb, John S. (fl. 1847), Streaks of Squatter Life, and Far-West
    Scenes. F; Kaam; or, Daylight . . . A Tale of the Rocky
    Mountains. F
Sabine, Lorenzo (1803), The American Loyalists . . . (rev. as
    Biographical Sketches of the Loyalists of the American
    Revolution, 1864). NF
Sargent, Epes (1813), Songs of the Sea with Other Poems. V
Simms, William Gilmore (1806), The Life of the Chevalier
    Bayard. NF
Story, William Wetmore (1819), Poems. V
Thompson, Daniel Pierce (1795), Locke Amsden; or, The
    Schoolmaster. F; The Shaker Lovers, and Other Tales. F
Thorpe, T. B. (1815), Our Army at Monterey. NF

Maria Mitchell (Nantucket astronomer)
    discovered a comet.
The Chicago Tribune, 1847–.

Great Britain and Ireland disputed
    union.
United Presbyterian Church of Scotland
    founded.
Charlotte Brontë's *Jane Eyre.*
Emily Brontë's *Wuthering Heights.*
Anne Brontë's *Agnes Grey.*
Disraeli's *Tancred.*
Marryat's *The Children of the New
    Forest.*
Keble's *Sermons.*
Tennyson's *The Princess.*
Trollope's *The Macdermotts of
    Ballycloran.*

1848

Adams, John Quincy (d. 1848), Poems of Religion and Society.
    V
Arthur, Timothy Shay (1809), Agnes; or, The Possessed. A
    Revelation of Mesmerism. F
Baker, Benjamin A. (1818), A Glance at New York. D
Barnes, Charlotte Mary Sanford (1818), The Forest Princess. D
Bennett, Emerson (1822), Mike Fink. F
Boker, George Henry (1823), The Lesson of Life and Other
    Poems. V; Calaynos: A Tragedy. D
Bryant, Edwin (1805), What I Saw in California (repub. as
    Rocky Mountain Adventures, 1885). NF

Wisconsin admitted to the Union.
Mexico relinquished present-day
    California, New Mexico, and parts of
    Arizona and Nevada to U.S. for $15
    million.
Discovery of gold in California.
Free-Soil Party (antislavery) formed.
American Association for the
    Advancement of Science established,
    in Philadelphia.
Oneida Community founded, 1848–79.

Bunce, Oliver Bell (1828), The Morning of Life. D

Burton, William Evans (1804), Waggeries and Vagaries. F

Carey, Henry Charles (1793), Past, Present, and Future. NF

Channing, William Henry (1810), Memoir of William Ellery Channing. NF

Chivers, Thomas Holley (1809), Search After Truth; or, A New Revelation of the Psycho-Physiological Nature of Man. NF

Cooper, James Fenimore (1789), The Crater; or, Vulcan's Peak: A Tale of the Pacific. F; Jack Tier; or, The Florida Reef. F; The Oak Openings; or, The Bee-Hunter. F

Hall, James (1793), The West: Its Commerce and Navigation. NF

Hart, Joseph C. (1798), The Romance of Yachting. NF

Hedge, Frederic Henry (1805), Prose Writers of Germany. NF

Hirst, Henry Beck (1817), Endymion. V

Hoffman, Charles Fenno (1806), The Pioneers of New York. NF

Lee, Eliza Buckminster (1794), Naomi; or, Boston Two Hundred Years Ago. F

Leslie, Eliza (1787), Amelia, or a Young Lady of Vicissitudes. F

Lowell, James Russell (1819), Poems: Second Series. V; A Fable for Critics. V; The Biglow Papers (1st ser.). V; The Vision of Sir Launfal. V

Mathews, Cornelius (1817), Jacob Leisler. D

Myers, Peter Hamilton (1812), The First of the Knickerbockers. F

Neal, Joseph Clay (1807), Charcoal Sketches: Second Series. F

Noyes, John Humphrey (1811), Bible Communism. NF; Male Continence. NF

Parker, Theodore (1810), A Letter to the People of the United States Touching the Matter of Slavery. NF

Poe, Edgar Allan (1809), Eureka: A Prose Poem. NF; "The Poetic Principle" (pub. 1850). NF

Rouquette, Adrien Emmanuel (1813), Wild Flowers: Sacred Poetry. V

Simms, William Gilmore (1806), Lays of the Palmetto. V; The Cassique of Accabee. V; Charleston, and Her Satirists: A Scribblement. V

Smith, Elizabeth Oakes (1806), The Salamander: A Legend for Christmas. F

Squier, Ephraim George (1821), Ancient Monuments of the Mississippi Valley. NF

Thompson, Daniel Pierce (1795), Lucy Hosmer; or, The Guardian and the Ghost. F

Thompson, William Tappan (1812), Major Jones's Sketches of Travel. F

Thorpe, T. B. (1815), The Taylor Anecdote Book. NF

Wallace, William Ross (1819), Alban the Pirate. V

Webber, Charles Wilkins (1819), Old Hicks, the Guide. F

First woman's rights convention, in Seneca Falls, N.Y.

The Independent (New York), 1848–1928.

Stephen Foster's "Oh! Susanna."

Revolutions in France, Italy, Germany, Denmark, Hungary.

Marx and Engels published *Communist Manifesto*.

Formation of the Pre-Raphaelite Brotherhood.

Frederick Marryat d.

Joris Karl Huysmans b.

Thackeray's *Vanity Fair*.

Dicken's *Dombey and Son*.

Trollope's *The Kellys and the O'Kellys*.

Gaskell's *Mary Barton*.

John Stuart Mill's *Principles of Political Economy*.

Dumas fils' *Camille*.

Chateaubriand's *Memoirs from Beyond the Grave*.

1849

Bennett, Emerson (1822), Prairie Flower. F; Leni-Leoti. F

Brougham, John (1810), Temptation, or the Irish Immigrant. D

Bushnell, Horace (1802), God in Christ. NF

Channing, William Ellery (1818), The Woodman. V

Cooper, James Fenimore (1789), The Sea Lions; or, The Lost Sealers. F; The Works of J. Fenimore Cooper: Author's Revised Edition (12 vols., 1849–51). F, NF

Eastman, Mary H. (1818), Dacotah, or Life and Legends of the Sioux Around Fort Snelling. NF

Creation of Minnesota Territory.

U.S. Department of the Interior established.

Slavery debated in California and New Mexico.

Edgar Allan Poe d.

The Spirit of the Age (New York), 1849–50.

Notes and Queries (London), 1849–.

Anne Brontë d.

Gilman, Caroline Howard (1794), Verses of a Life-time. V
Griswold, Rufus Wilmot (1815), The Female Poets of America (editor). V, NF
Henson, Josiah (1789), The Life of Josiah Henson. NF
Herbert, Henry William (1807), The Deerstalkers. F
Hildreth, Richard (1807), History of the United States (6 vols., 1849–52). NF
Hirst, Henry Beck (1817), The Penance of Roland. V
Holmes, Oliver Wendell (1809), Poems. V
Irving, Washington (1783), A Book of the Hudson. NF; Mahomet and His Successors (2 vols., 1849–50). NF
Jones, John Beauchamp (1810), The Western Merchant. F
Kennedy, John Pendleton (1795), Memoirs of the Life of William Wirt. NF
Logan, Cornelius Ambrosius (1806), Chloroform; or New York a Hundred Years Hence. D
Longfellow, Henry Wadsworth (1807), Kavanagh: A Tale. F
Mayo, William Starbuck (1811), Kaloolah; or, Journeyings to the Djébel Kumri. F
Melville, Herman (1819), Redburn: His First Voyage. F; Mardi: And a Voyage Thither. F
Motley, John Lothrop (1814), Merry-Mount: A Romance of the Massachusetts Colony. F
Myers, Peter Hamilton (1812), The Young Patroon. F
Owen, Robert Dale (1801), Hints on Public Architecture. NF
Parkman, Francis (1823), The California and Oregon Trail. NF
Paulding, James Kirke (1778), The Puritan and His Daughter. F
Peterson, Charles Jacobs (1819), Grace Dudley; or, Arnold at Saratoga. F
Ross, Alexander (1783), Adventures of the First Settlers on the Oregon or Columbia River. NF
Simms, William Gilmore (1806), Sabbath Lyrics; or, Songs from Scripture. V; The Life of Nathaniel Greene. NF
Southworth, E. D. E. N. (1819), Retribution. F
Stoddard, Richard Henry (1825), Foot-Prints. V
Street, Alfred Billings (1811), Frontenac. V
Taylor, Bayard (1825), Rhymes of Travel, Ballads and Poems. V
Thomas, Frederick William (1806), Sketches of Character, and Tales Founded on Fact. NF
Thoreau, Henry David (1817), A Week on the Concord and Merrimack Rivers. NF; "Resistance to Civil Government" (repub. as "Civil Disobedience," 1894). NF
Ticknor, George (1791), History of Spanish Literature (3 vols., rev. 1872). NF
Tuckerman, Henry Theodore (1813), Characteristics of Literature (2 vols., 1849–51). NF
Webber, Charles Wilkins (1819), The Gold Mines of the Gila. F
Whittier, John Greenleaf (1807), Poems. V; Leaves from Margaret Smith's Journal in the Province of Massachusetts Bay, 1678–79.
Willis, N. P. (1806), Rural Letters and Other Records of Thought at Leisure. NF
Wise, Henry Augustus (1819), Los Gringos; or, An Inside View of Mexico and California. . . . F

Maria Edgeworth d.
William Ernest Henley b.
Coleridge's Notes and Lectures upon Shakespeare (posth.; ed. Sara Coleridge).
Charlotte Brontë's Shirley.
Thackeray's The History of Pendennis (1849–50).
Arnold's The Strayed Reveller and Other Poems.
Ruskin's The Seven Lamps of Architecture.
Macaulay's The History of England from the Accession of James II (1849–55).
Harriet Martineau's The History of England during the Thirty Years' Peace, 1816–46.
James Anthony Froude's The Nemesis of Faith.
Clough's Ambarvalia.
Scribe's Adrienne Lecouvreur.
Hebbel's Herod and Marianne.

1850

Adams, John (d. 1826), The Works of John Adams (10 vols., 1850–56). NF
Allston, Washington (d. 1843), Lectures on Art and Poems. NF

President Taylor died sixteen months after taking office.
Compromise of 1850: California admitted as a free state; New Mexico

Arthur, Timothy Shay (1809), The Debtor's Daughter; or, Life and Its Changes. F

Boker, George Henry (1823), Anne Boleyn: A Tragedy. D; The Betrothal (pub. 1856). D

Bryant, William Cullen (1794), Letters of a Traveller; or, Notes of Things Seen in Europe and America. NF

Bunce, Oliver Bell (1828), Marco Bozzaris. D

Cannon, Charles James (1800), The Oath of Office. D

Cobb, Joseph B. (1819), The Creole; or, Siege of New Orleans. F

Colton, Walter (1797), Deck and Port. NF; Three Years in California. NF

Cooper, James Fenimore (1789), The Ways of the Hour: A Tale. F

Cooper, Susan Fenimore (1813), Rural Hours. NF

Copway, George (1818), Traditional History of the Ojibway Nation. NF; The Ojibway Conquest. V

Davis, Andrew Jackson (1826), The Great Harmonia. NF

Drake, Daniel (1785), Systematic Treatise . . . on the Principal Diseases of the Interior Valley of North America (2 vols., 1850–54). NF

Dupuy, Eliza Ann (1814), The Conspirator. F

Emerson, Ralph Waldo (1803), Representative Men: Seven Lectures. NF

Garrard, Lewis H. (1829), Wah-to'-yah, and the Taos Trail. NF

Grayson, William J. (1788), Letter to Governor Seabrook. NF

Hare, Robert (1781), Standish the Puritan. F

Hawthorne, Nathaniel (1804), The Scarlet Letter. F

Hentz, Caroline Lee Whiting (1800), Linda. F

Holmes, Oliver Wendell (1809), Astraea: The Balance of Illusions. V

"Ik Marvel" (1822), Reveries of a Bachelor; or, A Book of the Heart. NF/F

Judd, Sylvester (1813), Richard Edney and the Governor's Family. F; Philo, An Evangeliad. V

Lewis, Henry Clay (1825), Odd Leaves from the Life of a Louisiana "Swamp Doctor." F

Lippincott, Sara Jane (1823), Greenwood Leaves. NF

Longfellow, Henry Wadsworth (1807), The Seaside and the Fireside. V

Mathews, Cornelius (1817), Moneypenny; or, The Heart of the World. F; Chanticleer: A Thanksgiving Story of the Peabody Family. F

Melville, Herman (1819), White-Jacket; or, The World in a Man-of-War. F

Miles, George Henry (1824), Mohammed, The Arabian Prophet (prod. 1851). D

Myers, Peter Hamilton (1812), The King of the Hurons. F

Poe, Edgar Allan (d. 1849), The Works of the Late Edgar Allan Poe: With a Memoir by Rufus Wilmot Griswold and Notices of His Life and Genius by N. P. Willis and J. R. Lowell (4 vols., 1850–56). F, NF, V

Reid, Mayne (1818), The Rifle Rangers. F

Saxe, John Godfrey (1816), Humorous and Satirical Poems. V

Simms, William Gilmore (1806), The Lily and the Totem; or, The Huguenots in Florida. F; Flirtation at the Moultrie House. F; The City of the Silent. V

Taylor, Bayard (1825), Eldorado; or, Adventures in the Path of Empire. NF

Tuckerman, Henry Theodore (1813), The Optimist. NF

Warner, Susan Bogert (1819), The Wide, Wide World. F

and Utah organized as territories; Fugitive Slave Act.

Clayton-Bulwer Treaty with Great Britain (neutrality of Panama Canal project).

Mrs. Amelia Bloomer donned "bloomers."

Jenny Lind toured U.S., managed by P.T. Barnum.

J. Merritt Ives joined Nathaniel Currier.

Mathew Brady's photographs (pub. as *Gallery of Illustrious Americans*).

Margaret Fuller d.

Harper's Monthly Magazine (New York), 1850–.

Stephen Foster's "Camptown Races."

Alfred, Lord Tennyson named poet laureate of England.

Richard Wagner's *Lohengrin*.

Household Words (London), 1850–59.

William Wordsworth d.

Honoré de Balzac d.

Wordsworth's *The Prelude*.

Tennyson's *In Memoriam*.

Dickens's *David Copperfield*.

E.B. Browning's *Sonnets from the Portuguese*.

Carlyle's *Latter-Day Pamphlets*.

Turgenev's *A Month in the Country*.

Whittier, John Greenleaf (1807), Old Portraits and Modern
Sketches. NF; Songs of Labor and Other Poems. V
Willis, N. P. (1806), People I Have Met. F; Life Here and
There. F

1851

Andrews, Stephen Pearl (1812), The Science of Society.
NF; Cost the Limit of Price. NF
Audubon, John James (1785), The Quadrupeds of North
America (with John Bachman; octavo edition, 1851–54). NF
Blood, Benjamin Paul (1832), The Philosophy of Justice. NF
Boker, George Henry (1823), The World a Mask. D
Bryant, William Cullen (1794), Reminiscences of The Evening
Post. NF
Bushnell, Horace (1802), The Age of Homespun. NF
Calhoun, John C. (d. 1850), A Disquisition on Government
and a Discourse on the Constitution and Government of the
United States. NF; The Works of John C. Calhoun (6 vols.,
1851–56). NF
Chivers, Thomas Holley (1809), Eonchs of Ruby: A Gift of
Love. V
Cobb, Sylvanus, Jr. (1823), The King's Talisman. F
Curtis, George William (1824), Nile Notes of a Howadji. NF
Deering, Nathaniel (1791), Bozzaris. D
De Forest, John William (1826), History of the Indians of
Connecticut. NF
Duganne, Augustine Joseph Hickey (1823), Parnassus in
Pillory. V
Fay, Theodore Sedgwick (1807), Ulric; or, The Voices. V
Gayarré, Charles Etienne Arthur (1805), History of Louisiana
(4 vols., 1851–66). NF
Godwin, Parke (1816), Vala. F
Grayson, William J. (1788), Letters of Curtius. NF
Hawthorne, Nathaniel (1804), The House of the Seven Gables.
F; True Stories from History and Biography. NF
Hollister, Gideon Hiram (1817), Mount Hope. F
Hooper, Johnson Jones (1815), The Widow Rugby's Husband,
A Night at the Ugly Man's and Other Tales of Alabama. F
"Ik Marvel" (1822), Dream Life. NF, F
Kelly, Jonathan Falconbridge (1817), Dan Marble: A
Biographical Sketch of That Famous and Diverting Humorist.
NF
Kendall, George Wilkins (1809), The War Between the United
States and Mexico. NF
Longfellow, Henry Wadsworth (1807), The Golden Legend
(repub. as Christus, 1872). V
Lord, William Wilberforce (1819), Christ in Hades. V
Mayo, William Starbuck (1811), Romance Dust from the
Historic Placer (repub. as Flood and Field, 1855). F
Melville, Herman (1819), Moby-Dick; or, The Whale. F
Morgan, Lewis Henry (1818), League of the Ho-dé-no-sau-nee,
or Iroquois. NF
Parkman, Francis (1823), History of the Conspiracy of Pontiac
and the War of the North American Tribes. NF
Phelps, Elizabeth Stuart (1815), The Sunny Side; or, The
Country Minister's Wife. F
Reid, Mayne (1818), The Scalp Hunters. F

Gen. Narciso López's expedition to free
Cubans from Spanish rule.
Isaac Singer patented sewing machine.
U.S. schooner-yacht America won first
"America's Cup."
American YMCA founded, in Boston.
Northwestern University founded.
James Fenimore Cooper d.
The New York Times, 1851–.
The Carpet-Bag (Boston), 1851–53.
Stephen Foster's "Old Folks at Home."

Coup d'état by Louis Napoleon, in
France.
The Great Exhibition in Hyde Park,
London.
Thomas Cook's first guided tour from
England to the Continent.
Ruskin's The Stones of Venice (1851–
53).
Meredith's Poems.
Borrow's Lavengro.
Hunt's Table-Talk
E.B. Browning's Casa Guidi Windows.
Bulwer-Lytton's Not So Bad As We
Seem.
Fitzgerald's Euphranor: A Dialogue on
Youth.
Spencer's Social Statistics.

Schoolcraft, Henry Rowe (1793), Historical and Statistical Information Respecting the History, Condition, and Prospect of the Indian Tribes of the United States (6 vols., 1851–57). NF

Simms, William Gilmore (1806), Katharine Walton; or, The Rebel of Dorchester. F; Norman Maurice; or, The Man of the People. NF

Smith, Elizabeth Oakes (1806), Woman and Her Needs. NF

Squier, Ephraim George (1821), Aboriginal Monuments of the State of New York. NF

Stearns, Oliver (1807), The Gospel as Applied to the Fugitive Slave Law. NF

Thompson, Daniel Pierce (1795), The Rangers; or, The Tory's Daughter. F; History of Vermont, and the Northern Campaign of 1777. NF

Tuckerman, Henry Theodore (1813), Poems. V

Victor, Frances Fuller (1826), Poems of Sentiment and Imagination (with Metta Victoria Victor). V

Wallace, William Ross (1819), Meditations in America, and Other Poems. V

Webber, Charles Wilkins (1819), The Hunter-Naturalist. NF

Willis, N. P. (1806), Hurry-graphs. NF

1852

Aiken, George L. (1830), Uncle Tom's Cabin [adapted from Harriet Beecher Stowe's novel (1852)]. D

Beecher, Lyman (1775), Beecher's Works. NF

Boker, George Henry (1823), The Podesta's Daughter and Other Poems. V; The Widow's Marriage (pub. 1856). D

Brownson, Orestes (1803), Essays and Reviews. NF

Bryant, William Cullen (1794), A Discourse on the Life and Genius of James Fenimore Cooper. NF

Clark, Lewis Gaylord (1808), Knick-Knacks from an Editor's Table. NF

Curtis, George William (1824), The Howadji in Syria. NF; Lotus Eating. NF

Eastman, Mary H. (1818), The Romance of Indian Life. NF; Aunt Phillis's Cabin; or Southern Life as It Is. F

Farley, Harriet (1817), Happy Nights at Hazel Nook. NF

Hale, Sara Josepha (1788), Northwood; or, Life North and South. F

Hawthorne, Nathaniel (1804), The Blithedale Romance. F; A Wonder-Book for Girls and Boys. F; The Snow-Image and Other Twice-Told Tales. F; The Life of Franklin Pierce. NF

Herbert, Henry William (1807), The Quorndon Hounds; or, A Virginian at Melton Mowbray. F

Holmes, Oliver Wendell (1809), The Poetical Works of Oliver Wendell Holmes. V

Jarvis, James Jackson (1818), Parisian Sights. NF

Jones, Joseph Stevens (1809), The Silver Spoon. D

Meeker, Nathan Cook (1817), The Adventures of Captain Armstrong. F

Melville, Herman (1819), Pierre; or, The Ambiguities. F

Miles, George Henry (1824), Hernando de Soto. D

Norton, Andrews (1786), Tracts on Christianity. NF

Olmsted, Frederick Law (1822), Walks and Talks of an American Farmer in England. NF

Parker, Theodore (1810), Speeches, Addresses, and Occasional Sermons. NF

"Young America" movement.

American Geographical Society founded.

William Makepeace Thackeray lectured in U.S.

Daniel Webster d.

The Golden Era (San Francisco), 1852–93.

Dwight's Journal of Music (Boston), 1852–81.

President Louis Napoleon proclaimed himself Emperor Napoleon III.

Anglo-Burmese War began.

Thomas Moore d.

George Moore b.

Arnold's *Empedocles on Etna.*

Newman's *The Scope and Nature of University Education.*

Thackeray's *The History of Henry Esmond.*

Tennyson's *Ode on the Death of the Duke of Wellington.*

Gautier's *Enamels and Cameos.*

Turgenev's A *Sportman's Sketches.*

Peterson, Charles Jacobs (1819), History of the United States Navy. NF

Phelps, Elizabeth Stuart (1815), A Peep at Number Five. F; The Angel Over the Right Shoulder. F

Realf, Richard (1834), Guesses at the Beautiful. V

Reid, Mayne (1818), The Boy Hunters. F

Reynolds, John (1788), Pioneer History of Illinois. NF

Rouquette, Adrien Emmanuel (1813), La Thebaïde en Amérique, ou Apologie de la vie solitaire et contemplative. NF

Shea, Joseph Dawson Gilmary (1824), Discovery and Exploration of the Mississippi Valley. NF

Simms, William Gilmore (1806), The Golden Christmas: A Chronicle of St. John's, Berkeley. F; The Sword and the Distaff; or, "Fair, Fat, and Forty" (repub. as Woodcraft, 1854). F; As Good as a Comedy; or, The Tennesseean's Story. F; Michael Bonham; or, The Fall of Bexar. NF

Southworth, E. D. E. N. (1819), The Curse of Clifton; or, The Widowed Bride. F

Squier, Ephraim George (1821), Nicaragua. NF

Stoddard, Richard Henry (1825), Poems. V

Stowe, Harriet Beecher (1811), Uncle Tom's Cabin; or, Life Among the Lowly. F

Thomas, Frederick William (1806), An Autobiography of William Russell. F

Ware, William (1797), Lectures on . . . Washington Allston. NF

Warner, Susan Bogert (1819), Queechy. F

Webber, Charles Wilkins (1819), Tales of the Southern Border. F

1853

Baldwin, Joseph Glover (1815), The Flush Times of Alabama and Mississippi. F

Boker, George Henry (1823), Leonor de Guzman (pub. 1856). D

Bremer, Fredrika (1801), The Homes of the New World. NF

Browne, J. Ross (1821), Yusef . . . a Crusade in the East. NF

Chivers, Thomas Holley (1809), Memoralia; or, Phials of Amber Full of the Tears of Love. V; Virginalia, or Songs of My Summer Nights. V

Curtis, George William (1824), The Potiphar Papers. NF

De Bow, James Dunwoody Brownson (1820), Industrial Resources of the Southern and Western States. NF

Delano, Alonzo (1802?), Pen-Knife Sketches, or Chips of the Old Block. NF

Duganne, Augustine Joseph Hickey (1823), A Sound Literature the Safeguard of Our National Institutions. NF; Art's True Mission in America. NF

"Fanny Fern" (1811), Fern Leaves from Fanny's Portfolio. NF

Gayarré, Charles Etienne Arthur (1805), Address of Charles Gayarré, to the People of the State, on the Late Frauds Perpetrated at the Election Held on the 7th Nov., 1853, in the City of New Orleans. NF

Hammett, Samuel Adams (1816), A Stray Yankee in Texas. F, NF

Hawthorne, Nathaniel (1804), Tanglewood Tales for Girls and Boys. F

Hedge, Frederic Henry (1805), Hymns for the Church of Christ. V

Hildreth, Richard (1807), Theory of Politics. NF

Creation of the Washington Territory.

Gadsden Purchase from Mexico (completed the present borders).

Commodore Perry and the U.S. fleet arrived in Tokyo Bay.

Second Grinnell Arctic Expedition.

New York Central Railroad founded.

Charles Lewis Tiffany established a jewelry company.

Gail Borden condensed milk.

Putnam's Monthly Magazine (New York), 1853–1910.

Stephen Foster's "My Old Kentucky Home."

Crimean War (Turkey vs. Russia), 1853–56.

Baron Haussmann began reconstruction of Paris city plan.

Compulsory smallpox vaccination in England.

First railroad through the Alps.

Dickens's *Bleak House*.

Charlotte Brontë's *Villette*.

Charles Kingsley's *Hypatia*.

Arnold's *Poems*.

Thackeray's *The Newcomes* (1853–55).

Gaskell's *Cranford*.

Reade's *Peg Woffington*.

Kane, Elisha Kent (1820), The U.S. Grinnell Expedition in Search of Sir John Franklin. NF

Lieber, Francis (1800), On Civil Liberty and Self-Government. NF

Lippard, George (1822), New York: Its Upper Ten and Lower Million. F

Longfellow, Samuel (1819), Thalatta: A Book for the Sea-side (compiled with Thomas Wentworth Higginson). V

Mathews, Cornelius (1817), A Pen-and-Ink Panorama of New York City. NF

Melville, Herman (1819), "Bartleby the Scrivener: A Story of Wall Street" (pub. anon.; repub. in The Piazza Tales, 1856). F

Parker, Theodore (1810), Ten Sermons on Religion. NF; Sermons on Theism, Atheism, and the Popular Theology. NF

Reynolds, John (1788), The Life and Adventures of John Kelly. F

Sigourney, Lydia Huntley (1791), The Faded Hope. V

Simms, William Gilmore (1806), Marie de Berniere. F; Vasconselos: A Romance of the New World. F; Egeria; or, Voices of Thought and Counsel for the Woods and the Wayside. NF; South Carolina in the Revolutionary War. NF

Stowe, Harriet Beecher (1811), A Key to Uncle Tom's Cabin. NF; Uncle Sam's Emancipation . . . and Other Tales and Sketches. F

Tuckerman, Henry Theodore (1813), Leaves from the Diary of a Dreamer. NF

Whitman, Sarah Helen (1803), Hours of Life. V

Whittier, John Greenleaf (1807), The Chapel of the Hermits. V

Willis, N. P. (1806), Health Trip to the Tropics. NF; Fun-Jottings. F

1854

Arthur, Timothy Shay (1809), Ten Nights in a Bar-room and What I Saw There. F

Ballou, Adin (1803), Practical Christian Socialism. NF

Benton, Thomas Hart (1782), Thirty Years' View; or, A History of the Working of the American Government . . . 1820 to 1850 (2 vols., 1854–55). NF

Blood, Benjamin Paul (1832), The Bride of the Iconoclast. V

Brownson, Orestes (1803), The Spirit-Rapper: An Autobiography. F

Bryant, William Cullen (1794), Poems. V

Cary, Phoebe (1824), Poems and Parodies. V

Clappe, Louise Amelia Knapp Smith (1819), Dame Shirley Letters (pub. in Pioneer Magazine, 1854–55; coll. 1922). NF

Clarke, James Freeman (1810), The Christian Doctrine of Prayer. NF

Cooke, John Esten (1830), Leather Stocking and Silk; or, Hunter John Myers and His Times. F; The Virginia Comedians; or, Old Days in the Old Dominion. F

Cummins, Maria Susanna (1827), The Lamplighter. F

Delano, Alonzo (1802?), Life on the Plains and Among the Diggings. NF

Eastman, Mary H. (1818), Chicora, and Other Regions of the Conquerors and Conquered. NF

Fitzhugh, George (1806), Sociology for the South; or, The Failure of Free Society. NF

Gayarré, Charles Etienne Arthur (1805), The School for Politics: A Dramatic Novel. F; Influence of Mechanic Arts on the Human Race; Two Lectures. . . . NF

Ostend Manifesto (American-Cuban-Spanish contretemps).

Treaty of Kanagawa (opening of Japan to the Occident).

Kansas-Nebraska Act (repealed the Missouri Compromise).

Know-Nothing Party reached its apogee.

Republican Party formed.

The Chicago Times, 1854–1918.

Stephen Foster's "Jeanie with the Light Brown Hair."

Battle of Balaclava; siege of Sevastopol.

Florence Nightingale nursed British soldiers in Turkey.

Pope Pius IX declared doctrine of Immaculate Conception.

Oscar Wilde b.

Dickens's *Hard Times.*

Tennyson's "The Charge of the Light Brigade."

Yonge's *Heartsease.*

Ferrier's *The Institutes of Metaphysics.*

Nerval's *Girls of Fire.*

Grayson, William J. (1788), The Hireling and the Slave. V

Hale, Sarah Josepha (1788), Woman's Record. NF

Hentz, Caroline Lee Whiting (1800), The Planter's Northern
Bride. F

Hosmer, William H. C. (1814), Poetical Works. V

Howe, Julia Ward (1819), Passion Flowers. V

Jones, John Beauchamp (1810), Freaks of Fortune; or, The
History of Ned Lorn. F

Lippincott, Sara Jane (1823), Haps and Mishaps of a Tour in
Europe. NF

Melville, Herman (1819), "The Encantadas, or Enchanted Isles"
(by "Salvator R. Tarnmoor"; repub. in The Piazza Tales,
1856). F

Moulton, Louise Chandler (1835), This, That, and the Other. F

Mowatt, Anna Cora (1819), Autobiography of an Actress. NF

Neal, John (1793), One Word More. NF

O'Brien, Fitz-James (c. 1828), The Gentleman from Ireland. D

"Oliver Optic" (1822), Boat Club Series. F

Pike, Mary Hayden (1824), Ida May. F

Quincy, Edmund (1808), Wensley, a Story Without a Moral. F

Ridge, John Rollin (1827), The Life and Adventures of Joaquin
Murieta, the Celebrated California Bandit. F

Robinson, Solon (1803), Hot Corn: Life Scenes in New York
Illustrated. F

Sargent, Epes (1813), The Priestess. D

Shea, John Dawson Gilmary (1824), History of the Catholic
Missions Among the Indian Tribes of the United States, 1529–
1854. NF

Shillaber, Benjamin Penhallow (1814), Life and Sayings of
Mrs. Partington. F

Simms, William Gilmore (1806), Southward Ho! A Spell of
Sunshine. F

Smith, Elizabeth Oakes (1806), Bertha and Lily. F; The
Newsboy. F

Smith, Seba (1792), 'Way Down East, or Portraitures of Yankee
Life. F

Smith, Solomon Franklin (1801), The Theatrical Journey . . .
of Sol Smith. F, NF

Southworth, E. D. E. N. (1819), The Missing Bride. F

Stephens, Ann Sophia (1813), Fashion and Famine. F

Stowe, Harriet Beecher (1811), Sunny Memories of Foreign
Lands. NF

Taylor, Bayard (1825), A Journey to Central Africa. NF

Thoreau, Henry David (1817), Walden; or, Life in the Woods.
NF; "Slavery in Massachusetts." NF

Thorpe, T. B. (1815), The Hive of the Bee-Hunter. NF; The
Master's House. F

Webber, Charles Wilkins (1819), Wild Scenes and Song Birds.
NF

Whittier, John Greenleaf (1807), Literary Recreations and
Miscellanies. NF

Willis, N. P. (1806), Famous Persons and Famous Places. NF

Young, Brigham (1801), Journal of Discourses (26 vols., 1854–
86). NF

1855

Alcott, Louisa May (1832), Flower Fables. F

Aldrich, Thomas Bailey (1836), The Bells: A Collection of
Chimes. V

Baldwin, Joseph Glover (1815), Party Leaders. NF

"Kansas Question" (pro- vs. anti-
slavery factions).
William Walker's filibustering
expeditions in Nicaragua.

Bancroft, George (1800), Literary and Historical Miscellanies. NF

Barnum, P. T. (1810), The Life of P. T. Barnum, Written by Himself. NF

Bartlett, John (1820), Familiar Quotations (editor). NF, F, V, D

Beecher, Henry Ward (1813), Star Papers; or, Experiences of Art and Nature. NF

Boker, George Henry (1823), Francesca da Rimini (pub. 1856). D; The Bankrupt. D

Brougham, John (1810), Po-ca-hon-tas! or, Ye Gentle Savage. D

Bulfinch, Thomas (1796), The Age of Fable. F

Cannon, Charles James (1800), Ravellings from the Web of Life. F

Clay, Henry (d. 1852), The Private Correspondence of Henry Clay (ed. by Calvin Colton). NF

Coggeshall, William Turner (1824), Oakshaw. F

Derby, George Horatio (1823), Phoenixiana: A Collection of Burlesques and Sketches. F

Duganne, Augustine Joseph Hickey (1823), Poetical Works. V

Evans, Augusta Jane (1835), Inez: A Tale of the Alamo. F

"Fanny Fern" (1811), Ruth Hall. F

Griswold, Rufus Wilmot (1815), The Republican Court, or American Society in the Days of Washington. NF

Hammett, Samuel Adams (1815), The Wonderful Adventures of Captain Priest. F

Hare, Robert (1781), Experimental Investigation of the Spirit Manifestations. . . . NF

Hayne, Paul Hamilton (1830), Poems. V

Helper, Hinton Rowan (1829), Land of Gold: Reality Versus Fiction. NF

Ingraham, Joseph Holt (1809), The Prince of the House of David. F

Irving, Washington (1783), The Life of George Washington (5 vols., 1855–59). NF; Wolfert's Roost and Other Papers. NF

Leland, Charles Godfrey (1824), Meister Karl's Sketch-Book. F

Longfellow, Henry Wadsworth (1807), The Song of Hiawatha. V

Mathews, Cornelius (1817), False Pretences; or, Both Sides of Good Society: A Comedy. D

Melville, Herman (1819), Israel Potter: His Fifty Years of Exile. F

Moulton, Louise Chandler (1835), Juno Clifford. F

Nichols, Mary Sargeant (1810), Mary Lyndon; or, Revelations of a Life. F

Nordhoff, Charles (1830), Man-of-War Life. NF

Norton, Andrews (d. 1853), Internal Evidences of the Genuineness of the Gospels. NF

Parker, Theodore (1810), Additional Speeches, Addresses, and Occasional Sermons. NF; The Trial of Theodore Parker, for the "Misdemeanor" of a Speech in Faneuil Hall Against Kidnapping. NF

Parton, James (1822), The Life of Horatio Greeley. NF

Peck, John Mason (1789), Father Clark; or, The Pioneer Preacher. NF

Peterson, Charles Jacobs (1819), Kate Aylesford, A Story of the Refugees. F

Prescott, William Hickling (1796), History of the Reign of Philip the Second (3 vols., 1855–58; incomplete). NF

"Q. K. Philander Doesticks, P. B." (1831), Doesticks, And What He Says. F

Ross, Alexander (1783), The Fur Hunters of the Far West. NF

First U.S. Court of Claims established.
Boston Philharmonic Orchestra organized.
The New York Ledger, 1855–1903.
Frank Leslie's Illustrated Newspaper (New York), 1855–1922.

Alexander II proclaimed czar of Russia.
Ferdinand de Lesseps granted concession by France to build the Suez Canal.
The Daily Telegraph (London), 1855–.
Charlotte Brontë d.
Trollope's *The Warden.*
Tennyson's *Maud and Other Poems.*
Arnold's *Poems, Second Series.*
Charles Kingsley's *Westward Ho!*
Robert Browning's *Men and Women.*
Spencer's *Principles of Psychology.*

Sargent, Winthrop (1825), The History of an Expedition against Fort Du Quesne. . . . NF

Simms, William Gilmore (1806), The Forayers; or, The Raid of the Dog-Days. F

Southworth, E. D. E. N. (1819), The Missing Bride. F

Taylor, Bayard (1825), The Lands of the Saracen. NF; Poems of the Orient. V; A Visit to India, China, and Japan in the Year 1853. NF; Poems of Home and Travel. V

Wallace, Horace Binney (d. 1852), Art, Scenery, and Philosophy in Europe. NF

Whitman, Walt (1819), Leaves of Grass. V

Willis, N. P. (1806), Out-Doors at Idlewild. NF; The Rag-Bag: A Collection of Ephemera. NF

Wise, Henry Augustus (1819), Tales for the Marines. F

1856

Adams, John Turvill (1805), The Lost Hunter. F

Bateman, Sidney Frances (1823), Self. D

Beckwourth, James P. (1798), The Life and Adventures of James P. Beckwourth, Mountaineer, Scout, and Pioneer and Chief of the Crow Nation of Indians. NF

Boker, George Henry (1823), Plays and Poems. D, V

Brooks, Charles T. (1813), Faust (trans. from German). D

Brougham, John (1810), Dred [adapted from the novel by Harriet Beecher Stowe (1856)]. D

Calvert, George Henry (1803), Introduction to Social Science. NF

Channing, Edward Tyrrell (d. 1856), Lectures Read to the Seniors in Harvard College. NF

Chivers, Thomas Holley (1809), Birth-Day Song of Liberty. V

Clemens, Jeremiah (1814), Bernard Lile. F

Cranch, Christopher Pearse (1813), The Last of the Huggermuggers. F

Curtis, George William (1824), Prue and I. NF; The Duty of the American Scholar to Politics and the Times. NF

De Forest, John William (1826), Oriental Acquaintance; or, Letters from Syria. NF

Delano, Alonzo (1802?), Old Block's Sketch Book. NF

Dupuy, Eliza Ann (1814), The Huguenot Exiles. F

Emerson, Ralph Waldo (1803), English Traits. NF

Fuller, Margaret (d. 1850), At Home and Abroad. NF

Goodrich, Samuel Griswold (1793), Recollections of a Lifetime. NF

Hentz, Caroline Lee Whiting (1800), Ernest Linwood. F

Holmes, Mary Jane (1825), Lena Rivers. F

Holmes, Oliver Wendell (1809), Oration Delivered Before the New England Society. NF

Jarves, James Jackson (1818), Italian Sights. NF

Kelly, Jonathan Falconbridge (d. 1855), The Humors of Falconbridge. NF

Lord, William Wilberforce (1819), André. V

Mathews, Cornelius (1817), The Indian Fairy Book (repub. as The Enchanted Moccasins and Other Legends of the American Indians, 1877). F

Melville, Herman (1819), The Piazza Tales. F

Motley, John Lothrop (1814), The Rise of the Dutch Republic. NF

"Bleeding Kansas" (five-year border war).

John Brown's Pottawatomie massacre.

Charles Sumner's "Crime Against Kansas" speech; Sumner assaulted in Senate chamber by Preston Brooks.

Harold Frederic b.

Porter's Spirit of the Times (New York), 1856–61

Congress of Paris and end of Crimean War.

The Saturday Review (London), 1856–1938.

Oxford and Cambridge Magazine, 1856.

Heinrich Heine d.

George Bernard Shaw b.

Sigmund Freud b.

Reade's *It Is Never Too Late to Mend.*

James Anthony Froude's *History of England from the Fall of Wolsey to the Death of Elizabeth* (1856–70).

Hugo's *Contemplations.*

Turgenev's *Rudin.*

Mowatt, Anna Cora (1819), Mimic Life. F
Neal, Joseph Clay (d. 1847), The Misfortunes of Peter Faber, and Other Sketches. F
Nordhoff, Charles (1830), Whaling and Fishing. NF
Olmsted, Frederick Law (1822), A Journey in the Seaboard Slave States. NF
Parkman, Francis (1823), Vassall Morton. F
Perry, Matthew Calbraith (1794), Narrative of the Expedition of an American Squadron to the China Seas and Japan. NF
Pike, Mary Hayden (1824), Caste. F
Poole, William Frederick (1821), The Battle of the Dictionaries. NF
"Q. K. Philander Doesticks, P. B." (1831), Plu-ri-bus-tah, A Song That's by No Author. V
Reid, Mayne (1818), The Quadroon (adapted for the stage by Reid, 1856). F
Robinson, Charles (1818), Kansas: Its Interior and Exterior Life. NF
Ross, Alexander (1783), The Red River Settlement. NF
Rouquette, François Dominique (1810), Fleurs d'Amérique. V
Simms, William Gilmore (1806), Charlemont; or, The Pride of the Village. F; Eutaw. F
Stowe, Harriet Beecher (1811), Dred: A Tale of the Great Dismal Swamp. F
Taylor, Bayard (1825), Cyclopaedia of Modern Travel. NF
Tucker, George (1775), History of the United States (4 vols., 1856–57). NF
Wallace, Horace Binney (d. 1852), Literary Criticisms and Other Papers. NF
Whitcher, Frances Miriam (d. 1852), The Widow Bedott Papers (adapted for the stage by "Petroleum V. Nasby," 1879). F
Whitman, Walt (1819), Leaves of Grass. Second edition. V
Whittier, John Greenleaf (1807), The Panorama and Other Poems. V

1857

Agassiz, Louis (1807), Contributions to the Natural History of the United States (4 vols., 1857–62). NF
Aldrich, Thomas Bailey (1836), Daisy's Necklace: And What Came of It. F
Bacon, Delia Salter (1811), Philosophy of the Plays of Shakespeare Unfolded. NF
Boucicault, Dion (1820), The Poor of New York. D
Brougham, John (1810), Columbus. D
Brownson, Orestes (1803), The Convert; or, Leaves from My Experience. NF
Bunce, Oliver Bell (1828), Love in '76. D
Butler, William Allen (1825), Nothing to Wear (first pub. anon. in Harper's Weekly, 1857). V
Cartwright, Peter (1785), Autobiography. NF
Catlin, George (1796), Life Amongst the Indians. NF
Cooke, Philip St. George (1809), Scenes and Adventures in the Army. NF
Cranch, Christopher Pearse (1813), Kobboltozo. F
Cummins, Maria Susanna (1827), Mabel Vaughan. F
Delano, Alonzo (1802?), A Live Woman in the Mines. D
Fitzhugh, George (1806), Cannibals All; or, Slaves Without Masters. NF

Lecompton constitution (Kansas pro-slavery act).
Dred Scott decision.
Economic panic widespread.
Frederick Law Olmsted and Calvert Vaux designed Central Park.
The Atlantic Monthly (Boston), 1857–.
Harper's Weekly (New York), 1857–1916.
Russell's Magazine (Charleston), 1857–60.

Great Mutiny in India.
The Standard (London), 1857–1916.
The Christian World (London), 1857–1961.
Joseph Conrad b.
Trollope's Barchester Towers,
Dickens's Little Dorrit.
Hughes's Tom Brown's Schooldays.
E.B. Browning's Aurora Leigh.
Borrow's The Romany Rye.
Livingstone's Missionary Travels in South Africa.

Gayarré, Charles Etienne Arthur (1805), A Sketch of General Jackson, by Himself. NF
Hayne, Paul Hamilton (1830), Sonnets and Other Poems. V
Helper, Hinton Rowan (1829), The Impending Crisis of the South: How to Meet It. NF
Holland, Josiah Gilbert (1819), The Bay-Path. F
Key, Francis Scott (d. 1843), Poems. V
Lawson, James (1799), Poems. V
Ludlow, Fitz Hugh (1836), The Hasheesh Eater. NF
Meek, Alexander Beaufort (1814), Romantic Passages in Southwestern History. NF; Songs and Poems of the South. V
Melville, Herman (1819), The Confidence-Man: His Masquerade. F
Mowatt, Anna Cora (1819), Twin Roses. F
Nordhoff, Charles (1830), Stories of the Island World. NF; Nine Years a Sailor (reprint of his first three books). NF
Olmsted, Frederick Law (1822), A Journey Through Texas. NF
Parton, James (1822), Aaron Burr. NF
"Q. K. Philander Doesticks, P. B." (1831), Nothing to Say: A Slight Slap at Mobocratic Snobbery, Which Has "Nothing to Do" with "Nothing to Wear." V
Sedgwick, Catharine Maria (1789), Married or Single? F
Stoddard, Richard Henry (1825), Songs of Summer. V
Thompson, Daniel Pierce (1795), Gaut Gurley; or, The Trappers of Umbabog. F
Townsend, Mary Ashley (1832), The Brother Clerks. F
Trowbridge, J. T. (1827), Neighbor Jackwood (adapted for the stage by Trowbridge, 1857; rev. 1895). F
Whittier, John Greenleaf (1807), The Sycamores. V; The Poetical Works of John Greenleaf Whittier. V
Willis, N. P. (1806), Paul Fane. F

Flaubert's *Madame Bovary*.
Baudelaire's *The Flowers of Evil*.

1858

Aldrich, Thomas Bailey (1836), The Course of True Love Never Did Run Smooth. V
Allibone, S. Austin (1816), A Critical Dictionary of English Literature and British and American Authors (3 vols., 1858–71). NF
Brougham, John (1810), The Mustard Ball; Or, Love at the Academy. D
Bulfinch, Thomas (1796), The Age of Chivalry. F
Bushnell, Horace (1802), Nature and the Supernatural. NF
Carey, Henry Charles (1793), The Principles of Social Science (3 vols., 1858–59). NF
Cartwright, Peter (1785), The Backwoods Preacher. NF
Chivers, Thomas Holley (1809), The Sons of Usna: A Tragi-Apotheosis in Five Acts. D
Cobb, Joseph B. (1819), Leisure Labors. NF
De Forest, John William (1826), European Acquaintance. NF
English, Thomas Dunn (1819), The Mormons. D
Fields, James T. (1817), A Few Verses for a Few Friends. V
Grayson, William J. (1788), The Country. V
"Gustave Aimard" (1818), Loyal Heart; or, The Trappers of Arkansas. F; The Pirates of the Prairies. F
Hammett, Samuel Adams (1816), Piney Woods Tavern, or Sam Slick in Texas. F
Holland, Josiah Gilbert (1819), Bitter-Sweet. V; Letters to Young People. NF

Minnesota admitted to the Union.
Lincoln-Douglas debates.
Lincoln's "A House Divided" speech.
William Henry Seward's "Irrepressible Conflict" speech.
First transatlantic telegraph cable.
Thomas Holley Chivers d.
The Saturday Press (New York), 1858–66.

End of Mogul Empire in India.
Charles Dickens began public lectures.
Robert Owen d.
George Eliot's *Scenes of Clerical Life*.
Morris's The *Defence of Guenevere*.
Carlyle's *History of Frederick the Great* (1858–65).
Trelawny's *Recollections of the Last Days of Shelley and Byron*.
Tom Taylor's *Our American Cousin*.
Trollope's *Doctor Thorne*.
Arnold's *Merope*, a Tragedy.
Goncharov's *Oblomov*.

Holmes, Oliver Wendell (1809), Valedictory Address . . .
March 10, 1858. NF; The Autocrat of the Breakfast-Table. V,
NF
Hooper, Johnson Jones (1815), Dog and Gun, A Few Loose
Chapters on Shooting. NF
Jones, John Beauchamp (1810), The War Path. F
Longfellow, Henry Wadsworth (1807), The Courtship of Miles
Standish and Other Poems. V
Lowell, Robert Traill Spence (1816), The New Priest in
Conception Bay. F
O'Brien, Fitz-James (c. 1828), "The Diamond Lens." F
Pike, Mary Hayden (1824), Agnes. F
Pratt, William W. (?), Ten Nights in a Bar-room [adapted from
the novel by T. S. Arthur (1854.)]. D
Stevens, Abel (1815), The History of the Religious Movement of
the Eighteenth Century, Called Methodism (3 vols., 1858–61).
NF
Stowe, Harriet Beecher (1811), Our Charley and What to Do
with Him. F
Taylor, Bayard (1825), Northern Travel. NF
Taylor, William (1821), California Life Illustrated. NF
Thorpe, T. B. (1815), Colonel Thorpe's Scenes in Arkansaw. F

1859

Adams, John Turvill (1805), The White Chief Among the Red
Men; or, Knight of the Golden Melice. F
Aldrich, Thomas Bailey (1836), The Ballad of Babie Bell and
Other Poems. V
Bateman, Sidney Frances (1823), Geraldine. D
Beecher, Henry Ward (1813), New Star Papers; or, Views and
Experiences of Religious Subjects. NF; Plain and Pleasant
Talk About Fruits, Flowers, and Farming. NF
Boucicault, Dion (1820), The Octoroon; or, Life in Louisiana
[adapted from Mayne Reid's novel The Quadroon (1856)]. D
Brinton, Daniel Garrison (1837), Notes on the Floridian
Peninsula. NF
Bryant, William Cullen (1794), Letters of a Traveller: Second
Series. NF
Cobb, Sylvanus, Jr. (1823), The Patriot Cruiser. F
Cooke, John Esten (1830), Henry St. John, Gentleman. F
Dana, Richard Henry, Jr. (1815), To Cuba and Back. NF
De Forest, John William (1826), Seacliff; or, The Mystery of
the Westervelts. F
De Smet, Pierre Jean (1801), Western Missions and
Missionaries. NF
Evans, Augusta Jane (1835), Beulah. F
Fuller, Margaret (d. 1850), Life Without and Life Within. NF
Ingraham, Joseph Holt (1809), The Pillar of Fire. F
Miles, George Henry (1824), Señor Valiente. D
Neal, John (1793), True Womanhood. F
"Q. K. Philander Doesticks, P. B." (1831), The Witches,
Prophets, and Planet Readers of New York. NF
Parton, James (1822), Andrew Jackson (3 vols., 1859–60). NF
Redpath, James (1833), The Roving Editor; or, Talks with
Slaves in the Southern States. NF; A Handbook to Kansas
Territory. NF
Shillaber, Benjamin Penhallow (1814), Mrs. Partington's
Knitting Work. F
Simms, William Gilmore (1806), The Cassique of Kiawah. F
Smith, Seba (1792), My Thirty Years Out of the Senate. F

Oregon admitted to the Union.
John Brown's raid on Harpers Ferry, his
trial and execution.
Comstock Lode (silver deposits in
Nevada).
Washington Irving d.
William Hickling Prescott d.
George Wilkes' Spirit of the Times
(New York), 1859–1902.
Dan Emmett's "Dixie" and "Turkey in
the Straw."

War of Italian Liberation.
All the Year Round (London), 1859–95.
Macmillan's Magazine (London),
1859–1907.
Sporting Life (London), 1859–.
Thomas Babington Macaulay d.
Thomas de Quincey d.
Dickens's *A Tale of Two Cities*.
George Eliot's *Adam Bede*.
Meredith's *The Ordeal of Richard
Feverel*.
Tennyson's *Idylls of the King* (1859–
85).
Thackeray's *The Virginians*.
John Stuart Mill's *On Liberty*.
Darwin's *On the Origin of Species*.
Marx's *Critique of Political Economy*.
Turgenev's *Home of the Gentry*.

Southworth, E. D. E. N. (1819), The Hidden Hand. F
Spofford, Harriet (1835), "In a Cellar." F
Stoddard, Richard Henry (1825), The Life, Travels and Books
    of Alexander von Humboldt. NF
Stowe, Harriet Beecher (1811), The Minister's Wooing. F
Taliaferro, Harden E (1818), Fisher's River (North Carolina)
    Scenes and Characters. NF
Taylor, Bayard (1825), Travels in Greece and Russia. NF
Tucker, George (1775), Political Economy for the People. NF
Willis, N. P. (1806), The Convalescent. F

1860

Bateman, Sidney Francis (1823), Evangeline [adapted from
    Henry Wadsworth Longfellow's poem (1847)]. D
Blood, Benjamin Paul (1822), Optimism. NF
Boucicault, Dion (1820), The Colleen Bawn. D
Bryant, William Cullen (1794), A Discourse on the Life,
    Character, and Genius of Washington Irving. NF
Clemens, Jeremiah (1814), The Rivals. F
Coggleshall, William Turner (1824), Poets and Poetry of the
    West (editor). V, NF
Craft, William (?), Running a Thousand Miles for Freedom, or
    the Escape of William and Ellen Craft from Slavery
    (attrib.; pub. in London), NF
Cummins, Maria Susanna (1827), El Fureidis. F
Custis, George Washington Parke (d. 1857), Recollections and
    Private Memoirs of Washington. NF
Ellis, Edward S. (1840), Seth Jones; or, The Captives of the
    Frontier. F
Emerson, Ralph Waldo (1803), The Conduct of Life. NF
Gilpin, William (1813), The Central Gold Region (repub. as The
    Mission of the North American People, 1873). NF
"Gustave Aimard" (1818), Lynch Law (trans. from French).
    F; The Tiger Slayer (trans. from French). F
Hawthorne, Nathaniel (1804), The Marble Faun. F
Hayne, Paul Hamilton (1830), Avolio: A Legend of the Island of
    Cos. V
Holland, Josiah Gilbert (1819), Miss Gilbert's Career. F
Holmes, Oliver Wendell (1809), The Professor at the Breakfast-
    Table. F, NF, V
Howells, William Dean (1837), Poems of Two Friends (with
    John James Piatt). V; Lives and Speeches of Abraham Lincoln
    and Hannibal Hamlin. NF
Ingraham, Joseph Holt (1809), The Throne of David. F
King, Thomas Starr (1824), The White Hills. NF
Motley, John Lothrop (1814), History of the United Netherlands
    (4 vols., 1860–67). NF
O'Connor, William Douglas (1832), Harrington. F
Olmsted, Frederick Law (1822), A Journey in the Back
    Country. NF
Parker, Jane Marsh (1836), Barley Wood. F
Redpath, James (1833), The Public Life of Captain John Brown.
    NF; Echoes of Harpers Ferry. NF; A Guide to Hayti. NF
Rouquette, Adrien Emmanuel (1813), L'Antoniade, ou la
    solitude avec Dieu. V
Spofford, Harriet Prescott (1835), Sir Rohan's Ghost. F
Stedman, Edmund Clarence (1833), Poems, Lyrical and Idyllic.
    V
Stephens, Ann Sophia (1810), Malaeska: The Indian Wife of the
    White Hunter. F

Crittenden Compromise; South
    Carolina seceded.
Pony Express (1860–61).
U.S. Secret Service established.
Oliver Winchester developed first
    repeating rifle.
Elizabeth Peabody established first
    kindergarten, in Boston.
First Beadle dime novel.
Theodore Parker d.
Hamlin Garland b.
Owen Wister b.
The Dial (Cincinnati), 1860.
Stephen Foster's "Old Black Joe."

Florence Nightingale founded first
    nursing school, in England.
The Cornhill Magazine (London),
    1860–1975.
James M. Barrie b.
Anton Chekhov b.
Jules Laforgue b.
Collins's *The Woman in White.*
Meredith's *Evan Harrington.*
George Eliot's *The Mill on the Floss.*
Turgenev's *On the Eve.*
Burckhardt's *The Civilization of the
    Renaissance in Italy.*

Thoreau, Henry David (1817), "A Plea for Captain John Brown." NF
Timrod, Henry (1828), Poems. V
Tuckerman, Frederick Goddard (1821), Poems. V
Whitman, Walt (1819), Leaves of Grass. Third edition. V
Whittier, John Greenleaf (1807), Home Ballads, Poems, and Lyrics. V

1861

Aldrich, Thomas Bailey (1836), Pampinea and Other Poems. V
Andrews, Jane (1833), The Seven Little Sisters Who Live on the Round Ball That Floats in the Air. F
Curtis, George William (1824), Trumps. F
Davis, Rebecca Harding (1831), "Life in the Iron Mills." F
Du Chaillu, Paul Belloni (1835), Explorations and Adventures in Equatorial Africa. NF
"Gustave Aimard" (1818), The Gold Seekers (trans. from French). F; The Freebooters, (trans. from French). F; The Indian Chief (trans. from French). F; The Prairie Flower (trans. from French). F
Holmes, Oliver Wendell (1809), Elsie Venner: A Romance of Destiny. F
Kennedy, John Pendleton (1795), The Border States. NF
"Oliver Optic" (1822), Woodville Series (1861–67). F
Olmsted, Frederick Law (1822), The Cotton Kingdom (condensation of three travel books, 1856, 1857, 1860). NF
Sargent, Lucius Manlius (1786), The Ballad of the Abolition Blunderbuss. V
Sargent, Winthrop (1825), Life and Career of Major John André. NF
Stedman, Edmund Clarence (1833), The Battle of Bull Run. V

Jefferson Davis elected president of Confederate States of America.
Bombardment of Fort Sumter in Charleston harbor.
First Battle of Bull Run.
Richmond made capital of Confederate States.
Kansas admitted to the Union.
Creation of the Nevada, Colorado, and Dakota Territories.
First federal income tax.
Vassar College founded.
Massachusetts Institute of Technology founded.
Mathew Brady began photographing the Civil War.

Victor Emmanuel II proclaimed king of Italy.
Elizabeth Barrett Browning d.
Palgrave's The Golden Treasury of Songs and Lyrics.
Dickens's Great Expectations.
George Eliot's Silas Marner.
Reade's The Cloister and the Hearth.
Wood's East Lynne.
Dostoevsky's Memoirs from the House of the Dead (1861–62).

1862

Aldrich, Thomas Bailey (1836), Out of His Head. F
"Artemus Ward" (1834), Artemus Ward: His Book. F
Beecher, Henry Ward (1813), Eyes and Ears. NF
Brownlow, William Gannaway (1805), Sketches of the Rise, Progress, and Decline of Secession. NF
Dana, James Dwight (1813), Manual of Geology. NF
Davis, Rebecca Harding (1831), Margaret Howth. F
Dodge, Mary Abigail (1833), Country Living and Country Thinking. NF
"Gustave Aimard" (1818), The Last of the Incas (trans. from French). F
Holmes, Oliver Wendell (1809), Songs in Many Keys. V; The Poems of Oliver Wendell Holmes. V
Howe, Julia Ward (1819), "The Battle Hymn of the Republic." V
"Orpheus C. Kerr" (1836), The Orpheus C. Kerr Papers (5 vols., 1862–71). F
Story, William Wetmore (1819), Roba di Roma. NF
Stowe, Harriet Beecher (1811), The Pearl of Orr's Island. F; Agnes of Sorrento. F
Victor, Metta Victoria (1831), Maum Guinea and Her Plantation Children. F
Wallace, William Ross (1819), The Liberty Bell. V

Second Battle of Bull Run.
Lee's invasion of North halted at Antietam.
Siege of Vicksburg (1861–62).
Richard Gatling patented machine gun.
Homestead Act induced westward migration.
Morrill Land Grant Act (college endowments).
Union Pacific Railroad chartered.
Henry David Thoreau d.
Edith Wharton b.
Julia Ward Howe's "The Battle Hymn of the Republic."

Sarah Bernhardt made debut, in Paris.
Arthur Schnitzler b.
Maurice Maeterlinck b.
Gerhart Hauptmann b.
Meredith's Modern Love.
Ruskin's Unto This Last.
Anthony Trollope's North America.
Collins's No Name.
Christina Rossetti's Goblin Market.
Spencer's A System of Synthetic Philosophy (10 vols., 1862–96).

Winthrop, Theodore (1828), John Brent. F; Edwin Brothertoft. F

Flaubert's *Salammbô*.
Hugo's *Les Misérables*.
Turgenev's *Fathers and Sons*.

1863

Alcott, Louisa May (1832), Hospital Sketches. NF
Aldrich, Thomas Bailey (1836), Poems. V
Beecher, Henry Ward (1813), Freedom and War. NF
Brown, William Wells (1816?), The Black Man: His Antecedents. His Genius, and His Achievements (expanded as The Rising Son, 1874). NF
Calvert, George Henry (1803), The Gentleman. NF
Cooke, John Esten (1830), Life of Stonewall Jackson. NF
De Smet, Pierre Jean (1801), New Indian Sketches. NF
Hawthorne, Nathaniel (1804), Our Old Home. NF
"Ik Marvel" (1822), My Farm of Edgewood. NF
Lieber, Francis (1800), A Code for the Government of Armies. NF
Longfellow, Henry Wadsworth (1807), Tales of a Wayside Inn. V
Morford, Henry (1823), The Days of Shoddy. F; Shoulder-Straps. F
Owen, Robert Dale (1801), The Policy of Emancipation. NF
Sargent, Lucius Manlius (1786), The Temperance Tales (6 vols., 1863–64). NF
Spofford, Harriet Prescott (1835), The Amber Gods and Other Stories. F
Stephens, Ann Sophia (1810), The Rejected Wife. F
Stowe, Harriet Beecher (1811), A Reply . . . in Behalf of the Women of America. NF
Taylor, Bayard (1825), Hannah Thurston. F
Thoreau, Henry David (d. 1862), Excursions. NF; "Life Without Principle." NF
Winthrop, Theodore (1828), The Canoe and the Saddle. NF; Life in the Open Air. NF

Emancipation Proclamation signed.
Battles of Chancellorsville, Gettysburg, and Chattanooga.
Lincoln's Gettysburg Address.
West Virginia admitted to the Union.
National Bank Act.
Thanksgiving Day proclaimed national holiday.
George Santayana b.
The Round Table (New York), 1863–69.
Thomas Bishop's "When Johnny Comes Marching Home."

English Football Association founded.
William Makepeace Thackeray d.
Gabriele D'Annunzio b.
Charles Kingsley's *The Water Babies*.
John Stuart Mill's *Utilitarianism*.
Reade's *Hard Cash*.
George Eliot's *Romola*.
Le Fanu's *The House by the Churchyard*.
Lyell's *Geological Evidence of the Antiquity of Man*.
Tolstoy's *The Cossacks*
Verne's *Five Weeks in a Balloon*.
Renan's *Life of Jesus*.

1864

Alcott, Louisa May (1832), On Picket Duty and Other Tales. F; The Rose Family. F; Moods. F
Boker, George Henry (1823), Poems of the War. V
Brown, William Wells (1816?), Clotelle: A Tale of the Southern States. F
Browne, J. Ross (1821), Crusoe's Island . . . with Sketches of Adventures in California and Washoe. NF
Bryant, William Cullen (1794), Thirty Poems. V; Hymns. V
Calvert, George Henry (1803), Arnold and André. D
Cobb, Sylvanus, Jr. (1823), Ben Hamed. F
Cummins, Maria Susanna (1827), Haunted Hearts. F
Dodge, Mary Mapes (1831), Irvington Stories. F
Evans, Augusta Jane (1835), Macaria; or, Altars of Sacrifice. F
Greeley, Horace (1811), The American Conflict (2 vols., 1864–65). NF
Halpine, Charles Graham (1829), The Life and Adventures . . . of Private Miles O'Reilly. F
Holmes, Oliver Wendell (1809), Soundings from the Atlantic. NF
Johnston, Richard Malcolm (1822), Georgia Sketches. F

Battles of the Wilderness, Spotsylvania, and Mobile Bay.
Ulysses Grant named commander of Union armies.
Gen. William T. Sherman's march to the sea ended at Savannah.
Nevada admitted to the Union.
Creation of the Montana Territory.
George Pullman patented railroad sleeping-car (1864–65).
Nathaniel Hawthorne d.
Richard Harding Davis b.
Paul Elmer More b.

Emperor Maximilian's regime in Mexico (1864–67).
Metropolitan Railway opened in London.
Louis Pasteur developed pasteurization method for wine.
Early English Text Society founded.
Walter Savage Landor d.

Longstreet, Augustus Baldwin (1790), Master William Mitten. F

Lowell, James Russell (1819), Fireside Travels. NF

Marsh, George Perkins (1801), Man and Nature (rev. as The Earth as Modified by Human Action, 1874). NF

Morford, Henry (1823), The Coward. F; Red-Tape and Pigeon-Hole Generals As Seen from the Ranks (attrib.). NF

"Petroleum V. Nasby" (1833), The Nasby Papers. F

Sargent, Epes (1813), Peculiar: A Tale of the Great Transition. F

Spofford, Harriet Prescott (1835), Azarian: An Episode. F

Stedman, Edmund Clarence (1833), Alice of Monmouth: An Idyll of the Great War and Other Poems. V

Stevens, Abel (1815), History of the Methodist Episcopalian Church in the United States (4 vols., 1864–67). NF

Taylor, Bayard (1825), John Godfrey's Fortunes. F

Thompson, Daniel Pierce (1795), Centeola and Other Tales. F

Thoreau, Henry David (d. 1862), The Maine Woods. NF

Trowbridge, J. T. (1827), Cudjo's Cave. F

Tuckerman, Henry Theodore (1813), America and Her Commentators. NF

Whittier, John Greenleaf (1807), In War Time and Other Poems. V

Frank Wedekind b.
Miguel de Unanumo b.
Tennyson's *Enoch Arden*.
Robert Browning's *Dramatis Personae*.
Newman's *Apologia pro vita sua*.
Le Fanu's *Uncle Silas*.
Dostoevsky's *Notes from the Underground*.
Verne's *Journey to the Center of the Earth*.

1865

Aldrich, Thomas Bailey (1836), Poems. V

"Artemus Ward" (1834), Artemus Ward: His Travels. F

Barnum, P. T. (1810), The Humbugs of the World. NF

Boucicault, Dion (1820), Rip Van Winkle [adapted with Joseph Jefferson from Washington Irving's tale (1819).] D

Bowles, Samuel (1826), Across the Continent. NF

Brownson, Orestes (1803), The American Republic: Its Constitution, Tendencies, and Destiny. NF

Clemens, Jeremiah (1814), Tobias Wilson. F

Derby, George Horatio (1823), Squibob Papers. NF

Dodge, Mary Abigail (1833), A New Atmosphere. NF

Dodge, Mary Mapes (1831), Hans Brinker; or, The Silver Skates. F

Duganne, Augustine Joseph Hickey (1823), Camps and Prisons. NF

Gayarré, Charles Etienne Arthur (1805), Dr. Bluff in Russia; or, The Emperor Nicholas and the American Doctor. D

Hale, Edward Everett (1822), The Man Without a Country. F

Halleck, Fitz-Greene (1790), Young America: A Poem. V

Holmes, Oliver Wendell (1809), Humorous Poems. V

Kennedy, John Pendleton (1795), Mr. Ambrose's Letters on the Rebellion. NF

Longfellow, Henry Wadsworth (1807), The Divine Comedy of Dante Aligheri (2 vols., 1865–67). V; Household Poems. V

Lowell, James Russell (1819), Ode Recited at the Commemoration of the Living and Dead Soldiers of Harvard University. V

"Oliver Optic" (1822), Army and Navy Series (1865–94). F

Parkman, Francis (1823), Pioneers of France in the New World. NF

Saxe, John Godfrey (1816), Clever Stories of Many Nations Rendered in Rhyme. V

Stoddard, Richard Henry (1825), Abraham Lincoln: An Horatian Ode. V

Stowe, Harriet Beecher (1811), House and Home Papers. NF

Gen. Lee's surrender at Appomattox.
President Lincoln assassinated.
13th Amendment (abolishing slavery) ratified.
Freedmen's Bureau created (1865–74) to assist liberated Negroes.
Ku Klux Klan organized (1865–69).
Molly Maguires (strong-arm Irish miners) active (1865–67).
Opening of Union stockyards, in Chicago.
Cornell University founded.
Tony Pastor opened first variety theatre, in New York City.
The Nation (New York), 1865–.
The Radical (Boston), 1865–72.
Henry Clay Work's "Marching Through Georgia".

Leopold II proclaimed king of the Belgians.
Manet's "Olympia" called an obscene painting.
Marquis of Queensberry established boxing rules.
The Pall Mall Gazette (London), 1865–1923.
The Fortnightly Review (London), 1865–1954.
Dickens's *Our Mutual Friend*.
Carroll's *Alice's Adventures in Wonderland*.
Meredith's *Rhoda Fleming*.
Ruskins's *Sesame and Lilies*.
Swinburne's *Atalanta in Calydon*.
Arnold's *Essays in Criticism, First Series*.
Tolstoy's *War and Peace* (1865–69).

Thoreau, Henry David (d. 1862), Cape Cod. NF
Ward, Samuel (1814), Lyrical Recreations. V
Whitman, Walt (1819), Drum-Taps. V
Whittier, John Greenleaf (1807), National Lyrics. V

1866

Akers, Elizabeth (1832), Poems. V
Arnold, George (d. 1865), Drift: A Sea-Shore Idyl. V
Baker, William M. (1825), Inside: A Chronicle of Secession. F
"Bill Arp" (1826), Bill Arp, So-Called. F
Burritt, Elihu (1810), Lectures and Speeches. NF
Bushnell, Horace (1802), The Vicarious Sacrifice. NF
Cooke, John Esten (1830), Surry of Eagle's Nest. F
Gayarré, Charles Etienne Arthur (1805), Philip II of Spain. NF
Halleck, Fitz-Greene (1790), Lines to the Recorder. V
Hollister, Gideon Hiram (1817), Thomas à Becket. D
Howells, William Dean (1837), Venetian Life. NF
"Ik Marvel" (1822), Dr. Johns. F
Irving, Washington (d. 1859), Spanish Papers and Other
    Miscellanies. NF
Jones, John Beauchamp (1810), A Rebel War Clerk's Diary at
    the Confederate Capital. NF
"Josh Billings" (1818), Josh Billings: Hiz Sayings. F
Melville, Herman (1819), Battle-Pieces and Aspects of the War.
    V
Miles, George Henry (1824), Christine. V
O'Connor, William Douglas (1832), The Good Gray Poet. NF
Parkman, Francis (1823), The Book of Roses. NF
"Petroleum V. Nasby" (1833), Divers Views, Opinions, and
    Prophecies. NF
Poole, William Frederick (1821), The Popham Colony. NF
Sigourney, Lydia (1791), Letters of Life. NF
Taylor, Bayard (1825), The Story of Kennett. F
Thoreau, Henry David (d. 1862), A Yankee in Canada, with
    Anti-Slavery and Reform Papers. NF
Tuckerman, Henry Theodore (1813), The Criterion. NF
Whittier, John Greenleaf (1807), Snow-Bound. V

Civil Rights Act passed by Congress.
Grand Army of the Republic formed.
Fisk University founded.
First YWCA opened, in Boston.
ASPCA chartered, in New York City.
Lincoln Steffens b.
The Galaxy (New York), 1866–78.
The New York World, 1866–1931.

Carol I became first king of Rumania.
Second Atlantic cable laid (England–
    U.S.).
Thomas Love Peacock d.
Jane Welsh Carlyle d.
George Eliot's *Felix Holt*.
Swinburne's *Poems and Ballads*.
Charles Kingsley's *Hereward the Wake*.
Reade's *Griffith Gaunt*.
Ruskin's *The Crown of Wild Olive*.
Ouida's *Chandos*.
Ibsen's *Brand*.
Dostoevsky's *Crime and Punishment*.
Hugo's *Toilers of the Sea*.
Verlaine's *Saturnian Poems*.

1867

Alcott, Louisa May (1832), The Mysterious Key and What It
    Opened. F
Alger, Horatio, Jr. (1832), Ragged Dick Series (1867 ff.). F
Arnold, George (d. 1865), Poems, Grave and Gay. V
"Artemus Ward" (1834), Artemus Ward in London and Other
    Papers. F
Bancroft, George (1800), Joseph Reed: A Historical Essay. NF
Beecher, Henry Ward (1813), Norwood; or, Village Life in New
    England. F
Burroughs, John (1837), Notes on Walt Whitman as Poet and
    Person. NF
Catlin, George (1796), Last Rambles Amongst the Indians of the
    Rocky Mountains and the Andes. NF
Daly, Augustin (1838), Under the Gaslight. D
De Forest, John William (1826), Miss Ravenel's Conversion
    from Secession to Loyalty. F
Emerson, Ralph Waldo (1803), May-Day and Other Pieces. V
Evans, Augusta Jane (1835), St. Elmo. F

Nebraska admitted to the Union.
Three Reconstruction acts passed by
    Congress.
U.S. purchased Alaska from Russia.
Granger Movement begun.
First elevated railroad, in New York
    City.
The Johns Hopkins University chartered
    (opened in 1876).
Howard University founded.
Harper's Bazar (New York), 1867–.
*Oliver Optic's Magazine for Boys and
    Girls* (Boston), 1867–75.
Journal of Speculative Philosophy (St.
    Louis), 1867–93.

Dominion of Canada constituted.
Benito Juárez elected president of
    Mexico.
The Mikado restored to power in Japan.

Finley, Martha Farquharson (1828), Elsie Dinsmore Series (28 vols., 1867–1905). F
Harris, George Washington (1814), Sut Lovingood Yarns. F
Harte, Bret (1836), The Lost Galleon. V; Condensed Novels and Other Papers. F
Holland, Josiah Gilbert (1819), Kathrina: Her Life and Mine, in a Poem. V
Holmes, Oliver Wendell (1809), The Guardian Angel. F
Howells, William Dean (1837), Italian Journeys. NF
"Ik Marvel" (1822), Rural Studies. NF
Kellogg, Elijah (1813), Good Old Times. F
Lanier, Sidney (1842), Tiger-Lilies. F
Lazarus, Emma (1849), Poems and Translations. V
Longfellow, Henry Wadsworth (1807), Flower-de-Luce. V
Lowell, James Russell (1819), The Biglow Papers (2nd ser.). V
Ludlow, Fitz Hugh (1836), Little Brother and Other Genre-Pictures. F
"Mark Twain" (1835), The Celebrated Jumping Frog of Calaveras County and Other Sketches. F
May, Samuel Joseph (1797), A Brief Account of His Ministry. NF
"Oliver Optic" (1822), Starry Flag Series (1867–69). F
Parkman, Francis (1823), The Jesuits in North America in the Seventeenth Century. NF
"Petroleum V. Nasby" (1833), Swingin Round the Cirkle. F
Richardson, Albert Deane (1833), Beyond the Mississippi. NF
Robinson, Solon (1803), Me-Won-I-Toc, A Tale of Frontier Life and Indian Character. NF
Stowe, Calvin Ellis (1802), Origin and History of the Books of the Bible. NF
Stowe, Harriet Beecher (1811), Religious Poems. V; Queer Little People. F; The Daisy's First Winter and Other Stories. F
Thorpe, Rose Hartwick (1850), "Curfew Must Not Ring Tonight." V
Whitcher, Frances Miriam (1814), Widow Spriggins, Mary Elmer, and Other Sketches. F
Whitman, Walt (1819), Leaves of Grass. Fourth edition. V
Whittier, John Greenleaf (1807), The Tent on the Beach. V

Alfred Nobel patented dynamite.
Charles Baudelaire d.
Arnold Bennett b.
Luigi Pirandello b.
Arnold's *New Poems*.
Ouida's *Under Two Flags*.
Ruskin's *Time and Tide*.
Ibsen's *Peer Gynt*.
Marx's *Das Kapital* (3 vols., 1867–94).
Turgenev's *Smoke*.
Zola's *Thérèse Raquin*.

1868

Alcott, Bronson (1799), Tablets. NF
Alcott, Louisa May (1832), Little Women; or Meg, Jo, Beth and Amy. F; Morning-Glories. F; Kitty's Class Day. F; Aunt Kipp. F
"Bill Arp" (1826), Bill Arp's Letters. F
Blood, Benjamin Paul (1832), The Colonnades. V
Cary, Phoebe (1824), Poems of Faith, Hope, and Love. V
Cooke, John Esten (1830), Fairfax. F
Davis, Rebecca Harding (1831), Waiting for the Verdict. F
Dodge, Mary Abigail (1833), Woman's Wrongs: A Counter-Irritant. NF
Greeley, Horace (1811), Recollections of a Busy Life. NF
Hale, Edward Everett (1822), If, Yes, and Perhaps. F
Hawthorne, Nathaniel (d. 1864), Passages from the American Note-Books. NF
"Josh Billings" (1818), Josh Billings on Ice, and Other Things. F
Longfellow, Henry Wadsworth (1807), The New England Tragedies. D

President Johnson impeached, tried, acquitted.
14th Amendment (Negro citizenship) ratified.
Creation of the Wyoming Territory.
Eight-hour working day for government employees.
University of California founded.
Hampton Institute founded.
First successful typewriter patented.
Memorial Day (May 30) celebrated nationally.
W.E.B. DuBois b.
Lippincott's Magazine (Phila.), 1868–1916.
Overland Monthly (San Francisco), 1868–75; 1883–1935.
Hearth and Home (New York), 1868–75.
Phillips Brooks's "O Little Town of Bethlehem."

Menken, Adah Isaacs (1835), Infelicia. V
Miller, Joaquin (1841?), Specimens. V
"Petroleum V. Nasby" (1833), The Impendin Crisis uv the
    Democracy. F
Ridge, John Rollin (d. 1867), Poems. V
Sill, Edward Rowland (1841), The Hermitage and Other Poems.
    V
Story, William Wetmore (1819), Graffiti d'Italia. V
Stowe, Harriet Beecher (1811), The Chimney-Corner. NF; Men
    of Our Times. NF
Ward, Elizabeth Stuart Phelps (1844), The Gates Ajar. F

Royal Historical Society founded in
   London.
Vanity Fair (London), 1868–1929.
Robert Browning's The Ring and the
   Book (1868–69).
Collins's The Moonstone.
Morris's The Earthly Paradise (1868–
   70).
Swinburne's William Blake.
Dostoevsky's The Idiot (1868–69).

1869

Alcott, Louisa May (1832), Little Women: Part Second. F
Alger, Horatio, Jr. (1832), Luck and Pluck Series (1869ff.). F
"Artemus Ward" (d. 1867), Artemus Ward's Panorama. F
Beecher, Henry Ward (1813), Sermons. NF
Boker, George Henry (1823), Königsmark: The Legend of the
    Hounds. V
Bowles, Samuel (1826), The Switzerland of America. NF
Browne, J. Ross (1821), Adventures in Apache Country. NF
Bryant, William Cullen (1794), Hymns. V; Some Notices of the
    Life and Writings of Fitz-Greene Halleck. NF; Letters from
    the East. NF
Cooke, John Esten (1830), Hilt to Hilt. F; Mohun. F
Darley, Felix Octavius Carr (1822), Sketches Abroad with Pen
    and Pencil. NF
Hale, Edward Everett (1822), Sybaris and Other Homes. F
Holmes, Oliver Wendell (1809), The Medical Profession in
    Massachusetts. NF
Howells, William Dean (1837), No Love Lost: A Romance of
    Travel. V
Lowell, James Russell (1819), Under the Willows and Other
    Poems. V
"Mark Twain" (1835), The Innocents Abroad. NF
May, Samuel Joseph (1797), Some Recollections of Our Anti-
    Slavery Conflict. NF
Miller, Joaquin (1841?), Joaquin et al. V
Neal, John (1793), Wandering Recollections of a Somewhat
    Busy Life. NF
Parkman, Francis (1823), The Discovery of the Great West. NF
Prentiss, Elizabeth Payson (1818), Stepping Heavenward. F
Southworth, E. D. E. N. (1819), The Fatal Marriage. F
Stedman, Edmund Clarence (1833), The Blameless Prince and
    Other Poems. V
Stowe, Harriet Beecher (1811), Oldtown Folks. F; The
    American Woman's Home (with Catharine Beecher). NF
Whittier, John Greenleaf (1807), Among the Hills. V

Tweed Ring (political corruption) in
   New York City (1869–71).
Prohibition Party founded in Chicago.
Knights of Labor organized in
   Philadelphia.
"Black Friday" (gold speculation) in
   Wall Street.
First transcontinental railroad
   completed.
First intercollegiate football game
   (Rutgers vs. Princeton).
Mathew Brady's National Photographic
   Collection of War Views.
Appleton's Journal (New York), 1869–
   81.

Suez Canal opened.
First Vatican Council in Rome.
Vanity Fair Album (London), 1869–
   1912.
Alphonse de Lamartine d.
Charles Augustin Sainte-Beuve d.
Arnold's Culture and Anarchy.
John Stuart Mill's On the Subjection of
   Women.
Tennyson's The Holy Grail.
Blackmore's Lorna Doone.
Trollope's Phineas Finn.
Ibsen's The League of Youth.
Baudelaire's Paris Spleen (posth.).
Verlaine's Gallant Parties.
Daudet's Letters from My Mill.

1870

Alcott, Louisa May (1832), An Old-Fashioned Girl. F
Aldrich, Thomas Bailey (1836), Pansy's Wish: A Christmas
    Fantasy. F; The Story of a Bad Boy. F
Baker, William M. (1825), The New Timothy. F
Ballou, Adin (1803), Primitive Christianity and Its Corruptions.
    NF

15th Amendment (Negro's right to vote)
   ratified.
Congress created Department of
   Justice.
U.S. Weather Bureau established.
Standard Oil Co. of Ohio founded.

Beecher, Henry Ward (1813), The Life of Jesus, the Christ (Part I). NF

Bigelow, John (1817), Beaumarchais the Merchant. NF

Brownson, Orestes (1803), Conversations on Liberalism and the Church. NF

Bryant, William Cullen (1794), A Discourse on the Life, Character, and Writings of Gulian Crommelin Verplanck. NF

Cooke, John Esten (1830), The Heir of Gaymount. F

Drake, Daniel (1785), Pioneer Life in Kentucky. NF

Emerson, Ralph Waldo (1803), Society and Solitude. NF

Harte, Bret (1836), The Luck of Roaring Camp and Other Sketches. F; Plain Language from Truthful James (pirated as The Heathen Chinee). V

Hawthorne, Nathaniel (d. 1864), Passages from the English Note-Books. NF

Higginson, Thomas Wentworth (1823), Army Life in a Black Regiment. NF

Howard, Bronson (1842), Saratoga. D

Lowell, James Russell (1819), The Cathedral. V; Among My Books. NF

Ludlow, Fitz Hugh (1836), The Heart of the Continent. NF

"Oliver Optic" (1822), Onward and Upward Series (1870). F

Sargent, Epes (1813), The Woman Who Dared. V

Stockton, Frank R. (1834), Ting-a-Ling. F

Stowe, Harriet Beecher (1811), Lady Byron Vindicated. NF; Little Pussy Willow. F

Taylor, Bayard (1825), Joseph and His Friend. F

Donkey first used as symbol of Democratic Party.

William Gilmore Simms d.

Frank Norris b.

Scribner's Monthly (New York), 1870–81.

The Outlook (New York), 1870–1935.

Woman's Journal (Boston; Chicago), 1870–1917.

Franco-Prussian War began (1870–71).

France proclaimed Third Republic after fall of Napoleon III.

Charles Dickens d.

Alexandre Dumas père d.

Prosper Mérimée d.

Dickens's *The Mystery of Edwin Drood.*

Ouida's *Puck.*

Disraeli's *Lothair.*

D.G. Rossetti's *Poems.*

Verne's *Twenty Thousand Leagues Under the Sea.*

Flaubert's *A Sentimental Education.*

1871

Adams, Henry (1838), Chapters of Erie, and Other Essays (with Charles Francis Adams). NF

Alcott, Louisa May (1832), Little Men: Life at Plumfield with Jo's Boys. F

Alger, Horatio, Jr. (1832), Tattered Tom Series (1871 ff.). F

Beecher, Catharine Esther (1800), Women Suffrage. NF

Bigelow, John (1817), France and Hereditary Monarchy. NF

Bryant, William Cullen (1794), Poems. V

Burroughs, John (1837), Wake-Robin. NF

Cartwright, Peter (1785), Fifty Years as a Presiding Elder. NF

Channing, William Ellery (1818), The Wanderer. V

Clarke, James Freeman (1810), Ten Great Religions (2 parts, 1871, 1883). NF

Cooke, John Esten (1830), Hammer and Rapier. F

Daly, Augustin (1838), Horizon. D; Divorce. D

De Forest, John William (1826), Overland. F

Eggleston, Edward (1837), The Hoosier Schoolmaster. F

George, Henry (1839), Our Land and Land Policy. NF

Hale, Edward Everett (1822), Ten Times One Is Ten. F

Harte, Bret (1836), Poems. V; East and West Poems. V

Hawthorne, Nathaniel (d. 1864), Passages from the French and Italian Note-Books. NF

Hay, John (1838), Jim Bludso of the Prairie Belle, and Little Breeches. V; Castilian Days. NF; Pike County Ballads. V

Holmes, Oliver Wendell (1809), Mechanism in Thought and Morals. NF

Johnston, Richard Malcolm (1822), Dukesborough Tales. F

Lazarus, Emma (1849), Admetus and Other Poems. V

Longfellow, Henry Wadsworth (1807), The Divine Tragedy. D

Lowell, James Russell (1819), My Study Windows. NF

Treaty of Washington (convenant with Great Britain).

William Marcy "Boss" Tweed indicted for fraud.

Fire destroyed over three acres of Chicago.

Smith College founded.

P.T. Barnum's circus founded.

H.H. Furness's *Variorum Shakespeare* begun.

Theodore Dreiser b.

Stephen Crane b.

James Weldon Johnson b.

France ceded Alsace-Lorraine to Germany.

German Empire framed by Bismarck; Wilhelm I declared emperor.

Rome became capital of Italy.

James Millington Synge b.

Marcel Proust b.

Paul Valéry b.

George Eliot's *Middlemarch* (1871–72).

Meredith's *The Adventures of Harry Richmond.*

Ruskin's *Fors Clavigera* (1871–84).

Lear's *Nonsense Songs, Stories, Botany, and Alphabets.*

Swinburne's *Songs Before Sunrise.*

Darwin's *The Descent of Man.*

Dostoevsky's *The Possessed* (1871–72).

Zola's *Les Rougon-Macquart* (20 vols., 1871–93).

"Mark Twain" (1835), Mark Twain's (Burlesque)
Autobiography. F
Miller, Joaquin (1841?), Songs of the Sierras. V; Pacific Poems.
V
Morgan, Lewis Henry (1818), Systems of Consanguinity and
Affinity of the Human Family. NF
Spofford, Harriet Prescott (1835), New-England Legends. F
Stowe, Harriet Beecher (1811), Pink and White Tyranny. F; My
Wife and I. F
Whitman, Walt (1819), Leaves of Grass. Fifth edition.
V; Democratic Vistas. NF; Passage to India. V
Whittier, John Greenleaf (1807), Miriam and Other Poems. V
Woodhull, Victoria (1838), Origin, Tendencies, and Principles
of Government. NF

1872

Alcott, Bronson (1799), Concord Days. NF
Alcott, Louisa May (1832), Aunt Jo's Scrap-Bag (6 vols., 1872–
82). F
Andrews, Stephen Pearl (1812), Basic Outline of Universology.
NF
Appleton, Thomas Gold (1812), Faded Leaves. V
Barr, Amelia Edith (1831), Romance and Reality. F
Beecher, Henry Ward (1813), Yale Lectures on Preaching (3
vols., 1872–74). NF; Lecture Room Talks. NF
De Forest, John William (1826), Kate Beaumont. F
Eggleston, Edward (1837), The End of the World. F
Fields, James T. (1817), Yesterdays with Authors. NF
Gayarré, Charles Etienne Arthur (1805), Fernando de Lemos—
Truth and Fiction. F
Harte, Bret (1836), Stories of the Sierras. F
Hawthorne, Nathaniel (d. 1864), Septimius Felton; or The Elixir
of Life. F
Hayne, Paul Hamilton (1830), Legends and Lyrics. V
Holmes, Oliver Wendell (1809), The Poet at the Breakfast-
Table. F, NF, V
Howells, William Dean (1837), Their Wedding Journey. F
Ingraham, Prentiss (1843), The Masked Spy. F
Longfellow, Henry Wadsworth (1807), Three Books of Song.
V; Christus: A Mystery. D
"Mark Twain" (1835), Roughing It. NF
"Oliver Optic" (1822), Yacht Club Series (1872–1900). F
Pike, Albert (1809), Hymns to the Gods. V
Roe, E. P. (1838), Barriers Burned Away. F
Stanley, Henry Morton (1841), How I Found Livingstone. NF
Stowe, Harriet Beecher (1811), Sam Lawson's Oldtown Fireside
Stories. F
Taylor, Bayard (1872), Beauty and the Beast and Tales of
Home. F
Thaxter, Celia (1835), Poems. V

Crédit Mobilier scandal (1872–73).
National Labor Reform Party founded.
Jehovah's Witnesses organized, in
Pittsburgh, Penna.
Yellowstone Park Timberland Reserve
established.
Susan B. Anthony arrested for leading
women voters to the polls.
Montgomery Ward & Co. founded.
Publishers' Weekly (New York), 1872–.
Popular Science Monthly (New York),
1872–.
Eadweard Muybridge's photographs of
animal locomotion.

Germany, Russia, and Austria-Hungary
alliance.
Théophile Gautier d.
Franz Grillparzer d.
Butler's *Erewhon.*
Hardy's *Under the Greenwood Tree.*
Carroll's *Through the Looking Glass.*
Lear's *More Nonsense Pictures,
Rhymes, Botany.*
Tennyson's *Gareth and Lynette.*
Ruskin's *Munera Pulveris.*
Nietzsche's *The Birth of Tragedy.*

1873

Alcott, Louisa May (1832), Work. F
Aldrich, Thomas Bailey (1836), Marjorie Daw and Other
People. F
Bierce, Ambrose (1842), The Fiend's Delight. F, NF; Nuggets
and Dust. F, NF

Financial panic, precipitated by failure
of Jay Cooke & Co.
Slaughterhouse cases (states' rights).
"Boss" Tweed convicted of fraud.
Cable streetcar first used in San
Francisco.

"Bill Arp" (1826), Bill Arp's Peace Papers. NF
Carleton, Will (1845), Farm Ballads. V
Channing, William Ellery (1818), Thoreau, the Poet-Naturalist.
  NF
Cooke, John Esten (1830), Her Majesty the Queen. F
De Forest, John William (1826), The Wetherel Affair. F
Eggleston, Edward (1837), The Mystery of Metropolisville. F
Fawcett, Edgar (1847), Purple and Fine Linen. F
Harte, Bret (1836), Mrs. Skagg's Husbands and Other Stories. F
Higginson, Thomas Wentworth (1823), Oldport Days. F
Holland, Josiah Gilbert (1819), Arthur Bonnicastle. F
Howells, William Dean (1837), A Chance Acquaintance.
  F; Poems. V
Longfellow, Henry Wadsworth (1807), Aftermath. V
"Mark Twain" (1835), The Gilded Age (with Charles Dudley
  Warner). F
Mayo, William Starbuck (1811), Never Again. F
Miller, Joaquin (1841?), Life Amongst the Modocs. NF
"Ned Buntline" (1823), The Scouts of the Plains. D
Shillaber, Benjamin Penhallow (1814), Partingtonian
  Patchwork. F
Stowe, Harriet Beecher (1811), Palmetto-Leaves. NF; Woman
  in Sacred History. NF
Taylor, Bayard (1825), Lars: A Pastoral of Norway. V
Timrod, Henry (d. 1867), Poems. V
Wallace, Lew (1827), The Fair God. F

Remington Arms Co. perfected the
  typewriter.
The Delineator (New York), 1873–
  1937).
Woman's Home Companion
  (Springfield, Ohio), 1873–1957.
St. Nicholas (New York), 1873–1940.
The Congressional Record
  (Washington, D.C.), 1873–.

First Spanish Republic proclaimed.
New Shakespeare Society founded.
Edward Bulwer-Lytton d.
John Stuart Mill d.
Arnold's Literature and Dogma.
John Stuart Mill's Autobiography.
Pater's Studies in the History of the
  Renaissance.
Trollope's The Eustace Diamonds.
Hardy's A Pair of Blue Eyes.
Verne's Around the World in Eighty
  Days.
Rimbaud's A Season in Hell.
Ibsen's The Emperor and the Galilean.

1874

Adams, John Quincy (d. 1848), The Memoirs of John Quincy
  Adams (12 vols., 1874–77). NF
Aldrich, Thomas Bailey (1836), Prudence Palfrey. F; Cloth of
  Gold and Other Poems. V
Bancroft, Hubert Howe (1832), The Native Races of the Pacific
  States of North America (5 vols., 1874–75). NF
Beecher, Catharine Esther (1800), Educational Reminiscences
  and Suggestions. NF
Bierce, Ambrose (1842), Cobwebs from an Empty Skull. F
Blood, Benjamin Paul (1832), The Anaesthetic Revelation and
  the Gist of Philosophy. NF
Boyesen, Hjalmar Hjorth (1848), Gunnar. F
Bryant, William Cullen (1794), Among the Trees. V
Clark, Charles Heber (1841), Out of the Hurly-Burly. F
Clarke, James Freeman (1810), Common Sense in Religion. NF
Custer, George Armstrong (1839), My Life on the Plains. NF
Davis, Rebecca Harding (1831), John Andross. F
Dodge, Mary Mapes (1831), Rhymes and Jingles. V
Eggleston, Edward (1837), The Circuit Rider. F
Fiske, John (1842), The Outlines of Cosmic Philosophy. NF
Hale, Edward Everett (1822), In His Name. F
Howe, Julia Ward (1819), Sex and Education. NF
"Josh Billings" (1818), Everybody's Friend. NF
Lawson, James (1799), Liddlesdale. D
Lazarus, Emma (1849), Alide: An Episode in Goethe's Life. F
Longfellow, Henry Wadsworth (1807), The Hanging of the
  Crane. V
"Mark Twain" (1835), Colonel Sellers [adapted with G. S.
  Densmore from Twain and Warner's novel The Gilded Age
  (1873); prod.]. D
Motley, John Lothrop (1814), The Life and Death of John of
  Barneveld. NF

Women's Christian Temperance Union
  founded in Cleveland.
Young Men's Hebrew Association
  organized in New York City.
Chautauqua Assembly established.
Joseph Glidden marketed barbed wire.
Tiffany glass factory opened.
Elephant first used as symbol of
  Republican Party.
Ellen Glasgow b.
Gertrude Stein b.
Robert Frost b.

Alfonso XII proclaimed king of Spain.
First exhibition of Impressionist
  paintings, in Paris.
Somerset Maugham b.
Hugo von Hoffmansthal b.
Green's Short History of the English
  People.
Hardy's Far from the Madding Crowd.
Swinburne's Bothwell, a Tragedy.
Thomson's "The City of Dreadful
  Night."
Flaubert's The Temptation of Saint
  Anthony.
Verlaine's Romances Without Words.
Alarcón's The Three-Cornered Hat.

Neal, John (1793), Portland Illustrated. NF
Parkman, Francis (1823), The Old Regime in Canada. NF
Roe, E. P. (1838), Opening of a Chestnut Burr. F
Tilton, Theodore (1835), Tempest-Tossed. F
Tourgée, Albion W. (1838), 'Toinette. F
Townsend, Mary Ashley (1832), The Captain's Story. V

1875

Alcott, Louisa May (1832), Eight Cousins; or, The Aunt-Hill. F
Appleton, Thomas Gold (1812), A Sheaf of Papers. NF
Boyesen, Hjalmar Hjorth (1848), A Norseman's Pilgrimage. F
Bryant, William Cullen (1794), Poems. V
Carleton, Will (1845), Farm Legends. V
Cranch, Christopher Pearse (1813), The Bird and the Bell. V
Croly, Jane Cunningham (1829), For Better or Worse: A Book for Some Men and All Women. NF
De Forest, John William (1826), Honest John Vane. F; Playing the Mischief. F
Eddy, Mary Baker (1821), Science and Health with Key to the Scriptures. NF
Gilder, Richard Watson (1844), The New Day. V
Harte, Bret (1836), Tales of the Argonauts. F; Echoes of the Foot-Hills. F
Hayne, Paul Hamilton (1830), The Mountain of the Lovers. V
Holland, Josiah Gilbert (1819), Sevenoaks. F
Holmes, Oliver Wendell (1809), Songs of Many Seasons. V
Howells, William Dean (1837), A Foregone Conclusion. F
Hunt, William Morris (1824), Talks About Art (2 vols., 1875, 1883). NF
James, Henry (1843), A Passionate Pilgrim and Other Tales. F; Transatlantic Sketches. NF
Jones, Joseph Stevens (1809), Paul Revere and the Sons of Liberty. D
Longfellow, Henry Wadsworth (1807), The Masque of Pandora and Other Poems. V
"Mark Twain" (1835), Mark Twain's Sketches: New and Old. F
"Oliver Optic" (1822), Great Western Series (1875–92). F
"Petroleum V. Nasby" (1833), Inflation at the Cross-Roads. F
Saxe, John Godfrey (1816), Leisure-Day Rhymes. V
Stedman, Edmund Clarence (1833), Victorian Poets. NF
Stowe, Harriet Beecher (1811), We and Our Neighbors. F
Taylor, Bayard (1825), Home Pastorals, Ballads, and Lyrics. V
Whittier, John Greenleaf (1807), Hazel-Blossoms. V

Congress passed new Civil Rights Acts.
Andrew Carnegie built first factory to produce Bessemer steel.
Luther Burbank established a plant nursery in Santa Rosa, Calif.
Hebrew Union College founded.
First Kentucky Derby at Churchill Downs.
The Chicago Daily News, 1875–1929.

Beginning of Irish independence movement.
Gilbert and Sullivan comic operas (1875–96).
Paris Opera opened.
Charles Kingsley d.
Thomas Mann b.
Symond's *History of the Renaissance in Italy* (7 vols., 1875–86).
Palgrave's *The Children's Treasury of English Song.*
Trollope's *The Way We Live Now.*
Tennyson's *Queen Mary.*
Swinburne's *Essays and Studies.*
Dostoevsky's *A Raw Youth.*
Tolstoy's *Anna Karenina* (1875–77).

1876

Adams, Henry (1838), Essays in Anglo-Saxon Law. NF
Alcott, Louisa May (1832), Silver Pitchers. F; Rose in Bloom. F
Appleton, Thomas Gold (1812), A Nile Journey. NF
Baker, William M. (1825), Carter Quarterman. F
Boyesen, Hjalmar Hjorth (1848), Tales from Two Hemispheres. F
Brisbane, Albert (1809), General Introduction to Social Sciences. NF
Burroughs, John (1837), Winter Sunshine. NF
Clark, Charles Heber (1841), Elbow-Room. F
Coffin, Charles Carleton (1823), The Boys of '76. F
Emerson, Ralph Waldo (1803), Letters and Social Aims. NF; Selected Poems. V

Colorado admitted to the Union.
Centennial Exposition in Philadelphia.
Greenback Party held first national convention.
Custer's last stand at Battle of Little Big Horn.
Alexander Graham Bell patented telephone.
American Library Association established.
Orestes Brownson d.
Jack London b.
Frank Leslie's Popular Monthly (New York), 1876–1904.

Finney, Charles Grandison (d. 1875), Memoirs. NF

Harte, Bret (1836), Two Men of Sandy Bar. D; Gabriel Conroy. F

Hawthorne, Nathaniel (d. 1864), The Dolliver Romance and Other Pieces. F

Howells, William Dean (1837), Sketch of the Life and Character of Rutherford B. Hayes. NF; A Day's Pleasure and Other Sketches. NF; The Parlor Car. D

Jackson, Helen Hunt (1830), Mercy Philbrick's Choice. F

James, Henry (1843), Roderick Hudson. F

Lowell, James Russell (1819), Among My Books: Second Series. NF

"Mark Twain" (1835), The Adventures of Tom Sawyer. F

Melville, Herman (1819), Clarel: A Poem and Pilgrimage in the Holy Land. V

Miller, Joaquin (1841?), The One Fair Woman. F

Moore, Julia A. (1847), The Sweet Singer of Michigan Salutes the Public (repub. as The Sentimental Song Book). V

Southworth, E. D. E. N. (1819), Self-Raised. F

Stowe, Harriet Beecher (1811), Betty's Bright Idea. F; Footsteps of the Master. NF

Taylor, Bayard (1825), The Echo Club and Other Literary Diversions. V

Ticknor, George (1791), Life, Letters and Journals. NF

Warner, Charles Dudley (1829), My Winter on the Nile. NF

Whitman, Walt (1819), Leaves of Grass. Sixth edition. V

Whittier, John Greenleaf (1807), Mabel Martin. V

Queen Victoria assumed title of Empress of India.

Heinrich Schliemann excavated Mycenae in Greece.

Wagner's The Ring of the Nibelungen performed in Bayreuth.

Harriet Martineau d.

George Sand d.

Trollope's The Prime Minister.

Meredith's Beauchamp's Career.

Carroll's The Hunting of the Snark.

Hardy's The Hand of Ethelberta.

George Eliot's Daniel Deronda.

Huysmans's Martha, Story of a Prostitute.

1877

Adams, Henry (1838), Documents Relating to New-England Federalism, 1800–1815. NF

Alcott, Bronson (1799), Table-Talk. NF

Alcott, Louisa May (1832), A Modern Mephistopheles. F

Aldrich, Thomas Bailey (1836), Flower and Thorn. V; The Queen of Sheba. F; A Midnight Fantasy and the Little Violinist. F

Bierce, Ambrose (1842), The Dance of Death. NF

Blavatsky, Helena Petrovna Hahn (1831), Isis Unveiled. NF

Brooks, Phillips (1835), Lectures on Preaching. NF

Burnett, Frances Hodgson (1849), That Lass o' Lowrie's. F

Burroughs, John (1837), Birds and Poets. NF

Chapman, Maria Weston (1806), Life of Harriet Martineau. NF

Cooke, John Esten (1830), Canolles. F

"Dan DeQuille" (1829), History of the Big Bonanza. NF

Fields, James T. (1817), Underbrush. NF

Hale, Edward Everett (1822), Philip Nolan's Friends. F

Hedge, Frederic Henry (1805), Ways of the Spirit and Other Essays. NF

Holland, Josiah Gilbert (1819), Nicholas Minturn. F

Holmes, Oliver Wendell (1809), Poetical Works. V

Howells, William Dean (1837), Out of the Question. D; A Counterfeit Presentment. D

James, Henry (1843), The American. F

Jewett, Sarah Orne (1849), Deephaven. F

"Josh Billings" (1818), Josh Billings' Trump Kards. F

Lanier, Sidney (1842), Poems. V

Lawson, James (1799), The Maiden's Oath. D

Lowell, James Russell (1819), Three Memorial Poems. V

"Mark Twain" (1835), Ah Sin (with Bret Harte; pub. 1961). D

End of carpetbag rule in the South.

Railroad and coal strikes across the country.

Socialist-Labor Party organized.

Nez Percé Indians at war with U.S.

American Humane Association founded.

John Lothrop Motley d.

Puck (New York), 1877–1918.

Russo-Turkish War (1877–78),

Porfirio Díaz became president of Mexico.

Warwick Deeping b.

Harley Granville-Barker b.

Hermann Hesse b.

Sewell's Black Beauty.

Harriet Martineau's Autobiography (posth.).

Ibsen's The Pillars of Society.

Zola's The Dram-Shop.

Flaubert's A Simple Heart.

Turgenev's Virgin Soil.

Miller, Joaquin (1841?), The Danites of the Sierras (pub. 1882). D

Morgan, Lewis Henry (1818), Ancient Society; or Researches in the Lines of Human Progress. NF

Parkman, Francis (1823), Count Frontenac and New France under Louis XIV. NF

Squier, Ephraim George (1821), Peru. NF

Stedman, Edmund Clarence (1833), Hawthorne and Other Poems. V

Thompson, Denman (1833), Joshua Whitcomb. D

1878

Adams, Charles Francis (1835), Railroads: Their Origins and Problems. NF

Alcott, Louisa May (1832), Under the Lilacs. F

Baker, William M. (1825), The Virginians in Texas. F; A Year Worth Living. F

Bellamy, Edward (1850), Six to One: A Nantucket Idyl. F

Bryant, William Cullen (1794), The Flood of Years. V

Clarke, James Freeman (1810), Essentials and Non-Essentials in Religion. NF

Cooke, Philip St. George (1809), Conquest of New Mexico and California. NF

Eggleston, Edward (1837), Roxy. F

Emerson, Ralph Waldo (1803), Fortune of the Republic. NF

Green, Anna Katharine (1846), The Leavenworth Case. F

Harrigan, Edward (1845), The Mulligan Guard Picnic. D

Harte, Bret (1836), An Heiress of Red Dog. F; The Story of a Mine. F; Drift from Two Shores. F

Hayne, Paul Hamilton (1830), Lives of Robert Young Hayne and Hugh Swinton Legaré. NF

Howard, Bronson (1842), Old Love Letters. D; The Banker's Daughter. D; Only a Tramp. D

James, Henry (1843), Watch and Ward. F; The Europeans. F; French Poets and Novelists. NF

Longfellow, Henry Wadsworth (1807), Kéramos and Other Poems. V

"Mark Twain" (1835), Punch, Brothers, Punch! F

Stanley, Henry Morton (1841), Through the Dark Continent. NF

Stowe, Harriet Beecher (1811), Poganuc People. F

Tyler, Moses Coit (1835), History of American Literature, 1607–1765. NF

Whittier, John Greenleaf (1807), The Vision of Echard. V

Bland-Allison Silver Act.
Edison patented phonograph.
First copper refinery, in Connecticut.
First electric light company formed.
A.A. Pope made first bicycles.
William Cullen Bryant d.
Bayard Taylor d.
Carl Sandburg b.
Upton Sinclair b.
St. Louis Post-Dispatch, 1878–.

Britain and Afghanistan at war.
John Masefield b.
Oliver St. John Gogarty b.
Georg Kaiser b.
Ferenc Molnár b.
Grove's *Dictionary of Music and Musicians* (4 vols., 1878–89).
Hardy's *The Return of the Native*.
Stevenson's *An Inland Voyage*.
Trollope's *Is He Popenjoy?*

1879

Adams, Henry (1838), The Life of Albert Gallatin. NF

Alcott, Louisa May (1832), Meadow Blossoms. F; Sparkles for Bright Eyes. F; Water-Cresses. F

Beers, Ethel Lynn (1827), All Quiet Along the Potomac and Other Poems. V

Boyesen, Hjalmar Hjorth (1848), Falconberg. F

Brooks, Phillips (1835), The Influence of Jesus. NF

Burroughs, John (1837), Locusts and Wild Honey. NF

Cable, George Washington (1844), Old Creole Days. F

Campbell, Bartley (1843), My Partner. D

De Forest, John William (1826), Irene the Missionary. F

George, Henry (1839), Progress and Poverty. NF

Herne, James A. (1839), Hearts of Oak (with David Belasco). D

Uprising of Ute Indians.
Mary Baker Eddy founded the Church of Christ, Scientist, in Boston.
Edison invented incandescent lamp.
Radcliffe College founded.
Carlisle Indian School founded (1879–1918).
First Woolworth 5-and-10-cent store.
First Madison Square Garden, in New York City.
Gilbert and Sullivan operas first performed, in New York City.
Wallace Stevens b.

Holmes, Oliver Wendell (1809), John Lothrop Motley: A
  Memoir. NF; The School-Boy. V
Howells, William Dean (1837), The Lady of the Aroostook. F
James, Henry (1843), Daisy Miller. F; An International
  Episode. F; The Madonna of the Future and Other Tales.
  F; Hawthorne. NF
Jewett, Sarah Orne (1849), Old Friends and New. F
"Josh Billings" (1818), Old Probability: Perhaps Rain—Perhaps
  Not. F
Longfellow, Henry Wadsworth (1807), From My Arm-Chair.
  NF
Rouquette, Adrien Emmanuel (1813), La nouvelle Atala. F
Stedman, Edmund Clarence (1833), Lyrics and Idylls, with
  Other Poems. V
Stockton, Frank R. (1834), Rudder Grange. F
Thaxter, Celia (1835), Drift-Weed. V
Thompson, William Tappan (1812), Rancy Cottem's Courtship.
  F
Tourgée, Albion W. (1838), Figs and Thistles. F; A Fool's
  Errand. F

Austro-German Alliance.
La Nouvelle Revue (Paris), 1879–1940.
Albert Einstein b.
E.M. Forster b.
Robert Browning's *Dramatic Idyls*
  (1879–80).
Meredith's *The Egoist.*
Stevenson's *Travels with a Donkey in
  the Cevennes.*
Arnold's *Mixed Essays.*
Dostoevsky's *The Brothers Karamazov*
  (1879–80).
Ibsen's *A Doll's House.*
Büchner's *Woyzeck.*

1880

Adams, Henry (1838), Democracy: An American Novel. F
Alcott, Louisa May (1832), Jack and Jill: A Village Story. F
Aldrich, Thomas Bailey (1836), The Stillwater Tragedy. F
Baker, William M. (1825), His Majesty: Myself. F
Bellamy, Edward (1850), Dr. Heidenhoff's Process. F
Cable, George Washington (1844), The Grandissimes. F
Dodge, Mary Abigail (1833), Our Common School System. NF
Emerson, Ralph Waldo (1803), The Preacher. NF
Fawcett, Edgar (1847), The False Friend. D; Our First Families.
  D
Hale, Lucretia Peabody (1820), The Peterkin Papers. F
Harte, Bret (1836), Jeff Brigg's Love Story. F; Poetical Works.
  V
Holmes, Oliver Wendell (1809), The Iron Gate and Other
  Poems. V
Howells, William Dean (1837), The Undiscovered Country. F
James, Henry (1843), Confidence. F; The Diary of a Man of
  Fifty and A Bundle of Letters. F
Lanier, Sidney (1843), The Science of English Verse. NF
Longfellow, Henry Wadsworth (1809), Ultima Thule. V
MacKaye, Steele (1842), Hazel Kirke. D
"Mark Twain" (1835), A Tramp Abroad. NF
Mitchell, S. Weir (1829), Hephzibah Guinness. F
Rouquette, Adrien Emmanuel (1813), Critical Dialogue
  Between Aboo and Caboo. NF
Stoddard, Richard Henry (1825), Poems. V
Tourgée, Albion W. (1838), Bricks Without Straw. F
Wallace, Lew (1827), Ben-Hur. F

Chinese Immigration Treaty (limiting
  immigration) signed.
First major gold strike in Alaska.
National Farmers' Alliance organized.
Metropolitan Museum of Art opened in
  Central Park, in New York City.
Sarah Bernhardt made American debut.
The Dial (Chicago; New York), 1880–
  1929.

Gladstone succeeded Disraeli as British
  prime minister.
George Eliot d.
Gustave Flaubert d.
Sean O'Casey b.
Hardy's *The Trumpet-Major.*
Meredith's *The Tragic Comedians.*
Tennyson's *Ballads and Other Poems.*
Disraeli's *Endymion.*
Ouida's *Moths.*
Zola's *Nana.*

1881

Aldrich, Thomas Bailey (1836), Friar Jerome's Beautiful Book.
  V
Anthony, Susan B. (1820), History of Woman Suffrage (with
  others; 4 vols., 1881–87). NF
"Bill Nye" (1850), Bill Nye and Boomerang. F

President Garfield shot in Washington,
  died 11 weeks later.
Adolphus Washington Greely's Arctic
  expedition (1881–84).
Marshall Field and Co. opened in
  Chicago.

Boyesen, Hjalmar Hjorth (1848), Queen Titania. F; Ilka on the Hilltop. F

Bunce, Oliver Bell (1828), The Opinions and Disputations of Bachelor Bluff. NF

Burnett, Frances Hodgson (1849), Esmeralda (with William Gillette). D; A Fair Barbarian. F

Burroughs, John (1837), Pepacton. NF

Cable, George Washington (1844), Madame Delphine. F

Coffin, Charles Carleton (1823), The Boys of '61. F

Cooke, Rose Terry (1827), Somebody's Neighbors. F

Coolbrith, Ina (1842), A Perfect Day. V

Davis, Jefferson (1808), The Rise and Fall of the Confederacy. NF

De Forest, John William (1826), The Bloody Chasm. F

Falkner, William Clark (1825), The White Rose of Memphis. F

George, Henry (1839), The Irish Land Question. NF

Harris, Joel Chandler (1848), Uncle Remus: His Songs and His Sayings. F, V

Howard, Bronson (1842), Baron Rudolph. D

Howe, Julia Ward (1819), Modern Society. NF

Howells, William Dean (1837), Dr. Breen's Practice. F; A Fearful Responsibility and Other Stories. F

Jackson, Helen Hunt (1830), A Century of Dishonor. NF

James, Henry (1843), Washington Square. F; The Portrait of a Lady. F

Jewett, Sarah Orne (1849), Country By-Ways. F

"Josh Billings" (1818), Josh Billings Struggling with Things. F

MacKaye, Steele (1842), A Fool's Errand [adapted from Albion W. Tourgée's novel (1879)]. D

"Margaret Sidney" (1844), Five Little Peppers and How They Grew. F

O'Brien, Fitz-James (d. 1862), Poems and Stories. V, F

"Petroleum V. Nasby" (1833), The Diary of an Office Seeker. F

Redpath, James (1833), Talks About Ireland. NF

Stockton, Frank R. (1834), The Floating Prince and Other Fairy Tales. F

Story, William Wetmore (1819), Vallombrosa. NF

Stowe, Harriet Beecher (1811), A Dog's Mission. F

Tourgée, Albion W. (1838), Zouri's Christmas. F

Whitman, Walt (1819), Leaves of Grass. Seventh edition. F

Whittier, John Greenleaf (1807), The King's Missive. V

Tuskegee Institute founded.
Barnum and Bailey Circus founded.
Clara Barton organized American National Red Cross.
Sidney Lanier d.
American Men of Letters series (1881–1904), ed. by Charles Dudley Warner.
The Century Illustrated Magazine (New York), 1881–1930.
Judge (New York), 1881–1939.
The Critic (New York), 1881–1906.

Czar Alexander II assassinated; Alexander III crowned.
Richard D'Oyly Carte built Savoy Theatre in London.
Thomas Carlyle d.
Benjamin Disraeli d.
Feodor Dostoevsky d.
Stefan Zweig b.
Hardy's *A Laodicean.*
D.G. Rossetti's *Ballads and Sonnets.*
Stevenson's *Virginibus Puerisque.*
Swinburne's *Mary Stuart, A Tragedy.*
Wilde's *Poems.*
Rutherford's *Autobiography.*
Ibsen's *Ghosts.*
France's *The Crime of Sylvester Bonnard.*
Verga's *The House by the Medlar Tree.*
Verlaine's *Wisdom.*
Machado de Assis's *Epitaph for a Small Winner.*

1882

Adams, Henry (1838), John Randolph. NF

Alcott, Bronson (1799), Ralph Waldo Emerson. V, NF; Sonnets and Canzonets. V

Alcott, Louisa May (1832), Proverb Stories. F

Aldrich, Thomas Bailey (1836), Poems. V

Bancroft, George (1800), History of the Formation of the Constitution of the United States. NF

Bancroft, Hubert Howe (1832), History of the Pacific States (34 vols., 1882–90). NF

Benson, Eugene (1837), Art and Nature in Italy. NF

Bigelow, John (1817), Molinos the Quietist. NF

Boker, George Henry (1823), The Book of the Dead. V

Boyesen, Hjalmar Hjorth (1848), Idyls of Norway. V

Brinton, Daniel Garrison (1837), Library of Aboriginal American Literature (editor; 8 vols., 1882–90). NF, F, V, D

Campbell, Bartley (1843), The White Slave. D

Immigration of Chinese labor suspended.
Knights of Columbus founded.
Standard Oil Trust organized.
Clara Barton established National Society of the Red Cross.
American School of Classical Studies founded in Athens.
Lily Langtry's first visit to Broadway.
Ralph Waldo Emerson d.
Henry Wadsworth Longfellow d.

Germany, Italy, and Austria-Hungary formed Triple Alliance.
St. Gotthard Tunnel (Switzerland to Italy) opened.
Charles Darwin d.
D.G. Rossetti d.

Crawford, Francis Marion (1854), Mr. Isaacs. F
Gayarré, Charles Etienne Arthur (1805), Aubert Dubayet, or
  The Two Sister Republics. F
Hayne, Paul Hamilton (1830), Collected Poems. V
Hollister, Gideon Hiram (1817), Kinley Hollow. F
Holmes, Oliver Wendell (1809), Medical Highways and By-
  Ways. NF
Howells, William Dean (1837), A Modern Instance. F
Lazarus, Emma (1849), Songs of a Semite. V, D
Longfellow, Henry Wadsworth (1807), In the Harbor: Ultima
  Thule, Part II. V
"Mark Twain" (1835), The Prince and the Pauper. F
"Petroleum V. Nasby" (1833), Nasby in Exile; or, Six Months
  of Travel. F
Tourgée, Albion W. (1838), John Eax and Mamelon. F
Townsend, Mary Ashley (1832), Down the Bayou and Other
  Poems. V
Whitman, Walt (1819), Specimen Days and Collect. NF
Woolson, Constance Fenimore (1840), Anne. F

Anthony Trollope d.
Virginia Woolf b.
James Joyce b.
Jean Giraudoux b.
Arnold's *Irish Essays and Others.*
Hardy's *Two on a Tower.*
Swinburne's *Tristram of Lyonesse.*
Ouida's *In Maremma.*
Ibsen's *An Enemy of the People.*

1883

Aldrich, Thomas Bailey (1836), From Ponkapog to Pesth. NF
Bates, Arlo (1850), Mr. Jacobs. F
Boyesen, Hjalmar Hjorth (1848), A Daughter of the Philistines.
  F
Bucke, Richard Maurice (1837), Walt Whitman. NF
Child, Francis James (1825), English and Scottish Popular
  Ballads (editor; 5 vols., 1883–98). V
Cooke, John Esten (1830), Fanchette. F; Virginia. NF
Cooper, Peter (1791), Ideas for a Science of Good Government.
  NF
Crawford, Francis Marion (1854), Dr. Claudius. F
Eggleston, Edward (1837), The Hoosier Schoolboy. F
Foote, Mary Hallock (1843), The Led-Horse Claim: A Romance
  of a Mining Camp. F
Freeman, Mary E. Wilkins (1852), Decorative Plaques. V
George, Henry (1839), Social Problems. NF
Grant, Robert (1852), An Average Man. F
Harris, Joel Chandler (1848), Nights with Uncle Remus. F
Hawthorne, Nathaniel (d. 1864), Dr. Grimshawe's Secret.
  F; The Ancestral Footstep. F
Holmes, Oliver Wendell (1809), Pages from an Old Volume of
  Life. NF; Medical Essays. NF
Howe, E. W. (1853), The Story of a Country Town. F
Howells, William Dean (1837), A Woman's Reason. F; The
  Sleeping Car. D
James, Henry (1843), Portraits of Places. NF; The Siege of
  London. F
Jewett, Sarah Orne (1849), The Mate of the Daylight and
  Friends Ashore. F
Lanier, Sidney (d. 1881), The English Novel. NF
Longfellow, Henry Wadsworth (d. 1882), Michael Angelo. V
"Mark Twain" (1835), Life on the Mississippi. NF
Peck, George Wilbur (1840), Peck's Bad Boy and His Pa. F
Pillsbury, Parker (1809), Acts of the Anti-Slavery Apostles. NF
Riley, James Whitcomb (1849), The Old Swimmin'-Hole and
  'Leven More Poems. V

Civil Service Commission established.
Brooklyn Bridge completed.
"Buffalo Bill" Cody organized first
  Wild West show.
Metropolitan Opera Association
  organized in New York City.
Joseph Pulitzer bought New York
  World.
B.F. Keith opened first Boston
  vaudeville theatre.
Modern Language Association
  organized.
William Carlos Williams b.
Ladies' Home Journal (Phila.), 1883–
  1968.
Life (New York), 1883–1936.

Explosion of Krakatoa, an island in
  Indonesia.
Hiram Maxim invented machine gun.
Ivan Turgenev d.
José Ortega y Gasset b.
Franz Kafka b.
Nikos Kazantzakis b.
Stevenson's *Treasure Island.*
Meredith's *Poems and Lyrics of the Joy
  of Earth.*
Trollope's *Autobiography.*
Schreiner's *The Story of an African
  Farm.*
Nietzsche's *Thus Spake Zarathustra* (4
  vols., 1883–85).
Maupassant's *A Life.*

Thompson, William Tappan (1812), John's Alive . . . and
  Other Sketches. F
Tourgée, Albion W. (1838), Hot Plowshares. F
Very, Jones (d. 1880), Poems. V
Whittier, John Greenleaf (1807), The Bay of Seven Islands. V
Wilcox, Ella Wheeler (1850), Poems of Passion. V
Willard, Frances E. (1839), Women and Temperance. NF
Woolson, Constance Fenimore (1840), For the Major. F

1884

Adams, Henry (1838), Esther: A Novel. F
Alcott, Louisa May (1832), Spinning-Wheel Stories. F
Aldrich, Thomas Bailey (1836), Mercedes and Later Lyrics. V
Altgeld, John Peter (1847), Our Penal Machinery and Its
  Victims. NF
Bates, Arlo (1850), The Pagans. F
Bellamy, Edward (1850), Miss Ludington's Sister. F
"Bill Arp" (1826), Bill Arp's Scrap Book. F
Cable, George Washington (1844), The Creoles of Louisiana.
  NF
Carleton, Henry Guy (1856), The Thompson Street Poker Club.
  NF
"Charles Egbert Craddock" (1850), In the Tennessee
  Mountains. F; Where the Battle Was Fought. F
Crawford, Francis Marion (1854), A Roman Singer. F; To
  Leeward. F
Emerson, Ralph Waldo (d. 1882), Lectures and Biographical
  Sketches. NF; The Senses and the Soul. NF
Fiske, John (1842), Excursions of an Evolutionist. NF; The
  Destiny of Man. NF
Guiney, Louise Imogen (1861), Songs at the Start. V
Harris, Joel Chandler (1848), Mingo and Other Sketches in
  Black and White. F
Hay, John (1838), The Bread-Winners. F
Hearn, Lafcadio (1850), Stray Leaves from Strange Literature. F
Hedge, Frederic Henry (1805), Atheism in Philosophy. NF
Howells, William Dean (1837), Three Villages. NF; A Little
  Girl Among the Old Masters. NF; Niagara Revisited. NF; The
  Register. D
Jackson, Helen Hunt (1830), Ramona. F
James, Henry (1843), Tales of Three Cities. F
Jewett, Sarah Orne (1849), A Country Doctor. F
Lanier, Sidney (d. 1881), Poems. V
"Mark Twain" (1835), The Adventures of Huckleberry Finn. F
Miller, Joaquin (1841?), Memorie and Rime. NF, V
Parkman, Francis (1823), Montcalm and Wolfe. NF
Stedman, Edmund Clarence (1833), Songs and Ballads. V
Stockton, Frank R. (1834), The Lady or the Tiger? and Other
  Stories. F
Stowe, Harriet Beecher (1811), Our Famous Women. NF
Timrod, Henry (d. 1867), Katie. V
Tourgée, Albion W. (1838), An Appeal to Caesar. F

Bureau of Labor created.
Equal Rights Party formed by
  suffragettes.
"Mugwumps" bolted Republican Party.
First long distance telephone line.
Lewis Waterman patented fountain
  pen.
Ottmar Mergenthaler patented linotype
  machine.
Mississippi State College for Women
  chartered.
American Historical Association
  founded.
Grolier Club founded, in New York
  City.
First newspaper syndicate (S.S.
  McClure's) founded.
PMLA: Publications of the Modern
  Language Association (Baltimore;
  New York), 1884–.

Fabian Society founded, in London.
First underground railway, in London.
Charles Reade d.
Hugh Walpole b.
Percy Wyndham Lewis b.
The Oxford English Dictionary (10
  vols., 1884–1928).
Tennyson's Becket; The Cup and the
  Falcon.
Spencer's The Man versus the State.
Ibsen's The Wild Duck.
Huysmans's Against the Grain.

1885

Aldrich, Thomas Bailey (1836), Poems. V
Arnold, Matthew (1822), Discourses in America. NF
Barr, Amelia Edith (1831), Jan Vedder's Wife. F

Apache Indians resumed war against
  whites.
Washington Monument dedicated.

Bates, Arlo (1850), A Wheel of Fire. F
Beecher, Henry Ward (1813), Evolution and Religion. NF
Brinton, Daniel Garrison (1837), The Lenâpé and Their
    Legends. NF
Burroughs, John (1837), Fresh Fields. NF
Cable, George Washington (1844), Dr. Sevier. F; The Silent
    South. NF
Carleton, Will (1845), City Ballads. V
Channing, William Ellery (1818), Eliot. V
"Charles Egbert Craddock" (1850), Down the Ravine. F; The
    Prophet of the Great Smoky Mountains. F
Cooke, John Esten (1830), My Lady Pokahontas. F
Cooke, Rose Terry (1827), Root-Bound. F
Crawford, Francis Marion (1854), Zoroaster. F
Grant, Ulysses S. (1822), Personal Memoirs (2 vols., 1885–86).
    NF
Hayne, Paul Hamilton (1830), The Broken Battalions. V
Hearn, Lafcadio (1850), Gombo Zhêbes. NF
Holmes, Oliver Wendell (1809), A Mortal Antipathy. F; Ralph
    Waldo Emerson. NF; Illustrated Poems. V
Howard, Bronson (1842), One of Our Girls. D
Howells, William Dean (1837), The Rise of Silas Lapham.
    F; The Elevator. D
James, Henry (1843), A Little Tour in France. NF
Jewett, Sarah Orne (1849), A Marsh Island. F
Keenan, Henry Francis (1850), The Money-Makers. F
Mitchell, S. Weir (1829), In War Time. F
Royce, Josiah (1855), The Religious Aspect of Philosophy. NF
Stedman, Edmund Clarence (1883), The Poets of America. NF

New Orleans Exposition opened.
Stanford University founded.
Bryn Mawr College founded.
American Economic Association
    organized.
Ezra Pound b.
Ring Lardner b.
Sinclair Lewis b.

Congo Free State organized by Leopold
    II of Belgium.
The Rijksmuseum opened in
    Amsterdam.
Victor Hugo d.
D.H. Lawrence b.
François Mauriac b.
The Dictionary of National Biography
    (63 vols., 1885–1900).
Meredith's *Diana of the Crossways*.
Moore's *A Mummer's Wife*.
Pater's *Marius the Epicurean*.
Ruskin's *Praeterita* (1885–89).
Stevenson's *A Child's Garden of Verses*.
Hudson's *The Purple Land,*
Burton's *Arabian Nights Entertainments*
    (16 vols., 1885–88).
Zola's *Germinal*.
Maupassant's *Bel-Ami*.

1886

Alcott, Louisa May (1832), Jo's Boys and How They Turned
    Out. F; Lulu's Library (3 vols., 1886–89). F
Bancroft, George (1800), A Plea for the Constitution of the
    United States. NF
Barr, Amelia Edith (1831), The Bow of Orange Ribbon. F
Boyesen, Hjalmar Hjorth (1848), The Story of Norway. NF
Bunner, H. C. (1855), The Midge. F
Burnett, Frances Hodgson (1849), Little Lord Fauntleroy. F
Carnegie, Andrew (1835), Triumphant Democracy. NF
Channing, William Ellery (1818), John Brown and the Heroes
    of Harpers Ferry. V
"Charles Egbert Craddock" (1850), In the Clouds. F
Cooke, Rose Terry (1827), The Sphinx's Children. F
Freeman, Mary E. Wilkins (1852), The Adventure of Ann. F
George, Henry (1839), Protection of Free Trade. NF
Gillette, William (1855), Held by the Enemy. D
Grant, Robert (1852), Face to Face. F
Hale, Lucretia Peabody (1820), The Last of the Peterkins. F
Howells, William Dean (1837), Indian Summer. F; Tuscan
    Cities. NF; The Garroters. D
James, Henry (1843), The Bostonians. F; The Princess
    Casamassima. F
Jewett, Sarah Orne (1849), A White Heron and Other Stories. F
"Mark Twain" (1835), Colonel Sellers (with William Dean
    Howells; prod.). D
Mitchell, S. Weir (1829), Roland Blake. F
Parker, Jane Marsh (1836), The Midnight Cry. F

Presidential Succession Act.
Continuing labor unrest, especially
    railroad workers.
Haymarket Square riots in Chicago.
American Federation of Labor
    organized.
Statue of Liberty dedicated.
Emily Dickinson d.
The Cosmopolitan Magazine (New
    York), 1886–.
The Forum (New York), 1886–1940.
Modern Language Notes (Baltimore),
    1886–.

Auguste Rodin exhibited sculpture
    titled "The Kiss" in Paris.
English Historical Review (London),
    1886–.
Siegfried Sassoon b.
Hermann Broch b.
Hardy's *The Mayor of Casterbridge*.
Kipling's *Departmental Ditties*.
Shaw's *Cashel Byron's Profession*.
Stevenson's *The Strange Case of Dr.
    Jekyll and Mr. Hyde*.
Tolstoy's *The Death of Ivan Ilyich*.
Rimbaud's *Illuminations*.
Ibsen's *Rosmersholm*.
Nietzsche's *Beyond Good and Evil*.
Krafft-Ebing's *Psychopathia Sexualis*.

Peabody, Elizabeth Palmer (1804), A Last Evening with
    Allston. NF
Shea, John Dawson Gilmary (1824), History of the Catholic
    Church in the United States (4 vols., 1886–92). NF
Stockton, Frank R. (1834), The Casting Away of Mrs. Lecks
    and Mrs. Aleshine. F
Story, William Wetmore (1819), Fiammetta: A Summer Idyl.
    NF
Thaxter, Celia (1835), Idyls and Pastorals. V
Thompson, Denman (1833), The Old Homestead. D
Very, Jones (d. 1880), Poems and Essays. V, NF
Whittier, John Greenleaf (1807), St. Gregory's Guest. V
Woolson, Constance Fenimore (1840), East Angels. F

1887

Adams, Brooks (1848), The Emancipation of Massachusetts. NF
Alcott, Bronson (1799), New Connecticut. V
Bates, Arlo (1850), Sonnets in Shadow. V
Baylor, Frances Courtenay (1848), Behind the Blue Ridge. F
Beecher, Henry Ward (1813), Patriotic Addresses in America
    and England. NF
Brown, Alice (1857), Fools of Nature. F
Boyesen, Hjalmar Hjorth (1848), The Modern Vikings. F
Bunner, H. C. (1855), The Story of a New York House. F
"Charles Egbert Craddock" (1850), The Story of Keedon
    Bluffs. F
Coffin, Charles Carleton (1823), Drum-Beat of the Nation. NF
Conway, Moncure D. (1832), Pine and Palm. F
Cox, Palmer (1840), The Brownies: Their Book (1887 ff.). V
Crawford, Francis Marion (1854), Saracinesca. F; Marzio's
    Crucifix. F
Dewey, John (1859), Psychology. NF
Frederic, Harold (1856), Seth's Brother's Wife. F
Freeman, Mary E. Wilkins (1852), A Humble Romance and
    Other Stories. F
Gunter, Archibald Clavering (1847), Mr. Barnes of New York.
    F
Harris, Joel Chandler (1848), Free Joe, and Other Georgian
    Sketches. F
Hearn, Lafcadio (1850), Some Chinese Ghosts. F
Holmes, Oliver Wendell (1809), Our Hundred Days in Europe.
    NF
Howard, Bronson (1842), The Henrietta. D
Howells, William Dean (1837), The Minister's Charge.
    F; Modern Italian Poets. NF
Kirkland, Joseph (1830), Zury: The Meanest Man in Spring
    County. F
Lazarus, Emma (1849), By The Waters of Babylon. V
Le Gallienne, Richard (1866), My Ladies' Sonnets. V
Lowell, James Russell (1819), Democracy and Other Addresses.
    NF
MacKaye, Steele (1842), Paul Kauvar. D
"Nelly Bly" (1867), Ten Days in a Mad House. NF
Page, Thomas Nelson (1853), In Ole Virginia. F
Reese, Lizette Woodworth (1856), A Branch of May. V
Riley, James Whitcomb (1849), Afterwhiles. V
Saltus, Edgar (1855), Mr. Incoul's Misadventure. F
Stockton, Frank R. (1834), The Bee Man of Orn and Other
    Fanciful Tales. F

Interstate Commerce Act.
First electric surface trolley line.
Golf introduced to U.S. by Joseph
    Mickle Fox.
Henry Ward Beecher d.
Marianne Moore b.
Robinson Jeffers b.
Scribner's Magazine (New York),
    1887–1939.

Queen Victoria's Golden Jubilee.
Reinsurance Treaty allied Russia with
    Germany.
Jules Laforgue d.
Edwin Muir b.
Georg Trakl b.
Hardy's *The Woodlanders*.
Meredith's *Ballads and Poems of Tragic
    Life*.
Pater's *Imaginary Portraits*.
Doyle's *A Study in Scarlet*.
Haggard's *She*.
Strindberg's *The Father*.
Zola's *The Soil*.
Chekhov's *Ivanov*.

Tourgée, Albion W. (1838), Button's Inn. F
Wiggin, Kate Douglas (1856), The Birds' Christmas Carol. F

1888

Alcott, Louisa May (1832), A Garland for Girls. F
Aldrich, Thomas Bailey (1836), The Second Son. F
Arnold, Matthew (1822), Civilization in the United States. NF
Bancroft, Hubert Howe (1832), California Pastoral.
   NF; California Inter Pocula. NF
Bangs, John Kendrick (1862), New Waggings of Old Tales
   (with F. D. Sherman). F
Bates, Arlo (1850), Prince Vance (with Harriet L. Vose). F
Baylor, Frances Courtenay (1848), Juan and Juanita. F
Belasco, David (1859), Lord Chumley (with Henry C. DeMille).
   D
Bellamy, Edward (1850), Looking Backward: 2000–1887. F
Blavatsky, Helena Petrovna Hahn (1831), The Secret Doctrine.
   NF
Burnett, Frances Hodgson (1849), Sara Crewe. F; Editha's
   Burglar. F
Cable, George Washington (1844), Bonaventure. F
"Charles Egbert Craddock" (1850), The Despot of
   Broomsedge Cove. F
Conwell, Russell Herman (1843), Acres of Diamonds. NF
Deland, Margaret (1857), John Ward, Preacher. F
Eggleston, Edward (1837), The Graysons. F
Hedge, Frederic Henry (1805), Martin Luther and Other Essays.
   NF
Holmes, Oliver Wendell (1809), Before the Curfew and Other
   Poems. V
Howard, Bronson (1846), Shenandoah. D
Howells, William Dean (1837), April Hopes. F; A Sea-Change;
   or, Love's Stowaway. D
James, Henry (1843), The Aspern Papers. F; The Reverberator.
   F; Partial Portraits. NF
Jewett, Sarah Orne (1849), The King of Folly Island and Other
   People. F
Kirkland, Joseph (1830), The McVeys. F
Lowell, James Russell (1819), The English Poets; Lessing,
   Rousseau. NF; Political Essays. NF; Heartsease and Rue. V
Melville, Herman (1819), John Marr and Other Sailors. V
Page, Thomas Nelson (1853), Befo' de War (with A. C.
   Gordon). V
Repplier, Agnes (1858), Books and Men. NF
Riley, James Whitcomb (1849), Pipes o' Pan at Zekesbury. NF,
   V; Old-Fashioned Roses. V
Saltus, Edgar (1855), The Truth About Tristrem Varick. F
Stockton, Frank R. (1834), The Dusantes. F
Tourgée, Albion W. (1838), Letters to a King. F; Black Ice. F
Whitman, Walt (1819), November Boughs. V, NF
Woodhull, Victoria (1838), Stirpiculture. NF

Department of Labor established.
William Burroughs patented adding
   machine.
George Eastman perfected box camera
   and roll film.
Great March Blizzard in New York
   City.
American Folk-Lore Society founded.
Bronson Alcott d.
Louisa May Alcott d.
Eugene O'Neill b.
T.S. Eliot b.
Maxwell Anderson b.
John Crowe Ransom b.
Collier's (Springfield, Ohio), 1888–
   1957.
National Geographic Magazine
   (Washington, D.C.), 1888–.

Wilhelm II crowned emperor of
   Germany.
Suez Canal declared neutral and open.
Matthew Arnold d.
Joyce Cary b.
T.E. Lawrence b.
Kipling's *Soldiers Three.*
Arnold's *Essays in Criticism: Second
   Series.*
Meredith's *A Reading of Earth.*
Ward's *Robert Elsmere.*
Hardy's *Wessex Tales.*
Zola's *The Dream.*
Tolstoy's *The Power of Darkness.*
Strindberg's *Miss Julie.*
Maupassant's *Pierre and Jean.*
Dujardin's *We'll to the Woods No
   More.*

1889

Adams, Henry (1838), History of the United States of America
   During the Administration of Thomas Jefferson and James
   Madison (9 vols., 1889–91). NF
Alcott, Louisa May (d. 1888), A Modern Mephistopheles and A
   Whisper in the Dark. F

North Dakota, South Dakota, Montana,
   and Washington admitted to the
   Union.
Oklahoma opened to white settlers.
First Pan-American Congress in
   Washington.

Austin, Jane Goodwin (1831), Standish of Standish. F
Bancroft, George (1800), Martin Van Buren to the End of His Public Career. NF
Bates, Arlo (1850), The Philistines. F
Brownell, William C. (1851), French Traits: An Essay in Comparative Criticism. NF
Burroughs, John (1837), Indoor Studies. NF
Cable, George Washington (1844), Strange True Stories of Louisiana. NF
Carnegie, Andrew (1835), The Gospel of Wealth. NF
Catherwood, Mary (1847), The Romance of Dollard. F
Crawford, Francis Marion (1854), Sant' Ilario. F; Greifenstein. F
Field, Eugene (1850), A Little Book of Western Verse. V; A Little Book of Profitable Tales. F
Harris, Joel Chandler (1848), Daddy Jake the Runaway. F
Hearn, Lafcadio (1850), Chita: A Memory of Last Island. F
Herne, James A. (1839), The Hawthornes. D
Howells, William Dean (1837), Annie Kilburn. F; The Mouse-Trap and Other Farces. D
James, Henry (1843), A London Life. F
Kemble, Frances Anne (1809), Far Away and Long Ago. F
Lowell, James Russell (1819), Books and Libraries, and Other Papers. NF
"Mark Twain" (1835), A Connecticut Yankee in King Arthur's Court. F
Moulton, Louise Chandler (1835). Poems. V
Roosevelt, Theodore (1858), The Winning of the West (4 vols., 1889–96). NF
Saltus, Edgar (1855), The Pace That Kills. F; A Transient Guest and Other Episodes. F
Warner, Charles Dudley (1829), A Little Journey in the World. F
Whitman, Walt (1819), Leaves of Grass. Eighth edition. V
Willard, Frances E. (1839), Glimpses of Fifty Years. NF
Woolson, Constance Fenimore (1840), Jupiter Lights. F

Johnstown, Penna., flood killed 2,295 persons.
Jane Addams established Hull-House, in Chicago.
Introduction of motion pictures in U.S. (1889–91) by W.K.L. Dickson
American Academy of Political and Social Science founded.
General Federation of Women's Clubs founded.
The Wall Street Journal (New York), 1889–.
The Arena (Boston), 1889–1909.
Munsey's Magazine (New York), 1889–1929.
Poet Lore (Phila. et al.), 1889–.

Robert Browning d.
Wilkie Collins d.
Gerard Manley Hopkins d.
Kipling's *Wee Willie Winkie and Other Stories.*
Pater's *Appreciations.*
Yeats's *The Wanderings of Oisin.*
Chekhov's *The Wood Demon.*
Bergson's *Time and Free Will*

1890

Adams, Charles Francis (1835), Richard Henry Dana. NF
Aldrich, Thomas Bailey (1836), Wyndham Towers. V
Bancroft, Hubert Howe (1832), Literary Industries. NF
Boyesen, Hjalmar Hjorth (1848), A Fearless Trio. F; Against Heavy Odds. F
Cable, George Washington (1844), The Negro Question. NF
Cawein, Madison (1865), Lyrics and Idyls. V
Chopin, Kate (1851), At Fault. F
Crawford, Francis Marion (1854), A Cigarette-Maker's Romance. F
Davis, Jefferson (1808), A Short History of the Confederate States of America. NF
Dickinson, Emily (d. 1886), Poems. V
Fiske, John (1842), The War of Independence. NF; Civil Government in the United States. NF
Fitch, Clyde (1865), Beau Brummell. D
Frederic, Harold (1856), The Lawton Girl. F; In the Valley. F
Fuller, Henry Blake (1857), The Chevalier of Pensieri Vani. F
Garland, Hamlin (1860), Under the Wheel. D
Gilpin, William (1813), The Cosmopolitan Railway. NF
Harte, Bret (1836), A Ward of the Golden Gate. F; A Waif of the Plains. F

Idaho and Wyoming admitted to the Union.
Sherman Silver Purchase Act.
McKinley Tariff Act.
Sherman Anti-Trust Act.
Child labor increased in the South.
University of Chicago founded.
Madison Square Garden rebuilt in New York City.
Katherine Anne Porter b.
Literary Digest (New York), 1890–1938.
Review of Reviews (New York), 1890–1937,

Resignation of Chancellor Bismarck in Germany.
Free elementary education introduced in England.
John Henry Newman d.
Franz Werfel b.
Boris Pasternak b.
Frazer's *The Golden Bough* (12 vols., 1890–1915).

Hay, John (1838), Poems. V; Abraham Lincoln: A History (10 vols., with John G. Nicolay). NF
Hearn, Lafcadio (1850), Two Years in the French West Indies. NF; Youma. F
Herne, James A. (1839), Margaret Fleming. D
Howells, William Dean (1837), A Hazard of New Fortunes. F; The Shadow of a Dream. F; A Boy's Town. NF
James, Henry (1843), The Tragic Muse. F
James, William (1842), The Principles of Psychology. NF
Jefferson, Joseph (1829), Autobiography. NF
Jewett, Sarah Orne (1849), Strangers and Wayfarers. F
Mahan, Alfred Thayer (1840), The Influence of Sea Power Upon History, 1660–1783. NF
Miller, Joaquin (1841?), In Classic Shades and Other Poems. V
Riis, Jacob August (1849), How the Other Half Lives. NF
Riley, James Whitcomb (1849), Rhymes of Childhood. V
Saltus, Edgar (1855), Love and Lore. NF
Stanley, Henry Morton (1841), In Darkest Africa. NF
Stoddard, Richard Henry (1825), The Lion's Cub; with Other Verse. V
Tourgée, Albion W. (1838), Pactolus Prime. F
Whittier, John Greenleaf (1807), At Sundown. V

Kipling's *The Light That Failed*.
Gissing's *The Emancipated*.
Whistler's *The Gentle Art of Making Enemies*.
France's *Thaïs*.
Ibsen's *Hedda Gabler*.
Hamsun's *Hunger*.

1891

Adams, Henry (1838), Historical Essays. NF
Aldrich, Thomas Bailey (1836), The Sisters' Tragedy. V
Allen, James Lane (1849), Flute and Violin. F
Ames, Nathaniel (d. 1864), The Essays, Humor, and Poems of Nathaniel Ames. F. NF, V
Austin, Jane Goodwin (1831), Betty Alden. F
Bancroft, George (1800), History of the Battle of Lake Erie and Miscellaneous Papers. NF
Bangs, John Kendrick (1862), Tiddledywink Tales. F
Bierce, Ambrose (1842), Tales of Soldiers and Civilians (repub. as In the Midst of Life, 1892). F
Boyesen, Hjalmar Hjorth (1848), The Mammon of Unrighteousness. F
Brinton, Daniel Garrison (1837), The American Race. NF
"Charles Egbert Craddock" (1850), In the "Stranger People's" Country. F
Cooke, Rose Terry (1827), Huckleberries Gathered from New England Hills. F
Davis, Richard Harding (1864), Gallegher and Other Stories. F
Dewey, John (1859), Outlines of a Critical Theory of Ethics. NF
Dickinson, Emily (d. 1886), Poems: Second Series. V
Donnelly, Ignatius (1831), Caesar's Column: A Story of the Twentieth Century. F
Eggleston, Edward (1837), The Faith Doctor. F
Frederic, Harold (1856), The Young Emperor: William II of Germany. NF
Freeman, Mary E. Wilkins (1852), A New England Nun and Other Stories. F
Garland, Hamlin (1860), Main-Travelled Roads. F
George, Henry (1839), The Condition of Labor. NF
Harte, Bret (1836), A Sappho of Green Springs, and Other Stories. F
Holmes, Oliver Wendell (1809), Over the Teacups. F, NF, V
Howells, William Dean (1837), Criticism and Fiction. NF

Circuit Courts of Appeal established.
Forest Reserve Act.
Office of Superintendent of Immigration created.
Thomas Alva Edison granted patent for motion picture camera.
Edwin Booth retired from stage.
First correspondence school, in Scranton, Penna.
James Russell Lowell d.
Herman Melville d.
George Bancroft d.

Germany, Italy, and Austria-Hungary renewed Triple Alliance.
Widespread famine in Russia.
International Copyright Act.
Arthur Rimbaud d.
Morris's *News from Nowhere*.
Barrie's *The Little Minister*.
Hardy's *Tess of the D'Urbervilles*.
Wilde's *The Picture of Dorian Gray*.
Shaw's *The Quintessence of Ibsenism*.
Gissing's *New Grub Street*.
George du Maurier's *Peter Ibbetson*.
Tolstoy's *The Kreutzer Sonata*.
Wedekind's *Spring's Awakening*.

Kirkland, Joseph (1830), The Captain of Company K. F
Lowell, James Russell (1819), Latest Literary Essays and
    Addresses. NF
Melville, Herman (1819), Timoleon. V
Monroe, Harriet (1860), Valeria and Other Poems. V
Norris, Frank (1870), Yvernelle: A Tale of Feudal France. V
Page, Thomas Nelson (1853), Elsket and Other Stories. F; On
    Newfound River. F
"Petroleum V. Nasby" (1833), The Demagogue. F
Reese, Lizette Woodworth (1856), A Handful of Lavender. V
Repplier, Agnes (1858), Points of View. NF
Smith, Francis Hopkinson (1838), Colonel Carter of
    Cartersville. F
Stockton, Frank R. (1834), The Rudder Grangers Abroad. F
Story, William Wetmore (1819), Excursions in Art and Letters.
    NF
Thomas, Augustus (1857), Alabama. D

1892

Adams, Charles Francis (1835), Three Episodes of
    Massachusetts History. NF
Allen, James Lane (1849), Sister Dolorosa and Posthumous
    Fame. F; The Blue-Grass Region of Kentucky. NF
Balestier, Wolcott (1861), The Naulahka (with Rudyard
    Kipling). F; Benefits Forgot. F
Bierce, Ambrose (1842), The Monk and the Hangman's
    Daughter (with G. A. Danziger, trans. from the German of
    Richard Voss). F; Black Beetles in Amber. V, NF, D
Boyesen, Hjalmar Hjorth (1848), The Golden Calf. F
Brooks, Phillips (1835), Essays and Addresses. NF
Brownell, William C. (1851), French Art: Classic and
    Contemporary Painting and Sculpture. NF
Carleton, Henry Guy (1856), The Gilded Fool. D
Crawford, Francis Marion (1854), Don Orsino. F; The Three
    Fates. F
Davis, Richard Harding (1864), Van Bibber and Others. F
Foote, Mary Hallock (1847), The Chosen Valley. F
Frederic, Harold (1856), The Return of the O'Mahony. F
Freeman, Mary E. Wilkins (1852), The Pot of Gold. F; Young
    Lucretia. F
Garland, Hamlin (1860), A Member of the Third House.
    F; Jason Edwards: An Average Man. F; A Little Norsk; or, Ol'
    Pap's Flaxen. F; A Spoil of Office. F
George, Henry (1839), A Perplexed Philosopher. NF
Harris, Joel Chandler (1848), Balaam and His Friends. F; On
    the Plantation. F; Uncle Remus and His Friends. F
Harte, Bret (1836), Colonel Starbottle's Client, and Some Other
    People. F
Herne, James A. (1839), Shore Acres [revision of The
    Hawthornes (1889)].D
Howard, Bronson (1842), Aristocracy. D
Howells, William Dean (1837), An Imperative Duty. F; The
    Quality of Mercy. F; A Little Swiss Sojourn. NF; The Albany
    Depot. D; A Letter of Introduction. D
James, Henry (1843), The Lesson of the Master. F.
Lowell, James Russell (d. 1891), The Old English Dramatists.
    NF

Continuing labor unrest and strikes.
Populist Party met in national
    convention.
Ellis Island opened as immigration
    station.
Boll weevil first appeared in Texas.
American Fine Arts Society founded.
American Psychological Association
    organized.
Ward McAllister first used the
    designation "The Four Hundred."
John Greenleaf Whittier d.
Walt Whitman d.
The Sewanee Review (Sewanee, Tenn.),
    1892–.
The Yale Review (New Haven), 1892–.
Charles K. Harris's "After the Ball is
    Over."

Gladstone fought for Home Rule for
    Ireland.
Rudolf Diesel patented an internal
    combustion engine.
Alfred Lord Tennyson d.
Yeats's *The Countess Cathleen.*
Doyle's *The Adventures of Sherlock
    Holmes.*
Kipling's *Barrack-Room Ballads.*
Wilde's *Lady Windermere's Fan.*
Shaw's *Widowers' Houses.*
Gissing's *Born in Exile.*
Chekhov's *Ward 6.*
Maeterlinck's *Pelléas and Mélisande.*
Hauptmann's *The Weavers.*
Zola's *The Downfall.*
Ibsen's *The Master Builder.*

"**Mark Twain**" (1835), The American Claimant. F; Merry Tales. F
Mitchell, S. Weir (1829), Characteristics. F
Page, Thomas Nelson (1853), The Old South. NF
Parkman, Francis (1823), A Half-Century of Conflict. NF
Repplier, Agnes (1858), Essays in Miniature. NF
Riis, Jacob August (1849), The Children of the Poor. NF
Riley, James Whitcomb (1849), Green Fields and Running Brooks. V
Royce, Josiah (1855), The Spirit of Modern Philosophy. NF
Saltus, Edgar (1855), Imperial Purple. NF
Stedman, Edmund Clarence (1833), The Nature and Elements of Poetry. NF
Whitman, Walt (1819), Leaves of Grass. Ninth edition. V
Woodhull, Victoria (1838), Humanitarian Money. NF

1893

Adams, Henry (1838), Memoirs of Marau Taaroa, Last Queen of Tahiti (rev. 1901). NF
Aldrich, Thomas Bailey (1836), An Old Town by the Sea. NF
Allen, James Lane (1849), John Gray. F
Belasco, David (1853), The Girl I Left Behind Me (with Franklin Fyles; pub. 1941). D
Bierce, Ambrose (1842), Can Such Things Be? F
Boyesen, Hjalmar Hjorth (1848), The Social Strugglers. F
Bucke, Richard Maurice (1837), In Re Walt Whitman (editor). NF
Carman, Bliss (1861), Low Tide on Grand Pré. V
Crane, Stephen (1871), Maggie: A Girl of the Streets (pub. under the pseudonym "Johnston Smith"; pub. under his own name, 1896). F
Crawford, Francis Marion (1854), Pietro Ghisleri. F; The Novel—What It Is. NF
Dazey, Charles T. (1855), In Old Kentucky (pub. 1897). D
Dunbar, Paul Laurence (1872), Oak and Ivy. V
Eggleston, Edward (1837), Duffels. F
Emerson, Ralph Waldo (d. 1882), Natural History of the Intellect and Other Papers. NF
Frederic, Harold (1856), The Copperhead. F; The New Exodus: A Study of Israel in Russia. NF
Freeman, Mary E. Wilkins (1852), Jane Field. F; Giles Corey, Yeoman. D
Fuller, Henry Blake (1857), The Cliff-Dwellers. F
Garland, Hamlin (1860), Prairie Folks. F; Prairie Songs. V
Guiney, Louise Imogen (1861), A Roadside Harp. V
Howells, William Dean (1837), The World of Chance. F; The Coast of Bohemia. F; My Year in a Log Cabin. NF; The Unexpected Guests. D; Evening Dress. D
James, Henry (1843), The Private Life. F; The Real Thing and Other Tales. F; The Wheel of Time. F; Picture and Text. NF; Essays in London and Elsewhere. NF
Jewett, Sarah Orne (1849), A Native of Wimby and Other Tales. F
"**Mark Twain**" (1835), The £1,000,000 Bank Note. F
Monroe, Harriet (1860), The Columbian Ode. V
"**Octave Thanet**" (1850), Stories of a Western Town. F
Repplier, Agnes (1858), Essays in Idleness. NF
Riley, James Whitcomb (1849), Poems Here at Home. V
Saltus, Edgar (1855), Madame Sapphira. F

Financial panic (gold and silver).
Repeal of Sherman Silver Purchase Act.
World's Columbian Exposition in Chicago.
Mormon Temple dedicated in Salt Lake City.
Edison's film studio in West Orange, N.J.
Anti-Saloon League organized.
Frank Lloyd Wright built his Chicago house.
Francis Parkman d.
J.P. Marquand b.
S.N. Behrman b.
McClure's Magazine (New York), 1893–1929.
Katherine Lee Bates's "America the Beautiful."

France and Russia signed dual alliance.
The Panama scandal, in France.
Guy de Maupassant d.
Wilfred Owen b.
Ernst Toller b.
Vladimir Mayakovsky b.
Pater's *Plato and Platonism*.
Pinero's *The Second Mrs. Tanqueray*.
Wilde's *Salomé; A Woman of No Importance*.
Yeats's *The Celtic Twilight*.
Francis Thompson's *Poems*.
Hauptmann's *The Beaver Coat*.

Shillaber, Benjamin Penhallow (1814), Mrs. Partington's Grab Bag. F
Thomas, Augustus (1857), In Mizzoura. D
Wilson, Woodrow (1856), Division and Reunion, 1829–1889. NF

1894

Allen, James Lane (1849), A Kentucky Cardinal. F
Atherton, Gertrude (1857), Before the Gringo Came. F
Baylor, Frances Courtenay (1848), Claudia Hyde. F
Berenson, Bernard (1865), Venetian Painters of the Renaissance. NF
"Bill Nye" (1850), History of the United States. F
Boyesen, Hjalmar Hjorth (1848), Norseland Tales. F; Literary and Social Silhouettes. NF
Burroughs, John (1837), Riverby. NF
Cable, George Washington (1844), John March, Southerner. F
Carleton, Henry Guy (1856), The Butterflies. D
Carman, Bliss (1861), Songs from Vagabondia (with Richard Hovey). V
Chambers, Robert W. (1865), In the Quarter. F
"Charles Egbert Craddock" (1850), His Vanished Star. F
Chopin, Kate (1851), Bayou Folk. F
Coolbrith, Ina (1842), The Singer of the Sea. V
Crawford, Francis Marion (1854), Katherine Lauderdale. F
Foote, Mary Hallock (1847), Coeur d'Alene. F
Ford, Paul Leicester (1865), The Honorable Peter Stirling. F
Frederic, Harold (1856), Marsena, and Other Stories of the Wartime. F
Garland, Hamlin (1860), Crumbling Idols. NF
Gillette, William (1855), Too Much Johnson. D
Harris, Joel Chandler (1848), Little Mr. Thimblefinger and His Queer Country. F
Hearn, Lafcadio (1850), Glimpses of Unfamiliar Japan. NF
Howells, William Dean (1837), A Traveler from Altruria. F; A Likely Story. D
James, Henry (1843), Theatricals: Two Comedies. D
Lloyd, Herbert Demarest (1847), Wealth Against Commonwealth. NF
"Mark Twain" (1835), Tom Sawyer Abroad. F; The Tragedy of Pudd'nhead Wilson. F
Muir, John (1838), The Mountains of California. NF
Page, Thomas Nelson (1853), The Burial of the Guns. F
Repplier, Agnes (1858), In the Dozy Hours. NF
Saltus, Edgar (1855), Enthralled. F
Santayana, George (1863), Sonnets and Other Verses. V
Spofford, Harriet Prescott (1835), A Scarlet Poppy and Other Stories. F
Stockton, Frank R. (1834), Pomona's Travels. F
Tabb, John B. (1845), Poems. V
Warner, Charles Dudley (1829), The Golden House. F
Woolson, Constance Fenimore (1840), Horace Chase. F

Wilson-Gorman Tariff Act.
U.S. recognized Republic of Hawaii.
Bureau of Immigration created.
March of "Coxey's Army" on Washington.
Pullman Car Co. strike began railway and mining labor unrest.
Labor Day established as national holiday.
Sunday comics first appeared.
Oliver Wendell Holmes d.
E.E. Cummings b.
Mark Van Doren b.
The Chap-Book (Chicago), 1894–98.
Billboard (Cincinnati; Los Angeles), 1894–.
Charles Lawler's "The Sidewalks of New York."

Nicholas II crowned czar of Russia.
Sino-Japanese War (1894–95).
Dreyfus Affair (1894–1906).
The Yellow Book (London), 1894–97.
Robert Louis Stevenson d.
Walter Pater d.
Christina Rossetti d.
Aldous Huxley b.
Yeats's The Land of Heart's Desire.
Kipling's The Jungle Book.
Moore's Esther Waters.
Shaw's Arms and the Man.
George du Maurier's Trilby.
Hope's The Prisoner of Zenda.
Ibsen's Little Eyolf.
Feydeau's Hotel Paradiso.
Hamsun's Pan.

1895

Adams, Brooks (1848), The Law of Civilization and Decay. NF
Aldrich, Thomas Bailey (1836), Unguarded Gates. V
Bangs, John Kendrick (1862), The Idiot. F; Mr. Bonaparte of Corsica. F

Income tax law declared unconstitutional.
Venezuelan boundary dispute.

Belasco, David (1859), The Heart of Maryland. D
Brown, Alice (1857), Meadow-Grass. F
Carman, Bliss (1865), Behind the Arras: A Book of the Unseen.
  V
Chambers, Robert W. (1865), The Red Republic. F
"Charles Egbert Craddock" (1850), The Mystery of Witch-
  Face Mountain. F; The Phantoms of the Foot-Bridge. F
Coolbrith, Ina (1842), Songs from the Golden Gate. V
Crane, Stephen (1871), The Red Badge of Courage. F; The
  Black Riders and Other Lines. V
Crawford, Francis Marion (1854), The Ralstons. F; Casa
  Braccio. F
Davis, Richard Harding (1864), About Paris. NF
Dunbar, Paul Laurence (1872), Majors and Minors. V
Freeman, Mary E. Wilkins (1852), Comfort Pease and Her Gold
  Ring. F
Fuller, Henry Blake (1857), With the Procession. F
Garland, Hamlin (1860), Rose of Dutcher's Coolly. F
Gillette, William (1855), Secret Service. D
Harris, Joel Chandler (1848), Mr. Rabbit at Home. F
Hearn, Lafcadio (1850), Out of the East. NF
Howells, William Dean (1837), Stops of Various Quills. V; My
  Literary Passions. NF
James, Henry (1843), Theatricals, Second Series. D;
  Terminations. F
Jewett, Sarah Orne (1849), The Life of Nancy. F
Lowell, James Russell (d. 1891), Last Poems. V
Mitchell, John Ames (1845), Amos Judd. F
Thomas, Augustus (1857), The Capitol. D
Thoreau, Henry David (d. 1862), Poems of Nature. V
Townsend, Edward W. (1855), "Chimmie Fadden," Major
  Max, and Other Stories. F

National Association of Manufacturers
  founded.
Yerkes Observatory established, in
  Chicago.
New York Public Library consolidated.
Guglielmo Marconi's first wireless
  telegraph.
Wilhelm Roentgen discovered X-rays.
Sears, Roebuck and Co. opened mail-
  order business.
Edmund Wilson b.
William Allan White purchased the
  Emporia Gazette.
The Lark (San Francisco), 1895–97.
The Bookman (New York), 1895–1933.
M'lle New York (New York), 1895–99.

Cuba fought Spain for independence.
Lumière brothers pioneered movie
  production, in France.
Thomas Henry Huxley d.
Alexandre Dumas fils d.
Robert Graves b.
Hardy's Jude the Obscure.
Conrad's Almayer's Folly.
Meredith's The Amazing Marriage.
Pinero's The Notorious Mrs. Ebbsmith.
Wells's The Time Machine.
Wilde's The Importance of Being
  Earnest.
Yeats's Poems.
Hauptmann's Florian Geyer.
Wedekind's Earth Spirit.

1896

Abbott, Lyman (1835), Christianity and Social Problems. NF
Ade, George (1866), Artie. F
Aldrich, Thomas Bailey (1836), Judith and Holofernes. V; Later
  Lyrics. V
Allen, James Lane (1849), Aftermath. F; Summer in Arcady. F
Bangs, John Kendrick (1862), A Houseboat on the Styx. F
Berenson, Bernard (1865), Florentine Painters of the
  Renaissance. NF
"Bill Nye" (1850), History of England. F
Burroughs, John (1837), Whitman: A Study. NF
Cahan, Abraham (1860), Yekl, a Tale of the New York Ghetto.
  F
Carman, Bliss (1861), More Songs from Vagabondia (with
  Richard Hovey). V
Crane, Stephen (1871), The Little Regiment. F; George's
  Mother. F
Crawford, Francis Marion (1854), Corleone. F; Adam
  Johnstone's Son. F
Dickinson, Emily (d. 1886), Poems: Third Series. V
Dunbar, Paul Laurence (1872), Lyrics of Lowly Life. V
Frederic, Harold (1856), The Damnation of Theron Ware.
  F; March Hares. F
Harris, Joel Chandler (1848), Sister Jane: Her Friends and
  Acquaintances. F; Stories of Georgia. F; The Story of Aaron.
  F

Utah admitted to the Union.
William Jennings Bryan's "Cross of
  Gold" speech.
Klondike gold discovered; stampede
  began in 1897.
Start of "Jim Crow" (legalized
  segregation) era.
First Ford automobile assembled.
First motion pictures at Koster & Bial's
  Music Hall, in New York City.
Billy Sunday began evangelical
  preaching.
Harriet Beecher Stowe d.
John Dos Passos b.
F. Scott Fitzgerald b.
Theodore Metz's "There'll Be a Hot
  Time in the Old Town Tonight."

First modern Olympic games held, in
  Athens.
Alfred Austin named poet laureate of
  England.
Henri Becquerel discovered
  radioactivity in uranium.
The Daily Mail (London), 1896–.
William Morris d.
Conrad's An Outcast of the Islands.
A.E. Housman's A Shropshire Lad.

Hearn, Lafcadio (1850), Kokoro. NF
Howells, William Dean (1837), The Day of Their Wedding.
    F; A Parting and a Meeting. F; Impressions and Experiences.
    NF
James, Henry (1843), Embarrassments. F; The Other House. F
Jewett, Sarah Orne (1849), The Country of the Pointed Firs. F
Le Gallienne, Richard (1866), The Quest of the Golden Girl. F
"Mark Twain" (1835), Personal Recollections of Joan of Arc.
    F; Tom Sawyer, Detective. F
Reese, Lizette Woodworth (1856), A Quiet Road. V
Robinson, Edwin Arlington (1869), The Torrent and the Night
    Before. V
Santayana, George (1863), The Sense of Beauty. NF
Van Dyke, Henry (1852), The Story of the Other Wise Man. NF
Wilson, Woodrow (1856), Mere Literature and Other Essays. NF
Wister, Owen (1860), Red Men and White. F

Wells's The Island of Doctor Moreau.
Ibsen's John Gabriel Borkman.
Valery's Monsieur Teste (1896–1946).
Sienkiewicz's Quo Vadis.
Chekhov's The Sea Gull.
Jarry's Ubu Roi.
Hauptmann's The Sunken Bell.

1897

Abbott, Lyman (1835), The Theology of an Evolutionist. NF
Ade, George (1866), Pink Marsh. F
Allen, James Lane (1849), The Choir Invisible [revision of John
    Gray (1893)]. F
Bangs, John Kendrick (1862), The Pursuit of the Houseboat. F
Baylor, Frances Courtenay (1848), Miss Nina Barrow. F
Bellamy, Edward (1850), Equality. F
Berenson, Bernard (1865), Central Italian Painters of the
    Renaissance. NF
Brinton, Daniel Garrison (1837), Religions of Primitive
    People. NF
Bucke, Richard Maurice (1837), Walt Whitman, Man and Poet.
    NF
Carman, Bliss (1861), Ballads of Lost Haven: A Book of the
    Sea. V
Catherwood, Mary (1847), The Spirit of an Illinois Town. F
"Charles Egbert Craddock" (1850), The Young Mountaineers.
    F; The Juggler. F
Chopin, Kate (1851), A Night in Acadie. F
Crane, Stephen (1871), The Third Violet. F
Davis, Richard Harding (1864), Soldiers of Fortune. F
Ford, Paul Leicester (1865), The Great K & A Train Robbery. F
Freeman, Mary E. Wilkins (1852), Jerome, a Poor Man. F
Garland, Hamlin (1860), Wayside Courtships. F
George, Henry (1839), The Science of Political Economy. NF
Glasgow, Ellen (1874), The Descendant. F
Harris, Joel Chandler (1848), Aaron in the Wildwoods. F
Hearn, Lafcadio (1850), Gleanings in Buddha-Fields. NF
Hough, Emerson (1857), The Story of the Cowboy. NF
Howells, William Dean (1837), The Landlord at Lion's Head.
    F; An Open-Eyed Conspiracy: An Idyl at Saratoga. F; Stories
    of Ohio. NF; A Previous Engagement. D
James, Henry (1843), The Spoils of Poynton. F; What Maisie
    Knew. F
James, William (1842), The Will To Believe, and Other Essays
    in Popular Psychology. NF
"Mark Twain" (1835), Following the Equator. NF; How to Tell
    a Story and Other Essays. NF
Mitchell, S. Weir (1829), Hugh Wynne, Free Quaker. F
Page, Thomas Nelson (1853), The Old Gentleman of the Black
    Stock. F; Social Life in Old Virginia. NF
Riley, James Whitcomb (1849), Neighborly Poems. V

Dingley Tariff increased duties on
    imports.
U.S. anti-Spanish sentiment increased.
Coal miners' strike.
Klondike gold rush (Yukon territory).
Thornton Wilder b.
William Faulkner b.
Louise Bogan b.
Paul Dresser's "On the Banks of the
    Wabash."

Greece and Turkey at war.
Severe famine in India.
Alphonse Daudet d.
Meredith's The Idea of Comedy.
Kipling's Captains Courageous.
Yeats's The Secret Rose.
Shaw's Candida; The Devil's Disciple.
Stoker's Dracula.
Ellis's Studies in the Psychology of Sex
    (7 vols., 1897–1928).
Rostand's Cyrano de Bergerac.
Tolstoy's What is Art?
Gide's The Fruits of the Earth.
France's Contemporary History (4 vols.,
    1897–1901).

Robinson, Edwin Arlington (1869), The Children of the Night. V

Royce, Josiah (1855), The Conception of God. NF

Sheldon, Charles M. (1857), In His Steps. F

Tabb, John B. (1845), Lyrics. V

Tyler, Moses Coit (1835), The Literary History of the American Revolution, 1763–1783. NF

Wharton, Edith (1862), The Decoration of Houses (with Ogden Codman, Jr.). NF

1898

Atherton, Gertrude (1857), The Californians. F

Belasco, David (1859), Zaza. D

Bellamy, Edward (1850), The Blindman's World. F

Bierce, Ambrose (1842), In the Midst of Life [revision of Tales of Soldiers and Civilians (1891)]. F

Cahan, Abraham (1860), The Imported Bridegroom and Other Stories. F

Chapman, John Jay (1862), Emerson and Other Essays. NF

Churchill, Winston (1871), The Celebrity: An Episode. F

Crane, Stephen (1871), The Open Boat and Other Stories. F

Crawford, Francis Marion (1854), Via Crucis. F

Croly, Jane Cunningham (1829), The History of the Women's Club Movement in America. NF

De Forest, John William (1826), A Lover's Revolt. F

Deland, Margaret (1857), Old Chester Tales. F

Dunbar, Paul Laurence (1872), Folks from Dixie. V; The Uncalled. V

Dunne, Finley Peter (1867), Mr. Dooley in Peace and in War. F

Fox, John, Jr. (1863), The Kentuckians. F

Frederic, Harold (1856), The Deserter and Other Stories. F; Gloria Mundi. F

Garland, Hamlin (1860), The Spirit of Sweetwater. F; Ulysses S. Grant: His Life and Character. NF

Glasgow, Ellen (1874), Phases of an Inferior Planet. F

Guiney, Louise Imogen (1861), England and Yesterday. V

Harris, Joel Chandler (1848), Tales of the Home Folks in Peace and War. F

Hearn, Lafcadio (1850), Exotics and Retrospectives. NF

Herrick, Robert (1868), The Gospel of Freedom. F

Higginson, Thomas Wentworth (1823), Cheerful Yesterdays. NF

Hovey, Richard (1864), Along the Trail: A Book of Lyrics. V

Howells, William Dean (1837), The Story of a Play. F

James, Henry (1843), In the Cage. F; The Two Magics. F

James, William (1842), Human Immortality: Two Supposed Objections to the Doctrine. NF

Johnston, Mary (1870), Prisoners of Hope. F

Major, Charles (1856), When Knighthood Was in Flower. F

Masters, Edgar Lee (1868), A Book of Verses. V

Mitchell, S. Weir (1829), The Adventures of François. F

Norris, Frank (1870), Moran of the Lady Letty. F

Page, Thomas Nelson (1853), Red Rock. F

Parker, Lottie Blair (1859), Way Down East (pub. 1899). D

Peabody, Josephine Preston (1874), The Wayfarers. V

Riis, Jacob August (1849), Out of Mulberry Street. NF

Royce, Josiah (1855), Studies of Good and Evil. NF

Stockton, Frank R. (1834), The Great Stone of Sardis. F

Westcott, Edward Noyes (1846), David Harum; A Story of American Life. F

Wister, Owen (1860), Lin McLean. F

Annexation of the Hawaiian Islands.

Battleship Maine exploded in Havana harbor; ten-week Spanish-American War.

Annexation of Cuba, Puerto Rico, Guam, and the Philippine Islands.

First Food and Drug Act.

National Institute of Arts and Letters founded.

Harold Frederic d.

Social Democratic Party formed in Russia.

Moscow Art Theatre founded.

Pierre and Marie Curie discovered radium, in Paris.

Aubrey Beardsley d.

Lewis Carroll d.

Stéphane Mallarmé d.

Erich Maria Remarque b.

Bertolt Brecht b.

Federico García Lorca b.

Hardy's Wessex Poems.

Wells's The War of the Worlds.

Pinero's Trelawny of the "Wells."

Conrad's The Nigger of the "Narcissus."

Wilde's The Ballad of Reading Gaol.

Bridges's Poetical Works (1898–1905).

Svevo's As a Man Grows Older.

Zola's "J'accuse."

Hamsun's Victoria.

Huysmans's The Cathedral.

1899

Ade, George (1866), Doc' Horne. F; Fables in Slang. F
Antin, Mary (1881), From Plotzk to Boston. NF
Bierce, Ambrose (1842), Fantastic Fables. F
Brown, Alice (1847), Tiverton Tales. F
Cable, George Washington (1844), Strong Hearts. F
"Charles Egbert Craddock" (1850), The Bushwackers. F; The
    Story of Old Fort Loudon. F
Chesnutt, Charles Waddell (1858), The Conjure Woman.
    F; The Wife of His Youth. F; Frederick Douglass. NF
Chopin, Kate (1851), The Awakening. F
Churchill, Winston (1871), Richard Carvel. F
Crane, Stephen (1871), Active Service. F; War Is Kind. V; The
    Monster and Other Stories. F
Dewey, John (1859), The School and Society. NF
Dunbar, Paul Laurence (1872), Lyrics of the Hearthside. V
Fiske, John (1842), Through Nature to God. NF
Ford, Paul Leicester (1865), Janice Meredith. F
Frederic, Harold (d. 1898), The Market-Place. F
Garland, Hamlin (1860), Boy Life on the Prairie. F; The Trail
    of the Goldseekers. NF, V
Gillette, William (1855), Sherlock Holmes [adapted from the
    novels of Arthur Conan Doyle (1889–93)]. D
Guiney, Louise Imogen (1861), The Martyrs' Idyl. V
Harris, Joel Chandler (1848), Plantation Pageants. F; The
    Chronicles of Aunt Minervy Ann. F
Hearn, Lafcadio (1850), In Ghostly Japan. NF
Herne, James A. (1839), Sag Harbor [revision of Hearts of Oak
    (1879)]. D; The Reverend Griffith Davenport (pub. 1940). D
Higginson, Thomas Wentworth (1823), Old Cambridge. NF
Howells, William Dean (1837), Ragged Lady. F; Their Silver
    Wedding Journey. F
Hubbard, Elbert (1856), A Message to Garcia. NF
Huneker, James Gibbons (1857), Mezzotints in Modern Music.
    NF
James, Henry (1843), The Awkward Age. F
James, William (1842), Talks to Teachers on Psychology. NF
Jewett, Sarah Orne (1849), The Queen's Twin and Other
    Stories. F
Markham, Edwin (1852), The Man with the Hoe and Other
    Poems. V
Norris, Frank (1870), McTeague. F; Blix. F
Santayana, George (1863), Lucifer: A Theological Tragedy. D
Tarkington, Booth (1869), The Gentleman from Indiana. F
Thomas, Augustus (1857), Arizona. D
Timrod, Henry (d. 1867), Complete Poems. V
Veblen, Thorstein (1857), The Theory of the Leisure Class. NF
Warner, Charles Dudley (1829), That Fortune. F
Washington, Booker T. (1856), The Future of the American
    Negro. NF
Wharton, Edith (1862), The Greater Inclination. F

Annexation of Wake Island.
Beginning of "Open Door Policy" with
    China.
Philippines insurrection (1899–1901).
Gideons (international Bible society)
    organized.
Who's Who in America first published.
Charles Dana Gibson's sketches of "the
    Gibson Girl."
Ernest Hemingway b.
Allen Tate b.
Hart Crane b.
Pearson's Magazine (New York),
    1899–1925.
The American Boy (Detroit), 1899–
    1929.
Scott Joplin's "Maple Leaf Rag."

Boer War began in South Africa (1899–
    1902).
First Hague Peace Conference.
Action Française (anti-republican
    group) founded in France.
Elizabeth Bowen b.
Vladimir Nabokov b.
Jorge Luis Borges b.
Shaw's You Never Can Tell.
Kipling's Stalky & Co.
Yeats's The Wind Among the Reeds.
Symons's The Symbolist Movement in
    Literature.
Feydeau's The Lady from Maxim's.
Tolstoy's Resurrection.
Chekhov's Uncle Vanya.
Ibsen's When We Dead Awaken.
Machado de Assis's Dom Casmurro.

1900

Adams, Brooks (1848), America's Economic Supremacy. NF
Adams, Charles Francis (1835), Charles Francis Adams [1807–
    1886]. NF
Ade, George (1866), More Fables. F
Allen, James Lane (1849), Chimney Corner Graduates. F; The
    Reign of Law. F
Atherton, Gertrude (1857), Senator North. F

Gold Standard Act passed by Congress.
International Ladies' Garment Worker's
    Union established.
Carry Nation began crusade against
    saloons.
Hall of Fame founded, in New York
    City.

129

Bacheller, Irving (1859), Eben Holden. F
Baum, L. Frank (1856), The Wonderful Wizard of Oz. F
Belasco, David (1853), Madame Butterfly [adapted from John
  Luther Long's short story (1898), pub. 1917]. D
Bellamy, Edward (d. 1898), The Duke of Stockbridge: A
  Romance of Shays' Rebellion. F
Burgess, Gelett (1866), Goops and How to Be Them. F, V
Burroughs, John (1837), Squirrels and Other Fur-Bearers.
  NF; The Light of Day. NF
Chesnutt, Charles Waddell (1858), The House Behind the
  Cedars. F
Crane, Stephen (1871), Wounds in the Rain, F, NF;
  Whilomville Stories. F
Crawford, Francis Marion (1854), In the Palace of the King. F
De Forest, John William (1826), The DeForests of Avesnes. NF
Dreiser, Theodore (1871), Sister Carrie (printed but withheld;
  reissued in 1907). F
Dunbar, Paul Laurence (1872), The Strength of Gideon and
  Other Stories. F; The Love of Landry. F
Dunne, Finley Peter (1867), Mr. Dooley's Philosophy. F
Freeman, Mary E. Wilkins (1852), The Heart's Highway. F
Garland, Hamlin (1860), The Eagle's Heart. F
Glasgow, Ellen (1874), The Voice of the People. F
Grant, Robert (1852), Unleavened Bread. F
Harland, Henry (1861), The Cardinal's Snuff-Box. F
Harris, Joel Chandler (1848), On the Wing of Occasions. F
Hearn, Lafcadio (1850), Shadowings. NF
Herrick, Robert (1868), The Web of Life. F
Howells, William Dean (1837), Literary Friends and
  Acquaintance. NF; Room Forty-five. D; Bride Roses. D; The
  Smoking Car. D; An Indian Giver. D
Huneker, James Gibbons (1857), Chopin: The Man and His
  Music. NF
James, Henry (1843), The Soft Side. F
Johnston, Mary (1870), To Have and To Hold. F
London, Jack (1876), The Son of the Wolf. F
"Mark Twain" (1835), The Man That Corrupted Hadleyburg
  and Other Stories and Essays. F, NF
Mitchell, S. Weir (1829), Dr. North and His Friends. F
Moody, William Vaughn (1869), The Masque of Judgment. D
Norris, Frank (1870), A Man's Woman. F
Peabody, Josephine Preston (1874), Fortune and Men's Eyes. D
Santayana, George (1863), Interpretations of Poetry and
  Religion. NF
Slocum, Joshua (1844), Sailing Alone Around the World. NF
Tarkington, Booth (1869), Monsieur Beaucaire. F
Thompson, Maurice (1844), Alice of Old Vincennes. F
Torrence, Ridgely (1875), The House of a Hundred Lights. V
Wharton, Edith (1862), The Touchstone. F
Wister, Owen (1860), The Jimmyjohn Boss. F

Stephen Crane d.
Thomas Wolfe b.
World's Work (New York), 1900–32.
Smart Set (New York), 1900–30.

Boxer Rebellion in China (1900–01).
World Exposition opened in Paris.
Umberto I assassinated; Victor
  Emmanuel III crowned king of Italy.
Max Planck proposed quantum theory.
Niels Bohr proposed theory of atomic
  structure.
Prix Goncourt established in France.
Friedrich Nietzsche d.
John Ruskin d.
Oscar Wilde d.
Antoine de Saint-Exupéry b.
Conrad's *Lord Jim.*
Wells's *Love and Mr. Lewisham.*
Shaw's *Captain Brassbound's
  Conversion.*
Saintsbury's *A History of Criticism and
  Literary Taste in Europe* (3 vols.,
  1900–04).
Freud's *The Interpretation of Dreams.*
Colette's *Claudine at School.*

1901

Ade, George (1866), Forty Modern Fables. F
Belasco, David (1853), Du Barry (pub. 1928). D
Berenson, Bernard (1865), Study and Criticism of Italian Art.
  NF
Brownell, William C. (1851), Victorian Prose Masters. NF
Cable, George Washington (1844), The Cavalier. F

President McKinley shot at Buffalo
  Exposition, died eight days later.
Socialist Party founded by Eugene V.
  Debs and others.
Walter Reed discovered cause and
  transmission of yellow fever.

Carman, Bliss (1861), Last Songs from Vagabondia (with Richard Hovey). V

Chesnutt, Charles Waddell (1858), The Marrow of Tradition. F

Churchill, Winston (1871), The Crisis. F

Crane, Stephen (d. 1900), Great Battles of the World. NF

Crawford, Francis Marion (1854), Marietta. F

De Forest, John William (1826), The Downing Legends. NF

Dunbar, Paul Laurence (1872), The Fanatics. F

Dunne, Finley Peter (1867), Mr. Dooley's Opinions. F

Fitch, Clyde (1865), The Climbers. D; Captain Jinks of the Horse Marines. D

Freeman, Mary E. Wilkins (1852), The Portion of Labor. F

Fuller, Henry Blake (1857), Under the Skylights. F

Garland, Hamlin (1860), Her Mountain Lover. F

Grant, Robert (1852), Unleavened Bread [with Leo Ditrichstein, adapted from Grant's novel (1900)]. D

Hearn, Lafcadio (1850), A Japanese Miscellany. NF

Herrick, Robert (1868), The Real World. F

Howells, William Dean (1837), A Pair of Patient Lovers. F; Heroines of Fiction. NF

James, Henry (1843), The Sacred Fount. F

Jewett, Sarah Orne (1849), The Tory Lover. F

London, Jack (1876), The God of His Fathers. F

McCutcheon, George Barr (1866), Graustark. F

Markham, Edwin (1852), Lincoln and Other Poems. V

Mitchell, S. Weir (1829), Circumstance. F

Moody, William Vaughn (1869), Poems. V

Muir, John (1838), Our National Parks. NF

Norris, Frank (1870), The Octopus. F

Paine, Albert Bigelow (1861), The Great White Way. D

Peabody, Josephine Preston (1874), Marlowe. D

Phillips, David Graham (1867), The Great God Success. F

Repplier, Agnes (1858), The Fireside Sphinx. NF

Rice, Alice Hegan (1870), Mrs. Wiggs of the Cabbage Patch. F

Riis, Jacob August (1849), The Making of an American. NF

Santayana, George (1863), A Hermit of Carmel and Other Poems. V

Sinclair, Upton (1878), Springtime and Harvest (repub. as King Midas, 1901). F

Tarkington, Booth (1869), Monsieur Beaucaire. D

Washington, Booker T. (1856), Up from Slavery. NF

Wharton, Edith (1862), Crucial Instances. F

J.P. Morgan founded U.S. Steel Corp.

Oil deposits discovered in Texas.

Marconi's first transatlantic radio signal.

James A. Herne d.

Glenway Wescott b.

Death of Victoria; accession of Edward VII.

Social Revolutionary Party founded in Russia.

First Nobel prizes awarded.

André Malraux b.

Salvatore Quasimodo b.

Butler's *Erewhon Revisited.*

Hardy's *Poems of the Past and Present.*

Kipling's *Kim.*

Meredith's *A Reading of Life.*

Barrie's *Quality Street.*

Thomas Mann's *Buddenbrooks.*

Chekhov's *Three Sisters.*

Schnitzler's *None But the Brave.*

Lagerlöf's *Jerusalem.*

Strindberg's *Dance of Death.*

1902

Adams, Brooks (1848), The New Empire. NF

Addams, Jane (1860), Democracy and Social Ethics. NF

Ade, George (1866), The Girl Proposition. F; The Sultan of Sulu (pub. 1903). D

Akers, Elizabeth (1832), The Sunset Song. V

Aldrich, Thomas Bailey (1836), A Sea Turn and Other Matters. F

Atherton, Gertrude (1857), The Conqueror. F; The Splendid Idle Forties [revision of her short stories Before the Gringo Came (1894)]. F

Belasco, David (1853), The Darling of the Gods (with John Luther Long; pub. 1928). D

Cable, George Washington (1844), Bylow Hill. F

Carnegie, Andrew (1835), The Empire of Business. NF

Cawein, Madison (1865), Kentucky Poems. V

Pennsylvania anthracite coal strike.

Republic of Cuba proclaimed.

Telegraph cable from California to Hawaii.

The Life of an American Fireman, Edwin S. Porter's first dramatic film.

Bret Harte d.

Frank Norris d.

John Steinbeck b.

Langston Hughes b.

The South Atlantic Quarterly (Durham, N.C.), 1902–.

First international Court of Arbitration (The Hague).

Edward VII established the Order of Merit.

Crane, Stephen (d. 1900), Last Words. F, NF
Crawford, Francis Marion (1854), Francesca da Rimini. D
Davis, Richard Harding (1864), Ranson's Folly. F; Captain
  Macklin. F
De Forest, John William (1826), Poem: Medley and Palestrina.
  V
Dewey, John (1859), The Educational Situation. NF
Dixon, Thomas (1864), The Leopard's Spots. F
Dunbar, Paul Laurence (1872), The Sport of the Gods. F
Fitch, Clyde (1865), The Girl with the Green Eyes (pub. 1905).
  D
Garland, Hamlin (1860), The Captain of the Gray-Horse Troop.
  F
Glasgow, Ellen (1874), The Freeman and Other Poems. V; The
  Battle-Ground. F
Harris, Joel Chandler (1848), Gabriel Tolliver. F; The Making
  of a Statesman. F
Harte, Bret (1836), Condensed Novels: Second Series. F
Hearn, Lafcadio (1850), Kottō. NF
Howells, William Dean (1837), The Kentons. F; The Flight of
  Pony Baker. F; Literature and Life. NF
Huneker, James Gibbons (1857), Melomaniacs. NF
James, Henry (1843), The Wings of the Dove. F
James, William (1842), The Varieties of Religious Experience.
  NF
Johnston, Mary (1870), Audrey. F
Keller, Helen (1880), The Story of My Life. NF
London, Jack (1876), A Daughter of the Snows. F; Children of
  the Frost. F; The Cruise of the Dazzler. F
Lorimer, George Horace (1867), Letters from a Self-Made
  Merchant to His Son. NF
McCutcheon, George Barr (1866), Brewster's Millions. F
Major, Charles (1856), Dorothy Vernon of Haddon Hall. F
"Mark Twain" (1835), A Double-Barrelled Detective Story. F
Masters, Edgar Lee (1868), Maximilian. D
Riis, Jacob August (1849), The Battle with the Slum. NF
Riley, James Whitcomb (1849), The Book of Joyous Children.
  V
Robinson, Edwin Arlington (1869), Captain Craig. V
Stickney, Trumbull (1874), Dramatic Verses. V
Tabb, John B. (1845), Later Lyrics. V
Wharton, Edith (1862), The Valley of Decision. F
Whitlock, Brand (1869), The 13th District. F
Wister, Owen (1860), The Virginian. F

Samuel Butler d.
Lionel Johnson d.
Emile Zola d.
Carlo Levi b.
TLS: Times Literary Supplement
  (London), 1902–.
Barrie's The Admirable Crichton.
Conrad's Youth and Two Other Stories.
Kipling's Just So Stories.
Doyle's The Hound of the Baskervilles.
Masefield's Salt-Water Ballads.
Bennett's Anna of the Five Towns.
Shaw's Mrs. Warren's Profession.
Yeats's Cathleen ni Houlihan.
Gide's The Immoralist.
Gorky's The Lower Depths.

1903

Abbott, Lyman (1835), Henry Ward Beecher. NF
Adams, Andy (1859), The Log of a Cowboy. F
Ade, George (1866), In Babel. F; People You Knew. F; The
  County Chairman (pub. 1924). D
Allen, James Lane (1849), The Mettle of the Pasture. F
Austin, Mary (1868), The Land of Little Rain. NF
Bierce, Ambrose (1842), Shapes of Clay. V
"Bill Arp" (1826), Bill Arp: From the Uncivil War to Date. F
Cather, Willa (1873), April Twilights. V
"Charles Egbert Craddock" (1850), A Spectre of Power. F
Crane, Stephen (d. 1900), The O'Ruddy (completed by Robert
  Barr). F
Crawford, Francis Marion (1854), The Heart of Rome. F
Davis, Richard Harding (1864), The Bar Sinister. F

Departments of Commerce and Labor
  established.
U.S. recognized Republic of Panama.
Pacific cable opened from San
  Francisco to Manila.
Wright brothers' first successful flight at
  Kitty Hawk, N.C.
Ford Motor Co. founded.
First transcontinental automobile trip.
The Great Train Robbery, Edwin S.
  Porter's first "Western" film.
Kay Boyle b.
Erskine Caldwell b.
James Gould Cozzens b.
Camera Work (New York), 1903–17.
Modern Philology (Chicago), 1903–.

Deland, Margaret (1857), Dr. Lavendar's People. F
Dewey, John (1859), Studies in Logical Theory. NF
DuBois, William E. B. (1868), The Souls of Black Folk. F, V
Dunbar, Paul Laurence (1872), Lyrics of Love and Laughter.
  V; In Old Plantation Days. F
Fox, John, Jr. (1863), The Little Shepherd of Kingdom Come. F
Freeman, Mary E. Wilkins (1852), The Wind in the Rose-Bush.
  F
Garland, Hamlin (1860), Hesper. F
Harris, Joel Chandler (1848), Wally Wanderoon and His Story-
  Telling Machine. F
Howells, William Dean (1837), Questionable Shapes. F; Letters
  Home. F
James, Henry (1843), The Ambassadors. F; The Better Sort.
  F; William Wetmore Story and His Friends. NF
London, Jack (1876), The Call of the Wild. F; The Kempton-
  Wace Letters (with Anna Strunsky). F, NF; The People of the
  Abyss. NF
"Mark Twain" (1835), My Debut as a Literary Person. NF
Mencken, H. L. (1880), Ventures into Verse. V
Monroe, Harriet (1860), The Passing Show. D
Norris, Frank (d. 1902), The Pit. F; A Deal in Wheat. F; The
  Responsibilities of the Novelist. NF
Page, Thomas Nelson (1853), Gordon Keith. F
Peabody, Josephine Preston (1874), The Singing Leaves. V
Phillips, David Graham (1867), Golden Fleece. F; The Master-
  Rogue. F
Saltus, Edgar (1855), Purple and Fine Women. F
Sinclair, Upton (1878), Prince Hagen. F; The Journal of Arthur
  Stirling. F
Sterling, George (1869), The Testimony of the Suns. V
Torrence, Ridgely (1875), El Dorado. D
Trowbridge, J. T. (1827), Poetical Works. V; My Own Story.
  NF
Wharton, Edith (1862), Sanctuary. F
Wiggin, Kate Douglas (1856), Rebecca of Sunnybrook Farm. F
Wister, Owen (1860), Philosophy 4. F

Russian Social Democratic Party split
  into Mensheviks and Bolsheviks.
William Ernest Henley d.
George Gissing d.
Evelyn Waugh b.
Alan Paton b.
Conrad's *Typhoon and Other Stories*.
Yeats's *Ideas of Good and Evil; In the
  Seven Woods*.
Russell's *Principles of Mathematics*.
Butler's *The Way of All Flesh*.
Thomas Mann's *Tonio Kröger*.
Hauptmann's *Rose Bernd*.
Hofmannsthal's *Electra*.

1904

Adams, Henry (1838), Mont-Saint-Michel and Chartres. NF
Ade, George (1866), Breaking into Society. F; True Bills.
  F; The College Widow (pub. 1924). D
Aldrich, Thomas Bailey (1836), Judith of Bethulia. D
Belasco, David (1853), Adrea (with John Luther Long; pub.
  1928). D
Braithwaite, William Stanley (1878), Lyrics of Life and Love.
  V
Burroughs, John (1837), Far and Near. NF
Cabell, James Branch (1879), The Eagle's Shadow. F
"Charles Egbert Craddock" (1850), The Frontiersmen. F
Churchill, Winston (1871), The Crossing. F
Conway, Moncure D. (1854), Autobiography. NF
Darrow, Clarence (1857), Farmington. F
Davis, Richard Harding (1864), The Dictator (pub. 1909).
  D; Ranson's Folly[adapted from his short stories (1902)]. D
Debs, Eugene V. (1855), Unionism and Socialism, a Plea for
  Both. NF; The American Movement. NF
Garland, Hamlin (1860), The Light of the Star. F
Glasgow, Ellen (1874), The Deliverance. F

Panama Canal project begun under
  American auspices (opened 1914).
St. Louis Exposition.
New York City subway opened.
First Olympic Games held in America
  (St. Louis).
Frank Lloyd Wright designed first
  poured concrete building, in
  Chicago.
American Academy of Arts and Letters
  founded.
Lafcadio Hearn d.
James T. Farrell b.
Isaac Bashevis Singer b.

France and Britain signed Entente
  Cordiale.
Russo-Japanese War (1904–05).
Abbey Theatre (Dublin) opened.
Anton Chekhov d.
Christopher Isherwood b.
Graham Greene b.

Grant, Robert (1852), The Undercurrent. F
Harris, Joel Chandler (1848), A Little Union Scout. F; The Tar Baby and Other Rhymes of Uncle Remus. V
Hearn, Lafcadio (1850), Kwaidan. NF; Japan: An Attempt at Interpretation. NF
Herrick, Robert (1868), The Common Lot. F
Howells, William Dean (1837), The Son of Royal Langbrith. F
Huneker, James Gibbons (1857), Overtones. NF
James, Henry (1843), The Golden Bowl. F
London, Jack (1876), The Faith of Men. F; The Sea-Wolf. F
"Mark Twain" (1835), Extracts from Adam's Diary. F; A Dog's Tale. F
Moody, William Vaughn (1869), The Fire-Bringer. D
More, Paul Elmer (1864), Shelburne Essays (14 vols., 1904–36). NF
Nation, Carry (1846), The Use and Need of the Life of Carry A. Nation. NF
"O. Henry" (1862), Cabbages and Kings. F
Page, Thomas Nelson (1853), Bred in the Bone. F
Peabody, Josephine Preston (1874), Pan, A Choric Idyl. V
Phillips, David Graham (1867), The Cost. F
Pollock, Channing (1880), The Pit [adapted from Frank Norris's novel (1903)]. D
Repplier, Agnes(1858), Compromises. NF
Saltus, Edgar (1855), The Pomps of Satan. F
Sandburg, Carl (1878), In Reckless Ecstasy. V
Sinclair, Upton (1878), Manassas: A Novel of the War.F
Steffens, Lincoln (1866), The Shame of the Cities. NF
Stratton-Porter, Gene (1863), Freckles. F
Tabb, John B. (1845), The Rosary in Rhyme. V
Tarbell, Ida M. (1857), The History of the Standard Oil Company. NF
Veblen, Thorstein (1857), The Theory of Business Enterprise. NF
Wharton, Edith (1862), Italian Villas and Their Gardens. NF; The Descent of Man. F

Conrad's Nostromo.
Hardy's The Dynasts (1904–08).
Hudson's Green Mansions.
Barrie's Peter Pan.
Shaw's John Bull's Other Island.
Yeats's On Bailie's Strand
Synge's Riders to the Sea.
Bradley's Shakespearean Tragedy.
Corvo's Hadrian the Seventh.
Chekhov's The Cherry Orchard.
Rolland's Jean-Christophe (10 vols., 1904–12).
Blok's Verses About the Lady Beautiful.

1905

Adams, Andy (1859), The Outlet. F
Ade, George (1866), Just Out of College (pub. 1924). D
Austin, Mary (1868), Isidro. F
Belasco, David (1853), The Girl of the Golden West (pub. 1915. D
Burroughs, John (1837), Ways of Nature. NF
Cabell, James Branch (1879), The Line of Love. F
Cather, Willa (1873), The Troll Garden. F
Cawein, Madison (1865), Vale of Tempe. V
"Charles Egbert Craddock" (1850), The Storm Centre. F
Chesnutt, Charles Waddell (1858), The Colonel's Dream. F
Debs, Eugene V. (1855), Industrial Unionism. NF
DeLeon, Daniel (1852), Socialist Reconstruction of Society. NF
Dixon, Thomas (1864), The Clansman. F
Dunbar, Paul Laurence (1872), Lyrics of Sunshine and Shadow. V
Garland, Hamlin (1860), The Tyranny of the Dark. F
Gillette, William (1885), Clarice. D
Grant, Robert (1852), The Orchid. F
Harris, Joel Chandler (1848), Told by Uncle Remus: New Stories of the Old Plantation. F

Yellow fever epidemic in New Orleans.
Industrial Workers of the World founded, in Chicago.
Niagara Movement organized to protest discrimination against Negroes.
First Rotary Club meeting, in Chicago.
Alfred Stieglitz opened "291" Gallery, in New York City.
First motion picture theatre (nickelodeon) opened, in Pittsburgh.
George Pierce Baker's "47 Workshop" at Harvard (1905–25).
Shaw's Mrs. Warren's Profession banned in New York City.
John O'Hara b.
Lillian Hellman b.
Robert Penn Warren b.
Variety (New York), 1905–.
The American Magazine (New York), 1905–56.
───────────
Sinn Fein (Irish Nationalists) organized in Dublin.

Herrick, Robert (1868), The Memoirs of an American Citizen. NF

Howells, William Dean (1837), Miss Bellard's Inspiration. F; London Films. NF

Huneker, James Gibbons (1857), Iconoclasts, a Book of Dramatists. NF; Visionaries. F

James, Henry (1843), The Question of Our Speech, and The Lesson of Balzac. NF; English Hours. NF

James, William (1842), The Sentiments of Rationality. NF

London, Jack (1876), War of the Classes. NF; The Game. F; Tales of the Fish Patrol. F

"Mark Twain" (1835), King Leopold's Soliloquy. F

Mencken, H. L. (1880), George Bernard Shaw: His Plays. NF

Mitchell, S. Weir (1829), Constance Trescot. F

"Octave Thanet" (1850), The Man of the Hour. F

Peabody, Josephine Preston (1874), The Wings. D

Phillips, David Graham (1867), The Deluge. F; The Plum Tree. F

Saltus, Edgar (1855), The Perfume of Eros. F

Santayana, George (1863), The Life of Reason (5 vols., 1905–06). NF

Stickney, Trumbull (d. 1904), Poems. V

Tarkington, Booth (1869), The Conquest of Canaan. F

Wharton, Edith (1862), The House of Mirth. F; Italian Backgrounds. NF

Wheelock, John Hall (1886), Verses by Two Undergraduates (with Van Wyck Brooks). V

Fauvists stirred Parisian art circles.
Haakon VII elected king of Norway.
Czar Nicholas granted Russia a constitution after a revolutionary uprising.
Einstein proposed the theory of relativity.
Jules Verne d.
Anthony Powell b.
Arthur Koestler b.
Jean-Paul Sartre b.
Mikhail Sholokhov b.
Forster's *Where Angels Fear to Tread.*
Shaw's *Major Barbara; Man and Superman.*
Synge's *The Well of the Saints.*
Wilde's *De Profundis.*
Doyle's *The Return of Sherlock Holmes.*
Barrie's *Alice-Sit-by-the-Fire.*
Orczy's *The Scarlet Pimpernel.*

1906

Adams, Andy (1859), Cattle Brands. F

Adams, Samuel Hopkins (1871), The Great American Fraud. NF

Ade, George (1866), In Pastures New. F

Atherton, Gertrude (1857), Rezánov. F

Beach, Rex (1877), The Spoilers. F

Bierce, Ambrose (1842), The Cynic's Word Book. NF

Burgess, Gelett (1866), Are You a Bromide? F, V

Burroughs, John (1837), Bird and Bough. NF

Butler, Ellis Parker (1869), Pigs Is Pigs. F

"Charles Egbert Craddock" (1850), The Amulet. F

Churchill, Winston (1871), Coniston. F

Cohan, George M. (1878), Forty-Five Minutes from Broadway. D

Crothers, Rachel (1878), The Three of Us. D

Davis, Owen (1874), Nellie, the Beautiful Cloak Model. D

Davis, Richard Harding (1864), Miss Civilization. D

Deland, Margaret (1857), The Awakening of Helena Richie. F

Dunne, Finley Peter (1867), Dissertations by Mr. Dooley, F

Gale, Zona (1874), Romance Island. F

Glasgow, Ellen (1874), The Wheel of Life. F

Howells, William Dean (1837), Certain Delightful English Towns. NF

Leonard, William Ellery (1876), Sonnets and Poems. V

London, Jack (1876), Moon-Face and Other Stories. F; White Fang. F; Scorn of Women. D; Before Adam. F; Love of Life and Other Stories. F

MacKaye, Percy (1875), Jeanne d'Arc. D

"Mark Twain" (1835), Eve's Diary. F; The $30,000 Bequest. F

Mitchell, Langdon (1862), The New York Idea (pub. 1908). D

Moody, William Vaughn (1860), A Sabine Woman (prod.). D

Norris, Frank (d. 1902), The Joyous Miracle. F

San Francisco earthquake and fire.
Severe anti-Negro riots in Atlanta.
Series of coal mine disasters (1906–10).
Pure Food and Drug Act.
President Roosevelt first used the word "muckraker."
First radio transmission of speech and music.
Ruth St. Denis introduced modern dance.
New First Church of Christ Scientist dedicated, in Boston.
Clifford Odets b.
George M. Cohan's "Forty five Minutes from Broadway."

First Russian parliament (Duma) opened.
Simplon Tunnel connected Switzerland and Italy.
Henrik Ibsen d.
Samuel Beckett b.
Galsworthy's *The Man of Property.*
Kipling's *Puck of Pook's Hill.*
Shaw's *The Doctor's Dilemma.*
Conrad's *The Mirror of the Sea.*
Yeats's *Poems 1899–1905.*
Blok's *The Puppet Show.*
Hauptmann's *And Pippa Dances.*
Hofmannsthal's *Oedipus and the Sphinx.*
Musil's *The Confusions of Young Törless*

"O. Henry" (1862), The Four Million. F
Poole, Ernest (1880), The Voice of the Street. F
Saltus, Edgar (1855), Vanity Square. F
Sinclair, Upton (1878), The Jungle. F; A Captain of Industry. F
Smith, Winchell (1871), Brewster's Millions [adapted with
  Byron Ongley from George Barr McCutcheon's novel (1902)].
  D
Steffens, Lincoln (1866), The Struggle for Self-Government. NF
Thoreau, Henry David (d. 1862), Journal (14 vols., ed.
  Bradford Torrey and Francis H. Allen). NF
Traubel, Horace L. (1858), With Walt Whitman in Camden (5
  vols., 1906–64). NF
Williams, Jesse Lynch (1871), The Stolen Story. D
Wister, Owen (1860), Lady Baltimore. F

1907

Adams, Andy (1859), Reed Anthony, Cowman. F
Adams, Henry (1838), The Education of Henry Adams: An
  Autobiography (privately printed; pub. posth., 1918). NF
Ade, George (1866), The Slim Princess. F
Baum, L. Frank (1856), Ozma of Oz. F
Bynner, Witter (1881), An Ode to Harvard and Other Poems. V
Cabell, James Branch (1879), Gallantry. F
"Charles Egbert Craddock" (1850), The Windfall. F
Cohan, George M. (1878), The Talk of New York. D
Dixon, Thomas (1864), The Traitor. F
Fisher, Dorothy Canfield (1879), Gunhild. F
Gale, Zona (1874), The Loves of Pelleas and Etarre. F
Garland, Hamlin (1860), The Long Trail. F; Money Magic. F
Harris, Joel Chandler (1848), Uncle Remus and Brer Rabbit. F
Howells, William Dean (1837), Through the Eye of a Needle.
  F; Between the Dark and the Daylight. F
James, Henry (1843), The American Scene. NF
James, William (1842), Pragmatism: A New Name for Some Old
  Ways of Thinking. NF
London, Jack (1876), The Road. NF
MacKaye, Percy (1875), Sappho and Phaon. D
Mitchell, S. Weir (1829), The Red City. F
Neihardt, John G. (1881), The Lonesome Trail. F
"O. Henry" (1862), The Trimmed Lamp. F; Heart of the West.
  F
Phillips, David Graham (1867), Light-Fingered Gentry. F; The
  Second Generation. F
Teasdale, Sara (1884), Sonnets to Duse and Other Poems. V
Thomas, Augustus (1857), The Witching Hour. D
Torrence, Ridgely (1875), Abelard and Héloïse. D
Wharton, Edith (1862), Madame de Treymes. F; The Fruit of
  the Tree. F
Whitlock, Brand (1869), The Turn of the Balance. F
Wister, Owen (1860), The Seven Ages of Washington. NF
Wright, Harold Bell (1872), The Shepherd of the Hills. F

U.S. Marines landed in Honduras.
Brief financial panic.
Oklahoma admitted to the Union.
American fleet sent around the world
  (1907–09).
Japanese laborers denied entry into
  U.S.
Albert Michelson became first
  American Nobel laureate (physics).
Lee De Forest patented the "Audion"
  (vacuum tube).
First Ziegfeld Follies.
Strauss's *Salomé* outraged New York
  City.

Second Hague Peace Conference.
Robert Baden-Powell founded Boy
  Scouts in England.
Beginning of Cubism in modern art.
Francis Thompson d.
Alfred Jarry d.
W.H. Auden b.
Cambridge History of English Literature
  (14 vols., 1907–16).
Conrad's *The Secret Agent.*
Forster's *The Longest Journey.*
Joyce's *Chamber Music.*
Shaw's *Ceasar and Cleopatra.*
Synge's *The Playboy of the Western
  World.*
Yeats's *Deirdre.*
Gorky's *Mother.*
Rilke's *New Poems.*
Feydeau's *A Flea in Her Ear.*
Strindberg's *The Ghost Sonata.*
Bergson's *Creative Evolution.*

1908

Ade, George (1866), Father and the Boys (pub. 1924). D
Beers, Clifford (1876), A Mind That Found Itself. NF
Braithwaite, William Stanley (1878), The House of Falling
  Leaves. V

Unemployment followed financial
  panic.
Child labor laws.
First Model T Ford produced.

Cable, George Washington (1844), Kincaid's Battery. F
"Charles Egbert Craddock" (1850), The Fair Mississippian. F
Chester, George Randolph (1869), Get-Rich-Quick
  Wallingford. F
Churchill, Winston (1871), Mr. Crewe's Career. F
Fox, John, Jr. (1863), The Trail of the Lonesome Pine. F
Gale, Zona (1874), Friendship Village. F
Garland, Hamlin (1860), The Shadow World. NF
Glasgow, Ellen (1874), The Ancient Law. F
Herrick, Robert (1868), The Master of the Inn. F; Together. F
Howells, William Dean (1837), Fennel and Rue. F; Roman
  Holidays and Others. NF
James, Henry (1843), Views and Reviews. NF
Lewisohn, Ludwig (1882), The Broken Snare. F
London, Jack (1876), The Iron Heel. F
MacKaye, Percy (1875), The Scarecrow. D; Mater. D
"O. Henry" (1862), The Voice of the City. F; The Gentle
  Grafter. F
Page, Thomas Nelson (1853), The Old Dominion: Her Making
  and Her Manners. NF
Phillips, David Graham (1867), Old Wives for New. F; The
  Worth of a Woman. D
Pound, Ezra (1885), A Lume Spento. V
Rinehart, Mary Roberts (1876), The Circular Staircase. F
Sheldon, Edward (1886), Salvation Nell. D
Sinclair, Upton (1878), The Metropolis. F
Walter, Eugene (1874), Paid in Full. D
Wharton, Edith (1862), A Motor-Flight Through France.
  NF; The Hermit and the Wild Woman. F
Wilson, Woodrow (1856), Constitutional Government in the
  United States. NF

Beginning of film censorship.
Singer Building in New York City, first
  U.S. skyscraper.
Isadora Duncan's second American
  dance tour.
Ashcan School of realistic painters, in
  New York City.
Joel Chandler Harris d.
Theodore Roethke b.
Richard Wright b.
The Christian Science Monitor (Boston),
  1908–.

First Balkan crisis.
Carlos I of Portugal assassinated.
Sir Robert Baden-Powell founded the
  Boy Scouts, in England.
The English Review (London), 1908–
  37.
Cesare Pavese b.
Simone de Beauvoir b.
Forster's *A Room with a View*.
Barrie's *What Every Woman Knows*.
Bennett's *The Old Wives' Tale*.
Grahame's *The Wind in the Willows*.
Shaw's *Getting Married*.
France's *Penguin Island*.

1909

Allen, James Lane (1849), The Bride of the Mistletoe. F
Armstrong, Paul (1869), Alias Jimmy Valentine [adapted from
  O. Henry's short story "A Retrieved Reformation" (1903)]. D
Baum, L. Frank (1856), The Road to Oz. F
Bierce, Ambrose (1842), The Shadow on the Dial. NF; Write it
  Right. NF; Collected Works (12 vols., 1909–12). F, NF, V
Brooks, Van Wyck (1886), The Wine of the Puritans. NF
Brownell, William C. (1851), American Prose Masters. NF
Cabell, James Branch (1879), Chivalry. F; The Cords of
  Vanity. F
Cable, George Washington (1844), "Posson Jone'" and Père
  Raphaël. F
Crawford, Francis Marion (1854), Stradella. F
Croly, Herbert (1869), The Promise of American Life. NF
Crothers, Rachel (1878), A Man's World (pub. 1915). D
Dewey, John (1859), Moral Principles in Education. NF
DuBois, William E. B. (1868), John Brown. NF
Fitch, Clyde (1865), The City. D
Gale, Zona (1874), Friendship Village Love Stories. F
Garland, Hamlin (1860), Moccasin Ranch: A Story of Dakota. F
Glasgow, Ellen (1874), The Romance of a Plain Man. F
Grant, Robert (1852), The Chippendales. F
Guiney, Louise Imogen (1861), Happy Ending. V
Harris, Joel Chandler (d. 1908), The Bishop and the
  Boogerman. F; The Shadow Between His Shoulder-Blades. F
Howells, William Dean (1837), The Mother and the Father:
  Dramatic Passages. V; Seven English Cities. NF

Payne-Aldrich Tariff Act (high
  protective rates).
Rise of the "Progressive" movement.
"Dollar diplomacy" supported U.S.
  commercial enterprises abroad.
U.S. Copyright Act adopted.
Admiral Peary reached North Pole.
National Association for the
  Advancement of Colored People
  (NAACP) founded.
First issue of Lincoln penny.
Francis Marion Crawford d.
Sarah Orne Jewett d.
Nelson Algren b.
Eudora Welty b.

Albert I crowned king of the Belgians.
Sergei Diaghilev founded Ballet Russe,
  in Paris.
Charles Pathé produced first newsreels,
  in Paris.
La Nouvelle Revue Française (Paris),
  1909–43.
John Millington Synge d.
Algernon Charles Swinburne d.
George Meredith d.
Stephen Spender b.
Wells's *Tono-Bungay*.
Synge's *The Tinker's Wedding*.
Meredith's *Last Poems*.

Huneker, James Gibbons (1857), Egoists, A Book of Supermen. NF
James, Henry (1843), Julia Bride. F; Italian Hours. NF
James, William (1842), A Pluralistic Universe. NF; The Meaning of the Truth. NF
Lindsay, Vachel (1879), The Tramp's Excuse and Other Poems. V
London, Jack (1876), Martin Eden. F
"Mark Twain" (1835), Extract from Captain Stormfield's Visit to Heaven. F; Is Shakespeare Dead? NF
Moody, William Vaughn (1869), The Great Divide [revision of A Sabine Woman (1906)]. D; The Faith Healer. D
Muir, John (1838), Stickeen. F
Norris, Frank (d. 1902), The Third Circle. F
"O. Henry" (1862), Roads of Destiny. F; Options. F
Oppenheim, James (1882), Dr. Rast. F; Monday Morning. V
Page, Thomas Nelson (1853), John Marvel, Assistant. F
Phillips, David Graham (1867), The Fashionable Adventures of Joshua Craig. F; The Hungry Heart. F
Pound, Ezra (1885), Personae. V; Exultations. V
Reese, Lizette Woodworth (1856), A Wayside Lute. V
Rinehart, Mary Roberts (1876), The Man in Lower Ten. F
Sheldon, Edward (1886), The Nigger. D
Steffens, Lincoln (1866), Upbuilders. NF
Stein, Gertrude (1874), Three Lives. F
Sterling, George (1869), A Wine of Wizardry. V
Stratton-Porter, Gene (1863), A Girl of the Limberlost. F
Thomas, Augustus (1857), The Harvest Moon. D
Walter, Eugene (1874), The Easiest Way. D
Washington, Booker T. (1856), The Story of the Negro. NF
Wharton, Edith (1862), Artemis to Acteon. V
White, William Allen (1868), A Certain Rich Man. F
Williams, William Carlos (1883), Poems. V
Wright, Harold Bell (1872), The Calling of Dan Matthews. F

Galsworthy's *Strife*.
Molnár's *Liliom*.
Gide's *Strait Is the Gate*.
Thomas Mann's *Royal Highness*.
Bely's *The Silver Dove* (1909–10).

1910

Adams, Charles Follen (1842), Yawcob Strauss and Other Poems. V
Addams, Jane (1860), Twenty Years at Hull-House. NF
Allen, James Lane (1849), The Doctor's Christmas Eve. F
Babbitt, Irving (1865), The New Laokoön. NF
Chapman, John Jay (1862), Learning and Other Essays. NF; The Treason and Death of Benedict Arnold. D
Churchill, Winston (1871), A Modern Chronicle. F
Davis, Richard Harding (1864), Notes of a War Correspondent. NF
Dunne, Finley Peter (1867), Mr. Dooley Says. F
Garland, Hamlin (1860), Other Main-Travelled Roads. F; Cavanagh, Forest Ranger. F
Harris, Joel Chandler (d. 1908), Uncle Remus and the Little Boy. F
Herrick, Robert (1868), A Life for a Life. F
Howells, William Dean (1837), Imaginary Interviews. NF; My Mark Twain. NF
Huneker, James Gibbons (1857), Promenades of an Impressionist. NF
James, Henry (1843), The Finer Grain. F
Johnson, Owen (1878), The Varmint. F
Johnson, Robert Underwood (1853), Saint-Gaudens, an Ode. V
Le Gallienne, Richard (1866), Orestes. D

President Roosevelt's proclamation of "New Nationalism" and "Square Deal" policies.
Mann-Elkins Act bolstered Interstate Commerce Commission.
Boy Scouts of America and Camp Fire Girls founded.
Mann Act (combating white slave traffic).
Carnegie Endowment for International Peace established.
Alfred Stieglitz showed young American artists at "291" Gallery.
Mark Twain d.
O. Henry d.
William James d.
The Crisis (New York), 1910–.

Death of Edward VII; accession of George V.
Portugese Republic proclaimed.
Abstract Expressionist movement in modern art.
Leo Tolstoy d.
Jean Anouilh b.
Bennett's *Clayhanger*.
Barrie's *The Twelve-Pound Look*.

Lomax, John A. (1872), Cowboy Songs and Other Frontier Ballads. V

London, Jack (1876), Revolution and Other Essays. NF; Lost Face. F; Burning Daylight. F; Theft. D

MacKaye, Percy (1875), Anti-Matrimony. D

Mulford, Clarence E. (1883), Hopalong Cassidy. F

Neihardt, John G. (1881), The River and I. NF

"O. Henry" (1862), Strictly Business. F; Whirligigs. F; Let Me Feel Your Pulse. F

Peabody, Josephine Preston (1874), The Piper. D

Phillips, David Graham (1867), The Husband's Story. F

Pound, Ezra (1885), Provença. V; The Spirit of Romance. NF

Robinson, Edwin Arlington (1869), The Town Down the River. V

Santayana, George (1863), Three Philosophical Poets: Lucretius, Dante, and Goethe. NF

Wharton, Edith (1862), Tales of Men and Ghosts. F

Wells's *The History of Mr. Polly.*
Synge's *Deirdre of the Sorrows.*
Galsworthy's *Justice.*
Forster's *Howard's End.*
Shaw's *Misalliance.*
Yeats's *The Green Helmet and Other Poems.*
Granville-Barker's *The Madras House.*
Wodehouse's *Psmith in the City.*
Walpole's *Maradick at Forty.*
Rilke's *The Notebook of Malte Laurids Brigge.*
Bunin's *The Village.*
Molnár's *The Guardsman.*
Claudel's *The Tidings Brought to Mary.*
Hauptmann's *The Fool in Christ.*

1911

Adams, Charles Francis (1835), Studies: Military and Diplomatic. NF

Adams, Franklin P. (1881), Tobogganing on Parnassus. V

Adams, Henry (1838), The Life of George Cabot Lodge. NF

Belasco, David (1853), The Return of Peter Grimm (with Cecil B. DeMille; pub. 1915). D

Bierce, Ambrose (1842), The Devil's Dictionary [revision of The Cynic's Word Book (1906)]. NF

Crawford, Francis Marion (d. 1909), Wandering Ghosts. F

Crothers, Rachel (1878), He and She. D

Deland, Margaret (1857), The Iron Woman. F

Dreiser, Theodore (1871), Jennie Gerhardt. F

Ferber, Edna (1887), Dawn O'Hara. F

Gale, Zona (1874), Mothers to Men. F

Garland, Hamlin (1860), Victor Ollnee's Discipline. F

Glasgow, Ellen (1874), The Miller of Old Church. F

Herrick, Robert (1868), The Healer. F

Howells, William Dean (1837), Parting Friends. D

Huneker, James Gibbons (1857), Franz Liszt. NF

James, Henry (1843), The Outcry. F

James, William (d. 1910), Some Problems of Philosophy. NF; Memories and Studies. NF

Johnson, Owen (1878), Stover at Yale. F; The Tennessee Shad. F

Johnston, Mary (1870), The Long Roll. F

London, Jack (1876), When God Laughs and Other Stories. F; Adventure. F; The Cruise of the Snark. NF; South Sea Tales. F

Mitchell, S. Weir (1829), John Sherwood, Iron Master. F

Muir, John (1838), My First Summer in the Sierra. NF

"O. Henry" (d. 1910), Sixes and Sevens. F

Page, Thomas Nelson (1853), Robert E. Lee: Man and Soldier. NF

Phillips, David Graham (1867), The Conflict. F

Pound, Ezra (1885), Canzoni. V

Sheldon, Edward (1886), The Boss. D; The Princess Zim-Zim. D

Spingarn, J. E. (1875), The New Criticism. NF

Stedman, Edmund Clarence (1833), Genius and Other Essays. NF

Sterling, George (1869), The House of Orchids. V

Mexican Revolution started.
Carnegie Corporation of New York founded.
National Progressive Republican League founded.
David Graham Phillips d.
Elizabeth Bishop b.
Tennessee Williams b.
The Masses (New York), 1911–17.
Drama Magazine (Chicago), 1911–31.
Irving Berlin's "Alexander's Ragtime Band."
W. C. Handy's "Memphis Blues."

Second Moroccan and second Balkan crises.
Chinese Revolution began.
Roald Amundsen reached South Pole.
W. S. Gilbert d.
Terrence Rattigan b.
William Golding b.
D. H. Lawrence's *The White Peacock.*
Masefield's *The Everlasting Mercy.*
Shaw's *Fanny's First Play.*
Chesterton's *The Innocence of Father Brown.*
Wells's *The New Machiavelli.*
Hugh Walpole's *Mr. Perrin and Mr. Traill.*
Conrad's *Under Western Eyes.*
Beerbohm's *Zuleika Dobson.*
Mansfield's *In a German Pension.*
Hofmannsthal's *Everyman.*
Claudel's *The Hostage.*
Mori's *The Wild Geese.*

Stratton-Porter, Gene (1863), The Harvester. F
Teasdale, Sara (1884), Helen of Troy. V
Thomas, Augustus (1857), As a Man Thinks. D
Wharton, Edith (1862), Ethan Frome. F
Wheelock, John Hall (1886), The Human Fantasy. V
Wiggin, Kate Douglas (1856), Mother Carey's Chickens. F
Wright, Harold Bell (1872), The Winning of Barbara Worth. F

1912

Addams, Jane (1860), A New Conscience and an Ancient Evil. NF
Ade, George (1866), Knocking the Neighbors. F
Allen, James Lane (1849), The Heroine in Bronze. F
Antin, Mary (1881), The Promised Land. NF
Atherton, Gertrude (1857), Julia France and Her Times. F
Babbitt, Irving (1865), The Masters of Modern French Criticism. NF
Bradford, Gamaliel (1863), Lee, the American. NF
Cather, Willa (1873), Alexander's Bridge. F
"Charles Egbert Craddock" (1850), The Raid of the Guerilla. F; The Ordeal. F
Dreiser, Theodore (1871), The Financier. F
Fisher, Dorothy Canfield (1879), The Squirrel-Cage. F
Grey, Zane (1872), Riders of the Purple Sage. F
James, William (d. 1910), Essays in Radical Empiricism. NF
Jeffers, Robinson (1887), Flagons and Apples. V
Johnson, James Weldon (1871), The Autobiography of an Ex-Colored Man. F
Johnston, Mary (1870), Cease Firing. F
Leonard, William Ellery (1876), The Vaunt of Man. V
Lewis, Sinclair (1885), Hike and the Aeroplane. F
Lindsay, Vachel (1879), Rhymes to be Traded for Bread. V
London, Jack (1876), A Son of the Sun. F; The House of Pride and Other Tales of Hawaii. F; Smoke Bellew. F
Lowell, Amy (1874), A Dome of Many-Coloured Glass. V
Manners, J. Hartley (1870), Peg o' My Heart. D
Muir, John (1838), The Yosemite. NF
"O. Henry" (d. 1910), Rolling Stones. F
Paine, Albert Bigelow (1861), Mark Twain, A Biography. NF
Phillips, David Graham (1867), George Helm. F; The Price She Paid. F
Pound, Ezra (1885), Ripostes. V; The Sonnets and Ballate of Guido Cavalcanti. V
Repplier, Agnes (1858), Americans and Others. NF
Saltus, Edgar (1855), The Monster. F
Sheldon, Edward (1886), Egypt. D; The High Road. D
Webster, Jean (1876), Daddy-Long-Legs. F
Wharton, Edith (1862), The Reef. F
Wheelock, John Hall (1886), The Beloved Adventure. V
Wylie, Elinor (1885), Incidental Numbers. V

New Mexico and Arizona admitted to the Union.
Taft-Wilson-Roosevelt election debates.
First Progressive ("Bull Moose") Party created.
Eight-hour day adopted for federal employees.
Girl Scouts founded by Juliette Low, in Savannah, Ga.
Leopold Stokowski musical director of the Philadelphia Orchestra (1912–36).
Authors' League of America founded.
John Cheever b.
Poetry: A Magazine of Verse (Chicago), 1912–.
The English Journal (Chicago et al.), 1912–.

First Balkan War (against Turkey).
Christian X crowned king of Denmark.
Sinking of S. S. *Titanic*.
Creation of Republic of China.
August Strindberg d.
Lawrence Durrell b.
Patrick White b.
Georgian Poetry 1911–1912.
Beerbohm's *A Christmas Garland*.
Shaw's *Androcles and the Lion*.
Bridges's *Poetical Works*.
James Stephens's *The Crock of Gold*.
Saki's *The Unbearable Bassington*.
Thomas Mann's *Death in Venice*.
Schnitzler's *Professor Bernhardi*.
Jung's *Psychology of the Unconscious*.
Claudel's *The Tidings Brought to Mary*.
Bunin's *Dry Valley*.
Akhmatova's *Evening*.

1913

Adams, Brooks (1848), Theory of Social Revolution. NF
Beard, Charles A. (1874), An Economic Interpretation of the Constitution of the United States. NF
Beecher, Henry Ward (d. 1887), Lectures and Orations. NF
Biggers, Earl Derr (1884), Seven Keys to Baldpate. F

16th Amendment (income tax) and 17th Amendment (popular election of U.S. senators) ratified.
Federal Reserve Bank Act.
Underwood Tariff Act lowered duties.

Bourne, Randolph (1886), Youth and Life. NF
Burroughs, John (1837), The Summit of the Years. NF
Bynner, Witter (1881), Tiger. V
Cabell, James Branch (1879), The Soul of Melicent. F
Cather, Willa (1873), O Pioneers! F
Chapman, John Jay (1862), William Lloyd Garrison. NF
Churchill, Winston (1871), The Inside of the Cup. F
Crothers, Rachel (1878), Ourselves. D
Dewey, John (1859), Interest and Effort in Education. NF
Dreiser, Theodore (1871), A Traveler at Forty. NF
Dunbar, Paul Laurence (d. 1906), Complete Poems. V
Eastman, Max (1883), The Enjoyment of Poetry. NF
Fletcher, John Gould (1886), Fire and Wine. V; Fool's Gold
    V; The Book of Nature. V; The Dominant City. V; Visions
    of the Evening. V
Frost, Robert (1874), A Boy's Will. V
Gale, Zona (1874), When I Was a Little Girl. NF
Glasgow, Ellen (1874), Virginia. F
Herrick, Robert (1868), His Great Adventure. F; One Woman's
    Life. F
Howells, William Dean (1837), New Leaf Mills. F; Familiar
    Spanish Travels. NF
Huneker, James Gibbons (1857), The Pathos of Distance.
    NF; Old Fogy. NF
James, Henry (1843), A Small Boy and Others. NF
Le Gallienne, Richard (1866), The Lonely Dancer. V
Lindsay, Vachel (1879), General William Booth Enters into
    Heaven and Other Poems. V
Lippmann, Walter (1889), A Preface to Politics. NF
London, Jack (1876), John Barleycorn. NF; The Night-Born.
    F; The Abysmal Brute. F; The Valley of the Moon. F
MacKaye, Percy (1875), Tomorrow. D
Mitchell, S. Weir (1829), Westways. F
Muir, John (1838), The Story of My Boyhood and Youth. NF
Peabody, Josephine Preston (1874), The Wolf of Gubbio. D
Santayana, George (1863), Winds of Doctrine. NF
Sheldon, Edward (1886), Romance. D
Walter, Eugene (1874), Fine Feathers. D
Wharton, Edith (1862), The Custom of the Country. F
Wheelock, John Hall (1886), Love and Liberation. V
Williams, William Carlos (1883), The Tempers. V
Wilson, Woodrow (1856), The New Freedom. NF

Henry Ford started first moving
    assembly line for car production.
New York Armory Show of modern art.
Joaquin Miller d.
Karl Shapiro b.
Delmore Schwartz b.
William Inge b.
Muriel Rukeyser b.
Reedy's Mirror (St. Louis), 1913–20.

Second Balkan War.
King George of Greece assassinated.
Robert Bridges named poet laureate of
    England.
The New Statesman (London), 1913–.
Baron Corvo d.
Angus Wilson b.
Albert Camus b.
D. H. Lawrence's Sons and Lovers.
Mackenzie's Sinister Street (1913–14).
Conrad's Chance.
Shaw's Pygmalion.
Proust's Remembrance of Things Past
    (7 vols., 1913–27).
Apollinaire's Alcools.
Unamuno's The Tragic Sense of Life.
Gorky's My Childhood.
Fournier's The Wanderer.
Mandelstam's Stone.

1914

Adams, Samuel Hopkins (1871), The Clarion. F
Ade, George (1866), Ade's Fables. F
Aiken, Conrad (1889), Earth Triumphant. V
Allen, James Lane (1849), The Last Christmas Tree. F
Brandeis, Louis (1856), Other People's Money. NF
Brownell, William C. (1851), Criticism. NF
Burroughs, Edgar Rice (1875), Tarzan of the Apes. F
Cable, George Washington (1844), Gideon's Band. F; The
    Amateur Garden. NF
"Charles Egbert Craddock" (1850), The Story of Duciehurst. F
Croly, Herbert (1869), Progressive Democracy. NF
Dickinson, Emily (d. 1886), The Single Hound. V
Dreiser, Theodore (1871), The Titan. F
Frost, Robert (1874), North of Boston. V
Garland, Hamlin (1860), The Forester's Daughter. F

World War I began; American
    declaration of neutrality.
Financial crisis accelerated.
Federal Trade Commission established.
Panama Canal opened.
Margaret Sanger indicted for mailing
    birth control pamphlets.
Ralph Ellison b.
Randall Jarrell b.
John Berryman b.
Bernard Malamud b.
Vanity Fair (New York), 1914–36;
    1983–.
The Little Review (Chicago; New York;
    Paris), 1914–29.
The New Republic (New York;
    Washington), 1914–.

Hergesheimer, Joseph (1880), The Lay Anthony. F
Herrick, Robert (1868), Clark's Field. F
Howells, William Dean (1837), The Seen and the Unseen at Stratford-on-Avon. NF
James, Henry (1843), Notes on Novelists. NF; Notes of a Son and Brother. NF
Kilmer, Joyce (1886), Trees and Other Poems. V
Lewis, Sinclair (1885), Our Mr. Wrenn. F
Lindsay, Vachel (1879), Adventures While Preaching the Gospel of Beauty. NF; The Congo and Other Poems. V
London, Jack (1876), The Strength of the Strong. F; The Mutiny of the Elsinore. F
Lowell, Amy (1874), Sword Blades and Poppy Seed. V
Mencken, H. L. (1880), Europe After 8:15 (with George Jean Nathan and Willard Huntington Wright). NF
Neihardt, John G. (1881), Life's Lure. F
Norris, Frank (d. 1902), Vandover and the Brute. F
O'Neill, Eugene (1888), Thirst and Other One-Act Plays. D
Oppenheim, James (1882), Songs for the New Age. V
Reed, John (1887), Insurgent Mexico. NF
Rice, Elmer (1892), On Trial. D
Robinson, Edwin Arlington (1869), Van Zorn. D
Sheldon, Edward (1886), The Song of Songs [adapted from Hermann Sudermann's novel Das hohe Lied (1908)]. D
Stein, Gertrude (1874), Tender Buttons. V
Tarkington, Booth (1869), Penrod. F
Veblen, Thorstein (1857), The Instinct of Workmanship. NF

The Unpopular Review (New York), 1914–21.
W. C. Handy's "St. Louis Blues."

Assassination of Archduke Ferdinand at Sarajevo.
Allies (Britain, France, Russia, Belgium, Serbia) at war with Central Powers (Austria-Hungary and Germany).
The Egoist (London), 1914–19.
Charles Péguy d.
Jules Lemaitre d.
Dylan Thomas b.
Octavio Paz b.
Hardy's Satires of Circumstance.
D. H. Lawrence's The Prussian Officer.
Yeats's Responsibilities.
Joyce's Dubliners.
Gide's Lafcadio's Adventures.

1915

Abbott, Lyman (1835), Reminiscences. NF
Allen, James Lane (1849), The Sword of Youth. F
Beard, Charles A. (1874), Economic Origins of Jeffersonian Democracy. NF
Benét, Stephen Vincent (1898), Five Men and Pompey. V
Brooks, Van Wyck (1886), America's Coming-of-Age. NF
Burroughs, John (1837), The Breath of Life. NF
Cabell, James Branch (1879), The Rivet in Grandfather's Neck. F
Cather, Willa (1873), The Song of the Lark. F
Chapman, John Jay (1862), Memories and Milestones. NF; Greek Genius, and Other Essays. NF
Churchill, Winston (1871), A Far Country. F
Cobb, Irwin S. (1876), Old Judge Priest. F
Crapsey, Adelaide (1878), Verse. V
Dreiser, Theodore (1871), The "Genius." F
DuBois, William E. B. (1868), The Negro. NF
Fisher, Dorothy Canfield (1879), The Bent Twig. F; Hillsboro People. F
Fletcher, John Gould (1886), Irradiations: Sand and Spray. V
Grant, Robert (1852), The High Priestess. F
Hergesheimer, Joseph (1880), Mountain Blood. F
Huneker, James Gibbons (1857), Ivory Apes and Peacocks. NF; New Cosmopolis. NF
Lardner, Ring (1885), Bib Ballads. V
Lewis, Sinclair (1885), The Trail of the Hawk. F
Lindsay, Vachel (1879), The Art of the Moving Picture. NF
London, Jack (1876), The Scarlet Plague. F; The Star Rover. F
Lowell, Amy (1874), Six French Poets. NF
MacLeish, Archibald (1892), Songs for a Summer's Day. V

Preparedness movement in U.S.
Revival of the Ku Klux Klan, in Georgia.
Panama-Pacific International Exposition in San Francisco.
Taxi industry began.
Provincetown Players founded.
Washington Square Players founded.
D. W. Griffith's The Birth of a Nation opened.
Saul Bellow b.
Arthur Miller b.
Jean Stafford b.
The Midland (Iowa City; Chicago), 1915–33.
Southwest Review (Austin; Dallas), 1915.

German submarine sank SS Lusitania; blockade of Britain; heavy fighting on Eastern front.
Rupert Brooke d.
Georgian Poetry 1913–1915.
Conrad's Victory.
Ford's The Good Soldier.
D. H. Lawrence's The Rainbow.
Maugham's Of Human Bondage.
Woolf's The Voyage Out.
Buchan's The Thirty-Nine Steps.
Brooke's 1914 and Other Poems.
Dorothy Richardson's Pilgrimage (12 vols., 1915–38).
Trakl's Sebastian Dreaming.
Andreyev's He Who Gets Slapped.

Masters, **Edgar Lee** (1868), Spoon River Anthology. V
Muir, **John** (d. 1914), Travels in Alaska. NF
Neihardt, **John G.** (1881), The Song of Hugh Glass. V
Poole, **Ernest** (1880), The Harbor. F
Pound, **Ezra** (1885), Cathay. V
Richards, **Laura Elizabeth** (1850), Julia Ward Howe (with
    Maud Howe Elliott). NF
Roberts, **Elizabeth Madox** (1886), In the Great Steep's Garden.
    V
Robinson, **Edwin Arlington** (1869), The Porcupine. D
Tarkington, **Booth** (1869), The Turmoil. F
Teasdale, **Sara** (1884), Rivers to the Sea. V
Wharton, **Edith** (1862), Fighting France, From Dunkerque to
    Belfort. NF
Wilson, **Harry Leon** (1867), Ruggles of Red Gap. F
Wister, **Owen** (1860), The Pentecost of Calamity. NF

Blok's *Poems About Russia.*
Ryunosuke's *Rashomon.*

1916

Adams, **Charles Francis** (d. 1915), Charles Francis Adams,
    1835–1915: An Autobiography. NF
Aiken, **Conrad** (1889), Turns and Movies. V; The Jig of Forslin.
    V
Allen, **James Lane** (1849), A Cathedral Singer. F
Anderson, **Sherwood** (1876), Windy McPherson's Son. F
Bourne, **Randolph** (1886), The Gary Schools. NF
Cabell, **James Branch** (1879), From the Hidden Way. V; The
    Certain Hour. F
Dewey, **John** (1859), Democracy and Education. NF
Dreiser, **Theodore** (1871), Plays of the Natural and Supernatural.
    D; A Hoosier Holiday. NF
"**Emanuel Morgan**" (1881) **and "Anne Knish"** (1883),
    Spectra: A Book of Poetic Experiments. V
Fletcher, **John Gould** (1886), Goblins and Pagodas. V
Frost, **Robert** (1874), Mountain Interval. V
Garland, **Hamlin** (1860), They of the High Trails. F
Glasgow, **Ellen** (1874), Life and Gabriella. F
Guest, **Edgar A.** (1881), A Heap o' Livin'. V
"**H.D.**" (1886), Sea Garden. V
Howells, **William Dean** (1837), The Daughter of the Storage.
    F; The Leatherwood God. F; Years of My Youth. NF
Jeffers, **Robinson** (1887), Californians. V
Jewett, **Sarah Orne** (d. 1909), Verses. V
Kreymborg, **Alfred** (1883), Mushrooms. V
Lardner, **Ring** (1885), You Know Me Al: A Busher's Letters. F
Lindsay, **Vachel** (1879), A Handy Guide for Beggars. NF
London, **Jack** (1876), The Little Lady of the Big House. F; The
    Turtles of Tasman. F
Lowell, **Amy** (1874), Men, Women and Ghosts. V
"**Mark Twain**" (d. 1910), The Mysterious Stranger. F
Masters, **Edgar Lee** (1868), Songs and Satires. V; The Great
    Valley. V
Mencken, **H. L.** (1880), A Book of Burlesques. NF
Muir, **John** (d. 1914), A Thousand-Mile Walk to the Gulf. NF
O'Neill, **Eugene** (1888), Bound East for Cardiff. D; Before
    Breakfast. D
Oppenheim, **James** (1882), War and Laughter. V
Peabody, **Josephine Preston** (1874), Harvest Moon. V

American expedition against Pancho
    Villa in Mexico.
National Park Service established.
Margaret Sanger opened first birth
    control clinic, in Brooklyn.
Eight-hour day adopted for railroad
    workers.
Henry James d.
Alan Seeger d.
Jack London d.
James Whitcomb Riley d.
The Seven Arts (New York et al.),
    1916–17.
Theatre Arts (New York), 1916–64.
Journal of Negro History (Lancaster,
    Penna., Washington, D.C.), 1916–.

Battles of Verdun, the Somme, and
    Jutland; German warships ravaged
    Allied commerce.
Easter rebellion in Dublin.
David Lloyd George elected British
    prime minister.
Tristan Tzara and others founded Dada
    movement, in Zurich.
Saki d.
Henryk Sienkiewicz d.
Joyce's *A Portrait of the Artist as a
    Young Man.*
Wells's *Mr. Britling Sees It Through.*
D. H. Lawrence's *Twilight in Italy.*
Kaiser's *From Morn to Midnight.*
Barbusse's *Under Fire.*
Mayakovsky's *War and the World.*
Gorky's *In the World.*
Brod's *The Redemption of Tycho
    Brahe.*
Bely's *Petersburg.*

Pound, Ezra (1885), Lustra. V; Gaudier-Brzeska. NF; Noh—or,
Accomplishment. D; Certain Noble Plays of Japan. D
Reed, John (1887), The War in Eastern Europe. NF
Repplier, Agnes (1858), Counter-Currents. NF
Robinson, Edwin Arlington (1869), The Man Against the Sky.
V
Royce, Josiah (1855), The Hope of the Great Community. NF
Sandburg, Carl (1878), Chicago Poems. V
Santayana, George (1863), Egotism in German Philosophy. NF
Seeger, Alan (1888), Poems. V
Tarkington, Booth (1869), Penrod and Sam. F; Seventeen. F
Wharton, Edith (1862), Xingu and Other Stories. F
Wright, Harold Bell (1872), When a Man's a Man. F

1917

Aiken, Conrad (1889), Nocturne of Remembered Spring. V
Anderson, Sherwood (1876), Marching Men. F
Asch, Sholem (1880), Mottke, the Vagabond. D
Austin, Mary (1868), The Ford. F
Bishop, John Peale (1891), Green Fruit. V
Bourne, Randolph (1886), Education and Living. NF
Brownell, William C. (1851), Standards. NF
Bynner, Witter (1881), Grenstone Poems. V
Cabell, James Branch (1879), The Cream of the Jest. F
Cahan, Abraham (1860), The Rise of David Levinsky. F
Churchill, Winston (1871), The Dwelling-Place of Light. F
Eliot, T. S. (1888), Prufrock and Other Observations. V; Ezra
Pound: His Metric and Poetry. NF
Garland, Hamlin (1860), A Son of the Middle Border. NF
Guest, Edgar A. (1881), Just Folks. V
Hergesheimer, Joseph (1880), The Three Black Pennys. F
Huneker, James Gibbons (1857), Unicorns. NF; The
Philharmonic Society of New York. NF
James, Henry (d. 1916), The Ivory Tower. F; The Sense of the
Past. F; The Middle Years. NF
Johnson, James Weldon (1871), Fifty Years and Other Poems.
V
Lardner, Ring (1885), Gullible's Travels, Etc. F
Lewis, Sinclair (1885), The Job. F; The Innocents. F
Lindsay, Vachel (1879), The Chinese Nightingale and Other
Poems. V
London, Jack (d. 1916), The Human Drift. NF; Jerry of the
Islands. F; Michael, Brother of Jerry. F
Lowell, Amy (1874), Tendencies in Modern American Poetry.
NF
MacLeish, Archibald (1892), Tower of Ivory. V
"Mark Twain" (d. 1910), What Is Man? and Other Essays. NF
Mencken, H. L. (1880), A Book of Prefaces. NF
Millay, Edna St. Vincent (1892), Renascence and Other Poems.
V
Morley, Christopher (1890), Parnassus on Wheels. F
"O. Henry" (d. 1910), Waifs and Strays. F
O'Neill, Eugene (1888), The Sniper (prod.). D; In the Zone
(pub. 1919). D; Ile (pub. 1919). D; The Long Voyage Home
(pub. 1919). D
Oppenheim, James (1882), The Book of Self. V
Phillips, David Graham (d. 1911), Susan Lenox: Her Fall and
Rise. F
Poole, Ernest (1880), His Family. F

U.S. declared war on Germany.
Virgin Islands purchased from
Denmark.
Puerto Ricans became American
citizens.
Immigration Act (excluding Asiatic
workers).
Lions Club founded.
First Pulitzer prizes awarded.
Jeannette Rankin became first woman
in House of Representatives.
Sarah Bernhardt's last tour of the U.S.
Robert Lowell b.
Carson McCullers b.
*Cambridge History of American
Literature* (4 vols., 1917–21).
Negro World (New York), 1917–33.
George M. Cohan's "Over There."

Germany began unrestricted submarine
warfare; British and French suffer
heavy losses on Western front.
Czar Nicholas II abdicated.
Proclamation of Russian Republic.
Emergence of Lenin and Trotsky.
Balfour Declaration (Palestinian home
for Jewish people).
Edward Thomas d.
T. E. Hulme d.
Heinrich Böll b.
Georgian Poetry 1916–1917.
Barrie's *Dear Brutus.*
Yeats's *The Wild Swans at Coole.*
Douglas's *South Wind.*
Sassoon's *The Old Huntsman.*
Valéry's *The Young Parca.*
Hamsun's *Growth of the Soil.*
Pirandello's *Right You Are If You Think
You Are.*
Stefan Zweig's *Jeremiah.*
Pasternak's *Above the Barriers.*
Mayakovsky's *Man.*
Akhmatova's *White Flock.*
Jiménez's *The Diary of a Newly
Married Poet.*

Rice, Elmer (1892), The Home of the Free. D
Robinson, Edwin Arlington (1869), Merlin. V
Seeger, Alan (d. 1916), Letters and Diary. NF
Sinclair, Upton (1878), King Coal. F
Sterling, George (1869), Thirty-five Sonnets. V
Teasdale, Sara (1884), Love Songs. V
Torrence, Ridgely (1875), Granny Maumee, The Rider of
Dreams, and Simon the Cyrenian. D
Wharton, Edith (1862), Summer. F
Wiggin, Kate Douglas (1856), Mother Carey's Chickens
[adapted with Rachel Crothers from Wiggin's novel (1911)]. D
Williams, Jesse Lynch (1871), Why Marry? D
Williams, William Carlos (1883), A Book of Poems: Al Que
Quiere! V
Woollcott, Alexander (1887), Mrs. Fiske. NF

1918

Adams, Henry (d. 1918), The Education of Henry Adams: An
Autobiography. NF
Aiken, Conrad (1889), The Charnel Rose, Senlin: A Biography,
and Other Poems. V
Allen, James Lane (1849), The Kentucky Warbler. F
Anderson, Sherwood (1876), Mid-American Chants. V
Asch, Sholem (1880), The God of Vengeance. D
Benét, Stephen Vincent (1898), Young Adventure. V
Burt, Struthers (1882), John O'May and Other Stories. F
Cable, George Washington (1844), The Flower of the
Chapdelaines. F; Lovers of Louisiana. F
Cather, Willa (1873), My Ántonia. F
Dreiser, Theodore (1871), Free and Other Stories. F; The Hand
of the Potter. D
Fletcher, John Gould (1886), The Tree of Life. V
Freeman, Mary E. Wilkins (1852), Edgewater People. F
Fuller, Henry Blake (1857), On the Stairs. F
Gale, Zona (1874), Birth. F
Harris, Joel Chandler (d. 1908), Uncle Remus Returns. F
Hergesheimer, Joseph (1880), Gold and Iron. F
James, Henry (d. 1916), Within the Rim and Other Essays.
NF; Gabrielle de Bergerac. F
Lardner, Ring (1885), Treat 'em Rough. F; My Four Weeks in
France. NF
London, Jack (d. 1916), The Red One. F
Lowell, Amy (1874), Can Grande's Castle. V
Masters, Edgar Lee (1868), Toward the Gulf. V
Mencken, H. L. (1880), Damn! A Book of Calumny. NF; In
Defense of Women. NF
O'Neill, Eugene (1888), The Moon of the Caribees (pub. 1919).
D; The Rope (pub. 1919). D; Where the Cross Is Made (pub.
1919). D
Poole, Ernest (1880), His Second Wife. F
Pound, Ezra (1885), Pavannes and Divisions. NF
Ridge, Lola (1871), The Ghetto and Other Poems. V
Sandburg, Carl (1878), Cornhuskers. V
Sinclair, Upton (1878), The Profits of Religion. NF
Smith, Thorne (1892), Biltmore Oswald: The Diary of a Hapless
Recruit. F
Smith, Winchell (1871), Lightnin' (with Frank Bacon). D
Steele, Wilbur Daniel (1886), Land's End. F
Streeter, Edward (1891), Dere Mable: Love Letters of a Rookie.
F

Armistice declared November 11.
President Wilson's Fourteen Points
outlined to Congress.
Eugene V. Debs jailed for sedition.
Theatre Guild established.
Carolina Playmakers founded.
O. Henry Memorial Award established.
Henry Adams d.
The Stars and Stripes (Washington,
D.C.), 1918–26.
The Liberator (New York), 1918–24.

Proclamation of German Republic;
abdication of Kaiser Wilhelm.
Czar Nicholas and family executed.
Civil War between Bolsheviks and
White Russians began.
International influenza epidemic.
Edmond Rostand d.
Frank Wedekind d.
Wilfred Owen d.
Joyce's *Exiles*.
D. H. Lawrence's *New Poems*.
Hopkins's *Poems* (posth.; ed. by Robert
Bridges).
Strachey's *Eminent Victorians*.
Wyndham Lewis's *Tarr*.
Hudson's *Far Away and Long Ago*.
Kaiser's *Gas I*.
Spengler's *The Decline of the West*
(1918–1922).
Blok's *The Twelve*.
Maurois's *The Silence of Colonel
Bramble*.
Mayakovsky's *Mystery-Bouffe*.

Tarkington, Booth (1869), The Magnificent Ambersons. F
Thomas, Augustus (1857), The Copperhead. D
Veblen, Thorstein (1857), The Higher Learning in America. NF
Wharton, Edith (1862), The Marne. F

1919

Adams, Brooks (1848) and Henry Adams (d. 1918), The
  Degradation of the Democratic Dogma. NF
Aiken, Conrad (1889), Scepticisms. NF
Akins, Zoë (1886), Déclassée. D
Allen, James Lane (1849), The Emblems of Fidelity. F
Anderson, Sherwood (1876), Winesburg, Ohio. F
Babbitt, Irving (1865), Rousseau and Romanticism. NF
Bourne, Randolph (d. 1918), Untimely Papers. NF
Cabell, James Branch (1879), Jurgen. F; Beyond Life. NF
Chapman, John Jay (1862), Songs and Poems. V
Churchill, Winston (1871), Dr. Jonathan. D
Deutsch, Babette (1895), Banners. V
Dreiser, Theodore (1871), Twelve Men. NF
Dunne, Finley Peter (1867), Mr. Dooley on Making a Will. F
Eliot, T. S. (1888), Poems. V
Frank, Waldo (1889), Our America. NF
Fuller, Henry Blake (1857), Bertram Cope's Year. F
Glasgow, Ellen (1874), The Builders. F
Glaspell, Susan (1882), Bernice. D
Hergesheimer, Joseph (1880), Java Head. F; Linda Condon.
  F; The Happy End. F
Hopwood, Avery (1882), The Gold Diggers. D
Huneker, James Gibbons (1857), The Steinway Collection of
  Paintings. NF
James, Henry (d. 1916), Travelling Companions. F
Lardner, Ring (1885), Own Your Own Home. F; Regular
  Fellows I Have Met. V; The Real Dope. F
Lewis, Sinclair (1885), Free Air. F
London, Jack (d. 1916), On the Makaloa Mat. F
Lowell, Amy (1874), Pictures of a Floating World. V
Masters, Edgar Lee (1868), Starved Rock. V
Mencken, H. L. (1880), The American Language (rev. 1921,
  1923, 1936; sup. vols. 1945, 1948). NF; Prejudices. NF
Morley, Christopher (1890), The Haunted Bookshop. F
Nathan, Robert (1894), Peter Kindred. F
Neihardt, John G. (1881), The Song of Three Friends. V
O'Brien, Frederick (1869), White Shadows in the South Seas.
  NF
O'Neill, Eugene (1888), The Dreamy Kid (pub. 1922). D
Pound, Ezra (1885), Quia Pauper Amavi. V
Ransom, John Crowe (1888), Poems About God. V
Reed, John (1887), Red Russia. NF; Ten Days That Shook the
  World. NF
Saltus, Edgar (1855), The Paliser Case. F
Sinclair, Upton (1878), Jimmie Higgins. F
Streeter, Edward (1891), "Same Old Bill, eh Mable!" F
Tarkington, Booth (1869), Clarence (pub. 1921). D
Wharton, Edith (1862), French Ways and Their Meaning. NF
Wheelock, John Hall (1886), Dust and Light. V

18th Amendment (prohibition of
  alcoholic beverages) ratified.
President Wilson received Nobel Peace
  Prize.
Boston police and U.S. steel workers
  on strike.
Savage race riots in Chicago and
  Washington, D.C.
American Legion founded in Paris.
U.S. Communist Labor Party organized.
Institute for International Education
  established.
New School for Social Research
  founded, in New York City.
Daily airmail service between New
  York and Chicago.
J. D. Salinger b.

Treaty of Versailles (not signed by
  U.S.).
League of Nations created, seated in
  Geneva in 1920.
Weimar Constitution adopted in
  Germany.
Civil war spread in Russia.
Walter Gropius established Bauhaus
  school of architecture.
John Alcock and Arthur Brown, English
  aviators, flew nonstop across the
  Atlantic.
Littérature [Dada review] (Paris),
  1919–24.
W. M. Rossetti d.
Iris Murdoch b.
Doris Lessing b.
Georgian Poetry 1918–1919.
Beerbohm's Seven Men.
Hardy's Poetical Works (1919–21).
Firbank's Valmouth.
Maugham's The Moon and Sixpence.
Keynes's The Economic Consequences
  of the Peace.
Hesse's Demian.
Mayakovsky's 150,000,000 (1919–20).
Gide's The Pastoral Symphony.
Lenormand's Time Is a Dream.

1920

Ade, George (1866), Hand-Made Fables. F
Aiken, Conrad (1889), The House of Dust. V

19th Amendment (woman suffrage)
  ratified.

146

Anderson, Sherwood (1876), Poor White. F
Asch, Sholem (1880), Uncle Moses. F
Benét, Stephen Vincent (1898), Heavens and Earth. V
Bok, Edward William (1863), The Americanization of Edward
  Bok. NF
Bourne, Randolph (d. 1918), History of a Literary Radical. NF
Brooks, Van Wyck (1886), The Ordeal of Mark Twain. NF
Bynner, Witter (1881), A Canticle of Pan. V
Cabell, James Branch (1879), Domnei [revision of The Soul of
  Melicent (1913)]. F
Carnegie, Andrew (d. 1919), Autobiography. NF
Cather, Willa (1873), Youth and the Bright Medusa. F
Day, Clarence (1874), This Simian World. NF
Dell, Floyd (1887), Moon-Calf. F
Dewey, John (1859), Reconstruction in Philosophy. NF
Dos Passos, John (1896), One Man's Initiation—1917 (pub. in
  London; American edition 1922). F
Dreiser, Theodore (1871), Hey Rub-a-Dub-Dub. NF
DuBois, William E. B. (1868), Darkwater. F, V
Eliot, T. S. (1888), Poems. V; The Sacred Wood. NF
Fitzgerald, F. Scott (1896), This Side of Paradise. F; Flappers
  and Philosophers. F
Gale, Zona (1874), Miss Lulu Bett. F; Miss Lulu Bett (adapted
  from her novel). D
Hergesheimer, Joseph (1880), San Cristóbal de la Habana. NF
Hopwood, Avery (1882), The Bat [adapted with Mary Roberts
  Rinehart from her novel The Circular Staircase (1908)]. D
Howells, William Dean (1837), The Vacation of the Kelwyns. F
Huneker, James Gibbons (1857), Painted Veils. F; Bedouins.
  NF; Steeplejack. NF
Lardner, Ring (1885), The Young Immigrunts. F
Leonard, William Ellery (1876), The Lynching Bee. V
Lewis, Sinclair (1885), Main Street. F
Lindsay, Vachel (1879), The Golden Whales of California.
  V; The Golden Book of Springfield. NF
London, Jack (d. 1916), Hearts of Three. F
Masters, Edgar Lee (1868), Domesday Book. V; Mitch Miller.
  F
Mencken, H. L. (1880), Heliogabalus (with George Jean
  Nathan). D; The American Credo (with George Jean Nathan).
  NF; Prejudices: Second Series. NF
Millay, Edna St. Vincent (1892), A Few Figs from Thistles. V
Neihardt, John G. (1881), The Splendid Wayfaring. NF
O'Neill, Eugene (1888), Beyond the Horizon. D; The Emperor
  Jones (pub. 1921). D; Diff'rent (pub. 1921). D
Poole, Ernest (1880), Blind. F
Pound, Ezra (1885), Hugh Selwyn Mauberley. V; Umbra.
  V; Instigations. NF
Reese, Lizette Woodworth (1856), Spicewood. V
Ridge, Lola (1871), Sun-Up. V
Robinson, Edwin Arlington (1869), Lancelot. V; The Three
  Taverns. V
Royce, Josiah (1855), Fugitive Essays. NF
Sandburg, Carl (1878), Smoke and Steel. V
Santayana, George (1863), Character and Opinion in the United
  States. NF
Sinclair, Upton (1878), 100%: The Story of a Patriot. F; The
  Brass Check. NF
Streeter, Edward (1891), As You Were, Bill. F
Teasdale, Sara (1884), Flame and Shadow. V
Train, Arthur (1875), Tutt and Mr. Tutt. F
Turner, Frederick Jackson (1861), The Frontier in American
  History. NF

"Red scare" led to mass arrests.
Beginning of Sacco-Vanzetti case in
  Massachusetts.
American Civil Liberties Union
  founded
KDKA (Pittsburgh) first commercial
  radio station.
John Reed d.
William Dean Howells d.
Howard Nemerov b.
The Frontier and Midland (Missoula,
  Mont.), 1920–39.
The Freeman (New York), 1920–24.

Home Rule Bill established separate
  northern and southern Irish
  parliaments.
Nazi Party founded in Germany.
Russian-Polish War.
Chinese Civil War (1920–36).
Olive Schreiner d.
Galsworthy's *In Chancery*.
D. H. Lawrence's *Women in Love*.
Edward Thomas's *Collected Poems*.
Wells's *The Outline of History*.
Shaw's *Heartbreak House*.
Yeats's *Michael Robartes and the
  Dancer*.
de la Mare's *Poems*.
Mansfield's *Bliss*.
Undset's *Kristin Lavransdatter* (1920–
  22).
Colette's *Chéri*.
Kaiser's *Gas II*.
Breton and Soupault's *The Magnetic
  Fields*.

Van Vechten, Carl (1880), The Tiger in the House. NF
Wescott, Glenway (1901), The Bitterns. V
Wharton, Edith (1862), The Age of Innocence. F; In Morocco.
NF
Williams, William Carlos (1883), Kora in Hell: Improvisations.
NF
Yezierska, Anzia (1885), Hungry Hearts. F

1921

Abbott, Lyman (1835), What Christianity Means to Me. NF
Adams, James Truslow (1878), The Founding of New England.
NF
Adams, Samuel Hopkins (1871), Success. F
Aiken, Conrad (1889), Punch: The Immortal Liar. V
Anderson, Sherwood (1876), The Triumph of the Egg. F, V
Atherton, Gertrude (1857), The Sisters-in-Law. F
Benét, Stephen Vincent (1898), The Beginning of Wisdom. F
Broun, Heywood (1888), Seeing Things at Night. NF
Burt, Struthers (1882), Chance Encounters. F
Cabell, James Branch (1879), The Jewel Merchants. D; Figures
of Earth. F
Crane, Stephen (d. 1900), Men, Women, and Boats. F
Davis, Owen (1874), The Detour (pub. 1922). D
Dell, Floyd (1887), The Briary-Bush. F
Dos Passos, John (1896), Three Soldiers. F
Fisher, Dorothy Canfield (1879), The Brimming Cup. F
Fletcher, John Gould (1886), Breakers and Granite. V
Gale, Zona (1874), The Secret Way. V
Garland, Hamlin (1860), A Daughter of the Middle Border. NF
Glaspell, Susan (1882), The Inheritors. D; The Verge. D
"H.D." (1886), Hymen. V
Harris, Joel Chandler (d. 1908), The Witch Wolf. F
Hecht, Ben (1894), Erik Dorn. F
Hopwood, Avery (1882), Getting Gertie's Garter (with Wilson
Collison). D
Howard, Sidney (1891), Swords. D
Howells, William Dean (d. 1920), Mrs. Farrell. F; Eighty Years
and After. NF
Huneker, James Gibbons (1857), Variations. NF
James, Henry (d. 1916), Notes and Reviews. NF
Kaufman, George S. (1889), Dulcy (with Marc Connelly). D
Lardner, Ring (1887), The Big Town. F; Symptoms of Being
35. NF
Lowell, Amy (1874), Legends. V
Marquis, Don (1878), The Old Soak. NF
Millay, Edna St. Vincent (1892), Second April. V; The Lamp
and the Bell. D; Aria da Capo. D; Two Slatterns and a King.
D
Moore, Marianne (1887), Poems V
Neihardt, John G. (1891), Two Mothers. D
O'Neill, Eugene (1888), "Anna Christie" (pub. 1922). D; The
Straw. D; Gold. D
Poole, Ernest (1880), Beggars' Gold. F
Pound, Ezra (1885), Poems 1918–1921. V
Robinson, Edwin Arlington (1869), Avon's Harvest.
V; Collected Poems. V
Robinson, James Harvey (1863), The Mind in the Making. NF
Stearns, Harold E. (1891), America and the Young Intellectual.
NF

Separate U.S. peace treaty signed with
Germany, Austria, and Hungary.
Armistice Day (November 11)
proclaimed national holiday.
Tomb of the Unknown Soldier erected.
Washington Conference on the
Limitation of Armament (1921–22).
Industrial depression and wage cuts.
Albert Einstein on lecture tour of the
U.S.
American Birth Control League
founded by Margaret Sanger.
Richard Wilbur b.
James Jones b.
The Reviewer (Richmond), 1921–25.
Broom (Rome; Berlin; New York),
1921–24.
The Double-Dealer (New Orleans),
1921–26.

Lenin's New Economic Policy.
Mussolini organized Fascist political
party in Italy.
P.E.N. (international association of
writers) founded by John Galsworthy
et al., in London.
Aleksandr Blok d.
Friedrich Dürrenmatt b.
Galsworthy's *To Let.*
Aldous Huxley's *Crome Yellow.*
Strachey's *Queen Victoria.*
Sabatini's *Scaramouche.*
Lubbock's *The Craft of Fiction.*
Dane's *A Bill of Divorcement.*
Karel Čapek's *R.U.R.*.
Pirandello's *Six Characters in Search of
an Author.*
Toller's *Man and the Masses.*
Bely's *First Meeting.*
Vsevolod Ivanov's *Partisans.*

Stewart, Donald Ogden (1894), A Parody Outline of History. F
Tarkington, Booth (1869), Alice Adams. F
Williams, William Carlos (1883), Sour Grapes. V
Winters, Yvor (1900), The Immobile Wind. V
Wylie, Elinor (1885), Nets to Catch the Wind. V

1922

Addams, Jane (1860), Peace and Bread in Time of War. NF
Ade, George (1866), Single Blessedness and Other Observations. F
Aiken, Conrad (1889), Priapus and the Pool. V
Benét, Stephen Vincent (1898), Young People's Pride. F
Bishop, John Peale (1891), The Undertaker's Garland (with Edmund Wilson). V
Broun, Heywood (1888), Pieces of Hate, and Other Enthusiasms. NF
Cabell, James Branch (1879), The Lineage of Lichfield. NF
Cather, Willa (1873), One of Ours. F
Colton, John (1889), Rain [adapted with Clemence Randolph from Somerset Maugham's short story "Miss Thompson" (1921); pub. 1923]. D
Cummings, E. E. (1894), The Enormous Room. F, NF
Dos Passos, John (1896), A Pushcart at the Curb. V; Rosinante to the Road Again. NF
Dreiser, Theodore (1871), A Book About Myself. NF
Eliot, T. S. (1888), The Waste Land. V
Fitzgerald, F. Scott (1896), The Beautiful and Damned. F; Tales of the Jazz Age. F
Frank, Waldo (1889), Rahab. F
Glasgow, Ellen (1874), One Man in His Time. F
Hergesheimer, Joseph (1880), Cytherea. F; The Bright Shawl. F
Hough, Emerson (1857), The Covered Wagon. F
Kaufman, George S. (1889), To the Ladies (with Marc Connelly). D; Merton of the Movies [adapted with Marc Connelly from Harry Leon Wilson's novel (1922)]. D
Kelly, George (1889), The Torch-Bearers. D
Lewis, Sinclair (1885), Babbitt. F
Lewisohn, Ludwig (1882), Up Stream: An American Chronicle. NF
London, Jack (d. 1916), Dutch Courage and Other Stories. F
Lowell, Amy (1874), A Critical Fable. NF
Marquand, J. P. (1893), The Unspeakable Gentleman. F
Masters, Edgar Lee (1868), Children of the Market Place. F
Mencken, H. L. (1880), Prejudices: Third Series. NF
Morley, Christopher (1890), Where the Blue Begins. F
Nichols, Anne (1891), Abie's Irish Rose (pub. 1924). D
O'Neill, Eugene (1888), "The Hairy Ape." D; The First Man. D
Peabody, Josephine Preston (1874), Portrait of Mrs. W. D
Pollock, Channing (1880), The Fool. D
Poole, Ernest (1880), Millions. F
Pound, Louise (1872), American Ballads and Songs. V
Roberts, Elizabeth Madox (1886), Under the Tree. V
Sandburg, Carl (1878), Slabs of the Sunburnt West. V; Rootabaga Stories. F
Santayana, George (1863), Soliloquies in England and Later Soliloquies. NF; Poems. V
Sinclair, Upton (1878), They Call Me Carpenter. F

Coal mines and railway strikes.
Oklahoma under martial law after KKK terrorism.
Lincoln Memorial dedicated in Washington.
First experiments in radar research.
Anne Nichols's *Abie's Irish Rose* opened in New York (closed in 1927).
Thomas Nelson Page d.
Secession (Vienna et al.), 1922–24.
The Fugitive (Nashville), 1922–25.
The Reader's Digest (Pleasantville, N.Y.), 1922–.
Philological Quarterly (Iowa City), 1922–.

Mussolini became dictator of Italy.
Kemal Atatürk elected president of Turkish republic.
Mahatma Gandhi jailed for civil disobedience.
The Criterion (London), 1922–39.
Georgian Poetry 1920–1922.
Marcel Proust d.
W. H. Hudson d.
Philip Larkin b.
Alain Robbe-Grillet b.
A. E. Housman's *Last Poems*.
Woolf's *Jacob's Room*.
Shaw's *Back to Methusaleh*.
Joyce's *Ulysses*.
Mansfield's *The Garden Party*.
Yeats's *Later Poems*.
Galsworthy's *The Forsyte Saga*.
Edith Sitwell's *Facade*.
Hesse's *Siddhartha*.
Pirandello's *Henry IV*.
Mauriac's *The Kiss of the Leper*.
Martin du Gard's *The World of the Thibaults* (8 vols., 1922–40).
Pasternak's *My Sister, Life and Other Poems*.
Vsevolod Ivanov's *Armored Train No. 14–69*.
Mandelstam's *Tristia*.
Akhmatova's *Anno Domini MCMXXI*.

Stein, Gertrude (1874), Geography and Plays. NF, D
Van Vechten, Carl (1880), Peter Whiffle. F
Wharton, Edith (1862), The Glimpses of the Moon. F
Wheelock, John Hall (1886), The Black Panther. V
Williams, Jesse Lynch (1871), Why Not? D
Wilson, Harry Leon (1867), Merton of the Movies. F
Winters, Yvor (1900), The Magpie's Shadow. V
Woollcott, Alexander (1887), Shouts and Murmurs. NF

1923

Adams, James Truslow (1878), Revolutionary New England. NF
Ade, George (1866), The Mayor and the Manicure. D; Nettie. D; Speaking to Father. D
Aiken, Conrad (1889), The Pilgrimage of Festus. V
Allen, James Lane (1849), The Alabaster Box. F
Anderson, Sherwood (1876), Many Marriages. F; Horses and Men. F
Atherton, Gertrude (1857), Black Oxen. F
Barry, Philip (1896), You and I. D
Benét, Stephen Vincent (1898), King David. V; The Ballad of William Sycamore, 1790–1880. V; Jean Huguenot. F
Bogan, Louise (1897), Body of This Death. V
Boyd, Thomas (1898), Through the West. F
Bradford, Gamaliel (1863), Damaged Souls. NF
Cabell, James Branch (1879), The High Place. F
Cather, Willa (1873), A Lost Lady. F
Cohan, George M. (1878), The Song and Dance Man. D
Connelly, Marc (1890), Helen of Troy. D
Cummings, E. E. (1894), Tulips and Chimneys. V
Davis, Owen (1874), Icebound. D
Dell, Floyd (1887), Janet Marsh. F
Dos Passos, John (1896), Streets of Night. F
Dreiser, Theodore (1871), The Color of a Great City. NF
Fitzgerald, F. Scott (1896), The Vegetable; or, From President to Postman. D
Frost, Robert (1874), New Hampshire. V
Gale, Zona (1874), Faint Perfume. F
Garland, Hamlin (1860), The Book of the American Indian. F
Glasgow, Ellen (1874), The Shadowy Third and Other Stories. F
Hemingway, Ernest (1899), Three Stories & Ten Poems (pub. in Paris). F, V
Hergesheimer, Joseph (1880), The Presbyterian Child. F
Herrick, Robert (1868), Homely Lilla. F
Johnson, Robert Underwood (1853), Remembered Yesterdays. NF
Kelley, Edith Summers (1884), Weeds. F
Lardner, Ring (1885), Say It with Oil. NF
Lawson, John Howard (1895), Roger Bloomer. D
Leonard, William Ellery (1876), Red Bird. D
Lewisohn, Ludwig (1882), Don Juan. F
Lindsay, Vachel (1879), Going-to-the-Sun. V
Marquand, J. P. (1893), Four of a Kind. F
Masters, Edgar Lee (1868), Skeeters Kirby. F
Millay, Edna St. Vincent (1892), The Harp-Weaver and Other Poems. V
"O. Henry" (1862), Postscripts. F
Poole, Ernest (1880), Danger. F
Prouty, Olive Higgins (1882), Stella Dallas. F
Reese, Lizette Woodworth (1856), Wild Cherry. V

President Harding died suddenly, in San Francisco.
Teapot Dome Scandal (1921–23) involving Wyoming oil preserves.
Lee De Forest demonstrated first sound-on-film motion pictures.
Norman Mailer b.
Denise Levertov b.
James Purdy b.
Time (New York), 1923–.
The Modern Quarterly (Baltimore), 1923–40.

Hitler's abortive "Beerhall Putsch" in Munich.
Miguel Primo de Rivera became dictator of Spain.
Nonesuch Press (London) founded.
Katherine Mansfield d.
Bennett's *Riceyman Steps*.
Aldous Huxley's *Antic Hay*.
Shaw's *Saint Joan*.
D. H. Lawrence's *Studies in Classic American Literature*.
O'Casey's *The Shadow of a Gunman*.
Macauley's *Told by an Idiot*.
Svevo's *The Confessions of Zeno*.
Rilke's *The Duino Elegies; Sonnets to Orpheus*.
Radiguet's *The Devil in the Flesh*.
Mauriac's *Génitrix*.
Pasternak's *Themes and Variations*.
Feuchtwanger's *The Ugly Duchess*.
Gorky's *My Universities*.

Rice, Elmer (1892), The Adding Machine. D
Robinson, Edwin Arlington (1869), Roman Bartholow. V
Sandburg, Carl (1878), Rootabaga Pigeons. F
Santayana, George (1863), Scepticism and Animal Faith. NF
Sinclair, Upton (1878), The Goose-Step: A Study of American
   Education. NF
Steele, Wilbur Daniel (1886), The Shame Dance. F
Sterling, George (1869), Selected Poems. V
Stevens, Wallace (1879), Harmonium. V
Stewart, Donald Ogden (1894), Aunt Polly's Story of Mankind.
   F
Toomer, Jean (1894), Cane. F, V, D
Van Vechten, Carl (1880), The Blind Bow-Boy. F
Wharton, Edith (1862), A Son at the Front. F
Williams, William Carlos (1883), Spring and All. V, NF; The
   Great American Novel. NF, F
Woollcott, Alexander (1887), Mr. Dickens Goes to the Play. NF
Wylie, Elinor (1885), Black Armour. V; Jennifer Lorn. F

1924

Anderson, Maxwell (1888), What Price Glory? (with Laurence
   Stallings; pub. 1926). D
Anderson, Sherwood (1876), A Story Teller's Story. NF
Babbitt, Irving (1865), Democracy and Leadership. NF
Behrman, S. N. (1893), Bedside Manners (with Kenyon
   Nicholson). D
Bromfield, Louis (1896), The Green Bay Tree. F
Broun, Heywood (1888), Sitting on the World. NF
Brownell, William C. (1851), The Genius of Style. NF
Burke, Kenneth (1897), The White Oxen and Other Stories. F
Burt, Struthers (1882), The Interpreter's House. F
Cabell, James Branch (1879), Straws and Prayer Books. NF
Chapman, John Jay (1862), Letters and Religion. NF
Cozzens, James Gould (1903), Confusion. F
Eliot, T. S. (1888), Homage to John Dryden. NF
Faulkner, William (1897), The Marble Faun. V
Ferber, Edna (1887), So Big. F
"H.D." (1886), Heliodora and Other Poems. V
Hemingway, Ernest (1899), in our time (pub. in Paris). F
Hergesheimer, Joseph (1880), Balisand. F
Herrick, Robert (1868), Waste. F
Howard, Sidney (1891), They Knew What They Wanted (pub.
   1925). D
Jeffers, Robinson (1887), Tamar and Other Poems. V
Kaufman, George S. (1889), Beggar on Horseback (with Marc
   Connelly). D; Minick (with Edna Ferber). D
Kelly, George (1887), The Show-Off. D
Lardner, Ring (1885), How to Write Short Stories (with
   Samples). F
Leonard, William Ellery (1876), Tutankhamen and After. V
MacLeish, Archibald (1892), The Happy Marriage and Other
   Poems. V
"Mark Twain" (d. 1910), Autobiography. NF
Masters, Edgar Lee (1868), The New Spoon River. V; Mirage.
   F
Melville, Herman (d. 1891), Billy Budd and Other Prose Pieces.
   F

Industrial depression deepened.
Second Progressive Party formed.
Soldiers' Bonus Bill passed by
   Congress.
Henry Ford sold his 10-millionth
   automobile.
DuPont produced cellophane.
James Baldwin b.
The New York Herald-Tribune,
   1924–66.
The American Mercury (New York et
   al.), 1924–
The Commonweal (New York), 1924–.
The Saturday Review (New York),
   1924–.
George Gershwin's "Rhapsody in Blue."

Death of Lenin.
Stalin/Trotsky antagonism began.
André Breton published his first
   Surrealist Manifesto, in Paris.
Joseph Conrad d.
Anatole France d.
Franz Kafka d.
Forster's A Passage to India.
O'Casey's Juno and the Paycock.
Webb's Precious Bane.
Coward's The Vortex.
Kennedy's The Constant Nymph.
Ford's Some Do Not. . . .
Arlen's The Green Hat.
Wodehouse's The Inimitable Jeeves
Thomas Mann's The Magic Mountain.
Gide's Corydon.
Saint-John Perse's Anabasis.
Mayakovsky's Vladimir Ilyich Lenin.
Kafka's A Hunger Artist.
Musil's Three Women.
Neruda's Twenty Love Poems and a
   Song of Despair.
Tanizaki's A Fool's Love.

Mencken, H. L. (1880), Prejudices: Fourth Series. NF
Millay, Edna St. Vincent (1892), Distressing Dialogues. NF
Moore, Marianne (1887), Observations. V
Mulford, Clarence E. (1883), Hopalong Cassidy Returns. F
Mumford, Lewis (1895), Sticks and Stones. NF
O'Neill, Eugene (1888), All God's Chillun Got Wings.
　　D; Welded (pub. 1925). D; Desire Under the Elms (pub.
　　1925). D
Oppenheim, James (1882), The Sea. V
Peterkin, Julia (1880), Green Thursday. F
Pound, Ezra (1885), Antheil and the Treatise on Harmony. NF
Ransom, John Crowe (1888), Chills and Fever. V
Repplier, Agnes (1858), Under Dispute. NF
Rice, Elmer (1892), Close Harmony; or, The Lady Next Door
　　(with Dorothy Parker; pub. 1929). D
Robinson, Edwin Arlington (1869), The Man Who Died Twice.
　　V
Seldes, Gilbert (1893), The Seven Lively Arts. NF
Sheldon, Edward (1886), Bewitched (with Sidney Howard;
　　prod.). D
Sinclair, Upton (1878), The Goslings: A Study of American
　　Schools. NF
Stewart, Donald Ogden (1894), Mr. and Mrs. Haddock Abroad.
　　F
Suckow, Ruth (1892), Country People. F
Van Doren, Mark (1894), Spring Thunder. V
Van Vechten, Carl (1880), The Tattooed Countess. F
Wescott, Glenway (1901), The Apple of the Eye. F
Wharton, Edith (1862), Old New York. F
Woollcott, Alexander (1887), Enchanted Aisles. NF

1925

Adams, Léonie (1899), Those Not Elect. V
Aiken, Conrad (1889), Bring! Bring! F
Allen, James Lane (1849), The Landmark. F
Anderson, Maxwell (1888), You Who Have Dreams. V
Anderson, Sherwood (1876), Dark Laughter. F; The Modern
　　Writer. NF
Benét, Stephen Vincent (1898), Tiger Joy. V
Bodenheim, Maxwell (1893), Replenishing Jessica. F
Boyd, James (1888), Drums. F
Bromfield, Louis (1896), Possession. F
Brooks, Van Wyck (1886), The Pilgrimage of Henry James. NF
Bryan, William Jennings (1860), Memoirs. NF
Calverton, V. F. (1920), The Newer Spirit. NF
Cather, Willa (1873), The Professor's House. F
Cozzens, James Gould (1903), Michael Scarlett. F
Cullen, Countee (1903), Color. V
Cummings, E. E. (1894), &. V; XLI Poems. V
Deutsch, Babette (1895), Honey Out of the Rock. V
Dos Passos, John (1896), Manhattan Transfer. F
Dreiser, Theodore (1871), An American Tragedy. F
Eliot, T. S. (1888), Poems 1909–1925. V
Erskine, John (1879), The Private Life of Helen of Troy. F
Fitzgerald, F. Scott (1896), The Great Gatsby. F
Fletcher, John Gould (1886), Parables. V, NF
Gale, Zona (1874), Mister Pitt [adapted from her novel Birth
　　(1918)]. D

Scopes trial in Dayton, Tenn.
Florida land boom.
Court martial of Col. William ("Billy")
　　Mitchell and Air Force controversy.
Standard Oil Co. adopted eight-hour
　　work day.
Trinity College (N.C.) became Duke
　　University.
Nellie Tayloe Ross of Wyoming first
　　woman governor.
Charleston dance craze.
Guggenheim Fellowships established.
George Washington Cable d.
Flannery O'Connor b.
William Styron b.
Gore Vidal b.
The New Yorker (New York), 1925–.
American Speech (Baltimore et al.),
　　1925–.
This Quarter (Paris), 1925–32.
The Virginia Quarterly Review
　　(Charlottesville), 1925–.

Irish Free State declared the Republic of
　　Ireland.
Paul von Hindenburg elected president
　　of Germany.
Rider Haggard d.
Woolf's *Mrs. Dalloway*.

Glasgow, Ellen (1874), Barren Ground. F
Grant, Robert (1852), The Bishop's Granddaughter. F
"H.D." (1886), Collected Poems. V
Halliburton, Richard (1900), The Royal Road to Romance. NF
Hemingway, Ernest (1899), In Our Time: Stories (rev. and enl. edition). F
Hergesheimer, Joseph (1880), From an Old House. NF
Heyward, DuBose (1885), Porgy. F
Hillyer, Robert (1895), The Halt in the Garden. V
Howard, Sidney (1891), Lucky Sam McCarver (pub. 1926). D
Jeffers, Robinson (1887), Roan Stallion, Tamar and Other Poems. V
Kelly, George (1887), Craig's Wife (pub. 1926). D
Kreymborg, Alfred (1883), Troubadour. NF
Lardner, Ring (1885), What of It? NF
Lawson, John Howard (1895), Processional. D
Le Gallienne, Richard (1866), The Romantic '90s. NF
Leonard, William Ellery (1876), Two Lives. V
Lewis, Sinclair (1885), Arrowsmith. F
Loos, Anita (1893), Gentleman Prefer Blondes. F
Lowell, Amy (1874), What's O'Clock? V; John Keats. NF
MacLeish, Archibald (1892), The Pot of Earth. V
Marquand, J. P. (1893), The Black Cargo. F; Lord Timothy Dexter of Newburyport, Mass. NF
Morley, Christopher (1890), Thunder on the Left. F
Neihardt, John G. (1881), The Song of the Indian Wars. V; Poetic Values. NF
O'Neill, Eugene (1888), The Fountain (pub. 1926). D
Pollock, Channing (1880), The Enemy. D
Pound, Ezra (1885), A Draft of XVI Cantos. V
Robinson, Edwin Arlington (1869), Dionysus in Doubt. V
Santayana, George (1863), Dialogues in Limbo. NF
Stein, Gertrude (1874), The Making of Americans. F, NF
Suckow, Ruth (1892), The Odyssey of a Nice Girl. F
Torrence, Ridgely (1875), Hesperides. V
Van Druten, John (1901), Young Woodley. D
Van Vechten, Carl (1880), Firecrackers. F; Red: Papers on Musical Subjects. NF
Wharton, Edith (1862), The Mother's Recompense. F; The Writing of Fiction. NF
Williams, Jesse Lynch (1871), Lovely Lady. D
Williams, William Carlos (1883), In the American Grain. NF
Wylie, Elinor (1885), The Venetian Glass Nephew. F

Yeats's A Vision.
Deeping's Sorrell and Son.
Maugham's The Painted Veil.
Walpole's Portrait of a Man with Red Hair.
Coward's Hay Fever.
Ford's No More Parades.
O'Flaherty's The Informer.
Bunin's Mitya's Love.
Mandelstam's The Noise of Time.
Feuchtwanger's Power.
Kafka's The Trial.
Montale's Cuttlefish Bones.
Borges's Inquiries.
Hitler's Mein Kampf (1925–27).

1926

Adams, Franklin P. (1881), The Conning Tower Book. NF
Adams, James Truslow (1878), New England in the Republic. NF
Adams, Samuel Hopkins (1871), Revelry. F
Allen, Hervey (1889), Israfel: The Life and Times of Edgar Allan Poe. NF
Anderson, Sherwood (1876), Tar: A Midwest Childhood. F
Barry, Philip (1896), In a Garden. D; White Wings (pub. 1927). D
Beer, Thomas (1889), The Mauve Decade. NF
Behrman, S. N. (1893), A Night's Work (with Kenyon Nicholson). D
Benét, Stephen Vincent (1898), Spanish Bayonet. F

U.S. Marines in Nicaragua (1926–33).
Army Air Corps created by Congress.
Ford introduced eight-hour day, five-day work week.
Transatlantic wireless telephone.
Admiral Byrd flew over North Pole.
First International Eucharistic Congress, in Chicago.
Gene Tunney defeated Jack Dempsey for heavyweight boxing title.
Gertrude Ederle first woman to swim English Channel.
Book-of-the-Month Club founded.
Allen Ginsberg b.

Bromfield, Louis (1896), Early Autumn. F
Cabell, James Branch (1879), The Silver Stallion. F: The Music from Behind the Moon. F
Cather, Willa (1873), My Mortal Enemy. F
Colton, John (1889), The Shanghai Gesture. D
Crane, Hart (1899), White Buildings. V
Cummings, E. E. (1894), Is 5. V
De Kruif, Paul (1890), Microbe Hunters. NF
Dos Passos, John (1896), The Garbage Man (prod. under the title The Moon Is a Gong). D
Durant, Will (1885), The Story of Philosophy. NF
Eastman, Max (1873), Marx, Lenin, and the Science of Revolution. NF
Faulkner, William (1897), Soldiers' Pay. F
Ferber, Edna (1887), Show Boat. F
Fisher, Dorothy Canfield (1897), Her Son's Wife. F
Fitzgerald, F. Scott (1896), All the Sad Young Men. F
Fletcher, John Gould (1886), Branches of Adam. V
Forbes, Esther (1891), O Genteel Lady! F
Gale, Zona (1874), Preface to a Life. F
Garland, Hamlin (1860), Trail-Makers of the Middle Border. NF; Memories of the Middle Border. NF
Glasgow, Ellen (1874), The Romantic Comedians. F
Green, Paul (1894), In Abraham's Bosom (pub. 1927). D
"H.D." (1886), Palimpsest. F
Hemingway, Ernest (1899), The Torrents of Spring. F; The Sun Also Rises. F
Hergesheimer, Joseph (1880), Tampico. F
Herrick, Robert (1868), Chimes. F
Heyward, DuBose (1885), Angel. F
Howard, Sidney (1891), Ned McCobb's Daughter. D; The Silver Cord (pub. 1927). D
Hughes, Langston (1902), The Weary Blues. V
Kelly, George (1887), Daisy Mayme. D
Lardner, Ring (1885), The Love Nest. F
Lewis, Sinclair (1885), Mantrap. F
Lewisohn, Ludwig (1882), The Case of Mr. Crump. F
Lindsay, Vachel (1879), Going-to-the-Stars. V; The Candle in the Cabin. V
Loos, Anita (1893), Gentlemen Prefer Blondes [adapted from her novel (1925)]. D
Lowell, Amy (d. 1925), East Wind. V
MacLeish, Archibald (1892), Nobodaddy. D; Streets in the Moon. V
Masters, Edgar Lee (1868), Lee: A Dramatic Poem. V
Mencken, H. L. (1880), Prejudices: Fifth Series. NF; Notes on Democracy. NF
Neihardt, John G. (1881), Collected Poems. V; Indian Tales, and Others. F
O'Neill, Eugene (1888), The Great God Brown. D
Parker, Dorothy (1893), Enough Rope. V
Pound, Ezra (1885), Personae: The Collected Poems. V
Roberts, Elizabeth Madox (1886), The Time of Man. F
"S. S. Van Dine" (1888), The Benson Murder Case. F
Sandburg, Carl (1878), Abraham Lincoln: The Prairie Years. NF
Sheldon, Edward (1886), Lulu Belle (with Charles MacArthur). D
Smith, Thorne (1892), Topper. F
Steele, Wilbur Daniel (1886), Urkey Island. F
Stein, Gertrude (1874), Composition as Explanation. NF
Stewart, Donald Ogden (1894), Mr. and Mrs. Haddock in Paris, France. F

W. D. Snodgrass b.
New Masses (New York), 1926–48.

Germany admitted to League of Nations.
Józef Pilsudski became premier of Poland.
Rainer Maria Rilke d.
Ronald Firbank d.
D. H. Lawrence's *The Plumed Serpent.*
T. E. Lawrence's *The Seven Pillars of Wisdom.*
O'Casey's *The Plough and the Stars.*
Ford's *A Man Could Stand Up.*
Yeats's *Autobiographies.*
Milne's *Winnie-the-Pooh.*
Christie's *The Murder of Roger Ackroyd.*
Thomas Mann's *Disorder and Early Sorrow.*
Babel's *Red Cavalry.*
Gide's *The Counterfeiters.*
Sholokov's *Tales of the Don.*
Brecht's *A Man's a Man.*
Kafka's *The Castle.*
Kawabata's *The Izu Dancer.*
Borges's *The Measure of My Hope.*

Stribling, T. S. (1881), Teeftallow. F
Suckow, Ruth (1892), Iowa Interiors. F
Sullivan, Mark (1874), Our Times: The United States, 1900–1925 (6 vols., 1926–35). NF
Teasdale, Sara (1884), Dark of the Moon. V
Van Vechten, Carl (1880), Excavations. NF; Nigger Heaven. F
Wescott, Glenway (1901), Like a Lover. F
Wharton, Edith (1862), Here and Beyond. F; Twelve Poems. V
Wilder, Thornton (1897), The Cabala. F
Wilson, Edmund (1895), Discordant Encounters. D
Wylie, Elinor (1885), The Orphan Angel. F

1927

Adams, James Truslow (1878), Provincial Society, 1690–1763. NF
Aiken, Conrad (1889), Blue Voyage. F
Anderson, Maxwell (1888), Saturday's Children. D
Anderson, Sherwood (1876), A New Testament. V
Baker, Ray Stannard (1870), Woodrow Wilson: Life and Letters (8 vols., 1927–39). NF
Barry, Philip (1896), Paris Bound (pub. 1929). D
Beard, Charles A. (1874) and Mary R. Beard (1876), The Rise of American Civilization (4 vols., 1927–42). NF
Behrman, S. N. (1893), The Second Man. D
Boyd, James (1888), Marching On. F
Bromfield, Louis (1896), A Good Woman. F
Brownell, William C. (1851), Democratic Distinction in America. NF
Burt, Struthers (1882), The Delectable Mountains. F
Cabell, James Branch (1879), Something About Eve. F
Cather, Willa (1873), Death Comes for the Archbishop. F
Cullen, Countee (1903), Copper Sun. V; The Ballad of the Brown Girl. V
Cummings, E. E. (1894), Him. D
Davidson, Donald (1893), The Tall Men. V
Dos Passos, John (1896), Orient Express. NF
Dreiser, Theodore (1871), Chains. F
Eliot, T. S. (1888), Journey of the Magi. V; Shakespeare and the Stoicism of Seneca. NF
Erskine, John (1879), Adam and Eve. F
Faulkner, William (1897), Mosquitoes. F
Green, Paul (1894), The Field God. D
"H.D." (1886), Hippolytus Temporizes. D
Halliburton, Richard (1900), The Glorious Adventure. NF
Hemingway, Ernest (1899), Men Without Women. F
Heyward, DuBose (1885), Porgy [adapted with Dorothy Heyward from his novel (1925)]. D
Hughes, Langston (1902), Fine Clothes to the Jew. V
Jeffers, Robinson (1887), The Women at Point Sur. V
Johnson, James Weldon (1871), God's Trombones. V
Kaufman, George S. (1889), The Royal Family (with Edna Ferber). D
Lardner, Ring (1885), The Story of a Wonder Man. NF, F
Lawson, John Howard (1895), Loud Speaker. D
Leonard, William Ellery (1876), The Locomotive-God. NF
Lewis, Sinclair (1885), Elmer Gantry. F
Lewisohn, Ludwig (1882), Roman Summer. F
Lindbergh, Charles A. (1902), "We." NF
Lowell, Amy (d. 1925), Ballads for Sale. V
Marquis, Don (1878), archy and mehitabel. V

Sacco and Vanzetti executed.
Lindbergh's solo flight, New York to Paris.
First television transmission, New York to Washington.
Holland Tunnel opened between New Jersey and New York.
Academy of Motion Picture Arts and Sciences established.
The Jazz Singer, first successful talking motion picture.
Hound and Horn (Portland, Me.; Cambridge; New York), 1927–34.
transition (Paris et al.), 1927–38.
Books Abroad (Norman, Okla.), 1927–76.
American Caravan (New York), 1927–36.

Trotsky expelled from Communist Party.
Günter Grass b.
Wyndham Lewis' *Time and Western Man.*
T. E. Lawrence's *Revolt in the Desert.*
Granville-Barker's *Prefaces to Shakespeare* (5 vols., 1927–48).
Bowen's *The Hotel.*
Joyce's *Pomes Pennyeach.*
Woolf's *To the Lighthouse.*
Forster's *Aspects of the Novel.*
Milne's *Now We are Six.*
de la Roche's *Jalna.*
Lehmann's *Dusty Answer.*
Hesse's *Steppenwolf.*
Mauriac's *Thérèse Desqueyroux.*
Mayakovsky's *Good!*
Kafka's *Amerika.*
Lenormand's *Mixture.*

Mencken, H. L. (1880), Prejudices: Sixth Series. NF
Millay, Edna St. Vincent (1892), The King's Henchman (libretto
    of an opera by Deems Taylor). D
O'Neill, Eugene (1888), Lazarus Laughed (prod. 1928).
    D; Marco Millions (prod. 1928). D
Parrington, V. L. (1871), Main Currents in American Thought
    (3 vols., 1927–30).
Peterkin, Julia (1880), Black April. F
Ransom, John Crowe (1888), Two Gentlemen in Bonds. V
Reese, Lizette Woodworth (1856), Little Henrietta. V
Ridge, Lola (1871), Red Flag. V
Riding, Laura (1901), A Survey of Modernist Poetry (with
    Robert Graves). NF
Roberts, Elizabeth Madox (1886), My Heart and My Flesh. F
Robinson, Edwin Arlington (1869), Tristram. V
Rölvaag, O. E. (1876), Giants in the Earth. F
Sandburg, Carl (1878), The American Songbag. V
Santayana, George (1863), Platonism and the Spiritual Life.
    NF; The Realm of Essence. NF
Sherwood, Robert E. (1896), The Road to Rome. D
Sinclair, Upton (1878), Oil! F
Steele, Wilbur Daniel (1886), The Man Who Saw Through
    Heaven. F
Tarkington, Booth (1869), The Plutocrat. F
Wescott, Glenway (1901), The Grandmothers. F
Wharton, Edith (1862), Twilight Sleep. F
Wheelock, John Hall (1886), The Bright Doom. V
Wilder, Thornton (1897), The Bridge of San Luis Rey. F
Winters, Yvor (1900), The Bare Hills. V

1928

Ade, George (1866), Bang! Bang! F
Aiken, Conrad (1889), Costumes by Eros. F
Aldrich, Bess Streeter (1881), Lantern in Her Hand. F
Anderson, Maxwell (1888), Gods of the Lightning (with Harold
    Hickerson). D
Auden, W. H. (1907), Poems. V
Barnes, Djuna (1892), Ryder. F
Barry, Philip (1896), Holiday (pub. 1929). D
Benchley, Robert (1889), 20,000 Leagues Under the Sea; or,
    David Copperfield. NF
Benét, Stephen Vincent (1898), John Brown's Body. V
Bradford, Roark (1896), Ol' Man Adam an' His Chillun. F
Braithwaite, William Stanley (1878), Frost on the Green Tree. F
Bromfield, Louis (1896), The Strange Case of Miss Annie
    Spragg. F
Burt, Struthers (1882), They Could Not Sleep. F
Byrd, Richard E. (1888), Skyward. NF
Cabell, James Branch (1879), The White Robe. F
Cozzens, James Gould (1903), Cock Pit. F
Cummings, E. E. (1894), Christmas Tree. V
De Kruif, Paul (1890), Hunger Fighters. NF
Delmar, Viña (1905), Bad Girl. F
Dos Passos, John (1896), Airways, Inc. (prod. 1929). D
Dreiser, Theodore (1871), Dreiser Looks at Russia. NF
Eliot, T. S. (1888), A Song for Simeon. V; For Lancelot
    Andrewes. NF
Fletcher, John Gould (1886), The Black Rock. V; John Smith—
    Also Pocahontas. NF
Forbes, Esther (1891), A Mirror for Witches. F

Kellogg-Briand Pact to outlaw war
    signed by 15 nations.
First Admiral Byrd explorations from
    Little America, in Antarctica.
The Lights of New York, first all-talking
    motion picture.
George Eastman introduced a color
    photography process.
Elinor Wylie d.
Edward Albee b.
The New England Quarterly
    (Brunswick, Me.; Boston), 1928–.
Dictionary of American Biography (20
    vols., 1928–36).

Stalin's first Five-Year Plan.
Thomas Hardy d.
Hermann Sudermann d.
Italo Svevo d.
Alan Sillitoe b.
Gabriel García Márquez b.
Carlos Fuentes b.
Evelyn Waugh's *Decline and Fall.*
D. H. Lawrence's *Lady Chatterley's
    Lover.*
Aldous Huxley's *Point Counter Point.*
Wyndham Lewis's *The Childermass.*
Hall's *The Well of Loneliness.*
Woolf's *Orlando.*
Ford's *The Last Post.*
Yeats's *The Tower.*
Sassoon's *Memoirs of a Fox-Hunting
    Man.*

Frank, Waldo (1889), The Rediscovery of America. NF
Frost, Robert (1874), West-Running Brook. V
Gale, Zona (1874), Portage, Wisconsin and Other Essays. NF
Garland, Hamlin (1860), Back-Trailers of the Middle Border. NF
"H.D." (1886), Hedylus. F
Hecht, Ben (1894), The Front Page (with Charles MacArthur). D
Hergesheimer, Joseph (1880), Quiet Cities. F
Hillyer, Robert (1895), The Seventh Hill. V
Howard, Sidney (1891), Salvation (with Charles MacArthur). D
Jeffers, Robinson (1887), Cawdor and Other Poems. V
Lawson, John Howard (1895), The International. D
Leonard, William Ellery (1876), A Son of Earth. V
Lewis, Sinclair (1885), The Man Who Knew Coolidge. F
Lewisohn, Ludwig (1882), The Island Within. F
Loos, Anita (1893), But Gentlemen Marry Brunettes. F
MacLeish, Archibald (1892), The Hamlet of A. MacLeish. V
Marquand, J. P. (1893), Do Tell Me, Dr. Johnson. F
Masters, Edgar Lee (1868), Jack Kelso: A Dramatic Poem. V
Millay, Edna St. Vincent (1892), The Buck in the Snow. V
Nathan, Robert (1894), The Bishop's Wife. F
O'Neill, Eugene (1888), Strange Interlude. D
Parker, Dorothy (1893), Sunset Gun. V
Peterkin, Julia (1880), Scarlet Sister Mary. F
Pollock, Channing (1880), Mr. Moneypenny. D
Pound, Ezra (1885), A Draft of the Cantos 17–27. V
Rice, Elmer (1892), Cock Robin (with Philip Barry; pub. 1929). D
Riding, Laura (1901), Contemporaries and Snobs. NF
Roberts, Elizabeth Madox (1886), Jingling in the Wind. F
Robinson, Edwin Arlington (1869), Sonnets, 1889–1927. V
Sandburg, Carl (1878), Good Morning, America. V
Sherwood, Robert E. (1896), The Queen's Husband. D
Sinclair, Upton (1878), Boston. F
Stein, Gertrude (1874), Useful Knowledge. NF
Suckow, Ruth (1892), The Bonney Family. F
Tate, Allen (1899), Mr. Pope and Other Poems. V; Stonewall Jackson, the Good Soldier. NF
Thompson, Dorothy (1894), The New Russia. NF
Van Vechten, Carl (1880), Spider Boy. F
Wescott, Glenway (1901), Goodbye, Wisconsin. F
Wharton, Edith (1862), The Children. F
Wilder, Thornton (1897), The Angel That Troubled the Waters and Other Plays. D
Williams, William Carlos (1883), A Voyage to Pagany. F
Woollcott, Alexander (1887), Going to Pieces. NF
Wylie, Elinor (1885), Mr. Hodge & Mr. Hazard. F; Trivial Breath. V

Milne's The House at Pooh Corner.
Sholokov's The Quiet Don (4 vols., 1928–40).
Brecht and Weill's The Threepenny Opera.
García Lorca's The Gypsy Ballads.
Malraux's The Conquerors.
Soupault's Last Nights of Paris.
Mandelstam's The Egyptian Stamp; Poems.
Guillén's Cántico.
Tanizaki's Some Prefer Nettles.

1929

Adams, Léonie (1899), High Falcon. V
Aiken, Conrad (1889), Selected Poems. V
Beer, Thomas (1889), Hanna. NF
Behrman, S. N. (1893), Meteor (pub. 1930). D
Bogan, Louise (1897), Dark Summer. V
Bradford, Roark (1896), This Side of Jordan. F
Burnett, W. R. (1899), Little Caesar. F
Bynner, Witter (1881), Indian Earth. V
Cabell, James Branch (1879), Sonnets from Antan. V; The Way of Ecben. F

Stock market collapsed; beginning of Great Depression.
"St. Valentine's Day Massacre" in Chicago.
Admiral Byrd flew over South Pole.
Museum of Modern Art founded, in New York City.
Academy Awards ("Oscars") presented for best film work.
O'Neill's Strange Interlude banned in Boston.

Caldwell, Erskine (1903), The Bastard. F
Cowley, Malcolm (1898), Blue Juniata. V
Cozzens, James Gould (1903), The Son of Perdition. F
Cullen, Countee (1903), The Black Christ. V
Dahlberg, Edward (1900), Bottom Dogs (pub. in London). F
Delmar, Viña (1905), Kept Woman. F; Loose Ladies. F
Dewey, John (1857), The Quest for Certainty. NF
Dickinson, Emily (d. 1886), Further Poems. V
Douglas, Lloyd C. (1877), Magnificent Obsession. F
Dreiser, Theodore (1871), A Gallery of Women. F
Edmonds, Walter D. (1903), Rome Haul. F
Eliot, T. S. (1888), Animula. V; Dante. NF
"Ellery Queen" (1905), The Roman Hat Mystery. F
Faulkner, William (1897), Sartoris. F; The Sound and the Fury. F
Fearing, Kenneth (1902), Angel Arms. V
Gale, Zona (1874), Borgia. F
Glasgow, Ellen (1874), They Stooped to Folly. F
"H.D." (1886), Red Roses for Bronze. V
Halliburton, Richard (1900), New Worlds to Conquer. NF
Hammett, Dashiell (1894), The Dain Curse. F; Red Harvest. F
Hemingway, Ernest (1899), A Farewell to Arms. F
Hergesheimer, Joseph (1880), Swords and Roses. F
Heyward, DuBose (1885), Mamba's Daughters. F
Jeffers, Robinson (1888), Dear Judas and Other Poems. V
Kaufman, George S. (1889), June Moon (with Ring Lardner). D
Kelly, George (1887), Maggie the Magnificent. D
Kreymborg, Alfred (1883), Our Singing Strength. NF
Krutch, Joseph Wood (1893), The Modern Temper. NF
La Farge, Oliver (1901), Laughing Boy. F
Lardner, Ring (1885), Round Up. F
Lewis, Sinclair (1885), Dodsworth. F
Lewisohn, Ludwig (1882), Mid-Channel: An American Chronicle. NF
Lindsay, Vachel (1879), The Litany of Washington Street. NF; Every Soul Is a Circus. V
Lippmann, Walter (1889), A Preface to Morals. NF
Lynd, Robert S. (1892) **and Helen Merrell Lynd** (1896), Middletown—A Study in Contemporary American Culture. NF
Masters, Edgar Lee (1868), The Fate of the Jury. V
"Michael Gold" (1893), 120 Million. NF
O'Neill, Eugene (1888), Dynamo. D
Perelman, S. J. (1904), Dawn Ginsbergh's Revenge. F
Rice, Elmer (1892), Street Scene. D; The Subway. D; See Naples and Die (pub. 1930). D
Ridge, Lola (1871), Firehead. V
Robinson, Edwin Arlington (1869), Cavender's House. V
Rölvaag, O. E. (1876), Peder Victorious. F
Sandburg, Carl (1878), Steichen the Photographer. NF
Scott, Evelyn (1893), The Wave. F
Sheldon, Edward (1886), Jenny (with Margaret Ayer Barnes). D
Steele, Wilbur Daniel (1886), Tower of Sand. F
Steinbeck, John (1902), Cup of Gold. F
Stewart, Donald Ogden (1894), Father William. NF
Suckow, Ruth (1892), Cora. F
Tarkington, Booth (1869), Penrod Jashber. F
Tate, Allen (1899), Jefferson Davis: His Rise and Fall. NF
Thurber, James (1894), Is Sex Necessary? (with E. B. White). NF
Warren, Robert Penn (1905), John Brown, the Making of a Martyr. NF
Wharton, Edith (1862), Hudson River Bracketed. F

"Amos 'n' Andy" began radio serialization.
American Literature (Durham, N.C.), 1929–.

Trotsky exiled from Soviet Union.
Heinrich Himmler appointed head of Nazi SS troops.
Henry Arthur Jones d.
Hugo von Hofmannsthal d.
John Osborne b.
Graves's *Goodbye to All That*.
Priestley's *The Good Companions*.
Sherriff's *Journey's End*.
Hughes's *A High Wind in Jamaica*.
Woolf's *A Room of One's Own*.
Bridges's *The Testament of Beauty*.
Henry Green's *Living*.
Coward's *Bitter Sweet*.
Bowen's *The Last September*.
de la Roche's *Whiteoaks of Jalna*.
Remarque's *All Quiet on the Western Front*.
Pagnol's *Marius*.
Mayakovsky's *The Bedbug*.
Giraudoux's *Amphitryon 38*.
Döblin's *Berlin Alexanderplatz*.
Giono's *Hill of Destiny*
Cocteau's *Enfants Terribles*.
Claudel's *The Satin Slipper*.
Moravia's *The Indifferent Ones*.

White, E. B. (1899), The Lady Is Cold. V
Wilson, Edmund (1895), I Thought of Daisy. F; Poets,
    Farewell. V, NF
Wolfe, Thomas (1900), Look Homeward, Angel. F
Wylie, Elinor (d. 1928), Angels and Earthly Creatures. V

1930

Adams, James Truslow (1878), The Adams Family. NF
Adams, Samuel Hopkins (1871), The Godlike Daniel. NF
Addams, Jane (1860), The Second Twenty Years at Hull-House.
    NF
Aiken, Conrad (1889), John Deth: A Metaphysical Legend and
    Other Poems. V; Gehenna. F
Anderson, Margaret (?), My Thirty Years' War. NF
Anderson, Maxwell (1888), Elizabeth the Queen. D
Asch, Sholem (1880), Sabbatai Zevi. D; The Mother. F
Auden, W. H. (1907), Poems. V
Barnes, Margaret Ayer (1886), Years of Grace. F
Barry, Philip (1896), Hotel Universe. D
Benchley, Robert (1889), The Treasurer's Report. NF
Boyle, Kay (1902), Wedding Day and Other Stories. F
Bradford, Roark (1896), Ol' King David an' the Philistine Boys.
    F
Buck, Pearl (1892), East Wind, West Wind. F
Byrd, Richard E. (1888), Little America. NF
Cabell, James Branch (1879), Some of Us: An Essay in
    Epitaphs. NF
Caldwell, Erskine (1903), Poor Fool. F
Connelly, Marc (1890), The Green Pastures [adapted from Roark
    Bradford's Ol' Man Adam an' His Chillun (1928)]. D
Crane, Hart (1899), The Bridge V
Deutsch, Babette (1895), Fire for the Night. V
Dos Passos, John (1896), The 42nd Parallel. F
Eberhart, Richard (1904), A Bravery of Earth. V
Eliot, T. S. (1888), Ash-Wednesday. V; Marina. V
Faulkner, William (1897), As I Lay Dying. F
Ferber, Edna (1887), Cimarron. F
Fisher, Dorothy Canfield (1897), The Deepening Stream. F
Fletcher, John Gould (1886), The Two Frontiers: A Study in
    Historical Psychology. NF
Frost, Robert (1874), Collected Poems. V
Garland, Hamlin (1860), Roadside Meetings. NF
Glaspell, Susan (1882), Alison's House. D
Gregory, Horace (1898), Chelsea Rooming House. V
Hammett, Dashiell (1894), The Maltese Falcon. F
Hergesheimer, Joseph (1880), The Party Dress. F
Hughes, Langston (1902), Not Without Laughter. F
Johnson, James Weldon (1871), Black Manhattan. NF
Kaufman, George S. (1889), Once in a Lifetime (with Moss
    Hart). D
Kunitz, Stanley J. (1905), Intellectual Things. V
Leonard, William Ellery (1876), This Midland City. V
Lewisohn, Ludwig (1882), Stephen Escott. F
Lowell, Amy (d. 1925), Poetry and Poets. NF
MacLeish, Archibald (1892), New Found Land. V
Marquand, J. P. (1893), Warning Hill. F
Masters, Edgar Lee (1868), Lichee Nuts. V
Mencken, H. L. (1880), Treatise on the Gods. NF

Economic crisis deepened.
Hawley-Smoot Tariff Act raised levels
    to new highs.
Veterans' Administration established.
New York Customs seized copies of
    Joyce's *Ulysses*.
Sinclair Lewis became first American to
    receive Nobel Prize in literature.
Fortune (New York), 1930–.

Worldwide economic depression.
London Naval Treaty (partial
    disarmament).
John Masefield named poet laureate of
    England.
Robert Bridges d.
D. H. Lawrence d.
Sir Arthur Conan Doyle d.
Vladimir Mayakovsky d.
Wyndham Lewis's *The Apes of God*.
Coward's *Private Lives*.
Evelyn Waugh's *Vile Bodies*.
Edith Sitwell's *Collected Poems*.
Rhys's *After Leaving Mr. Mackenzie*.
Maugham's *Cakes and Ale*.
Priestley's *Angel Pavement*.
Sassoon's *Memoirs of an Infantry
    Officer*.
Thomas Mann's *Mario and the
    Magician*.
Silone's *Fontamara*.
Brecht's *The Measures Taken*.
Musil's *The Man Without Qualities* (3
    vols., 1930–43).
Bunin's *The Well of Days*.
Mayakovsky's *The Bath-House*.
Ortega y Gasset's *The Revolt of the
    Masses*.

"Michael Gold" (1893), Jews Without Money. NF
Osborn, Paul (1901), The Vinegar Tree (pub. 1931). D
Parker, Dorothy (1893), Laments for the Living. F
Perelman, S. J. (1904), Parlor, Bedlam, and Bath (with Q. J. Reynolds). F
Poole, Ernest (1880), The Car of Croesus. F
Porter, Katherine Anne (1890), Flowering Judas and Other Stories. F
Pound, Ezra (1885), A Draft of XXX Cantos. V
Ransom, John Crowe (1888), God Without Thunder: An Unorthodox Defense of Orthodoxy. NF
Reese, Lizette Woodworth (1856), White April. V
Rice, Elmer (1892), A Voyage to Purilia. F
Riggs, Lynn (1899), Roadside. D
Roberts, Elizabeth Madox (1886), The Great Meadow. F
Roberts, Kenneth (1885), Arundel. F
Robinson, Edwin Arlington (1869), The Glory of the Nightingales. V
Rölvaag, O. E. (1876), Pure Gold. F
Sandburg, Carl (1878), Potato Face. F
Santayana, George (1863), The Realm of Matter. NF
Sheldon, Edward (1886), Dishonored Lady (with Margaret Ayer Barnes). D
Sherwood, Robert E. (1896), Waterloo Bridge. D
Sinclair, Upton (1878), Mountain City. F
Smith, Thorne (1892), Did She Fall? F
Stein, Gertrude (1874), Lucy Church Amiably. F
Stewart, Donald Ogden (1894), Rebound. D
Stone, Grace Zaring (1896), The Bitter Tea of General Yen. F
Suckow, Ruth (1892), The Kramer Girls. F
Tate, Allen (1894), Three Poems. V
Teasdale, Sara (1884), Stars To-night. V
Train, Arthur (1875), The Adventures of Ephraim Tutt. F
Twelve Southerners, I'll Take My Stand: The South and the Agrarian Tradition. NF
Van Vechten, Carl (1880), Parties. F
Wescott, Glenway (1901), The Babe's Bed. F
Wharton, Edith (1862), Certain People. F
Wilder, Thornton (1897), The Woman of Andros. F
Winters, Yvor (1900), The Proof. V

1931

Adamic, Louis (1899), Dynamite: The Story of Class Violence in America. NF
Adams, Franklin P. (1881), Christopher Columbus. V
Adams, James Truslow (1878), The Epic of America. NF
Aiken, Conrad (1889), The Coming Forth by Day of Osiris Jones. V; Preludes for Memnon. V
Aldrich, Bess Streeter (1881), White Bird Flying. F
Allen, Frederick Lewis (1890), Only Yesterday. NF
Anderson, Sherwood (1876), Perhaps Women. NF
Barry, Philip (1896), Tomorrow and Tomorrow. D
Behrman, S. N. (1893), Brief Moment. D
Bishop, John Peale (1891), Many Thousands Gone. F
Bontemps, Arna (1902), God Sends Sunday. F
Boyle, Kay (1902), Plagued by the Nightingale. F
Bradford, Roark (1896), John Henry. F
Buck, Pearl (1892), The Good Earth. F
Burke, Kenneth (1897), Counter-Statement. NF
Caldwell, Erskine (1903), American Earth. F
Canby, Henry Seidel (1878), Classic Americans. NF
Cantwell, Robert (1908), Laugh and Lie Down. F

Increasing financial panic and unemployment.
First Scottsboro, Ala., trial of nine young Negroes.
New York City's Empire State Building completed.
"The Star-Spangled Banner" declared national anthem.
Vachel Lindsay d.
David Belasco d.
Story (Vienna; Majorca; New York), 1931–53.

Proclamation of the Second Spanish Republic.
Japan invaded Manchuria.
Arnold Bennett d.
Arthur Schnitzler d.
Yeats's *Words for Music Perhaps.*
Woolf's *The Waves.*
D. H. Lawrence's *The Man Who Died.*
Dane's *Broome Stages.*

Cather, Willa (1873), Shadows on the Rock. F
Cozzens, James Gould (1903), S. S. San Pedro. F
Cummings, E. E. (1894), W (Viva). V
Dreiser, Theodore (1871), Dawn: A History of Myself.
    NF; Tragic America. NF
Eliot, T. S. (1888), Triumphal March. V; Thoughts After
    Lambeth. NF; Charles Whibley: A Memoir. NF
Faulkner, William (1897), Sanctuary. F; These 13. F
Garland, Hamlin (1860), Companions on the Trail. NF
Gordon, Caroline (1895), Penhally. F
Grant, Robert (1852), The Dark Horse. F
Green, Paul (1894), The House of Connelly. D
Hammett, Dashiell (1894), The Glass Key. F
Hergesheimer, Joseph (1830), The Limestone Tree.
    F; Sheridan: A Military Narrative. NF
Hughes, Langston (1902), The Negro Mother. V
Hurst, Fannie (1889), Back Street. F
Kelly, George (1887), Philip Goes Forth.D
La Farge, Oliver (1901), Sparks Fly Upward. F
Lytle, Andrew (1902), Bedford Forrest. NF
Masters, Edgar Lee (1868), Godbey: A Dramatic Poem.
    V; Lincoln the Man. NF
Millay, Edna St. Vincent (1892), Fatal Interview. V
Nash, Ogden (1902), Free Wheeling. V; Hard Lines. V
"Nathanael West" (1903), The Dream Life of Balso Snell. F
O'Neill, Eugene (1888), Mourning Becomes Electra. D
Parker, Dorothy (1893), Death and Taxes. V
Pershing, John J. (1860), My Experiences in the World War. NF
Pollock, Channing (1880), The House Beautiful. D
Pound, Ezra (1885), How to Read. NF
Rice, Elmer (1892), Counsellor-at-Law. D; The Left Bank. D
Richards, Laura Elizabeth (1850), Stepping Westward. NF
Riggs, Lynn (1899), Green Grow the Lilacs. D
Roberts, Elizabeth Madox (1886), A Buried Treasure. F
Roberts, Kenneth (1885), The Lively Lady. F
Robinson, Edwin Arlington (1869), Matthias at the Door. V
Rölvaag, O. E. (1876), Their Fathers' God. F
Rourke, Constance (1885), American Humor. NF
Santayana, George (1863), The Genteel Tradition at Bay. NF
Sherwood, Robert E. (1896), Reunion in Vienna. D; The
    Virtuous Knight. F
Sinclair, Upton (1878), The Wet Parade. F
Smith, Thorne (1892), The Night Life of the Gods.
    F; Turnabout. F
Steffens, Lincoln (1866), Autobiography. NF
Stein, Gertrude (1874), How to Write. NF
Stribling, T. S. (1881), The Forge. F
Suckow, Ruth (1892), Children and Older People. F
Thurber, James (1894), The Owl in the Attic and Other
    Perplexities. F, NF
Toomer, Jean (1894), Essentials. NF
Van Doren, Mark (1894), Jonathan Gentry. V
Wilder, Thornton (1897), The Long Christmas Dinner and Other
    Plays. D
Wilson, Edmund (1895), Axel's Castle. NF
Winters, Yvor (1900), The Journey. V

Dodie Smith's *Autumn Crocus.*
Coward's *Cavalcade.*
Rhys's *After Leaving Mr. Mackenzie.*
Compton-Burnett's *Men and Wives.*
Broch's *The Sleepwalkers* (1931–32).
Saint-Exupéry's *Night Flight.*
Tzara's *Approximate Man.*
Seferis's *Turning Point.*
Pagnol's *Fanny.*

1932

Adamic, Louis (1899), Laughing in the Jungle. NF
Adams, James Truslow (1878), The March of Democracy
    (2 vols., 1932–33). NF

Depression and unemployment
    rampant.
March of "Bonus Army" on
    Washington.

Anderson, Maxwell (1888), Night Over Taos. D
Anderson, Sherwood (1876), Beyond Desire. F
Auden, W. H. (1907), The Orators. V, NF
Babbitt, Irving (1865), On Being Creative. NF
Barry, Philip (1896), The Animal Kingdom. D
Becker, Carl (1873), The Heavenly City of the Eighteenth
   Century Philosophers. NF
Behrman, S. N. (1893), Biography (pub. 1933). D
Buck, Pearl (1892), Sons. F
Burke, Kenneth (1897), Towards a Better Life. F
Cabell, James Branch (1879), These Restless Heads. NF
Caldwell, Erskine (1903), Tobacco Road. F
Calverton, V. F. (1900), The Liberation of American Literature.
   NF
Cather, Willa (1873), Obscure Destinies. F
Chapman, John Jay (1862), New Horizons in American Life.
   NF
Chodorov, Edward (1904), Wonder Boy. D
Dahlberg, Edward (1900), From Flushing to Calvary. F
Day, Clarence (1874), God and My Father. NF
De Kruif, Paul (1890), Men Against Death. NF
De Voto, Bernard (1897), Mark Twain's America. NF
Dos Passos, John (1896), 1919. F
Eliot, T. S. (1888), Sweeney Agonistes. D; John Dryden, the
   Poet, the Dramatist, the Critic. NF; Selected Essays 1917–
   1932. NF
Farrell, James T. (1904), Young Lonigan: A Boyhood in
   Chicago Streets. F
Faulkner, William (1897), Light in August. F
Fisher, Vardis (1895), In Tragic Life. F
Garland, Hamlin (1860), My Friendly Contemporaries. NF
Glasgow, Ellen (1874), The Sheltered Life. F
Hale, Nancy (1908), The Young Die Good. F
Halliburton, Richard (1900), The Flying Carpet. NF
Hammett, Dashiell (1894), The Thin Man. F
Hecht, Ben (1894), 20th Century (with Charles MacArthur). D
Hemingway, Ernest (1899), Death in the Afternoon. NF
Hergesheimer, Joseph (1880), Berlin. NF; Love in the United
   States and the Big Shot. F
Herrick, Robert (1868), The End of Desire. F
Heyward, Du Bose (1885), Peter Ashley. F
Hughes, Langston (1902), Scottsboro Limited. V, D; The
   Dream Keeper. V
Jeffers, Robinson (1887), Thurso's Landing and Other Poems. V
Kaufman, George S. (1889), Dinner at Eight (with Edna Ferber).
   D
Lawson, John Howard (1895), Success Story. D
Lewisohn, Ludwig (1882), Expression in America. NF
Luhan, Mabel Dodge (1879), Lorenzo in Taos. NF
Lumpkin, Grace (?), To Make My Bread. F
MacLeish, Archibald (1892), Conquistador. V
Mencken, H. L. (1880), Making a President. NF
Millay, Edna St. Vincent (1892), The Princess Marries the Page.
   D
Nordhoff, Charles Bernard (1887) and James Norman Hall
   (1887), Mutiny on the Bounty. F
Peterkin, Julia (1880), Bright Skin. F
Repplier, Agnes (1858), To Think of Tea! NF
Rice, Elmer (1892), The House in Blind Alley. D; Black Sheep
   (pub. 1938). D
Roberts, Elizabeth Madox (1886), The Haunted Mirror. F
Robinson, Edwin Arlington (1869), Nicodemus. V

Norris–La Guardia Anti-Injunction Act.
Reconstruction Finance Corp.
   established.
Lindbergh kidnapping.
Folger Shakespeare Memorial Library
   dedicated, in Washington.
Hart Crane d.
John Updike b.
Sylvia Plath b.
Common Sense (New York), 1932–46.
The American Scholar (New York;
   Washington), 1932–.
The American Spectator (New York),
   1932–37.

Antonio Salazar became virtual dictator
   of Portugal.
Scrutiny (Cambridge), 1932–53.
Lytton Strachey d.
V. S. Naipaul b.
Evelyn Waugh's *Black Mischief.*
Aldous Huxley's *Brave New World.*
Shaw's *Too True To Be Good.*
D. H. Lawrence's *Last Poems.*
Bowen's *To the North.*
Greene's *Stamboul Train.*
Gibbons's *Cold Comfort Farm.*
Romains's *Men of Good Will* (27 vols.,
   1932–46).
Sholokhov's *Virgin Soil Upturned* (2
   vols., 1932–60).
Céline's *Journey to the End of Night.*
Giono's *Blue Boy.*
Seferis's *The Cistern.*
Tanizaki's *Ashikari.*

Runyon, Damon (1884), Guys and Dolls. F
Sandburg, Carl (1878), Mary Lincoln, Wife and Widow (with Paul Angle). NF
Sherwood, Robert E. (1896), Reunion in Vienna. D; Unending Crusade. F
Sinclair, Upton (1878), American Outpost. NF
Skinner, Cornelia Otis (1901), Tiny Garments. NF
Smith, Thorne (1892), The Bishop's Jaegers. F; Topper Takes A Trip. F
Stein, Gertrude (1874), Operas and Plays. D
Steinbeck, John (1902), The Pastures of Heaven. F
Stong, Phil (1899), State Fair. F
Stribling, T. S. (1881), The Store. F
Tate, Allen (1899), Poems: 1928–1931. V
Teasdale, Sara (1884), A Country House. V
Thompson, Dorothy (1894), ''I Saw Hitler!'' NF
Van Vechten, Carl (1880), Sacred and Profane Memories. NF
Wescott, Glenway (1901), Fear and Trembling. NF; A Calendar of Saints for Unbelievers. NF
Wharton, Edith (1862), The Gods Arrive. F
Williams, William Carlos (1883), The Knife of the Times. F; A Novelette and Other Prose. F, NF
Wilson, Edmund (1895), The American Jitters: A Year of the Slump. NF

1933

Adams, James Truslow (1878), Henry Adams. NF
Adams, Léonie (1899), This Measure. V
Agar, Herbert (1897), The People's Choice. NF
Aiken, Conrad (1889), Great Circle. F
Allen, Hervey (1889), Anthony Adverse. F
Anderson, Maxwell (1888), Both Your Houses. D; Mary of Scotland. D
Anderson, Sherwood (1876), Death in the Woods. F
Asch, Sholem (1880), Three Cities. NF
Auden, W. H. (1907), The Dance of Death. D
Benét, Stephen Vincent (1898), A Book of Americans (with Rosemary Carr Benét). V
Bishop, John Peale (1891), Now with His Love. V
Boyle, Kay (1902), The First Lover. F; Gentlemen, I Address You Privately. F
Buck, Pearl (1892), First Wife. F
Burman, Ben Lucien (1895), Steamboat Round the Bend. F
Cabell, James Branch (1879), Special Delivery: A Packet of Replies. F, NF
Caldwell, Erskine (1903), God's Little Acre. F; We Are the Living. F
Carroll, Gladys Hasty (1904), As the Earth Turns. F
Coffin, Robert P. Tristram (1892), Ballads of Square-Toed Americans. V
Cozzens, James Gould (1903), The Last Adam. F
Crane, Hart (d. 1932), Collected Poems. V
Cummings, E. E. (1894), Eimi. NF
Eliot, T.S. (1888), The Use of Poetry and the Use of Criticism. NF
Farrell, James T. (1904), Gas-House McGinty. F
Faulkner, William (1897), A Green Bough. V
Gale, Zona (1874), Papa La Fleur. F
Gardner, Erle Stanley (1899), The Case of the Velvet Claws. F; The Case of the Sulky Girl. F

20th Amendment (abolishing ''Lame Duck'' Congress) and 21st Amendment (repeal of prohibition) ratified.
Closing of banks and stock exchanges.
''Hundred Days'' of the New Deal.
National Industrial Recovery Act.
Tennessee Valley Authority established to conserve area resources.
U.S. recognized Soviet Union.
Frances Perkins became first woman Cabinet member (Secretary of Labor).
Century of Progress Exposition in Chicago.
Institute for Advanced Study opened in Princeton, N.J.
Ban on importation of Ulysses lifted.
Ring Lardner d.
Sara Teasdale d.
Philip Roth b.
The American Review (New York), 1933–37.
Esquire (Chicago; New York), 1933–.
Newsweek (Dayton; New York), 1933–.

Adolf Hitler appointed chancellor of Germany.
Nazis burned Reichstag building.
Einstein and other émigrés fled to U.S.
Stalin began purge of the Communist Party (1933–39).
John Galsworthy d.
George Moore d.
Yevgeny Yevtushenko b.
Andrei Voznesensky b.
Spender's Poems.
O'Casey's Within the Gates.

Gregory, Horace (1898), No Retreat. V
Guest, Edgar A. (1881), Life's Highway. V
Halper, Albert (1904), Union Square. F
Hemingway, Ernest (1899), Winner Take Nothing. F
Herbst, Josephine (1897), Pity Is Not Enough. F
Hergesheimer, Joseph (1880), Tropical Winter. F
Herrick, Robert (1868), Sometime. F
Hicks, Granville (1901), The Great Tradition. NF
Hillyer, Robert (1901), Collected Verse. V
Horgan, Paul (1903), The Fault of Angels. F
Howard, Sidney (1891), Alien Corn. D
Hurst, Fannie (1889), Imitation of Life. F
Jeffers, Robinson (1887), Give Your Heart to the Hawks. V
Johnson, James Weldon (1871), Along This Way. NF
Kingsley, Sidney (1906), Men in White. D
Kirkland, Jack (1902), Tobacco Road [adapted from Erskine Caldwell's novel (1932)]. D
Lardner, Ring (1885), Lose with a Smile. F
Lewis, Sinclair (1885), Ann Vickers. F
Luhan, Mabel Dodge (1879), Intimate Memories: Background. NF
MacLeish, Archibald (1892), Frescoes for Mr. Rockefeller's City. V; Poems. V
Marquand, J. P. (1893), Haven's End. F
Masters, Edgar Lee (1868), The Tale of Chicago. NF
Nash, Ogden (1902), Happy Days. V
Nathan, Robert (1894), One More Spring. F
"Nathanael West" (1903), Miss Lonelyhearts. F
O'Neill, Eugene (1888), Ah, Wilderness! D
Parker, Dorothy (1893), After Such Pleasures. F
Pound, Ezra (1885), ABC of Economics. F
Rawlings, Marjorie Kinnan (1896), South Moon Under. F
Reese, Lizette Woodworth (1856), Pastures. V
Rice, Elmer (1892), We, the People. D
Roberts, Kenneth (1885), Rabble in Arms. F
Robinson, Edwin Arlington (1869), Talifer. V
Rölvaag, O. E. (1876), The Boat of Longing. F
Santayana, George (1863), Five Essays. NF
Smith, Thorne (1892), Skin and Bones. F
Stein, Gertrude (1874), The Autobiography of Alice B. Toklas. NF; Matisse Picasso and Gertrude Stein with Two Shorter Stories. NF, F
Steinbeck, John (1902), To a God Unknown. F
Teasdale, Sara (1884), Strange Victory. V
Thurber, James (1894), My Life and Hard Times. NF
Wharton, Edith (1862), Human Nature. F
White, E. B. (1899), Alice Through the Cellophane. NF
"William March" (1894), Company K. F
Woollcott, Alexander (1887), The Dark Tower (with George S. Kaufman). D

Yeats's Collected Poems.
Wells's The Shape of Things to Come.
Coward's Design for Living.
Hilton's Lost Horizon.
O'Faolain's A Nest of Simple Folk.
Malraux's Man's Fate.
Thomas Mann's Joseph and His Brothers (4 vols., 1933–43).
Werfel's The Forty Days of Musa Dagh.
Mandelstam's Journey to Armenia.
García Lorca's Blood Wedding.
Neruda's Residence on Earth (3 vols., 1933–47).
Tanizaki's A Portrait of Shunkin.

1934

Adamic, Louis (1899), The Native's Return. NF
Agee, James (1909), Permit Me Voyage. V
Aiken, Conrad (1889), Among the Lost People. F
Anderson, Maxwell (1888), Valley Forge. D
Anderson, Sherwood (1876), No Swank. NF
Asch, Sholem (1880), Salvation. F
Auden, W. H. (1907), Poems. V

Employment rose, business failures declined.
Federal Communications Commission established.
Securities and Exchange Commission established.
Tydings-McDuffie Act (granted the Philippines independence in 1946).

"**B. Traven**" (?), The Death Ship. F
Barry, Philip (1896), The Joyous Season. D
Behrman, S. N. (1893), Rain from Heaven (pub. 1935). D
Benchley, Robert (1889), From Bed to Worse. NF
Benét, Stephen Vincent (1898), James Shore's Daughter. F
Brandeis, Louis (1856), The Curse of Bigness. NF
Cabell, James Branch (1879), Ladies and Gentlemen. F, NF:
  Smirt: An Urban Nightmare. F
Cain, James M. (1892), The Postman Always Rings Twice. F
Cantwell, Robert (1908), The Land of Plenty. F
Carmer, Carl (1893), Stars Fell on Alabama. F
Chase, Mary Ellen (1887), Mary Peters. F
Connelly, Marc (1890), The Farmer Takes a Wife [adapted with
  F. B. Elser from Walter Edmonds's novel Rome Haul (1929)].
  D
Cowley, Malcolm (1898), Exile's Return: A Narrative of Ideas
  (rev. 1951). NF
Cozzens, James Gould (1903), Castaway. F
Dahlberg, Edward (1900), Those Who Perish. F
Dewey, John (1859), Art as Experience. NF
Dos Passos, John (1896), In All Countries. NF; Three Plays. D
Eliot, T. S. (1888), After Strange Gods. NF; The Rock: A
  Pageant Play. D; Elizabethan Essays. NF
Engle, Paul (1908), American Song. V
Farrell, James T. (1904), The Young Manhood of Studs
  Lonigan. F; Calico Shoes and Other Stories. F
Faulkner, William (1898), Doctor Martino and Other Stories. F
Fisher, Vardis (1895), Passions Spin the Plot. F
Fitzgerald, F. Scott (1896), Tender Is the Night. F
Freeman, Douglas Southall (1886), R. E. Lee (4 vols., 1934–
  35). NF
Fuchs, Daniel (1909), Summer in Williamsburg. F
Gale, Zona (1874), Faint Perfume [adapted from her novel
  (1923)]. D
Garland, Hamlin (1860), Afternoon Neighbors. NF
Gordon, Caroline (1895), Aleck Maury, Sportsman. F
Grant, Robert (1852), Fourscore. NF
Hale, Nancy (1908), Never Any More. F
Hellman, Lillian (1905), The Children's Hour. D
Herbst, Josephine (1897), The Executioner Waits. F
Hergesheimer, Joseph (1880), The Foolscap Rose. F
Howard, Sidney (1891), Dodsworth [adapted with Sinclair Lewis
  from Lewis's novel (1929).]. D; Yellow Jack. D
Hughes, Langston (1902), The Ways of White Folks. F
Johnson, Josephine (1910), Now in November. F
Josephson, Matthew (1899), The Robber Barons. NF
Kantor, MacKinlay (1904), Long Remember. F
Kaufman, George S. (1889), Merrily We Roll Along (with Moss
  Hart). D
Lardner, Ring (d. 1933), First and Last. F
Lawson, John Howard (1895), The Pure in Heart.
  D; Gentlewoman. D
Lewis, Sinclair (1885), Work of Art. F
Lincoln, Victoria (1904), February Hill. F
Lomax, John A. (1872), American Ballads and Folk Songs
  (compiler, with Alan Lomax). V
Maxwell, William (1908), Bright Center of Heaven. F
Mencken, H. L. (1880), Treatise on Right and Wrong. NF
Millay, Edna St. Vincent (1892), Wine From These Grapes. V
Miller, Henry (1891), Tropic of Cancer (pub. in Paris). F
Mumford, Lewis (1895), Technics and Civilization. NF

Death penalty enacted for kidnapping
  across state lines.
The Partisan Review (New York;
  Boston), 1934–.
*ELH: A Journal of English Literary
  History* (Baltimore), 1934–.

___

Nazi storm troopers began purges.
Soviet Union joined League of Nations.
Italian-Ethiopian War (1934–35).
SS *Queen Mary* launched.
Sir Arthur Wing Pinero d.
Andrei Bely d.
Graves's *I, Claudius.*
Hilton's *Goodbye, Mr. Chips.*
Sayers's *The Nine Tailors.*
Dylan Thomas's *18 Poems.*
Corvo's *The Desire and Pursuit of the
  Whole.*
Evelyn Waugh's *A Handful of Dust.*
Orwell's *Burmese Days.*
Laurence Housman's *Victoria Regina.*
Snow's *The Search.*
Toynbee's *A Study of History* (12 vols.,
  1934–61).
Cocteau's *The Infernal Machine.*
García Lorca's *Yerma.*
Giono's *The Song of the World.*
Beckett's *More Pricks Than Kicks.*
Dinesen's *Seven Gothic Tales.*
Vsevolod Ivanov's *The Adventures of a
  Fakir* (1934–35).

"Nathanael West" (1903), A Cool Million. F
Nordhoff, Charles Bernard (1887) and Charles Norman Hall
    (1887), Pitcairn's Island. F; Men Against the Sea. F
O'Hara, John (1905), Appointment in Samarra. F
O'Neill, Eugene (1888), Days Without End. D
Poole, Ernest (1880), One of Us. F
Pound, Ezra (1885), Eleven New Cantos: XXXI–XLI. V; ABC
    of Reading. NF; Make It New. NF
Rice, Elmer (1892), Judgment Day. D; The Passing of Chow-
    Chow. D; Three Plays Without Words. D; Between Two
    Worlds (pub. 1935). D
Roberts, Kenneth (1885), Captain Caution. F
Robinson, Edwin Arlington (1869), Amaranth. V
Roth, Henry (1906), Call It Sleep. F
Saroyan, William (1908), The Daring Young Man on the Flying
    Trapeze and Other Stories. F
Stein, Gertrude (1874), Four Saints in Three Acts. D; Portraits
    and Prayers. D, NF
Stribling, T. S. (1881), Unfinished Cathedral. F
Stuart, Jesse (1907), Man with a Bull-Tongue Plow. V
Suckow, Ruth (1892), The Folks. F
Wharton, Edith (1862), A Backward Glance. NF
White, E. B. (1899), Everyday Is Saturday. NF
Wilder, Thornton (1897), Heaven's My Destination (pub. in
    London). F
Williams, William Carlos (1883), Collected Poems 1921–1931.
    V
Winters, Yvor (1900), Before Disaster. V
Woollcott, Alexander (1887), While Rome Burns. NF

1935

Adamic, Louis (1899), Grandsons: A Story of American Lives. F
Adams, Franklin P. (1881), The Diary of Our Own Samuel
    Pepys. NF
Agar, Herbert (1897), Land of the Free. NF
Aiken, Conrad (1889), King Coffin. F
Akins, Zoë (1886), The Old Maid [adapted from Edith Wharton's
    novella (1924)]. D
Aldrich, Bess Streeter (1881), Spring Came On Forever. F
Algren, Nelson (1909), Somebody in Boots. F
Allen, Frederick Lewis (1890), The Lords of Creation. NF
Anderson, Maxwell (1888), Winterset. D
Anderson, Sherwood (1876), Puzzled America. NF
Asch, Sholem (1880), In the Beginning. NF
Auden, W. H. (1907), The Dog Beneath the Skin (with
    Christopher Isherwood). D
"B. Traven" (?), The Treasure of the Sierra Madre. F
Barnes, Margaret Ayer (1886), Edna, His Wife. F
Barry, Philip (1896), Bright Star. D
Bishop, John Peale (1891), Minute Particulars. V; Act of
    Darkness. F
Blackmur, R. P. (1904), The Double Agent. NF
Buck, Pearl (1892), A House Divided. F
Burke, Kenneth (1897), Permanence and Change: An Anatomy
    of Purpose. NF
Cabell, James Branch (1879), Smith: A Sylvan Interlude. F
Caldwell, Erskine (1903), Journeyman. F; Kneel to the Rising
    Sun. F; Some American People. NF
Cather, Willa (1873), Lucy Gayheart. F
Chase, Mary Ellen (1887), Silas Crockett. F

National Recovery Administration
    declared unconstitutional.
Social Security Act passed by Congress.
Works Projects Administration
    established.
Transpacific air service established.
Gershwin and Heyward's Porgy and
    Bess opened.
Edwin Arlington Robinson d.
The Southern Review (Baton Rouge),
    1935–42; 1965–.

Jews lost civil rights in Germany.
Start of Germany's expansion under
    Hitler.
T. E. Lawrence d.
Bowen's The House in Paris.
Emlyn Williams's Night Must Fall.
George Barker's Poems.
Cronin's The Stars Look Down.
MacNeice's Poems
Bagnold's National Velvet.
Wodehouse's Blandings Castle.
Forester's The African Queen.
Giraudoux's The Trojan War Will Not
    Take Place.
Seferis's Myth-History.
Tzara's Grains and By-Products.
Troyat's False Light.
Giono's Joy of Man's Desiring.
Canetti's Auto-da-Fé.

Chodorov, Edward (1904), Kind Lady. D
Coffin, Robert P. Tristram (1892), Strange Holiness. V
Cullen, Countee (1903), The Medea and Some Poems. D, V
Cummings, E. E. (1894), Tom: A Ballet. D; No Thanks. V
Day, Clarence (1874), Life with Father. NF
Dewey, John (1859), Liberalism and Social Action. NF
Douglas, Lloyd C. (1877), Green Light. F
DuBois, William E. B. (1868), Black Reconstruction. NF
Durant, Will (1885) **and Ariel Durant** (1898), The Story of
　Civilization (11 vols., 1935–68). NF
Eliot, T. S. (1888), Murder in the Cathedral. D
Farrell, James T. (1904), Judgment Day. F; Guillotine Party
　and Other Stories. F
Faulkner, William (1897), Pylon. F
Fearing, Kenneth (1902), Poems. V
Field, Rachel (1894), Time Out of Mind. F
Fisher, Vardis (1895), We Are Betrayed. F
Fitzgerald, F. Scott (1896), Taps at Reveille. F
Fitzgerald, Robert (1910), Poems. V
Fletcher, John Gould (1886), XXIV Elegies. V
Forbes, Esther (1891), Miss Marvel. F
Garland, Hamlin (1860), Iowa, O Iowa! V
Glasgow, Ellen (1874), Vein of Iron. F
Green, Paul (1894), This Body the Earth. F
Gregory, Horace (1898), Chorus for Survival. V
Halliburton, Richard (1900), Seven League Boots. NF
Hemingway, Ernest (1899), Green Hills of Africa. NF
Horgan, Paul (1903), No Quarter Given. F
Howard, Sidney (1891), Paths of Glory (adapted from Humphrey
　Cobb's novel (1935)]. D
Hughes, Langston (1902), Mulatto (pub. 1963). D
Isherwood, Christopher (1904), The Last of Mr. Norris. F
Jeffers, Robinson (1887), Solstice and Other Poems. V
Johnson, James Weldon (1871), Selected Poems. V
Johnson, Josephine (1910), Winter Orchard. F
Kantor, MacKinlay (1904), The Voice of Bugle Ann. F
Kaufman, George S. (1889), First Lady (with Katherine
　Dayton). F
Kingsley, Sidney (1906), Dead End (pub. 1936). D
Lewis, Sinclair (1885), It Can't Happen Here. F; Selected Short
　Stories. F; Jayhawker (with Lloyd Lewis). D
Lindbergh, Anne Morrow (1906), North to the Orient. NF
Luhan, Mabel Dodge (1879), Winter in Taos. NF; European
　Experiences. NF
Lumpkin, Grace (?), A Sign for Cain. F
McCoy, Horace (1897), They Shoot Horses, Don't They? F
MacLeish, Archibald (1892), Panic. D
Marquand, J. P. (1893), Ming Yellow. F; No Hero. F
Masters, Edgar Lee (1868), Invisible Landscapes. V; Vachel
　Lindsay. NF
Melville, Herman (d. 1891), Journal Up the Straits. NF
Miller, Henry (1891), Aller Retour New York. NF
Moore, Marianne (1887), Selected Poems. V
Neihardt, John G. (1881), The Song of the Messiah. V
Odets, Clifford (1906), Awake and Sing! D; Waiting for Lefty.
　D; Till the Day I Die. D; Paradise Lost (pub. 1936). D
O'Hara, John (1905), The Doctor's Son and Other Stories.
　F; Butterfield 8. F
Perry, Bliss (1860), And Gladly Teach. NF
Pound, Ezra (1885), Jefferson and/or Mussolini. NF; Social
　Credit: An Impact. NF
Prokosch, Frederic (1908), The Asiatics. F

Rand, Ayn (1905), The Night of January 16th. D
Rawlings, Marjorie Kinnan (1896), Golden Apples. F
Rice, Elmer (1892), Not for Children. D
Ridge, Lola (1871), Dance of Fire. V
Roberts, Elizabeth Madox (1886), He Sent Forth a Raven. F
Robinson, Edwin Arlington (1869), King Jasper. V
Rukeyser, Muriel (1913), Theory of Flight. V
Runyon, Damon (1884), A Slight Case of Murder (with Howard
    Lindsay). D
Sandoz, Mari (1896), Old Jules. NF
Santayana, George (1863), The Last Puritan. F
Schorer, Mark (1908), A House Too Old. F
Shapiro, Karl (1913), Poems. V
Sheean, Vincent (1899), Personal History. NF
Sherwood, Robert E. (1895), The Petrified Forest. D
Spewack, Samuel (1899), Boy Meets Girl (with Bella Spewack;
    pub. 1936). D
Stein, Gertrude (1874), Narration. NF; Lectures in America. NF
Steinbeck, John (1902), Tortilla Flat. F
Stout, Rex (1886), The League of Frightened Men. F
Thurber, James (1894), The Middle Aged Man on the Flying
    Trapeze. F, NF
Van Doren, Mark (1894), The Transients. F
Warren, Robert Penn (1905), Thirty-Six Poems. V
Williams, William Carlos (1883), An Early Martyr. V
Wolfe, Thomas (1900), Of Time and the River. F; From Death
    to Morning. F

1936

Adamic, Louis (1899), Cradle of Life: The Story of One Man's
    Beginnings. F
Aiken, Conrad (1889), Time in the Rock. V
Aldrich, Bess Streeter (1881), The Man Who Caught the
    Weather. F
Anderson, Maxwell (1888), The Masque of Kings. D; The
    Wingless Victory. D
Anderson, Sherwood (1876), Kit Brandon. F
Asch, Sholem (1880), The War Goes On. F
Auden, W. H. (1907), The Ascent of F6 (with Christopher
    Isherwood). D
Barnes, Djuna (1892), Nightwood (pub. in London; American
    edition, 1937). F
Behrman, S. N. (1893), End of Summer. D
Benchley, Robert (1889), My Ten Years in a Quandary and How
    They Grew. NF
Benét, Stephen Vincent (1898), Burning City. V
Bontemps, Arna (1902), Black Thunder. F
Boothe, Clare (1903), The Women. D
Boyle, Kay (1902), The White Horses of Vienna and Other
    Stories. F; Death of a Man. F
Brooks, Van Wyck (1886), The Flowering of New England. NF
Cain, James M. (1892), Double Indemnity. F
Caldwell, Erskine (1903), The Sacrilege of Alan Kent. F
Carmer, Carl (1893), Listen for a Lonesome Drum. F
Carnegie, Dale (1888), How to Win Friends and Influence
    People. NF
Cather, Willa (1873), Not Under Forty. NF
Cozzens, James Gould (1903), Men and Brethren. F

Passage of "Bonus Act" (cash payment
    to World War I veterans).
Dust bowl drought caused havoc for
    farmers.
Inter-American Peace Conference in
    Buenos Aires.
Boulder (Hoover) Dam on Colorado
    River completed.
Labor discovered efficacy of sit-down
    strikes.
Eugene O'Neill awarded Nobel Prize in
    literature.
Ford Foundation (worldwide charity)
    established.
Lincoln Steffens d.
Life (Chicago), 1936–72; 1978– .
Science and Society (New York),
    1936– .

Spanish Civil War (1936–39).
Death of George V; accession and
    abdication of Edward VIII; accession
    of George VI.
Proclamation of "Rome-Berlin Axis."
Rudyard Kipling d.
A. E. Housman d.
Federico García Lorca d.
Maxim Gorky d.
Luigi Pirandello d.
Miguel de Unamuno d.
Shaw's The Millionairess.
Aldous Huxley's Eyeless in Gaza.

Cummings, E. E. (1894), 1/20. V
Davenport, Marcia (1903), Of Lena Geyer. F
Dickinson, Emily (d. 1886), Unpublished Poems. V
Dos Passos, John (1896), The Big Money. F
Eastman, Max (1873), Enjoyment of Laughter. NF
Edmonds, Walter D. (1903), Drums Along the Mohawk. F
Eliot, T. S. (1888), Collected Poems 1909–1935. V
Engle, Paul (1908), Break the Heart's Anger. V
Farrell, James T. (1904), A World I Never Made. F
Faulkner, William (1897), Absalom, Absalom! F
Fisher, Vardis (1895), No Villain Need Be. F
Fletcher, John Gould (1886), The Epic of Arkansas. V
Frost, Robert (1874), A Further Range. V
Fuchs, Daniel (1909), Homage to Blenholt. F
Garland, Hamlin (1860), Forty Years of Psychic Research. NF
Green, Paul (1894), Hymn to the Rising Sun. D
Gunther, John (1910), Inside Europe. NF
"H.D." (1886), The Hedgehog. F
Hellman, Lillian (1905), Days to Come (pub. 1937). D
Heyward, DuBose (1885), Lost Morning. F
Horgan, Paul (1903), Main Line West. F
Hutchins, Robert (1899), The Higher Learning in America. NF
Jeffers, Robinson (1887), The Beaks of Eagles. V
Kaufman, George S. (1889), Stage Door (with Edna Ferber).
    D; You Can't Take It With You (with Moss Hart). D
Kelly, George (1887), Reflected Glory. D
Kingsley, Sidney (1906), Ten Million Ghosts. D
Lewis, Sinclair (1885), It Can't Happen Here (with John C.
    Moffitt). D
Luhan, Mabel Dodge (1879), Movers and Shakers. NF
Lytle, Andrew (1902), The Long Night. F
MacLeish, Archibald (1892), Public Speech. V
Marquand, J. P. (1893), Thank You, Mr. Moto. F
Masters, Edgar Lee (1868), Poems of People. V; Across Spoon
    River. NF
"Michael Gold" (1893), Battle Hymn (with Michael Blankfort).
    D
Miller, Henry (1891), Black Spring (pub. in Paris). F
Mitchell, Margaret (1900), Gone with the Wind. F
Moore, Marianne (1897), The Pangolin and Other Verse. V
Nash, Ogden (1902), The Bad Parents' Garden of Verse. V
Nin, Anaïs (1903), The House of Incest. F
Parker, Dorothy (1893), Not So Deep As a Well: Collected
    Poems. V
Patchen, Kenneth (1911), Before the Grave. V
Prokosch, Frederic (1908), The Assassins. V
Rand, Ayn (1905), We, the Living. F
Reese, Lizette Woodworth (1856), The Old House in the
    Country. V
Richter, Conrad (1890), Early Americana. F
Riggs, Lynn (1899), Russet Mantle. D; The Cherokee
    Night. D
Sandburg, Carl (1878), The People, Yes. V
Santayana, George (1863), Obiter Scripta. NF
Saroyan, William (1908), Inhale and Exhale. F; Three Times
    Three. F
Scott, Winfield Townley (1910), Elegy for Robinson. V
Shaw, Irwin (1913), Bury the Dead. D
Sherwood, Robert E. (1896), Idiot's Delight. D; Tovarich
    [adapted from Jacques Deval's play (1934)]. D
Stein, Gertrude (1874), The Geographical History of America.
    NF

Daphne du Maurier's Jamaica Inn.
Sassoon's Sherston's Progress.
Holtby's South Riding.
Silone's Bread and Wine.
Bernanos's Diary of a Country Priest.
García Lorca's The House of Bernarda
    Alba (prod. posth., 1945).
Amado's Dead Sea.
Pagnol's César.
Céline's Death on the Installment Plan.
Montherlant's The Girls (4 vols.,
    1936–39).

Steinbeck, John (1902), In Dubious Battle. F
Stevens, Wallace (1879), Owl's Clover. V; Ideas of Order. V
Stuart, Jesse (1907), Head o' W-Hollow. F
Tate, Allen (1899), The Mediterranean and Other Poems.
  V; Reactionary Essays on Poetry and Ideas. NF
Train, Arthur (1875), Mr. Tutt's Case Book. F
Wharton, Edith (1862), The World Over. F
Wheelock, John Hall (1886), Poems, 1911–1936. V
Williams, William Carlos (1883), Adam & Eve & The City. V
Wilson, Edmund (1895), Travels in Two Democracies. NF
Wolfe, Thomas (1900), The Story of a Novel. NF

1937

Adamic, Louis (1899), The House in Antigua. NF
Anderson, Maxwell (1888), High Tor. D; The Star-Wagon. D
Auden, W. H. (1907), Letters from Iceland (with Louis
  MacNeice). NF, V
Behrman, S. N. (1893), Amphitryon 38 (adapted from a French
  version of a Greek legend). D
Bemelmans, Ludwig(1898), My War with the United States. NF
Benét, Stephen Vincent (1898), Thirteen O'Clock. F; The Devil
  and Daniel Webster. F; The Headless Horseman. D
Blackmur, R. P. (1904), From Jordan's Delight. V
Bogan, Louise (1897), The Sleeping Fury. V
Bromfield, Louis (1896), The Rains Came. F
Burke, Kenneth (1897), Attitudes Toward History. NF
Cabell, James Branch (1879), Smire: An Acceptance in the
  Third Person. F
Cain, James M. (1892), Serenade. F
Caldwell, Erskine (1903), You Have Seen Their Faces (with
  Margaret Bourke-White). NF
Crothers, Rachel (1878), Susan and God (pub. 1938). D
Davis, Clyde Brion (1894), The Anointed. F
Day, Clarence (1874), Life with Mother. NF
Eberhart, Richard (1904), Reading the Spirit. V
Farrell, James T. (1904), Can All This Grandeur Perish? F
Fletcher, John Gould (1886), Life Is My Song. F
Forbes, Esther (1891), Paradise. F
Fuchs, Daniel (1909), Low Company. F
Gordon, Caroline (1895), The Garden of Adonis. F; None Shall
  Look Back. F
Green, Paul (1894), The Lost Colony. D
Hecht, Ben (1894), To Quito and Back. D
Hemingway, Ernest (1899), To Have and Have Not. F
Hillyer, Robert (1895), A Letter to Robert Frost and Others. V
Horgan, Paul (1903), Lamp on the Plains. F
Howard, Sidney (1891), The Ghost of Yankee Doodle. D
Hurston, Zora Neale (1901), Their Eyes Were Watching God. F
Jeffers, Robinson (1887), Such Counsels You Gave to Me. V
Johnson, Josephine (1910), Jordanstown. F; Years's End. V
Kaufman, George S. (1889), I'd Rather Be Right (with Moss
  Hart). D
Kober, Arthur (1900), Having a Wonderful Time. D
La Farge, Oliver (1901), The Enemy Gods. F
Lawson, John Howard (1895), Marching Song. D
"Leonard Q. Ross" (1908), The Education of H∗Y∗M∗A∗N
  K∗A∗P∗L∗A∗N. F
Levin, Meyer (1905), The Old Bunch. F
Luhan, Mabel Dodge (1879), Edge of Taos Desert. NF

Economic "recession" and industrial
  unrest.
U.S. Neutrality Act prohibited export of
  arms.
Drought intensified migrant workers'
  problems.
Farm Security Administration
  established.
Dirigible Hindenburg exploded at
  Lakehurst, N.J.
Golden Gate Bridge dedicated in San
  Francisco.
Edith Wharton d.

Emergence of Franco's dictatorship in
  Spain.
Neville Chamberlain elected prime
  minister of Great Britain.
Picasso painted Guernica mural.
Sir James M. Barrie d.
Woolf's The Years.
Cronin's The Citadel.
Bottome's The Mortal Storm.
Muir's Journeys and Places.
David Jones's In Parenthesis.
Wyndham Lewis's Blasting and
  Bombardiering.
Sharp's The Nutmeg Tree.
Koestler's Spanish Testament.
Charles Williams's Descent into Hell.
Tolkien's The Hobbit; or, There and
  Back Again.
Rex Warner's The Wild Goose Chase.
Malraux's Man's Hope.
Dinesen's Out of Africa.
Paz's Root of Man.
Kawabata's Snow Country.
Neruda's Spain in the Heart.

Lynd, Robert S. (1892), **and Helen Merrell Lynd** (1896), Middletown in Transition. NF

McCoy, Horace (1897), No Pockets in a Shroud. F

MacLeish, Archibald (1892), The Fall of the City. D

Marquand, J. P. (1893), The Late George Apley. F; Think Fast, Mr. Moto. F

Masters, Edgar Lee (1868), The Tide of Time. F; Whitman. NF; The New World. V

Maxwell, William (1908), They Came Like Swallows. F

"Michael Gold" (1893), Change the World. NF

Millay, Edna St. Vincent (1892), Conversation at Midnight. V

Odets, Clifford (1906), Golden Boy. D

Paul, Elliot (1891), The Life and Death of a Spanish Town. NF

Perelman, S. J. (1904), Strictly from Hunger. F

Pound, Ezra (1885), The Fifth Decad of Cantos. V; Polite Essays. NF

Prokosch, Frederic (1908), The Seven Who Fled. F

Repplier, Agnes (1858), Eight Decades. NF

Rice, Elmer (1892), Imperial City. F

Richter, Conrad (1890), The Sea of Grass. F

Roberts, Kenneth (1885), Northwest Passage. F

Roosevelt, Eleanor (1884), This Is My Story. NF

Sandoz, Mari (1901), Slogum House. F

Santayana, George (1863), The Realm of Truth. NF

Saroyan, William (1908), Little Children. F

Sarton, May (1912), Encounter in April. V

Shaw, Irwin (1913), Siege. D

Sinclair, Upton (1878), The Flivver King. NF

Stearns, Harold E. (1891), America: A Reappraisal. NF

Stegner, Wallace (1909), Remembering Laughter. F

Stein, Gertrude (1874), Everybody's Autobiography. NF

Steinbeck, John (1902), Of Mice and Men. F; The Red Pony. F

Stevens, Wallace (1879), The Man with the Blue Guitar. V

Stout, Rex (1886), The Hand in the Glove. F

Tate, Allen (1899), Selected Poems. V

Thurber, James (1894), Let Your Mind Alone. F, NF

Weidman, Jerome (1913), I Can Get It for You Wholesale. F

Wharton, Edith (1862), Ghosts. F

Williams, William Carlos (1883), White Mule. F

Wilson, Edmund (1895), This Room and This Gin and These Sandwiches. D

Winters, Yvor (1900), Primitivism and Decadence. NF

1938

Adams, James Truslow (1878), Building the British Empire. NF

Adler, Mortimer (1902), What Man Has Made of Man. NF; St. Thomas and the Gentiles. NF

Agar, Herbert (1897), The Pursuit of Happiness. NF

Allen, Hervey (1889), Action at Aquila. F

Anderson, Maxwell (1888), The Feast of Ortolans. D; Knickerbocker Holiday. D

Asch, Sholem (1880), Three Novels: Uncle Moses, Chaim Lederer's Return, Judge Not. F

Auden, W. H. (1907), On the Frontier (with Christopher Isherwood). D

"B. Traven" (?), The Bridge in the Jungle. F

Baker, Dorothy (1907), Young Man with a Horn. F

Stock market "recession."

Formation of House Committee on Un-American Activities.

Wages and Hours Law benefited labor.

Congress of Industrial Organizations created.

DuPont began manufacture of nylon.

Pearl Buck received Nobel Prize in literature.

Playwrights' Company founded.

Orson Welles's radio play, "Invasion from Mars."

Dictionary of American English (4 vols., 1938–44).

Barnes, Margaret Ayer (1886), Wisdom's Gate. F
Barry, Philip (1896), Here Come the Clowns (pub. 1939). D
Behrman, S. N. (1893), Wine of Choice. D
Benchley, Robert (1889), After 1903—What? NF
Benét, Stephen Vincent (1898), Johnny Pye and the Fool-Killer.
  F
Boothe, Clare (1903), Kiss the Boys Goodbye. D
Byrd, Richard E. (1888), Alone. NF
Cabell, James Branch (1879), The King Was in His Counting
  House. F
Caldwell, Erskine (1903), Southways. F
Chase, Mary Ellen (1887), Dawn in Lyonesse. F
Chase, Stuart (1888), The Tyranny of Words. NF
Cummings, E. E. (1894), Collected Poems. V
Daniels, Jonathan (1902), A Southerner Discovers the South. NF
Davidson, Donald (1895), The Attack on Leviathan. NF; Lee in
  the Mountains. V
Davis, Clyde Brion (1894), The Great American Novel. F
Dewey, John (1859), Logic: The Theory of Inquiry.
  NF; Experience and Education. NF
Dos Passos, John (1896), U.S.A. (trilogy; first pub. 1930–
  36); Journeys Between Wars. NF
Farrell, James T. (1904), No Star Is Lost. F
Faulkner, William (1897), The Unvanquished. F
Fearing, Kenneth (1902), Dead Reckoning. V
Field, Rachel (1894), All This, and Heaven Too. F
Fletcher, John Gould (1886), Selected Poems. V
Forbes, Esther (1891), The General's Lady. F
Hemingway, Ernest (1899), The Spanish Earth. NF; The Fifth
  Column and the First Forty-Nine Stories. D, F
Hicks, Granville (1901), I Like America. NF
Horgan, Paul (1903), Far From Cibola. F
Lewis, Sinclair (1885), The Prodigal Parents. F
Lindbergh, Anne Morrow (1906), Listen! the Wind. NF
McAlmon, Robert (1895), Being Geniuses Together. NF
McKenney, Ruth (1911), My Sister Eileen. NF
MacLeish, Archibald (1892), Air Raid. D; Land of the Free. V
Marquand, J. P. (1893), Mr. Moto Is Sorry. F
Masters, Edgar Lee (1868), Mark Twain. NF
Miller, Henry (1891), Max and the White Phagocytes. NF
Mumford, Lewis (1895), The Culture of the Cities. NF
Nabokov, Vladimir (1899), Laughter in the Dark (rev. and trans.
  from Russian). F
Nash, Ogden (1902), I'm a Stranger Here Myself. V
Nathan, Robert (1894), Journey of Tapiola. F
Odets, Clifford (1906), Rocket to the Moon (pub. 1939). D
O'Hara, John (1905), Hope of Heaven. F
Osborn, Paul (1901), On Borrowed Time [adapted from
  Lawrence Edward Watkin's novel (1937)]. D
Pound, Ezra (1885), Guide to Kulcher (rev. 1952). NF
Prokosch, Frederic (1908), The Carnival. F
Ransom, John Crowe (1888), The World's Body. NF
Rawlings, Marjorie Kinnan (1896), The Yearling. F
Rice, Elmer (1892), American Landscape (pub. 1939). F
Riding, Laura (1901), Collected Poems. V
Roberts, Elizabeth Madox (1886), Black Is My Truelove's Hair.
  F
Rukeyser, Muriel (1913), U.S. 1. V
Runyon, Damon (1884), Take It Easy. F
Saroyan, William (1908), Love, Here Is My Hat. F; A Native
  American. F; The Trouble with Tigers. F
Sarton, May (1912), The Single Hound. F

Thomas Wolfe d.
Owen Wister d.
Joyce Carol Oates b.
Twice a Year (New York), 1938–48.

Hitler invaded Austria.
Munich Pact (Hitler, Mussolini,
  Daladier, Chamberlain).
Nazi opponents began to be sent to
  concentration camps.
Karel Čapek d.
Osip Mandelstam d.
Yeats's New Poems.
Greene's Brighton Rock.
Graves's Collected Poems.
Bowen's The Death of the Heart.
Daphne du Maurier's Rebecca.
Dodie Smith's Dear Octopus.
Spring's My Son, My Son!
Emlyn Williams's The Corn Is Green.
Richard Hughes's In Hazard.
Beckett's Murphy.
Sartre's Nausea.
Troyat's The Spider.
Kazantzakis's The Odyssey: A Modern
  Sequel.

Schwartz, Delmore (1913), In Dreams Begin Responsibilities. V
Sherwood, Robert E. (1896), Abe Lincoln in Illinois (pub. 1939). D
Snow, Edgar (1905), Red Star Over China. NF
Stein, Gertrude (1874), Picasso. NF.
Steinbeck, John (1902), Their Blood Is Strong. NF; The Long Valley. F
Stewart, George R. (1895), East of the Giants. F
Stout, Rex (1886), Too Many Cooks. F
Stuart, Jesse (1907), Beyond Dark Hills. NF
Tate, Allen (1899), The Fathers. F
Weidman, Jerome (1913), What's in It for Me? F
Wharton, Edith (d. 1937), The Buccaneers (unfinished). F
White, E. B. (1899), The Fox of Peapack. V
Wilder, Thornton (1897), Our Town. D; The Merchant of Yonkers [adapted from Johann Nestroy's Einen Jux will er sich machen (1842); pub. 1939]. D
Williams, William Carlos (1883), Life Along the Passaic River. F; The Complete Collected Poems. V
Winters, Yvor (1900), Maule's Curse. NF
Wright, Richard (1908), Uncle Tom's Children (enl. 1940). F

1939

Adams, Samuel Hopkins (1871), Incredible Era. NF
Aldrich, Bess Streeter (1881), Song of Years. F
Anderson, Maxwell (1888), Key Largo. D; The Essence of Tragedy. NF
Asch, Sholem (1880), Song of the Valley. F; The Nazarene. F
Auden, W. H. (1907), Journey to a War (with Christopher Isherwood). V, NF
Barry, Philip (1896), The Philadelphia Story. D
Beard, Charles A. (1874), and Mary R. Beard (1876), America in Mid-Passage. NF
Behrman, S. N. (1893), No Time for Comedy. D
Benét, Stephen Vincent (1898), Tales Before Midnight. F; The Ballad of the Duke's Mercy. V; The Devil and Daniel Webster. D
Bontemps, Arna (1902), Drums at Dusk. F
Boothe, Clare (1903), Margin for Error. D
Caldwell, Erskine (1903), North of the Danube (with Margaret Bourke-White). NF
Canby, Henry Seidel (1878), Thoreau. NF
Chandler, Raymond (1888), The Big Sleep. F
Crouse, Russel (1893), Life with Father [adapted with Howard Lindsay from Clarence Day's novel (1935)]. D
Di Donato, Pietro (1911), Christ in Concrete. F
Dos Passos, John (1896), Adventures of a Young Man. F
Douglas, Lloyd C. (1877), Disputed Passage. F
Dowdey, Clifford (1904), Bugles Blow No More. F
Eliot, T. S. (1888), The Family Reunion. D; The Idea of a Christian Society. NF; Old Possum's Book of Practical Cats. V
Engle, Paul (1908), Corn. V
Farrell, James T. (1904), Tommy Gallagher's Crusade. F
Faulkner, William (1897), The Wild Palms. F
Fisher, Vardis (1895), Children of God. F
Frost, Robert (1874), Collected Poems. V
Gale, Zona (d. 1938), Magna. F
Garland, Hamlin (1860), The Mystery of the Buried Crosses. NF

Declaration of national emergency.
Neutrality Act emended repealing of arms embargo.
George VI and Elizabeth visited U.S.
First regular transatlantic air service.
New York City and San Francisco World Fairs.
Gone with the Wind opened.
Zane Grey d.
The Kenyon Review (Gambier, Ohio), 1939–70; 1979–.
College English (Chicago et al.), 1939–.

Germany invaded Poland; World War II began.
German-Russian nonaggression pact.
Soviet Union invaded Finland.
Italy annexed Albania.
Poetry London (London), 1939–45.
Horizon (London), 1939–50.
Ford Madox Ford d.
William Butler Yeats d.
Sigmund Freud d.
Joyce's *Finnegans Wake*.
Struther's *Mrs. Miniver*.
Household's *Rogue Male*.
Godden's *Black Narcissus*.
Ambler's *The Mask of Dimitrios*.
Forester's *Captain Hornblower, R.N.*
MacNeice's *Autumn Journal*.
Aldous Huxley's *After Many a Summer*.
Thomas Mann's *Lotte in Weimar*.
Sartre's *The Wall*.
Saint-Exupéry's *Wind, Sand and Stars*.
Bunin's *Lika*.
Montale's *The Occasions*.
Patrick White's *Happy Valley*.

Hecht, Ben (1894), Ladies and Gentlemen (with Charles MacArthur). D

Hellman, Lillian (1905), The Little Foxes. D

Herbst, Josephine (1897), Rope of Gold. F

Heyward, DuBose (1885), Mamba's Daughters (with Dorothy Heyward). D

Hicks, Granville (1901), Figures of Transition. NF

Horgan, Paul (1903), The Habit of Empire. F

Isherwood, Christopher (1904), Goodbye to Berlin. F

Kaufman, George S. (1889), The American Way (with Moss Hart). D; The Man Who Came to Dinner (with Moss Hart). D

Keith, Agnes Newton (1901), Land Below the Wind. NF

Kingsley, Sidney (1906), The World We Make [adapted from Millen Brand's novel The Outward Room (1937)]. D

Lewisohn, Ludwig (1882), Forever Wilt Thou Love. F

Lovecraft, Howard Phillips (1890), The Outsider and Others. F

Lumpkin, Grace (?), The Wedding. F

MacLeish, Archibald (1892), America Was Promises. V

McWilliams, Carey (1905), Factories in the Fields. NF

Marquand, J. P. (1893), Wickford Point. F

Miles, Josephine (1911), Lines at Intersection. V

Millay, Edna St. Vincent (1892), Huntsman, What Quarry? V

Miller, Henry (1891), Tropic of Capricorn (pub. in Paris) F; The Cosmological Eye. F; NF; Hamlet (2 vols., 1939–41). NF

Morley, Christopher (1890), Kitty Foyle. F

"Nathanael West" (1903), The Day of the Locust. F

Nin, Anaïs (1903), The Winter of Artifice. F

O'Hara, John (1905), Files on Parade. F

Osborn, Paul (1901), Morning's at Seven (pub. 1940). D

Parker, Dorothy (1893), Here Lies: Collected Stories. F

Patchen, Kenneth (1911), First Will and Testament. V

Porter, Katherine Anne (1890), Pale Horse, Pale Rider: Three Short Novels. F

Prokosch, Frederic (1908), Night of the Poor, F

Rukeyser, Muriel (1913), A Turning Wind. V

Sandburg, Carl (1878), Abraham Lincoln: The War Years. NF

Sandoz, Mari (1896), Capital City. F

Saroyan, William (1908), My Heart's in the Highlands (pub. 1940). D; The Time of Your Life (pub. 1940). D; The Hungerers. D; Peace, It's Wonderful. F

Sarton, May (1912), Inner Landscape. V

Shaw, Irwin (1913), The Gentle People. D; Sailor off the Bremen. F

Sheean, Vincent (1899), Not Peace but a Sword. NF

Steinbeck, John (1902), The Grapes of Wrath. F

Stewart, George (1895), Doctor's Oral. F

Stout, Rex (1886), Some Buried Caesar. F

Taylor, Edward (d. 1729), The Poetical Works (ed. Thomas H. Johnson). V

Thompson, Dorothy (1894), Let the Record Speak. NF

Van Doren, Mark (1894), Collected Poems. V

Waln, Nora (1895), Reaching for the Stars. F

Warren, Robert Penn (1905), Night Rider. F

Weidman, Jerome (1913), The Horse That Could Whistle "Dixie." F

White, E. B. (1899), Quo Vadimus? or, The Case for the Bicycle. F, NF

Wolfe, Thomas (d. 1938), The Web and the Rock. F; The Face of a Nation. V, F

1940

Adler, Mortimer (1902), How to Read a Book. NF
Agar, Herbert (1897), Beyond German Victory. NF
Aiken, Conrad (1889), And in the Human Heart.
V; Conversation; or, Pilgrims' Progress. F
Allen, Frederick Lewis (1890), Since Yesterday. NF
Anderson, Maxwell (1888), Journey to Jerusalem. D; Second
Overture. D
Anderson, Sherwood (1876), Home Town. NF
Auden, W. H. (1907), Another Time. V
Bacon, Leonard (1887), Sunderland Capture. V
Bellamy, Edward (d. 1898), The Religion of Solidarity. NF
Benét, Stephen Vincent (1898), Nightmare at Noon. V
Blackmur, R. P. (1904), The Expense of Greatness. NF
Boyle, Kay (1902), The Crazy Hunter and Other Stories. F
Bromfield, Louis (1896), Night in Bombay. F
Brooks, Van Wyck (1886), New England: Indian Summer. NF
Bynner, Witter (1881), Against the Cold. V
Cabell, James Branch (1879), Hamlet Had an Uncle. F
Caldwell, Erskine (1903), Trouble in July. F; Jackpot. F
Cather, Willa (1873), Sapphira and the Slave Girl. F
Chandler, Raymond (1888), Farewell, My Lovely. F
Chodorov, Jerome (1911), My Sister Eileen [adapted with
Joseph Fields from Ruth McKenney's sketches (1938)]. D
Ciardi, John (1916), Homeward to America. V
Clark, Walter Van Tilburg (1909), The Ox-Bow Incident. F
Cozzens, James Gould (1903), Ask Me Tomorrow. F
Cummings, E. E. (1894), 50 Poems. V
Daniels, Jonathan (1902), A Southerner Discovers New
England. NF
Day, Clarence (1874), Father and I. NF
Eberhart, Richard (1940), Song and Idea. V
Edmonds, Walter D. (1903), Chad Hanna. F
Eliot, T. S. (1888), East Coker. V
Farrell, James T. (1904), Father and Son. F
Faulkner, William (1897), The Hamlet. F
Fearing, Kenneth (1902), Collected Poems. V
Hayden, Robert (1913), Heart-Shape in the Dust. V
Hemingway, Ernest (1899), For Whom the Bell Tolls. F
Horgan, Paul (1903), Figures in a Landscape. F
Hughes, Langston (1902), The Big Sea. NF
Kaufman, George S. (1889), George Washington Slept Here
(with Moss Hart). D
La Farge, Oliver (1901), As Long As the Grass Shall Grow. NF
Lewis, Sinclair (1885), Bethel Merriday. F
Lewisohn, Ludwig (1882), Haven. F
Lindbergh, Anne Morrow (1906), The Wave of the Future. NF
McCullers, Carson (1917), The Heart Is a Lonely Hunter. F
McGinley, Phyllis (1905), A Pocketful of Wry. V
MacLeish, Archibald (1892), The Irresponsibles: A Declaration.
NF
Mencken, H. L. (1880), Happy Days, 1880–1892. NF
Millay, Edna St. Vincent (1892), Make Bright the Arrows. V
Nash, Ogden (1902), The Face Is Familiar. V
Nathan, Robert (1894), Portrait of Jennie. F
Odets, Clifford (1906), Night Music. D
O'Hara, John (1905), Pal Joey. F; Pal Joey (with Lorenz Hart
and Richard Rodgers; pub. 1952). D
Perelman, S. J. (1904), Look Who's Talking. F
Pound, Ezra (1885), Cantos LII-LXXI. V
Prokosch, Frederic (1908), Death at Sea. V

Selective Service Act passed by
Congress.
Destroyer exchange with Great Britain.
Alien Registration Act.
Forty-hour work week adopted
nationally.
First successful helicopter flight.
Dictionary of American History (6
vols., 1940–61).
America's Lost Plays Series (1940–41).
F. Scott Fitzgerald d.
Nathanael West d.
Hamlin Garland d.
Accent (Urbana, Ill.), 1940–60.
Common Ground (New York), 1940–
49.
Phylon (Atlanta), 1940–.
Modern Language Quarterly (Seattle),
1940–.

Germany invaded Norway, Denmark,
Low Countries, and France.
Battle of Britain began.
Winston Churchill became British
prime minister.
Selma Lagerlöf d.
Joseph Brodsky b.
Greene's *The Power and the Glory.*
O'Casey's *Purple Dust.*
Snow's *Strangers and Brothers* (11
vols., 1940–70).
Ambler's *Journey into Fear.*
Llewellyn's *How Green Was My
Valley.*
Dylan Thomas's *Portrait of the Artist as
a Young Dog.*
Spring's *Fame Is the Spur.*
Yeats's *Last Poems and Plays.*
García Lorca's *Poet in New York*
(posth.).
Koestler's *Darkness at Noon.*
Seferis's *Logbook I.*

Rawlings, Marjorie Kinnan (1896), When the Whippoorwill. F
Rexroth, Kenneth (1905), In What Hour. V
Rice, Elmer (1892), Two on an Island. D
Richter, Conrad (1890), The Trees. F
Roberts, Elizabeth Madox (1886), Song in the Meadow. V
Roberts, Kenneth (1885), Oliver Wiswell. F
Runyon, Damon (1884), My Wife Ethel. F
Santayana, George (1863), The Realm of Spirit. NF
Saroyan, William (1908), My Name Is Aram. F; The Ping-Pong
  Game. D; Subway Circus. D
Shaw, Irwin (1913), Retreat to Pleasure. D
Sherwood, Robert E. (1896), There Shall Be No Night. D
Sinclair, Upton (1878), World's End. F
Stead, Christina (1902), The Man Who Loved Children. F
Stegner, Wallace (1909), On a Darkling Plain. F
Stein, Gertrude (1874), Paris France. NF; What Are
  Masterpieces. NF
Stuart, Jesse (1907), Trees of Heaven. F
Thurber, James (1894), The Male Animal (with Elliott Nugent).
  D; Fables for Our Time, and Famous Poems Illustrated. F
Van Doren, Mark (1894), Windless Cabins. F
Van Druten, John (1901), Old Acquaintance. D
Wescott, Glenway (1901), The Pilgrim Hawk. F
Williams, Tennessee (1911), Battle of Angels (pub. 1945). D
Williams, William Carlos (1883), In the Money. F
Wilson, Edmund (1895), To the Finland Station. NF
Wolfe, Thomas (d. 1938), You Can't Go Home Again. F
Wright, Richard (1908), Native Son. F
Zinsser, Hans (1878), As I Remember Him. NF

1941

Adamic, Louis (1899), Two-Way Passage. NF
Adler, Mortimer (1902), A Dialectic of Morals. NF
Agee, James (1909), Let Us Now Prasie Famous Men (with
  Walker Evans). NF
Anderson, Maxwell (1888), Candle in the Wind. D
Asch, Sholem (1880), What I Believe. NF
Auden, W. H. (1907), The Double Man. V
Behrman, S. N. (1893), The Talley Method. D
Bemelmans, Ludwig (1898), Hotel Splendide. F
Benét, Stephen Vincent (1898), Listen to the People. D; A
  Summons to the Free. V, NF
Benson, Sally (1900), Junior Miss. F
Bishop, John Peale (1891), Selected Poems. V
Bogan, Louise (1897), Poems and New Poems. V
Brooks, Van Wyck (1886), The Opinions of Oliver Allston. NF
Buck, Pearl (1892), Today and Forever. F
Burke, Kenneth (1897), The Philosophy of Literary Form. NF
Cain, James M. (1892), Mildred Pierce. F
Caldwell, Erskine (1903), Say! Is This the U.S.A.? (with
  Margaret Bourke-White). NF
Carmer, Carl (1893), Genesee Fever. F
Chase, Mary Ellen (1887), Windswept. F
Chodorov, Jerome (1911), Junior Miss [adapted with Joseph
  Fields from Sally Benson's stories (1941)]. D
Daniels, Jonathan (1902), Tar Heels, A Portrait of North
  Carolina. NF
Dos Passos, John (1896), The Ground We Stand On. NF
Dreiser, Theodore (1871), America Is Worth Saving. NF

Japan attacked U.S. at Pearl Harbor.
U.S. declared war on Japan.
Germany and Italy declared war on
  U.S.
U.S. occupied Greenland.
Lend-Lease Bill aided anti-Axis powers.
Office of Price Administration
  established.
National Gallery of Art opened in
  Washington.
Sherwood Anderson d.
Elizabeth Madox Roberts d.
The Antioch Review (Yellow Springs,
  Ohio), 1941–.

Balkan countries overrun by Germany.
Germany invaded Soviet Union.
Britain started clothes rationing.
James Joyce d.
Virginia Woolf d.
Hugh Walpole d.
Henri Bergson d.
Woolf's *Between the Acts.*
MacNeice's *Plant and Phantom.*
Coward's *Blithe Spirit.*
Cronin's *The Keys of the Kingdom.*
Bowen's *Look at All Those Roses.*
Cary's *Herself Surprised.*
Koestler's *Scum of the Earth.*
Werfel's *The Song of Bernadette.*
Borges's *The Garden of the Forking
  Paths.*

Eliot, T. S. (1888), Burnt Norton. V; The Dry Salvages. V

Engle, Paul (1908), West of Midnight. V

Farrell, James T. (1904), Ellen Rogers. F

Fast, Howard (1914), The Last Frontier. F

Fearing, Kenneth (1902), Dagger of the Mind. V

Ferber, Edna (1887), Saratoga Trunk. F

Fitzgerald, F. Scott (d. 1940), The Last Tycoon: An Unfinished Novel. F

Fletcher, John Gould (1886), South Star. V

Freeman, Douglas Southall (1886), Lee's Lieutenants: A Study in Command (3 vols., 1942–44). NF

Glasgow, Ellen (1874), In This Our Life. F

Gordon, Caroline (1895), Green Centuries. F

Green, Paul (1894), Native Son [adapted from Richard Wright's novel (1940)]. D

Hart, Moss (1904), Lady in the Dark (with Kurt Weill and Ira Gershwin). D

Hellman, Lillian (1905), Watch on the Rhine. D

Jeffers, Robinson (1887), Be Angry at the Sun. V

Kaufman, George S. (1889), The Land Is Bright (with Edna Ferber). D

Lytle, Andrew (1902), At the Moon's Inn. F

McCullers, Carson (1917), Reflections in a Golden Eye. F

MacInnes, Helen (1907), Above Suspicion. F

MacLeish, Archibald (1892), The American Cause. NF; A Time to Speak. NF

Marquand, J. P. (1893), H. M. Pulham, Esquire. F; Don't Ask Questions. F

Masters, Edgar Lee (1868), Illinois Poems. V

Mencken, H. L. (1880), Newspapers Days, 1899–1906. NF

"Michael Gold" (1893), The Hollow Men. NF

Miles, Josephine (1911), Poems on Several Occasions. V

Millay, Edna St. Vincent (1892), Collected Sonnets. V

Miller, Henry (1891), The Wisdom of the Heart. F, NF; The Colossus of Maroussi. NF.

Moore, Marianne (1887), What Are Years. V

Nabokov, Vladimir (1899), The Real Life of Sebastian Knight. F

Nathan, Robert (1894), They Went On Together. F

Neihardt, John G. (1881), The Song of Jed Smith. V

Niebuhr, Reinhold (1892), The Nature and Destiny of Man (2 vols., 1941–43). NF

Nordhoff, Charles Bernard (1887) **and Charles Norman Hall** (1887), Botany Bay. F

Odets, Clifford (1906), Clash by Night. D

Patchen, Kenneth (1911), The Journal of Albion Moonlight. F

Percy, William Alexander (1885), Lanterns on the Levee. NF

Prokosch, Frederic (1908), The Skies of Europe. F

Pyle, Ernie (1900), Ernie Pyle in England. NF

Ransom, John Crowe (1888), The New Criticism. NF

Rice, Elmer (1892), Flight to the West. D

Roberts, Elizabeth Madox (1886), Not by Strange Gods. F

Roethke, Theodore (1908), Open House. V

Saroyan, William (1908), Saroyan's Fables. F; Three Plays: The Beautiful People, Sweeney in the Trees, and Across the Board on Tomorrow Morning. D

Schorer, Mark (1908), The Hermit Place. F

Schulberg, Budd (1914), What Makes Sammy Run? F

Schwartz, Delmore (1913), Shenandoah. D

Scott, Winfield Townley (1910), Wind the Clock. V

Seton, Anya (1916), My Theodosia. F

Shaw, Irwin (1913), Welcome to the City. F

Shirer, William L. (1904), Berlin Diary. NF

Silone's *The Seed Beneath the Snow.*

Brecht's *Mother Courage and Her Children.*

Mauriac's *A Woman of the Pharisees.*

Valéry's *My Faust.*

Emmanuel's *The Tomb of Orpheus.*

Ekelöf's *Ferry Song.*

Sinclair, Upton (1878), Between Two Worlds. F
Skinner, Cornelia Otis (1901), Soap Behind the Ears. NF
Stegner, Wallace (1909), Fire and Ice. F
Stein, Gertrude (1874), Ida, a Novel. F
Steinbeck, John (1902), Sea of Cortez (with Edward F.
   Ricketts). NF
Stewart, George (1895), Storm. F
Stuart, Jesse (1907), Men of the Mountains. F
Tarkington, Booth (1869), The Heritage of Hatcher Ide. F
Tate, Allen (1899), Reason in Madness. NF
Torrence, Ridgely (1875), Poems. V
Van Doren, Mark (1894), The Mayfield Deer. V
Welty, Eudora (1909), A Curtain of Green. F
White, William L. (1900), Journey for Margaret. NF
Williams, William Carlos (1883), The Broken Span. V
Wilson, Edmund (1895), The Wound and the Bow. NF; The
   Boys in the Back Room. NF
Wolfe, Thomas (d. 1938), The Hills Beyond. F
Wolff, Maritta (1918), Whistle Stop. F
Wright, Richard (1908), 12 Million Black Voices. NF; Native
   Son [adapted with Paul Green from Wright's novel (1940)]. D

1942

Adamic, Louis (1899), What's Your Name? NF; Inside
   Yugoslavia. NF
Adams, Samuel Hopkins (1871), The Harvey Girls. F
Agar, Herbert (1897), A Time for Greatness. NF
Aiken, Conrad (1889), Brownstone Eclogues. V
Aldrich, Bess Streeter (1881), The Lieutenant's Lady. F
Algren, Nelson (1909), Never Come Morning. F
Anderson, Maxwell (1888), The Eve of St. Mark. D
Anderson, Sherwood (d. 1941), Memoirs. NF
Asch, Sholem (1880), Children of Abraham. F
Beard, Charles A. (1874), **and Mary R. Beard** (1876), The
   American Spirit. NF
Bemelmans, Ludwig (1898), I Love You, I Love You, I Love
   You, F
Benchley, Robert (1889), Inside Benchley. NF
Benét, Stephen Vincent (1898), They Burned the Books.
   V; Dear Adolph. NF; A Child Is Born. D
Benson, Sally (1900), Meet Me in St. Louis. F
Berryman, John (1914), Poems. V
Blackmur, R. P. (1904), The Second World. V
Boyle, Kay (1902), Primer for Combat. F
Brinnin, John Malcolm (1916), The Garden Is Political. V; The
   Lincoln Lyrics. V
Buck, Pearl (1892), Dragon Seed. F
Burt, Struthers (1882), Along These Streets. F
Cabell, James Branch (1879), The First Gentleman of America.
   F
Cain, James M. (1892), Love's Lovely Counterfeit. F
Caldwell, Erskine (1903), All Night Long. F; All-Out on the
   Road to Smolensk. NF
Cowley, Malcolm (1898), A Dry Season. V
Cozzens, James Gould (1903), The Just and the Unjust. F
DeVoto, Bernard (1897), Mark Twain at Work. NF
Douglas, Lloyd C. (1877), The Robe. F
Eliot, T. S. (1888), Little Gidding. V; The Music of Poetry.
   NF; The Classics and the Man of Letters. NF

Nationwide rationing of essential
   goods.
Fall of Singapore; loss of Philippines to
   Japan.
American-British invasion of North
   Africa.
First American bombing of Tokyo.
Office of War Information established.
WAVES and WAACS organized.
First American jet plane (XP-59) tested.
First nuclear reaction recorded, in
   Chicago.
Congress of Racial Equality (CORE)
   established.
The Stars and Stripes revived (1942–
   45), U.S. Armed Forces newspaper.
Yank (New York), 1942–45.
Negro Digest (Chicago), 1942–51;
   1961–70. Renamed *Black World*
   (Chicago), 1970–76.

Germany fighting in North Africa,
   France, and Soviet Union.
Gen. Francisco Franco kept Spain
   neutral.
Evelyn Waugh's *Put Out More Flags.*
Rebecca West's *Black Lamb and Grey
   Falcon.*
Coward's *Present Laughter.*
Bowen's *Bowen's Court.*
C. S. Lewis's *The Screwtape Letters.*
Dinesen's *Winter's Tales.*
Quasimodo's *And It Is Suddenly
   Evening.*
Amado's *The Violent Land.*
Camus's *The Stranger; The Myth of
   Sisyphus.*
Montherlant's *Queen After Death.*
Vercors's *The Silence of the Sea.*

Farrell, James T. (1904), $1,000 a Week and Other Stories. F
Fast, Howard (1914), The Unvanquished. F
Faulkner, William (1897), Go Down, Moses and Other Stories. F
Field, Rachel (1894), And Now Tomorrow. F
Forbes, Esther (1891), Paul Revere and the World He Lived In. NF
Frost, Robert (1874), A Witness Tree. V
Hale, Nancy (1908), The Prodigal Women. F
Hargrove, Marion (1919), See Here, Private Hargrove. NF
Hersey, John (1914), Men on Bataan. NF
Hicks, Granville (1901), Only One Storm. F
Horgan, Paul (1903), The Common Heart. F
Hughes, Langston (1902), Shakespeare in Harlem. V
Jarrell, Randall (1914), Blood for a Stranger. V
Kazin, Alfred (1915), On Native Grounds. NF
McCarthy, Mary (1912), The Company She Keeps. F
McWilliams, Carey (1905), Ill Fares the Land. NF
Marquand, J. P. (1893), Last Laugh, Mr. Moto. F
Masters, Edgar Lee (1868), The Sangamon. NF
Millay, Edna St. Vincent (1892), The Murder of Lidice. V
Morris, Wright (1910), My Uncle Dudley. F
Patchen, Kenneth (1911), The Teeth of the Lion. V
Paul, Elliot (1891), The Last Time I Saw Paris. NF
Rawlings, Marjorie Kinnan (1896), Cross Creek. NF
Richter, Conrad (1890), Tacey Cromwell. F
Rukeyser, Muriel (1913), Wake Island. V; Willard Gibbs, American Genius. NF
Sandoz, Mari (1901), Crazy Horse. NF
Saroyan, William (1908), Razzle Dazzle. D
Shapiro, Karl (1913), Person, Place and Thing. V; The Place of Love. V
Sinclair, Upton (1878), Dragon's Teeth. F
Skinner, Cornelia Otis (1901), Our Hearts Were Young and Gay (with Emily Kimbrough). NF
Stegner, Wallace (1909), Mormon Country. NF
Steinbeck, John (1902), The Moon Is Down. F; Bombs Away. NF
Stevens, Wallace (1879), Parts of a World. V;
Suckow, Ruth (1892), New Hope. F
Thurber, James (1894), My World—and Welcome to It. F, NF
Van Doren, Mark (1894), Private Reader. NF; Liberal Education. NF; Our Lady Peace. V
Van Druten, John (1901), The Damask Cheek (with Lloyd Morris). D
Walker, Margaret (1915), For My People. V
Warren, Robert Penn (1905), Eleven Poems on the Same Theme. V
Welty, Eudora (1909), The Robber Bridegroom. F
White, E. B. (1899), One Man's Meat. NF
White, William L. (1900), They Were Expendable. NF
Wilder, Thornton (1897), The Skin of Our Teeth. D
Wilson, Edmund (1895), Notebooks of Night. V, NF
Wolff, Maritta (1918), Night Shift. F
Wylie Philip (1902), Generation of Vipers. NF

1943

Adamic, Louis (1899), My Native Land. NF
Adams, James Truslow (1878), The American: The Making of a New Man. NF

Roosevelt, Churchill, and Stalin met at Teheran.
Race riots in Detroit and Harlem.

Allen, Hervey (1889), The Forest and the Fort. F
Asch, Sholem (1880), The Apostle. F
Bacon, Leonard (1887), Day of Fire. V
Baker, Dorothy (1907), Trio. F
Barzun, Jacques (1907), Romanticism and the Modern Ego. NF
Benchley, Robert (1915), Benchley Beside Himself. NF
Benét, Stephen Vincent (1898), Western Star. V
Bromfield, Louis (1896), Mrs. Parkington. F
Cabell, James Branch (1879), The St. Johns: A Parade of Diversities (with A. J. Hanna). NF
Cain, James M. (1892), Three of a Kind. F
Caldwell, Erskine (1903), Georgia Boy. F
Canby, Henry Seidel (1878), Whitman. NF
Chandler, Raymond (1888), The Lady in the Lake. F
Cheever, John (1912), The Way Some People Live. F
Chodorov, Edward (1904), Those Endearing Young Charms. D
Davenport, Marcia (1903), The Valley of Decision. F
DeVoto, Bernard (1897), The Year of Decision: 1846. NF
Dos Passos, John (1896), Number One. F.
Eliot, T. S. (1888), Four Quartets, V
Farrell, James T. (1904), My Days of Anger. F
Fast, Howard (1914), Citizen Tom Paine. F
Fearing, Kenneth (1902), Afternoon of a Pawnbroker. V
Fitzgerald, Robert (1910), A Wreath for the Sea. V
Flavin, Martin (1883), Journey in the Dark. F
Glasgow, Ellen (1874), A Certain Measure: An Interpretation of Prose Fiction. NF
Hart, Moss (1904), Winged Victory (with others). D
Hersey, John (1914), Into the Valley. NF
Hughes, Langston (1902), Freedom's Plow. V
Janeway, Elizabeth (1913), The Walsh Girls. F
Kantor, MacKinlay (1904), Happy Land. F
Kees, Weldon (1914), The Last Man. V
Kingsley, Sidney (1906), The Patriots (with Madge Evans). D
Laurents, Arthur (1918), The Way We Were. F
Lewis, Sinclair (1885), Gideon Planish. F
Lovecraft, Howard Phillips (1890), Beyond the Wall of Sleep. F
MacLeish, Archibald (1892), A Time to Act. NF; Colloquy for the States. V.
McWilliams, Carey (1905), Brothers Under the Skin. NF
Marquand, J. P. (1893), So Little Time. F;
Mencken, H. L. (1880), Heathen Days, 1890–1936. NF
Millay, Edna St. Vincent (1892), Collected Lyrics. V
Patchen, Kenneth (1911), Cloth of the Tempest. V
Perelman, S. J. (1904), The Dream Department. F; One Touch of Venus (with Ogden Nash). D
Prokosch, Frederic (1908), The Conspirators. F
Pyle, Ernie (1900), Here Is Your War. NF
Rand, Ayn (1905), The Fountainhead. F
Richter, Conrad (1890), The Free Man. F
Sandburg, Carl (1878), Home Front Memo. V, NF
Saroyan, William (1908), Get Away, Old Man (pub. 1944). D; The Human Comedy. F
Schwartz, Delmore (1913), Genesis: Book One. V
Sheean, Vincent (1899), Between the Thunder and the Sun. NF
Sinclair, Upton (1878), Wide Is the Gate. F
Smith, Betty (1904), A Tree Grows in Brooklyn. F
Stegner, Wallace (1909), The Big Rock Candy Mountain. F
Stuart, Jesse (1907), Taps for Private Tussie. F
Tarkington, Booth (1869), Kate Fennigate. F
Train, Arthur (1875), Yankee Lawyer: The Autobiography of Ephraim Tutt. F

Churchill addressed U.S. Congress.
Radar detection devices in use.
Rodgers and Hammerstein's *Oklahoma!* an instant success.
Zoot suits and the jitterbug introduced.
Stephen Vincent Benét d.
ETC: Review of General Semantics (Chicago; San Francisco), 1943–.
Quarterly Review of Literature (Chapel Hill; New Haven; Annandale-on-Hudson; Princeton), 1943–.

German troops surrendered in North Africa.
Soviet armies relieved 17-month siege of Leningrad.
Fall of Mussolini after Allied bombings of Rome.
Chiang Kai-shek made president of Chinese Nationalist Republic.
Simone Weil d.
Greene's *The Ministry of Fear.*
Dylan Thomas's *New Poems.*
Henry Green's *Caught.*
Koestler's *Arrival and Departure.*
Hesse's *The Glass Bead Game (Magister Ludi).*
Vercors's *Guiding Star.*
Brecht's *The Good Woman of Setzuan; The Life of Galileo.*
Saint-Exupéry's *The Little Prince.*
Stefan Zweig's *The World of Yesterday.*
Beauvoir's *She Came to Stay.*
Tanizaki's *The Makioka Sisters* (1943–48).

Van Druten, John (1901), The Voice of the Turtle (pub. 1944).
D
Wallace, Henry A. (1888), The Century of the Common Man.
NF
Warren, Robert Penn (1905), At Heaven's Gate. F
Welty, Eudora (1909), The Wide Net. F
White, William L. (1900), Queens Die Proudly. NF
Willkie, Wendell (1892), One World. NF
Winters, Yvor (1900), The Giant Weapon. V; The Anatomy of
Nonsense. NF
Wolfert, Ira (1908), Battle for the Solomons. NF; Tucker's
People. F
Woollcott, Alexander (1887), Long, Long Ago. NF
Wylie, Elinor (d. 1928), Last Poems. V

1944

Adams, Franklin P. (1881), Nods and Becks. V, NF
Adams, James Truslow (1878), Frontiers of American Culture.
NF
Adams, Samuel Hopkins (1871), Canal Town. F
Adler, Mortimer (1902), How to Think About War and Peace.
NF
Aiken, Conrad (1889), The Soldier. V
Allen, Hervey (1889), Bedford Village. F
Anderson, Maxwell (1888), Storm Operation. D
Auden, W. H. (1907), For the Time Being. V
Behrman, S. N. (1893), Jacobowsky and the Colonel (with Franz
Werfel). D
Bellow, Saul (1915), Dangling Man. F
Benét, Stephen Vincent (d. 1943), America. NF
Brooks, Van Wyck (1886), The World of Washington Irving. NF
Brown, Harry (1917), A Walk in the Sun. F
Caldwell, Erskine (1903), Tragic Ground. F
Chase, Mary Coyle (1907), Harvey. D
Cummings, E. E. (1894), 1 × 1. V
Deutsch, Babette (1895), Take Them, Stranger. V
Dos Passos, John (1896), State of the Nation. NF
Farrell, James T. (1904), To Whom It May Concern. F
Fast, Howard (1914), Freedom Road. F
Feikema, Feike (1912), The Golden Bowl. F
Gordon, Caroline (1895), The Women on the Porch. F
"H.D." (1886), The Walls Do Not Fall. V
Hellman, Lillian (1905), The Searching Wind. D
Hersey, John (1914), A Bell for Adano. F
Jackson, Charles (1903), The Lost Weekend. F
Kaufman, George S. (1889), The Late George Apley [adapted
with J. P. Marquand from Marquand's novel (1937); pub.
1946]. D
Kunitz, Stanley J. (1905), Passport to the War. V
Lewisohn, Ludwig (1882), Breathe Upon These. F
Lindbergh, Anne Morrow (1906), Steep Ascent. F
Lowell, Robert (1917), Land of Unlikeness. V
MacLeish, Archibald. (1892), The American Story. NF
Meredith, William (1919), Love Letter from an Impossible
Land. V
Miller, Arthur (1915), The Man Who Had All the Luck.
D; Situation Normal. NF
Miller, Henry (1891), Sunday After the War. F
Moore, Marianne (1887), Nevertheless. V
Mumford, Lewis (1895), The Condition of Man. NF

Allied invasion of Normandy under
Gen. Dwight D. Eisenhower.
Reconquest of the Philippines by Gen.
Douglas MacArthur.
"G.I. Bill of Rights" adopted.
Plans laid for United Nations, World
Bank, and International Monetary
Fund.
Ezra Pound arrested by U.S. Army on
charges of treason.
United Negro College Fund
established.
Penicillin proved to be miracle drug.

Rumania and Bulgaria surrendered to
Soviets.
Massive air bombardment of Berlin.
Jean Giraudoux d.
Romain Rolland d.
Antoine de Saint-Exupéry d.
Max Jacob d.
Cary's The Horse's Mouth.
Rosamond Lehmann's The Ballad and
the Source.
Maugham's The Razor's Edge.
H. E. Bates's Fair Stood the Wind for
France.
Sharp's Cluny Brown.
Aldous Huxley's Time Must Have a
Stop.
Joyce's Stephen Hero.
Camus's Caligula.
Sartre's No Exit.
Genet's Our Lady of the Flowers.
Bunin's Dark Avenues.
Borges's Ficciones.
Anouilh's Antigone.
Werfel's Jakobowsky and the Colonel.
Lagerkvist's The Dwarf.

Nabokov, Vladimir (1899), Nikolai Gogol. NF
Nin, Anaïs (1903), Under a Glass Bell. F
Osborn, Paul (1901), A Bell for Adano [adapted from John
  Hersey's novel (1944); pub. 1945]. D
Pennell, Joseph Stanley (1908), The History of Rome Hanks. F
Porter, Katherine Anne (1890), The Leaning Tower and Other
  Stories. F
Pyle, Ernie (1900), Brave Men. NF
Rexroth, Kenneth (1905), The Phoenix and the Tortoise. V
Rukeyser, Muriel (1913), Beast in View. V
Runyon, Damon (1884), Runyon à la Carte. F
Santayana, George (1863), Persons and Places: The Background
  of My Life. NF
Saroyan, William (1908), Dear Baby. F
Seton, Anya (1916), Dragonwyck. F
Shapiro, Karl (1913), V-Letter and Other Poems. V
Shaw, Irwin (1913), Sons and Soldiers. D; The Assassin. D
Sinclair, Upton (1878), Presidential Agent. F
Smith, Lillian (1897), Strange Fruit. F
Stafford, Jean (1915), Boston Adventure. F
Stout, Rex (1886), Not Quite Dead Enough. F
Stuart, Jesse (1907), Album of Destiny. V; Mongrel Mettle. F
Van Doren, Mark (1894), Seven Sleepers. V
Van Druten, John (1901), I Remember Mama [adapted from
  Kathryn Forbes's short stories, Mama's Bank Account (1943)].
  D
Warren, Robert Penn (1905), Selected Poems, 1923–1943. V
Winsor, Kathleen (1919), Forever Amber. F

1945

Adamic, Louis (1899), A Nation of Nations. NF
Adams, James Truslow (1878), Big Business in a Democracy.
  NF
Auden, W. H. (1907), The Collected Poetry. V
Barzun, Jacques (1907), Teacher in America. NF
Behrman, S. N. (1893), Dunnigan's Daughter. D
Brinnin, John Malcolm (1916), No Arch, No Triumph. V
Bromfield, Louis (1896), Pleasant Valley. NF
Brooks, Gwendolyn (1917), A Street in Bronzeville. V
Burke, Kenneth (1897), A Grammar of Motives. NF
Clark, Walter Van Tilburg (1909), The City of Trembling
  Leaves. F
Cousins, Norman (1912), Modern Man Is Obsolete. NF
Crouse, Russel (1893), State of the Union (with Howard
  Lindsay; pub. 1946). D
Cummings, E. E. (1894), Anthropos: The Future of Art. NF
Dickinson, Emily (d. 1886), Bolts of Melody. V
Eliot, T. S. (1888), What Is a Classic? NF
Farrell, James T. (1904), The League of Frightened Philistines
  and Other Papers. NF
Feikema, Feike (1912), Boy Almighty. F
Fitzgerald, F. Scott (d. 1940), The Crack-Up, (ed. Edmund
  Wilson). NF
Frost, Robert (1874), A Masque of Reason. D
Gordon, Caroline (1895), The Forest of the South. F
"H.D." (1886), Tribute to the Angels. V
Hardwick, Elizabeth (1916), The Ghostly Lover. F
Haydn, Hiram (1907), Manhattan Furlough. F
Himes, Chester (1909), If He Hollers Let Him Go. F
Isherwood, Christopher (1904), Prater Violet. F

Roosevelt, Churchill, and Stalin met in
  Yalta.
Roosevelt died at Warm Springs, Ga.
Germany surrendered May 7.
First atomic bomb dropped on
  Hiroshima August 6.
Japan surrendered August 14.
United Nations charter written in San
  Francisco.
United Nations Educational, Scientific,
  and Cultural Organization
  (UNESCO) created.
Medal of Freedom established.
Robert Benchley d.
Theodore Dreiser d.
Ellen Glasgow d.
Commentary (New York), 1945–.
Ebony (Chicago), 1945–.

Mussolini captured and executed.
Hitler committed suicide.
Clement Attlee became British prime
  minister.
Charles de Gaulle elected provisional
  president of France.
Les Temps Modernes (Paris), 1945–.
Paul Valéry d.
Georg Kaiser d.
Franz Werfel d.
Orwell's Animal Farm.
Evelyn Waugh's Brideshead Revisited.
Henry Green's Loving.
Charles Williams's All Hallows' Eve.

Jarrell, Randall (1914), Little Friend, Little Friend. V
"John Patrick" (1905), The Hasty Heart. D
Laurents, Arthur (1918), Home of the Brave (pub. 1946). D
Leonard, William Ellery (d. 1944), A Man Against Time. V
Lewis, Sinclair (1885), Cass Timberlane. F
MacDonald, Betty (1908), The Egg and I. NF
Marquand, J. P. (1893), Repent in Haste. F
Maxwell, William (1908), The Folded Leaf. F
Miller, Arthur (1915), Focus. F
Miller, Henry (1891), The Air-Conditioned Nightmare. NF
Morris, Wright (1910), The Man Who Was There. F
Nash, Ogden (1902), Many Long Years Ago. V
Nin, Anaïs (1903), This Hunger. F
O'Hara, John (1905), Pipe Night. F
Patchen, Kenneth (1911), An Astonished Eye Looks Out of the
     Air. V; The Memoirs of a Shy Pornographer. F
Pinckney, Josephine (1895), Three O'Clock Dinner. F
Prokosch, Frederic (1908), Age of Thunder. F
Ransom, John Crowe (1888), Selected Poems. V
Rice, Elmer (1892), Dream Girl (pub. 1946). D
Santayana, George (1863), The Middle Span. NF
Shapiro, Karl (1913), Essay on Rime. V
Sinclair, Upton (1878), Dragon Harvest. F
Stegner, Wallace (1909), One Nation. NF
Stein, Gertrude (1874), Wars I Have Seen. NF
Steinbeck, John (1902), Cannery Row. F
Tarkington, Booth (1869), Image of Josephine. F
Train, Arthur (1875), Mr. Tutt Finds a Way. F
Ullman, James Ramsey (1907), The White Tower. F
Wescott, Glenway (1901), Apartment in Athens. F
West, Jessamyn (1907), The Friendly Persuasion. F
White, E. B. (1899), Stuart Little. F
White, William L. (1900), Report on the Russians. NF
Williams, Tennessee (1911), The Glass Menagerie. D; You
     Touched Me! [with Donald Windham, suggested by D. H.
     Lawrence's short story (1922); pub. 1947]. D
Wolfert, Ira (1908), American Guerilla in the Philippines. NF
Wright, Richard (1908), Black Boy: A Record of Childhood and
     Youth. NF

Koestler's The Yogi and the Commissar.
Balchin's Mine Own Executioner.
Broch's The Death of Vergil.
Levi's Christ Stopped at Eboli.
Waltari's The Egyptian.
Giraudoux's The Madwoman of
     Chaillot.
Peyrefitte's Special Friendships.
Andrić's The Bridge on the Drina.
Ekelöf's I Will Not Serve.
Moravia's Agostino.

1946

Adamic, Louis (1899), Dinner at the White House. NF
Anderson, Maxwell (1888), Joan of Lorraine. D
Asch, Sholem (1880), East River. F
Bemelmans, Ludwig (1898), Hotel Bemelmans. F
Benét, Stephen Vincent (d. 1943), The Last Circle. V, F
Bishop, Elizabeth (1911), North & South. V
Boyle, Kay (1902), A Frenchman Must Die. F; Thirty Stories. F
Brown, Harry (1917), A Sound of Hunting. D
Buck, Pearl (1892), Pavilion of Women. F
Cabell, James Branch (1879), There Were Two Pirates. F
Cain, James M. (1892), Past All Dishonor. F
Caldwell, Erskine (1903), A House in the Uplands. F
Cummings, E. E. (1894), Santa Claus: A Morality. D
Dodson, Owen (1914), Powerful Long Ladder. V
Dos Passos, John (1896), Tour of Duty. NF
Dreiser, Theodore (d. 1945), The Bulwark. F
Farrell, James T. (1904), Bernard Clare. F; When Boyhood
     Dreams Come True. F
Fearing, Kenneth (1902), The Big Clock. F

First meetings of United Nations and
     UNESCO.
Coal mines and railroad strikes.
U.S. Atomic Energy Commission
     established.
Atomic bomb tests in the Pacific.
Ezra Pound committed to mental
     hospital.
Gertrude Stein d.
Booth Tarkington d.
Edward Sheldon d.
Damon Runyon d.

Beginning of the "Cold War" and the
     "Iron Curtain."
Chinese civil war continued between
     Nationalists and Communists.
Arts Council of Great Britain
     established.
H. G. Wells d.
Gerhart Hauptmann d.

Fletcher, John Gould (1886), The Burning Mountain. V
"H.D." (1886), The Flowering of the Rod. V
Hayes, Alfred (1911), All Thy Conquests. F
Heggen, Thomas (1919), Mr. Roberts. F
Hellman, Lillian (1905), Another Part of the Forest (pub. 1947).
    D
Hersey, John (1914), Hiroshima. NF
Hicks, Granville (1901), Small Town. NF
Jackson, Charles (1903), The Fall of Valor. F
Jeffers, Robinson (1887), Medea. D
Johnson, Josephine (1910), Wildwood. F
Kanin, Garson (1912), Born Yesterday. D
Kelly, George (1887), The Fatal Weakness. D
Levertov, Denise (1923), The Double Image. V
Lowell, Robert (1917), Lord Weary's Castle. V
McCullers, Carson (1917), The Member of the Wedding. F
McGinley, Phyllis (1905), Stones from a Glass House. V
Marquand, J. P. (1893), B. F.'s Daughter. F
Miles, Josephine (1911), Local Measures. V
Morris, Wright (1910), The Inhabitants. F
Moss, Howard (1922), The Wound and the Weather. V
Nin, Anaïs (1903), Ladders to Fire. F; Realism and Reality. NF
O'Neill, Eugene (1888), The Iceman Cometh. D
Patchen, Kenneth (1911), Sleepers Awake. V
Perelman, S. J. (1904), Keep It Crisp. F
Petry, Ann (1911), The Street. F
Prokosch, Frederic (1908), The Idols of the Cave. F
Pyle, Ernie (d. 1945), Last Chapter. NF
Rand, Ayn (1905), Anthem. F
Richter, Conrad (1890), The Fields. F
Runyon, Damon (1884), In Our Town. F; Short Takes. F
Santayana, George (1863), The Idea of Christ in the Gospels.
    NF
Saroyan, William (1908), The Adventures of Wesley Jackson. F
Sarton, May (1912), The Bridge of Years. F
Seton, Anya (1916), The Turquoise. F
Shaw, Irwin (1913), Act of Faith. F
Sheean, Vincent (1899), This House Against This House. NF
Sinclair, Upton (1878), A World to Win. F
Stein, Gertrude (1874), Brewsie and Willie. NF
Stuart, Jesse (1907), Tales from the Plum Grove Hills.
    F; Foretaste of Glory. F
Van Doren, Mark (1894), The Country New Year. V
Vidal, Gore (1925), Williwaw. F
Warren, Robert Penn (1905), All the King's Men.
    F; Blackberry Winter. F
Welty, Eudora (1909), Delta Wedding. F
White, E. B. (1899), The Wild Flag. NF
White, William Allen (d. 1944), Autobiography. NF
Williams, Tennessee (1911), 27 Wagons Full of Cotton and
    Other One-Act Plays. D
Williams, William Carlos (1883), Paterson (Book One). V
Wilson, Edmund (1895), Memoirs of Hecate County. F
Winters, Yvor (1900), Edwin Arlington Robinson. NF

Dylan Thomas's *Deaths and Entrances.*
Fry's *A Phoenix Too Frequent.*
Larkin's *Jill.*
Beerbohm's *Mainly on the Air.*
Aldous Huxley's *The Perennial
    Philosophy.*
Read's *Collected Poems.*
Rattigan's *The Winslow Boy.*
Koestler's *Thieves in the Night.*
Anouilh's *Medea.*
Genet's *Miracle of the Rose.*
Jiménez's *Total Season.*
Kazantzakis's *Zorba the Greek.*
Sartre's *The Respectful Prostitute.*
Nekrasov's *Front-Line Stalingrad.*

1947

Aiken, Conrad (1889), The Kid. V
Algren, Nelson (1909), The Neon Wilderness. F
Amory, Cleveland (1917), The Proper Bostonians. NF

Truman Doctrine aided foreign nations.
Marshall Plan attempted to foster
    European recovery.

Auchincloss, Louis (1917), The Indifferent Children. F
Auden, W. H. (1907), The Age of Anxiety. V
Bellow, Saul (1915), The Victim. F
Blackmur, R. P. (1904), The Good European. V
Bourjaily, Vance (1922), The End of My Life. F
Brooks, Van Wyck (1886), The Times of Melville and Whitman. NF
Buck, Pearl (1892), Far and Near. F
Burns, John Horne (1916), The Gallery. F
Bynner, Witter (1881), Take Away the Darkness. V
Cabell, James Branch (1879), Let Me Lie. NF
Cain, James M. (1892), The Butterfly. F
Caldwell, Erskine (1903), The Sure Hand of God, F
Canby, Henry Seidel (1878), American Memoir. NF
Ciardi, John (1916), Other Skies. V
Coxe, Louis (1918), The Sea Faring. V
Davenport, Marcia (1903), East Side, West Side. F
DeVoto, Bernard (1897), Across the Wide Missouri. NF
Dreiser, Theodore (d. 1945), The Stoic. F
Duncan, Robert (1919), Heavenly City, Earthly City. V
Eberhart, Richard (1904), Burr Oaks. V
Eliot, T. S. (1888), On Poetry. NF; Milton. NF
Farrell, James T. (1904), The Life Adventurous. F; Literature and Morality. NF
Fletcher, John Gould (1886), Arkansas. NF
Frost, Robert (1874), A Masque of Mercy. D; Steeple Bush. V
Garrigue, Jean (1914), The Ego and the Centaur. V
Green, Paul (1894), The Common Glory. D
Guthrie, A. B., Jr. (1901), The Big Sky. F
Haines, William Wister (1908), Command Decision. F; Command Decision (pub. 1948). D
Hayes, Alfred (1911), Shadow of Heaven. F
Himes, Chester (1909), Lonely Crusade. F
Hobson, Laura (1900), Gentleman's Agreement. F
Hughes, Langston (1902), Fields of Wonder. V
Inge, William (1913), Farther Off from Heaven. D
Kantor, MacKinlay (1904), But Look, the Morn. NF
Kees, Weldon (1914), The Fall of the Magicians. V
Lewis, Sinclair (1885), Kingsblood Royal. F
Loos, Anita (1893), Happy Birthday. D
Lytle, Andrew (1902), A Name for Evil. F
Michener, James A. (1907), Tales of the South Pacific. F
Miller, Arthur (1915), All My Sons. D
Miller, Henry (1891), Remember to Remember. NF
Motley, Willard (1912), Knock on Any Door. F
Nabokov, Vladimir (1899), Nine Stories. F; Bend Sinister. F
Nemerov, Howard (1920), The Image and the Law. V
Nims, John Frederick (1913), The Iron Pastoral. V
Nin, Anaïs (1903), On Writing. NF
O'Hara, John (1905), Hellbox. F
O'Neill, Eugene (1888), A Moon for the Misbegotten (pub. 1952). D
Patchen, Kenneth (1911), Panels for the Walls of Heaven. V
Petry, Ann (1911), Country Place. F
Powers, J. F. (1917), The Prince of Darkness and Other Stories. F
Richter, Conrad (1890), Always Young and Fair. F
Roberts, Kenneth (1885), Lydia Bailey. F
Ruark, Robert (1915), Grenadine Etching. F
Sandoz, Mari (1896), The Tom-Walker. F
Saroyan, William (1908), Jim Dandy. D
Sarton, May (1912), The Underground River. D
Schorer, Mark (1908), The State of Mind. F

Taft-Hartley Labor Relations Act limited union power.
Creation of unified Department of Defense.
Housing shortage was a major problem.
Rocket-powered airplane reached supersonic speed.
Jackie Robinson became first Negro major-league baseball player.
Willa Cather d.
The Pacific Spectator (Stanford), 1947–56.

Communist parties in Europe established Cominform.
Pakistan established as independent state.
Lowry's Under the Volcano.
Larkin's A Girl in Winter.
Hartley's Eustace and Hilda.
MacKenzie's Whisky Galore.
Trevor-Roper's The Last Days of Hitler.
Potter's The Theory and Practice of Gamesmanship.
Camus's The Plague.
Anouilh's Ring Round the Moon.
Moravia's The Woman of Rome.
Pavese's Dialogues with Leucò.
Quasimodo's Day After Day.
Thomas Mann's Doctor Faustus.
Genet's The Maids.
Frank's The Diary of a Young Girl.

Schulberg, Budd (1914), The Harder They Fall. F
Shapiro, Karl (1913), Trial of a Poet. V
Shirer, William L. (1904), End of a Berlin Diary. NF
Sinclair, Upton (1878), Presidential Mission. F
Smith, William Jay (1918), Poems. V
Spillane, Mickey (1918), I, the Jury. F
Stafford, Jean (1915), The Mountain Lion. F
Stegner, Wallace (1909), Second Growth. F
Stein, Gertrude (d. 1946), Four in America. NF; The Mother of
    Us All (with Virgil Thomson). D
Steinbeck, John (1902), The Wayward Bus. F; The Pearl. F
Stevens, Wallace (1879), Transport to Summer. V
Trilling, Lionel (1905), The Middle of the Journey. F
Vidal, Gore (1925), In a Yellow Wood. F
Warren, Robert Penn (1905), The Circus in the Attic and Other
    Stories. F
White, William L. (1900), Report on the Germans. NF
Wilbur, Richard (1921), The Beautiful Changes. V
Williams, Tennessee (1911), A Streetcar Named Desire. D
Willingham, Calder (1922), End as a Man. F
Wilson, Edmund (1895), Europe without Baedecker. NF
Winters, Yvor (1900), In Defense of Reason. NF
Wouk, Herman (1915), Aurora Dawn. F

1948

Allen, Hervey (1889), Toward the Morning. F
Anderson, Maxwell (1888), Anne of the Thousand Days. D
Asch, Sholem (1880), Tales of My People. F
Berryman, John (1914), The Dispossessed. V
Bishop, John Peale (d. 1944), Collected Essays. NF; Collected
    Poems. V
Bontemps, Arna (1902), The Story of the Negro. NF
Bromfield, Louis (1896), Malabar Farm. NF
Cain, James M. (1892), The Moth. F
Caldwell, Erskine (1903), This Very Earth. F
Capote, Truman (1924), Other Voices, Other Rooms. F
Cather, Willa (d. 1947), The Old Beauty and Others. F
Cozzens, James Gould (1903), Guard of Honor. F
Eisenhower, Dwight D. (1890), Crusade in Europe. NF
Eliot, T. S. (1888), Notes Toward a Definition of Culture.
    NF; From Poe to Valery. NF
Faulkner, William (1897), Intruder in the Dust. F
Freeman, Douglas Southall (1886), George Washington (6
    vols., 1948–54). NF
Haydn, Hiram (1907), The Time Is Noon. F
Jackson, Charles (1903), The Outer Edges. F
Jackson, Shirley (1919), The Road Through the Wall. F
Jarrell, Randall (1914), Losses. V
Jeffers, Robinson (1887), The Double Axe and Other Poems. V
Lewisohn, Ludwig (1882), Anniversary. F
Lindbergh, Charles A. (1902), Of Flight and Life. NF
Lockridge, Ross (1914), Raintree County. F
Logan, Joshua (1908), Mr. Roberts [adapted with Thomas
    Heggen from Heggen's novel (1946)]. D
McCoy, Horace (1897), Kiss Tomorrow Goodbye. F
MacLeish, Archibald (1892), Actfive, and Other Poems. V
McWilliams, Carey (1905), A Mask for Privilege. NF
Mailer, Norman (1923), The Naked and the Dead. F
Maxwell, William (1908), Time Will Darken It. F
Melville, Herman (d. 1891), Journal of a Visit to London and the
    Continent. NF

First peacetime Selective Service Act.
Organization of American States
    chartered at Bogotá.
Investigations by House Committee on
    Un-American Activities.
Cortisone introduced for rheumatoid
    arthritis.
T. S. Eliot awarded Nobel Prize in
    literature.
The Hudson Review (New York),
    1948–.
Masses and Mainstream (New York),
    1948–56.

West Berlin blockade and airlift.
Mahatama Gandhi assassinated.
Proclamation of the state of Israel.
World Council of Churches organized.
Greene's *The Heart of the Matter*.
Rattigan's *The Browning Version*.
Graves's *The White Goddess*.
C. Day-Lewis's *Collected Poems*.
Evelyn Waugh's *The Loved One*.
Fry's *The Lady's Not for Burning*.
Betjeman's *Selected Poems*.
Toynbee's *Civilization on Trial*.
Sylvia Townsend Warner's *The Corner
    That Held Them*.
Gary's *Company of Men*.
Sarraute's *Portrait of a Man Unknown*.
Benn's *Static Poems*.
Sartre's *Dirty Hands*.
Paton's *Cry, the Beloved Country*.
Brecht's *The Caucasian Chalk Circle*.
Moravia's *Luca*.

Meredith, William (1919), Ships and Other Figures. V
Merton, Thomas (1915), The Seven Storey Mountain. NF
Miller, Henry (1891), The Smile at the Foot of the Ladder. F
Morris, Wright (1910), The Home Place. F
Patchen, Kenneth (1911), See You in the Morning. F
Pennell, Joseph Stanley (1908), The History of Nora Beckham. F
Perelman, S. J. (1904), Westward Ha! F
Pound, Ezra (1885), The Pisan Cantos. V; The Cantos of Ezra Pound. V
Prokosch, Frederic (1908), Storm and Echo. F
Roethke, Theodore (1908), The Lost Son and Other Poems. V
Rukeyser, Muriel (1913), The Green Wave. V
Sandburg, Carl (1878), Remembrance Rock. F
Sarton, May (1912), The Lion and the Rose. V
Schwartz, Delmore (1913), The World Is a Wedding. F
Scott, Winfield Townley (1910), Mr. Whittier. V
Shaw, Irwin (1913), The Young Lions. F
Sherwood, Robert E. (1896), Roosevelt and Hopkins: An Intimate History. NF
Sinclair, Upton (1878), One Clear Call. F
Skinner, Cornelia Otis (1901), Family Circle. NF
Smith, Betty (1904), Tomorrow Will Be Better. F
Smith, William Gardner (1926), Last of the Conquerors. F
Snow, Edgar (1905), The Pattern of Soviet Power. NF
Spencer, Elizabeth (1921), Fire in the Morning. F
Stein, Gertrude (d. 1946), Blood on the Dining Room Floor. F
Steinbeck, John (1902), A Russian Journal (with Robert Capa). NF
Stewart, George R. (1895), Fire. F
Tate, Allen (1899), Poems 1922–1947. V; On the Limits of Poetry. NF
Taylor, Peter (1917), A Long Fourth and Other Stories. F
Thurber, James (1894), The Beast in Me and Other Animals. F, NF
Van Doren, Mark (1894), New Poems. V
Vidal, Gore (1925), The City and the Pillar (rev. 1965). F
Viereck, Peter (1916), Terror and Decorum. V
Wilder, Thornton (1897), The Ides of March. F
Williams, Tennessee (1911), Summer and Smoke. D; One Arm and Other Stories. F
Williams, William Carlos (1883), Paterson (Book Two). V; A Dream of Love. D
Wolfe, Thomas (d. 1938), Mannerhouse. D
Wouk, Herman (1915), The City Boy. F

1949

Aiken, Conrad (1889), The Divine Pilgrim. V; Skylight One. V
Algren, Nelson (1909), The Man with the Golden Arm. F
Asch, Sholem (1880), Mary. F
Bowles, Paul (1910), The Sheltering Sky. F
Boyle, Kay (1902), His Human Majesty. F
Brooks, Gwendolyn (1917), Annie Allen. V
Burnett, W. R. (1899), The Asphalt Jungle. F
Burns, John Horne (1916), Lucifer with a Book. F
Cabell, James Branch (1879), The Devil's Own Dear Son. F
Caldwell, Erskine (1903), A Place Called Estherville. F
Capote, Truman (1924), A Tree of Night. F
Chase, Mary Ellen (1887), The Plum Tree. F
Ciardi, John (1916), Live Another Day. V
Clark, Walter Van Tilburg (1909), The Track of the Cat. F

U.N. headquarters dedicated, in New York City.
North Atlantic Treaty Organization (NATO) signed by 12 nations.
American Communist leaders convicted of conspiracy.
Philip Barry d.
American Heritage (New York), 1949–.
American Quarterly (Minneapolis; ·Phila.), 1949–.
The Reporter (New York), 1949–68.
Comparative Literature (Eugene, Ore.), 1949–.

Soviet Union tested atomic bomb.
People's Republic of China proclaimed.

Dos Passos, John (1896), The Grand Design. F
Douglas, Lloyd C. (1877), The Big Fisherman. F
Eliot, T. S. (1888), The Aims of Poetic Drama. NF
Farrell, James T. (1904), The Road Between. F
Faulkner, William (1897), Knight's Gambit. F
Fearing, Kenneth (1902), Stranger at Coney Island. V
Feikema, Feike (1912), The Primitive. F
Foote, Shelby (1916), Tournament. F
Frost, Robert (1874), Complete Poems. V
Goodman, Paul (1911), The Break-Up of Our Camp. F
Gunther, John (1901), Death Be Not Proud. NF
Guthrie, A. B., Jr. (1901), The Way West. F
"H.D." (1886), By Avon River. V, NF
Hawkes, John (1925), The Cannibal. F
Hayes, Alfred (1911), The Girl on the Via Flaminia. F
Hellman, Lillian (1905), Montserrat [adapted from Emmanuel
    Roblès's play (1949); pub. 1950]. D
Hughes, Langston (1902), One-Way Ticket. V
Isherwood, Christopher (1904), The Condor and the Cows. NF
Jackson, Shirley (1919), The Lottery or, The Adventures of
    James Harris. F
Kanin, Garson (1912), The Rat Race (pub. 1950). D
Kingsley, Sidney (1906), Detective Story. D
Krutch, Joseph Wood (1893), The Twelve Seasons. NF
Lea, Tom (1907), The Brave Bulls. F
Lewis, Sinclair (1885), The God-Seeker. F
McCarthy, Mary (1912), The Oasis. F
MacKaye, Percy (1875), The Mystery of Hamlet, King of
    Denmark; or, What We Will (pub. 1950). D
McWilliams, Carey (1905), North from Mexico. NF
Marquand, J. P. (1893), Point of No Return. F
Michener, James A. (1907), The Fires of Spring. F
Miller, Arthur (1915), Death of a Salesman. D
Miller, Henry (1891), Sexus (pub. in Paris). F, NF
Morris, Wright (1910), The World in the Attic. F
Nemerov, Howard (1920), The Melodramatists. F
Odets, Clifford (1906), The Big Knife. D
O'Hara, John (1905), A Rage to Live. F
Patchen, Kenneth (1911), Red Wine & Yellow Hair. V; To Say
    If You Love Someone. V
Perelman, S. J. (1904), Listen to the Mocking Bird. F
Pound, Ezra (1885), Selected Poems. V
Rexroth, Kenneth (1905), The Signature of All Things. V
Rice, Elmer (1892), The Show Must Go On. F
"Ross Macdonald" (1915), The Moving Target. F
Rukeyser, Muriel (1913), Orpheus. V; The Life of Poetry. NF
Saroyan, William (1908), Don't Go Away Mad, and Two Other
    Plays: Sam Ego's House and A Decent Birth, A Happy
    Funeral. D
Simpson, Louis (1923), The Arrivistes. V
Sinclair, Upton (1878), O Shepherd, Speak! F
Smith, Lillian (1897), Killers of the Dream (rev. 1961). NF
Stein, Gertrude (d. 1946), Last Operas and Plays. D
Stewart, George R. (1895), Earth Abides. F
Streeter, Edward (1891), Father of the Bride. F
Stuart, Jesse (1907), The Thread That Runs So True. NF
Tate, Allen (1899), The Hovering Fly. NF
Vidal, Gore (1925), The Season of Comfort. F
Welty, Eudora (1909), The Golden Apples. F
White, E. B. (1899), Here Is New York. NF
Williams, William Carlos (1883), Selected Poems. V; Paterson
    (Book Three). V
Wylie, Philip (1902), Opus 21. NF

Sigrid Undset d.
Bowen's *The Heat of the Day.*
Nancy Mitford's *Love in a Cold
    Climate.*
Orwell's *Nineteen Eighty-Four.*
Cary's *A Fearful Joy.*
Rebecca West's *The Meaning of
    Treason.*
MacNeice's *Collected Poems 1925–
    1948.*
Genet's *Deathwatch; The Thief's
    Journal.*
Borges's *The Aleph.*
Pavese's *The Beautiful Summer.*
Böll's *The Train Was on Time.*
Gordimer's *Face to Face.*
Mishima's *Confessions of a Mask.*
Beauvoir's *The Second Sex.*
Quasimodo's *Life Is No Dream.*
Betti's *Corruption in the Palace of
    Justice.*

1950

Agar, Herbert (1897), The Price of Union. NF
Aiken, Conrad (1889), The Short Stories of Conrad Aiken. F
Archibald, William (1924), The Innocents [adapted from Henry James's novella The Turn of the Screw (1898)]. D
Auden, W. H. (1907), Collected Shorter Poems, 1930–1944. V; The Enchafèd Flood. NF
Berryman, John (1914), Stephen Crane. NF
Bowles, Paul (1910), The Delicate Prey. F
Bradbury, Ray (1920), The Martian Chronicles. F
Buechner, Frederick (1926), A Long Day's Dying. F
Burke, Kenneth (1897), A Rhetoric of Motives. NF
Caldwell, Erskine (1903), Episode in Palmetto. F
Capote, Truman (1924), Local Color. NF
Cassill, R. V. (1919), The Eagle on the Coin. F
Clark, Walter Van Tilburg (1909), The Watchful Gods. F
Cummings, E. E. (1894), XAIPE: 71 Poems. V
Dahlberg, Edward (1900), Flea of Sodom. NF
Demby, William (1922), Beetlecreek. F
Dos Passos, John (1896), The Prospect Before Us. F
Duncan, Robert (1919), Medieval Scenes. V
Eberhart, Richard (1904), An Herb Basket. V
Eliot, T. S. (1888), The Cocktail Party. D
Farrell, James T. (1904), An American Dream Girl. F
Faulkner, William (1897), Collected Stories. F
Feikema, Feike (1912), The Brother. F
Foote, Shelby (1916), Follow Me Down. F
Gill, Brendan (1914), The Trouble of One House. F
Goyen, William (1915), The House of Breath. F
Hemingway, Ernest (1899), Across the River and into the Trees. F
Hersey, John (1914), The Wall. F
Hughes, Langston (1902), Simple Speaks His Mind. F
Inge, William (1913), Come Back, Little Sheba. D
Kerouac, Jack (1922), The Town and the City. F
Laurents, Arthur (1918), The Bird Cage. D
McCarthy, Mary (1912), Cast a Cold Eye. F
McCullers, Carson (1917), The Member of the Wedding [adapted from her novel (1946); pub. 1951]. D
MacLeish, Archibald (1892), Poetry and Opinion. NF
McWilliams, Carey (1905), Witch Hunt. NF
Morrison, Theodore (1901), The Dream of Alcestis. V
Nemerov, Howard (1920), Guide to the Ruins. V
Nims, John Frederick (1913), A Fountain in Kentucky. V
Nin, Anaïs (1903), The Four-Chambered Heart. F
Odets, Clifford (1906), The Country Girl. D
Richter, Conrad (1890), The Town. F
"Ross Macdonald" (1915), The Drowning Pool. F
Sandburg, Carl (1878), Complete Poems. V
Sarton, May (1912), Shadow of a Man. F
Schulberg, Budd (1914), The Disenchanted. F
Schwartz, Delmore (1913), Vaudeville for a Princess. V, NF
Shaw, Irwin (1913), Mixed Faith. F
Singer, Isaac Bashevis (1904), The Family Moskat. F
Smith, William Jay (1918), Celebration at Dark. V
Spillane, Mickey (1918), My Gun Is Quick. F; Vengeance Is Mine. F
Stegner, Wallace (1909), The Women on the Wall. F; The Preacher and the Slave. F
Stein, Gertrude (d. 1946), Things As They Are. F
Steinbeck, John (1902), Burning Bright. F
Stevens, Wallace (1879), The Auroras of Autumn. V

Proclamation of national emergency.
U.S. troops landed in South Korea (July), invaded North Korea (October).
Truman approved development of hydrogen bomb.
Senator McCarthy began attacks on Communist infiltration.
Alger Hiss sentenced to prison for perjury.
National Book Awards established.
William Faulkner awarded Nobel Prize in literature.
Edgar Lee Masters d.
Edna St. Vincent Millay d.

India proclaimed a republic.
George Bernard Shaw d.
George Orwell d.
Cesare Pavese d.
Heinrich Mann d.
Greene's The Third Man
William Cooper's Scenes from Provincial Life.
Sherriff's Home at Seven.
Sansom's The Passionate North.
Angus Wilson's Such Darling Dodos.
Wyndham Lewis's Rude Assignment.
Betti's Crime on Goat Island.
Pavese's The Moon and the Bonfires.
Paz's The Labyrinth of Solitude.
Lessing's The Grass Is Singing.
Böll's Traveler, If You Come to Spa.
Ionesco's The Bald Soprano.
Neruda's General Song.
Lagerkvist's Barabbas.
Mishima's Thirst for Love.

Stuart, Jesse (1907), Hie to the Hunters. F
Taylor, Peter (1917), A Woman of Means. F
Van Druten, John (1901), Bell, Book, and Candle. D
Vidal, Gore (1925), A Search for the King. F; Dark Green, Bright Red. F
Viereck, Peter (1916), Strike Through the Mask! V
Warren, Robert Penn (1905). World Enough and Time. F
Wilbur, Richard (1921), Ceremony and Other Poems. V
Williams, Tennessee (1911), The Roman Spring of Mrs. Stone. F
Williams, William Carlos (1883), The Collected Later Poems. V; Make Light of It. F
Willingham, Calder (1922), Geraldine Bradshaw. F
Wilson, Edmund (1895), Classics and Commercials. NF; The Little Blue Light. D

1951

Abbott, George (1887), A Tree Grows in Brooklyn [adapted with Betty Smith from her novel (1943)]. D
Agee, James (1909), The Morning Watch. F
Algren, Nelson (1909), Chicago: City on the Make. NF
Anderson, Maxwell (1888), Barefoot in Athens. D
Asch, Sholem (1880), Moses. F
Auden, W. H. (1907), Nones. V; The Rake's Progress (with Chester Kallmann). D
Bowen, Robert O. (1920), The Weight of the Cross. F
Brinnin, John Malcolm (1916), The Sorrows of Cold Stone. V
Caldwell, Erskine (1903), Call It Experience: The Years of Learning How to Write. NF
Calisher, Hortense (1911), In the Absence of Angels. F
Capote, Truman (1924), The Grass Harp. F
Carson, Rachel (1907), The Sea Around Us. NF
Catton, Bruce (1899), Mr. Lincoln's Army. NF
Ciardi, John (1916), From Time to Time. V
Coxe, Louis (1918), Billy Budd [adapted with Robert Chapman from Herman Melville's novella (1924)]. D
Dodson, Owen (1914), Boy at the Window. F
Dos Passos, John (1896), Chosen Country. F
Eliot, T. S. (1888), Poetry and Drama. NF
Farrell, James T. (1904), This Man and This Woman. F
Faulkner, William (1897), Requiem for a Nun. F
Feikema, Feike (1912), The Giant. F
Foote, Shelby (1916), Love in a Dry Season. F
Gold, Herbert (1924), Birth of a Hero. F
Gordon, Caroline (1895), The Strange Children. F
Hawkes, John (1925), The Beetle Leg. F
Hellman, Lillian (1905), The Autumn Garden. D
Hughes, Langston (1902), Montage of a Dream Deferred. V
Jackson, Shirley (1919), Hangsaman. F
Jarrell, Randall (1914), The Seven-League Crutches. V
Jones, James (1921), From Here to Eternity. F
Kazin, Alfred (1915), A Walker in the City. NF
Kingsley, Sidney (1906), Darkness at Noon [adapted from Arthur Koestler's novel (1941)]. D
Laurents, Arthur (1918), A Clearing in the Woods (pub. 1957). D
Lewis, Sinclair (1885), World So Wide. F

22nd Amendment (limiting president to two terms in office) ratified.
Selective Service Act extended to 1955.
Gen. Dwight D. Eisenhower assumed command of SHAPE.
Gen. Douglas MacArthur recalled from Far East commands.
American Studies Association founded.
Columbia Broadcasting System offered first commercial color television.
Sinclair Lewis d.

Chinese Communist troops supported North Korean army.
Occupation of Tibet by Chinese.
Winston Churchill became British prime minister.
Hermann Broch d.
Henri René Lenormand d.
André Gide d.
Powell's A Dance to the Music of Time (12 vols., 1951–75).
Pritchett's Mr. Beluncle.
Spender's World Within World.
Monsarrat's The Cruel Sea.
Greene's The End of the Affair.
Ionesco's The Lesson.
Camus's The Rebel.
Yourcenar's Hadrian's Memoirs.
Betti's The Queen and the Rebels.
Malraux's The Voices of Silence.
Böll's Adam, Where Art Thou?
Giono's The Horseman on the Roof.
Beckett's Molloy; Malone Dies.
Paz's Eagle or Sun?

Lowell, Robert (1917), The Mills of the Kavanaughs. V
McCullers, Carson (1917), The Ballad of the Sad Café. F
MacLeish, Archibald (1892), Freedom Is the Right to Choose.
   NF
Mailer, Norman (1923), Barbary Shore. F
Marquand, J. P. (1893), Melville Goodwin, USA. F
Merrill, James (1926), First Poems. V
Michener, James A. (1907), Return to Paradise. F, NF; The
   Voice of Asia. NF
Moore, Marianne (1887), Collected Poems. V
Morris, Wright (1910), Man and Boy. F
Motley, Willard (1912), We Fished All Night. F
Mumford, Lewis (1895), The Conduct of Life. NF
Nash, Ogden (1902), Parents Keep Out. V
Neihardt, John G. (1881), When the Tree Flowered. F
O'Connor, Edwin (1918), The Oracle. F
O'Hara, John (1905), The Farmers Hotel. F
Osborn, Paul (1901), Point of No Return [adapted from J. P.
   Marquand's novel (1949); pub. 1952]. D
Rice, Elmer (1892), The Grand Tour (pub. 1952). D
Rich, Adrienne (1929), A Change of World. V
Roethke, Theodore (1908), Praise to the End! V
Salinger, J. D. (1919), The Catcher in the Rye. F
Saroyan, William (1908), Tracy's Tiger. F; Rock Wagram. F
Shaw, Irwin (1913), The Troubled Air. F
Sherwood, Robert E. (1896), Second Threshold [revised from a
   manuscript by Philip Barry (d. 1949)]. D
Spillane, Mickey (1918), The Big Kill. F
Stein, Gertrude (d. 1946), Two: Gertrude Stein and Her Brother,
   and Other Early Portraits (1908–1912). NF
Stevens, Wallace (1879), The Necessary Angel. NF
Stout, Rex (1886), Murder by the Book. F
Styron, William (1925), Lie Down in Darkness. F
Tillich, Paul (1886), Systematic Theology (3 vols., 1951–63).
   NF
Van Druten, John (1901), I Am a Camera [adapted from
   Christopher Isherwood's sketches Goodbye to Berlin (1939)].
   D
Warren, Robert Penn (1905), William Faulkner and His South.
   NF
Weiss, Theodore (1916), The Catch. V
West, Jessamyn (1907), The Witch Diggers. F
Williams, Tennessee (1911), The Rose Tattoo. D
Williams, William Carlos (1883), Paterson (Book Four). V; The
   Collected Earlier Poems. V; The Autobiography of William
   Carlos Williams. NF
Willingham, Calder (1922), The Gates of Hell. F; Reach to the
   Stars. F
Wouk, Herman (1915), The Caine Mutiny. F

1952

Agar, Herbert (1897), A Declaration of Faith. NF
Aiken, Conrad (1889), Ushant: An Essay. NF
Allen, Frederick Lewis (1890), The Big Change. NF
Auchincloss, Louis (1917), Sybil. F
"B. Traven" (?), The Rebellion of the Hanged. F
Behrman, S. N. (1893), Jane [adapted from Somerset
   Maugham's story (1923)]. D; Duveen. NF
Blackmur, R. P. (1904), Language as Gesture. NF
Bowles, Paul (1910), Let It Come Down. F

Truce negotiations continued in Korea.
Unemployment reached record high.
Prolonged steel strike over higher wage
   demands.
Anti-Communism investigations
   increased.
Atomic Energy Commission announced
   hydrogen bomb tests.
McCarran-Walter Act codified
   immigration laws.

Brooks, Van Wyck (1886), The Confident Years. NF
Brossard, Chandler (1922), Who Walk in Darkness. F
Buechner, Frederick (1926), The Seasons' Difference. F
Burns, John Horne (1916), A Cry of Children. F
Cabell, James Branch (1879), A Lamp for Nightfall. F; The Courting of Susie Brown. F
Capote, Truman (1924), The Grass Harp [adapted from his novel (1951)]. D
Catton, Bruce (1899), Glory Road. NF
Clark, Eleanor (1913), Rome and a Villa. NF
Conrad, Barnaby (1922), Matador. F
De Vries, Peter (1910), No, But I Saw the Movie. F
Dos Passos, John (1896), District of Columbia (trilogy; first pub. 1939–49). F
Eliot, T. S. (1888), The Complete Poems and Plays. D, V
Ellison, Ralph (1914), Invisible Man. F
Farrell, James T. (1904), Yet Other Waters. F
Fast, Howard (1914), Spartacus. F
Ferber, Edna (1887), Giant. F
Foote, Shelby (1916), Shiloh. F
Goyen, William (1915), Ghost and Flesh. F
Hemingway, Ernest (1899), The Old Man and the Sea. F
Holmes, John Clellon (1926), Go. F
Hughes, Langston (1902), Laughing to Keep from Crying. F
Kramm, Joseph (1908), The Shrike. D
Laurents, Arthur (1918), The Time of the Cuckoo (pub. 1953). D
Loos, Anita (1893), Gigi [adapted from Colette's novel (1946)]. D
Macauley, Robie (1919), The Disguises of Love. F
McCarthy, Mary (1912), The Groves of Academe. F
MacLeish, Archibald (1892), The Trojan Horse. D; Collected Poems 1917–1952. V
Malamud, Bernard (1914), The Natural. F
Merwin, W. S. (1927), A Mask for Janus. V
Miller, Henry (1891), The Books in My Life. NF
Morris, Wright (1910), The Works of Love. F
O'Connor, Flannery (1925), Wise Blood. F
O'Hara, Frank (1926), A City Winter and Other Poems. V
Porter, Katherine Anne (1890), The Days Before. NF
Saroyan, William (1908), The Bicycle Rider in Beverly Hills. NF
Sarton, May (1912), A Shower of Summer Days. F
Spencer, Elizabeth (1921), This Crooked Way. F
Spillane, Mickey (1918), Kiss Me Deadly. F
Stafford, Jean (1915), The Catherine Wheel. F
Stein, Gertrude (d. 1946), Mrs. Reynolds and Five Earlier Novelettes (1931–1942). F
Steinbeck, John (1902), East of Eden. F
Stuart, Jesse (1907), Kentucky Is My Land. V
Suckow, Ruth (1892), Some Others and Myself. F, NF
Tillich, Paul (1886), The Courage to Be. NF
Vidal, Gore (1925), The Judgment of Paris. F
Viereck, Peter (1916), The First Morning. V
Vonnegut, Kurt, Jr. (1922), Player Piano. F
White, E. B. (1899), Charlotte's Web. F
Williams, William Carlos (1883), The Build-Up. F
Willingham, Calder (1922), Natural Child. F
Wilson, Edmund (1895), The Shores of Light. NF
Winter, Yvor (1900), Collected Poems. V
Wolff, Maritta (1918), Back of Town. F

Wave of UFO's (unidentified flying objects) reported.
John Dewey d.
George Santayana d.

Death of George VI; accession of Elizabeth II.
Increasing racial tensions in Africa.
Norman Douglas d.
Ferenc Molnár d.
Knut Hamsun d.
Angus Wilson's *Hemlock and After.*
Cary's *Prisoner of Grace.*
Dylan Thomas's *Collected Poems: 1934–1952.*
Evelyn Waugh's *Men at Arms.*
David Jones's *The Anathemata.*
Muir's *Collected Poems.*
Rattigan's *The Deep Blue Sea.*
Ionesco's *The Chairs.*
Borges's *Other Inquisitions.*
Boulle's *The Bridge Over the River Kwai.*
Anouilh's *The Waltz of the Toreadors.*
Silone's *A Handful of Blackberries.*
Adamov's *The Parody.*
Yevtushenko's *Prospectors of the Future.*
Calvino's *The Cloven Viscount.*
Kawabata's *A Thousand Cranes.*
Lessing's *Children of Violence* (5 vols., 1952–69).

1953

Aiken, Conrad (1889), Collected Poems. V

Anderson, Robert (1917), Tea and Sympathy. D; All Summer Long [adapted from Donald Wetzel's novel A Wreath and a Curse (1950); pub. 1955]. D

Asch, Sholem (1880), A Passage in the Night. F

Ashbery, John (1927), Turandot and Other Poems. V

Auchincloss, Louis (1917), A Law for the Lion. F

Baldwin, James (1924), Go Tell It on the Mountain. F

Bellow, Saul (1915), The Adventures of Augie March. F

Bissell, Richard (1913), 7½ Cents. F

Bowles, Jane (1917), In the Summer House (pub. 1954). D

Bradbury, Ray (1920), The Golden Apples of the Sun. F; Fahrenheit 451. F

Cain, James M. (1892), Galatea. F

Carter, Hodding (1907), Where Main Street Meets the River. NF

Catton, Bruce (1899), A Stillness at Appomattox. NF

Chayefsky, Paddy (1923), Marty (pub. 1955). D

Cheever, John (1912), The Enormous Radio. F

Cummings, E. E. (1894), i: six nonlectures. NF

Eberhart, Richard (1904), Undercliff: Poems 1946–1953. V

Eliot, T. S. (1888), The Three Voices of Poetry. NF; The Confidential Clerk (pub. 1954). D

Farrell, James T. (1904), The Face of Time. F

Garrigue, Jean (1914), The Monument Rose. V

Harris, Mark (1922), The Southpaw. F

Hayes, Alfred (1911), In Love. F

Hersey, John (1914), The Marmot Drive. F

Hughes, Langston (1902), Simple Takes a Wife. F

Humphrey, William (1924), The Last Husband. F

Inge, William (1913), Picnic. D

Jackson, Charles (1903), Earthly Creatures. F

Jackson, Shirley (1919), Life Among the Savages. NF

Jarrell, Randall (1914), Poetry and the Age. NF

"John Patrick" (1905), The Teahouse of the August Moon [adapted from Vern Sneider's novel (1951)]. D

Kaufman, George S. (1889), The Solid Gold Cadillac (with Howard Teichmann). D

Koch, Kenneth (1925), Poems. V

Lindbergh, Charles A. (1902), The Spirit of St. Louis. NF

MacLeish, Archibald (1892), This Music Crept by Me Upon the Waters. D

Michener, James A. (1907), The Bridges at Toko-ri. F

Miller, Arthur (1915), The Crucible. D

Miller, Henry (1891), Plexus (pub. in Paris). F, NF

Morris, Wright (1910), The Deep Sleep. F

Morrison, Theodore (1901), The Stones of the House. F

Neihardt, John G. (1881), Eagle Voice. F

Parker, Dorothy (1893), The Ladies of the Corridor (with Arnaud d'Usseau; pub. 1954). D

Perelman, S. J. (1904), The Ill-Tempered Clavichord. F

Peterson, Louis (1922), Take a Giant Step (pub. 1954). D

Petry, Ann (1911), The Narrows. F

Prokosch, Frederic (1908), Nine Days to Mukulla. F

Pound, Ezra (1885), The Translations of Ezra Pound. D, V

Rawlings, Marjorie Kinnan (1896), The Sojourner. F

Richter, Conrad (1890), The Light in the Forest. F

Roethke, Theodore (1908), The Waking: Poems 1933–1953. V

Salinger, J. D. (1919), Nine Stories. F

Sandburg, Carl (1878), Always the Young Strangers. NF

Korean War armistice signed in Panmunjom.

Department of Health, Education, and Welfare created.

Lifting of all wage and price controls.

"McCarthyism" synonymous with attacks on the "Red menace."

Eugene O'Neill d.

John Horne Burns d.

The Paris Review (Paris et al.), 1953–.

Death of Stalin.

Egypt proclaimed a republic.

Encounter (London), 1953–.

La Nouvelle Nouvelle Revue Française (Paris), 1953–.

Dylan Thomas d.

Ugo Betti d.

Ivan Bunin d.

Hartley's *The Go-Between.*

Wain's *Hurry on Down.*

Renault's *The Charioteer.*

Beckett's *Watt; Waiting for Godot.*

Anouilh's *The Lark.*

Bonnefoy's *On the Motion and Immobility of Douve.*

Lessing's *Five.*

Sarraute's *Martereau.*

Barthes's *Writing Degree Zero.*

Betti's *The Burnt Flower-Bed.*

Adamov's *Professor Taranne.*

Gordimer's *The Lying Days.*

Santayana, George (1952), My Host the World. NF; The Poet's Testament. V, D
Sarton, May (1912), The Land of Silence. V
Schulberg, Budd (1914), Some Faces in the Crowd. F
Shapiro, Karl (1913), Poems 1940–1953. V; Beyond Criticism. NF
Sinclair, Upton (1878), The Return of Lanny Budd. F
Stafford, Jean (1915), Children Are Bored on Sunday. F
Stuart, Jesse (1953), The Good Spirit of Laurel Ridge. F
Stein, Gertrude (d. 1946), Bee Time Vine and Other Pieces (1913–1927). F, V
Tate, Allen (1899), The Forlorn Demon. NF
Tolson, Melvin B. (1900), Libretto for the Republic of Liberia. V
Van Doren, Mark (1874), Nobody Say a Word. F
Wagoner, David (1926), Dry Sun, Dry Wind. V
Warren, Robert Penn (1905), Brother to Dragons. V
West, Jessamyn (1907), Cress Delahanty. F
White, William L. (1900), Back Down the Ridge. NF
Williams, Tennessee (1911), Camino Real. D
Wright, Richard (1908), The Outsider. F

1954

Adams, Léonie (1899), Poems. V
Arnow, Harriette (1908), The Dollmaker. F
Auchincloss, Louis (1917), The Romantic Egoists. F
Basso, Hamilton (1904), The View from Pompey's Head. F
Behrman, S. N. (1893), The Worcester Account. NF
Bogan, Louise (1897), Collected Poems, 1923–1953. V
Brooks, John (1920), A Pride of Lions. F
Caldwell, Erskine (1903), Love and Money. F
Capote, Truman (1924), House of Flowers. D
Chandler, Raymond (1888), The Long Goodbye. F
Chayefsky, Paddy (1923), The Bachelor Party (pub. 1955). D
Chodorov, Jerome (1911), Anniversary Waltz (with Joseph Fields). D
Cummings, E. E. (1894), Poems, 1923–1954. V
Daniels, Jonathan (1902), The End of Innocence. NF
Davis, Elmer (1890), But We Were Born Free. NF
Deutsch, Babette (1895), Animal, Vegetable, Mineral. V
De Vries, Peter (1910), The Tunnel of Love. F
Dos Passos, John (1896), Most Likely to Succeed. F; The Head and Heart of Thomas Jefferson. NF
Farrell, James T. (1904), Reflections at Fifty and Other Essays. NF
Faulkner, William (1897), A Fable. F
Foote, Shelby (1916), Jordan County: A Landscape in Narrative. F
Glasgow, Ellen (d. 1945), The Woman Within. NF
Gold, Herbert (1924), The Prospect Before Us. F
Hawkes, John (1925), The Goose on the Grave. F
Hecht, Anthony (1923), A Summoning of Stones. V
Hecht, Ben (1894), A Child of the Century. NF
Hicks, Granville (1901), Where We Came Out. NF
Himes, Chester (1909), The Third Generation. F
Hoffman, Daniel G. (1923), An Armada of Thirty Whales. V
Horgan, Paul (1903), Great River: The Rio Grande in North American History. NF
Isherwood, Christopher (1904), The World in the Evening. F

Supreme Court ruled racial segregation in public schools unconstitutional.
Army-McCarthy hearings and Senate's vote to censure McCarthy.
Southeast Asia Treaty Organization (SEATO) established.
Jonas Salk developed poliomyelitis vaccine.
Aliens deported on charge of Communist Party membership.
Ernest Hemingway awarded Nobel Prize in literature.

End of French power in Indochina.
Gamal Abdel Nasser seized power in Egypt.
The London Magazine (London), 1954–.
James Hilton d.
Sidonie-Gabrielle Colette d.
Kinglsey Amis's Lucky Jim.
Rattigan's Separate Tables.
Spender's Collected Poems.
Sansom's A Bed of Roses.
Murdoch's Under the Net.
Tolkien's The Lord of the Rings (3 vols., 1954–55).
Behan's The Quare Fellow.
Fry's The Dark Is Light Enough.
Golding's Lord of the Flies.
Dylan Thomas's Under Milk Wood.
Thomas Mann's Confessions of Felix Krull.
Beauvoir's The Mandarins.
Mishima's The Sound of Waves.
Sagan's Bonjour Tristesse.
Nekrasov's In the Home Town.
Neruda's Elementary Odes.
Fuentes's The Masked Days.

Jackson, Shirley (1919), The Bird's Nest. F
Jarrell, Randall (1914), Pictures from an Institution. F
Jeffers, Robinson (1887), Hungerfield and Other Poems. V
Kees, Weldon (1914), Poems 1947–1954. V
Kingsley, Sidney (1906), Lunatics and Lovers. D
Krutch, Joseph Wood (1893), The Measure of Man. NF
MacLeish, Archibald (1892), Songs for Eve. V
Manfred, Frederick (Feike Feikema) (1917), Lord Grizzly. F
Marquand, J. P. (1893), Thirty Years. F, NF
Matthiessen, Peter (1927), Race Rock. F
Merwin, W. S. (1927), The Dancing Bears. V
Michener, James A. (1907), Sayonara. F; The Floating World.
  NF
Millay, Edna St. Vincent (d. 1950), Mine the Harvest. V
Moore, Marianne (1887), The Fables of La Fontaine. V
Morris, Wright (1910), The Huge Season. F
Moss, Howard (1922), The Toy Fair. V
Nash, N. Richard (1913), The Rainmaker. D
Nemerov, Howard (1920), Federigo, or, The Power of Love. F
Nin, Anaïs (1903), A Spy in the House of Love. F
Odets, Clifford (1906), The Flowering Peach (prod.). D
O'Hara, John (1905), Sweet and Sour. NF
Patchen, Kenneth (1911), The Famous Boating Party. V
Pound, Ezra (1885), Literary Essays. NF; The Classic
  Anthology Defined by Confucius. V
Rice, Elmer (1892), The Winner. D
Sandoz, Mari (1896), The Buffalo Hunters. NF
Schorer, Mark (1908), The Wars of Love. F
Seton, Anya (1916), Katherine. F
Smith, Lillian (1897), The Journey. NF
Stafford, Jean (1915), A Winter's Tale. F
Stegner, Wallace (1909), Beyond the Hundredth Meridian. NF
Stein, Gertrude (d. 1946), As Fine as Melanctha (1914–1930).
  NF, F
Steinbeck, John (1902), Sweet Thursday. F
Stevens, Wallace (1879), The Collected Poems. V
Swenson, May (1919), Another Animal. V
Taylor, Peter (1917), The Widows of Thornton. F
Vidal, Gore (1925), Messiah. F
Wagoner, David (1926), The Man in the Middle. F
Welty, Eudora (1909), The Ponder Heart. F
White, E. B. (1899), The Second Tree from the Corner, V, NF
Wilder, Thornton (1897), The Matchmaker [revision of The
  Merchant of Yonkers (1938); pub. 1957.]. D
"William March" (1894), The Bad Seed. F
Williams, Tennessee (1911), Hard Candy. F
Williams, William Carlos (1883), The Desert Music.
  V; Selected Essays. NF
Wilson, Edmund (1895), Five Plays. D
Wouk, Herman (1915), The Caine Mutiny Court-Martial
  [adapted from his novel The Caine Mutiny (1951)]. D
Wright, Richard (1908), Black Power. NF

1955

Adams, Samuel Hopkins (1871), Grandfather Stories. F
Aiken, Conrad (1889), A Letter from Li Po. V
Ammons, A. R. (1926), Ommateum with Doxology. V
Anderson, Maxwell (1888), The Bad Seed [adapted from
  William March's novel (1954)]. D

Selective Service Act extended to 1959.
AFL and CIO merged.
Beginning of Negro boycott of buses in
  Alabama.
Robert E. Sherwood d.

Asch, Sholem (1880), The Prophet. F
Auden, W. H. (1907), The Shield of Achilles. V
Baldwin, James (1924), Notes of a Native Son. NF
Bishop, Elizabeth (1911), Poems: North & South. A Cold
Spring. V
Blackmur, R. P. (1904), The Lion and the Honeycomb. NF
Bogan, Louise (1897), Selected Criticism. NF
Bourjaily, Vance (1922), The Hound of Earth. F
Bowles, Paul (1910), The Spider's House. F
Brinnin, John Malcolm (1916), Dylan Thomas in America. NF
Burke, Kenneth (1897), Book of Moments: Poems 1915–1954.
V
Cabell, James Branch (1879), As I Remember It. NF
Caldwell, Erskine (1903), Gretta. F
Carson, Rachel (1907), The Edge of the Sea. NF
Chayefsky, Paddy (1923), The Catered Affair. D
Ciardi, John (1916), As If. V
Corso, Gregory (1930), The Vestal Lady on Brattle. V
Coxe, Louis (1918), The Second Man. V
Davis, Elmer (1890), Two Minutes Till Midnight. NF
Dickinson, Emily (d. 1886), The Complete Poems (3 vols.). V
Donleavy, J. P. (1926), The Ginger Man (pub. in Paris; rev.
1958, 1965). F
Faulkner, William (1897), Big Woods. F
Ferlinghetti, Lawrence (1920), Pictures of the Gone World. V
Gaddis, William (1922), The Recognitions. F
Goyen, William (1915), In a Farther Country. F
Grau, Shirley Ann (1929), The Black Prince. F
Hackett, Albert (1900), The Diary of Anne Frank [adapted with
Frances Goodrich from Anne Frank: Diary of a Young Girl
(1952)]. D
Hall, Donald (1928), Exiles and Marriages. V
Hardwick, Elizabeth (1916), The Simple Truth. F
Hellman, Lillian (1905), The Lark [adapted from Jean Anouilh's
play L'Alouette (1953); pub. 1956]. D
Himes, Chester (1909), The Primitive. F
Inge, William (1913), Bus Stop. D
Jarrell, Randall (1914), Selected Poems. V
Kantor, MacKinlay (1904), Andersonville. F
Kazin, Alfred (1915), The Inmost Leaf. NF
Lindbergh, Anne Morrow (1906), Gift from the Sea. NF
McCarthy, Mary (1912), A Charmed Life. F
Mailer, Norman (1923), The Deer Park. F
Marquand, J. P. (1893), Sincerely, Willis Wayde. F
Matthiessen, Peter (1927), Partisans. F
Melville, Herman (d. 1891), Journal of a Visit to Europe and the
Levant. NF
Miles, Josephine (1911), Prefabrications. V
Miller, Arthur (1915), A Memory of Two Mondays. D; A View
from the Bridge. D
Moore, Marianne (1887), Predilections. NF
Nabokov, Vladimir (1899), Lolita (pub. in Paris; American
edition, 1958). F
Nemerov, Howard (1920), The Salt Garden. V
O'Connor, Flannery (1925), A Good Man Is Hard to Find. F
O'Hara, John (1905), Ten North Frederick. F
Prokosch, Frederic (1890), A Tale for Midnight. F
Ransom, John Crowe (1888), Poems and Essays. V, NF
Rich, Adrienne (1929), The Diamond Cutters. V
Richter, Conrad (1890), The Mountain on the Desert. NF
Sarton, May (1912), Faithful Are the Wounds. F

National Review (New York), 1955–.
Daedalus (Boston; Cambridge), 1955–.
Modern Fiction Studies (Lafayette, Ind.),
1955–.
TDR: Tulane Drama Review (New
Orleans; New York), 1955–.
Twentieth Century Literature (Denver;
Los Angeles; Hempstead, N.Y.),
1955–.

"Big Four" conference in Geneva
(U.S., Soviet Union, France, Britain).
Sir Anthony Eden became British prime
minister.
Warsaw Pact formed (Soviet bloc's
answer to NATO).
Thomas Mann d.
Paul Claudel d.
José Ortega y Gasset d.
Golding's *The Inheritors.*
Bagnold's *The Chalk Garden.*
Dennis's *Cards of Identity.*
Evelyn Waugh's *Officers and
Gentlemen.*
Dylan Thomas's *Adventures in the Skin
Trade.*
Compton-Burnett's *Mother and Son.*
Kingsley Amis's *That Uncertain Feeling.*
Bowen's *A World of Love.*
Larkin's *The Less Deceived.*
Greene's *The Quiet American.*
Wain's *Living in the Present.*
Peyrefitte's *The Keys of St. Peter.*
Patrick White's *The Tree of Man.*
Robbe-Grillet's *The Voyeur.*
Pasolini's *The Ragazzi.*
Yevtushenko's *The Third Snow.*
Teilhard de Chardin's *The
Phenomenon of Man.*
Rama Rau's *Remember the House.*
Adamov's *Ping-Pong.*

Schulberg, Budd (1914), Waterfront [adapted from his
    screenplay On the Waterfront (1954)]. F
Simpson, Louis (1923), Good News of Death. V
Singer, Isaac Bashevis (1904), Satan in Goray. F
Smith, Lillian (1897), Now Is the Time. NF
Stegner, Wallace (1909), This Is Dinosaur. NF
Stein, Gertrude (d. 1946), Painted Lace and Other Pieces (1914–
    1937). NF
Stewart, George R. (1895), The Years of the City. F
Swados, Harvey (1920), Out Went the Candle. F
Tate, Allen (1899), The Man of Letters in the Modern World. NF
Wagoner, David (1926), Money Money Money. F
Warren, Robert Penn (1905), Band of Angels. F
Welty, Eudora (1909), The Bride of the Innisfallen. F
Wilder, Thornton (1897), A Life in the Sun [adapted from
    Euripides' play Alcestis (438 B.C.)]. D
Williams, Tennessee (1911), Cat on a Hot Tin Roof. D
Williams, William Carlos (1883), Journey to Love. V
Willingham, Calder (1922), To Eat a Peach. F
Wilson, Edmund (1895), The Scrolls from the Dead Sea. NF
Wilson, Sloan (1920), The Man in the Gray Flannel Suit. F
Wouk, Herman (1915), Marjorie Morningstar. F
Zinsser, Hans (1878), Rats, Lice and History. NF

1956

Algren, Nelson (1909), A Walk on the Wild Side. F
Ashbery, John (1927), Some Trees. V
Auchincloss, Louis (1917), The Great World and Timothy Colt.
    F
Baldwin, James (1924), Giovanni's Room. F
Barth, John (1930), The Floating Opera. F
Bellow, Saul (1915), Seize the Day. F
Berryman, John (1914), Homage to Mistress Bradstreet. V
Blackmur, R. P. (1904), Anni Mirabiles: 1921–1925. NF
Buck, Pearl (1892), Imperial Woman. F
Bynner, Witter (1881), A Book of Lyrics. V
Caldwell, Erskine (1903), Gulf Coast Stories. F
Capote, Truman (1924), The Muses Are Heard. NF
Chayefsky, Paddy (1923), The Middle of the Night (pub. 1957).
    D
De Vries, Peter (1910), Comfort Me with Apples F
Dos Passos, John (1896), The Theme Is Freedom. NF
Fearing, Kenneth (1902), New and Selected Poems. V
Fitzgerald, Robert (1910), In the Rose of Time: Poems 1931–
    1956. V
Ginsberg, Allen (1926), Howl and Other Poems. V
Gold, Herbert (1924), The Man Who Was Not With It. F
Gordon, Caroline (1895), The Malefactors. F
Guthrie, A. B. Jr. (1901), These Thousand Hills. F
Harris, Mark (1922), Bang the Drum Slowly. F
Heinlein, Robert A. (1907), Double Star. F
Hellman, Lillian (1905), Candide [adapted with Richard Wilbur
    and Leonard Bernstein from Voltaire's tale (1759); pub.
    1957]. D
Hersey, John (1914), A Single Pebble. F
Horgan, Paul (1903), The Centuries of Santa Fe. NF
Hughes, Langston (1902), I Wonder As I Wander: An
    Autobiographical Journey. NF

Supreme Court ruled segregation on
    buses unconstitutional.
First transcontinental helicopter flight.
First transatlantic telephone cable
    (Newfoundland-Scotland).
Lerner and Loewe's My Fair Lady
    opened.
H. L. Mencken d.
Percy MacKaye d.
Critique (Minneapolis; Atlanta), 1956–.

Anti-Soviet uprising in Hungary
    crushed by Soviets.
"De-Stalinization" period begun by
    Nikita Khrushchev.
Gamal Abdel Nasser elected president
    of Egypt.
Pakistan became an Islamic republic.
Sir Max Beerbohm d.
A. A. Milne d.
Walter de la Mare d.
Angus Wilson's Anglo-Saxon Attitudes.
Colin Wilson's The Outsider.
Golding's Pincher Martin.
Osborne's Look Back in Anger.
Macaulay's The Towers of Trebizond.
Sansom's A Contest of Ladies.
Renault's The Last of the Wine.
Bedford's A Legacy.
Gabriel Fielding's In the Time of
    Greenbloom.
Genet's The Balcony.
Camus's The Fall.
Gary's The Roots of Heaven.
Butor's Passing Time.
Calvino's Italian Folktales.
Yevtushenko's Zima Junction.

Levin, Ira (1929), No Time for Sergeants [adapted from Mac Hyman's novel (1954)]. D
Levin, Meyer (1905), Compulsion. F
Lindbergh, Anne Morrow (1906), The Unicorn. V
Loos, Anita (1893), This Brunette Prefers Work. NF
McCarthy, Mary (1912), Sights and Spectacles, 1937–1956. NF; Venice Observed. NF
Mencken, H. L. (1880), Minority Report. NF
Merwin, W. S. (1927), Green with Beasts. V
Millay, Edna St. Vincent (d. 1950), Collected Poems. V
Miller, Henry (1891), Quiet Days in Clichy (pub. in Paris). F
Moore, Marianne (1887), Like a Bulwark. V
Morris, Wright, (1910), The Field of Vision. F
O'Connor, Edwin (1918), The Last Hurrah. F
O'Hara, John (1905), A Family Party. F
O'Neill, Eugene (d. 1953), Long Day's Journey into Night. D
Pound, Ezra (1885), Section: Rock-Drill, 85–95 de los cantares. V; Sophokles: Women of Trachis. D
Powers, J. F. (1917), The Presence of Grace. F
Roberts, Kenneth (1885), Boon Island. F
Saroyan, William (1908), Mama, I Love You. F; The Whole Voyald, and Other Stories. F
Shaw, Irwin (1913), Lucy Crown. F
Spencer, Elizabeth (1921), The Voice at the Back Door. F
Stegner, Wallace (1909), The City of the Living. F
Stein, Gertrude (d. 1946), Stanzas in Meditation and Other Poems (1929–1933). V
Stuart, Jesse (1907), Year of My Rebirth. NF
Styron, William (1925), The Long March. F
Taylor, Peter (1917), Tennessee Day in St. Louis. D
Thurber, James (1894), Further Fables for Our Times. F
Vidal, Gore (1925), A Thirsty Evil. F
Viereck, Peter (1916), The Persimmon Tree. V
Warren, Robert Penn (1905), Segregation: The Inner Conflict in the South. NF
Wheelock, John Hall (1886), Poems Old and New. V
Whittemore, Reed (1917), An American Takes a Walk. V
Wilbur, Richard (1921), Things of This World. V
Williams, Tennessee (1911), In the Winter of Cities. V
Wilson, Edmund (1895), Red, Black, Blond, and Olive. NF; A Piece of My Mind. NF
Wright, Richard (1908), The Color Curtain. NF

Montale's *The Storm.*
Dürrenmatt's *The Visit.*
Bassani's *Five Stories of Ferrara.*
Lagerkvist's *The Sybil.*
Mishima's *The Temple of the Golden Pavilion.*
Tanizaki's *The Key.*

1957

Agar, Herbert (1897), The Price of Power. NF
Agee, James (d. 1955), A Death in the Family. F
Booth, Philip (1925), Letter from a Distant Land. V
Caldwell, Erskine (1903), Certain Women. F
Chase, Mary Ellen (1887), The Edge of Darkness. F
Cheever, John (1912), The Wapshot Chronicle. F
Chodorov, Jerome (1911), The Ponder Heart [adapted with Joseph Fields from Eudora Welty's novel (1954)]. D
Connell, Evan S., Jr. (1924), The Anatomy Lesson. F
Cozzens, James Gould (1903), By Love Possessed. F
Dahlberg, Edward (1900), The Sorrows of Priapus. NF
Davidson, Donald (1893), Still Rebels, Still Yankees. NF
Dos Passos, John (1896), The Men Who Made the Nation. NF
Eberhart, Richard (1904), Great Praises. V
Eliot, T. S. (1888), On Poetry and Poets. NF

Eisenhower Doctrine established (protection of Middle East against Communist aggression).
U.S. troops sent to Little Rock, Ark., to guard Negro students.
Nuclear power plant opened in Pennsylvania.
Kenneth Roberts d.
John Van Druten d.
The Evergreen Review (New York), 1957–73.

European Economic Community (Common Market) formed.
Soviet Union launched first artificial satellite and first ICBM.
International Geophysical Year.

Farrell, James T. (1904), A Dangerous Woman and Other Stories, F; My Baseball Diary. NF
Fast, Howard (1914), The Naked God. NF
Faulkner, William (1897), The Town. F
Frings, Ketti (1915), Look Homeward, Angel [adapted from Thomas Wolfe's novel (1929); pub. 1958]. D
Garrett, George (1929), The Reverend Ghost. V
Gill, Brendan (1914), The Day the Money Stopped. F
Gordon, Caroline (1895), How to Read a Novel. NF
Harris, Mark (1922), A Ticket for a Seamstitch. F
Hine, Daryl (1936), The Carnal and the Crane. V
Horgan, Paul (1903), Give Me Possession. F
Hughes, Langston (1902), Simple Stakes a Claim. F; Simply Heavenly (pub. 1958). D
Inge, William (1913), The Dark at the Top of the Stairs. D
Jackson, Shirley (1919), Raising Demons. NF
Jones, James (1921), Some Came Running. F
Kerouac, Jack (1922), On the Road. F
Kerr, Jean (1923), Please Don't Eat the Daisies. NF
Laurents, Arthur (1918), A Clearing in the Woods. D
Levertov, Denise (1923), Here and Now. V
Lytle, Andrew (1902), The Velvet Horn. F
Macauley, Robie (1919), The End of Pity. F
McCarthy, Mary (1912), Memories of a Catholic Girlhood. NF
McCullers, Carson (1917), The Square Root of Wonderful (pub. 1958). D
Macdonald, Dwight (1906), Memoirs of a Revolutionist. NF
Mailer, Norman (1923), The White Negro. NF
Malamud, Bernard (1914), The Assistant. F
Marquand, J. P. (1893), Stopover: Tokyo. F; Life at Happy Knoll. F
Merrill, James (1926), The Seraglio. F
Michener, James A. (1907), The Bridge at Andau. NF
Miller, Henry (1891), Big Sur and the Oranges of Hieronymus Bosch. NF
Morris, Wright (1910), Love Among the Cannibals. F
Moss, Howard (1922), A Swimmer in the Air. V
Nabokov, Vladimir (1899), Pnin. F
Nash, Ogden (1902), You Can't Get There from Here. V
Nemerov, Howard (1920), The Homecoming Game. F
O'Hara, Frank (1926), Meditations in an Emergency. V
O'Neill, Eugene (d. 1953), A Touch of the Poet (prod. in Stockholm). D
Patchen, Kenneth (1911), Hurrah for Anything. V
Perelman, S. J. (1904), The Road to Miltown; or, Under the Spreading Atrophy. F
Purdy, James (1923), Color of Darkness. F
Rand, Ayn (1905), Atlas Shrugged. F
Richter, Conrad (1890), The Lady. F
Rukeyser, Muriel (1913), One Life. V, NF
Saroyan, William (1908), Papa, You're Crazy. F; The Cave Dwellers (pub. 1958). D
Sarton, May (1912), In Time Like Air. V; The Birth of a Grandfather. F
Shaw, Irwin (1913), Tip on a Dead Jockey. F
Sherwood, Robert E. (1896), Small War on Murray Hill. D
Singer, Isaac Bashevis (1904), Gimpel the Fool. F
Smith, William Jay (1918), Poems 1947–1957. V
Stein, Gertrude (d. 1946), Alphabets and Birthdays. NF
Steinbeck, John (1902), The Short Reign of Pippin IV. F
Stevens, Wallace (d. 1955), Opus Posthumous. V, D, NF
Swados, Harvey (1920), On the Line. F

Percy Wyndham Lewis d.
Joyce Cary d.
Dorothy Richardson d.
Nikos Kazantzakis d.
Durrell's *The Alexandria Quartet* (1957–60).
Shute's *On the Beach.*
Braine's *Room at the Top.*
Ted Hughes's *The Hawk in the Rain.*
Colin MacInnes's *City of Spades.*
Osborne's *The Entertainer.*
MacLean's *The Guns of Navarone.*
Beckett's *Endgame.*
Pasternak's *Doctor Zhivago.*
Moravia's *Two Women.*
Djilas's *The New Class.*
Robbe-Grillet's *Jealousy.*
Naipaul's *The Mystic Masseur.*
Pasolini's *The Ashes of Gramsci.*
Calvino's *The Baron in the Trees.*
Paz's *Sun Stone.*
Donoso's *Coronation.*
Walser's *The Gadarene Club.*
Camus's *Exile and the Kingdom.*

Van Doren, Mark (1894), Home with Hazel. F
Vidal, Gore (1925), Visit to a Small Planet. D
Warren, Robert Penn (1905), Promises: Poems 1954–1956. V
Wilbur, Richard (1921), Poems 1943–1956. V
Williams, Tennessee (1911), Orpheus Descending [revision of Battle of Angels (1940); pub. 1958]. D
Winters, Yvor (1900), The Function of Criticism. NF
Wright, James (1927), The Green Wall. V
Wright, Richard (1908), Pagan Spain. NF; White Man, Listen! NF

1958

Adler, Mortimer (1902), The Idea of Freedom. NF
Agee, James (d. 1955), Agee on Film. NF
Aiken, Conrad (1889), Sheepfold Hill. V; A Reviewer's ABC: Collected Criticism. NF
Asch, Sholem (d. 1957), From Many Countries: Collected Short Stories. F
Auchincloss, Louis (1917), Venus in Sparta. F
Barth, John (1930), The End of the Road. F
Behrman, S. N. (1893), The Cold Wind and the Warm [adapted from his autobiographical sketches The Worcester Account (1954)]. D
Berger, Thomas (1924), Crazy in Berlin. F
Berryman, John (1914), His Thoughts Made Pockets & the Plane Buckt. V
Bourjaily, Vance (1922), The Violated. F
Buechner, Frederick (1926), The Return of Ansel Gibbs. F
Caldwell, Erskine (1903), Claudelle Inglish. F
Capote, Truman (1924), Breakfast at Tiffany's. F
Cheever, John (1912), The Housebreaker of Shady Hill. F
Ciardi, John (1916), I Marry You. V
Corso, Gregory (1930), Gasoline. V; Bomb. V
Coxe, Louis (1918), The Wilderness and Other Poems. V
Cummings, E. E. (1894), 95 Poems. V
De Vries, Peter (1910), The Mackerel Plaza. F
Donleavy, J. P. (1926), The Ginger Man (pub. in Paris, 1955). F
Dos Passos, John (1896), The Great Days. F
Eliot, T. S. (1888), The Elder Statesman (pub. 1959). D
Farrell, James T. (1904), It Has Come to Pass. NF
Faulkner, William (1897), New Orleans Sketches. F
Ferlinghetti, Lawrence (1920), A Coney Island of the Mind. V
Fitzgerald, F. Scott (d. 1940), Afternoon of an Author. F, NF
Foote, Shelby (1916), The Civil War: A Narrative (3 vols., 1958–74). NF
Garrett, George (1929), The Sleeping Gypsy. V; King of the Mountain. F
Gill, Brendan (1914), The Day the Money Stopped [adapted with Maxwell Anderson from Gill's novel (1957)]. D
Golden, Harry (1902), Only in America. NF
Grau, Shirley Ann (1929), The Hard Blue Sky. F
Hall, Donald (1928), The Dark Houses. V
Hecht, Anthony (1923), The Seven Deadly Sins. V
Hollander, John (1929), A Crackling of Thorns. V
Holmes, John Clellon (1926), The Horn. F
Hughes, Langston (1902), Tambourines to Glory. F
Humphrey, William (1924), Home from the Hill. F
Jackson, Shirley (1919), The Sundial. F
Kerouac, Jack (1922), The Dharma Bums. F

U.S. launched first "talking satellite."
John Birch Society formed.
Xerox produced first commercial copying machine.
Ezra Pound released from mental hospital.
Van Cliburn won Moscow piano competition.
James Branch Cabell d.
Mary Roberts Rinehart d.
Modern Drama (Lawrence, Kan.), 1958–.
Texas Quarterly (Austin), 1958–.
Tri-Quarterly (Evanston, Ill.), 1958–.
Yugen (New York), 1958–62.

Iraq proclaimed a republic.
Suez Canal reopened.
Nikita Khrushchev became premier of Soviet Union.
Boris Pasternak declined Nobel Prize in literature.
Brussels World Fair.
Lion Feuchtwanger d.
Roger Martin du Gard d.
Betjeman's *Collected Poems.*
Sillitoe's *Saturday Night and Sunday Morning.*
Pinter's *The Birthday Party.*
Abse's *Tenants of the House.*
Behan's *The Hostage.*
T. H. White's *The Once and Future King.*
Wesker's *Chicken Soup with Barley.*
Peter Shaffer's *Five Finger Exercise.*
William Cooper's *Young People.*
Greene's *Our Man in Havana.*
Murdoch's *The Bell.*
O'Faolain's *The Short Stories of Sean O'Faolain.*
Beckett's *Krapp's Last Tape.*
Tomasi di Lampedusa's *The Leopard.*
Quasimodo's *The Incomparable Land.*
Kazakov's *Manka.*
Gordimer's *A World of Strangers.*
Fuentes's *Where the Air Is Clear.*
Beauvoir's *Memoirs of a Dutiful Daughter.*
Amado's *Gabriela, Clove and Cinnamon.*
Donoso's *Coronation.*
Neruda's *Extravagaria.*

Kunitz, Stanley (1905), Selected Poems:1928–1958. V
Levertov, Denise (1923), Overland to the Islands. V
Lytle, Andrew (1902), A Novel, a Novella, and Four Stories. F
MacLeish, Archibald (1892), J.B. D
Malamud, Bernard (1914), The Magic Barrel. F
Marquand, J. P. (1893), Women and Thomas Harrow. F
Meredith, William (1919), The Open Sea and Other Poems. V
Morris, Wright (1910), The Territory Ahead. NF
Motley, Willard (1912), Let No Man Write My Epitaph. F
Nabokov, Vladimir (1899), Nabokov's Dozen. F
Nemerov, Howard (1920), Mirrors & Windows. V
O'Hara, John (1905), From the Terrace. F
O'Neill, Eugene (d. 1953), Hughie (prod. in Stockholm; pub. 1959). D
Pound, Ezra (1885), Pavannes and Divagations. NF
Rice, Elmer (1892), Cue for Passion (pub. 1959). D
"Robert Traver" (1903), Anatomy of a Murder. F
Roethke, Theodore (1908), Words for the Wind. V
Rukeyser, Muriel (1913), Body of Waking. V
Seton, Anya (1916), The Winthrop Woman. F
Shapiro, Karl (1913), Poems of a Jew. V
Sinclair, Upton (1878), It Happened to Didymus. F
Stein, Gertrude (d. 1946), A Novel of Thank You. F
Steinbeck, John (1902), Once There Was a War. NF
Stuart, Jesse (1907), Plowshare in Heaven. F
Swenson, May (1919), A Cage of Spines. V
Taylor, Robert Lewis (1912), The Travels of Jamie McPheeters. F
Thoreau, Henry David (d. 1862), Consciousness in Concord: The Text of Thoreau's Hitherto "Lost Journal," 1840–1841 (ed. Perry Miller). NF
Updike, John (1932), The Carpentered Hen and Other Tame Creatures. V
Uris, Leon (1924), Exodus. F
Van Doren, Mark (1894), Autobiography. NF
Van Duyn, Mona (1921), Valentines to the Wide World. V
Wagoner, David (1926), A Place to Stand. V; Rock. F
Warren, Robert Penn (1905), Selected Essays. NF
Williams, Tennessee (1911), Garden District: Something Unspoken and Suddenly Last Summer (pub. 1959). D
Williams, William Carlos (1883), Paterson (Book Five). V; I Wanted to Write a Poem. NF
Wilson, Edmund (1895), The American Earthquake. NF
Wright, Richard (1908), The Long Dream. F

1959

Adams, Samuel Hopkins (d. 1958), Tenderloin. F
Albee, Edward (1928), The Zoo Story (pub. 1960). D
Anderson, Robert (1917), Silent Night, Lonely Night. D
Auden, W. H. (1907), Selected Poetry. V
Barzun, Jacques (1907), The House of Intellect. NF
Basso, Hamilton (1904), Light Infantry Ball. F
Bellow, Saul (1915), Henderson the Rain King. F
Boyle, Kay (1902), Generation Without Farewell. F
Brinnin, John Malcolm (1914), The Third Rose: Gertrude Stein and Her World. NF
Burroughs, William S. (1914), The Naked Lunch (pub. in Paris; repub. in the U.S. as Naked Lunch, 1962). F
Caldwell, Erskine (1903), When You Think of Me. F

Nixon visited Moscow; Khrushchev visited U.S.
Alaska and Hawaii admitted as 49th and 50th states.
Prolonged steelworkers' strike.
St. Lawrence Seaway (U.S. and Canada) opened.
First U.S. weather station in space.
First U.S. nuclear-powered submarine commissioned.
Travel by Americans to Red China banned.
Lawrence's *Lady Chatterley's Lover* published after 30-year ban.

Carruth, Hayden (1921), The Crow and the Heart. V
Chayefsky, Paddy (1923), The Tenth Man (pub. 1960). D
Condon, Richard (1915), The Manchurian Candidate. F
Connell, Evan S., Jr. (1924), Mrs. Bridge. F
Crouse, Russel (1893), Tall Story [adapted with Howard Lindsay from Howard Nemerov's novel The Homecoming Game (1957)]. D
Deutsch, Babette (1895), Coming of Age. V
De Vries, Peter (1920), The Tents of Wickedness. F
Dos Passos, John (1896), Prospects of a Golden Age. NF
Drury, Allen (1918), Advise and Consent. F
Duncan, Robert (1919), Selected Poems. V
Fast, Howard (1914), The Winston Affair. F
Faulkner, William (1897), The Mansion. F; Requiem for a Nun [adapted with Ruth Ford from Faulkner's novel (1951)]. D
Garrett, George (1929), The Finished Man. F
Garrigue, Jean (1914), A Water Walk by Villa d'Este. V
Gelber, Jack (1932), The Connection (pub. 1960). D
Gellhorn, Martha (1908), The Face of War. NF
Gold, Herbert, (1924), The Optimist. F
Hansberry, Lorraine (1930), A Raisin in the Sun. D
Harris, Mark (1922), Wake Up, Stupid. F
Hart, Moss (1904), Act One. NF
Heinlein, Robert A. (1907), Starship Troopers. F
Hersey, John (1914), The War Lover. F
Horgan, Paul (1903), Rome Eternal. NF
Hughes, Langston (1902), Selected Poems. V
Inge, William (1913), A Loss of Roses (pub. 1960). D
Jackson, Shirley (1919), The Haunting of Hill House. F
Jones, James (1921), The Pistol. F
Kerouac, Jack (1922), Doctor Sax. F; Maggie Cassidy. F; Mexico City Blues. V
Koch, Kenneth (1925), Ko, or a Season on Earth. V
"Leonard Q. Ross" (1908), The Return of H*Y*M*A*N K*A*P*L*A*N. F
Levertov, Denise (1923), With Eyes at the Back of Our Heads. V
Lowell, Robert (1917), Life Studies. V
McCarthy, Mary (1912), The Stones of Florence. NF
McGinley, Phyllis (1905), Province of the Heart. NF
Mailer, Norman (1923), Advertisements for Myself. NF
Merrill, James (1926), The Country of a Thousand Years of Peace. V
Merwin, W. S. (1927), Poem of the Cid. V
Michener, James A. (1907), Hawaii. F; Japanese Prints. NF
Moore, Marianne (1887), O To Be a Dragon. V
Nabokov, Vladimir (1899), Invitation to a Beheading (trans. from Russian). F; Poems. V
Nash, Ogden (1902), Verses from 1929 On. V
Nemerov, Howard (1920), A Commodity of Dreams. F
Nin, Anaïs (1903), Cities of the Interior. F
Paley, Grace (1922), The Little Disturbances of Man. F
Pound, Ezra (1885), Thrones: 96–109 de los cantares. V
Purdy, James (1923), Malcolm. F
Rexroth, Kenneth (1905), Bird in the Bush. NF
Rice, Elmer (1892), The Living Theatre. NF
"Ross Macdonald"(1915), The Galton Case. F
Roth, Philip (1933), Goodbye, Columbus. F
Sarton, May (1912), I Knew a Phoenix. NF
Schwartz, Delmore (1913), Summer Knowledge. V
Simpson, Louis (1923), A Dream of Governors. V
Smith, Lillian (1897), One Hour. F
Snodgrass, W. D. (1926), Heart's Needle. V

Maxwell Anderson d.
Criticism (Detroit), 1959–.

———

Charles de Gaulle became president of France.
Cyprus declared a republic.
Fidel Castro toppled Batista regime in Cuba.
Edwin Muir d.
Spark's Memento Mori.
Snow's The Two Cultures.
Golding's Free Fall.
Wesker's Roots.
Sillitoe's The Loneliness of the Long Distance Runner.
Waterhouse's Billy Liar.
Bradbury's Eating People Is Wrong.
Geoffrey Hill's For the Unfallen.
Genet's The Blacks.
Böll's Billiards at Half-Past Nine.
Grass's The Tin Drum.
Anouilh's Becket.
Ionesco's Rhinoceros.
Richler's The Apprenticeship of Duddy Kravitz.
Sartre's The Condemned of Altona.
Robbe-Grillet's In the Labyrinth.
Pasolini's A Violent Life.
Sarraute's The Planetarium.
Naipaul's Miguel Street.
Fuentes's The Good Conscience.

Snyder, **Gary** (1930), Riprap. V
Suckow, **Ruth** (1892), The John Wood Case. F
Tate, **Allen** (1899), Collected Essays. NF
Taylor, **Peter** (1917), Happy Families Are All Alike. F
Thurber, **James** (1894), The Years with Ross. NF
Updike, **John** (1932), The Poorhouse Fair. F; The Same Door. F
Vonnegut, **Kurt, Jr.** (1922), The Sirens of Titan. F
Warren, **Robert Penn** (1905), The Cave. F
West, **Jessamyn** (1907), Love, Death, and the Ladies' Drill
    Team. F; Love Is Not What You Think. NF
Williams, **Tennessee** (1911), Sweet Bird of Youth. D
Williams, **William Carlos** (1883), Yes, Mrs. Williams. NF
Wouk, **Herman** (1915), This Is My God. NF
Wright, **James** (1927), Saint Judas. V
Zukofsky, **Louis** (1904), "A" 1–12. V

1960

Agar, **Herbert** (1897), The Saving Remnant. NF
Agee, **James** (d. 1955), Agee on Film: Volume Two: Five Film
    Scripts. D
Aiken, **Conrad** (1889), Collected Short Stories. F
Albee, **Edward** (1928), The Death of Bessie Smith. D; The
    Sandbox. D; FAM and YAM (pub. 1963). D; The American
    Dream (pub. 1961). D
Ashbery, **John** (1927), The Poems. V
Auchincloss, **Louis** (1917), The House of Five Talents. F
Auden, **W. H.** (1907), Homage to Clio. V
Barth, **John** (1930), The Sot-Weed Factor. F
Behrman, **S. N.** (1893), Portrait of Max. NF
Bourjaily, **Vance** (1922), Confessions of a Spent Youth. F
Brooks, **Gwendolyn** (1917), The Bean Eaters. V
Burroughs, **William S.** (1914), The Exterminator. F
Bynner, **Witter** (1881), New Poems. V
Chase, **Mary Ellen** (1887), The Lovely Ambition. F
Condon, **Richard** (1915), Some Angry Angel. F
Connell, **Evan S., Jr.** (1924), The Patriot. F
Corso, **Gregory** (1930), The Happy Birthday of Death. V
Coxe, **Louis** (1918), The Middle Passage. V
Dickey, **James** (1923), Into the Stone. V
Doctorow, **E. L.** (1931), Welcome to Hard Times. F
Duncan, **Robert** (1919), The Opening of the Field. V
Eberhart, **Richard** (1904), Collected Poems 1930–1960. V
Epstein, **Seymour** (1917), Pillar of Salt. F
Gold, **Herbert** (1924), Love and Like. F; Therefore Be Bold. F
Goodman, **Paul** (1911), Growing Up Absurd. NF
Goyen, **William** (1915), The Faces of Blood Kindred. F
Guthrie, **A. B., Jr.** (1901), The Big It. F
"**H.D.**" (1886), Bid Me To Live. F
Hecht, **Anthony** (1923), A Bestiary. V
Hellman, **Lillian** (1905), Toys in the Attic. D
Herlihy, **James Leo** (1927), All Fall Down. F
Hersey, **John** (1914), The Child Buyer. F
Hine, **Daryl** (1936), The Devil's Picture Book. V
Hoffman, **Daniel G.** (1923), A Little Geste and Other Poems. V
Horgan, **Paul** (1903), A Distant Trumpet. F
Jarrell, **Randall** (1914), The Woman at the Washington Zoo. V
Justice, **Donald** (1925), The Summer Anniversaries. V

First Negro "sit-in" staged in North
    Carolina.
U.S. launched 17 space satellites and
    probes.
American U-2 reconnaissance plane
    shot down over Soviet Union.
Kennedy-Nixon pre-election television
    debates.
Richard Wright d.
John P. Marquand d.
Theatre Survey (Waltham, Mass.;
    Pittsburgh; Albany), 1960–.

France became fourth nuclear power.
Belgian Congo became independent
    state.
Boris Pasternak d.
Albert Camus d.
Betjeman's *Summoned by Bells.*
Bolt's *A Man for All Seasons.*
Dahl's *Kiss, Kiss.*
Kinglsey Amis's *Take a Girl Like You.*
Pinter's *The Caretaker; The Dumb
    Waiter.*
Ted Hughes's *Lupercal.*
Rattigan's *Ross.*
Barstow's *A Kind of Loving.*
Enright's *Some Men Are Brothers.*
Spark's *The Ballad of Peckham Rye.*
Storey's *This Sporting Life.*
O'Brien's *The Country Girls.*
Borges's *Dreamtigers.*
Butor's *Degrees.*
Brian Moore's *The Luck of Ginger
    Coffey.*
Canetti's *Crowds and Power.*
Walser's *Half-Time.*
Voznesensky's *Mosaic.*

Kerouac, Jack (1922), Tristessa. F; Lonesome Traveler. NF
Kerr, Jean (1923), The Snake Has All the Lines. NF
Kinnell, Galway (1927), What a Kingdom It Was. V
Knowles, John (1926), A Separate Peace. F
Kopit, Arthur (1937), Oh Dad, Poor Dad, Mama's Hung You in
    the Closet and I'm Feelin' So Sad (prod. 1962). D
Lee, Harper (1926), To Kill a Mockingbird. F
McGinley, Phyllis (1905), Times Three: Selected Verse from
    Three Decades. V
Marquand, J. P. (1893), Timothy Dexter Revisited. NF
Matthiessen, Peter (1927), Raditzer. F
Merwin, W. S. (1927), The Drunk in the Furnace. V
"Michael Gold" (1893), Life of John Brown. NF
Miles, Josephine (1911), Poems 1930–1960. V
Miller, Henry (1891), Nexus (pub. in Paris). F, NF
Morris, Wright (1910), Ceremony in Lone Tree. F
Mosel, Tad (1922), All the Way Home [adapted from James
    Agee's novel A Death in the Family (1957); pub. 1961]. D
Moss, Howard (1921), A Winter Come, A Summer Gone: Poems
    1946–1960. V
Nemerov, Howard (1920), New and Selected Poems. V
Nims, John Frederick (1913), Knowledge of the Evening. V
O'Connor, Flannery (1925), The Violent Bear It Away. F
O'Hara, John (1905), Ourselves to Know. F; Sermons and
    Sodawater. F
Olson, Charles (1910), The Maximus Poems. V; The Distances.
    V
Patchen, Kenneth (1911), Because It Is. V
Pound, Ezra (1885), Impact: Essays on Ignorance and the
    Decline of American Civilization. NF
Prokosch, Frederic (1908), A Ballad of Love. F
Purdy, James (1923), The Nephew. F
Richardson, Jack (1935), The Prodigal. D
Richter, Conrad (1890), The Waters of Kronos. F
Sandburg, Carl (1878), Wind Song. V
Sandoz, Mari (1896), Son of the Gamblin' Man. F
Sexton, Anne (1928), To Bedlam and Part Way Back. V
Shapiro, Karl (1913), In Defense of Ignorance. NF
Shaw, Irwin (1913), Two Weeks in Another Town. F
Shirer, William L. (1904), The Rise and Fall of the Third Reich.
    NF
Sinclair, Upton (1878), My Lifetime in Letters. NF
Singer, Isaac Bashevis (1904), The Magician of Lublin. F
Snyder, Gary (1930), Myths and Texts. V
Spencer, Elizabeth (1921), The Light in the Piazza. F
Stafford, William (1914), West of Your City. V
Stern, Richard G. (1928), Golk. F
Stuart, Jesse (1907), God's Oddling. NF
Styron, William (1925), Set This House on Fire. F
Tate, Allen (1899), Poems. V
Updike, John (1932), Rabbit, Run. F
Van Doren, Mark (1894), Morning Worship. V
Vidal, Gore (1925), The Best Man. D
Wallant, Edward Lewis (1926), The Human Season. F
Warren, Robert Penn (1905), You, Emperors, and Others.
    V; All the King's Men [adapted from his novel (1946)]. D
Weiss, Theodore (1916), Outlanders. V
West, Jessamyn (1907), South of the Angels. F
Williams, John A. (1925), The Angry Ones. F
Williams, Tennessee (1911), Period of Adjustment. D
Wilson, Edmund (1895), Apologies to the Iroquois. NF
Winters, Yvor (1900), Collected Poems. V

1961

Baldwin, James (1924), Nobody Knows My Name. NF
Booth, Philip (1925), The Islanders. V
Burke, Kenneth (1897), The Rhetoric of Religion. NF
Burroughs, William S. (1914), The Soft Machine (pub. in Paris; American edition, 1966). F
Caldwell, Erskine (1903), Jenny by Nature. F
Calisher, Hortense (1911), False Entry. F
Cassill, R. V. (1919), Clem Anderson. F
Chayefsky, Paddy (1923), Gideon (pub. 1962). D
Cheever, John (1912), Some People, Places, and Things That Will Not Appear in My Next Novel. F
Davidson, Donald (1893), The Long Street. V
Davis, Ossie (1917), Purlie Victorious. D
Donleavy, J. P. (1926), Fairy Tales of New York. D
Dos Passos, John (1896), Midcentury. F
Dugan, Alan (1923), Poems. V
Epstein, Seymour (1917), The Successor. F
Farrell, James T. (1904), Side Street and Other Stories. F; Boarding House Blues. F
Ferlinghetti, Lawrence (1920), Starting from San Francisco. V
Garrett, George (1929), Abraham's Knife. V; In the Briar Patch. F; Which Ones Are the Enemy? F
Ginsberg, Allen (1926), Empty Mirror: Early Poems. V; Kaddish and Other Poems. V
Grau, Shirley Ann (1929), The House on Coliseum Street. F
Gregory, Horace (1898), Medusa in Gramercy Park. V
"H.D." (1886), Helen in Egypt. V
Hawkes, John (1925), The Lime Twig. F
Heinlein, Robert A. (1907), Stranger in a Strange Land. F
Heller, Joseph (1923), Catch-22. F
Hine, Daryl (1936), Heroics. V; The Prince of Darkness & Co. F
Horgan, Paul (1903), Citizen of New Salem. NF
Hughes, Langston (1902), Ask Your Mama: 12 Moods for Jazz. V; The Best of Simple. F
Jones, LeRoi (1934), Preface to a Twenty Volume Suicide Note. V
Kantor, MacKinlay (1904), Spirit Lake. F
Kerouac, Jack (1922), Book of Dreams. NF
Kerr, Jean (1923), Mary, Mary. D
Kizer, Carolyn (1925), The Ungrateful Garden. V
Kumin, Maxine (1925), Halfway. V
Levertov, Denise (1923), The Jacob's Ladder. V
Levine, Philip (1928), On the Edge. V
Loos, Anita (1893), No Mother to Guide Her. F
Lowell, Robert (1917), Imitations. V; Phaedra. D
McCarthy, Mary (1912), On the Contrary. NF
McCullers, Carson (1917), Clock Without Hands. F
MacLeish, Archibald (1892), Poetry and Experience. NF
Malamud, Bernard (1914), A New Life. F
Marshall, Paule (1929), Soul Clap Hands and Sing. F
Matthiessen, Peter (1927), The Cloud Forest. NF
Maxwell, William (1908), The Chateau. F
Michener, James A. (1907), Report of the County Chairman. NF
Miller, Arthur (1915), The Misfits. F/D
O'Connor, Edwin (1918), The Edge of Sadness. F
O'Hara, John (1905), Assembly. F; Five Plays. D
Percy, Walker (1916), The Moviegoer. F
Perelman, S. J. (1904), The Rising Gorge. F
Rand, Ayn (1905), For the New Intellectual. F, NF

23rd Amendment (presidential vote to District of Columbia citizens) ratified.
Kennedy and Khrushchev met in Vienna.
U.S. Peace Corps established.
U.S. broke diplomatic relations with Cuba.
"Bay of Pigs," U.S. failure to invade Cuba.
First U.S.-manned suborbital space flight.
Freedom Riders challenged segregation from Washington, D.C., to New Orleans.
Ernest Hemingway d.
James Thurber d.
George S. Kaufman d.
Dashiell Hammett d.
Drama Survey (Minneapolis), 1961–69.

Soviet Yuri Gagarin became first man to orbit globe.
President Trujillo of Colombia assassinated.
Carl Jung d.
Louis-Ferdinand Céline d.
Spark's The Prime of Miss Jean Brodie.
Osborne's Luther.
Murdoch's A Severed Head.
Greene's A Burnt-Out Case.
Richard Hughes's The Fox in the Attic.
Evelyn Waugh's Unconditional Surrender.
Pritchett's When My Girl Comes Home.
William Cooper's Scenes from Married Life.
Le Carré's Call for the Dead.
John Fuller's Fairground Music.
Leonard Cohen's The Spice Box of Earth.
Patrick White's Riders in the Chariot.
Beckett's Happy Days.
Boulle's Planet of the Apes.
Genet's The Screens.
Kazakov's Along the Road.
Grass's Cat and Mouse.
Naipaul's A House for Mr. Biswas.
Amado's The Two Deaths of Quincas Wateryell.
Neruda's Ceremonial Songs.
García Márquez's No One Writes to the Colonel.
Borges's Personal Anthology.
Arrabal's The Automobile Graveyard.
Frisch's Andorra.
Fugard's The Blood Knot.

Rexroth, Kenneth (1905), Assays. NF
Richardson, Jack (1935), Gallows Humor. D
Roethke, Theodore (1908), I Am! Says the Lamb. V
Salinger, J. D. (1919), Franny and Zooey. F
Sandoz, Mari (1896), Love Song to the Plains. NF; These Were the Sioux. NF
Saroyan, William (1908), Here Comes, There Goes, You Know Who. NF
Sarton, May (1912), Cloud, Stone, Sun, Vine. V; The Small Room. F
Schwartz, Delmore (1913), Successful Love and Other Stories. F
Sheed, Wilfrid (1930), A Middle Class Education. F
Singer, Isaac Bashevis (1904), The Spinoza of Market Street. F
Stegner, Wallace (1909), A Shooting Star. F
Steinbeck, John (1902), The Winter of Our Discontent. F
Streeter, Edward (1891), Chairman of the Bored. F
Taylor, Robert Lewis (1912), A Journey to Matecumbe. F
Thurber, James (1894), Lanterns & Lances. F
Van Doren, Mark (1894), The Happy Critic. NF
Viereck, Peter (1916), The Tree Witch. D
Vonnegut, Kurt, Jr. (1922), Mother Night. F; Canary in a Cat House. F
Wallant, Edward Lewis (1926), The Pawnbroker. F
Warren, Robert Penn (1905), Wilderness: A Tale of the Civil War. F; The Legacy of the Civil War. NF
Weinstein, Arnold (1927), Red Eye of Love. D
Wheelock, John Hall (1886), The Gardener. V
Wilbur, Richard (1921), Advice to a Prophet. V
Williams, John A. (1925), Night Song. F
Williams, Tennessee (1911), The Night of the Iguana (pub. 1962). D
Williams, William Carlos (1883), Many Loves and Other Plays. D; The Farmer's Daughters. F
Wilson, Edmund (1895), Night Thoughts. V, NF
Wright, Richard (d. 1960). Eight Men. F
Yates, Richard (1926), Revolutionary Road. F

1962

Agee, James (d. 1955), Letters to Father Flye. NF
Albee, Edward (1928), Who's Afraid of Virginia Woolf? D
Ashbery, John (1927), The Tennis Court Oath. V
Auchincloss, Louis (1917), Portrait in Brownstone. F
Auden, W. H. (1907), The Dyer's Hand. NF
Baldwin, James (1924), Another Country. F
Berger, Thomas (1924), Reinhart in Love. F
Bly, Robert (1926), Silence in the Snowy Fields. V
Boyle, Kay (1902), Collected Poems. V
Burroughs, William S. (1914), The Ticket That Exploded (pub. in Paris; American edition, 1967). F
Cabell, James Branch (d. 1958), Between Friends: Letters of James Branch Cabell and Others. NF
Cain, James M. (1892), Mignon. F
Caldwell, Erskine (1903), Close to Home. F
Calisher, Hortense (1911), Tale for the Mirror. F
Carson, Rachel (1907), Silent Spring. NF
Corso, Gregory (1930), Long Live Man. V
Creeley, Robert (1926), For Love: Poems 1950–1960. V

Crisis over Soviet missile bases in Cuba.
Three American astronauts orbited earth.
Telstar 1, first private communications satellite.
U.S. troops to Vietnam; military aid to India.
Century 21 Exposition in Seattle.
Congressional medal to Robert Frost on his 88th birthday.
John Steinbeck received Nobel Prize in literature.
E. E. Cummings d.
William Faulkner d.
Robinson Jeffers d.

Pope John XXIII opened Ecumenical Council in Rome.
Hermann Hesse d.
Isak Dinesen d.

Dickey, James (1923), Drowning with Others. V
Dos Passos, John (1896), Mr. Wilson's War. NF
Eberhart, Richard (1904), Collected Verse Plays. D
Farrell, James T. (1904), Sound of a City. F
Faulkner, William (1897), The Reivers. F; Prose and Poetry. F, NF, V
Fitzgerald, F. Scott (d. 1940), The Pat Hobby Stories. F
Friedman, Bruce Jay (1930), Stern. F
Frost, Robert (1874), In the Clearing. V
Gilroy, Frank D. (1926), Who'll Save the Plowboy? D
Gold, Herbert (1924), The Age of Happy Problems. NF
Goodman, Paul (1911), The Community of Scholars. NF; The Lordly Hudson. V
Gover, Robert (1929), One Hundred Dollar Misunderstanding. F
Hanley, William (1931), Mrs. Dally Has a Lover. D
Hardwick, Elizabeth (1916), A View of My Own. NF
Hayden, Robert (1913), A Ballad of Remembrance. V
Hollander, John (1929), Movie-Going and Other Poems. V
Howard, Richard (1929), Quantities. V
Hughes, Langston (1902), Fight for Freedom: The Story of the NAACP. NF
Inge, William (1913), Summer Brave and Eleven Short Plays. D
Isherwood, Christopher (1904), Down There on a Visit. F
Jackson, Shirley (1919), We Have Always Lived in the Castle. F
Jarrell, Randall (1914), A Sad Heart at the Supermarket: Essays and Fables. NF
Jones, James (1921), The Thin Red Line. F
Kees, Weldon (d. 1955?), Collected Poems. V
Kelley, William Melvin (1937), A Different Drummer. F
Kerouac, Jack (1922), Big Sur. F
Kesey, Ken (1935), One Flew Over the Cuckoo's Nest. F
Knowles, John (1926), Morning in Antibes. F
Koch, Kenneth (1925), Thank You and Other Poems. V
Lindbergh, Anne Morrow (1906), Dearly Beloved. F
Lurie, Alison (1926), Love and Friendship. F
Mailer, Norman (1923), Death for the Ladies and Other Disasters. V
"Mark Twain" (d. 1910), Letters from the Earth. F
Merrill, James (1926), Water Street. V
Merwin, W. S. (1927), The Life of Lazarillo de Tormes. NF
Miller, Henry (1891), Stand Still Like a Hummingbird. NF
Morris, Wright (1910), What a Way To Go. F
Moss, Howard (1922), The Magic Lantern of Marcel Proust. NF
Nabokov, Vladimir (1899), Pale Fire. F
Nash, Ogden (1902), Everyone But Thee and Me. V
Nemerov, Howard (1920), The Next Room of the Dream. V, D
O'Hara, John (1905), The Big Laugh. F; The Cape Cod Lighter. F
O'Neill, Eugene (d. 1953), More Stately Mansions (prod. in Stockholm; pub. 1964). D
Plath, Sylvia (1932), The Colossus and Other Poems. V
Porter, Katherine Anne (1890), Ship of Fools. F
Powers, J. F. (1917), Morte d'Urban. F
Price, Reynolds (1933), A Long and Happy Life. F
Richter, Conrad (1890), A Simple Honorable Man. F
"Ross Macdonald" (1915), The Zebra-Striped Hearse. F
Roth, Philip (1933), Letting Go. F
Rukeyser, Muriel (1913), Waterlily Fire. V
Scott, Winfield Townley (1910), Collected Poems. V
Sexton, Anne (1928), All My Pretty Ones. V
Shapiro, Karl (1913), Prose Keys to Modern Poetry. NF

Pinter's The Collection.
Braine's Life at the Top.
Burgess's A Clockwork Orange.
Enright's Addictions.
Kinsella's Downstream.
Wesker's Chips with Everything.
Penelope Mortimer's The Pumpkin Eater.
Deighton's The Ipcress File.
O'Faolain's I Remember! I Remember!
Dürrenmatt's The Physicists.
Fuentes's The Death of Artemio Cruz.
Lessing's The Golden Notebook.
Ionesco's Exit the King.
Pinget's The Inquisitory.
Bassani's The Garden of the Finzi-Continis.
Solzhenitsyn's One Day in the Life of Ivan Denisovich.
Voznesensky's The Triangular Pear.
Yevtushenko's A Wave of the Hand.
Neruda's Full Powers.
Tanizaki's Diary of a Mad Old Man.
Abé's The Woman in the Dunes.

Simpson, Louis (1923), Riverside Drive. F; James Hogg, A
    Critical Study. NF
Sinclair, Upton (1878), Autobiography. NF
Stafford, William (1914), Traveling Through the Dark. V
Stegner, Wallace (1909), Wolf Willow. NF
Steinbeck, John (1902), Travels with Charley in Search of
    America. NF
Swados, Harvey (1920), A Radical's America. NF
Thurber, James (d. 1961), Credos and Curios. F, NF
Tuchman, Barbara W. (1912), The Guns of August. NF
Updike, John (1932), Pigeon Feathers. F
Vidal, Gore (1925), Rocking the Boat. NF
Wakoski, Diane (1937), Coins and Coffins. V
Weiss, Theodore (1916), Gunsight. V
Wescott, Glenway (1901), Images of Truth. NF
White, E. B. (1899), The Points of My Compass. NF
Williams, William Carlos (1883), Pictures from Brueghel. V
Wilson, Edmund (1895), Patriotic Gore. NF
Wouk, Herman (1915), Youngblood Hawke. F
Yates, Richard (1926), Eleven Kinds of Loneliness. F

1963

Aiken, Conrad (1889), The Morning Song of Lord Zero. V
Albee, Edward (1928), The Ballad of the Sad Café [adapted from
    Carson McCullers's novella (1951)]. D
Algren, Nelson (1909), Who Lost an American? NF
Baldwin, James (1924), The Fire Next Time. NF
Bourjaily, Vance (1922), The Unnatural Enemy. F
Brinnin, John Malcolm (1916), Selected Poems. V
Buck, Pearl (1892), The Living Reed. F
Burroughs, William S. (1917), The Yage Letters (with Allen
    Ginsberg). NF; Dead Fingers Talk (pub. in London). F
Caldwell, Erskine (1903), The Last Night of Summer. F
Calisher, Hortense (1911), Textures of Life. F
Carter, Hodding (1907), First Person Rural. NF
Cassill, R. V. (1919), Pretty Leslie. F
Ciardi, John (1916), In Fact. V; Dialogue with an Audience. NF
Connell, Evan S., Jr. (1924), Notes from a Bottle Found on the
    Beach at Carmel. V
Creeley, Robert (1926), The Island. F
Cummings, E. E. (d. 1962), 73 Poems. V
Didion, Joan (1934), Run River. F
Donleavy, J. P. (1926), A Singular Man. F
Dos Passos, John (1896), Brazil on the Move. NF
Duberman, Martin (1930), In White America (pub. 1964). D
Dugan, Alan (1923), Poems 2. V
Farrell, James T. (1904), The Silence of History. F
Friedan, Betty (1921), The Feminine Mystique. NF
Friedman, Bruce Jay (1930), Far from the City of Class. F
Ginsberg, Allen (1926), Reality Sandwiches. V
Gold, Herbert (1911), Salt. F
Goodman, Paul (1911), The Society I Live in Is Mine. NF
Gordon, Caroline (1895), Old Red and Other Stories. F
Goyen, William (1915), The Fair Sister. F
Hazzard, Shirley (1931), Cliffs of Fall and Other Stories. F
Hellman, Lillian (1905), My Mother, My Father, and Me.
    [adapted from Burt Blechman's novel How Much? (1961)]. D

President Kennedy assassinated in
    Dallas.
U.S., Great Britain, and Soviet Union
    initiated nuclear test ban treaty.
Washington-Moscow "hot line"
    established.
Widespread civil rights demonstrations.
Anti-segregation drives in Birmingham,
    Ala.
Armory Show of 1913 (modern art) re-
    created in New York City.
Robert Frost d.
William Carlos Williams d.
Clifford Odets d.
Theodore Roethke d.
Sylvia Plath d.
The New York Review of Books,
    1963–.
Studies in Short Fiction (Newberry,
    S.C.), 1963–.

France and Algeria end seven-year civil
    war.
Civil war between Greek and Turkish
    Cypriots.
Beatles dominate British pop music.
Louis MacNeice d.
Aldous Huxley d.
Tristan Tzara d.
Fowles's *The Collector.*
Burgess's *Honey for the Bears.*
Kingsley Amis's *One Fat Englishman.*
Spark's *The Girls of Slender Means.*
Le Carré's *The Spy Who Came in from
    the Cold.*
Böll's *The Clown.*
Grass's *Dog Years.*
Yevtushenko's *A Precocious
    Autobiography.*

Hersey, John (1914), Here to Stay. NF
Hoffman, Daniel G. (1923), The City of Satisfactions. V
Hollander, John (1929), Various Owls. V
Horgan, Paul (1903), Conquistadors in North American History. NF
Inge, William (1913), Natural Affection. F
Jeffers, Robinson (d. 1962), The Beginning and the End and Other Poems. V
Johnson, Josephine (1910), The Dark Traveler. F
Jones, LeRoi (1934), Blues People. NF
Justice, Donald (1925), A Local Storm. V
Kerouac, Jack (1922), Visions of Gerard. F
McCarthy, Mary (1912), The Group. F
Macdonald, Dwight (1906), Against the American Grain. NF
Mailer, Norman (1923), The Presidential Papers. NF
Malamud, Bernard (1914), Idiots First. F
Matthiessen, Peter (1927), Under the Mountain Wall. NF
Merwin, W. S. (1927), The Moving Target. V
Michener, James A. (1907), Caravans. F
Morris, Wright (1910), Cause for Wonder. F
Nemerov, Howard (1920), Poetry and Fiction. NF
Oates, Joyce Carol (1938), By the North Gate. F
O'Hara, John (1905), Elizabeth Appleton. F; The Hat on the Bed. F
Perelman, S. J. (1904), The Beauty Part. F
Plath, Sylvia (1932), The Bell Jar (pub. in London; American edition, 1971). F
Price, Reynolds, (1933), The Names and Faces of Heroes. F
Prokosch, Frederic (1908), The Seven Sisters. F
Pynchon, Thomas (1937), V. F
Ransom, John Crowe (1888), Selected Poems (rev. and enl.). V
Rechy, John (1934), City of Night. F
Rexroth, Kenneth (1905), Natural Numbers. V
Rice, Elmer (1892), Minority Report: An Autobiography. NF; Love Among the Ruins. D
Rich, Adrienne (1929), Snapshots of a Daughter-in-Law. V
Richardson, Jack (1935), Lorenzo. D
Roethke, Theodore (1908), Sequence, Sometimes Metaphysical. V
Salinger, J. D. (1919), Raise High the Roof Beam, Carpenters, and Seymour—An Introduction. F
Sandburg, Carl (1878), Honey and Salt. V
Saroyan, William (1908), Boys and Girls Together. F; Not Dying. NF
Schisgal, Murray (1926), Luv. D; The Tiger. D
Shaw, Irwin (1913), Children from Their Games. D
Sheed, Wilfrid (1930), The Hack. F
Simon, Neil (1927), Barefoot in the Park (pub. 1964). D
Simpson, Louis (1923), At the End of the Open Road. V
Sontag, Susan (1933), The Benefactor. F
Swados, Harvey (1920), The Will. F
Swenson, May (1919), To Mix with Time. V
Taylor, Peter (1917), Miss Leonora When Last Seen. F
Toklas, Alice B. (1877), What Is Remembered. NF
Updike, John (1932), The Centaur. F; Telephone Poles. V
Vonnegut, Kurt, Jr. (1922), Cat's Cradle. F
Wagoner, David (1926), The Nesting Ground. V
Wallant, Edward Lewis (d. 1962), The Tenants of Moonbloom. F
Wheelock, John Hall (1886), What Is Poetry? NF
Williams, John A. (1925), Sissie. F

Vargas Llosa's *The Time of the Hero*.
Le Clézio's *The Interrogation*.
Mishima's *The Sailor Who Fell from Grace with the Sea*.
Kazakov's *Blue and Green*.
Naipaul's *Mr. Stone and the Knights Companion*.
Akhmatova's *Requiem*.
Hochhuth's *The Deputy*.
Sarraute's *The Golden Fruits*.
Cortázar's *Hopscotch*.

Williams, Tennessee (1911), The Milk Train Doesn't Stop Here Anymore (pub. 1964). D
Williams, William Carlos (1883), Paterson. V
Willingham, Calder (1922), Eternal Fire. F
Wilson, Edmund (1895), The Cold War and the Income Tax. NF
Wright, James (1927), The Branch Will Not Break. V
Wright, Richard (d. 1960), Lawd Today! F

1964

Aiken, Conrad (1889), A Seizure of Limericks. V; The Collected Novels. F
Albee, Edward (1928), Tiny Alice (pub. 1965). D
Ammons, A. R. (1926), Expressions of Sea Level. V
Auchincloss, Louis (1917), The Rector of Justin. F
Auden, W. H. (1907), Selected Essays. NF
Baldwin, James (1924), Blues for Mister Charlie. D; The Amen Corner. D
Barthelme, Donald (1931), Come Back, Dr. Caligari. F
Behrman, S. N. (1893), But for Whom Charlie. D
Bellow, Saul (1915), Herzog. F; The Last Analysis (pub. 1965). D
Berger, Thomas (1924), Little Big Man. F
Berry, Wendell (1934), The Broken Ground. V
Berryman, John (1914), 77 Dream Songs. V
Blackmur, R. P. (1904), Eleven Essays in the European Novel. NF
Brautigan, Richard (1935), A Confederate General from Big Sur. F
Burroughs, William S. (1914), Nova Express. F
Caldwell, Erskine (1903), Around About America. NF
Calisher, Hortense (1911), Extreme Magic. F
Cassill, R. V. (1919), The President. F
Chayefsky, Paddy (1923), The Passion of Josef D. D
Cheever, John (1912), The Brigadier and the Golf Widow. F; The Wapshot Scandal. F
Ciardi, John (1916), Person to Person. V
Clark, Eleanor (1913), The Oysters of Locmariaquer. NF
Cozzens, James Gould (1903), Children and Others. F
Dahlberg, Edward (1900), Because I Was Flesh. NF
Davison, Peter (1928), The Breaking of the Day. V
De Vries, Peter (1910), Reuben, Reuben. F
Dickey, James (1923), Helmets. V; The Suspect in Poetry. NF
Dos Passos, John (1896), Occasions and Protests. NF
Duncan, Robert (1919), Roots and Branches. V
Eberhart, Richard (1904), The Quarry. V
Eliot, T. S. (1888), Knowledge and Experience in the Philosophy of F. H. Bradley. NF
Elkin, Stanley (1930), Boswell: A Modern Comedy. F
Ellison, Ralph (1914), Shadow and Act. NF
Epstein, Seymour (1917), Leah. F
Farrell, James T. (1904), What Time Collects. F
Friedman, Bruce Jay (1930), A Mother's Kisses. F
Gaines, Ernest J. (1933), Catherine Carmier. F
Garrett, George (1929), Cold Ground Was My Bed Last Night. F
Garrigue, Jean (1914), Country Without Maps. V

24th Amendment (outlawing poll taxes) ratified.
Gulf of Tonkin incident precipitated U.S.-North Vietnam warfare.
Race riots in Harlem, Brooklyn, and Rochester, N.Y.
Anti-poverty and civil rights legislation passed.
Major earthquake in Alaska.
New York World's Fair opened.
Martin Luther King awarded Nobel Peace Prize.
Rachel Carson d.
Carl Van Vechten d.
Flannery O'Connor d.

Aleksei Kosygin succeeded Khrushchev as Soviet premier.
Jean-Paul Sartre declined Nobel Prize in literature.
Sean O'Casey d.
Brendan Behan d.
Golding's *The Spire*.
Larkin's *The Whitsun Weddings*.
Murdoch's *The Italian Girl*.
Peter Shaffer's *The Royal Hunt of the Sun*.
Bagnold's *The Chinese Prime Minister*.
Osborne's *Inadmissible Evidence*.
Orton's *Entertaining Mr. Sloane*.
Drabble's *The Garrick Year*.
Trevor's *The Old Boys*.
Friel's *Philadelphia, Here I Come!*
Koestler's *The Act of Creation*.
Abé's *The Face of Another*.
Böll's *Absent Without Leave*.
Frisch's *A Wilderness of Mirrors*.
Yevtushenko's *The Bratsk Station* (1964–65).
Voznesensky's *Antiworlds*.
Weiss's *Marat/Sade*.
Mandelstam's *Collected Works* (3 vols. 1964–71).
Cabrera Infante's *View of a Tropical Dawn*.

Gilroy, Frank D. (1926), The Subject Was Roses (pub. 1965). D
Grau, Shirley Ann (1929), The Keepers of the House. F
Hall, Donald (1928), A Roof of Tiger Lilies. V
Hanley, William (1931), Slow Dance on the Killing Ground. D
Hansberry, Lorraine (1930), The Sign in Sidney Brustein's
  Window. D
Hawkes, John (1925), Second Skin. F
Hemingway, Ernest (d. 1961), A Moveable Feast. NF
Holmes, John Clellon (1926), Get Home Free. F
Horgan, Paul (1903), Things As They Are. F
Isherwood, Christopher (1904), A Single Man. F
Jones, LeRoi (1934), The Dead Lecturer. V; Dutchman. D; The
  Slave. D The Baptism (pub. 1967). D; The Toilet (pub.
  1967). D
Kennedy, Adrienne (1931), Funnyhouse of a Negro (pub. 1969).
  D
Kesey, Ken (1935), Sometimes a Great Notion. F
Kinnell, Galway (1927), Flower Herding on Mount Monadnock.
  V
Knowles, John (1926), Double Vision. NF
Larner, Jeremy (1937), Drive, He Said. F
Levertov, Denise (1923), O Taste and See. V
Lowell, Robert (1917), For the Union Dead. V; The Old Glory
  (pub. 1965). D
McGinley, Phyllis (1905), Sixpence in Her Shoe. NF
McNally, Terrence (1939), And Things That Go Bump in the
  Night (pub. 1966). D
Manfred, Frederick (Feike Feikema) (1912), Scarlet Plume. F
Markfield, Wallace (1926), To an Early Grave. F
Meredith, William (1919), The Wreck of the Thresher and Other
  Poems. V
Miller, Arthur (1915), After the Fall. D; Incident at Vichy (pub.
  1965). D
Nin, Anaïs (1903), Collages. F
Oates, Joyce Carol (1938), With Shuddering Fall. F
O'Connor, Edwin (1918), I Was Dancing. F
O'Hara, Frank (1926), Lunch Poems. V
O'Hara, John (1905), The Horse Knows the Way. F
Prokosch, Frederic (1908), The Dark Dancer. F
Purdy, James (1923), Cabot Wright Begins. F
Richter, Conrad. (1890), The Grandfathers. F
Roethke, Theodore (d. 1963). The Far Field. V
Sandoz, Mari (1896), The Beaver Men. NF
Saroyan, William (1908), One Day in the Afternoon of the
  World. F
Selby, Hubert, Jr. (1924), Last Exit to Brooklyn. F
Sexton, Anne (1928), Selected Poems. V
Shapiro, Karl (1913), The Bourgeois Poet. V
Shaw, Irwin (1913), In the Company of Dolphins. F
Singer, Isaac Bashevis (1904), Short Friday. F
Smith, Lillian (1897), Our Faces, Our Words. NF
Stafford, Jean (1915), Bad Characters. F
Stegner, Wallace (1909), The Gathering of Zion. NF
Strand, Mark (1934), Sleeping with One Eye Open. V
Stuart, Jesse (1907), Save Every Lamb. F
Taylor, Robert Lewis (1912), Two Roads to Guadalupé. F
Tyler, Anne (1941), If Morning Ever Comes. F
Updike, John (1932), Olinger Stories. F
Van Doren, Mark (1894), Collected and New Poems. V
Van Duyn, Mona (1921), A Time of Bees. V
Vidal, Gore (1925), Julian. F

Wallant, Edward Lewis (d. 1962), The Children at the Gate. F
Warren, Robert Penn (1905), Flood: A Romance of Our Time.
    F
Webb, Charles (1939), The Graduate. F
Wilson, Lanford (1938), Balm in Gilead (pub. 1965). D
Zinsser, William K. (1922), The Haircurl Papers and Other
    Searches for the Lost Individual. NF

1965

Alfred, William (1922), Hogan's Goat (pub. 1966). D
Algren, Nelson (1909), Notes from a Sea Diary: Hemingway All
    the Way. F, NF
Ammons, A. R. (1926), Corsons Inlet. V; Tape for the Turn of
    the Year. V
Auden, W. H. (1907), About the House. V
Baldwin, James (1924), Going to Meet the Man. F
Behrman, S. N. (1893), The Suspended Drawing Room. NF
Bishop, Elizabeth (1911), Questions of Travel. V
Brown, Claude (1937), Manchild in the Promised Land. NF
Bryan, C.D.B. (1936), P. S. Wilkinson. F
Buechner, Frederick (1926), The Final Beast. F
Caldwell, Erskine (1903), In Search of Bisco. NF
Calisher, Hortense (1911), Journal from Ellipsia. F
Carruth, Hayden (1921), Nothing for Tigers: Poems 1959–
    1964. V
Connell, Evan S., Jr. (1924), At the Crossroads. F
Creeley, Robert (1926), The Gold-Diggers and Other Stories. F
Demby, William (1922), The Catacombs. F
Dickey, James (1923), Buckdancer's Choice. V
Eberhart, Richard (1904), Selected Poems 1930–1965. V
Eliot, T. S. (1888), To Criticize the Critic and Other Writings.
    NF
Epstein, Seymour (1917), A Penny for Charity. F
Farrell, James T. (1904), Collected Poems. V
Faulkner, William (d. 1962), Essays, Speeches, and Public
    Letters. NF
Ford, Jesse Hill (1928), The Liberation of Lord Byron Jones. F
Garrett, George (1929), Do, Lord, Remember Me. F
Gelber, Jack (1932), Square in the Eye (pub. 1966). D
Herlihy, James Leo (1927), Midnight Cowboy. F
Hersey, John (1914), White Lotus. F
Hicks, Granville (1901), Part of the Truth. NF
Hine, Daryl (1936), The Wooden Horse. V
Hoagland, Edward (1932), The Peacock's Tail. NF
Hollander, John (1929), Visions from the Ramble. V
Horgan, Paul (1903), Songs After Lincoln. V
Howard, Maureen (1930), Bridgeport Bus. F
Hughes, Langston (1902), Simple's Uncle Sam. F
Humphrey, William (1924), The Ordways. F
Jarrell, Randall (1914), The Lost World. V
Jones, LeRoi (1934), The System of Dante's Hell. F
Kazin, Alfred (1915), Starting Out in the Thirties. NF
Kelley, William Melvin (1937), A Drop of Patience. F
Kerouac, Jack (1922), Desolation Angels. F
Kizer, Carolyn (1925), Knock Upon Silence. V
Kopit, Arthur (1937), The Day the Whores Came Out to Play
    Tennis. D
Kosinski, Jerzy (1933), The Painted Bird. F

Malcolm X assassinated.
Martin Luther King, Jr., led voter
    registration march from Selma to
    Montgomery, Ala.
Race riots in Watts section of Los
    Angeles.
Marines in Danang were first U.S.
    combat troops in South Vietnam.
Vietnam War escalated amid civilian
    protests.
First space walk by American astronaut.
National Endowment for the
    Humanities established.
Thornton Wilder received first National
    Medal for Literature.
T. S. Eliot d.
R. P. Blackmur d.
Randall Jarrell d.

Charles de Gaulle re-elected president
    of France.
Rolling Stones became major British
    rock group.
Sir Winston Churchill d.
Somerset Maugham d.
Pinter's *The Homecoming.*
Spark's *The Mandelbaum Gate.*
Angus Wilson's *Late Call.*
Murdoch's *The Red and the Green.*
Peter Shaffer's *Black Comedy.*
Bond's *Saved.*
LeCarré's *The Looking-Glass War.*
Bradbury's *Stepping Westward.*
Lodge's *The British Museum Is Falling
    Down.*
Enright's *Figures of Speech.*
Drabble's *The Millstone.*
Trevor's *The Boarding-House.*
Akhmatova's *The Flight of Time.*
Richler's *Cocksure.*
Pinget's *Someone.*
Le Clézio's *Fever.*
Weiss's *The Investigation.*
Bonnefoy's *Words in Stone.*
Calvino's *Cosmicomics.*
Gordimer's *Not for Publication.*

Kumin, Maxine (1925), The Privilege. V
Lurie, Alison (1926), The Nowhere City. F
McCarthy, Cormac (1933), The Orchard Keeper. F
McConkey, James (1921), Night Stand. F
MacLeish, Archibald (1892), The Eleanor Roosevelt Story. NF
McPhee, John (1931), A Sense of Where You Are. NF
Mailer, Norman (1923), An American Dream. F
"Malcolm X" (1921), Autobiography (with Alex Haley). NF
Matthiessen, Peter (1927), At Play in the Fields of the Lord. F
Merrill, James (1926), The (Diblos) Notebook. F
Michener, James A. (1907), The Source. F
Morris, Wright (1910), One Day. F
Moss, Howard (1922), Finding Them Lost. V
O'Connor, Flannery (1925), Everything That Rises Must
    Converge. F
O'Hara, John (1905), The Lockwood Concern. F
Porter, Katherine Anne (1890), Collected Stories. F
Ribman, Ronald (1932), Harry, Noon and Night (pub. 1967). D
Richardson, Jack (1935), Xmas in Las Vegas. D
Roethke, Theodore (d. 1963), On the Poet and His Craft. NF
Sarton, May (1912), Mrs. Stevens Hears the Mermaids Singing. F
Shaw, Irwin (1913), Voices of a Summer Day. F
Sheed, Wilfrid (1930), Square's Progress. F
Simon, Neil (1927), The Odd Couple (pub. 1966). D
Simpson, Louis (1923), Selected Poems. V
Snyder, Gary (1930), Six Sections from Mountains and Rivers
    Without End. V
Spencer, Elizabeth (1921), Knights and Dragons. F
Stern, Richard G. (1928), Stitch. F
Tolson, Melvin B. (1900), Harlem Gallery, Book I. V
Tyler, Anne (1941), The Tin Can Tree. F
Updike, John (1932), Of the Farm. F; Assorted Prose. NF
Vonnegut, Kurt, Jr. (1922), God Bless You, Mr. Rosewater; or
    Pearls Before Swine. F
Wagoner, David (1926), The Escape Artist. F
Ward, Douglas Turner (1930), Happy Ending (pub. 1966).
    D; Day of Absence (pub. 1966). D
Warren, Robert Penn (1905), Who Speaks for the Negro? NF
Weiss, Theodore (1916), The Medium. V
Williams, John A. (1925), This Is My Country, Too. NF
Wilson, Edmund (1895), O Canada. NF; The Bit Between My
    Teeth. NF
Wolfe, Thomas (d. 1938), The Lost Boy. F
Wolfe, Tom (1931), The Kandy Kolored Tangerine-Flake
    Streamline Baby. NF
Wouk, Herman (1915), Don't Stop the Carnival. F
Zukofsky, Louis (1904), All the Collected Short Poems, 1923–
    1958. V

1966

Adams, Alice (1926), Careless Love. F
Albee, Edward (1928), A Delicate Balance. D; Malcolm
    [adapted from James Purdy's novel (1959)]. D
Ammons, A. R. (1926), Northfield Poems. V
Ashbery, John (1927), Rivers and Mountains. V
Auden, W. H. (1907), Collected Shorter Poems, 1927–1957. V
Barth, John (1930), Giles Goat-Boy; or, The Revised New
    Syllabus. F
Booth, Philip (1925), Weathers and Edges. V

U.S. increased bombing raids in North
    Vietnam.
400,000 American troops in Southeast
    Asia.
Anti-war protests proliferated.
Race riots in major U.S. cities.
Stock market reached new low.
U.S. made first (unmanned) soft landing
    on the moon.
Drug use spread alarmingly.

Burke, Kenneth (1897), Language as Symbolic Action. NF
Calisher, Hortense (1911), The Railway Police and The Last Trolley Ride. F
Capote, Truman (1924), In Cold Blood. NF, F
Coover, Robert (1932), The Origin of the Brunists. F
Davison, Peter (1928), The City and the Island. V
Doctorow, E. L. (1931), Big as Life. F
Donleavy, J. P. (1926), The Saddest Summer of Samuel S. F
Dos Passos, John (1896), The Best Times: An Informal Memoir. NF; The Shackles of Power: Three Jeffersonian Decades. NF
Elkin, Stanley (1930), Criers and Kibitzers, Kibitzers and Criers. F
Farrell, James T. (1904), Lonely for the Future. F
Gardner, John (1933), The Resurrection. F
Garrigue, Jean (1910), The Animal Hotel. V
Gass, William H. (1924), Omensetter's Luck. F
Hayden, Robert (1913), Selected Poems. V
Hazzard, Shirley (1931), The Evening of the Holiday. F
Heinlein, Robert A. (1907), The Moon Is a Harsh Mistress. F
Hersey, John (1914), Too Far to Walk. F
Isherwood, Christopher (1904), Exhumations. F, NF, V
Jones, LeRoi (1934), Home: Social Essays. NF; A Black Mass (pub. 1969). D
Kerouac, Jack (1942), Satori in Paris. NF
Kinnell, Galway (1927), Black Light. F
Knowles, John (1926), Indian Summer. F
Lytle, Andrew (1902), The Hero with the Private Parts. NF
McMurty, Larry (1936), The Last Picture Show. F
McPhee, John (1931), The Headmaster. NF
Mailer, Norman (1923), Cannibals and Christians. NF
Malamud, Bernard (1914), The Fixer. F
Manfred, Frederick (Feike Feikema) (1912), King of Spades. F
Maxwell, William (1908), The Old Man at the Railroad Crossing. F
Merrill, James (1926), Nights and Days. V
Moore, Marianne (1887), Tell Me, Tell Me: Granite, Steel and Other Topics. V
Motley, Willard (1912), Let Noon Be Fair. F
Nabokov, Vladimir (1899), Speak, Memory (rev. edition; first pub. in London, 1951). NF
Oates, Joyce Carol (1938), Upon the Sweeping Flood. F
O'Connor, Edwin (1918), All in the Family. F
O'Hara, John (1905), Waiting for Winter. F; My Turn. NF
Ozick, Cynthia (1928), Trust. F
Percy, Walker (1916), The Last Gentleman. F
Plath, Sylvia (d. 1963), Ariel. V
Price, Reynolds (1933), A Generous Man. F
Pynchon, Thomas (1937), The Crying of Lot 49. F
Ribman, Ronald (1932), The Journey of the Fifth Horse (pub. 1967). D
Rich, Adrienne (1929), Necessities of Life. V
Richter, Conrad (1890), A Country of Strangers. F
Roethke, Theodore (d. 1963), Collected Poems. V
Saroyan, William (1908), Short Drive, Sweet Chariot. NF
Sexton, Anne (1928), Live or Die. V
Sheed, Wilfrid (1930), Office Politics. F
Singer, Isaac Bashevis (1904), In My Father's Court. NF
Smith, William Jay (1918), The Tin Can and Other Poems. V
Snyder, Gary (1930), A Range of Poems. V
Sontag, Susan (1933), Against Interpretation. NF
Stafford, Jean (1915), A Mother in History. NF
Steinbeck, John (1902), America and Americans. NF

Robert Weaver became first black Cabinet member (Housing and Urban Development).
Metropolitan Opera opened new house in Lincoln Center.
Delmore Schwartz d.
Lillian Smith d.

France withdrew from NATO.
Start of cultural revolution under Mao Tse-tung in China.
Indira Gandhi elected prime minister of India.
Evelyn Waugh d.
C. S. Forester d.
Anna Akhmatova d.
André Breton d.
Fowles's *The Magus.*
Greene's *The Comedians.*
Murdoch's *The Time of the Angels.*
Ballard's *The Crystal World.*
Heaney's *Death of a Nationalist.*
Kinsella's *Wormwood.*
Osborne's *A Patriot for Me.*
Renault's *The Mask of Apollo.*
Paul Scott's *The Raj Quartet* (1966–75).
Rebecca West's *The Birds Fall Down.*
Orton's *Loot.*
Leonard Cohen's *Beautiful Losers.*
Patrick White's *The Solid Mandala.*
Böll's *End of a Mission.*
Gordimer's *The Late Bourgeois World.*
Le Clézio's *The Flood.*
Donoso's *This Sunday.*
Vargas Llosa's *The Green House.*
Amado's *Doña Flor and Her Two Husbands.*
Walser's *The Unicorn.*
Voznesensky's *Achilles' Heart.*

Stevens, Wallace (d. 1955), The Letters of Wallace Stevens (ed. Holly Stevens). NF
Swenson, May (1919), Poems to Solve. V
Tuchman, Barbara W. (1912), The Proud Tower: A Portrait of the World Before the War, 1890–1914. NF
Updike, John (1932), The Music School. F
Van Itallie, Jean-Claude (1935), America Hurrah (pub. 1967). D
Wagoner, David (1926), Staying Alive. V
Wakoski, Diane (1937), Discrepancies and Apparitions. V
West, Jessamyn (1907), A Matter of Time. F
Williams, Tennessee (1911), Slapstick Tragedy: the Mutilated and The Gnädiges Fräulein (pub. 1967). D
Wilson, Lanford (1937), The Rimers of Eldritch (pub. 1967). D
Winters, Yvor (1900), The Early Poems. V
Zukofsky, Louis (1904), All the Collected Short Poems, 1956–1964. V

1967

Aiken, Conrad (1889), Thee. V
Albee, Edward (1928), Everything in the Garden [adapted from Giles Cooper's play (1963); pub. 1968]. D
Anderson, Robert (1917), You Know I Can't Hear You When the Water's Running. D
Barthelme, Donald (1931), Snow White. F
Berger, Thomas (1924), Killing Time. F
Berryman, John (1914), Berryman's Sonnets. V; Short Poems. V
Blackmur, R. P. (d. 1965), A Primer of Ignorance. NF
Bly, Robert (1926), The Light Around the Body. V
Bourjaily, Vance (1922), The Man Who Knew Kennedy. F
Brautigan, Richard (1935), Trout Fishing in America. F
Bullins, Ed (1935), In New England Winter (pub. 1969). D
Caldwell, Erskine (1903), Miss Mamma Aimee. F
Conroy, Frank (1936), Stop-time. NF
Creeley, Robert (1926), Words. V
Dickey, James (1923), Poems 1957–1967. V
Dugan, Alan (1923), Poems 3. V
Elkin, Stanley (1930), A Bad Man. F
Epstein, Seymour (1917), Caught in That Music. F
Feiffer, Jules (1929), Little Murders. D
Ferlinghetti, Lawrence (1919), An Eye on the World. V
Fox, Paula (1923), Poor George. F
Gaines, Ernest J. (1933), Of Love and Dust. F
Garrett, George (1929), For a Bitter Season. V
Garrigue, Jean (1914), New and Selected Poems. V
Gilroy, Frank D. (1925), That Summer—That Fall. D
Gold, Herbert (1924), Fathers. F
Hazzard, Shirley (1931), People in Glass Houses. F
Hecht, Anthony (1923), The Hard Hours. V
Heller, Joseph (1923), We Bombed in New Haven (pub. 1968). D
Hersey, John (1914), Under the Eye of the Storm. F
Holmes, John Clellon (1926), Nothing More to Declare. F
Horovitz, Israel (1939), Line (pub. 1968). D
Howard, Richard (1929), The Damages. V
Hughes, Langston (1902), The Panther and the Lash: Poems of Our Times. V
Isherwood, Christopher (1904), A Meeting by the River. F
Jackson, Charles (1903), A Second-Hand Life. F

25th Amendment (contingency plan for presidential succession) ratified.
Puerto Rico rejected statehood, remained a commonwealth.
First U.S.–U.S.S.R. consular treaty.
Johnson and Kosygin met in Glassboro, N.J.
U.S. planes bombed Hanoi, war intensified.
Anti-war protestors clashed with police.
Worst racial disturbances in U.S. history.
Thurgood Marshall became first black Supreme Court justice.
Negro Ensemble Company founded in New York City.
Langston Hughes d.
Elmer Rice d.
Carl Sandburg d.
Novel: A Forum on Fiction (Providence), 1967–.

Israeli-Arab six-day war.
Constantine II fled Greece after Papadopoulos junta seized power.
Journal of American Studies (London), 1967–.
John Masefield d.
André Maurois d.
Robert Shaw's *The Man in the Glass Booth.*
Stoppard's *Rosencrantz and Guildenstern Are Dead*
Kinsella's *Nightwalker.*
Golding's *The Pyramid.*
Bailey's *At the Jerusalem.*
Gunn's *Touch.*
Nichols's *A Day in the Death of Joe Egg.*
Drabble's *Jerusalem the Golden.*
Hochhuth's *Soldiers.*
Kundera's *The Joke.*
Calvino's *t zero.*
Butor's *Portrait of the Artist as a Young Monkey.*
Narayan's *The Vendor of Sweets.*

Jones, James (1921), Go to the Widow-Maker. F
Jones, LeRoi (1934), Tales. F; Slave Ship (pub. 1969). D
Justice, Donald (1925), Night Light. V
Kelley, William Melvin (1937), dem. F
Levertov, Denise (1923), The Sorrow Dance. V
Levin, Ira (1929), Rosemary's Baby. F
Lowell, Robert (1917), Near the Ocean. V; Prometheus Bound
    (pub. 1969). D
Lurie, Allison (1926), Imaginary Friends. F
McCarthy, Mary (1912), Vietnam. NF
MacLeish, Archibald (1892), Herakles. D
McNally, Terrence (1939), Next (pub. 1969). D
McPhee, John (1931), Oranges. NF
Mailer, Norman (1923), Why Are We in Vietnam? F; The
    Bullfight. NF; The Deer Park [adapted from his novel (1955)].
    D
Matthiessen, Peter (1927), Oomingmark. NF
Merwin, W. S. (1927), The Lice. V
Miles, Josephine (1911), Kinds of Affection. V
Miller, Arthur (1915), The Price (pub. 1968). D; I Don't Need
    You Any More. F
Moore, Marianne (1887), The Complete Poems. V
Morris, Wright (1910), In Orbit. F
Nemerov, Howard (1920), The Blue Swallows. V
Nims, John Frederick (1913), Of Flesh and Bone. V
Oates, Joyce Carol (1938), A Garden of Earthly Delights. F
O'Hara, John (1905), The Instrument. F
Olson, Charles (1910), Human Universe and Other Essays. F
Podhoretz, Norman (1930), Making It. NF
Purdy, James (1923), Eustace Chisholm and The Works. F
Rechy, John (1934), Numbers. F
Reed, Ishmael (1938), The Free-Lance Pallbearers. F
Ribman, Ronald (1932), The Ceremony of Innocence (pub.
    1968). D
Rich, Adrienne (1931), Selected Poems. V
Richter, Conrad (1890), Over the Blue Mountain. F
Roth, Philip (1933), When She Was Good. F
Shepard, Sam (1942), La Turista (pub. 1968). D
Singer, Isaac Bashevis (1904), The Manor. F
Snodgrass, W. D. (1926), Gallows Songs of Christian
    Morgenstern. V
Sontag, Susan (1933), Death Kit. F
Stegner, Wallace (1909), All the Little Live Things. F
Stone, Robert (1937), A Hall of Mirrors. F
Styron, William (1925), The Confessions of Nat Turner. F
Swenson, May (1919), Half Sun, Half Sleep. V
Tate, James (1943), The Lost Pilot. V
Theroux, Paul (1941), Waldo. F
Vidal, Gore (1925), Washington, D.C. F
Wakoski, Diane (1937), The George Washington Poems. V
Whittemore, Reed (1919), Poems New and Selected. V
Wideman, John Edgar (1941), A Glance Away. F
Wilder, Thornton (1897), The Eighth Day. F
Williams, John A. (1925), The Man Who Cried I Am. F
Williams, Tennessee (1911), The Knightly Quest. F
Wilson, Edmund (1895), A Prelude: Landscape, Characters, and
    Conversations. NF
Winters, Yvor (1900), Forms of Discovery. NF
Zukofsky, Louis (1904), Prepositions: The Collected Critical
    Essays. NF

Beauvoir's *The Woman Destroyed.*
Le Clézio's *Terra Amata.*
Cabrera Infante's *Three Trapped Tigers.*
García Márquez's *One Hundred Years
    of Solitude.*
Arrabal's *The Architect and the
    Emperor of Assyria.*
Naipaul's *The Mimic Men.*
Kuznetsov's *Babi Yar.*
Abé's *Friends.*

1968

Albee, Edward (1928), Box (pub. 1969). D; Quotations from Chairman Mao Tse-Tung (pub. 1969). D

Ammons, A. R. (1926), Selected Poems. V

Anderson, Robert (1917), I Never Sang for My Father. D

Ashbery, John (1927), Three Madrigals. V; Sunrise in Suburbia. V

Auchincloss, Louis (1917), A World of Profit. F

Auden, W. H. (1907), Collected Longer Poems. V; Secondary Worlds. NF

Baldwin, James (1924), Tell Me How Long the Train's Been Gone. F

Barth, John (1930), Lost in the Funhouse. F

Barthelme, Donald (1931), Unspeakable Practices, Unnatural Acts. F

Behrman, S. N. (1893), The Burning Glass. F

Bellow, Saul (1915), Mosby's Memoirs. F

Berry, Wendell (1934), Openings. V

Berryman, John (1914), His Toy, His Dream, His Rest. V

Bogan, Louise (1897), The Blue Estuaries: Poems 1923–1968. V

Brautigan, Richard (1935), In Watermelon Sugar. F

Brooks, Gwendolyn (1917), In the Mecca. V

Bullins, Ed (1935), In the Wine Time (pub. 1969); The Electronic Nigger (pub. 1969). D

Burke, Kenneth (1897), The Complete White Oxen: Collected Short Fiction. F; Collected Poems 1915–1967. V

Caldwell, Erskine (1903), Deep South: Memory and Observation. NF; Writing in America. NF

Cleaver, Eldridge (1935), Soul on Ice. NF

Coover, Robert (1932), The Universal Baseball Association, Inc., J. Henry Waugh, Prop. F

Cozzens, James Gould (1903), Morning Noon and Night. F

Dickey, James (1923), Babel to Byzantium. NF

Didion, Joan (1934), Slouching Towards Bethlehem. NF

Donleavy, J. P. (1926), The Beastly Beatitudes of Balthazar B. F

Duncan, Robert (1919), Bending the Bow. V

Eberhart, Richard (1904), Shifts of Being. V

Farrell, James T. (1904), A Brand New Life. F

Friedman, Bruce Jay (1930), Scuba Duba. D

Gaines, Ernest J. (1933), Bloodline. F

Gass, William H. (1924), In the Heart of the Heart of the Country. F

Gilroy, Frank D. (1925), The Only Game in Town. D

Ginsberg, Allen (1926), Planet News: 1961–1967. V

Giovanni, Nikki (1943), Black Judgment. V; Black Feeling, Black Talk. V

Guare, John (1938), Muzeeka (pub. 1969). D

Hayes, Alfred (1911), The End of Me. F

Hersey, John (1914), The Algiers Motel Incident. NF

Hine, Daryl (1936), Minutes. V

Hoffman, Daniel G. (1923), Striking the Stones. V

Hollander, John (1929), Types of Shape. V

Horgan, Paul (1903), Everything to Live For. F

Horovitz, Israel (1939), The Indian Wants the Bronx. D

Humphrey, William (1924), A Time and a Place. F

Jones, James (1921), The Ice-Cream Headache and Other Stories. F

Kennedy, Adrienne (1931), A Rat's Mass (prod. 1970). D

Kerouac, Jack (1922), Vanity of Duluoz. F

Kinnell, Galway (1927), Body Rags. V

Knowles, John (1926), Phineas. F

Robert F. Kennedy and Martin Luther King Jr., assassinated.

Sixty-two nations signed nuclear non-proliferation treaty.

North Korean patrol boat seized USS *Pueblo*.

U.S. astronauts made 10 orbits of the moon.

Violence erupted at Miami and Chicago political conventions.

Student militancy in anti-war protests rampant.

Drug abuse and economic inflation on the rise.

John Steinbeck d.

Upton Sinclair d.

Soviet troops invaded Czechoslovakia.

Cecil Day-Lewis named poet laureate of England.

Sir Herbert Read d.

Salvatore Quasimodo d.

Enright's *Unlawful Assembly*.

Murdoch's *The Nice and the Good*.

Arthur C. Clarke's *2001: A Space Odyssey*.

Gunn's *The Garden of the Gods*.

Stoppard's *The Real Inspector Hound*.

Bond's *Narrow Road to the Deep North*.

Gilliatt's *What's It Like Out?*

Geoffrey Hill's *King Log*.

Leonard Cohen's *Selected Poems*.

Sarraute's *Between Life and Death*.

Bassani's *The Heron*.

Adamov's *Off Limits*.

Arrabal's *The Automobile Graveyard*.

Solzhenitsyn's *The First Circle; The Cancer Ward*.

Borges's *The Book of Imaginary Beings*.

Cortázar's *62: A Model Kit*.

Mishima's *Sun and Steel*.

Kopit, Arthur (1937), Indians (pub. 1969). D
Kosinski, Jerzy (1933), Steps. F
Levine, Philip (1928), Not This Pig. V
McCarthy, Cormac (1933), Outer Dark. F
McCarthy, Mary (1912), Hanoi. NF
McConkey, James (1921), Crossroads. NF
MacLeish, Archibald (1892), The Wild Old Wicked Man and
  Other Poems. V; A Continuing Journey. V
McNally, Terrence (1939), Sweet Eros (pub. 1969). D
McPhee, John (1931), The Pine Barrens. NF; A Roomful of
  Hovings. NF
Mailer, Norman (1923), The Idol and the Octopus. NF; The
  Armies of the Night. NF; Miami and the Siege of Chicago.
  NF
Michener, James A. (1907), Iberia. NF
Momaday, N. Scott (1934), House Made of Dawn. F
Moody, Anne (1940), Coming of Age in Mississippi. NF
Morris, Wright (1910), God's Country and My People. NF
Moss, Howard (1922), Second Nature. V
Nabokov, Vladimir (1899), King, Queen, Knave (trans. from
  Russian). F
Oates, Joyce Carol (1938), Expensive People. F; Women in
  Love. V
O'Hara, John (1905), And Other Stories. F
Olson, Charles (1910), Maximus Poems IV, V, VI. V
Oppen, George (1908), On Being Numerous. V
Piercy, Marge (1936), Breaking Camp. V
Price, Reynolds (1933), Love and Work. F
Rukeyser, Muriel (1913), The Speed of Darkness. V
Sackler, Howard (1929), The Great White Hope. D
Saroyan, William (1908), I Used to Believe I Had Forever Now
  I'm Not So Sure. NF
Shapiro, Karl (1913), To Abolish Children. NF, F
Sheed, Wilfrid (1930), The Blacking Factory, & Pennsylvania
  Gothic. F
Simon, Neil (1927), Plaza Suite (pub. 1969). D
Singer, Isaac Bashevis (1904), The Séance. F
Snodgrass, W. D. (1926), After Experience. V
Snyder, Gary (1930), The Back Country. V
Sontag, Susan (1933), Trip to Hanoi. NF
Strand, Mark (1934), Reasons for Moving. V
Sukenick, Ronald (1932), Up. F
Tate, Allen (1899), Essays of Four Decades. NF
Tate, James (1943), Notes of Woe. V; The Torches. V
Theroux, Paul (1941), Fong and the Indians. F
Updike, John (1932), Couples. F
Vidal, Gore (1925), Myra Breckinridge. F
Vonnegut, Kurt, Jr. (1922), Welcome to the Monkey House. F
Wagoner, David (1926), Baby, Come On Inside. F
Wakoski, Diane (1937), Inside the Blood Factory. V
Walker, Alice (1944), Once. V
Warren, Robert Penn (1905), Incarnations: Poems 1966–1968.
  V
Weiss, Theodore (1916), The Last Day and the First. V
Williams, Tennessee (1911), Kingdom of Earth (prod. in 1969 in
  abbreviated form as The Seven Descents of Myrtle). D
Wilson, Edmund (1895), The Fruits of the MLA. NF
Wilson, Lanford (1937), The Gingham Dog (pub. 1969). D
Wolfe, Tom (1931), The Electric Kool-Aid Acid Test. NF; The
  Pump House Gang. NF
Wright, James (1927), Shall We Gather at the River? V

218

1969

Acheson, Dean (1893), Present at the Creation. NF
Ashbery, John (1927), Fragment. V
Auden, W. H. (1907), City Without Walls. V
Berry, Wendell (1934), Findings. V
Berryman, John (1914), The Dream Songs. V
Bishop, Elizabeth (1911), The Complete Poems. V
Brooks, Gwendolyn (1917), Riot. V
Brown, H. Rap (1943), Die, Nigger, Die. NF
Caldwell, Erskine (1903), The Weather Shelter. F
Calisher, Hortense (1911), The New Yorkers. F
Cheever, John (1912), Bullet Park. F
Connell, Evan S., Jr. (1924), Mr. Bridge. F
Coover, Robert (1932), Pricksongs and Descants. F
Creeley, Robert (1926), Pieces. V
Dos Passos, John (1896), The Portugal Story: Three Centuries of Exploration and Discovery. NF
Dugan, Alan (1923), Collected Poems. V
Elder, Lonne (1931), Ceremonies in Dark Old Men. D
Farrell, James T. (1904), Childhood Is Not Forever. F
Ferlinghetti, Lawrence (1919), The Secret Meaning of Things. V
Garrett, George (1929), A Wreath for Garibaldi. F
Ginsberg, Allen (1926), Compositions from Journals. V
Gold, Herbert (1924), The Great American Jackpot. F
Gordone, Charles (1927), No Place to Be Somebody. D
Hall, Donald (1928), The Alligator Bride. V
Hawkes, John (1925), Lunar Landscapes. F
Hellman, Lillian (1915), An Unfinished Woman. NF
Himes, Chester (1909), Blind Man with a Pistol. F
Hoagland, Edward (1932), Notes from the Century Before. NF
Howard, Richard (1929), Untitled Subjects. V; Alone with America. NF
Jarrell, Randall (d. 1965), The Complete Poems. V; The Third Book of Criticism. NF
Jones, LeRoi (1934), Black Magic: Poetry 1961–1967. V
Koch, Kenneth (1925), When the Sun Tries to Go On. V; The Pleasures of Peace. V
Lowell, Robert (1917), Notebook 1967–1968. V; The Voyage. V
Lurie, Alison (1926), Real People. F
McGuane, Thomas (1939), The Sporting Club. F
McPhee, John (1931), Levels of the Game. NF
McPherson, James Alan (1943), Hue and Cry. F
Malamud, Bernard (1914), Pictures of Fidelman. F
Marshall, Paule (1929), The Chosen Place, the Timeless People. F
Merrill, James (1926), The Fire Screen. V
Michaels, Leonard (1933), Going Places. F
Miller, Arthur (1915), In Russia (with Inge Morath). NF
Momaday, N. Scott (1934), The Way to Rainy Mountain. NF
Moss, Howard (1922), Writing Against Time. NF
Nabokov, Vladimir (1899), Ada or Ardor: A Family Chronicle. F
Oates, Joyce Carol (1938), them. F; Anonymous Sins. V
O'Connor, Flannery (d. 1964), Mystery and Manners: Occasional Prose. NF
O'Hara, John (1905), Lovey Childs: A Philadelphian's Story. F
Piercy, Marge (1936), Going Down Fast. F; Hard Loving. V
Pound, Ezra (1885), Drafts and Fragments of Cantos CX–CXVII. V

U.S.–Vietnam peace talks continued in Paris.
War protesters held Vietnam Moratorium Days.
First draft lottery since World War II.
Two American astronauts became first men to walk on the moon.
First SALT (strategic arms limitation) talks between U.S. and Soviet Union.
Airplane highjacking at new high.
Woodstock Music and Art Fair attracted over 400,000 youths.
Jack Kerouac d.

Chinese and Soviet troops clashed on Siberian border.
Charles de Gaulle replaced by Georges Pompidou as president of France.
Alexander Solzhenitsyn expelled from Soviet Union.
Ivy Compton-Burnett d.
Karl Jaspers d.
Fowles's *The French Lieutenant's Woman*.
Greene's *Travels with My Aunt*.
Orton's *What the Butler Saw*.
Enright's *Selected Poems*.
Storey's *The Contractor*.
Brophy's *In Transit*.
Drabble's *The Waterfall*.
Heaney's *Door into the Dark*.
Grass' *Local Anaesthetic*.
Calvino's *The Castle of Crossed Destinies*.
Arrabal's *And They Put Handcuffs on the Flowers*.
Fugard's *Boesman and Lena*.
Le Clézio's *Book of Flights*.
Kundera's *Laughable Loves*.
Vargas Llosa's *Conversation in the Cathedral*.
Abé's *The Ruined Map*.
Mishima's *The Sea of Fertility* (4 vols., 1969–71).

Reed, Ishmael (1938), Yellow Back Radio Broke-Down. F
Ribman, Ronald (1932), Passing Through from Exotic Places
   (pub. 1970). D
Rich, Adrienne (1929), Leaflets. V
Roth, Philip (1933), Portnoy's Complaint. F
Sexton, Anne (1928), Love Poems. V
Singer, Isaac Bashevis (1904), The Estate. F
Snyder, Gary (1930), Earth House Hold. V
Sontag, Susan (1933), Styles of Radical Will. NF
Stafford, Jean (1915), Collected Stories. F
Stegner, Wallace (1909), The Sound of Mountain Water. NF
Steinbeck, John (d. 1968), Journal of a Novel: The East of Eden
   Letters. NF
Sukenick, Ronald (1932), The Death of the Novel and Other
   Stories. F
Taylor, Peter (1917), Collected Stories. F
Theroux, Paul (1941), Girls at Play. F
Updike, John (1932), Midpoint. V
Van Itallie, Jean-Claude (1936), The Serpent: A Ceremony. D
Vidal, Gore (1925), Reflections Upon a Sinking Ship. NF
Vonnegut, Kurt, Jr. (1922), Slaughterhouse Five, or The
   Children's Crusade. F
Wagoner, David (1926), New and Selected Poems. V
Ward, Douglas Turner (1930), The Reckoning (pub. 1970). D
Warren, Robert Penn (1905), Audubon: A Vision. V
West, Jessamyn (1907), Except for Me and Thee. F
Wilbur, Richard (1921), Walking to Sleep. V
Williams, John A. (1925), Sons of Darkness, Sons of Light. F
Williams, Tennessee (1911), In the Bar of a Tokyo Hotel. D
Willingham, Calder (1922), Providence Island. F
Wilson, Edmund (1895), The Dead Sea Scrolls, 1947–1969.
   NF; The Duke of Palermo and Other Plays. D
Woiwode, Larry (1941), What I'm Going to Do, I Think. F
Wolff, Geoffrey (1937), Bad Debts. F
Yates, Richard (1926), A Special Providence. F
Zukofsky, Louis (1904), "A" 13–21. V

1970

Adler, Renata (1938), A Year in the Dark. NF; Toward a
   Radical Middle. NF
Aiken, Conrad (1889), Collected Poems. V
Ammons, A. R. (1926), Uplands. V
Angelou, Maya (1928), I Know Why the Caged Bird Sings. NF
Ashbery, John (1927), The Double Dream of Spring. V
Auden, W. H. (1907), A Certain World. NF
Barthelme, Donald (1931), City Life. F
Bellow, Saul (1915), Mr. Sammler's Planet. F
Berger, Thomas (1924), Vital Parts. F
Berryman, John (1914), Love & Fame. V
Bly, Robert (1926), The Teeth-Mother Naked at Last. V
Booth, Philip (1925), Margins. V
Bourjaily, Vance (1922), Brill Among the Ruins. F
Boyle, Kay (1902), The Long Walk at San Francisco State. NF
Brautigan, Richard (1935), Rommel Drives Deep into Egypt. V
Brinnin, John Malcolm (1916), Skin Diving in the Virgins. V
Buechner, Frederick (1926), The Entrance to Porlock. F
Bullins, Ed (1935), The Duplex (pub. 1971). D
Cassill, R. V. (1919), Dr. Cobb's Game. F
Corso, Gregory (1930), Elegiac Feelings American. V
Davison, Peter (1928), Pretending to Be Asleep. V

Attempted de-escalation of war in
   Indochina.
Bombing of Cambodia; student deaths
   in Kent State protest.
Economic crises and continued
   unemployment.
Increase in PLO airplane hijacking.
Velázquez painting brought record
   $5,544,000 at auction.
John Dos Passos d.
John O'Hara d.
Louise Bogan d.
Journal of Modern Literature (Phila.),
   1970–.

Death of President Nasser of Egypt;
   election of Anwar el-Sadat.
Soviet spacecraft landed on Venus.
E. M. Forster d.
Erich Maria Remarque d.
Bertrand Russell d.
Yukio Mishima d.
Abse's *Selected Poems*.
Larkin's *The Explosion*.

Dickey, James (1923), The Eye-Beaters, Blood, Victory, Madness, Buckhead and Mercy. V; Deliverance. F
Didion, Joan (1934), Play It As It Lays. F
Feiffer, Jules (1929), The White House Murder Case. D
Fox, Paula (1923), Desperate Characters. F
Gardner, John (1933), The Wreckage of Agathon. F
Gass, William H. (1924), Fiction and the Figures of Life. NF
Giovanni, Nikki (1943), Re-Creation. V
Godwin, Gail (1937), The Perfectionists. F
Hayden, Robert (1913), Words in the Mourning Time. V
Hazzard, Shirley (1931), The Bay of Noon. F
Hemingway, Ernest (d. 1961), Islands in the Stream. F
Hersey, John (1914), Letter to the Alumni. NF
Hoagland, Edward (1932), The Courage of Turtles. NF
Hoffman, Daniel G. (1923), Broken Laws. V
Inge, William (1913), Good Luck, Miss Wyckoff. F
Jackson, George (1941), Soledad Brother. NF
Kelley, William Melvin (1937), Dunfords Travels Everywhere. F
Kumin, Maxine (1925), The Nightmare Factory. V
Levertov, Denise (1923), Relearning the Alphabet. V
Lowell, Robert (1917), Notebook (rev. and enl). V
McCarthy, Mary (1912), The Writing on the Wall. NF
McPhee, John (1931), The Crofter and the Laird. NF
Mailer, Norman (1923), Of a Fire on the Moon. NF
Markfield, Wallace (1926), Teitelbaum's Window. F
Meredith, William (1919), Earth Walk: New and Selected Poems. V
Merwin, W. S. (1927), The Carrier of Ladders. V; The Miner's Pale Children. F, NF
Millett, Kate (1934), Sexual Politics. NF
Morrison, Toni (1931), The Bluest Eye. F
Nabokov, Vladimir (1899), Poems and Problems. V, NF
Oates, Joyce Carol (1938), The Wheel of Love. F; Love and Its Derangements. V
Pound, Ezra (1885), The Cantos [1–117]. V
Price, Reynolds (1933), Permanent Errors. F
Purdy, James (1923), Jeremy's Version. F
Schwartz, Delmore (d. 1966), Selected Essays. NF
Seale, Bobby (1936), Seize the Time. NF
Shaw, Irwin (1913), Rich Man, Poor Man. F
Sheed, Wilfrid (1930), Max Jamison. F
Shepard, Sam (1942), Operation Sidewinder. D
Singer, Isaac Bashevis (1904), A Friend of Kafka. F
Smith, William Jay (1918), New and Selected Poems. V
Snyder, Gary (1930), Regarding Wave. V
Sorrentino, Gilbert (1929), Steelwork. F
Strand, Mark (1934), Darker. V
Swados, Harvey (1920), Standing Fast. F
Swenson, May (1919), Iconographs. V
Tyler, Anne (1941), A Slipping-Down Life. F
Updike, John (1932), Bech: A Book. F
Van Duyn, Mona (1921), To See, To Take. V
Vidal, Gore (1925), Two Sisters. F
Vonnegut, Kurt, Jr. (1922), Happy Birthday, Wanda June (pub. 1971). D
Wagoner, David (1926), Working Against Time. V
Wakefield, Dan (1932), Going All the Way. F
Weiss, Theodore (1916), The World Before Us. V
Welty, Eudora (1909), Losing Battles. F
Wideman, John Edgar (1941), Hurry Home. F
Williams, William Carlos (d. 1963), Imaginations: Collected Earlier Prose. NF, F, V

Storey's *Home.*
Anthony Shaffer's *Sleuth.*
Deighton's *Bomber.*
Lodge's *Out of the Shelter.*
Gordimer's *A Guest of Honour.*
Beckett's *Mercier and Camier.*
Adamov's *If Summer Should Return.*
Beauvoir's *The Coming of Age.*
Voznesensky's *Shadow of Sound.*
Donoso's *The Obscene Bird of Night.*

Wilson, Lanford (1939), Serenading Louie (pub. 1976). D
Wolfe, Tom (1931), Radical Chic and Mau-mauing the Flak
  Catchers. NF
Zindel, Paul (1936), The Effect of Gamma Rays on Man-in-the-
  Moon Marigolds (pub. 1971). D
Zinsser, William K. (1922), The Lunacy Boom. NF

1971

Albee, Edward (1928), All Over. D
Ammons, A. R. (1926), Briefings: Poems Small and Easy. V
Anderson, Robert (1917), Solitaire & Double Solitaire (pub.
  1972), D
Baraka, Imamu Amiri (LeRoi Jones) (1934), Raise Race Rays
  Raze: Essays Since 1965. NF
Brinnin, John Malcolm (1916), The Sway of the Grand Saloon.
  NF
Brooks, Gwendolyn (1917), Aloneness. V
Buechner, Frederick (1926), Lion Country. F
Burroughs, William S. (1914), The Wild Boys: A Book of the
  Dead. F
Calisher, Hortense (1911), Queenie. F
Dahlberg, Edward (1900), Confessions. NF
Dickey, James (1923), Sorties. NF
Doctorow, E. L. (1931), The Book of Daniel. F
Donleavy, J. P. (1926), The Onion Eaters. F
Elkin, Stanley (1930), The Dick Gibson Show. F
Epstein, Seymour (1917), The Dream Museum. F
Fitzgerald, Robert (1910), Spring Shade: Poems 1931–1970. V
Friedman, Bruce Jay (1930), Steambath. D
Fuchs, Daniel (1909), West of the Rockies. F
Gaines, Ernest J. (1933), The Autobiography of Miss Jane
  Pittman. F
Gardner, John (1933), Grendel. F
Garrett, George (1929), Death of the Fox. F
Gass, William H. (1924), Willie Masters' Lonesome Wife. F
Giovanni, Nikki (1943), Gemini: An Extended Autobiographical
  Statement. NF
Gold, Herbert (1929), The Magic Will. F, NF
Grau, Shirley Ann (1929), The Condor Passes. F
Guare, John (1938), The House of Blue Leaves (pub. 1972). D
Guthrie, A. B., Jr. (1902), Arfive. F
Hawkes, John (1925), The Blood Oranges. F
Herlihy, James Leo (1927), The Season of the Witch. F
Hollander, John (1929), The Night Mirror. V
Horovitz, Israel (1939), Acrobats and Line: Two Plays. D
Howard, Richard (1939), Findings. V
Inge, William (1913), My Son Is a Splendid Driver. F
Jones, James (1921), The Merry Month of May. F
Kerouac, Jack (d. 1969), Pic. F
Kinnell, Galway (1927), The Book of Nightmares. V
Kizer, Carolyn (1926), Midnight Was My Cry. V
Knowles, John (1926), The Paragon. F
Kosinski, Jerzy (1933), Being There. F
Kumin, Maxine (1925), The Abduction. F
Kunitz, Stanley (1905), The Testing Tree. V
Levertov, Denise (1923), To Stay Alive. V
McCarthy, Mary (1912), Birds of America. F
McConkey, James (1921), A Journey to Sabalin. F
McGuane, Thomas (1939), The Bushwacked Piano. F

26th Amendment (voting age reduced
  to 18) ratified.
Active participation in Vietnam War
  gradually reduced.
Anti-war protests continued
  nationwide.
Two successful U.S. manned lunar
  landings.
New York Times published classified
  Pentagon Papers.
Kennedy Center for the Performing Arts
  opened in Washington.
Dance Theater of Harlem founded.
Ogden Nash d.
Walter Van Tilburg Clark d.
Reinhold Niebuhr d.

U.N. admitted Communist China and
  expelled Nationalist (Taiwan)
  Chinese.
George Seferis d.
Burgess's *MF.*
Pinter's *Old Times.*
Gray's *Butley.*
Storey's *The Changing Room.*
Kingsley Amis's *Girl, 20.*
Geoffrey Hill's *Mercian Hymns.*
Lessing's *Briefing for a Descent into
  Hell.*
Böll's *Group Portrait with Lady.*
Solzhenitsyn's *August 1914.*
Naipaul's *In a Free State.*
Hochhuth's *The Midwife.*
Butor's *Where.*
Montale's *Satura.*
Richler's *St. Urbain's Horseman.*

McHale, Tom (1942?), Farragan's Retreat. F
MacLeish, Archibald (1892), Scratch. D
McPhee, John (1931), Encounters with the Archdruid. NF
Mailer, Norman (1923), The Prisoner of Sex. NF
Malamud, Bernard (1914), The Tenants. F
Matthiessen, Peter (1927), Blue Meridian. NF
Morris, Wright (1910), Fire Sermon. F
Moss, Howard (1922), Selected Poems. V
Oates, Joyce Carol (1938), Wonderland. F
O'Connor, Flannery (d. 1964), The Complete Stories. F
Olson, Charles (d. 1970), The Archaeologist of Morning. V
Ozick, Cynthia (1928), The Pagan Rabbi. F
Percy, Walker (1916), Love in the Ruins. F
Plath, Sylvia (d. 1963), Crossing the Water. V
Rabe, David (1940), The Basic Training of Pavlo Hummel (pub.
    1973). D; Sticks and Bones (pub. 1973). D
Reeves, Donald (1952), Notes of a Processed Brother. NF
Ribman, Ronald (1932), Fingernails Blue as Flowers (pub.
    1973). D
Rich, Adrienne (1929), The Will to Change. V
"Ross Macdonald" (1915), The Underground Man. F
Roth, Philip (1933), Our Gang. F, NF
Selby, Hubert, Jr. (1928), The Room. F
Sexton, Anne (1928), Transformations. V
Shepard, Sam (1943), Mad Dog Blues. D
Simon, Neil (1927), The Prisoner of Second Avenue (pub. 1972).
    D
Simpson, Louis (1923), Adventures of the Letter I. V
Stegner, Wallace (1909), Angle of Repose. F
Swenson, May (1919), More Poems to Solve. V
Tate, Allen (1899), The Swimmers and Selected Poems. V
Theroux, Paul (1941), Jungle Lovers. F
Updike, John (1932), Rabbit Redux. F
Wakoski, Diane (1937), The Motorcycle Betrayal Poems. V
Warren, Robert Penn (1905), Meet Me in the Green Glen. F
Welty, Eudora (1909), One Time, One Place: Mississippi in the
    Depression. NF
Wilson, Edmund (1895), Upstate. NF
Wouk, Herman (1915), The Winds of War. F
Wright, James (1927), Collected Poems. V

1972

Ammons, A. R. (1926), Collected Poems 1951–1971. V
Ashbery, John (1927), Three Poems. V
Auden, W. H. (1907), Epistle to a Godson. V
Baldwin, James (1924), No Name in the Street. NF
Baraka, Imamu Amiri (LeRoi Jones) (1924), Spirit Reach. V
Barth, John (1930), Chimera. F
Barthelme, Donald (1931), Sadness. F
Behrman, S. N. (1893), People in a Diary: A Memoir. NF
Berryman, John (1914), Delusions, Etc. V
Buechner, Frederick (1926), Open Heart. F
Calisher, Hortense (1911), Standard Dreaming. F; Herself. NF
Conroy, Pat (1945), The Water Is Wide. F
Coover, Robert (1932), A Theological Position: Four Plays. D
Creeley, Robert (1926), A Day Book. V, NF
DeLillo, Don (1936), End Zone. F
Eberhart, Richard (1904), Fields of Grace. V
Elkin, Stanley (1930), The Making of Ashenden. F
Gardner, John (1933), The Sunlight Dialogues. F

U.S. ground troops removed from Vietnam.
Nixon visited Communist China and Soviet Union.
Governor George Wallace wounded in assassination attempt.
Ban on travel to China lifted.
Stockmarket closed above 1,000 for first time.
Edmund Wilson d.
Ezra Pound d.
Marianne Moore d.
John Berryman d.

Terrorists murdered eight Israeli athletes at Olympic Games in Munich.
Sir John Betjeman named poet laureate of England.
L. P. Hartley d.

Gelber, Jack (1932), Sleep. D
Ginsberg, Allen (1926), The Fall of America: Poems of These States, 1965–1971. V; The Gates of Wrath. V
Giovanni, Nikki (1943), My House. V
Godwin, Gail (1937), Glass People. F
Gold, Herbert (1924), My Last Two Thousand Years. NF
Gordon, Caroline (1895), The Glory of Hera. F
Halberstam, David (1934), The Best and the Brightest. NF
Hayden, Robert (1913), The Night-Blooming Cereus. V
Hollander, John (1929), Town & Country Matters. V
Irving, John (1942), The Water-Method Man. F
Isherwood, Christopher (1904), Kathleen and Frank. NF
Kerouac, Jack (1922), Visions of Cody. NF
Kumin, Maxine (1925), Up Country. V
Levertov, Denise (1923), Footprints. V
Levin, Ira (1929), The Stepford Wives. F.
Levine, Philip (1928), They Feed They Lion. V
MacLeish, Archibald (1982), The Human Season. V
Mailer, Norman (1923), St. George and the Godfather. NF; Existential Errands. NF
Matthiessen, Peter (1927), The Tree Where Man Was Born. NF
Merrill, James (1926), Braving the Elements. V
Miller, Arthur (1915), The Creation of the World and Other Business (pub. 1973). D
Miller, Jason (1939), The Championship Season. D
Millhauser, Steven (1943), Edwin Mullhouse: The Life and Death of an American Writer, 1943–1954, by Jeffrey Cartwright. F
Milosz, Czeslaw (1911), Selected Poems. V
Morgan, Frederick (1922), A Book of Change. V
Nabokov, Vladimir (1899), Transparent Things. F
Nemerov, Howard (1920), Reflections on Poetry and Politics. NF
Oates, Joyce Carol (1938), Marriages and Infidelities. F
O'Hara, Frank (d. 1966), The Collected Poems. V
O'Hara, John (d. 1970), The Ewings. F; The Time Element. F
Plath, Sylvia (d. 1963), Winter Trees. V
Price, Reynolds (1933), Things Themselves: Essays and Scenes. NF
Purdy, James (1923), I Am Elijah Thrush. F
Reed, Ishmael (1938), Mumbo Jumbo. F; Conjure. V
Ribman, Ronald (1938), A Break in the Skin. D
Roth, Philip (1933), The Breast. F
Sexton, Anne (1928), The Book of Folly. V
Shepard, Sam (1943), The Tooth of Crime (pub. 1974). D
Simpson, Louis (1923), North of Jamaica. NF
Singer, Isaac Bashevis (1904), Enemies: A Love Story. F
Spencer, Elizabeth (1921), The Snare. F
Styron, William (1925), In the Clap Shack (pub. 1973). D
Tate, James (1943), Absences. V
Theroux, Paul (1941), Sinning with Annie. F
Tyler, Anne (1941), The Clock Winder. F
Updike, John (1932), Museums and Women. F
Vidal, Gore (1925), Homage to Daniel Shays: Collected Essays 1952–1972. NF
Wagoner, David (1926), Riverbed. V
Walker, Joseph A. (1935), The River Niger (pub. 1973). D
Welty, Eudora (1909), The Optimist's Daughter. F
Williams, John A. (1925), Captain Blackman. F
Williams, Tennessee (1911), Small Craft Warnings. D
Willingham, Calder (1922), Rambling Rose. F

Henry de Montherlant d.
Jules Romains d.
Yasunari Kawabata d.
Stoppard's Jumpers.
Kinsella's Butcher's Dozen.
Adams's Watership Down.
Drabble's The Needle's Eye.
Renault's The Persian Boy.
Berger's G.
Gilliatt's Nobody's Business.
John Fuller's Cannibals and Missionaries.
Leonard Cohen's The Energy of Slaves.
Beauvoir's All Said and Done.
Calvino's Invisible Cities.
Naipaul's The Overcrowded Barracoon.
Yevtushenko's Under the Skin of the Statue of Liberty.
Voznesensky's The Glance.
Borges's The Gold of the Tigers.
Sarraute's Do You Hear Them?
Bonnefoy's The Country Beyond.

1973

Algren, Nelson (1909), The Last Carousel. F
Anderson, Robert (1917), After. F
Berger, Thomas (1924), Regiment of Women. F
Berry, Wendell (1934), The Country of Marriage. V
Berryman, John (d. 1972), Recovery. F
Bly, Robert (1926), Sleepers Joining Hands. V
Brodsky, Joseph (1940), Selected Poems. V
Burroughs, William S. (1914), Exterminator! F
Calisher, Hortense (1911), Eagle Eye. F
Carruth, Hayden (1921), From Snow and Rock, from Chaos: Poems 1965–1972. V
Cheever, John (1912), The World of Apples. F
Connell, Evan S., Jr. (1924), Points of a Compass Rose. V
Cowley, Malcolm (1898), A Second Flowering: Works and Days of the Lost Generation. NF
Davison, Peter (1928), Half Remembered: A Personal History. NF
DeLillo, Don (1936), Great Jones Street. F
Donleavy, J. P. (1926), A Fairy Tale of New York. F
Elkin, Stanley (1930), Searches and Seizures. F
Epstein, Seymour (1917), Looking for Fred Schmidt. F
Ferlinghetti, Lawrence (1919), Open Eye, Open Heart. V
Gardner, John (1933), Nickel Mountain. F; Jason and Medeia. V
Garrett, George (1929), The Magic Striptease. F
Grau, Shirley Ann (1929), The Wind Shifting West. F
Hazzard, Shirley (1931), Defeat of an Ideal: A Study of the Self-Destruction of the United States. NF
Hellman, Lillian (1905), Pentimento: A Book of Portraits. NF
Hoagland, Edward (1932), Walking the Dead Diamond River. NF
Humphrey, William (1924), Proud Flesh. F
Jones, James (1921), A Touch of Danger. F
Jong, Erica (1942), Fear of Flying. F
Justice, Donald (1925), Departures. V
Kazin, Alfred (1915), Bright Book of Life. NF
Kosinski, Jerzy (1933), The Devil Tree. F
Levertov, Denise (1923), The Poet in the World. NF
Lowell, Robert (1917), The Dolphin. V; History. V; For Lizzie and Harriet. V
McCarthy, Cormac (1933), Child of God. F
McGuane, Thomas (1939), Ninety-two in the Shade. F
McPhee, John (1931), The Deltoid Pumpkin Seed. NF
Mailer, Norman (1923), Marilyn. NF
Malamud, Bernard (1914), Rembrandt's Hat. F
Medoff, Mark (1940), When You Comin' Back, Red Ryder? (pub. 1974). D
Merwin, W. S. (1927), Writings to an Unfinished Accompaniment. V
Morris, Wright (1910), A Life. F
Morrison, Toni (1931), Sula. F
Nabokov, Vladimir (1899), A Russian Beauty, and Other Stories. F
Nemerov, Howard (1920), Gnomes & Occasions. V
Oates, Joyce Carol (1938), Do With Me What You Will. F; Angel Fire. V
Piercy, Marge (1936), Small Changes. F; To Be of Use. V
Pynchon, Thomas (1937), Gravity's Rainbow. F
Rabe, David (1940), The Orphan (pub. 1975). D

U.S.–Vietnam peace agreements signed in Paris.
Watergate scandals revealed high-level governmental corruption.
Vice-President Agnew resigned; Gerald R. Ford replaced him.
First U.S. liaison office opened in Communist China.
William Inge d.
Pearl Buck d.
W. H. Auden d.
Conrad Aiken d.
S. N. Behrman d.

Organization of Petroleum Exporting Countries (OPEC) formed.
Sir Noel Coward d.
Elizabeth Bowen d.
J. R. R. Tolkien d.
Pablo Neruda d.
Murdoch's The Black Prince.
Peter Shaffer's Equus.
Fowles's Poems.
John Fuller's Epistles to Several Persons.
Abse's Funland and Other Poems.
Frayn's Sweet Dreams.
Greene's The Honorary Consul.
Akhmatova's Tale Without a Hero (posth.).
Solzhenitsyn's The Gulag Archipelago (3 vols., 1973–75).
Kundera's Life Is Elsewhere.
Guillén's And Other Poems.
Montale's Diary of 1971–1972.
Cortázar's A Manual for Manuel.
Vargas Llosa's Captain Pantoja and the Special Service.
Donoso's Sacred Families: Three Novellas.
Abé's The Box Man.
Fugard's Sizwe Bansi Is Dead.

Reed, Ishmael (1938), Chattanooga. V
Rich, Adrienne (1929), Diving into the Wreck. V
Roth, Philip (1933), The Great American Novel. F
Sarton, May (1912), Journal of a Solitude. NF
Sheed, Wilfrid (1930), People Will Always Be Kind. F
Singer, Isaac Bashevis (1904), A Crown of Feathers. F
Stern, Richard G. (1928), Other Men's Daughters. F
Strand, Mark (1934), The Sargeantville Notebook. V; The Story
  of Our Lives. V
Sukenick, Ronald (1932), Out. F
Theroux, Paul (1941), Saint Jack. F
Van Duyn, Mona (1921), Merciful Disguises. V
Vidal, Gore (1925), Burr. F
Vonnegut, Kurt, Jr. (1922), Breakfast of Champions; or,
  Goodbye Blue Monday! F
Wakefield, Dan (1932), Starting Over. F
Walker, Alice (1944), Revolutionary Petunias. V
Wideman, John Edgar (1941), The Lynchers. F
Wilbur, Richard (1921), Opposites. V
Wilder, Thornton (1897), Theophilus North. F
Williams, John A. (1925), Flashbacks. NF
Williams, Tennessee (1911), Out Cry. D
Wilson, Lanford (1938), The Hot l Baltimore. D
Wolfe, Tom (1931), The New Journalism. NF
Wright, James (1927), Two Citizens. V

1974

Adams, Alice (1926), Families and Survivors. F
Ammons, A. R. (1926), Sphere: The Form of a Motion. V
Angelou, Maya (1928), Gather Together in My Name. NF
Auden, W. H. (d. 1973), Thank You, Fog. V
Baldwin, James (1924) If Beale Street Could Talk. F
Barthelme, Donald (1931), Guilty Pleasures. F
Benchley, Peter (1940), Jaws. F
Buechner, Frederick (1926), Love Feast. F
Condon, Richard (1915), Winter Kills. F
Connell, Evan S., Jr. (1924), The Connoisseur. F
Corso, Gregory (1934), Earth Egg. V
Davenport, Guy (1927), Tatlin! F
Davis, Angela (1944), Autobiography. NF
Davison, Peter (1928), Walking the Boundaries: Poems 1957–
  1974. V
Dillard, Annie (1945), Pilgrim at Tinker Creek. NF
Dugan, Alan (1925), Poems 4. V
Gardner, John (1933), The King's Indian: Stories and Tales. F
Gill, Brendan (1914), Ways of Loving. F
Godwin, Gail (1937), The Odd Woman. F
Goyen, William (1915), Come the Restorer. F
Grau, Shirley Ann (1929), Evidence of Love. F
Hawkes, John (1925), Death, Sleep & the Traveler. F
Heller, Joseph (1923), Something Happened. F
Hoagland, Edward (1932), The Moose on the Wall. NF
Hoffman, Daniel G. (1923), The Center of Attention. V
Hollander, John (1929), The Head of the Bed. V
Howard, Maureen (1930), Before My Time. F
Howard, Richard (1929), Two-Part Inventions. V; Preferences.
  NF
Irving, John (1942), The 158-Pound Marriage. F
Jones, James (1921), Viet Journal. NF

Watergate scandals forced Nixon's
  resignation.
President Ford appointed Nelson
  Rockefeller to vice-presidency.
FBI and CIA practices scrutinized by
  Justice Department.
Massive auto industry setbacks.
Expo '74 opened in Spokane.
Joseph H. Hirshhorn Museum opened
  in Washington.
John Crowe Ransom d.
Anne Sexton d.

Valéry Giscard d'Estaing became
  president of France.
Golda Meir resigned as prime minister
  of Israel.
Great Britain outlawed Irish Republican
  Army.
Henry Green d.
Cyril Connolly d.
Pär Lagerkvist d.
Marcel Pagnol d.
Larkin's *High Windows*.
Burgess's *Napoleon Symphony*.
Bainbridge's *The Bottle Factory Outing*.
Fowles's *The Ebony Tower*.
Ayckbourn's *The Norman Conquests*.
O'Brien's *A Scandalous Woman*.
Durrell's *Monsieur; or, The Prince of
  Darkness*.
Pritchett's *The Camberwell Beauty*.
Sisson's *In the Trojan Ditch*.
Stoppard's *Travesties*.
Böll's *The Lost Honor of Katharina
  Blum*.

Kinnell, Galway (1927), The Avenue Bearing the Initial of Christ into the New World. V

Knowles, John (1926), Spreading Fires. F

Kunitz, Stanley (1905), The Coat Without a Seam. V; The Terrible Threshold. V

Lurie, Alison (1926), The War Between the Tates. F

McCarthy, Mary (1912), The Mask of State: Watergate Portraits. NF

McNally, Terrence (1939), Bad Habits. D

McPhee, John (1931), The Curve of Binding Energy. NF

Madden, David (1933), Bijou. F

Mamet, David (1947), Sexual Perversity in Chicago (pub. 1978). D

Markfield, Wallace (1926), You Could Live If They Let You. F

Michener, James A. (1907), Centennial. F

Miles, Josephine (1911), To All Appearances. V

Millett, Kate (1934), Flying. NF

Nabokov, Vladimir (1899), Look at the Harlequins! F

Nims, John Frederick (1916), Western Wind. V

Oates, Joyce Carol (1938), The Hungry Ghosts. F; The Goddess and Other Women. F

O'Hara, John (d. 1970), Good Samaritan. F

Paley, Grace (1922), Enormous Changes at the Last Minute. F

Pirsig, Robert M. (1928), Zen and the Art of Motorcycle Maintenance. NF

Purdy, James (1923), The House of the Solitary Maggot. F

Rabe, David (1940), In the Boom Boom Room (pub. 1975). D

Reed, Ishmael (1938), The Last Days of Louisiana Red. F

Roth, Philip (1933), My Life as a Man. F

Sarton, May (1912), Collected Poems. V

Sexton, Anne (1928), The Death Notebooks. V

Shepard, Sam (1943), Geography of a Horse Dreamer. D

Snyder, Gary (1930), Turtle Island. V

Stone, Robert (1937), Dog Soldiers. F

Terkel, Studs (1912), Working. NF

Theroux, Paul (1941), The Black House. F

Trillin, Calvin (1935), American Fried. NF

Tyler, Anne (1941), Celestial Navigation. F

Updike, John (1932), Buchanan Dying. D

Vidal, Gore (1925), Myron. F

Vonnegut, Kurt, Jr. (1922), Wampeters, Foma and Granfalloons. NF

Wagoner, David (1926), Sleeping in the Woods. V; The Road to Many a Wonder. F

Warren, Robert Penn (1905), Or Else—Poem/Poems 1968–1974. V

Williams, Tennessee (1911), Eight Mortal Ladies Possessed. F

Wolff, Geoffrey (1937), The Sightseer. F

Arrabal's *The Ballad of the Ghost Train*.
Paz's *Children of the Mire*.
Canetti's *Earwitness: Fifty Characters*.
Yourcenar's *Pious Memories*.
Gordimer's *The Conservationist*.
Solzhenitsyn's *Prussian Nights*.
Voznesensky's *Set the Bird Free*.
Coetzee's *Dusklands*.

1975

Albee, Edward (1928), Seascape. D

Ammons, A. R. (1926), Diversifications. V

Ashbery, John (1927), The Vermont Notebook. V; Self-Portrait in a Convex Mirror. V

Barthelme, Donald (1931), The Dead Father. F

Bellow, Saul (1915), Humboldt's Gift. F

Berger, Thomas (1924), Sneaky People. F

Boyle, Kay (1902), The Underground Woman. F

Two attempted assassinations of President Ford.
U.S. and Soviet spaceships succeeded in first space linkage.
Court-ordered busing implemented school desegregation.
Elizabeth Ann Bayley Seton proclaimed first U.S.-born saint.
Lionel Trilling d.

Bullins, Ed (1935), The Taking of Miss Janie. D
Burroughs, William S. (1914), The Last Words of Dutch Schultz. F
Cain, James M. (1892), Rainbow's End. F
Calisher, Hortense (1911), Collected Stories. F
Clavell, James (1924), Shōgun. F
Doctorow, E. L. (1931), Ragtime. F
Dubus, Andre (1936), Separate Flights. F
Ford, Jesse Hill (1938), The Raider. F
Gaddis, William (1922), JR. F
Giovanni, Nikki (1943), The Women and the Men. V
Goyen, William (1915), The Collected Stories. F
Guthrie, A. B., Jr. (1901), The Last Valley. F
Hayden, Robert (1913), Angle of Ascent. V
Helprin, Mark (1947), A Dove of the East and Other Stories. F
Hollander, John (1929), Tales Told of the Father. V
Jones, James (1921), WW II. NF
Kennedy, William (1928), Legs. F
Koch, Kenneth (1925), The Act of Love. V
Kosinski, Jerzy (1933), Cockpit. F
Kumin, Maxine (1925), House, Bridge, Fountain, Gate. V
Kunitz, Stanley (1905), A Kind of Order, A Kind of Folly. NF
Levertov, Denise (1923), The Freeing of the Dust. V
Lytle, Andrew (1902), A Wake for the Living. NF
MacLeish, Archibald (1892), The Great American Fourth of July Parade. D
McNally, Terrence (1939), The Ritz (pub. 1976). D
McPhee, John (1931), Pieces of the Frame. NF; The Survival of the Bark Canoe. NF
Mailer, Norman (1923), The Fight. NF
Mamet, David (1947), American Buffalo (pub. 1977). D
Matthiessen, Peter (1927), Far Tortuga. F
Meredith, William (1919), Hazard the Painter. V
Michaels, Leonard (1933), I Would Have Saved Them If I Could. F
Moss, Howard (1922), Buried City. V
Nemerov, Howard (1920), The Western Approaches. V
Oates, Joyce Carol (1938), The Assassins. F; The Seduction and Other Stories. F
Olson, Charles (d. 1970), The Maximus Poems, Volume Three. V
Oppen, George (1908), The Collected Poems. V
Percy, Walker, (1916), The Message in the Bottle. NF
Price, Reynolds (1933), The Surface of the Earth. F
Purdy, James (1923), In a Shallow Grave. F
Rich, Adrienne (1929), Poems: Selected and New. V
Roth, Philip (1933), Reading Myself and Others. NF
Sarton, May (1912), Crucial Conversations. F
Sexton, Anne (d. 1974), The Awful Rowing Toward God. V
Shapiro, Karl (1913), The Poetry Wreck: Selected Essays 1950–1970. NF
Simpson, Louis (1923), Three on a Tower. NF
Singer, Isaac Bashevis (1904), Passions. F
Snodgrass, W. D. (1926), In Radical Pursuit. NF
Stewart, Donald Ogden (1894), By a Stroke of Luck: An Autobiography. NF
Sukenick, Ronald (1932), 98.6. F
Tate, Allen (1899), Memoirs & Opinions. F
Theroux, Paul (1941), The Great Railway Bazaar. NF
Updike, John (1932), A Month of Sundays. F; Picked-Up Pieces. NF
Wagoner, David (1926), Tracker. F

Thornton Wilder d.
Vincent Sheean d.

Helsinki Accord (peace and human rights) signed by 35 nations.
Juan Carlos I proclaimed king of Spain.
P. G. Wodehouse d.
Rex Stout d.
Saint-John Perse d.
Robert C. Sherriff d.
Graves's *Collected Poems.*
Gray's *Otherwise Engaged.*
Pinter's *No Man's Land.*
D. M. Thomas's *Love and Other Poems.*
Drabble's *The Realms of Gold.*
Bainbridge's *Sweet William.*
John Fuller's *The Mountain in the Sea.*
Sisson's *The Corridor.*
McIlvanney's *Docherty.*
Ballard's *High-Rise.*
B. S. Johnson's *See the Old Lady Decently.*
Lodge's *Changing Places.*
Heaney's *North.*
Bonnefoy's *In the Lure of the Threshold.*
Robbe-Grillet's *Topology of a Phantom City.*
Naipaul's *Guerrillas.*
Solzhenitsyn's *The Oak and the Calf.*
Handke's *A Moment of True Feeling.*
Frisch's *Montauk.*
Fuentes's *Terra Nostra.*
García Márquez's *The Autumn of the Patriarch.*
Voinovich's *The Life and Extraordinary Adventures of Private Ivan Chonkin.*
Vladimov's *Faithful Ruslan.*

Wakoski, Diane (1937), Virtuoso Literature for Two and Four
  Hands. V
Warren, Robert Penn (1905), Democracy and Poetry. NF
West, Jessamyn (1907), The Massacre at Fall Creek. F
Williams, John A. (1925), Mothersill and the Foxes. F
Williams, Tennessee (1911), Memoirs. NF; Moise and the
  World of Reason. F.
Willingham, Calder (1922), The Big Nickel. F
Wilson, Lanford (1937), The Mound Builders (pub. 1976). D
Woiwode, Larry (1941), Beyond the Bedroom Wall. F
Wolfe, Tom (1931), The Painted Word. NF
Wolff, Tobias (1945), Ugly Rumours. F
Yates, Richard (1926), Disturbing the Peace. F
Zukofsky, Louis (1904), "A" 22 & 23. V

1976

Adler, Renata (1938), Speedboat. F
Alther, Lisa (1944), Kinflicks. F
Angelou, Maya (1928), Singin' and Swingin' and Gettin' Merry
  Like Christmas. NF
Baldwin, James (1924), The Devil Finds Work. NF
Barthelme, Donald (1931), Amateurs. F
Beattie, Ann (1947), Chilly Scenes of Winter. F
Bellow, Saul (1915), To Jerusalem and Back. NF
Berryman, John (d. 1972), The Freedom of the Poet. NF
Bishop, Elizabeth (1911), Geography III. V
Booth, Philip (1925), Available Light. V
Bourjaily, Vance (1922), Now Playing at Canterbury. F
Brautigan, Richard (1935), Sombrero Fallout. F
Bryan, C.D.B. (1936), Friendly Fire. NF
Carver, Raymond (1938), Will You Please Be Quiet, Please? F
Connell, Evan S., Jr. (1924), Double Honeymoon. F
Conroy, Pat (1945), The Great Santini. F
Creeley, Robert (1926), Selected Poems. V
DeLillo, Don (1936), Ratner's Star. F
Dickey, James (1923), The Zodiac. V
Duberman, Martin (1930), Visions of Kerouac (pub. 1977). D
Elkin, Stanley (1930), The Franchiser. F
Feiffer, Jules (1929), Knock! Knock! D
Ferlinghetti, Lawrence (1920), Who Are We Now? V
Fox, Paula (1923), The Widow's Children. F
Gardner, John (1933), October Light. F
Gass, William H. (1924), On Being Blue. NF
Godwin, Gail (1937), Dream Children. F
Gray, Francine du Plessix (1930), Lovers and Tyrants. F
Guare, John (1938), Rich and Famous (pub. 1979). D
Haley, Alex (1921), Roots. NF
Hawkes, John (1925), Travesty. F
Hellman, Lillian (1905), Scoundrel Time. NF
Hoagland, Edward (1932), Red Wolves and Black Bears. NF
Hollander, John (1929), Reflecting on Espionage. V
Horovitz, Israel (1939), The Primary English Class (pub. 1979).
  D
Howard, Richard (1929), Fellow Feelings. V
Isherwood, Christopher (1904), Christopher and His Kind. NF
Kingston, Maxine Hong (1940), The Woman Warrior. F, NF
Levine, Philip (1928), The Names of the Lost. V
Lowell, Robert (1917), Selected Poems. V
McHale, Tom (1942?), School Spirit. F

U.S. withdrew remaining troops from
Thailand.
U.S. spaceship *Viking I* landed on
Mars.
First major reform of U.S. copyright
statutes.
The Village Voice (New York)
published congressional report on
intelligence agencies.
Bicentennial anniversary of U.S.
independence.
Nationwide activity of Equal Rights
Amendment for women.
Supersonic commercial airplanes
began transatlantic service.
Saul Bellow awarded Nobel Prize in
literature.

Dame Agatha Christie d.
André Malraux d.
Stoppard's *Dirty Linen; New-Found-
Land.*
Gunn's *Jack Straw's Castle.*
Bradbury's *Who Do You Think You
Are?*
Bainbridge's *A Quiet Life.*
Sisson's *Anchises.*
Robert Nye's *Falstaff.*
Stevenson's *A Man Called Intrepid.*
Brian Moore's *The Doctor's Wife.*
Hochhuth's *Death of a Hunter.*
Handke's *The Lefthanded Woman.*
Foucault's *The History of Sexuality.*
Kundera's *The Farewell Party.*
Kopelev's *To Be Preserved Forever.*
Bondarev's *The Shore.*
Zinoviev's *The Yawning Heights.*

Mailer, Norman (1923), Some Honorable Men: Political
Conventions, 1960–1972. NF
Manfred, Frederick (Feike Feikema) (1912), The Manly-
Hearted Woman. F
Merrill, James (1926), Divine Comedies. V
Momaday, N. Scott (1934), The Gourd Dancer. V; The Names.
NF
Morris, Wright (1910), Real Losses, Imaginary Gains. F.
Moss, Howard (1922), A Swim off the Rocks. V
Nabokov, Vladimir (1899), Details of a Sunset and Other
Stories. F
Oates, Joyce Carol (1938), Childwold. F; Crossing the Border.
F
Ozick, Cynthia (1928), Bloodshed and Three Novellas. F
Piercy, Marge (1936), Woman on the Edge of Time. F; Living
in the Open. V
Rabe, David (1940), Streamers (pub. 1977). D
Reed, Ishmael (1938), Flight to Canada. F
Ribman, Ronald (1932), The Poison Tree (pub. 1977). D
Rich, Adrienne (1929), Of Woman Born. NF
Selby, Hubert, Jr. (1928), The Demon. F
Shapiro, Karl (1913), Adult Bookstore. V
Simpson, Louis (1923), Searching for the Ox. V
Singer, Isaac Bashevis (1904), A Little Boy in Search of God.
NF
Stegner, Wallace (1909), The Spectator Bird. F
Strand, Mark (1934), Another Republic. V
Tate, James (1943), Viper Jazz. V
Theroux, Paul (1941), The Family Arsenal. F
Tyler, Anne (1941), Searching for Caleb. F
Updike, John (1932), Marry Me. F
Uris, Leon (1924), Trinity. F
Vidal, Gore (1925), 1876. F
Vonnegut, Kurt, Jr. (1922), Slapstick; or, Lonesome No More! F
Wagoner, David (1926), Collected Poems. V; Traveling Light. V
Wakefield, Dan (1932), All Her Children. F
Walker, Alice (1944), Meridian. F
Weiss, Theodore (1916), Fireweeds. V
Wilbur, Richard (1926), The Mind-Reader. V; Responses:
Prose Pieces 1948–1974. NF
Williams, John A. (1925), The Junior Bachelor Society. F
Wolfe, Tom (1931), Mauve Gloves and Madmen, Clutter and
Vine. F, NF
Wright, James (1927), Moments of the Italian Summer. V
Yates, Richard (1926), The Easter Parade. F

1977

Albee, Edward (1928), Counting the Ways; Listening. D
Ammons, A. R. (1926), The Snow Poems. V; The Selected
Poems, 1951–1977. V
Ashbery, John (1927), Houseboat Days. V
Berger, Thomas (1924), Who Is Teddy Villanova? F
Berry, Wendell (1934), Clearing. V
Berryman, John (d. 1972), Henry's Fate and Other Poems,
1967–1972. V
Bly, Robert (1926), This Body Is Made of Camphor and
Gopherwood V
Buechner, Frederick (1926), Treasure Hunt. F
Burroughs, William S. (1914), Junky. F
Calisher, Hortense (1911), On Keeping Women. F

President Carter pardoned Vietnam
War draft evaders.
James R. Schlesinger headed first
Department of Energy.
U.S. and Panama signed treaties
granting control of the Canal to
Panama in A.D. 2000
First National Women's Conference, in
Houston.
General Motors introduced first
American diesel-powered
automobile.
Spoleto Festival opened first American
season in Charleston, S.C.

Cheever, John (1912), Falconer. F
Coburn, Donald L. (1938), The Gin Game. D
Coover, Robert (1932), The Public Burning. F
Corman, Avery (1935), Kramer vs. Kramer. F
Cristofer, Michael (1945), The Shadow Box. D
Davison, Peter (1928), A Voice in the Mountain. V
DeLillo, Don (1936), Players. F
Didion, Joan (1934), A Book of Common Prayer. F
Dubus, Andre (1936), Adultery and Other Choices. F
Dunne, John Gregory (1932), True Confessions. F
French, Marilyn (1929), The Women's Room. F
Ginsberg, Allen (1926), Mind's Breath: Poems 1972–1977. V
Guare, John (1938), Landscape of the Body (pub. 1978). D
Hecht, Anthony (1923), Millions of Strange Shadows. V
Helprin, Mark (1947), Refiner's Fire: The Life and Adventures
    of Marshall Pearl, A Foundling. F
Herr, Michael (1940), Dispatches. NF
Hersey, John (1914), The Walnut Door. F
Hoffman, Daniel G. (1923), Able Was I Ere I Saw Elba. V.
Innaurato, Albert (1948), Gemini (pub. 1978),. D; The
    Transfiguration of Benno Blimpie (pub. 1978). D
Koch, Kenneth (1925), The Duplications. V
Kosinski, Jerzy (1933), Blind Date. F
Lowell, Robert (1917), Day by Day. V
McPhee, John (1931), Coming into the Country. NF
McPherson, James Alan (1943), Elbow Room. F
Mailer, Norman (1923), Genius and Lust. NF
Mamet, David (1947), A Life in the Theatre (pub. 1978).
    D; The Water Engine (pub. 1978). D
Maxwell, William (1908), Over by the River. F
Merwin, W. S. (1927), The Compass Flower. V; Houses and
    Travellers. NF
Millett, Kate (1934), Sita. NF
Millhauser, Steven (1943), Portrait of a Romantic. F
Morgan, Frederick (1922), Poems of the Two Worlds. V
Morris, Wright (1910), The Fork River Space Project. F
Morrison, Toni (1931), Song of Solomon. F
Nemerov, Howard (1920), Collected Poems. V
Oates, Joyce Carol (1938), Night-Side. F; The Triumph of the
    Spider Monkey. F
Percy, Walker (1916), Lancelot. F
Porter, Katherine Anne (1890), The Never-Ending Wrong. NF
Purdy, James (1923), A Day After the Fair. D, V
Ribman, Ronald (1932), Cold Storage (pub. 1978). D
Roth, Philip (1933), The Professor of Desire. F
Shaw, Irwin (1913), Beggar Man, Thief. F
Snodgrass, W. D. (1926), The Führer Bunker. V
Snyder, Gary (1930), The Old Ways. V
Sontag, Susan (1933), On Photography. NF
Stafford, William (1914), Stories That Could Be True. V
Tate, Allen (1899), Collected Poems. V
Theroux, Paul (1941), The Consul's File. F
Tyler, Anne (1941), Earthly Possessions. F
Updike, John (1932), Tossing and Turning. V
Vidal, Gore (1925), Matters of Fact and of Fiction: Essays 1973–
    1976. NF
Wakefield, Dan (1932), Home Free. F
Warren, Robert Penn (1905), A Place To Come To. F; Selected
    Poems, 1923–1975. V
Williams, Tennessee (1911), Vieux Carré (pub. 1979). D;
    Androgyne, Mon Amour. V
Willingham, Calder (1922), The Building of Venus Four. F

Alex Haley's Roots set new television
    records.
James M. Cain d.
Vladimir Nabokov d.
Robert Lowell d.
James Jones d.

Menachem Begin became prime
    minister of Israel.
Pompidou National Center of Art
    opened in Paris.
TLS: Times Literary Supplement
    (London) celebrated 75th
    anniversary.
Terence Rattigan d.
Jacques Prévert d.
Ted Hughes's Gaudete.
Fowles's Daniel Martin
Tolkien's The Silmarillion (posth.).
Drabble's The Ice Age.
Burgess's Abba Abba.
Paul Scott's Staying On.
Gilliatt's Splendid Lives.
Bainbridge's Injury Time.
Moorcock's The Condition of Muzak.
Trevor's The Children of Dynmouth.
O'Brien's Johnny, I Hardly Knew You.
Plunkett's Farewell Companions.
Grass's The Flounder.
Naipaul's India: A Wounded
    Civilization.
McCullough's The Thorn Birds.
Canetti's The Tongue Set Free.
Borges's History of Night.
Gustafsson's The Tennis Players.
Vargas Llosa's Aunt Julia and the
    Scriptwriter.
Coetzee's In the Heart of the Country.

Wilson, Edmund (d. 1972), Letters on Literature and Politics, 1912–1972. NF
Wilson, Lanford (1938), Brontosaurus (pub. 1978). D
Wolff, Geoffrey (1937), Inklings. F
Wright, James (1927), To a Blossoming Pear Tree. V

1978

Adams, Alice (1926), Listening to Billie. F
Anderson, Robert (1917), Getting Up and Going Home. F
Beattie, Ann (1947), Secrets and Surprises. F
Berger, Thomas (1924), Arthur Rex. F
Carroll, James (1943?), Mortal Friends. F
Cheever, John (1912), The Stories of John Cheever. F
Creeley, Robert (1926), Hello: A Journal, February 29–May 3, 1976. V
DeLillo, Don (1936), Running Dog. F
Doig, Ivan (1939), This House of Sky: Landscapes of a Western Mind. NF
Foote, Shelby (1916), September, September. F
Gaines, Ernest J. (1933), In My Father's House. F
Gardner, John (1933), On Moral Fiction. NF
Gass, William H. (1924), The World Within the Word. NF
Giovanni, Nikki (1943), Cotton Candy on a Rainy Day. V
Godwin, Gail (1937), Violet Clay. F
Gordon, Mary (1949), Final Payments. F
Hayden, Robert (1913), American Journal. V
Hollander, John (1929), In Place. V; Spectral Emenations. V
Howard, Maureen (1930), Facts of Life. NF
Innaurato, Albert (1948), Ulysses in Traction. D
Irving, John (1942), The World According to Garp. F
Jones, James (d. 1977), Whistle (completed by Willie Morris). F
Kazin, Alfred (1915), New York Jew. NF
Kennedy, William (1928), Billy Phelan's Greatest Game. F
Kinnell, Galway (1927), Walking Down the Stairs. NF
Kopit, Arthur (1937), Wings. D
Levertov, Denise (1923), Life in the Forest. V
Levin, Ira (1929), Deathtrap (pub. 1979). D
Lowell, Robert (d. 1977), The Oresteia of Aeschylus. V
McGuane, Thomas (1939), Panama. F
Madden, David (1933), The Suicide's Wife. F
Matthiessen, Peter (1927), The Snow Leopard. NF
Merrill, James (1926), Mirabell: Books of Number. V
Michener, James A. (1907), Chesapeake. F
Milosz, Czeslaw (1911), Bells in Winter. V
Mumford, Lewis (1895), My Works and Days. NF
Nemerov, Howard (1920), Figures of Thought. NF
Oates, Joyce Carol (1938), Women Whose Lives Are Food, Men Whose Lives Are Money. V; Son of the Morning. F
O'Brien, Tim (1946), Going After Cacciato. F
Piercy, Marge (1936), The High Cost of Living. F; The Twelve-Spoked Wheel Flashing. V
Purdy, James (1923), Narrow Rooms. F
Reed, Ishmael (1938), Shrovetide in Old New Orleans. NF
Rich, Adrienne (1929), The Dream of a Common Language. V
Sarton, May (1912), A Reckoning. F
Selby, Hubert, Jr. (1928), Requiem for a Dream. F
Shange, Ntozake (1948), Nappy Edges. V
Shapiro, Karl (1913), Collected Poems. V
Shaw, Irwin (1913), Five Decades. F

Camp David meeting (Carter, Sadat, Begin) led to peace treaty between Egypt and Israel.
Prolonged coal miners' strikes ended.
Anti-inflation measures sought by Congress.
Congress raised mandatory retirement age to 70.
Three American balloonists completed first transatlantic flight.
Isaac Bashevis Singer awarded Nobel Prize in literature.
James Gould Cozzens d.
John Hall Wheelock d.

Poland's Karol Cardinal Wojtyla became the first non-Italian pope elected since 1522.
F. R. Leavis d.
Sylvia Townsend Warner d.
Ignazio Silone d.
Brophy's *Palace Without Chairs*.
Greene's *The Human Factor*.
Murdoch's *The Sea, The Sea*.
Kingsley Amis's *Jake's Thing*.
Bainbridge's *Young Adolf*.
D. M. Thomas's *The Honeymoon Voyage*.
Follett's *Eye of the Needle*.
Bond's *The Bundle*.
Pinter's *Betrayal*.
Gilliatt's *The Cutting Edge*.
Farrell's *The Singapore Grip*.
Geoffrey Hill's *Tenebrae*.
MacDiarmid's *Complete Poems 1920–1976*.
Walser's *Runaway Horse*.
Bonnefoy's *Poems 1947–1974*.
Abé's *Secret Rendezvous*.
Handke's *Fantasies and Prejudices*.
Hochhuth's *A German Love Story*.
Fugard's *A Lesson from Aloes*.
Donoso's *A House in the Country*.
Fuentes's *The Hydra Head*.
Kopelev's *The Education of a True Believer*.

Sheed, Wilfrid (1930), Transatlantic Blues. F
Shepard, Sam (1943), Buried Child (pub. 1979). D; Curse of the
   Starving Class (pub. 1976). D
Simpson, Louis (1923), A Revolution in Taste. NF
Singer, Isaac Bashevis (1904), Shosha. F; A Young Man in
   Search of Love. NF
Sontag, Susan (1933), Illness as Metaphor. NF; I, Etcetera. F
Spackman, W. M. (1905), An Armful of Warm Girl. F
Stern, Richard G. (1928), Natural Shocks. F
Strand, Mark (1934), The Late Hour. V; The Monument. V
Theroux, Paul (1941), Picture Palace. F
Trillin, Calvin (1935), Alice, Let's Eat. NF
Updike, John (1932), The Coup. F
Vidal, Gore (1925), Kalki. F
Wagoner, David (1926), Who Shall Be the Sun? V
Wakoski, Diane (1937), The Man Who Shook Hands. V
Warren, Robert Penn (1905), Now and Then. V
Webb, James (1946), Fields of Fire. F
Weiss, Theodore (1916), Views and Spectacles. V
Welty, Eudora (1909), The Eye of the Story. NF
"William Wharton" (?), Birdy. F
Williams, Tennessee (1911), Where I Live: Selected Essays. NF
Wills, Gary (1934), Inventing America: Jefferson's Declaration
   of Independence. NF
Wilson, Lanford (1938), 5th of July. D
Wouk, Herman (1915), War and Remembrance. F
Yates, Richard (1926), A Good School. F

1979

Adams, Alice (1941), Beautiful Girl. F
Ashbery, John (1927), As We Know. V
Baldwin, James (1924), Just Above My Head. F
Baraka, Imamu Amiri (LeRoi Jones) (1934), Selected Plays
   and Prose. D, NF; Selected Poetry. V
Barth, John (1930), Letters. F
Barthelme, Donald (1931), Great Days. F
Bly, Robert (1926), This Tree Will Be Here for a Thousand
   Years. V
Bowles, Paul (1910), Collected Stories: 1939–1976. F
Connell, Evan S., Jr. (1924), A Long Desire. NF
Davenport, Guy (1927), DaVinci's Bicycle. F
Dickey, James (1923), The Strength of Fields. V
Didion, Joan (1934), The White Album. NF
Donleavy, J. P. (1926), Schultz. F
Elkin, Stanley (1930), The Living End. F
Ferlinghetti, Lawrence (1920), Landscapes of Living and Dying.
   V
Guare, John (1938), Bosoms and Neglect (pub. 1980), D
Halberstam, David (1934), The Powers That Be. NF
Hardwick, Elizabeth (1916), Sleepless Nights. F
Hawkes, John (1925), The Passion Artist. F
Hecht, Anthony (1923), The Venetian Vespers. V
Heller, Joseph (1923), Good as Gold. F
Henley, Beth (1952), Crimes of the Heart (pub. 1982). D
Hoagland, Edward (1932), African Calliope: A Journey to the
   Sudan. NF
Hollander, John (1929), Blue Wine. V
Howard, Richard (1929), Misgivings. V

U.S. and China established full
   diplomatic relations.
U.S. and Soviet Union completed SALT
   II treaty.
Accident at Three Mile Island nuclear
   power plant.
Gasoline supply diminished rapidly.
Shirley M. Hufstedler headed first
   Department of Education.
Allen Tate d.
James T. Farrell d.
Elizabeth Bishop d.
S. J. Perelman d.
Jean Stafford d.

Egypt and Israel signed peace treaty.
Soviet Union invaded Afghanistan.
Shah of Iran departed his country.
Ayatollah Khomeini returned to Iran
   from exile.
Iranian militants seized U.S. embassy in
   Teheran.
Margaret Thatcher became first woman
   prime minister of Great Britain.
Idi Amin deposed as president of
   Uganda.
Mika Waltari d.
Spark's *Territorial Rights*.
Enright's *A Faust Book*.
Kinsella's *Fifteen Dead*.
D. M. Thomas's *The Flute-Player*.
Peter Shaffer's *Amadeus*.
Golding's *Darkness Visible*.

Justice, Donald (1925), Selected Poems. V
Kissinger, Henry (1923), White House Years. NF
Knowles, John (1926), A Vein of Riches. F
Kosinski, Jerzy (1933), Passion Play. F
Kumin, Maxine (1925), To Make a Prairie: Essays on Poets, Poetry, and Country Living. NF
Kunitz, Stanley (1905), The Poems of Stanley Kunitz, 1928–1978. V
Lasch, Christopher (1932), The Culture of Narcissism: American Life in an Age of Diminishing Expectations. NF
Levertov, Denise (1923), Collected Earlier Poems, 1940–1960. V
Levine, Philip (1928), Seven Years from Somewhere. V
Lurie, Alison (1926), Only Children. F
McCarthy, Mary (1912), Cannibals and Missionaries. F
McConkey, James (1921), The Tree House Confessions. F
McPhee, John (1931), Giving Good Weight. NF
Madden, David (1933), Pleasure Dome. F
Mailer, Norman (1923), The Executioner's Song. F, NF
Malamud, Bernard (1914), Dubin's Lives. F
Miles, Josephine (1911), Coming to Terms. V
Miller, Arthur (1915), Chinese Encounters (with Inge Morath). NF
Millett, Kate (1934), The Basement: Meditations on a Human Sacrifice. NF
Morgan, Frederick (1922), Death Mother. V
O'Connor, Flannery (d. 1964), The Habit of Being. NF
Oates, Joyce Carol (1938), All the Good People I've Left Behind. F; Unholy Loves. F; Cybele. F
Phillips, Jayne Anne (1952), Black Tickets. F
Rich, Adrienne (1929), On Lies, Secrets, and Silence: Selected Prose. NF
Robison, Mary (1950?), Days. F
Roth, Philip (1933), The Ghost Writer. F
Rukeyser, Muriel (1913), Collected Poems. V
Schwartz, Delmore (d. 1966), The Last and Lost Poems. V
Shaw, Irwin (1913), The Top of the Hill. F
Sheed, Wilfrid (1930), The Good Word and Other Words. F
Singer, Isaac Bashevis (1904), Old Love. F
Sorrentino, Gilbert (1929), Mulligan Stew. F
Stegner, Wallace (1909), Recapitulation. F
Styron, William (1925), Sophie's Choice. F
Swenson, May (1919), New and Selected Things Taking Place. V
Theroux, Paul (1941), The Old Patagonian Express: By Train Through the Americas. NF
Updike, John (1932), Problems and Other Stories. F; Too Far to Go: The Maples Stories. F
Vonnegut, Kurt, Jr. (1922), Jailbird. F
Wagoner, David (1926), In Broken Country. V
West, Jessamyn (1907), The Life I Really Lived. F
Wilder, Thornton (d. 1975), American Characteristics and Other Essays. NF
Williams, Tennessee (1911), A Lovely Sunday for Crève Coeur (pub. 1980). D
Wilson, Lanford (1938), Talley's Folly (pub. 1980). D
Wilson, Sloan (1920), Ice Brothers. F
Wolfe, Tom (1931), The Right Stuff. NF
Wolff, Geoffrey (1937), The Duke of Deception. NF
Zukofsky, Louis (d. 1978), "A". V

Ballard's The Unlimited Dream Company.
A. N. Wilson's Kindly Light.
Heaney's Field Work.
Naipaul's A Bend in the River.
Carter's The Bloody Chamber.
Kundera's The Book of Laughter and Forgetting.
Calvino's If on a Winter's Night a Traveler.
Grass's The Meeting at Telgte.
Cabrera Infante's Infante's Inferno.
Cortázar's A Certain Lucas.
Voinovich's In Plain Russian.

1980

Adams, Alice (1926), Rich Rewards. F
Albee, Edward (1928), The Lady from Dubuque. D
Ammons, A. R. (1926), Selected Longer Poems. V
Auchincloss, Louis (1917), The House of the Prophet. F
Beattie, Ann (1947), Falling in Place. F
Berger, Thomas (1924), Neighbors. F
Bishop, Elizabeth (d. 1979), That Was Then. V
Bogan, Louise (d. 1970), Journey Around My Room. NF
Booth, Philip (1925), Before Sleep. V
Boyle, Kay (1902), Fifty Stories. F
Bradbury, Ray (1920), The Stories of Ray Bradbury. F
Brodsky, Joseph (1940), A Part of Speech. V
Buechner, Frederick (1926), Godric. F
Burroughs, William S. (1914), Port of Saints. F
Caldwell, Erskine (1903), Deep South: Memory and
    Observation. NF
Capote, Truman (1924), Music for Chameleons. F, NF
Carroll, James (1943?), Fault Lines. F
Cassill, R. V. (1919), Labors of Love. F
Connell, Evan S., Jr. (1924), The White Lantern. NF; St.
    Augustine's Pigeon: The Selected Stories. F
Conroy, Pat (1945), The Lords of Discipline. F
Coover, Robert (1932), A Political Fable. F
Corman, Avery (1935), The Old Neighborhood. F
Cowley, Malcolm (1898), The Dream of the Golden Mountains:
    Remembering the 1930s. NF
De Vries, Peter (1910), Consenting Adults; or, The Duchess
    Will Be Furious. F
Doctorow, E. L. (1935), Loon Lake. F
Doig, Ivan (1939), Winter Brothers. NF
Dubus, Andre (1936), Finding a Girl in America. F
French, Marilyn (1929), The Bleeding Heart. F
Fuller, Charles (1939), Zooman and the Sign (pub. 1982). D
Gardner, John (1932), Freddy's Book. F
Ginsberg, Allen (1926), Straight Hearts' Delight: Love Poems
    and Selected Letters, 1947–1980. V, NF
Hazzard, Shirley (1931), The Transit of Venus. F
Hellman, Lillian (1905), Maybe. NF
Hoban, Russell (1925), Riddley Walker. F
Hoffman, Daniel G. (1923), Brotherly Love. V
Innaurato, Albert (1948), Passione (pub. 1981). D
Isherwood, Christopher (1904), My Guru and His Disciple. NF
Jarrell, Randall (d. 1965), Kipling, Auden & Co. NF
Kinnell, Galway (1927), Mortal Acts, Mortal Words. V
Knowles, John (1926), Peace Breaks Out. F
McCarthy, Mary (1912), Ideas and the Novel. NF
McGinnis, Joe (1942), Going to Extremes. NF
McGuane, Thomas (1939), Outside Chance. NF
Mailer, Norman (1923), Of Women and Their Elegance. F, NF
Manfred, Frederick (Feike Feikema) (1912), Sons of Adam. F
Medoff, Mark (1940), Children of a Lesser God. D
Meredith, William (1919), The Cheer. V
Merrill, James (1926), Scripts for a Pageant. V
Michener, James A. (1907), The Covenant. F
Morris, Wright (1910), Plains Song, for Female Voices. F
Nabokov, Vladimir (d. 1977), Lectures on Literature. NF
Nemerov, Howard (1920), Sentences. V
Oates, Joyce Carol (1938), Bellefleur. F
Percy, Walker (1916), The Second Coming. F
Piercy, Marge (1936), The Moon Is Always Female. F; Vida. F

U.S. severed relations with Iran, sought
    hostages' release.
U.S. and NATO warned Soviets against
    invasion of Poland.
Cuban refugees flooded U.S.
U.S. banks raised prime lending rate to
    record 21.5%.
Czeslaw Milosz awarded Nobel Prize
    in literature.
Katherine Anne Porter d.
Marc Connelly d.
Henry Miller d.
Muriel Rukeyser d.

U.N. condemned Soviet aggression in
    Afghanistan.
Polish workers on strike, led by Lech
    Walesa.
Deaths of Tito and the Shah of Iran.
Olympic Games in Moscow boycotted
    by 65 nations.
C. P. Snow d.
Jean-Paul Sartre d.
Romain Gary d.
Roland Barthes d.
Pinter's The Hothouse.
Golding's Rites of Passage.
Greene's Doctor Fischer of Geneva; or,
    The Bomb Party.
Drabble's The Middle Ground.
Burgess's Earthly Powers.
Lodge's How Far Can You Go?
Le Carré's Smiley's People.
A. N. Wilson's The Healing Art.
John Fuller's The Illusionists.
Friel's Translations.
MacLaverty's Lamb.
Robert Nye's Faust.
D. M. Thomas's Birthstone.
MacLennan's Voices in Time.
Richler's Joshua Then and Now.
Beckett's Company.
Coetzee's Waiting for the Barbarians.
Walser's The Swan Villa.
Grass's Headbirths; or, The Germans
    Are Dying Out.
Eco's The Name of the Rose.
Canetti's The Torch in My Ear.
Fuentes's Distant Relations.
Cortázar's We Love Glenda So Much.
Aksyonov's The Burn.

Sarton, May (1912), Recovering. NF
Schulberg, Budd (1914), Everything That Moves. F
Seidel, Frederick (1936), Sunrise. V
Shepard, Sam (1943), True West (pub. 1981). D
Simpson, Louis (1923), Caviare at the Funeral. V
Singer, Isaac Bashevis (1904), Reaches of Heaven. F
Smith, William Jay (1918), Army Brat. NF
Sontag, Susan (1933), Under the Sign of Saturn. NF
Sorrentino, Gilbert (1929), Aberration of Starlight. F
Spackman, W. M. (1905), A Presence with Secrets. F
Stern, Richard G. (1928), Packages. F
Terkel, Studs (1912), American Dreams: Lost and Found. NF
Theroux, Paul (1941), World's End and Other Stories. F
Toole, John Kennedy (d. 1969), A Confederacy of Dunces. F
Trillin, Calvin (1935), Floater. F
Tyler, Anne (1941), Morgan's Passing. F
Warren, Robert Penn (1905), Being Here: Poetry 1977–1980. V
Welty, Eudora (1909), The Collected Stories. F
West, Jessamyn (1907), Double Discovery: A Journal. NF
Williams, Tennessee (1911), Clothes for a Summer Hotel (pub. 1983). D
Wilson, Edmund (d. 1972), The Thirties: From Notebooks and Diaries of the Period. NF
Wolfe, Tom (1931), In Our Time. NF

1981

Alther, Lisa (1944), Original Sins. F
Ammons, A. R. (1926), A Coast of Trees. V
Ashbery, John (1927), Shadow Train. V
Auchincloss, Louis (1917), The Cat and the King. F
Baraka, Imamu Amiri (LeRoi Jones) (1934), Reggae or Not! V
Barthelme, Donald (1931), Sixty Stories. F
Berger, Thomas (1924), Reinhart's Women. F
Bly, Robert (1926), The Man in the Black Coat Turns. V
Bowles, Paul (1911), Collected Stories. F; Next to Nothing: Collected Poems 1926–1977. V
Brinnin, John Malcolm (1916), Sextet: T. S. Eliot & Truman Capote & Others. NF
Burroughs, William S. (1914), Cities of the Red Night. F
Carver, Raymond (1938), What We Talk About When We Talk About Love. F
Clavell, James (1924), Noble House. F
Corso, Gregory (1930), Herald of the Autochthonic Spirit. V
Davison, Peter (1928), Barn Fever and Other Poems. V
De Vries, Peter (1910), Sauce for the Goose. F
Ferlinghetti, Lawrence (1920), Endless Life. V
Forché, Carolyn (1950), The Country Between Us. V
Friedan, Betty (1921), The Second Stage. NF
Fuller, Charles (1939), A Soldier's Play (pub. 1982). D
Gardner, John (1933), The Art of Living. F
Gold, Herbert (1924), Family. F; A Walk on the West Side. F, NF
Gordon, Caroline (1895), The Collected Stories. F
Gordon, Mary (1949), The Company of Women. F

Iran freed 52 U.S. hostages.
Assassination attempt on President Reagan.
U.S. launched world's first space shuttle, *Columbia.*
Sandra Day O'Connor became first woman Supreme Court justice.
Paul Green d.
William Saroyan d.

Egyptian President Sadat assassinated.
Pope John Paul II shot in St. Peter's Square.
Violence in Lebanon escalated.
Enid Bagnold d.
A. J. Cronin d.
Eugenio Montale d.
D. M. Thomas's *The White Hotel.*
Osborne's *A Better Class of Person.*
Lessing's *The Sirian Experiments.*
Rushdie's *Midnight's Children.*
Boyd's *A Good Man in Africa.*
Enright's *Collected Poems.*
Bainbridge's *A Weekend with Claude.*
Moorcock's *Byzantium Endures.*
Trevor's *Other People's Words.*
John Fuller's *The Ship of Sounds.*
A. N. Wilson's *Who Was Oswald Fish?*
Craig Raine's *A Free Translation.*
Naipaul's *Among the Believers: An Islamic Journey.*
Paton's *Ah, But Your Land Is Beautiful.*
Robbe-Grillet's *Djinn.*

Gray, Francine du Plessix (1930), World Without End. F
Helprin, Mark (1947), Ellis Island and Other Stories. F
Hemingway, Ernest (d. 1961), Selected Letters, 1917–1961. NF
Hine, Daryl (1936), Selected Poems. V
Hollander, John (1939), Rhyme's Reason: A Guide to English Verse. V, NF; The Figure of Echo. V
Irving, John (1942), The Hotel New Hampshire. F
Kauffman, Janet (?), The Weather Book. V
Levertov, Denise (1923), Light Up the Cave. V
Levine, Philip (1928), One for the Rose. V
Lurie, Alison (1926), The Language of Clothes. NF
McHale, Tom (1942?), Dear Friends. F
McPhee, John (1931), Basin and Range. NF
Matthiessen, Peter (1927), Sand Rivers. NF
Meschery, Joanne (1941), In a High Place. F
Michaels, Leonard (1933), The Men's Club. F
Morgan, Frederick (1922), Northbook. V
Morris, Wright (1910), Will's Boy: A Memoir. F
Morrison, Toni (1931), Tar Baby. F
Moss, Howard (1922), Whatever Is Moving. NF
Nabokov, Vladimir (d. 1977), Lectures on Russian Literature. NF
Oates, Joyce Carol (1938), Angel of Light. F; Contraries: Essays. NF
Perelman, S. J. (d. 1979), The Last Laugh. F, NF
Plath, Sylvia (d. 1963), The Collected Poems. V
Price, Reynolds (1933), The Source of Light. F
Purdy, James (1923), Mourners Below. F
Rich, Adrienne (1931), A Wild Patience Has Taken Me This Far. V
Robison, Mary (1950?), Oh! F
Roth, Philip (1933), Zuckerman Unbound. F
Schulberg, Budd (1914), Moving Pictures: Memories of a Hollywood Prince. NF
Sexton, Anne (d. 1974), The Complete Poems. V
Shaw, Irwin (1913), Bread Upon the Waters. F
Silko, Leslie M. (1948), Storyteller. F
Simpson, Louis (1923), A Company of Poets. NF
Singer, Isaac Bashevis (1940), Lost in America. NF
Sorrentino, Gilbert (1929), Selected Poems, 1958–1980. V; Crystal Vision. F
Spencer, Elizabeth (1921), Marilee. F; The Stories of Elizabeth Spencer. F
Stern, Gerald (1925), The Red Coal. V
Stone, Robert (1937), A Flag for Sunrise. F
Strand, Mark (1934), The Planet of Lost Things. V
Thurber, James (d. 1961), Selected Letters. NF
Tuchman, Barbara W. (1912), Practicing History. NF
Updike, John (1932), Rabbit Is Rich. F
Vidal, Gore (1925), Creation. F
Vonnegut, Kurt, Jr. (1922), Palm Sunday. NF
Wagoner, David (1926), Landfall. V
Wakoski, Diane (1937), The Magician's Feastletters. V
Walker, Alice (1944), You Can't Keep a Good Woman Down. F
Warren, Robert Penn (1905), Rumor Verified. V
Wilbur, Richard (1921), Seven Poems. V
"William Wharton" (?), Dad. F
Wilson, Lanford (1938), A Tale Told. D
Woiwode, Larry (1941), Poppa John. F
Wolfe, Tom (1931), From Bauhaus to Our House. NF

Bodard's Anne-Marie.
Simenon's Intimate Memoirs.
Gordimer's July's People.
Fuentes's Burnt Water.
García Márquez's Chronicle of a Death Foretold.
Vargas Llosa's The War of the End of the World.
Voinovich's Pretender to the Throne.

Wolff, Tobias (1945), In the Garden of the North American
   Martyrs. F
Yates, Richard (1926), Liars in Love. F

1982

Adams, Alice (1926), To See You Again. F
Ammons, A. R. (1926), Worldly Hopes. V
Baker, Russell (1925), Growing Up. NF
Barth, John (1930), Sabbatical: A Romance. F
Beattie, Ann (1947), The Burning House. F
Bellow, Saul (1915), The Dean's December. F
Carruth, Hayden (1921), The Sleeping Beauty. V
Cheever, John (1912), Oh What a Paradise It Seems. F
Christopher, Nicholas (1951), On Tour with Rita. V
Coover, Robert (1932), Spanking the Maid. F
Creeley, Robert (1926), The Collected Poems, 1945–1975. V
DeLillo, Don (1936), The Names. F
Del Vecchio, John (1948), The 13th Valley. F
Dickey, James (1923), Puella. V
Dillard, Annie (1945), Teaching a Stone to Talk: Expeditions and
   Encounters. NF
Doig, Ivan (1939), The Sea Runners. F
Dreiser, Theodore (d. 1945), American Diaries, 1902–1926. NF
Dunne, John Gregory (1932), Dutch Shea, Jr. F
Elkin, Stanley (1930), George Mills. F
Gardner, John (1933), Mickelsson's Ghosts. F
Ginsberg, Allen (1926), Plutonian Ode: Poems 1977–1980. V
Godwin, Gail (1937), A Mother and Two Daughters. F
Gold, Herbert (1924), True Love. F
Guthrie, A.B., Jr. (1901), Fair Land, Fair Land. F
Hawkes, John (1925), Virginie: Her Two Lives. F
Hoagland, Edward (1932), The Tugman's Passage. NF
Howard, Maureen (1930), Grace Abounding. F
Howard, Richard (1929), Les Fleurs du Mal: Charles
   Baudelaire. The Complete Text of The Flowers of Evil
   (translator). V
Kinnell, Galway (1927), Selected Poems. V
Kissinger, Henry (1923), Years of Upheaval. NF
Kosinski, Jerzy (1933), Pinball. F
Kumin, Maxine (1925), Our Ground Time Here Will Be Brief.
   V; Why Can't We Live Together Like Human Beings. F
Levertov, Denise (1923), Candles in Babylon. V
McGuane, Thomas (1939), Nobody's Angel. F
Mailer, Norman (1923), Pieces and Pontifications. NF
Malamud, Bernard (1914), God's Grace. F
Mamet, David (1947), Edmond (pub. 1983). D
Mason, Bobbie Ann (1940), Shiloh and Other Stories. F
Merrill, James (1926), The Changing Light at Sandover.
   V; From the First Nine Poems. V
Merwin, W. S. (1927), Unframed Originals. NF
Michener, James A. (1907), Space. F
Milosz, Czeslaw (1911), Visions from San Francisco Bay. NF
Morris, Wright (1910), Photographs and Words. NF
Mumford, Lewis (1895), Sketches from Life. NF
Oates, Joyce Carol (1938), A Bloodsmoor Romance. F
Ozick, Cynthia (1928), Levitation: Five Fictions. F
Pesetsky, Bette (1932), Stories Up to a Point. F
Piercy, Marge (1936), Braided Lives. F
Plath, Sylvia (d. 1963), The Journals. NF
Price, Reynolds (1933), Vital Provisions. V

Equal Rights Amendment failed
   ratification.
Braniff became first major airline to
   declare bankruptcy.
Growing concern over federal budget
   deficits.
First successful artificial heart implant.
John Cheever d.
Archibald MacLeish d.
John Gardner d.
The New Criterion (New York), 1982–.

Soviet premier Brezhnev died; Yuri
   Andropov elected general secretary.
Beginning of Iran-Iraq "border dispute."
Israel invaded Lebanon.
Argentina seized Falkland Islands in
   April; surrendered to British in June.
First formal constitution for Canada.
Burgess's *The End of the World News.*
Greene's *Monsignor Quixote.*
Lessing's *The Making of the
   Representative for Planet 8.*
Durrell's *Constance: or Solitary
   Practices.*
William Cooper's *Scenes from
   Metropolitan Life.*
Boyd's *An Ice-Cream War.*
Fowles's *Mantissa.*
Stoppard's *The Real Thing.*
Gunn's *The Passages of Joy.*
Fenton's *The Memory of War: Poems
   1968–1982.*
A. N. Wilson's *Wise Virgin.*
John Fuller's *Waiting for the Music.*
Christopher Reid's *Pea Soup.*
Keneally's *Schindler's Art.*
Fugard's *Master Harold and the Boys.*
Frisch's *Bluebeard.*
Bernhard's *Concrete.*
Yevtushenko's *Berry Patches.*
Yashushi Inoue's *Chronicle of My
   Mother.*
Nobuo Kojima's *Reasons for
   Separation.*
García Márquez's *The Fragrance of the
   Guava.*

Reeves, Richard (1936), American Journey: Traveling with
  Tocqueville in Search of Democracy in America. NF
Sarton, May (1912), Anger. F
Schell, Jonathan (1943), The Fate of the Earth. NF
Shange, Ntozake (1948), Sassafrass, Cypress, and Indigo. F
Shaw, Irwin (1913), Acceptable Losses. F.
Singer, Isaac Bashevis (1904), Collected Stories. F
Stegner, Wallace (1909), One Way to Spell Man. NF
Styron, William (1925), This Quiet Dust. NF
Theroux, Paul (1941), The Mosquito Coast. F
Trillin, Calvin (1935), Uncivil Liberties. NF
Tyler, Anne (1941), Dinner at the Homesick Restaurant. F
Updike, John (1932), Bech Is Back. F
Van Duyn, Mona (1921), Letters from a Father and Other
  Poems. V
Vidal, Gore (1925), The Second American Revolution and Other
  Essays: 1976–1982. NF
Walker, Alice (1944), The Color Purple. F
Weiss, Theodore (1916), Recoveries. V
Will, George F. (1941), The Pursuit of Virtue and Other Tory
  Notions. NF
"William Wharton" (?), A Midnight Clear. F
Williams, John A. (1925), Click Song. F
Wilson, Lanford (1938), Angels Fall. D
Wright, James (d. 1980), This Journey. V

1983

Adler, Renata (1938), Pitch Dark. F
Algren, Nelson (d. 1981), The Devil's Stocking. F
Ammons, A. R. (1926), Lake Effect Country. V
Auchincloss, Louis (1917), Exit Lady Masham. F
Barthelme, Donald (1931), Over Night to Many Distant Cities. F
Berger, Thomas (1924), The Feud. F
Bishop, Elizabeth (d. 1979), The Complete Poems, 1927–1979.
  V
Burroughs, William S. (1914), The Place of Dead Roads. F
Calisher, Hortense (1911), Mysteries of Motion. F
Carver, Raymond (1938), Cathedral. F
Chase, Joan (?), During the Reign of the Queen of Persia. F
Clampitt, Amy (1920), The Kingfisher. V
De Vries, Peter (1910), Slouching Toward Kalamazoo. F
Dickey, James (1923), The Central Motion. V
Didion, Joan (1934), Salvador. NF
Donleavy, J. P. (1926), Leila. F
Dreiser, Theodore (d. 1945), An Amateur Laborer. F
Dubus, Andre (1936), The Times Are Never So Bad. F
Ephron, Nora (1941), Heartburn. F
Farrell, James T. (d. 1979), Sam Holman. F
Garrett, George (1929), The Succession: A Novel of Elizabeth
  and James. F
Giovanni, Nikki (1943), Those Who Ride the Nightwinds. V
Godwin, Gail (1937), Mr. Bedford and the Muses. F
Goyen, William (1915), Arcadio. F
"H.D."(d. 1961), Collected Poems, 1912–1944. V
Hardwick, Elizabeth (1916), Bartleby in Manhattan and Other
  Essays. NF
Helprin, Mark (1947), Winter's Tale. F
Hollander, John (1929), Powers of Thirteen. V
Howard, Richard (1929), Lining Up. V

U.S. embassy in Beirut bombed: 241
  American soldiers killed by car
  bombs on Beirut airstrip.
U.S. troops invaded Grenada.
U.S. aid to Guatemala and El Salvador
  increased.
Harold Washington became first black
  mayor of Chicago.
Tennessee Williams d.
Ross Macdonald d.

Prime Minister Thatcher returned to
  office by large margin.
Prime Minister Begin of Israel resigned.
Soviets shot down unarmed South
  Korean airliner with 269 people
  aboard.
Yasser Arafat and PLO guerrillas left
  Lebanon.
Lech Walesa awarded Nobel Peace
  Prize.
Arthur Koestler d.
Rebecca West d.
Powell's How the Wheel Becomes It.
Pritchett's Collected Stories.
Lessing's The Sentimental Agents in the
  Volyen Empire.
Ted Hughes's The River.
Bradbury's Rates of Exchange.
Rushdie's Shame.
Le Carré's The Little Drummer Girl.
St. Aubin de Terán's The Keepers of the
  House.
Trevor's Fools of Fortune.
MacLaverty's Cal.
Geoffrey Hill's The Mystery of the
  Charity of Charles Péguy.

Karnow, Stanley (1925), Vietnam: A History. F
Kauffman, Janet (?), Places in the World a Woman Could Walk. F
Kennedy, William (1928), Ironweed. F
Knowles, John (1926), A Stolen Past. F
Kuniczak, W. S. (1930), Valedictory. F
Loewinsohn, Ron (1937), Magnetic Field(s). F
McConkey, James (1921), Court of Memory. NF
McPhee, John (1931), In Suspect Terrain. NF
Mailer, Norman (1923), Ancient Evenings. F; St. George and the Godfather. NF
Malamud, Bernard (1914), The Stories of Bernard Malamud. F
Mason, Robert (1946), Chickenhawk. NF
Matthiessen, Peter (1927), In the Spirit of Crazy Horse. NF
Merwin, W. S. (1927), Opening the Hand. V
Michener, James A. (1907), Poland. F
Milosz, Czeslaw (1911), The Witness of Poetry. NF
Morris, Wright (1910), Solo: An American Dream in Europe, 1933–1934. NF
Oates, Joyce Carol (1938), The Profane Art: Essays and Reviews. NF
Ozick, Cynthia (1928), The Cannibal Galaxy. F; Art and Ardor: Essays. NF
Pancake, Breece D'J (d. 1979), The Stories of Breece D'J Pancake. F
Pesetsky, Bette (1932), Author from a Savage People. F
Rich, Adrienne (1931), Sources. V
Robison, Mary (1950?), An Amateur's Guide to the Night. F
Rossner, Judith (1935), August. F
Roth, Philip (1933), The Anatomy Lesson. F
Saroyan, William (d. 1981), My Name Is Saroyan. F, NF, D, V
Schevill, James (1920), The American Fantasies: Collected Poems, 1945–1981. V
Shange, Ntozake (1948), A Daughter's Geography. V
Shepard, Sam (1943), Fool for Love. D
Simpson, Louis (1923), The Best Hour of the Night. V
Singer, Isaac Bashevis (1904), The Penitent. F
Snyder, Gary (1930), Axe Handles. V
Spackman, W. M. (1905), A Difference of Design. F
Steinem, Gloria (1934), Outrageous Acts and Everyday Rebellions. NF
Theroux, Paul (1941), The London Embassy. F
Trillin, Calvin (1935), Third Helpings. NF
Updike, John (1932), Hugging the Shore: Essays in Criticism. NF
Vidal, Gore (1925), Duluth. F
Wagoner, David (1926), First Light. V
Walker, Alice (1944), In Search of Our Mothers' Gardens. NF
Warren, Robert Penn (1905), Chief Joseph of the Nez Percé. V
Webb, James (1946), A Country Such as This. F
Wideman, John Edgar (1941), Sent for You Yesterday. F
"William Least Heat Moon" (1939), Blue Highways: A Journey into America. NF
Wright, Stephen (1946), Meditations in Green. F

John Fuller's *Flying to Nowhere.*
O'Faolain's *Collected Stories.*
Coetzee's *The Life and Times of Michael K.*
Aron's *Memoirs.*
Sarraute's *Childhood.*
Beauvoir's *Letters to Castor.*
Tournier's *Gilles and Joan.*
Barzini's *The Europeans.*
Wolf's *Cassandra.*
Tristan's *The Wanderers.*
Walser's *Letter to Lord Liszt.*
Galperin's *Bridge Over Lethe.*
Bykov's *Sign of Misfortune.*

INDEX

Abbott, George (1887–). A Tree Grows in Brooklyn [adapted with Betty Smith from her novel (1943)], 1951.

Abbott, Jacob (1803–79). The Young Christian, 1832. Rollo Series (28 vols., 1835ff.), 1835.

Abbott, Lyman (1835–1922). Christianity and Social Problems, 1896. The Theology of an Evolutionist, 1897. Henry Ward Beecher, 1903. Reminiscences, 1915. What Christianity Means to Me, 1921.

Accent (1940–60).

Acheson, Dean (1893–1971). Present at the Creation, 1969.

Acrelius, Israel (1714–1800). Beskrifning om Nya Swerige [Description of . . . New Sweden], 1759.

Adair, James (c. 1709–c. 1783). The History of the American Indians, 1775.

Adamic, Louis (1899–1951). Dynamite: The Story of Class Violence in America, 1931. Laughing in the Jungle, 1932. The Native's Return, 1934. Grandsons: A Story of American Lives, 1935. Cradle of Life: The Story of One Man's Beginnings, 1936. The House in Antigua, 1937. Two-Way Passage, 1941. What's Your Name? 1942. Inside Yugoslavia, 1942. My Native Land, 1943. A Nation of Nations, 1945. Dinner at the White House, 1946.

Adams, Abigail (1744–1818). Letters of Mrs. Adams, the Wife of John Adams, 1840.

Adams, Alice (1926–). Careless Love, 1966. Families and Survivors, 1974. Listening to Billie, 1978. Beautiful Girl, 1979. Rich Rewards, 1980. To See You Again, 1982.

Adams, Andy (1859–1935). The Log of a Cowboy, 1903. The Outlet, 1905. Cattle Brands, 1906. Reed Anthony, Cowman, 1907.

Adams, Brooks (1848–1927). The Emancipation of Massachusetts, 1887. The Law of Civilization and Decay, 1895. America's Economic Supremacy, 1900. The New Empire, 1902. Theory of Social Revolution, 1913.

Adams, Brooks (1848–1927) and Henry Adams (1838–1918). The Degradation of the Democratic Dogma, 1919.

Adams, Charles Follen (1842–1918). Yawcob Strauss and Other Poems, 1910.

Adams, Charles Francis (1835–1915). Railroads: Their Origins and Problems, 1878. Richard Henry Dana, 1890. Three Episodes of Massachusetts History, 1892. Charles Francis Adams [1807–1886], 1900. Studies: Military and Diplomatic, 1911. Charles Francis Adams, 1835–1915: An Autobiography, 1916.

Adams, Eliphalet (1677–1753). God Sometimes Answers His People by Terrible Things in Righteousness, 1735. A Sermon Preached on the Occasion of the Execution of Katherine Garret, an Indian-Servant (Who Was Condemned for the Murder of Her Spurious Child), 1738.

Adams, Franklin P. (1881–1960). Tobogganing on Parnassus, 1911. The Conning Tower Book, 1926. Christopher Columbus, 1931. The Diary of Our Own Samuel Pepys, 1935. Nods and Becks, 1944.

Adams, Hannah (1755–1831). Alphabetical Compendium of the Various Sects, 1784. A Summary History of New England, 1799. The Truth and Excellence of the Christian Religion Exhibited, 1804. The History of the Jews, 1812.

Adams, Henry (1838–1918). Chapters of Erie, and Other Essays (with Charles Francis Adams), 1871. Essays in Anglo-Saxon Law, 1876. Documents Relating to New-England Federalism, 1800–1815, 1877. The Life of Albert Gallatin, 1879. Democracy: An American Novel, 1880. John Randolph, 1882. Esther: A Novel, 1884. History of the United States of America During the Administration of Thomas Jefferson and James Madison, 1889. Historical Essays, 1891. Memoirs of Marau Taaroa, Last Queen of Tahiti, 1893. Mont-Saint-Michel and Chartres, 1904. The Education of Henry Adams: An Autobiography, privately printed, 1907. The Life of George Cabot Lodge, 1911. The Education of Henry Adams: An Autobiography, 1918.

Adams, James Truslow (1878–1949). The Founding of New England, 1921. Revolutionary New England, 1923. New England in the Republic, 1926. Provincial Society, 1690–1763, 1927. The Adams Family, 1930. The Epic of America, 1931. The March of Democracy (2 vols., 1932–33), 1932. Henry Adams, 1933. Building the British Empire, 1938. The American: The Making of a New Man, 1943. Frontiers of

gress, 1940. Brownstone Eclogues, 1942. The Soldier, 1944. The Kid, 1947. The Divine Pilgrim, 1949. Skylight One, 1949. The Short Stories of Conrad Aiken, 1950. Ushant: An Essay, 1952. Collected Poems, 1953. A Letter from Li Po, 1955. Sheepfold Hill, 1958. A Reviewer's ABC: 1958. Collected Short Stories, 1960. The Morning Song of Lord Zero, 1963. A Seizure of Limericks, 1964. The Collected Novels, 1964. Thee, 1967. Collected Poems, 1970.

Aiken, George L. (1830–76). Uncle Tom's Cabin [adapted from Harriet Beecher Stowe's novel (1852)], 1852.

Aikin, John (1747–1822). Letters from a Father to His Son; on Various Topics, Relative to Literature and the Conduct of Life, 1794.

"Aimard, Gustave." *See* Gloux, Oliver.

Ainslie, Hew (1792–1878). A Pilgrimage to the Land of Burns, 1822.

Akers, Elizabeth (1832–1911). Poems, 1866. The Sunset Song, 1902.

Akins, Zoë (1886–1958). Déclassée, 1919. The Old Maid [adapted from Edith Wharton's novella (1924)], 1935.

Albee, Edward (1928–   ). The Zoo Story, 1959. The Death of Bessie Smith, 1960. The Sandbox, 1960. FAM and YAM, 1960. The American Dream, 1960. Who's Afraid of Virginia Woolf? 1962. The Ballad of the Sad Café [adapted from Carson McCullers's novella (1951)], 1963. Tiny Alice, 1964. A Delicate Balance, 1966. Malcolm [adapted from James Purdy's novel (1959)], 1966. Everything in the Garden [adapted from Giles Cooper's play (1963)], 1967. Box, 1968. Quotations from Chairman Mao Tse-Tung, 1968. All Over, 1971. Seascape, 1975. Counting the Ways; Listening, 1977. The Lady from Dubuque, 1980.

Alcott, Bronson (1799–1888). Observations on the Principles and Methods of Infant Instruction, 1830. The Doctrine and Discipline of Human Culture, 1836. Conversations with Children on the Gospels (1836–37), 1836. "Orphic Sayings," 1840. Tablets, 1868. Concord Days, 1872. Table-Talk, 1877. Ralph Waldo Emerson, 1882. Sonnets and Canzonets, 1882. New Connecticut, 1887.

Alcott, Louisa May (1832–88). Flower Fables, 1855. Hospital Sketches, 1863. On Picket Duty and Other Tales, 1864. The Rose Family, 1864. Moods, 1864. The Mysterious Key and What It Opened, 1867. Little Women; or Meg, Jo, Beth and Amy, 1868. Morning-Glories, 1868. Kitty's Class Day, 1868. Aunt Kipp,

1868. Little Women: Part Second, 1869. An Old-Fashioned Girl, 1870. Little Men: Life at Plumfield with Jo's Boys, 1871. Aunt Jo's Scrap-Bag (6 vols., 1872–82), 1872. Work, 1873. Eight Cousins; or, The Aunt-Hill, 1875. Silver Pitchers, 1876. Rose in Bloom, 1876. A Modern Mephistopheles, 1877. Under the Lilacs, 1878. Meadow Blossoms, 1879. Sparkles for Bright Eyes, 1879. Water-Cresses, 1879. Jack and Jill: A Village Story, 1880. Proverb Stories, 1882. Spinning-Wheel Stories, 1884. Jo's Boys and How They Turned Out, 1886. Lulu's Library (3 vols., 1886–89), 1886. A Garland for Girls, 1888. A Modern Mephistopheles and A Whisper in the Dark, 1889.

Aldrich, Bess Streeter (1881–1954). Lantern in Her Hand, 1928. White Bird Flying, 1931. Spring Came On Forever, 1935. The Man Who Caught the Weather, 1936. Song of Years, 1939. The Lieutenant's Lady, 1942.

Aldrich, Thomas Bailey (1836–1907). The Bells: A Collection of Chimes, 1855. Daisy's Necklace: And What Came of It, 1857. The Course of True Love Never Did Run Smooth, 1858. The Ballad of Babie Bell and Other Poems, 1859. Pampinea and Other Poems, 1861. Out of His Head, 1862. Poems, 1863. Poems, 1865. Pansy's Wish: A Christmas Fantasy, 1870. The Story of a Bad Boy, 1870. Marjorie Daw and Other People, 1873. Prudence Palfrey, 1874. Cloth of Gold and Other Poems, 1874. Flower and Thorn, 1877. The Queen of Sheba, 1877. A Midnight Fantasy and the Little Violinist, 1877. The Stillwater Tragedy, 1880. Friar Jerome's Beautiful Book, 1881. Poems, 1882. From Ponkapog to Pesth, 1883. Mercedes and Later Lyrics, 1884. Poems, 1885. The Second Son, 1888. Wyndham Towers, 1890. The Sisters' Tragedy, 1891. An Old Town by the Sea, 1893. Unguarded Gates, 1895. Judith and Holofernes, 1896. Later Lyrics, 1896. A Sea Turn and Other Matters, 1902. Judith of Bethulia, 1904.

Alfred, William (1922–   ). Hogan's Goat, 1965.

Alger, Horatio, Jr. (1832–99). Ragged Dick Series (1867 ff.), 1867. Luck and Pluck Series (1869 ff.), 1869. Tattered Tom Series (1871 ff.), 1871.

Algren, Nelson (1909–81). Somebody in Boots, 1935. Never Come Morning, 1942. The Neon Wilderness, 1947. The Man with the Golden Arm, 1949. Chicago: City on the Make, 1951. A Walk on the Wild Side, 1956. Who Lost an American? 1963. Notes from a Sea Diary, 1965. The

Algren, Nelson (*continued*)
Last Carousel, 1973. The Devil's Stocking, 1983.

All the Year Round (1859–95).

Alleine, Richard (1611–81). A Companion for Prayer in Times of Extraordinary Danger, 1750.

Allen, Ethan (1738–89). An Animadversory Address to the Inhabitants of the State of Vermont, 1778. A Narrative of Colonel Ethan Allen's Captivity, 1779. The Present State of the Controversy Between the States of New-York and New-Hampshire on the One Part and the State of Vermont on the Other, 1782. Reason the Only Oracle of Man, 1784.

Allen, Frederick Lewis (1890–1954). Only Yesterday, 1931. The Lords of Creation, 1935. Since Yesterday, 1940. The Big Change, 1952.

Allen, Hervey (1889–1949). Israfel: The Life and Times of Edgar Allan Poe, 1926. Anthony Adverse, 1933. Action at Aquila, 1938. The Forest and the Fort, 1943. Bedford Village, 1944. Toward the Morning, 1948.

Allen, James Lane (1849–1925). Flute and Violin, 1891. Sister Dolorosa and Posthumous Fame, 1892. The Blue-Grass Region of Kentucky, 1892. John Gray, 1893. A Kentucky Cardinal, 1894. Aftermath, 1896. Summer in Arcady, 1896. The Choir Invisible [revision of John Gray (1893)], 1897. Chimney Corner Graduates, 1900. The Reign of Law, 1900. The Mettle of the Pasture, 1903. The Bride of the Mistletoe, 1909. The Doctor's Christmas Eve, 1910. The Heroine in Bronze, 1912. The Last Christmas Tree, 1914. The Sword of Youth, 1915. A Cathedral Singer, 1916. The Kentucky Warbler, 1918. The Emblems of Fidelity, 1919. The Alabaster Box, 1923. The Landmark, 1925.

Allen, Paul (1775–1826). Original Poems, Serious and Entertaining, 1801. History of the Expedition of Captains Lewis and Clark (with Nicholas Biddle), 1814. History of the American Revolution (largely revised by John Neal), 1819. Noah (rev. by John Neal), 1821.

Allen, William (1784–1868). American Biographical and Historical Dictionary (compiler), 1809.

Allibone, S. Austin (1816–89). A Critical Dictionary of English Literature and British and American Authors (3 vols., 1858–71), 1858.

Allin, John (1596–1671). Animadversions upon the Antisynodalia Americana, 1664. The Spouse of Christ Coming Out of Affliction, Leaning Upon Her Beloved, 1672.

Allston, Washington (1779–1843). The Sylphs of the Seasons, 1813. Monaldi, 1841. Lectures on Art and Poems, 1850.

Alsop, George (1638–?). A Character of the Province of Mary-Land, 1666.

Alsop, Richard (1761–1815). The Echo (with Theodore Dwight, Lemuel Hopkins, Elihu Hubbard Smith, and Mason Cogswell, 1791–1805), 1791. American Poems, 1793. The Political Greenhouse (with Lemuel Hopkins and Theodore Dwight), 1798. A Poem, Sacred to the Memory of George Washington, 1800.

Altgeld, John Peter (1847–1902). Our Penal Machinery and Its Victims, 1884.

Alther, Lisa (1944–   ). Kinflicks, 1976. Original Sins, 1981.

American Boy (1899–1929).

American Caravan (1927–36).

American Heritage (1949–   ).

American Law Journal (1808–17).

American Literature (1929–   ).

American Magazine (1741).

American Magazine (1905–56).

American Magazine and Historical Chronicle (1743–46).

American Mercury (1784–1833).

American Mercury (1924–   ).

American Museum (1787–92).

American Quarterly (1949–   ).

American Scholar (1932–   ).

American Spectator (1932–37).

American Speech (1925–   ).

American Review (1933–37).

American Weekly Mercury (1719–46).

American Whig Review (1845–52).

America's Lost Play Series (1940–41).

Ames, Fisher (1758–1808). Works, 1809.

Ames, Nathaniel (1708–64). An Astronomical Diary, or An Almanack (annually, 1725–64), 1725. The Essays, Humor, and Poems of Nathaniel Ames, 1891.

Amherst, Jeffrey (1717–97). A Journal of the Landing of His Majesty's Forces on the Island of Cape-Breton, 1758.

Ammons, A. R. (1926–   ). Ommateum, with Doxology, 1955. Expressions of Sea Level, 1964. Corsons Inlet, 1965. Tape for the Turn of the Year, 1965. Northfield Poems, 1966. Selected Poems, 1968. Uplands, 1970. Briefings: Poems Small and Easy, 1971. Collected Poems 1951–1971, 1972. Sphere: The Form of a Motion, 1974. Diversifications, 1975. The Snow Poems, 1977. The Selected Poems, 1951–1977, 1977. Selected Longer Poems, 1980. A Coast of Trees, 1981. Worldly Hopes, 1982. Lake Effect Country, 1983.

Arnow, Harriette (1908–). The Doll-maker, 1954.

"Arp, Bill." *See* Smith, Charles Henry.

"Artemus Ward." *See* Browne, Charles Farrar.

Arthur, Timothy Shay (1809–85). Temperance Tales, 1843. Agnes; or, The Possessed. A Revelation of Mesmerism, 1848. The Debtor's Daughter, 1850. Ten Nights in a Bar-room and What I Saw There, 1854.

Asch, Sholem (1880–1957). Mottke, the Vagabond, 1917. The God of Vengeance, 1918. Uncle Moses, 1920. Sabbatai Zevi, 1930. The Mother, 1930. Three Cities, 1933. Salvation, 1934. In the Beginning, 1935. The War Goes On, 1936. Three Novels: Uncle Moses, Chaim Lederer's Return, Judge Not, 1938. Song of the Valley, 1939. The Nazarene, 1939. What I Believe, 1941. Children of Abraham, 1942. The Apostle, 1943. East River, 1946. Tales of My People, 1948. Mary, 1949. Moses, 1951. A Passage in the Night, 1953. The Prophet, 1955. From Many Countries: Collected Short Stories, 1958.

Ashbery, John (1927–). Turandot and Other Poems, 1953. Some Trees, 1956. The Poems, 1960. The Tennis Court Oath, 1962. Rivers and Mountains, 1966. Three Madrigals, 1968. Sunrise in Suburbia, 1968. Fragment, 1969. The Double Dream of Spring, 1970. Three Poems, 1972. The Vermont Notebook, 1975. Self-Portrait in a Convex Mirror, 1975. Houseboat Days, 1977. As We Know, 1979. Shadow Train, 1981.

Athenaeum (1828–1921).

Athenian Gazette (1691–97).

Atherton, Gertrude (1857–1948). The Californians, 1898. Senator North, 1900. The Conqueror, 1902. The Splendid Idle Forties [revision of her short stories Before the Gringo Came (1894)], 1902. Rezánov, 1906. Julia France and Her Times, 1912. The Sisters-in-Law, 1921. Black Oxen, 1923.

Atlantic Monthly (1857–).

Auchincloss, Louis (1917–). The Indifferent Children, 1947. Sybil, 1952. A Law for the Lion, 1953. The Romantic Egoists, 1954. The Great World and Timothy Colt, 1956. Venus in Sparta, 1958. The House of Five Talents, 1960. Portrait in Brownstone, 1962. The Rector of Justin, 1964. A World of Profit, 1968. The House of the Prophet, 1980. The Cat and the King, 1981. Exit Lady Masham, 1983.

Auden, W. H. (1907–73). Poems, 1928. Poems, 1930. The Orators, 1932. The Dance of Death, 1933. Poems, 1934. The Dog Beneath the Skin (with Christopher Isherwood), 1935. The Ascent of F6 (with Christopher Isherwood), 1936. Letters from Iceland (with Louis MacNeice), 1937. On the Frontier (with Christopher Isherwood), 1938. Journey to a War (with Christopher Isherwood), 1939. Another Time, 1940. The Double Man, 1941. For the Time Being, 1944. The Collected Poetry, 1945. The Age of Anxiety, 1947. Collected Shorter Poems, 1930–1944, 1950. The Enchaféd Flood, 1950. Nones, 1951. The Rake's Progress (with Chester Kallmann), 1951. The Shield of Achilles, 1955. Selected Poetry, 1959. Homage to Clio, 1960. The Dyer's Hand, 1962. Selected Essays, 1964. About the House, 1965. Collected Shorter Poems, 1927–1957, 1966. Collected Longer Poems, 1968. Secondary Worlds, 1968. City Without Walls, 1969. A Certain World, 1970. Epistle to a Godson, 1972. Thank You, Fog, 1974.

Audubon, John James (1785–1851). The Birds of America from Original Drawings (folio edition, 1827–38), 1827. Ornithological Biography; or, An Account of the Habits of the Birds of the United States of America 1831. A Synopsis of the Birds of America, 1839. The Birds of America from Drawings Made in the United States and Their Territories (octavo edition, 1840–44), 1840. The Viviparous Quadrupeds of North America (with John Bachman; folio edition, 1845–54), 1845. The Quadrupeds of North America (with John Bachman; octavo edition, 1851–54), 1851.

Austin, Benjamin (1752–1820). Observations on the Pernicious Practice of the Law, 1786.

Austin, David (1760–1831). The American Preacher; or, A Collection of Sermons from Some of the Most Eminent Preachers Now Living in the United States (editor; 1791–93), 1791. The Voice of God to the People of These United States, 1796.

Austin, Jane Goodwin (1831–94). Standish of Standish, 1889. Betty Alden, 1891.

Austin, Mary (1868–1934). The Land of Little Rain, 1903. Isidro, 1905. The Ford, 1917.

Austin, William (1778–1841). Strictures on Harvard University, 1798. Letters from London, 1804. "Peter Rugg, the Missing Man," 1824.

"B. Traven" (?). The Death Ship, 1934. The Treasure of the Sierra Madre, 1935. The Bridge in the Jungle, 1938. The Rebellion of the Hanged, 1952.

Benét, Stephen Vincent (*continued*) ple's Pride, 1922. King David, 1923. The Ballad of William Sycamore, 1790–1880, 1923. Jean Huguenot, 1923. Tiger Joy, 1925. Spanish Bayonet, 1926. John Brown's Body, 1928. A Book of Americans (with Rosemary Carr Benét), 1933. James Shore's Daughter, 1934. Burning City, 1936. Thirteen O'Clock, 1937. The Devil and Daniel Webster, 1937. The Headless Horseman, 1937. Johnny Pye and the Fool-Killer, 1938. Tales Before Midnight, 1939. The Ballad of the Duke's Mercy, 1939. The Devil and Daniel Webster, 1939. Nightmare at Noon, 1940. Listen to the People, 1941. A Summons to the Free, 1941. They Burned the Books, 1942. Dear Adolph, 1942. A Child Is Born, 1942. Western Star, 1943. America, 1944. The Last Circle, 1946.

Benezet, Anthony (1713–84). Observations on the Inslaving, Importing, and Purchasing of Negroes, 1759. A Short Account of That Part of Africa Inhabited by the Negroes, 1762. A Caution to Great-Britain and Her Colonies, 1766. Some Historical Account of Guinea, 1771. A Mite Cast into the Treasury (attrib.), 1772. Some Necessary Remarks on the Education of the Youth, 1778.

Bennett, Emerson (1822–1905). The League of the Miami, 1845. Mike Fink, 1848. Prairie Flower, 1849. Leni-Leoti, 1849.

Benson, Eugene (1837–1908). Art and Nature in Italy, 1882.

Benson, Sally (1900–72). Junior Miss, 1941. Meet Me in St. Louis, 1942.

Benton, Thomas Hart (1782–1858). Thirty Years' View; or, A History of the Working of the American Government, 1820 to 1850, 1854.

Berenson, Bernard (1865–1959). Venetian Painters of the Renaissance, 1894. Florentine Painters of the Renaissance, 1896. Central Italian Painters of the Renaissance, 1897. Study and Criticism of Italian Art, 1901.

Berger, Thomas (1924–   ). Crazy in Berlin, 1958. Reinhart in Love, 1962. Little Big Man, 1964. Killing Time, 1967. Vital Parts, 1970. Regiment of Women, 1973. Sneaky People, 1975. Who Is Teddy Villanova? 1977. Arthur Rex, 1978. Neighbors, 1980. Reinhart's Women, 1981. The Feud, 1983.

Bernard, William Bayle (1807–75). The Dumb Belle, 1831. Rip Van Winkle [adapted from Washington Irving's short story (1819–20)], 1832. The Kentuckian; or, A Trip to New York [revision of James Kirke Paulding's The Lion of the West (1830)], 1833. His Last Legs, 1839.

Berry, Wendell (1934–   ). The Broken Ground, 1964. Openings, 1968. Findings, 1969. The Country of Marriage, 1973. Clearing, 1977.

Berryman, John (1914–72). Poems, 1942. The Dispossessed, 1948. Stephen Crane, 1950. Homage to Mistress Bradstreet, 1956. His Thoughts Made Pockets & the Plane Buckt, 1958. 77 Dream Songs, 1964. Berryman's Sonnets, 1967. Short Poems, 1967. His Toy, His Dream, His Rest, 1968. The Dream Songs, 1969. Love & Fame, 1970. Delusions, Etc, 1972. Recovery, 1973. The Freedom of the Poet, 1976. Henry's Fate and Other Poems, 1967–1972, 1977.

Beverley, Robert (c. 1673–c. 1722). The History and Present State of Virginia, 1705.

Bidwell, John (1819–1900). A Journey to California, 1842.

Bierce, Ambrose (1842–1914?). The Fiend's Delight, 1873. Nuggets and Dust, 1873. Cobwebs from an Empty Skull, 1874. The Dance of Death, 1877. Tales of Soldiers and Civilians (repub. as In the Midst of Life, 1892), 1891. The Monk and the Hangman's Daughter (with G. A. Danziger, trans. from the German of Richard Voss), 1892. Black Beetles in Amber, 1892. Can Such Things Be? 1893. In the Midst of Life [revision of Tales of Soldiers and Civilians (1891)], 1898. Fantastic Fables, 1899. Shapes of Clay, 1903. The Cynic's Word Book, 1906. The Shadow on the Dial, 1909. Write it Right, 1909. Collected Works (12 vols., 1909–12), 1909. The Devil's Dictionary [revision of The Cynic's Word Book (1906)], 1911.

Bigelow, John (1817–1911). Beaumarchais the Merchant, 1870. France and Hereditary Monarchy, 1871. Molinos the Quietist, 1882.

Biggers, Earl Derr (1884–1933). Seven Keys to Baldpate, 1913.

Bigland, John (1750–1832). A Geographical and Historical View of the World, 1811.

"Bill Arp." *See* Smith, Charles Henry.

"Bill Nye." *See* Nye, Edgar Wilson.

Billboard (1894–   ).

"Billings, Josh." *See* Shaw, Henry Wheeler.

Billings, William (1746–1800). The New England Psalm-Singer, 1770. Chester, 1778. The Singing Master's Assistant, or Key to Practical Music, 1778. The Psalm-Singers Amusement, Containing a Number of Fuging Pieces and Anthems, 1781.

Bingham, Caleb (1757–1817). The Young Lady's Accidence; or, A Short and Easy Introduction to English Grammar, 1785. The Child's Companion; Being a Concise Spelling Book, 1792. The American Pre-

Burroughs, John (*continued*)
The Light of Day, 1900. Far and Near, 1904. Ways of Nature, 1905. Bird and Bough, 1906. The Summit of the Years, 1913. The Breath of Life, 1915.

Burroughs, William S. (1914–   ). The Naked Lunch (pub. in Paris; repub. in the U.S. as Naked Lunch, 1962), 1959. The Exterminator, 1960. The Soft Machine (pub. in Paris; American edition, 1966), 1961. The Ticket That Exploded (pub. in Paris; American edition, 1967), 1962. The Yage Letters (with Allen Ginsberg), 1963. Dead Fingers Talk (pub. in London), 1963. Nova Express, 1964. The Wild Boys: A Book of the Dead, 1971. Exterminator! 1973. The Last Words of Dutch Schultz, 1975. Junky, 1977. Port of Saints, 1980. Cities of the Red Night, 1981. The Place of Dead Roads, 1983.

Burt, Struthers (1882–1954). John O'May and Other Stories, 1918. Chance Encounters, 1921. The Interpreter's House, 1924. The Delectable Mountains, 1927. They Could Not Sleep, 1928. Along These Streets, 1942.

Burton, William Evans (1804–60). Waggeries and Vagaries, 1848.

Bushnell, Horace (1802–76). Christian Nurture, 1847. God in Christ, 1849. The Age of Homespun, 1851. Nature and the Supernatural, 1858. The Vicarious Sacrifice, 1866.

Butler, Ellis Parker (1869–1937). Pigs Is Pigs, 1906.

Butler, James (1775?–1842). Fortune's Football; or, The Adventures of Mercutio (1797–98), 1797.

Butler, William Allen (1825–1902). Nothing to Wear (first pub. anon. in Harper's Weekly, 1857), 1857.

Byfield, Nathaniel (1653–1733). An Account of the Late Revolution in New-England, 1689. Seasonable Motives. To Our Duty and Allegiance, 1689.

Byles, Mather (1707–88). A Poem on the Death of His Late Majesty King George, of Glorious Memory, and the Accession of Our Present Sovereign, King George II, to the British Throne, 1727. The Character of the Perfect and Upright Man, 1729. A Discourse on the Present Vileness of the Body, and Its Future Glorious Change by Christ, 1732. To His Excellency Governeur Belcher, on the Death of His Lady. An Epistle, 1736. On the Death of the Queen, 1738. Affections on Things Above, 1740. Poems on Several Occasions, 1744. The Comet, 1744. The Conflagration, 1755.

Bynner, Witter (1881–1968). An Ode to Harvard and Other Poems, 1907. Tiger, 1913. Grenstone Poems, 1917. A Canticle of Pan, 1920. Indian Earth, 1929. Against the Cold, 1940. Take Away the Darkness, 1947. A Book of Lyrics, 1956. New Poems, 1960.

Byrd, Richard E. (1888–1957). Skyward, 1928. Little America, 1930. Alone, 1938.

Byrd, William (1674–1744). The Secret Diary . . . (1709–12, 1717–21, 1739–41; pub. 1941, 1942, 1958), 1709. History of the Dividing Line Betwixt Virginia and North Carolina (pub. 1841), 1729. A Progress to the Mines (pub. 1841), 1732. A Journey to the Land of Eden (pub. 1841), 1733.

Cabell, James Branch (1879–1958). The Eagle's Shadow, 1904. The Line of Love, 1905. Gallantry, 1907. Chivalry, 1909. The Cords of Vanity, 1909. The Soul of Melicent, 1913. The Rivet in Grandfather's Neck, 1915. From the Hidden Way, 1916. The Certain Hour, 1916. The Cream of the Jest, 1917. Jurgen, 1919. Beyond Life, 1919. Domnei [revision of The Soul of Melicent (1913)], 1920. The Jewel Merchants, 1921. Figures of Earth, 1921. The Lineage of Lichfield, 1922. The High Place, 1923. Straws and Prayer Books, 1924. The Silver Stallion, 1926. The Music from Behind the Moon, 1926. Something About Eve, 1927. The White Robe, 1928. Sonnets from Antan, 1929. The Way of Ecben, 1929. Some of Us: An Essay in Epitaphs, 1930. These Restless Heads, 1932. Special Delivery: A Packet of Replies, 1933. Ladies and Gentlemen, 1934. Smirt: An Urban Nightmare, 1934. Smith: A Sylvan Interlude, 1935. Smire: An Acceptance in the Third Person, 1937. The King Was in His Counting House, 1938. Hamlet Had an Uncle, 1940. The First Gentleman of America, 1942. The St. Johns: A Parade of Diversities (with A. J. Hanna), 1943. There Were Two Pirates, 1946. Let Me Lie, 1947. The Devil's Own Dear Son, 1949. A Lamp for Nightfall, 1952. The Courting of Susie Brown, 1952. As I Remember It, 1955. Between Friends: Letters of James Branch Cabell and Others, 1962.

Cable, George Washington (1844–1925). Old Creole Days, 1879. The Grandissimes, 1880. Madame Delphine, 1881. The Creoles of Louisiana, 1884. Dr. Sevier, 1885. The Silent South, 1885. Bonaventure, 1888. Strange True Stories of Louisiana, 1889. The Negro Question, 1890. John March, Southerner, 1894. Strong Hearts, 1899. The Cavalier, 1901. Bylow Hill, 1902. Kincaid's Battery, 1908.

Carey, Mathew (1760–1839). The Porcupiniad. A Hudibrastic Poem, 1799. The Olive Branch, 1814. Autobiographical
Sketches, 1829. Miscellaneous Essays,
1830.

Carleton, Henry Guy (1856–1910). The
Thompson Street Poker Club, 1884. The
Gilded Fool, 1892. The Butterflies, 1894.

Carleton, Will (1845–1912). Farm Ballads,
1873. Farm Legends, 1875. City Ballads,
1885.

Carman, Bliss (1861–1929). Low Tide on
Grand Pré, 1893. Songs from Vagabondia
(with Richard Hovey), 1894. Behind the
Arras: A Book of the Unseen, 1895. More
Songs from Vagabondia (with Richard
Hovey), 1896. Ballads of Lost Haven: A
Book of the Sea, 1897. Last Songs from
Vagabondia (with Richard Hovey), 1901.

Carmer, Carl (1893–1976). Stars Fell on
Alabama, 1934. Listen for a Lonesome
Drum, 1936. Genesee Fever, 1941.

Carnegie, Andrew (1835–1919). Triumphant
Democracy, 1886. The Gospel of Wealth,
1889. The Empire of Business, 1902. Autobiography, 1920.

Carnegie, Dale (1888–1955). How to Win
Friends and Influence People, 1936.

Carpet-Bag (1851–53).

Carroll, James (1943?–). Mortal Friends,
1978. Fault Lines, 1980.

Carroll, John (1735–1815). An Address to
the Roman Catholics of the United States
of America, 1784.

Carroll, Gladys Hasty (1904–). As the
Earth Turns, 1933.

Carruth, Hayden (1921–). The Crow
and the Heart, 1959. Nothing for Tigers:
Poems 1959–1964, 1965. From Snow and
Rock, from Chaos: Poems 1965–1972,
1973. The Sleeping Beauty, 1982.

Carson, Rachel (1907–64). The Sea Around
Us, 1951. The Edge of the Sea, 1955. Silent Spring, 1962.

Carter, Hodding (1907–72). Where Main
Street Meets the River, 1953. First Person
Rural, 1963.

Cartwright, John (1740–1824). American Independence the Interest and Glory of
Great Britain, 1776.

Cartwright, Peter (1785–1872). Autobiography, 1857. The Backwoods Preacher,
1858. Fifty Years as a Presiding Elder,
1871.

Caruthers, William Alexander (1802–46).
The Kentuckian in New York, 1834. The
Cavaliers of Virginia (1834–35), 1834.
The Knights of the Horse-Shoe, 1845.

Carver, Jonathan (1701–80). Travels
Through the Interior Part of North America, 1778.

Carver, Raymond (1938–). Will You
Please Be Quiet, Please? 1976. What We

Talk About When We Talk About Love,
1981. Cathedral, 1983.

Cary, Phoebe (1824–71). Poems and Parodies, 1854. Poems of Faith, Hope, and
Love, 1868.

Cassill, R. V. (1919–). The Eagle on
the Coin, 1950. Clem Anderson, 1961.
Pretty Leslie, 1963. The President, 1964.
Dr. Cobb's Game, 1970. Labors of Love,
1980.

Catesby, Mark (c. 1679–1749). The Natural
History of Carolina, Florida, and the Ba-
hama Islands (1731–43), 1731. Hortus
Britanno-Americanus (1763–67), 1763.

Cather, Willa (1873–1947). April Twilights,
1903. The Troll Garden, 1905. Alexander's Bridge, 1912. O Pioneers! 1913.
The Song of the Lark, 1915. My Ántonia,
1918. Youth and the Bright Medusa,
1920. One of Ours, 1922. A Lost Lady,
1923. The Professor's House, 1925. My
Mortal Enemy, 1926. Death Comes for
the Archbishop, 1927. Shadows on the
Rock, 1931. Obscure Destinies, 1932.
Lucy Gayheart, 1935. Not Under Forty,
1936. Sapphira and the Slave Girl, 1940.
The Old Beauty and Others, 1948.

Catherwood, Mary (1847–1902). The Romance of Dollard, 1889. The Spirit of an
Illinois Town, 1897.

Catlin, George (1796–1872). The Manners,
Customs, and Condition of the North
American Indians, 1841. Life Amongst
the Indians, 1857. Last Rambles Amongst
the Indians of the Rocky Mountains and
the Andes, 1867.

Catton, Bruce (1899–1978). Mr. Lincoln's
Army, 1951. Glory Road, 1952. A Stillness at Appomattox, 1953.

Cawein, Madison (1865–1914). Lyrics and
Idyls, 1890. Kentucky Poems, 1902. Vale
of Tempe, 1905.

Century Illustrated Magazine (1881–1930).

Chalkley, Thomas (1675–1741). Journal,
1747.

Chalmers, Lionel (1715?–77). An Essay on
Fevers, 1767.

Chambers, Robert W. (1865–1933). In
the Quarter, 1894. The Red Republic,
1895.

Champion (1739–43?)

Champion, Judah (1729–1810). A Brief
View of the Distresses, Hardships and
Dangers Our Ancestors Encounter'd in
Settling New-England, 1770.

Champlain, Samuel de (c. 1567–1635). Des
sauvages, ou, voyage de Samuel Champlain de Brouage fait en la France nouvelle, 1603. Voyages de la nouvelle
France, 1632.

Chandler, Elizabeth Margaret (1807–34). Essays, Philosophical and Moral, 1836. Poetical Works, 1836.

Chesnutt, Charles Waddell (1858–1932). The Conjure Woman, 1899. The Wife of His Youth, 1899. Frederick Douglass, 1899. The House Behind the Cedars, 1900. The Marrow of Tradition, 1901. The Colonel's Dream, 1905.

Chester, George Randolph (1869–1924). Get-Rich-Quick Wallingford, 1908.

Chicago Daily News (1875–1929).

Chicago Times (1854–1918).

Chicago Tribune (1847–   ).

Child, Francis James (1825–96). English and Scottish Popular Ballads (editor; 5 vols., 1883–98), 1883.

Child, John (?). New-Englands Jonas Cast Up at London, 1647.

Child, Lydia Maria (1802–80). Hobomok, 1824. The Rebels, or, Boston before the Revolution, 1825. An Appeal in Favor of that Class of Americans Called Africans, 1833. Philothea, 1836.

Chivers, Thomas Holley (1809–58). The Path of Sorrow, 1832. Conrad and Eudora, 1834. Nacoochee, 1837. The Lost Pleiad and Other Poems, 1845. Search After Truth; or, A New Revelation of the Psycho-Physiological Nature of Man, 1848. Eonchs of Ruby: A Gift of Love, 1851. Memoralia; or, Phials of Amber Full of the Tears of Love, 1853. Virginalia, or Songs of My Summer Nights, 1853. Birth-Day Song of Liberty, 1856. The Sons of Usna, 1858.

Chodorov, Edward (1904–   ). Wonder Boy, 1932. Kind Lady, 1935. Those Endearing Young Charms, 1943.

Chodorov, Jerome (1911–   ). My Sister Eileen [adapted with Joseph Fields from Ruth McKenney's sketches (1938)], 1940. Junior Miss [adapted with Joseph Fields from Sally Benson's stories (1941)], 1941. Anniversary Waltz (with Joseph Fields), 1954. The Ponder Heart [adapted with Joseph Fields from Eudora Welty's novel (1954)], 1957.

Chopin, Kate (1851–1904). At Fault, 1890. Bayou Folk, 1894. A Night in Acadie, 1897. The Awakening, 1899.

Christian Disciple (1813–23).

Christian Examiner (1824–69).

Christian Science Monitor (1908–   ).

Christian World (1857–1961).

Christopher, Nicholas (1951–   ). On Tour with Rita, 1982.

Church, Benjamin (1734–76). The Choice, 1757. The Times, 1765. Liberty and Property Vindicated and the St[am]pm[a]n Burnt, 1765. An Oration . . . to Commemorate the Bloody Tragedy of the Fifth of March, 1770, 1773.

Church, Thomas (1673–1748). Entertaining Passages Relating to Philip's War Which Began in the Month of June, 1675, 1716.

Churchill, Winston (1871–1947). The Celebrity: An Episode, 1898. Richard Carvel, 1899. The Crisis, 1901. The Crossing, 1904. Coniston, 1906. Mr. Crewe's Career, 1908. A Modern Chronicle, 1910. The Inside of the Cup, 1913. A Far Country, 1915. The Dwelling-Place of Light, 1917. Dr. Jonathan, 1919.

Ciardi, John (1916–   ). Homeward to America, 1940. Other Skies, 1947. Live Another Day, 1949. From Time to Time, 1951. As If, 1955. I Marry You, 1958. In Fact, 1963. Dialogue with an Audience, 1963. Person to Person, 1964.

City Mercury (1675–81).

Clampitt, Amy (1920–   ). The Kingfisher, 1983.

Clap, Thomas (1703–67). An Essay on the Nature and Foundation of Moral Virtue, 1765. The Annals or History of Yale-College, in New Haven, 1766.

Clapp, Henry (1814–75). The Pioneer; or, Leaves from an Editor's Portfolio, 1846.

Clappe, Louise Amelia Knapp Smith (1819–1906). Dame Shirley Letters (pub. in Pioneer Magazine, 1854–55; coll. 1922), 1854.

Clark, Charles Heber (1841–1915). Out of the Hurly-Burly, 1874. Elbow-Room, 1876.

Clark, Eleanor (1913–   ). Rome and a Villa, 1952. The Oysters of Locmariaquer, 1964.

Clark, Jonas (1730–1805). The Importance of Military Skill, Measures for Defence and a Martial Spirit, in a Time of Peace, 1768. The Use and Excellency of Vocal Music in Public Worship, 1770. The Fate of Blood-Thirsty Oppressors, and God's Tender Care for His Distressed People, 1776.

Clark, Lewis Gaylord (1808–73). Knick-Knacks from an Editor's Table, 1852.

Clark, Walter Van Tilburg (1909–71). The Ox-Bow Incident, 1940. The City of Trembling Leaves, 1945. The Track of the Cat, 1949. The Watchful Gods, 1950.

Clark, Willis Gaylord (1808–41). Literary Remains . . . Including the Ollipodiana Papers, 1844.

Clarke, James Freeman (1810–88). Hymn Book for the Church of the Disciples, 1844. The Christian Doctrine of Prayer, 1854. Ten Great Religions, 1871. Common Sense in Religion, 1874. Essentials and Non-Essentials in Religion, 1878.

Clarke, John (1609–76). Ill News from New England, 1652.

Clarke, McDonald (1798–1842). The Elixir of Moonshine . . . by the Mad Poet, 1822.

Clarke, William (?). Observations on the

novel The Homecoming Game (1957)], 1959.

Cullen, Countee (1903–46). Color, 1925. Copper Sun, 1927. The Ballad of the Brown Girl, 1927. The Black Christ, 1929. The Medea and Some Poems, 1935.

Cummings, E. E. (1894–1962). The Enormous Room, 1922. Tulips and Chimneys, 1923. &, 1925. XLI Poems, 1925. Is 5, 1926. Him, 1927. Christmas Tree, 1928. W (Viva), 1931. Eimi, 1933. Tom: A Ballet, 1935. No Thanks, 1935. 1/20, 1936. Collected Poems, 1938. 50 Poems, 1940. 1 × 1, 1944. Anthropos: The Future of Art, 1945. Santa Claus: A Morality, 1946. XAIPE: 71 Poems, 1950. i: six nonlectures, 1953. Poems, 1923–1954, 1954. 95 Poems, 1958. 73 Poems, 1963.

Cummins, Maria Susanna (1827–66). The Lamplighter, 1854. Mabel Vaughan, 1857. El Fureidis, 1860. Haunted Hearts, 1864.

Curtis, George William (1824–92). Nile Notes of a Howadji, 1851. The Howadji in Syria, 1852. Lotus Eating, 1852. The Potiphar Papers, 1853. Prue and I, 1856. The Duty of the American Scholar to Politics and the Times, 1856. Trumps, 1861.

Cushing, Jacob (1730–1809). Divine Judgments Upon Tyrants and Compassion to the Oppressed, 1778.

Custer, George Armstrong (1839–76). My Life on the Plains, 1874.

Custis, George Washington Parke (1781–1857). The Indian Prophecy, a National Drama in Two Acts, Founded on . . . the Life of George Washington, 1827. Pocahontas, 1830. The Railroad, 1830. North Point, 1833. The Eighth of January, 1834. Recollections and Private Memoirs of Washington, 1860.

Cutler, Timothy (1684–1765). The Firm Union of a People Represented, 1717.

Daedalus (1955–).

Daggett, David (1764–1851). The Life and Extraordinary Adventures of Joseph Mountain, a Negro, Who was Executed at New-Haven for a Rape, 1790.

Dahlberg, Edward (1900–77). Bottom Dogs (pub. in London), 1929. From Flushing to Calvary, 1932. Those Who Perish, 1934. Flea of Sodom, 1950. The Sorrows of Priapus, 1957. Because I Was Flesh, 1964. Confessions, 1971.

Daily Advertiser (1730–1808?).
Daily Courant (1702–35).
Daily Gazetteer (1735–48).
Daily Mail (1896–).
Daily News (1846–1930).
Daily Post (1719–46?).

Daily Telegraph (1855–).

Dalrymple, Sir John (1726–1810). The Rights of Great Britain Asserted Against the Claims of America (attrib.), 1776.

Daly, Augustin (1838–99). Under the Gaslight, 1867. Horizon, 1871. Divorce, 1871.

"Dan De Quille." *See* Wright, William.

Dana, James (1735–1812). An Examination of the Late Reverend President Edwards's Enquiry on Freedom of Will, 1770. The African Slave Trade. A Discourse, 1791.

Dana, James Dwight (1813–95). System of Mineralogy, 1837. Manual of Geology, 1862.

Dana, Richard Henry, Sr. (1787–1879). Poems and Prose Writings, 1833.

Dana, Richard Henry, Jr. (1815–82). "Cruelty to Seamen," 1839. Two Years Before the Mast, 1840. The Seaman's Friend (pub. in London as The Seaman's Manual), 1841. To Cuba and Back, 1859.

Danforth, John (1660–1730). The Right Christian Temper in Every Condition, 1702. The Blackness of Sins Against Light, 1710. A Poem, Upon the Much Honoured . . . Mrs. Maria Mather, 1714.

Danforth, Samuel (1626–74). A Brief Recognition of New-Englands Errand into the Wilderness, 1671.

Daniels, Jonathan (1902–). A Southerner Discovers the South, 1938. A Southerner Discovers New England, 1940. Tar Heels, A Portrait of North Carolina, 1941. The End of Innocence, 1954.

Darby, William (?). Ye Bare and Ye Cubb (with Cornelius Watkinson and Philip Howard), 1665.

Darley, Felix Octavius Carr (1822–88). Scenes in Indian Life, 1843. Sketches Abroad with Pen and Pencil, 1869.

Darrow, Clarence (1857–1938). Farmington, 1904.

Davenport, Guy (1927–). Tatlin! 1974. DaVinci's Bicycle, 1979.

Davenport, John (1597–1670). A Discourse about Civil Government in a New Plantation Whose Design is Religion, 1663. A Catechism Printed for the Use of the First Church in Boston, 1669. Gods Call to His People to Turn Unto Him, 1669.

Davenport, Marcia (1903–). Of Lena Geyer, 1936. The Valley of Decision, 1943. East Side, West Side, 1947.

Davidson, Donald (1893–1968). The Tall Men, 1927. The Attack on Leviathan, 1938. Lee in the Mountains, 1938. Still Rebels, Still Yankees, 1957. The Long Street, 1961.

Davidson, Robert (1750–1812). Geography Epitomized; or A Tour Round the World, 1784.

Davies, Samuel (1724–61). A Sermon on Man's Primitive State, 1748. The State of Religion Among the Protestant Dissenters in Virginia, 1751. Miscellaneous Poems, Chiefly on Divine Subjects, 1752. Virginia's Danger and Remedy, 1756. The Curse of Cowardice, 1759. An Ode on the Prospect of Peace, 1761.

Davis, Andrew Jackson (1826–1910). Principles of Nature, Her Divine Revelations, and A Voice of Mankind, 1847. The Great Harmonia, 1850.

Davis, Angela (1944–   ). Autobiography, 1974.

Davis, Charles Augustus (1795?–1868?). Letters Written During the President's Tour, "Down East," by Myself, Major Jack Downing, of Downingville, 1833. Letters of J. Downing, Major, Downingville Militia to Mr. Dwight of the New York Daily Advertiser, 1834.

Davis, Clyde Brion (1894–1962). The Anointed, 1937. The Great American Novel, 1938.

Davis, Elmer (1890–1958). But We Were Born Free, 1954. Two Minutes Till Midnight, 1955.

Davis, Jefferson (1808–89). The Rise and Fall of the Confederacy, 1881. A Short History of the Confederate States of America, 1890.

Davis, John (1775–1854). The Farmer of New Jersey; or, A Picture of Domestic Life, 1800. The Wanderings of William, 1801. Travels of Four Years and a Half in the United States, 1803. The Post Captain, 1805. The First Settlers of Virginia, 1805. Walter Kennedy, 1808.

Davis, Ossie (1917–   ). Purlie Victorious, 1961.

Davis, Owen (1874–1956). Nellie, the Beautiful Cloak Model, 1906. The Detour (pub. 1922), 1921. Icebound, 1923.

Davis, Rebecca Harding (1831–1910). "Life in the Iron Mills," 1861. Margaret Howth, 1862. Waiting for the Verdict, 1868. John Andross, 1874.

Davis, Richard Harding (1864–1916). Gallegher and Other Stories, 1891. Van Bibber and Others, 1892. About Paris, 1895. Soldiers of Fortune, 1897. Ranson's Folly, 1902. Captain Macklin, 1902. The Bar Sinister, 1903. The Dictator, 1904. Ranson's Folly [adapted from his short stories (1902)], 1904. Miss Civilization, 1906. Notes of a War Correspondent, 1910.

Davison, Peter (1928–   ). The Breaking of the Day, 1964. The City and the Island, 1966. Pretending to Be Asleep, 1970. Half Remembered: A Personal History, 1973. Walking the Boundaries:

Poems 1957–1974, 1974. A Voice in the Mountain, 1977. Barn Fever and Other Poems, 1981.

Dawes, Rufus (1803–59). Geraldine, Athenia of Damascus, and Miscellaneous Poems, 1839. Nix's Mate, 1839.

Dawes, Thomas (1757–1825). The Law Given at Sinai, 1777.

Dawson, William (1704–52). Poems on Several Occasions, 1736.

Day, Clarence (1874–1935). This Simian World, 1920. God and My Father, 1932. Life with Father, 1935. Life with Mother, 1937. Father and I, 1940.

Dazey, Charles T. (1855–1938). In Old Kentucky, 1893.

Dearborn, Henry (1751–1829). An Account of the Battle of Bunker Hill, 1818.

De Bow, James Dunwoody Brownson (1820–67). Industrial Resources of the Southern and Western States, 1853.

Debs, Eugene V. (1855–1926). Unionism and Socialism, a Plea for Both, 1904. The American Movement, 1904. Industrial Unionism, 1905.

Deering, Nathaniel (1791–1881). Carabasset, 1831. Bozzaris, 1851.

De Forest, John William (1826–1906). History of the Indians of Connecticut, 1851. Oriental Acquaintance; or, Letters from Syria, 1856. European Acquaintance, 1858. Seacliff; or, The Mystery of the Westervelts, 1859. Miss Ravenel's Conversion from Secession to Loyalty, 1867. Overland, 1871. Kate Beaumont, 1872. The Wetherel Affair, 1873. Honest John Vane, 1875. Playing the Mischief, 1875. Irene the Missionary, 1879. The Bloody Chasm, 1881. A Lover's Revolt, 1898. The DeForests of Avesnes, 1900. The Downing Legends, 1901. Poem: Medley and Palestrina, 1902.

De Kruif, Paul (1890–1971). Microbe Hunters, 1926. Hunger Fighters, 1928. Men Against Death, 1932.

Deland, Margaret (1857–1945). John Ward, Preacher, 1888. Old Chester Tales, 1898. Dr. Lavendar's People, 1903. The Awakening of Helena Richie, 1906. The Iron Woman, 1911.

Delano, Alonzo (1802?–74). Pen-Knife Sketches, or Chips of the Old Block, 1853. Life on the Plains and Among the Diggings, 1854. Old Block's Sketch Book, 1856. A Live Woman in the Mines, 1857.

Delano, Amasa (1763–1823). A Narrative of Voyages and Travels, in the Northern and Southern Hemispheres, 1817.

De La Warr, Thomas West, Baron (1577–1618). The relation of the Right Honourable the Lord De-La-Warre, lord gouernour

Dunbar, Paul Laurence (*continued*)
Lyrics of Lowly Life, 1896. Folks from
Dixie, 1898. The Uncalled, 1898. Lyrics
of the Hearthside, 1899. The Strength of
Gideon and Other Stories, 1900. The Love
of Landry, 1900. The Fanatics, 1901. The
Sport of the Gods, 1902. Lyrics of Love
and Laughter, 1903. In Old Plantation
Days, 1903. Lyrics of Sunshine and
Shadow, 1905. Complete Poems, 1913.

Duncan, Robert (1919–   ). Heavenly
City, Earthly City, 1947. Medieval
Scenes, 1950. Selected Poems, 1959. The
Opening of the Field, 1960. Roots and
Branches, 1964. Bending the Bow, 1968.

Dunlap, William (1766–1839). The Father;
or American Shandyism (rev. as The
Father of an Only Child, 1806), 1789.
Darby's Return, 1789. The Fatal Deception; or, The Progress of Guilt (pub. as
Leicester, 1807), 1794. Fontainville Abbey, 1795. The Archers; or, Mountaineers
of Switzerland, 1796. The Mysterious
Monk (pub. as Ribbemont; or, The Feudal
Baron, 1803), 1796. The Knight's Adventure, 1797. André. A Tragedy, 1798. The
Italian Father, 1799. The Glory of Columbia; Her Yeomanry [revision of André
(1798); pub. 1817], 1803. Yankee Chronology; or, Huzza for the Constitution!
1812. Memoirs of George Fred. Cooke,
1813. A Narrative of the Event Which
Followed Bonaparte's Campaign in Russia, 1814. The Life of Charles Brockden
Brown, 1815. A Trip to Niagara; or,
Travellers in America, 1828. The History
of the American Theatre, 1832. A History
of the Rise and Progress of the Arts of
Design in the United States, 1834. Thirty
Years Ago; or, The Memoirs of a Water
Drinker, 1836. A History of New York,
for Schools, 1837. History of the New
Netherlands, Province of New York, and
State of New York, 1839.

Dunne, Finley Peter (1867–1936). Mr.
Dooley in Peace and in War, 1898. Mr.
Dooley's Philosophy, 1900. Mr. Dooley's
Opinions, 1901. Dissertations by Mr.
Dooley, 1906. Mr. Dooley Says, 1910.
Mr. Dooley on Making a Will, 1919.

Dunne, John Gregory (1932–   ). True
Confessions, 1977. Dutch Shea, Jr, 1982.

Dunton, John (1659–1733). Life and Errors
of John Dunton, 1705.

Du Ponceau, Pierre Etienne (1760–1844).
English Phonology, 1817. A Discourse on
the Necessity and Means of Making Our
National Literature Independent, 1834.
Grammatical System of Some of the Lan-
guages of the Indian Nations of North
America, 1838.

Dupuy, Eliza Ann (1814–81). The Conspirator, 1850. The Huguenot Exiles, 1856.

Durant, Will (1885–1981). The Story of Philosophy, 1926.

Durant, Will (1885–1981) and Ariel Durant
(1898–1981). The Story of Civilization
(11 vols., 1935–68), 1935.

Dwight, Josiah (1671–1748). An Essay to
Silence the Outcry That Has Been Made
in Some Places Against Regular Singing,
1725.

Dwight, Marianne (1816–1901). Letters
from Brook Farm, 1844–1847 (pub.
1928), 1844.

Dwight, Theodore (1764–1846). The North-
ern Traveller, 1825. Sketches of Scenery
and Manners in the United States, 1829.
History of the Hartford Convention, 1833.
The Character of Thomas Jefferson, 1839.
The History of Connecticut, 1841.

Dwight, Timothy (1752–1817). A Dissertation on the History, Eloquence, and Poetry
of the Bible, 1772. America: or, A Poem
on the Settlement of the British Colonies
(attrib.), 1780. The Conquest of Canaan,
1785. The Triumph of Infidelity, 1788.
Virtuous Rulers a Natural Blessing, 1791.
Greenfield Hill, 1794. The True Means of
Establishing Public Happiness, Two Discourses on the Nature and Danger of Infidel Philosophy, 1798. The Duty of Americans, at the Present Crisis, 1798. Remarks
on the Review of Inchiquin's Letters,
1815. Theology, Explained and Defended,
1818. Travels in New-England and New-
York, 1821.

Dwight's Journal of Music (1852–81).

Eastman, Mary H. (1818–80). Dacotah, or
Life and Legends of the Sioux Around
Fort Snelling, 1849. The Romance of In-
dian Life, 1852. Aunt Phillis's Cabin; or
Southern Life as It Is, 1852. Chicora, and
Other Regions of the Conquerors and Con-
quered, 1854.

Eastman, Max (1883–1969). Enjoyment of
Poetry, 1913. Marx, Lenin, and the Sci-
ence of Revolution, 1926. Enjoyment of
Laughter, 1936.

Eberhart, Richard (1904–   ). A Bravery
of Earth, 1930. Reading the Spirit, 1937.
Song and Idea, 1940. Burr Oaks, 1947.
An Herb Basket, 1950. Undercliff: Poems
1946–1953, 1953. Great Praises, 1957.
Collected Poems 1930–1960, 1960. Collected Verse Plays, 1962. The Quarry,
1964. Selected Poems 1930–1965, 1965.
Shifts of Being, 1968. Fields of Grace,
1972.

Ebony (1945–   ).

Eckley, Joseph (1750–1811). Divine Glory,

menta (enl. as Elementa Philosophica, 1752), 1746.

Johnston, Mary (1870–1936). Prisoners of Hope, 1898. To Have and To Hold, 1900. Audrey, 1902. The Long Roll, 1911. Cease Firing, 1912.

Johnston, Richard Malcolm (1822–98). Georgia Sketches, 1864. Dukesborough Tales, 1871.

Jones, Hugh (c. 1670–1760). An Accidence to the English Tongue, 1724. The Present State of Virginia, 1724. A Protest Against Popery, 1745.

Jones, James (1921–77). From Here to Eternity, 1951. Some Came Running, 1957. The Pistol, 1959. The Thin Red Line, 1962. Go to the Widow-Maker, 1967. The Ice-Cream Headache and Other Stories, 1968. The Merry Month of May, 1971. A Touch of Danger, 1973. Viet Journal, 1974. WW II, 1975. Whistle (completed by Willie Morris), 1978.

Jones, James Athearn (1791–1854). The Refugee, 1825. Tales of an Indian Camp, 1829. Haverhill; or, Memoirs of an Officer in the Army of Wolfe, 1831.

Jones, John Beauchamp (1810–66). Wild Western Scenes, 1841. The Western Merchant, 1849. Freaks of Fortune; or, The History of Ned Lorn, 1854. The War Path, 1858. A Rebel War Clerk's Diary at the Confederate Capital, 1866.

Jones, Joseph Stevens (1809–77). The Liberty Tree, 1832. The People's Lawyer, 1839. The Carpenter of Rouen, 1840. The Silver Spoon, 1852. Paul Revere and the Sons of Liberty, 1875.

Jones, LeRoi (1934–). Preface to a Twenty Volume Suicide Note, 1961. Blues People, 1963. The Dead Lecturer, 1964. Dutchman, 1964. The Slave, 1964. The Baptism, 1964. The Toilet, 1964. The System of Dante's Hell, 1965. Home: Social Essays, 1966. A Black Mass, 1966. Tales, 1967. Slave Ship, 1967. Black Magic: Poetry 1961–1967, 1969. See also Baraka, Imamu Amiri.

Jong, Erica (1942–). Fear of Flying, 1973.

Jonson, Robert (fl. 1609–12). Nova Britannia: offeringe most excellent Fruites by Planting in Virginia, 1609. The New Life of Virginia (attrib.), 1612.

Josephson, Matthew (1899–1978). The Robber Barons, 1934.

"Josh Billings." See Shaw, Henry Wheeler.

Josselyn, John (fl. 1638–75). New-Englands Rarities Discovered, 1672. An Account of Two Voyages to New-England, 1674.

Journal de Paris (1777–1840).

Journal of American Studies (1967–).

Journal of Modern Literature (1970–).

Journal of Negro History (1916–).

Journal of Speculative Philosophy (1867–93).

Judd, Sylvester (1813–53). A Young Man's Account of His Conversion from Calvinism, 1838. Margaret: A Tale of the Real and Ideal, 1845. Richard Edney and the Governor's Family, 1850. Philo, An Evangeliad, 1850.

Judge (1881–1939).

Judson, David (1715–76). Timely Warning Against Surfeiting and Drunkenness, 1752.

Judson, Edward Zane Carroll ["Ned Buntline"] (1823–86). The Scouts of the Plains, 1873.

"Junius" Letters (1769–71).

Justice, Donald (1925–). The Summer Anniversaries, 1960. A Local Storm, 1963. Night Light, 1967. Departures, 1973. Selected Poems, 1979.

Kalm, Peter (1716–79). Travels into North America, 1770.

Kane, Elisha Kent (1820–57). The U.S. Grinnell Expedition in Search of Sir John Franklin, 1853.

Kanin, Garson (1912–). Born Yesterday, 1946. The Rat Race, 1949.

Kantor, MacKinlay (1904–77). Long Remember, 1934. The Voice of Bugle Ann, 1935. Happy Land, 1943. But Look, the Morn, 1947. Andersonville, 1955. Spirit Lake, 1961.

Karnow, Stanley (1925–). Vietnam: A History, 1983.

Kauffman, Janet (?). The Weather Book, 1981. Places in the World a Woman Could Walk, 1983.

Kaufman, George S. (1889–1961). Dulcy (with Marc Connelly), 1921. To the Ladies (with Marc Connelly), 1922. Merton of the Movies [adapted with Marc Connelly from Harry Leon Wilson's novel (1922)], 1922. Beggar on Horseback (with Marc Connelly), 1924. Minick (with Edna Ferber), 1924. The Royal Family (with Edna Ferber), 1927. June Moon (with Ring Lardner), 1929. Once in a Lifetime (with Moss Hart), 1930. Dinner at Eight (with Edna Ferber), 1932. Merrily We Roll Along (with Moss Hart), 1934. First Lady (with Katherine Dayton), 1935. Stage Door (with Edna Ferber), 1936. You Can't Take It With You (with Moss Hart), 1936. I'd Rather Be Right (with Moss Hart), 1937. The American Way (with Moss Hart), 1939. The Man Who Came to Dinner (with Moss Hart), 1939. George Washington Slept Here (with Moss Hart), 1940. The Land Is Bright (with

Lurie, Alison (1926–   ). Love and Friendship, 1962. The Nowhere City, 1965. Imaginary Friends, 1967. Real People, 1969. The War Between the Tates, 1974. Only Children, 1979. The Language of Clothes, 1981.

Luther, Seth (fl. 1817–46). An Address to the Working-Men of New England, 1832. An Address on the Right of Free Suffrage, 1833. An Address on the Origin and Progress of Avarice, 1834.

Lynd, Robert S. (1892–1970) and Helen Merrell Lynd (1896–1982). Middletown—A Study in Contemporary American Culture, 1929. Middletown in Transition, 1937.

Lyon, James (1735–94). Urania, or A Choice Collection of Psalm-Tunes, Anthems, and Hymns, 1761. The Lawfulness, Excellency, and Advantage of Instrumental Musick, in the Publick Worship of God, 1763.

Lytle, Andrew (1902–   ). Bedford Forrest, 1931. The Long Night, 1936. At the Moon's Inn, 1941. A Name for Evil, 1947. The Velvet Horn, 1957. A Novel, a Novella, and Four Stories, 1958. The Hero with the Private Parts, 1966. A Wake for the Living, 1975.

McAlmon, Robert (1895–1956). Being Geniuses Together, 1938.

Macauley, Robie (1919–   ). The Disguises of Love, 1952. The End of Pity, 1957.

McCarthy, Cormac (1933–   ). The Orchard Keeper, 1965. Outer Dark, 1968. Child of God, 1973.

McCarthy, Mary (1912–   ). The Company She Keeps, 1942. The Oasis, 1949. Cast a Cold Eye, 1950. The Groves of Academe, 1952. A Charmed Life, 1955. Sights and Spectacles, 1956. Venice Observed, 1956. Memories of a Catholic Girlhood, 1957. The Stones of Florence, 1959. On the Contrary, 1961. The Group, 1963. Vietnam, 1967. Hanoi, 1968. The Writing on the Wall, 1970. Birds of America, 1971. The Mask of State: Watergate Portraits, 1974. Cannibals and Missionaries, 1979. Ideas and the Novel, 1980.

McClure, David (1748–1820). An Oration on the Advantages of an Early Education, 1783.

McClure's Magazine (1893–1929).

McConkey, James (1921–   ). Night Stand, 1965. Crossroads, 1968. A Journey to Sabalin, 1971. The Tree House Confessions, 1979. Court of Memory, 1983.

McCoy, Horace (1897–1955). They Shoot Horses, Don't They? 1935. No Pockets in a Shroud, 1937. Kiss Tomorrow Goodbye, 1948.

McCullers, Carson (1917–67). The Heart Is a Lonely Hunter, 1940. Reflections in a Golden Eye, 1941. The Member of the Wedding, 1946. The Member of the Wedding [adapted from her novel (1946); pub. 1951], 1950. The Ballad of the Sad Café, 1951. The Square Root of Wonderful, 1957. Clock Without Hands, 1961.

McCutcheon, George Barr (1866–1928). Graustark, 1901. Brewster's Millions, 1902.

MacDonald, Betty (1908–1958). The Egg and I, 1945.

Macdonald, Dwight (1906–82). Memoirs of a Revolutionist, 1957. Against the American Grain, 1963.

"Macdonald, Ross." *See* Millar, Kenneth.

McGinley, Phyllis (1905–78). A Pocketful of Wry, 1940. Stones from a Glass House, 1946. Province of the Heart, 1959. Times Three: Selected Verse from Three Decades, 1960. Sixpence in Her Shoe, 1964.

McGinnis, Joe (1942–   ). Going to Extremes, 1980.

McGregore, David (1710–77). The Spirits of the Present Day Tried, 1742. The Christian Soldier, 1754.

McGuane, Thomas (1939–   ). The Sporting Club, 1969. The Bushwacked Piano, 1971. Ninety-two in the Shade, 1973. Panama, 1978. Outside Chance, 1980. Nobody's Angel, 1982.

McHale, Tom (1942?–   ). Faragan's Retreat, 1971. School Spirit, 1976. Dear Friends, 1981.

McHenry, James (1785–1845). The Pleasures of Friendship, 1822. Waltham, 1823. The Wilderness; or, Braddock's Times, 1823. The Spectre of the Forest, 1823.

MacInnes, Helen (1907–85). Above Suspicion, 1941 (the first of many mystery novels).

MacKaye, Percy (1875–1956). Jeanne d'Arc, 1906. Sappho and Phaon, 1907. The Scarecrow, 1908. Mater, 1908. Anti-Matrimony, 1910. Tomorrow, 1913. The Mystery of Hamlet, King of Denmark; or, What We Will, 1949.

MacKaye, Steele (1842–94). Hazel Kirke, 1880. A Fool's Errand [adapted from Albion W. Tourgée's novel (1879)], 1881. Paul Kauvar, 1887.

McKenney, Ruth (1911–72). My Sister Eileen, 1938.

MacKenzie, Henry (1745–1831). An Answer to Paine's Rights of Man, 1796.

MacLeish, Archibald (1892–1982). Songs

Miller, Henry (*continued*)
Paris), 1936. Max and the White Phago-
cytes, 1938. Tropic of Capricorn (pub. in
Paris), 1939. The Cosmological Eye,
1939. Hamlet, 1939. The Wisdom of
the Heart, 1941. The Colossus of Mar-
oussi, 1941. Sunday After the War, 1944.
The Air-Conditioned Nightmare, 1945.
Remember to Remember, 1947. The
Smile at the Foot of the Ladder, 1948.
Sexus (pub. in Paris), 1949. The Books in
My Life, 1952. Plexus (pub. in Paris),
1953. Quiet Days in Clichy (pub. in
Paris), 1956. Big Sur and the Oranges of
Hieronymus Bosch, 1957. Nexus (pub. in
Paris), 1960. Stand Still Like a Humming-
bird, 1962.
Miller, Jason (1939–   ). The Champion-
ship Season, 1972.
Miller, Joaquin (1841?–1913). Specimens,
1868. Joaquin et al, 1869. Songs of the
Sierras, 1871. Pacific Poems, 1871. Life
Amongst the Modocs, 1873. The One Fair
Woman, 1876. The Danites of the Sierras,
1877. Memorie and Rime, 1884. In Clas-
sic Shades and Other Poems, 1890.
Millett, Kate (1934–   ). Sexual Politics,
1970. Flying, 1974. Sita, 1977. The Base-
ment: Meditations on a Human Sacrifice,
1979.
Millhauser, Steven (1943–   ). Edwin
Mullhouse: The Life and Death of an
American Writer, 1943–1954, by Jeffrey
Cartwright, 1972. Portrait of a Romantic,
1977.
Milosz, Czeslaw (1911–   ). Selected
Poems, 1972. Bells in Winter, 1978. Vi-
sions from San Francisco Bay, 1982. The
Witness of Poetry, 1983.
Minot, George Richards (1758–1802). The
History of the Insurrections, in Massachu-
setts, in the Year 1786, 1788.
Miss Leslie's Magazine (1843–46).
Mitchel, Jonathan (1624–68). Nehemiah on
the Wall in Troublesome Times, 1671.
Mitchell, Donald Grant. ["Ik Marvel"]
(1822–1908). Reveries of a Bachelor; or,
A Book of the Heart, 1850. Dream Life,
1851. My Farm of Edgewood, 1863. Dr.
Johns, 1866. Rural Studies, 1867.
Mitchell, Isaac (c. 1759–1812). The Asy-
lum; or, Alonzo and Melissa, 1811.
Mitchell, John (fl. 1755–68). Map of the
British and French Dominions in North
America, 1755.
Mitchell, John Ames (1845–1918). Amos
Judd, 1895.
Mitchell, Langdon (1862–1935). The New
York Idea, 1906.
Mitchell, Margaret (1900–49). Gone with
the Wind, 1936.

Mitchell, S. Weir (1829–1914). Hephzibah
Guinness, 1880. In War Time, 1885. Ro-
land Blake, 1886. Characteristics, 1892.
Hugh Wynne, Free Quaker, 1897. The
Adventures of François, 1898. Dr. North
and His Friends, 1900. Circumstance,
1901. Constance Trescot, 1905. The Red
City, 1907. John Sherwood, Iron Master,
1911. Westways, 1913.
M'lle New York (1895–99).
Modern Drama (1958–   ).
Modern Fiction Studies (1955–   ).
Modern Language Notes (1886–   ).
Modern Language Quarterly (1940–   ).
Modern Philology (1903–   ).
Modern Quarterly (1923–40).
Mollineux, Mary Southworth (1651?–95).
Fruits of Retirement, 1730.
Momaday, N. Scott (1934–   ). House
Made of Dawn, 1968. The Way to Rainy
Mountain, 1969. The Gourd Dancer,
1976. The Names, 1976.
Monis, Judah (1683–1764). Proposals for
Printing by Subscription a Hebrew Gram-
mar, 1734. Dickdook Leshon Gnebreet. A
Grammar of the Hebrew Tongue, 1735.
Monitor (1755–65?).
Monk, Maria (c. 1817–50). Awful Disclo-
sures, 1836. Further Disclosures, 1837.
Monmouth, James Scott, Duke of (1649–
85). An Abridgment of the English Mili-
tary Discipline, 1690.
Monroe, Harriet (1860–1936). Valeria and
Other Poems, 1891. The Columbian Ode,
1893. The Passing Show, 1903.
Montefiore, Joshua (1762–1843). The Amer-
ican Trader's Compendium, 1811.
Monthly Review (1749–1844).
Moodey, Joshua (1633–97). A Practical Dis-
course Concerning the Choice Benefit of
Communion with God, 1685.
Moody, Anne (1940–   ). Coming of Age
in Mississippi, 1968.
Moody, Samuel (1676–1747). The Vain
Youth Summoned to Appear at Christ's
Bar, 1707. The Gospel Way of Escaping
the Doleful State of the Damned, 1710.
The Debtor's Monitor, Directory and
Comforter, 1715.
Moody, William Vaughn (1869–1910). The
Masque of Judgment, 1900. Poems, 1901.
The Fire-Bringer, 1904. A Sabine
Woman, 1906. The Great Divide [revision
of A Sabine Woman (1906)], 1909. The
Faith Healer, 1909.
"Moon, William Least Heat." *See* Trogdon,
William.
Moore, Clement Clarke (1779–1863). "A
Visit from St. Nicholas" (commonly
known as " 'Twas the Night Before
Christmas"), 1823.

Mosel, Tad (1922–   ). All the Way Home [adapted from James Agee's novel A Death in the Family (1957)], 1960.

Moss, Howard (1922–   ). The Wound and the Weather, 1946. The Toy Fair, 1954. A Swimmer in the Air, 1957. A Winter Come, A Summer Gone: Poems 1946–1960, 1960. The Magic Lantern of Marcel Proust, 1962. Finding Them Lost, 1965. Second Nature, 1968. Writing Against Time, 1969. Selected Poems, 1971. Buried City, 1975. A Swim off the Rocks, 1976. Whatever Is Moving, 1981.

Motley, John Lothrop (1814–77). Morton's Hope; or, The Memoirs of a Provincial, 1839. Merry-Mount: A Romance of the Massachusetts Colony, 1849. The Rise of the Dutch Republic, 1856. History of the United Netherlands, 1860. The Life and Death of John of Barneveld, 1874.

Motley, Willard (1912–65). Knock on Any Door, 1947. We Fished All Night, 1951. Let No Man Write My Epitaph, 1958. Let Noon Be Fair, 1966.

Moulton, Louise Chandler (1835–1908). This, That, and the Other, 1854. Juno Clifford, 1855. Poems, 1889.

Mowatt, Anna Cora (1819–70). The Fortune Hunter, 1844. Fashion; or, Life in New York, 1845. Evelyn; or, A Heart Unmasked, 1845. Armand, the Child of the People, 1847. Autobiography of an Actress, 1854. Mimic Life, 1856. Twin Roses, 1857.

Mucklow, William (1631–1713). The Spirit of the Hat: or, The Government of the Quakers Among Themselves, 1673.

Muir, John (1838–1914). The Mountains of California, 1894. Our National Parks, 1901. Stickeen, 1909. My First Summer in the Sierra, 1911. The Yosemite, 1912. The Story of My Boyhood and Youth, 1913. Travels in Alaska, 1915. A Thousand-Mile Walk to the Gulf, 1916.

Mulford, Clarence E. (1883–1956). Hopalong Cassidy, 1910. Hopalong Cassidy Returns, 1924.

Mumford, Lewis (1895–   ). Sticks and Stones, 1924. Technics and Civilization, 1934. The Culture of the Cities, 1938. The Condition of Man, 1944. The Conduct of Life, 1951. My Works and Days, 1978. Sketches from Life, 1982.

Munford, Robert (1730?–84). The Candidates; or, The Humours of a Virginia Election, 1798. The Patriots, 1798.

Munford, William (1775–1825). Prose on Several Occasions, 1798.

Munsey's Magazine (1889–1929).

Murat, Achille (1801–47). Lettres sur les États-Unis, 1830. Esquisse morale et politique des États-Unis, 1832. Exposition des principes du gouvernement républicain, tel qu'il a été perfectionné en Amérique, 1833.

Murdock, John (1748–1824). The Triumphs of Love, or Happy Reconciliation, 1795.

Murfree, Mary Noailles ["Charles Egbert Craddock"] (1850–1922). In the Tennessee Mountains, 1884. Where the Battle Was Fought, 1884. Down the Ravine, 1885. The Prophet of the Great Smoky Mountains, 1885. In the Clouds, 1886. The Story of Keedon Bluffs, 1887. The Despot of Broomsedge Cove, 1888. In the "Stranger People's" Country, 1891. His Vanished Star, 1894. The Mystery of Witch-Face Mountain, 1895. The Phantoms of the Foot-Bridge, 1895. The Young Mountaineers, 1897. The Juggler, 1897. The Bushwackers, 1899. The Story of Old Fort Loudon, 1899. A Spectre of Power, 1903. The Frontiersmen, 1904. The Storm Centre, 1905. The Amulet, 1906. The Windfall, 1907. The Fair Mississippian, 1908. The Raid of the Guerilla, 1912. The Ordeal, 1912. The Story of Duciehurst, 1914.

Murray, John (1741–1815). Letters and Sketches of Sermons, 1812.

Murray, Judith Sargent (1751–1820). The Gleaner, 1798.

Murray, Lindley (1745–1826). English Grammar (rev. edition, 1818), 1795. Extracts from the Writings of Divers Eminent Authors Representing the Evils and Pernicious Effects of Stage Plays, and Other Vain Amusements (editor), 1799. The English Reader; or, Pieces in Prose and Poetry Selected from the Best Writers (editor), 1799. Memoirs, 1826.

Muses Mercury (1707–08).

Museum (1746–47).

Myers, Peter Hamilton (1812–78). The First of the Knickerbockers, 1848. The Young Patroon, 1849. The King of the Hurons, 1850.

Nabokov, Vladimir (1899–1977). Laughter in the Dark, 1938. The Real Life of Sebastian Knight, 1941. Nikolai Gogol, 1944. Nine Stories, 1947. Bend Sinister, 1947. Lolita, 1955. Pnin, 1957. Nabokov's Dozen, 1958. Invitation to a Beheading, 1959. Poems, 1959. Pale Fire, 1962. Speak, Memory, 1966. King, Queen, Knave, 1968. Ada or Ardor: A Family Chronicle, 1969. Poems and Problems, 1970. Transparent Things, 1972. A Russian Beauty, and Other Stories, 1973. Look at the Harlequins! 1974. Details of a

Nichols, Thomas Low (1815–1901). Ellen Ramsay, 1843. The Lady in Black, 1844. Raffle for a Wife, 1845.

Niebuhr, Reinhold (1892–1971). The Nature and Destiny of Man (2 vols., 1941–43), 1941.

Niles, Samuel (1674–1762). Tristitiae Ecclesiarum, or a Brief and Sorrowful Account of the Present State of the Churches of New-England, 1745. A Brief and Plain Essay on God's Wonder Working Providence for New-England in the Reduction of Louisburg and Fortresses Thereto Belonging on Cape Breton, 1747.

Niles' Weekly Register (1811–49).

Nims, John Frederick (1913–   ). The Iron Pastoral, 1947. A Fountain in Kentucky, 1950. Knowledge of the Evening, 1960. Of Flesh and Bone, 1967. Western Wind, 1974.

Nin, Anaïs (1903–77). The House of Incest, 1936. The Winter of Artifice, 1939. Under a Glass Bell, 1944. This Hunger, 1945. Ladders to Fire, 1946. Realism and Reality, 1946. On Writing, 1947. The Four-Chambered Heart, 1950. A Spy in the House of Love, 1954. Cities of the Interior, 1959. Collages, 1964.

Noah, Mordecai Manuel (1785–1851). Paul and Alexis (retitled The Wandering Boys, 1821), 1812. She Would Be a Soldier, 1819. Travels in England, France, Spain, and the Barbary States, 1819. The Siege of Tripoli, 1820. Marion; or, The Hero of Lake George, 1821. The Grecian Captive, 1822. Gleanings from a Gathered Harvest, 1845.

Noble, Oliver (1734–92). Some Strictures Upon the Sacred Story Recorded in the Book of Esther, 1775.

Nordhoff, Charles (1830–1901). Man-of-War Life, 1855. Whaling and Fishing, 1856. Stories of the Island World, 1857. Nine Years a Sailor, 1857.

Nordhoff, Charles Bernard (1887–1947) and James Norman Hall (1887–1951). Mutiny on the Bounty, 1932. Pitcairn's Island, 1934. Men Against the Sea, 1934. Botany Bay, 1941.

Norris, Frank (1870–1902). Yvernelle: A Tale of Feudal France, 1891. Moran of the Lady Letty, 1898. McTeague, 1899. Blix, 1899. A Man's Woman, 1900. The Octopus, 1901. The Pit, 1903. A Deal in Wheat, 1903. The Responsibilities of the Novelist, 1903. The Joyous Miracle, 1906. The Third Circle, 1909. Vandover and the Brute, 1914.

North American Review (1815–1939).

North British Review (1844–71).

Norton, Andrews (1786–1853). A Discourse on Religious Education, 1818. The Evidences of the Genuineness of the Gospels, 1837. On the Latest Form of Infidelity, 1839. Tracts on Christianity, 1852. Internal Evidences of the Genuineness of the Gospels, 1855.

Norton, John (1606–63). Responsio ad Guliel, 1648. A Discussion of that Great Point in Divinity, the Sufferings of Christ, 1653. Abel Being Dead Yet Speaketh; or, The Life and Death of . . . John Cotton, 1658. The Heart of N-England rent at the Blasphemies of the Present Generation, 1659. A Brief Catechisme Containing the Doctrine of Godlines, or of Living Unto God, 1660. Three Choice and Profitable Sermons Upon Severall Texts of Scripture, 1664.

Norton, John (1716–78). The Redeemed Captive [of the French and Indians], 1748.

Notes and Queries (1849–   ).

Nott, Henry Junius (1797–1837). Novelettes of a Traveller; or, Odds and Ends from the Knapsack of Thomas Singularity, Journeyman Printer, 1834.

Nouvelle Nouvelle Revue Française (1953–   ).

Nouvelle Revue (1879–1940).

Nouvelle Revue Française (1909–43).

Novel: A Forum on Fiction (1967–   ).

Nowell, Samuel (1634–88). Abraham in Arms, 1678.

Noyes, John Humphrey (1811–86). The Berean, 1847. Bible Communism, 1848. Male Continence, 1848.

Nuttall, Thomas (1786–1859). The Genera of North American Plants, 1818.

"Nye, Bill." *See* Nye, Edgar Wilson.

Nye, Edgar Wilson ["Bill Nye"] (1850–96). Bill Nye and Boomerang, 1881. History of the United States, 1894. History of England, 1896.

"O. Henry." *See* Porter, William Sydney.

Oakes, Urian (1631–81). New-England Pleaded With, and Pressed to Consider the Things Which Concern Her Peace, 1673. The Unconquerable, All-Conquering & More-Than-Conquering Souldier, 1674. An Elegie Upon the Death of the Reverend Mr. Thomas Shepard, 1677. The Soveraign Efficacy of Divine Providence, 1682.

Oates, Joyce Carol (1938–   ). By the North Gate, 1963. With Shuddering Fall, 1964. Upon the Sweeping Flood, 1966. A Garden of Earthly Delights, 1967. Expensive People, 1968. Women in Love, 1968. them, 1969. Anonymous Sins, 1969. The Wheel of Love, 1970. Love and Its Derangements, 1970. Wonderland, 1971. Marriages and Infidelities, 1972. Do With Me What You Will, 1973. Angel Fire,

Squadron to the China Seas and Japan, 1856.

Pershing, John J. (1860–1948). My Experiences in the World War, 1931.

Pesetsky, Bette (1932–   ). Stories Up to a Point, 1982. Author from a Savage People, 1983.

Peterkin, Julia (1880–1961). Green Thursday, 1924. Black April, 1927. Scarlet Sister Mary, 1928. Bright Skin, 1932.

Peter (Peters?), Hugh (1598–1660). New Englands First Fruits (with Thomas Weld), 1643.

Peters, Richard (1704–76). A Sermon on Education, 1751.

Peters, Samuel Andrew (1735–1826). General History of Connecticut, by a Gentleman of the Province, 1781. A History of the Reverend Hugh Peters, 1807.

Peterson, Charles Jacobs (1819–87). Grace Dudley; or, Arnold at Saratoga, 1849. History of the United States Navy, 1852. Kate Aylesford, A Story of the Refugees, 1855.

Peterson, Louis (1922–   ). Take a Giant Step, 1953.

"Petroleum V. Nasby." See Locke, David Ross.

Petry, Ann (1911–   ). The Street, 1946. Country Place, 1947. The Narrows, 1953.

Phelps, Elizabeth Stuart (1815–52). The Sunny Side; or, The Country Minister's Wife, 1851. A Peep at Number Five, 1852. The Angel Over the Right Shoulder, 1852.

Philadelphia Public Ledger (1836–1934).

Phillips, David Graham (1867–1911). The Great God Success, 1901. Golden Fleece, 1903. The Master-Rogue, 1903. The Cost, 1904. The Deluge, 1905. The Plum Tree, 1905. Light-Fingered Gentry, 1907. The Second Generation, 1907. Old Wives for New, 1908. The Worth of a Woman, 1908. The Fashionable Adventures of Joshua Craig, 1909. The Hungry Heart, 1909. The Husband's Story, 1910. The Conflict, 1911. George Helm, 1912. The Price She Paid, 1912. Susan Lenox: Her Fall and Rise, 1917.

Phillips, Jayne Anne (1952–   ). Black Tickets, 1979.

Phillips, Samuel (1690–1771). Soldiers Counselled and Encouraged, 1741. The Sin of Suicide Contrary to Nature, 1767.

Philological Quarterly (1922–   ).

Phylon (1940–   ).

Pickering, John (1777–1846). Vocabulary of Words and Phrases Peculiar to the United States, 1816. Comprehensive Lexicon of the Greek Language, 1826. A Grammar of the Cherokee Language, 1830.

Piercy, Marge (1936–   ). Breaking

Camp, 1968. Going Down Fast, 1969. Hard Loving, 1969. Small Changes, 1973. To Be of Use, 1973. Woman on the Edge of Time, 1976. Living in the Open, 1976. The High Cost of Living, 1978. The Twelve-Spoked Wheel Flashing, 1978. The Moon Is Always Female, 1980. Vida, 1980. Braided Lives, 1982.

Pierpont, John (1785–1866). The Portrait, 1812. Airs of Palestine, 1816. The Anti-Slavery Poems of John Pierpont, 1843.

Pierson, Abraham (1608–78). Some Helps for the Indians, 1658.

Pike, Albert (1809–91). Prose Sketches and Poems, Written in the Western Country, 1834. Hymns to the Gods, 1872.

Pike, Mary Hayden (1824–1908). Ida May, 1854. Caste, 1856. Agnes, 1858.

Pike, Zebulon Montgomery (1779–1813). Account of Expeditions to the Sources of the Mississippi and through the Western Parts of Louisiana, 1810.

Pillsbury, Parker (1809–98). Acts of the Anti-Slavery Apostles, 1883.

Pinckney, Charles (1758–1824). Observations on the Plan of Government Submitted to the Federal Convention, 1787.

Pinckney, Josephine (1895–1957). Three O'Clock Dinner, 1945.

Pinkney, Edward Coote (1802–28). Poems, 1825.

Pirsig, Robert M. (1928–   ). Zen and the Art of Motorcycle Maintenance, 1974.

Plath, Sylvia (1932–63). The Colossus and Other Poems, 1962. The Bell Jar (pub. in London; American edition, 1971), 1963. Ariel, 1966. Crossing the Water, 1971. Winter Trees, 1972. The Collected Poems, 1981. The Journals, 1982.

PMLA: Publications of the Modern Language Association (1884–   ).

Podhoretz, Norman (1930–   ). Making It, 1967.

Poe, Edgar Allan (1809–49). Tamerlane and Other Poems, 1827. Al Aaraaf, Tamerlane and Minor Poems, 1829. Poems, 1831. "Ms. Found in a Bottle," 1833. "The Coliseum," 1833. Politian: A Tragedy, 1835. "Berenice," 1835. "Morella,"1835. The Narrative of Arthur Gordon Pym, of Nantucket, 1838. "Ligeia," 1838. "The Haunted Palace," 1839. "The Fall of the House of Usher," 1839. "William Wilson," 1839. "The Journal of Julius Rodman," 1840. Tales of the Grotesque and Arabesque, 1840. "A Descent into the Maelstrom," 1841. "The Murders in the Rue Morgue," 1841. "Eleonora," 1842. "The Masque of the Red Death," 1842. "The Mystery of Marie Roget," 1842. "The Black Cat," 1843. "The Gold Bug," 1843. "The Pit

the Nature of Civil Liberty . . . and the Justice and Policy of the War with America, 1776.

Priestley, Joseph (1733–1804). An Essay on the First Principles of Government, 1768. Letters to Edmund Burke, 1791. Unitarianism Explained and Defended, 1796.

Prime, Benjamin Youngs (1733–91). The Patriotic Muse, 1764. Columbia's Glory, or British Pride Humbled, 1791.

Prince, Nathan (1698–1748). The Constitution and Government of Harvard College, 1742.

Prince, Thomas (1687–1758). Earthquakes Are the Works of God and Tokens of His Just Displeasure, 1727. A Sermon on the Sorrowful Occasion of the Death of His Late Majesty King George, 1727. The Vade Mecum for America; or, A Companion for Traders and Travellers, 1731. A Chronological History of New England in the Form of Annals, 1736. The Christian History, 1744. The Pious Cry of the Lord for Help When the Godly & Faithful Fail Among Them, 1746. The Natural and Moral Government and Agency of God in Causing Droughts and Rains, 1749. The Psalms, Hymns, & Spiritual Songs of the Old and New Testaments, 1758.

Proceedings of the American Philosophical Society (1838–   ).

Prokosch, Frederic (1908–   ). The Asiatics, 1935. The Assassins, 1936. The Seven Who Fled, 1937. The Carnival, 1938. Night of the Poor, 1939. Death at Sea, 1940. The Skies of Europe, 1941. The Conspirators, 1943. Age of Thunder, 1945. The Idols of the Cave, 1946. Storm and Echo, 1948. Nine Days to Mukulla, 1953. A Tale for Midnight, 1955. A Ballad of Love, 1960. The Seven Sisters, 1963. The Dark Dancer, 1964.

Proud, Robert (1728–1813). The History of Pennsylvania, 1797.

Prouty, Olive Higgins (1882–1974). Stella Dallas, 1923.

Publick Occurrences (1690).

Publishers' Weekly (1872–   ).

Puck (1877–1918).

Punch (1841–   ).

Purchas, Samuel (1575?–1626). Purchas his Pilgrimage, or, Relations of the World and the Religions observed in all Ages and places discovered, from the Creation unto this Present, 1613. Purchas his Pilgrim. Microcosmus, or the histories of Man, 1619. Hakluytus Posthumus, or Purchas his Pilgrimes, contayning a History of the World in Sea Voyages and Lande Travells, by Englishmen and others, 1625.

Purdy, James (1923–   ). Color of Dark-

ness, 1957. Malcolm, 1959. The Nephew, 1960. Cabot Wright Begins, 1964. Eustace Chisholm and The Works, 1967. Jeremy's Version, 1970. I Am Elijah Thrush, 1972. The House of the Solitary Maggot, 1974. In a Shallow Grave, 1975. A Day After the Fair, 1977. Narrow Rooms, 1978. Mourners Below, 1981.

Pusey, Caleb (1650–1727). Satan's Harbinger Encountered, 1700. Daniel Leeds, Justly Rebuked for Abusing William Penn, 1702. George Keith Once More Brought to the Test, 1703. False News from Gath Rejected, 1704. The Bomb Search'd and Found Stuff'd with False Ingredients, 1705.

Putnam's Monthly Magazine (1853–1910).

Pyle, Ernie (1900–45). Ernie Pyle in England, 1941. Here Is Your War, 1943. Brave Men, 1944. Last Chapter, 1946.

Pynchon, Thomas (1937–   ). V, 1963. The Crying of Lot 49, 1966. Gravity's Rainbow, 1973.

"Q. K. Philander Doesticks, P. B." *See* Thomson, Mortimer Neal.

Quarterly Review of Literature (1943–   ).

"Queen, Ellery." *See* "Ellery Queen."

Quincy, Edmund (1808–77). Wensley, a Story Without a Moral, 1854.

Quincy, Josiah (1744–75). Observations on the Act of Parliament Commonly Called the Boston Port-Bill, 1744.

Quincy, Josiah (1772–1864). The History of Harvard University, 1840.

Rabe, David (1940–   ). The Basic Training of Pavlo Hummel, 1971. Sticks and Bones, 1971. The Orphan, 1973. In the Boom Boom Room, 1974. Streamers, 1976.

Radical (1865–72).

Rafinesque, Constantine Samuel (1783–1840). A History of Kentucky, 1824. A Life of Travels and Researches in North America and South Europe, 1836. The American Nations (incl. trans. of "Walam Olum"), 1836.

Rambler (1750–52).

Ramsay, David (1749–1815). An Oration on the Advantages of American Independence, 1778. A History of the Revolution of South Carolina, 1785. An Address to the Freemen of South-Carolina on the Subject of the Federal Constitution, 1788. The History of the American Revolution, 1789. A Dissertation on the Means of Preserving Health in Charleston, and the Adjacent Low Country, 1790. History of South Carolina from Its First Settlement in 1670 to the Year 1808, 1809. History of

Sewall, Samuel (*continued*)
of Joseph, 1700. Proposals Touching the Accomplishment of Prophecies, 1713. A Memorial Relating to the Kennebeck Indians, 1721.

Sewall, Stephen (1734–1804). A Hebrew Grammar (compiler and editor), 1763.

Sewanee Review (1892–   ).

Seward, Anna (1742–1809). Monody on Major André, 1781.

Seward, William (?). Journal of a Voyage from Savannah to Philadelphia, and from Philadelphia to England in 1740, 1740.

Sewel, William (1653–1720). The History of the Rise, Increase, and Progress of the Christian People Called Quakers, 1728.

Sexton, Anne (1928–74). To Bedlam and Part Way Back, 1960. All My Pretty Ones, 1962. Selected Poems, 1964. Live or Die, 1966. Love Poems, 1969. Transformations, 1971. The Book of Folly, 1972. The Death Notebooks, 1974. The Awful Rowing Toward God, 1975. The Complete Poems, 1981.

Shange, Ntozake (1948–   ). Nappy Edges, 1978. Sassafrass, Cypress, and Indigo, 1982. A Daughter's Geography, 1983.

Shapiro, Karl (1913–   ). Poems, 1935. Person, Place and Thing, 1942. The Place of Love, 1942. V-Letter and Other Poems, 1944. Essay on Rime, 1945. Trial of a Poet, 1947. Poems 1940–1953, 1953. Beyond Criticism, 1953. Poems of a Jew, 1958. In Defense of Ignorance, 1960. Prose Keys to Modern Poetry, 1962. The Bourgeois Poet, 1964. To Abolish Children, 1968. The Poetry Wreck: Selected Essays 1950–1970, 1975. Adult Bookstore, 1976. Collected Poems, 1978.

Sharp, Granville (1735–1813). An Essay on Slavery, 1773.

Shaw, Henry Wheeler ["Josh Billings"] (1826–85). Josh Billings, Hiz Sayings, 1866. Josh Billings on Ice, and Other Things, 1868. Everybody's Friend, 1874. Josh Billings' Trump Kards, 1877. Old Probability: Perhaps Rain—Perhaps Not, 1879. Josh Billings Struggling with Things, 1881.

Shaw, Irwin (1913–84). Bury the Dead, 1936. Siege, 1937. The Gentle People, 1939. Sailor off the Bremen, 1939. Retreat to Pleasure, 1940. Welcome to the City, 1941. Sons and Soldiers, 1944. The Assassin, 1944. Act of Faith, 1946. The Young Lions, 1948. Mixed Faith, 1950. The Troubled Air, 1951. Lucy Crown, 1956. Tip on a Dead Jockey, 1957. Two Weeks in Another Town, 1960. Children from Their Games, 1963. In the Company of Dolphins, 1964. Voices of a Summer

Day, 1965. Rich Man, Poor Man, 1970. Beggar Man, Thief, 1977. Five Decades, 1978. The Top of the Hill, 1979. Bread Upon the Waters, 1981. Acceptable Losses, 1982.

Shea, Joseph Dawson Gilmary (1824–92). Discovery and Exploration of the Mississippi Valley, 1852. History of the Catholic Missions Among the Indian Tribes of the United States. 1529–1854, 1854. History of the Catholic Church in the United States (4 vols., 1886–92), 1886.

Sheean, Vincent (1899–1975). Personal History, 1935. Not Peace but a Sword, 1939. Between the Thunder and the Sun, 1943. This House Against This House, 1946.

Sheed, Wilfrid (1930–   ). A Middle Class Education, 1961. The Hack, 1963. Square's Progress, 1965. Office Politics, 1966. The Blacking Factory, & Pennsylvania Gothic, 1968. Max Jamison, 1970. People Will Always Be Kind, 1973. Transatlantic Blues, 1978. The Good Word and Other Words, 1979.

Sheldon, Charles M. (1857–1946). In His Steps, 1897.

Sheldon, Edward (1886–1946). Salvation Nell, 1908. The Nigger, 1909. The Boss, 1911. The Princess Zim-Zim, 1911. Egypt, 1912. The High Road, 1912. Romance, 1913. The Song of Songs [adapted from Hermann Sudermann's novel Das hohe Lied (1908)], 1914. Bewitched (with Sidney Howard; prod.), 1924. Lulu Belle (with Charles MacArthur), 1926. Jenny (with Margaret Ayer Barnes), 1929. Dishonored Lady (with Margaret Ayer Barnes), 1930.

Shelton, Frederick William (1815–81). The Trollopiad; or Travelling Gentlemen in America, 1837.

Shepard, Jeremiah (1648–1720). A Sort of Believers Never Saved, 1711. God's Conduct of His Church Through the Wilderness, 1715.

Shepard, Sam (1942–   ). La Turista, 1967. Operation Sidewinder, 1970. Mad Dog Blues, 1971. The Tooth of Crime, 1972. Geography of a Horse Dreamer, 1974. Buried Child, 1978. Curse of the Starving Class, 1978. True West, 1980. Fool for Love, 1983.

Shepard, Thomas (1605–49). The Sincere Convert, Discovering the Paucity of True Believers, 1640. New Englands Lamentation for Old Englands Present Errours, 1645. The Sound Beleever, 1645. The Day-Breaking, 1647. Certain Select Cases Resolved, 1648. The Clear Sun-shine of the Gospel Breaking Forth upon the Indians, 1648. The First Principles of the Oracles of God, 1648. Theses Sabbaticae,

1649. Four Necessary Cases of Conscience, 1651. A Defence of the Answer (with John Allin), 1652. Subjection to Christ, 1652. A Short Catechism, 1654. The Parable of the Ten Virgins Opened and Applied, 1660. The Church-Membership of Children and Their Right to Baptisme, 1663. Wine for Gospel Wantons, 1668. Eye-Salve, or A Watch-Word from Our Lord Iesus Christ Unto His Churches, 1673. Three Valuable Pieces, 1747.

Sheridan, Thomas (1719–88). A Rhetorical Grammar of the English Language, 1783.

Sherwood, Robert E. (1896–1955). The Road to Rome, 1927. The Queen's Husband, 1928. Waterloo Bridge, 1930. The Virtuous Knight, 1931. Reunion in Vienna, 1931. Unending Crusade, 1932. The Petrified Forest, 1935. Idiot's Delight, 1936. Tovarich [adapted from Jacques Deval's play (1934)], 1936. Abe Lincoln in Illinois, 1938. There Shall Be No Night, 1940. Roosevelt and Hopkins: An Intimate History, 1948. Second Threshold [revised from a manuscript by Philip Barry (d. 1949)], 1951. Small War on Murray Hill, 1957.

Shillaber, Benjamin Penhallow (1814–90). Life and Sayings of Mrs. Partington, 1854. Mrs. Partington's Knitting Work, 1859. Partingtonian Patchwork, 1873. Mrs. Partington's Grab Bag, 1893.

Shirer, William L. (1904–   ). Berlin Diary, 1941. End of a Berlin Diary, 1947. The Rise and Fall of the Third Reich, 1960.

Shirley, William (1694–1771). The Antigonian and Bostonian Beauties: A Poem, 1754. Memoirs of the Principal Transactions of the Last War Between the English and French in North-America (attrib.), 1758.

"Sidney, Margaret." See Lothrop, Harriet Mulford Stone.

Sigourney, Lydia Huntley (1791–1865). Moral Pieces in Prose and Verse, 1815. Pocahontas and Other Poems, 1841. Poems, Religious and Elegiac, 1841. The Faded Hope, 1853. Letters of Life, 1866.

Silko, Leslie Marmon (1948–   ). Storyteller, 1981.

Sill, Edward Rowland (1841–87). The Hermitage and Other Poems, 1868.

Simms, William Gilmore (1806–70). Lyrical and Other Poems, 1827. Early Lays, 1827. The Vision of Cortes, Cain, and Other Poems, 1829. Atalantis, 1832. The Remains of Maynard Davis Richardson, 1833. The Book of My Lady, 1833. Martin Faber: The Story of a Criminal, 1833. Guy Rivers: A Tale of Georgia, 1834. The Yemassee: A Romance of Carolina, 1835.

The Partisan: A Tale of the Revolution, 1835. Mellichampe: A Legend of the Santee, 1836. Slavery in America, 1838. Richard Hurdis; or, The Avenger of Blood, 1838. Pelayo: A Story of the Goth, 1838. Carl Werner: An Imaginative Story, 1838. Southern Passages and Pictures, 1839. The Damsel of Darien, 1839. Border Beagles: A Tale of Mississippi, 1840. The History of South Carolina, 1840. The Kinsmen; or, The Black Riders of Congaree, 1841. Confession; or, The Blind Heart, 1841. Beauchampe; or, The Kentucky Tragedy, 1842. Castle Dismal; or, the Bachelor's Christmas, 1844. The Prima Donna: A Passage from City Life, 1844. The Life of Francis Marion, 1844. Helen Halsey; or, The Swamp State of Conelachita, 1845. Count Julian; or, The Last Days of the Goth, 1845. The Wigwam and the Cabin: First Series, 1845. The Wigwam and the Cabin: Second Series, 1845. Grouped Thoughts and Scattered Fancies, 1845. The Views and Reviews in American Literature, History, and Fiction, 1845. The Life of the Chevalier Bayard, 1847. Lays of the Palmetto, 1848. The Cassique of Accabee, 1848. Charleston, and Her Satirists: A Scribblement, 1848. Sabbath Lyrics; or, Songs from Scripture, 1849. The Life of Nathaniel Greene, 1849. The Lily and the Totem; or, The Huguenots in Florida, 1850. Flirtation at the Moultrie House, 1850. The City of the Silent, 1850. Katharine Walton; or, The Rebel of Dorchester, 1851. Norman Maurice; or, The Man of the People, 1851. The Golden Christmas: A Chronicle of St. John's, Berkeley, 1852. The Sword and the Distaff; or, "Fair, Fat, and Forty" (repub. as Woodcraft, 1854), 1852. As Good as a Comedy; or, The Tennesseean's Story, 1852. Michael Bonham; or, The Fall of Bexar, 1852. Marie de Berniere, 1853. Vasconselos: A Romance of the New World, 1853. Egeria; or, Voices of Thought and Counsel for the Woods and the Wayside, 1853. South Carolina in the Revolutionary War, 1853. Southward Ho! A Spell of Sunshine, 1854. The Forayers; or, The Raid of the Dog-Days, 1855. Charlemont; or, The Pride of the Village, 1856. Eutaw, 1856. The Cassique of Kiawah, 1859.

Simon, Neil (1927–   ). Barefoot in the Park, 1963. The Odd Couple, 1965. Plaza Suite, 1968. The Prisoner of Second Avenue, 1971.

Simpson, Louis (1923–   ). The Arrivistes, 1949. Good News of Death, 1955. A Dream of Governors, 1959. Riverside

Torrey, Samuel (1632–1707). An Exhortation unto Reformation, 1674. A Plea for the Life of Dying Religion, 1683. Man's Extremity, God's Opportunity, 1695.

Tourgée, Albion W. (1838–1905). 'Toinette, 1874. Figs and Thistles, 1879. A Fool's Errand, 1879. Bricks Without Straw, 1880. Zouri's Christmas, 1881. John Eax and Mamelon, 1882. Hot Plowshares, 1883. An Appeal to Caesar, 1884. Button's Inn, 1887. Letters to a King, 1888. Black Ice, 1888. Pactolus Prime, 1890.

Townsend, Edward W. (1855–1942). "Chimmie Fadden," Major Max, and Other Stories, 1895.

Townsend, Mary Ashley (1832–1901). The Brother Clerks, 1857. The Captain's Story, 1874. Down the Bayou and Other Poems, 1882.

Tracts for the Times (1833–41).

Train, Arthur (1875–1945). Tutt and Mr. Tutt, 1920. The Adventures of Ephraim Tutt, 1930. Mr. Tutt's Case Book, 1936. Yankee Lawyer: The Autobiography of Ephraim Tutt, 1943. Mr. Tutt Finds a Way, 1945.

Transactions of the American Philosophical Society (1771–   ).

transition (1927–38).

Traubel, Horace L. (1858–1919). With Walt Whitman in Camden (5 vols., 1906–64), 1906.

"Traven, B." *See* "B. Traven."

"Traver, Robert." *See* Voelker, John Donaldson.

Trillin, Calvin (1935–   ). American Fried, 1974. Alice, Let's Eat, 1978. Floater, 1980. Uncivil Liberties, 1982. Third Helpings, 1983.

Trilling, Lionel (1905–75). The Middle of the Journey, 1947.

Tri-Quarterly (1958–   ).

Trogdon, William ["William Least Heat-Moon"] (1939–   ). Blue Highways: A Journey into America, 1983.

Trotter, Thomas (1760–1832). An Essay, Medical, Philosophical, and Chemical, on Drunkenness and Its Effects on the Human Body, 1813.

Trowbridge, J. T. (1827–1916). Neighbor Jackwood, 1857. Cudjo's Cave, 1864. Poetical Works, 1903. My Own Story, 1903.

True Patriot (1745–46).

Trumbull, Benjamin (1735–1820). A Complete History of Connecticut, 1797. An Address to the Public on the Subjects of Prayer and Family Religion, 1807. General History of the United States, 1810.

Trumbull, John (1750–1831). An Essay on the Uses and Advantages of the Fine Arts 1770. An Elegy on the Death of Mr.

Buckingham St. John, 1771. The Progress of Dulness, 1772. An Elegy on the Times, 1774. M'Fingal: A Modern Epic Poem in Four Cantos, 1782. Autobiography, Reminiscences and Letters of John Trumbull, 1841.

Tuchman, Barbara W. (1912–   ). The Guns of August, 1962. The Proud Tower: A Portrait of the World Before the War, 1890–1914, 1966. Practicing History, 1981.

Tucker, George (1775–1861). Letters from Virginia, 1816. The Valley of Shenandoah, 1824. A Voyage to the Moon, 1827. The Life of Thomas Jefferson, 1837. The Law of Wages, Profits, and Rent Investigated, 1837. The Theory of Money and Banks Investigated, 1839. Progress of the United States, 1843. History of the United States (4 vols., 1856–57), 1856. Political Economy for the People, 1859.

Tucker, Nathaniel Beverley (1784–1851). George Balcombe, 1836. The Partisan Leader, 1836.

Tucker, St. George (1752–1827). Liberty, A Poem on the Independence of America, 1788. Dissertation on Slavery, 1796. The Probationary Odes of Jonathan Pindar, 1796.

Tuckerman, Frederick Goddard (1821–73). Poems, 1860.

Tuckerman, Henry Theodore (1813–71). Thoughts on the Poets, 1846. Characteristics of Literature, 1849. The Optimist, 1850. Poems, 1851. Leaves from the Diary of a Dreamer, 1853. America and Her Commentators, 1864. The Criterion, 1866.

Tudor, William (1779–1830). Letters on the Eastern States, 1820. Miscellanies, 1821. The Life of James Otis of Massachusetts, 1823. Gebel Teir, 1829.

Turell, Ebenezer (1702–78). The Life and Character of the Reverend Benjamin Colman, 1749.

Turnbull, Robert James (1775–1833). A Visit to the Philadelphia Prison, 1796.

Turner, Frederick Jackson (1861–1932). The Frontier in American History, 1920.

"Twain, Mark." *See* Clemens, Samuel Langhorne.

Twelve Southerners. I'll Take My Stand: The South and the Agrarian Tradition, 1930.

Twentieth Century Literature (1955–   ).

Twice a Year (1938–48).

Tyler, Anne (1941–   ). If Morning Ever Comes, 1964. The Tin Can Tree, 1965. A Slipping-Down Life, 1970. The Clock Winder, 1972. Celestial Navigation, 1974. Searching for Caleb, 1976. Earthly Pos-

DATE			

© THE BAKER & TAYLOR CO.